HANDBOOK OF MIDDLE AMERICAN INDIANS, VOLUME 14
Guide to Ethnohistorical Sources, Part 3

HANDBOOK OF MIDDLE AMERICAN INDIANS

EDITED AT MIDDLE AMERICAN RESEARCH INSTITUTE, TULANE UNIVERSITY, BY

ROBERT WAUCHOPE, *General Editor*
MARGARET A. L. HARRISON, *Associate Editor*
JOSEPHITA N. BODDIE, *Administrative Assistant*
JOSEPH C. WIEDEL, *Cartographical Consultant*

ASSEMBLED WITH THE AID OF A GRANT FROM THE NATIONAL SCIENCE FOUNDATION, AND UNDER THE SPONSORSHIP OF THE NATIONAL RESEARCH COUNCIL COMMITTEE ON LATIN AMERICAN ANTHROPOLOGY

Editorial Advisory Board

IGNACIO BERNAL, HOWARD F. CLINE, GORDON F. EKHOLM, NORMAN A. MCQUOWN, MANNING NASH, T. DALE STEWART, EVON Z. VOGT, ROBERT C. WEST, GORDON R. WILLEY

HANDBOOK OF MIDDLE AMERICAN INDIANS

ROBERT WAUCHOPE, General Editor

VOLUME FOURTEEN

Guide to Ethnohistorical Sources

PART THREE

HOWARD F. CLINE, Volume Editor

Charles Gibson and H. B. Nicholson,
Associate Volume Editors

UNIVERSITY OF TEXAS PRESS AUSTIN

Published in Great Britain by the
University of Texas Press, Ltd., London

International Standard Book Number 0–292–70154–3
Library of Congress Catalog Card No. 64–10316
Copyright © 1975 by the University of Texas Press

The preparation and publication of the
Handbook of Middle American Indians
have been assisted by grants from
the National Science Foundation.

Typesetting and printing by The University of
Texas Printing Division, Austin
Binding by Universal Bookbindery, Inc., San Antonio

C O N T E N T S (*Continued from Vol. 13*)

ABBREVIATIONS

AAMC	—	Anales Antiguos de Mexico y sus Contornos.
Acc.	—	Accession (date).
AGI	—	Archivo General de Indias, Seville.
AGG	—	Archivo General del Gobierno, Guatemala.
AGN	—	Archivo General de la Nación, Mexico.
AGN-C	—	AGN, Ramo de Civil.
AGN-H	—	AGN, Ramo de Historia.
AGN-HJ	—	AGN, Ramo Hospital de Jesús.
AGN-I	—	AGN, Ramo de Inquisición.
AGN-T	—	AGN, Ramo de Tierras.
AGN-V	—	AGN, Ramo de Vínculos.
AGS	—	Archivo General de Simancas.
AGT	—	Archivo General del Estado, Tlaxcala.
AMNH	—	American Museum of Natural History, New York.
BAN	—	Bancroft Library, University of California, Berkeley.
BAV	—	Biblioteca Apostolica Vaticana, Rome.
BF	—	Benjamin Franklin (series of microfilms, MNH/CD).
BLC	—	Berendt Linguistic Collection, University of Pennsylvania, Philadelphia.
BLO	—	Bodleian Library, Oxford.
BM	—	British Museum, London.
BNMA	—	Biblioteca Nacional, Madrid.
BNMex	—	Biblioteca Nacional, Mexico.
BNP	—	Bibliothèque Nationale, Paris.
BNP/FM	—	BNP, Fonds Mexicains.
BPN	—	Biblioteca del Palacio Nacional, Madrid.
BYU	—	Brigham Young University, Provo.
CA	—	Colección Antigua, MNA/AH.
CDG	—	Castañeda and Dabbs, *Guide*, 1939.
CMNE	—	Colección de Memorias de Nueva España.
CVM	—	Códices Vindobonenses Mexicani, NBV.
DGMH	—	Dirección de Geografía, Meteorología e Hidrología, Mexico.
DSB	—	Deutsche Staatsbibliothek, Berlin.
ESC	—	Biblioteca del Real Monasterio de El Escorial.
FM	—	Fonds Mexicains, BNP.
G	—	Genaro García Collection, UTX.
HSA	—	Hispanic Society of America, New York.
IAI	—	Ibero-Amerikanisches Institut, Berlin.
INAH	—	Instituto Nacional de Antropología e Historia, Mexico.
INAH/AF	—	INAH, Archivo Fotográfico.

JCB-AR	—	John Carter Brown Library, annual report.
JCBL	—	John Carter Brown Library, Providence.
JGI	—	Joaquín García Icazbalceta Collection.
JRL	—	John Rylands Library, Manchester.
LC	—	Library of Congress, Washington.
LC/HF	—	LC, Hispanic Foundation.
MAI/HF	—	Museum of the American Indian, Heye Foundation, New York.
MHP	—	Musée de l'Homme, Paris.
MMM	—	Museo Michoacano, Morelia.
MNA	—	Museo Nacional de Antropología, Mexico.
MNA/AH	—	MNA, Archivo Histórico del INAH.
MNA/AH-CA	—	Colección Antigua, MNA/AH.
MNA/BNA	—	MNA, Biblioteca Nacional de Antropología.
MNA 35	—	MNA, Codex collection.
MNH	—	Museo Nacional de Historia, Mexico.
MNH/CD	—	MNH, Centro de Documentación.
MS	—	Manuscript.
MVBA	—	Museum für Völkerkunde, Basle.
MVBE	—	Museum für Völkerkunde, Berlin.
MVH	—	Museum für Völkerkunde, Hamburg.
MVV	—	Museum für Völkerkunde, Vienna.
NBV	—	Osterreichische Nationalbibliothek, Vienna.
NLA	—	Newberry Library, Ayer Collection, Chicago.
NYPL	—	New York Public Library, New York.
PML	—	Peabody Museum Library, Harvard University, Cambridge.
PUL	—	Princeton University Library, Princeton.
RAH	—	Real Academia de la Historia, Madrid.
ROM	—	Royal Ontario Museum, Toronto.
SMGE	—	Sociedad Mexicana de Geografía y Estadística, Mexico.
SSPK	—	Staatsbibliothek Stiftung Preussischer Kulturbesitz, West Berlin.
TU	—	Tulane University, New Orleans.
TU/LAL	—	TU, Latin American Library.
TU/MARI	—	TU, Middle American Research Institute.
UBT	—	Universitätsbibliothek, Tübingen.
UP/UM	—	University of Pennsylvania, University Museum, Philadelphia.
UTX	—	University of Texas Library, Latin American Collection, Austin.

HANDBOOK OF MIDDLE AMERICAN INDIANS, VOLUME 14
Guide to Ethnohistorical Sources, Part 3

22. A Survey of Native Middle American Pictorial Manuscripts

JOHN B. GLASS

THE USE OF BOOKS, together with the related arts of hieroglyphic writing or other conventional means of painting, with a standardized syllabary of symbols and the manufacture of paper for use in the production of manuscripts, is a distinctive trait of the ancient cultures of Mesoamerica. Early chronicles of discovery and conquest provide abundant evidence for the trait from Central Mexico, Oaxaca, the Maya regions, and from as far south in Central America as Nicaragua. In terms of the regional divisions of Mesoamerica used herein the trait is unreported at Contact only for Western Mexico.

Picture writing on manuscripts of paper or animal skin is of unknown antiquity in Mesoamerica though the evidence of painted polychrome ceramics, bark beaters, murals, and hieroglyphic writing or calendrical symbols on stone or wood suggests that the art of manuscript painting may have been practiced as early as the Classic Period. Historical and calendrical records on some form of perishable media must have existed along with Early Classic monumental texts of the Maya and the murals of Teotihuacan. The date of the first manufacture of bark paper and of manuscript books in screenfold format in Mesoamerica is unknown. Both of these traits may be the result of diffusion from Asia.

Manuscripts painted in various native artistic traditions continued to be produced, particularly in Central Mexico and Oaxaca, throughout the 16th century. The continued production is explicable largely by the usefulness of the art. Secular authorities of the Spanish imperial regime provided a stimulation of the art by their patronage for both historical and administrative reasons. Scholarship of the mendicant Orders, particularly Franciscan ethnographic research designed to record Indian paganism (so that by understanding it, they could eradicate it), was an important source of patronage during the middle and later years of the 16th century. In civil and economic matters Indians and Spaniards alike found that maps, tribute registers, cadastral and census documents derived from native traditions met a common need.

3

There is little doubt that the manuscript art and writing systems of Central Mexico continued to develop under European influence at least into the last quarter of the 16th century. During that time the assimilation of Renaissance traits made extensive impact on manuscript format, composition, perspective, quality of line, and so forth. In other respects, particularly as a vehicle for the formal and symbolic expression of those aspects of Indian culture suppressed by the Spanish conquest, manuscript art quickly degenerated or came to an abrupt halt. From an artistic point of view the difference between colonial and preconquest drawings is considerable, a distinction that is sometimes blurred by the existence of colonial redactions of traditional subject matters and forms. By the early years of the 17th century the pictorial manuscript art as a traditional or even developing form was virtually extinct. Its decline parallels that of other traits of Indian culture under Spanish rule, but manuscript drawings in traditional forms may be said to have become unimportant when literacy in either written Spanish or Nahuatl spread to Indian administrators.

The survival of a significant corpus of manuscript drawings from both ancient and colonial Mesoamerica provides archaeologists and ethnohistorians with what is almost a unique body of materials in New World sources. The surviving pictorial manuscripts include calendars and religious books that are of incalculable importance in interpreting ancient practices and monuments. The historical manuscripts, which contain both preconquest and colonial annals, are of interest to both the archaeologist and historian. What may be called civil books, those dealing largely with the mundane affairs of colonial Mexico, provide ethnographic and historical information not only about Indians in acculturation but about the emerging colonial society.

The census of Mesoamerican pictorial manuscripts is intended to provide a comprehensive and descriptive inventory as well as a guide to the bibliography of the surviving corpus of Indian manuscript drawings and paintings that are in the native artistic and historical traditions. In the census are drawings on paper, cloth, and animal hide. Paintings on other media, such as murals, pottery, and stone monuments, are naturally not included although many of them are artistically comparable to executions in manuscript form. Printed items are also excluded unless they are the sole relic of a relevant manuscript. No attempt has been made to investigate easel paintings, although several late paintings on canvas are in the census. The criteria for inclusion are broad. No specific limitations of the ethnic origin of the artist (Spanish or Indian) or of content (colonial or preconquest) have been imposed. Most of the manuscripts that are described date from the 16th century, but a few are from the 18th century. Some may have been executed by Spaniards under Indian influence or be the product of creole or mestizo culture. The foremost criteria are that the paintings, drawings, or manuscripts display traits of pictorial content, style, composition, or formal symbolic conventions derived from indigenous traditions.

Generally speaking, the manuscripts in the census are those comprehended under the broad rubric of "codices" in the current ethnohistorical literature on Mesoamerica excepting, of course, those codices that are wholly textual in nature. Texts without drawings which describe or are based on lost pictorial sources are not included. In content the manuscripts that are surveyed deal with both the preconquest and early colonial Indian cultures.

Three categories of native pictorial documents have been segregated for separate treatment. The *pinturas* and maps of the *Relaciones geográficas* of 1579–85 are catalogued and discussed by Robertson and Robertson (Article 6). The Techialoyan codices of the late 17th or early 18th century are catalogued by Robertson and Robertson (Article 24), and the pictorial catechisms known as Testerian manuscripts by Glass (Article 25). Selected falsified pictorial manuscripts are listed by Glass (Article 26).

The different types are distinguished by different blocks of numbers. Numbers 1–599 are reserved for traditional pictorials; 701–799 for Techialoyans; 801–899 for Testerians; 901–999 for falsifications; and 1001– for nonpictorial texts. The numbers 601–699 were reserved for maps of the *Relaciones geográficas* but were not utilized in volume 12 of the *Handbook*. The addition of 600 to the numbers assigned by Robertson will convert them to the present scheme.

The scope of the census with regard to the collections in the various universities, museums, and libraries listed in the institutional checklist (Article 28) is discussed therein as is the special policy with regard to certain governmental archives.

The census includes most manuscripts in private or commercial possession that have come to our notice. Manuscripts in local Mexican village possession, however, have been listed only when their existence is a matter of published record.

We have included in the census a number of documents that have been listed in earlier catalogs, handlists, and bibliographies published since about 1890 even when we have determined that the item is otherwise unknown. This has been done to increase the usefulness of the census. It may save others the tedious task of studying such references or it may bring these unidentified items to the attention of some one in a position to identify them.

During preparation of the inventory our attention has frequently been drawn, particularly in the 19th-century literature, to references to pictorial manuscripts that have subsequently been lost to view. A similar situation exists with respect to many documents described in 19th- and even 20th-century sale catalogs. If they still exist,

such documents will eventually be found in private or institutional possession, but such references and descriptions when unaccompanied by illustrations have not been entered in the census with one or another exception. References to now unknown manuscripts in the literature of the 16th, 17th, and 18th centuries and in inventories of the Boturini collection have been completely omitted from the census, which is primarily concerned with available documents, subject to the foregoing remarks.

In a number of instances we have encountered drawings marginal to the native tradition. Depending on the nature of their bibliography some of these peripheral items have been included in the census; others are mentioned in the survey or listed in the insitutional checklist but excluded from the census.

Also excluded from the census are coats of arms of cities and individuals. Some of them, such as that granted to Texcoco (fig. 15), contain notable traditional iconographic or stylistic elements even though framed in the devices of European heraldry.[1] Although not lacking in interest, these curious fusions of different symbolic systems are somewhat removed from the main concern of ethnohistory.

Sixteenth-century drawings of the Indians of Mesoamerica, other than those by the Indians themselves and certain others surveyed herein, are rare. There is no corpus of ethnographic illustration comparable to that which exists, from later centuries, for the Indians in what is now the United States of America. The sketches that Cristoph Weiditz made of Indians transported to Spain in 1528 and a few of the drawings in the manuscript of Oviedo's general history are exceptional. The "Cortes" or "Nuremberg"

[1] The national coat of arms of Mexico—an eagle on a nopal cactus—is a famous and ubiquitous symbol of this nature that derives directly out of Indian iconography and may be related to manuscript sources. A curious version of it has been published by Barlow (1949f).

map of the City and Valley of Mexico first published in 1524 and an imaginative drawing of a double Mexican temple on a pyramid in the relation of the Anonymous Conqueror first published in 1556 are among the rare examples of such illustrations in 16th-century books. Fanciful portraits of Moctezuma (fig. 16) and the Inca Atahualpa published by Thevet in 1584 incorporate authentic details of costume based on Codex Mendoza, which Thevet owned.[2] To these examples might be added some of the engravings published by Valadés in Italy in 1579, one of which inspired the famous frontispiece in Torquemada's *Monarchia indiana*. A few further examples might be cited but most 16th- and 17th-century depictions in European books are simply imaginative or romantic; even those by Valadés, believed to be the son of an Indian mother, are so influenced by Renaissance classicism that their Mexican subjects are almost unrecognizable.[3] Illustrations in 16th-century Mexican books are almost exclusively concerned with Catholic religious themes (fig. 17).[4]

Religious art of the early colonial period, whether by Indians or Spaniards, often includes forms and elements of style that may be compared with colonial Indian manuscripts in the census. The recently uncovered allegorical convent murals at Ixmiquilpan, Hidalgo, contain numerous traditional Indian motifs. The Franciscan murals at Huexotzingo, Puebla, and elsewhere typify the colonial art of Mexico that influenced the artists of Códice de Tlatelolco and the Matrícula de Huexotzingo. At Tecamachalco, Puebla, the vault below the choir is covered with paintings on amatl paper (a distinctively Indian medium) by an Indian, Juan Gerson, that exhibit no traits of Indian composition or subject matter. Such examples lie outside the scope of the census and are mentioned only to indicate that the manuscripts in the census are but one source for the study of colonial Indian paintings and drawings.

Among preconquest sources of Indian paintings on media other than manuscripts there is an increasingly large body of murals and painted ceramics and a relatively small number of paintings on stone available for study. Murals from Santa Rita in British Honduras, Tulum in Yucatan, Teotihuacan in the Valley of Mexico, Tizatlan in Tlaxcala, and Mitla in Oaxaca are prominent examples that to one degree or another are comparable to preconquest manuscript painting. The notable Maya murals at Bonampak, Chiapas, and Chichen Itza, Yucatan, are examples of Maya painting that contrast strongly with the hieroglyphic writing of the three surviving Maya screenfold books.[5] From an archaeological discovery in Coahuila there is a painted piece of bark paper comparable to the Huaxtec murals at Tamuin, San Luis Potosi (Weitlaner de Johnson, 1959, fig. 38).

[2] The Weiditz drawings are reproduced in Weiditz (1927) and in Cline (1969b). Some of the drawings from the *Historia general y natural de las Indias* by Gonzalo Fernández de Oviedo y Valdés were first published by Ramusio (1556). The same work contains the first edition of the account of the Anonymous Conqueror and one of the many versions of the Nuremberg map that appeared in the 16th century. Bibliographical studies of the Nuremberg map are given by Carrera Stampa (1949b) and by Toussaint, Gómez de Orozco, and Fernández (1938). The portraits of Moctezuma and Atahualpa are published in Thevet (1584, ff. 641, 644).

[3] Both Palomera (1962, p. 216, note 11) and Anders (1965) have noted that details in one of Valadés' illustrations derive from Benzoni's *Historia del Mondo Nuovo* and thus do not even have a Mexican origin.

[4] The engraved title page of the *Constituciones del arzobispado y provincia de la muy insigne y muy leal ciudad de Tenuxtitlan Mexico de la Nueva España* (Mexico, 1556; reproduced in García Icazbalceta, 1954, pl. 36) contains the arms of the archbishopric of Mexico and an adaptation of the native place sign for Tenochtitlan (a stone and a nopal cactus).

[5] Details from most of the preconquest and colonial murals mentioned are reproduced in Edwards (1966).

Aztec low-relief sculpture, Mixteca-Puebla "tipo códice" pottery, Late Classic Maya polychrome ceramics decorated in figural styles (such as Chama Polychrome), and certain types of Ulua Polychrome pottery with human processional scenes from western Honduras are among other archaeological sources which afford material for iconographic or stylistic comparisons with the manuscript art.

The manuscript paintings and drawings of ancient and colonial Mesoamerica are at once a body of art—though few of the colonial examples are fine works of art—and a corpus of documentary ethnohistorical sources for the study of both periods. Few studies exist that have analyzed them from either point of view.

The manuscripts have frequently occupied a section in general studies of pre-Columbian art such as Kelemen (1943), Toscano (1944), Tentori (1961), and Kubler (1962). The most significant art-historical analysis in depth is that of colonial manuscripts from the Valley of Mexico by Donald Robertson (1959). This pioneer work, which will be cited frequently in these pages, makes important contributions (among other subjects) to such stylistic topics as page composition, perspective, and the treatment of space, line, color, and human and other forms in the colonial manuscripts. These are contrasted with preconquest practices in the Mixtec region, and the history, development, and decline of the colonial manuscript art are treated in detail. The definition of regional stylistic schools and their characteristics within the Valley of Mexico is an especially useful and important contribution that will affect future studies. The distinction that he draws between frame line and contour line is a useful analytical tool. The former is a line of unvarying width that defines form by outline and is the hallmark of the pure native style. Acculturated manuscripts utilize the European contour line that defines forms by

illusion through suggestive changes in width, continuity, and other traits. Of similar importance are his definitions of "scattered attributes" and "spaceless landscape" as traits of native style.[6]

Historiographic critique of the pictorial manuscripts—the analysis of their significance, contexts, and interrelationships—has been limited. Most broad efforts in this direction have usually been restricted to topical listings and simple generalizations. Certain notable exceptions are Kubler and Gibson's (1951) study of the sources on the 365-day calendar and the now outdated survey of the historical manuscripts by Radin (1920).

The depth and quality of Mexican ethnohistorical research will undoubtedly be related to the extent to which it can identify and make use of its sources. The present survey and census of one category of these sources—the visual record of human activity in ancient and colonial Mesoamerica for the period a century before and after the conquest—is intended as a contribution to the basis for the synthesizing and interpretive historiographic literature that currently is so lacking in Mesoamerican ethnohistorical studies. The regional and typological classifications and listings, around which the survey is organized, serve as a systematized guide to the manuscripts in the census.

NOMENCLATURE AND FORMAT TERMINOLOGY

Since the late 19th century archaeologists and other students of Mesoamerica have used the word "codex" or "códice" to designate any pictorial (or written) manuscript

---

[6] Earlier studies in art and style criticism in this field are Hoerschelmann (1922) and Sydow (1941). Gómez de Orozco (1939a) and Margáin Araujo (1943) are more popular treatments. An important but topically restricted analysis of central Mexican festival calendars is given by Kubler and Gibson (1951). Robertson's study of the *pinturas* of the *Relaciones geográficas* (Article 6) contrasts and summarizes preconquest and colonial styles of manuscript painting.

7

in the native tradition. In titles the word has been used in connection with the names of former owners (Codex Borgia), discoverers (Codex Nuttall), patrons (Códice Baranda), presumed provenience (Códice de Tlatelolco), location (Codex Dresden), or for some feature of content. It has been used without reference to the form of the manuscript and has thus been applied indiscriminately to preconquest screenfolds, to large paintings on cloth, to manuscripts in the form of a European book, and to isolated pages. The words "mapa" and "pintura" were similarly used by both Indians and Spaniards throughout the colonial period. In European biblical, classical, and library usages the term codex designates a manuscript book and, specifically, a gathering of leaves or signatures sewn along one side. Except in titles, the word is so used throughout the present work.

Present information indicates that the form or format of preconquest Mesoamerican manuscripts did not include the codex form in the sense just defined. Early colonial and preconquest manuscripts include the tira, the screenfold, the roll, the lienzo, and the single-panel formats. These terms require definition.

Tira. The tira is a manuscript painted or drawn on a long and relatively narrow strip composed of sheets of animal hide or paper glued together. It may be folded or rolled and may be read up, down, to the left, or to the right. More than 20 documents in the census have this format. Codices Baranda, Fernández Leal, Moctezuma, Saville, and de Tlatelolco are prominent examples. Some of this type that are now folded may once have been rolled.

Screenfold. The screenfold is a manuscript painted on a tira and folded, accordion-pleat-fashion, like a screen. The composition of individual pages may make allowance for the folds between each page so that the paintings do not run across the fold; otherwise, the manuscript is a tira

folded screenfold-fashion. Most screenfolds are composed horizontally; Códice de Azoyu no. 2, reverse, and Codex Selden are composed vertically. In some examples the composition of pages is such that they must be read boustrophedon- or meander-fashion. Screenfolds such as the Mixtec Codex Nuttall have guidelines for this purpose. The screenfold is the typical format of surviving preconquest Mesoamerican pictorial manuscripts. It may be made of amatl paper or skin and some examples have wooden or skin covers. The screenfold format has also been reported as a cultural trait from Europe, China, and southeastern Asia, where it is still used as a vehicle for Buddhist literature.

In a screenfold with an even number of leaves the covers (or blank exterior pages of the folded document) will fall on the same side of the document, and the number of pages on one side will be two less than on the other. When there is an odd number of leaves, the covers will fall on opposite sides of the document and the number of pages on each side will be the same. When the top of the pages on one side is along the same edge as the top of the pages on the other ("head-to-head"), and the manuscript is read in the same direction on both sides, the first page of one side will fall at the opposite end of the strip from the first page of the other side. When the top of the pages on one side falls along the bottom edge of the pages on the other side ("head-to-foot"), and the document is read in the same direction on both sides, the initial pages of each side will fall at the same end of the strip. Only when there are no covers and the pages exposed on the exterior when the manuscript is folded are painted, will terminal or initial pages of one side fall on the same leaf as those on the other.

Few published descriptions of screenfolds have taken cognizance of the variables that determine their particular realization of this rather complex form. These variables are: (1) the number of leaves including blank

8

leaves (and pages), (2) the presence or absence of covers or of blank exterior pages, (3) whether or not the pages are head-to-head or head-to-foot, (4) the direction it is read on both sides, and (5) the location of the first page of each side with respect to the cover (adjacent thereto or on the reverse thereof) or to the first exterior leaf (thereon or on the reverse thereof). In all cases the number of leaves given for a screenfold should include the covers. Accurate facsimile editions, of course, obviate the necessity of such description, but such information is unavailable for those that have not had such editions.

There are somewhat more than 24 screenfolds in the census. Eleven from Oaxaca and the five of the Borgia Group are all on skin. Two from Guerrero, three from the Maya region, the Tonalamatl Aubin from Tlaxcala, Codices Borbonicus and Boturini, and the Tira de Tepechpan from the Valley of Mexico are on paper.[7]

Roll. The roll is a tira that has been rolled rather than folded. The form loses its identity once it is folded and is rare. The Selden Roll and Codex Tulane, both from Western Oaxaca, are of this type.

Lienzo. The lienzo is a sheet of cloth, frequently of considerable size. In Spanish art-historical usage the word is similar to the English word "canvas." The lienzo is usually made of narrow strips of cloth sewn together; they may be of cotton, maguey fiber, or other material. No preconquest lienzo survives, but there is no doubt that it was also a preconquest form.

About 50 lienzos are reported in the census. They are most common from Oaxaca, Veracruz, and Michoacan; rare in surviving documents from the state of Mexico and the Distrito Federal; absent from Southeastern Mexico and Guatemala and Hidalgo. The

lienzo is the common medium for maps and documents recording village history and boundaries, especially those of the cartographic-historical type. During the later colonial period the use of European paper replaced it, much as the European form of book supplanted the screenfold.

No specific term designates the single panel or single sheet of animal hide or paper. One such example, Aubin Manuscript no. 20, is painted on a single panel of animal hide and is considered of preconquest date. There are numerous examples in the census of colonial manuscripts painted or drawn on a single expanse of paper; the single panel may be composed of various sheets of paper glued, sewn, or pressed together. Isolated leaves, pages, and fragments, frequently torn from a larger manuscript or removed from a codex, are commonplace among colonial documents.

The word "mapa," like the word "codex," has come to have a broad usage in titles, not necessarily referring to a map in the cartographic sense. As used in titles in the census the word has occasionally been substituted for the word "lienzo" when the document in question is on paper rather than on cloth or when the material of an original known only through a copy is unknown. In most cases it refers only to a single-panel manuscript.

PICTURE AND HIEROGLYPHIC WRITING

The present survey, census, and bibliography of Mesoamerican pictorial manuscripts are primarily concerned with their location, history, provenience, content, publication, commentaries, and bibliography bearing on these subjects. The interpretation of picture and hieroglyphic writing is a subject not specifically treated nor is its literature cited except when it bears on particular manuscripts.

Outside the Maya region (see "Southeastern Mexico and Guatemala," the last section in this survey, for comment on hiero-

---

[7] Lack of precise figures here is due to incomplete information and the difficulty in particular cases of distinguishing between tira and screenfold formats from deficient publications and descriptions.

glyphic writing in that region), the pictorial manuscript writing systems of Mexico are pictographic and ideographic. Place and personal names utilize a conventionalized rebus writing, a trait that, while also a preconquest one, is particularly developed in colonial manuscripts. The literature on the subject thus consists of generalizations, identification of specific signs, symbols, or "glyphs," and catalogs of their types. Few general works on Mexican archaeology have failed to give a brief exposition of the subject.

The identification of place glyphs and of their component rebus elements is a subject that has been well studied, frequently in connection with the etymology of Nahuatl place names. It has been greatly facilitated by the fact that in manuscripts having large numbers of such glyphs there are contemporary identifying glosses in Spanish or Nahuatl. Perhaps the earliest of such studies is that by Aubin (1849 and other editions) on Codex Vergara and other manuscripts in his collection. Orozco y Berra (1880) is another author who published numerous place and other glyphs. The compilation by Peñafiel (1885), based largely on Codex Mendoza and the Matrícula de Tributos, deserves mention. Its later enlargement (Peñafiel, 1897c), based on more than 20 manuscripts and on a collection of such glyphs made by J. F. Ramírez, is the standard dictionary of place glyphs. Barlow and McAfee (1949) give a dictionary of rebus elements derived from Codex Mendoza; Dibble (1940a) provides one based on Codex Xolotl. Nowotny (1959) has also contributed to Codex Mendoza place glyphs as have the authors of commentaries thereon cited in the census. For general comments on the subject see Dibble (1940a, 1955).

The decipherment of the Mixtec place glyphs has, until recently, proceeded very slowly but progress is now being made. Commentaries by Alfonso Caso on the major Western Oaxaca screenfolds and lienzos

contain a number of specific identifications as does the study by M. E. Smith (1966a).

The personal name glyphs for major personages in Aztec history are well identified (as in Codex Mendoza itself). The outstanding problems are in colonial names, particularly of Spaniards. Arreola (1920) comments on the subject of Spanish names and Seler in his study of the Humboldt Fragments (1893, 1902e, 1904f) and Codex Kingsborough (1915) also treats it. Galarza (1964, 1967) has identified the system utilized for given Christian and saints' names. Persons represented in some manuscripts, as from Puebla and Western Oaxaca, frequently have both personal and calendrical name glyphs; the latter can be read directly without any particular problems.

There is a large literature concerned with the identification of calendrical signs, especially day, month, and year glyphs. Seler (1902j), Waterman (1916), and García Granados (1942) are standard sources on day and year glyphs. Month glyphs are rare; their major occurrences are in Humboldt Fragment 1, Códice de Azoyu no. 2 (reverse), Matrícula de Tributos, Codex Ríos, some of the Códices de Tlaquiltenango, Veytia Calendar Wheel no. 4, and in manuscripts containing 18-month calendars (see Table 8). The bibliography given in the census for these manuscripts contains relevant identifications. Caso (1967, p. 36) and Kubler and Gibson (1951, fig. 11) illustrate examples of Central Mexican month glyphs.

The pictorial representation of the calendar and the 260-day divinatory almanac presents various problems in reading their graphic structure as do the symbolic systems surrounding particular rituals and ceremonies. The major studies of the Borgia Group manuscripts (treated separately in the survey), especially Nowotny (1961b), all contribute to this subject. The iconography of gods and their attributes has been the subject of a recent study by Spranz (1964) which systematizes the earlier work contained in the commentaries by Eduard Seler.

There have been numerous studies of particular types of pictorial forms. Aztec costumes and insignia are treated by Seler (1904b, 1904c); animals by Seler (1923) and Tozzer and Allen (1910); colonial land measurement units by Cline (1966a, 1972); Christian and phonetic symbolism by Galarza (1966); and the maguey plant by Gonçalves de Lima (1956). Numerous studies have treated Central Mexican numerals. This quite incomplete listing ignores important contributions contained in commentaries on specific manuscripts.

Glosses in such manuscripts as Codex Mendoza and Códice Osuna serve to identify many minor pictorial forms, particularly drawings of items of tribute—one of the most common types of forms in the colonial manuscripts. The works of Eduard Seler, including many not cited in the bibliography but published in his *Gesammelte Abhandlungen* (1902–23), are basic to any investigation into the identification of pictorial forms. His study of the Humboldt Fragments, previously cited, treats many minor forms. The collected works of Hermann Beyer, now in the course of publication, are of comparable importance to Central Mexican symbolism. Most works in this field are listed by Bernal (1962, pp. 143–68).

ORIGINS OF THE EXTANT MANUSCRIPTS

The typological classification presented in a subsequent section reflects the wide variety of topics represented in the extant pictorial manuscripts of Mesoamerica. No less diverse are their origins and the contexts in which they were created and have survived. A brief examination of them is necessary for the understanding of their nature and purposes, fundamental to any historiographic critique. They may be discussed as preconquest survivals, Spanish patronage, native colonial, and mixed colonial.[8] The first two of these categories, and to a certain extent the third as well, embrace manuscripts whose content is primarily concerned with indigenous institutions and customs. The mixed colonial category represents documents relating primarily to the colonial period.[9] In discussing the manuscripts of mixed colonial origin we comment on certain archival relationships.

Preconquest Survivals

Only a few pictorial manuscripts of preconquest date have survived the ravages of conquest, neglect, time and the political upheavals so devastating to the archives of all nations (see Table 1). Others were no doubt destroyed by, or hidden from, the systematic extirpation of native idolatry pursued during the 16th century by the authorities of the Inquisition.

From Central Mexico there is no manuscript of undisputed preconquest date. Codex Borbonicus and Tonalamatl Aubin are two ritual-calendrical manuscripts that exhibit attributes of preconquest style and composition but their dating is either controversial or in doubt.

The five ritual-calendrical manuscripts of the Borgia Group are universally conceded to antedate the conquest. It is no accident that they have survived through having reached Europe at an early date. Their provenience remains a matter of controversy but may be placed somewhere in the Puebla–Tlaxcala–Western Oaxaca region.

From Western Oaxaca the historical genealogies of the Mixtecs include an uncertain number of preconquest manuscripts. Among them are some of the skin screenfolds of the Nuttall Group: Codices Becker no. 1, Bodley, Colombino, Nuttall, and Vienna. Codex Selden would be considered preconquest on

---

[8] These distinctions and some of the ideas elaborated here have been stimulated by a comparable discussion by Robertson (1959, pp. 25–58).

[9] A distinction between manuscripts treating preconquest and colonial institutions is implied in the selective catalog by León-Portilla and Mateos Higuera (1957), which is limited to manuscripts in the former category.

TABLE 1—PRECONQUEST PICTORIAL MANUSCRIPTS OF MIDDLE AMERICA

The numbers in the first column in all tables are the census numbers as listed in Article 23. Ownership and location are indicated at the date of the first notice of their existence.

Manuscript	Date	Owner and Location
Central Mexico:		
15 Tonalamatl Aubin*	1743	Lorenzo Boturini, Mexico City[1]
32 Codex Borbonicus*	1777	El Escorial monastery, Madrid[2]
Borgia Group:		
33 Codex Borgia	1792–97	Cardinal Stephano Borgia, Rome[3]
79 Codex Cospi	1665	Ferdinando Cospi, Bologna, Italy[4]
118 Codex Féjérváry-Mayer	1829	Gabriel Féjérváry, Pest, Hungary[5]
185 Codex Laud	1636	William Laud, Oxford, England[6]
384 Codex Vaticanus B	1589	Vatican Library, Rome[7]
Western Oaxaca:		
14 Aubin Manuscript no. 20	1743	Lorenzo Boturini, Mexico City[8]
27 Codex Becker no. 1	1852	Pascual Almazán, Puebla, Mexico[9]
31 Codex Bodley	1603–05	Sir Thomas Bodley, Oxford, England[10]
72 Códice Colombino	1717	Local cacique, Tututepec, Oaxaca[11]
240 Codex Nuttall	1859	Dominican monastery of San Marco, Florence, Italy[12]
395 Codex Vienna	1521	King Emmanuel I of Portugal[13]
Maya region:		
113 Codex Dresden	1739	Johann Christian Götze, Vienna[14]
187 Codex Madrid:		
a. Códice Cortesiano	1867	Juan Palacios, Madrid[15]
b. Códice Troano	1866	Juan de Tro y Ortolano, Madrid[16]
247 Codex Paris	1829–37	Bibliothèque Imperiale, Paris[17]

* Date (preconquest or colonial) in dispute.

[1] Boturini collection inventory of 1743, no. 6-23 (P. López, 1925, p. 41).

[2] Examined by Waddilove in the Escorial (W. Robertson, 1778, 2: 477–78). Possibly listed in earlier inventories of the Escorial (Zarco Cuevas, 1924–29, 3: 474–75, no. 5; pp. 552–53, no. 13, the latter of 1600).

[3] Approximate date of the commentary by Fábrega (died 1797) in which a work of 1792 is cited. The editor of Barthelemy (1798) states that his notice was written in 1771 or shortly after Fábrega's arrival in Italy. Borson (1796) also refers to the manuscript.

[4] Inscription on the manuscript gives date acquired by Cospi from Valerio Zani (Lehmann, 1905a, p. 255).

[5] Copied by Aglio about this date (Lehmann, 1905a, pp. 256–57).

[6] Accession date by the Bodleian Library during Laud's life; intimates of Laud were in Spain in 1623 (Lehmann, 1905a, pp. 257–58).

[7] Possibly mentioned in a work of this date (Mercati, 1589). Lehmann speculates that it may have been acquired during the time that Cardinal Amulio was librarian, 1565–70. First unequivocal reference is an inventory of 1596–1600 (Lehmann, 1905a, pp. 253–54).

[8] Boturini collection inventory of 1743, no 6-24 (Lehmann, 1905a, p. 258).

[9] Date of copy made by Saussure. Almazán was an attorney and is said to have received the original from an Indian whom he represented (Lehmann, 1905a, pp. 259–60).

[10] Approximate date of accession by Bodleian Library, founded by Bodley in 1602 (Lehmann, 1905a, pp. 258, 271).

[11] Utilized in litigation in Jamiltepec, Oaxaca, by Indian owner (M. E. Smith, 1963, pp. 283–84). Subsequently claimed to have been seen about 1863 in Manuel Cardoso collection, Puebla, by Chavero (1901c, p. 4).

[12] Date purchased by John Temple Leader (British Museum, 1933, pp. 141–43).

[13] Emmanuel I died in 1521; his ownership is indicated by an inscription on the manuscript, believed to have been sent to Charles V of Spain, together with the Codex Nuttall, by Cortés in 1519 (Lehmann, 1905a, pp. 267–70).

[14] Date of acquisition from unknown source in Vienna (Götze, 1743–44, 1: 1–5; Förstemann, 1880).

[15] Offered in sale to the then Imperial Library of Paris (Núñez y Domínguez, 1947a, p. 360).

[16] Shown to Brasseur de Bourbourg in the Royal Academy of History, Madrid (Brasseur de Bourbourg, 1869–70, 1: iii).

[17] Copied by Aglio for Lord Kingsborough (died 1837) about this time; first clear published reference is by Aubin (1849). J. F. Ramírez (1855) seems to have had data indicating its purchase in 1832. It may have been part of the accession reported by Anonymous (1829, 1830a, 1830b).

the same stylistic grounds if there were not positive evidence for dating it close to the middle of the 16th century.

From the lowland Maya region three ritual-calendrical screenfolds—Codices Dresden, Paris, and Madrid—are preconquest and are the only Maya pictorial manuscripts extant aside from certain minor colonial documents.[10]

The inventory of preconquest manuscripts is thus small: perhaps 16 in all, probably less, hardly more. Most, by happy circumstance, are ritual-calendrical in content; the others are historical and genealogical. For all other categories of preconquest manuscripts scholarship is faced with substantially later redactions of the colonial period.

The history of the 16 possibly preconquest manuscripts is very poorly known. For several of the examples in Europe it does not extend even into the 18th century. Two of the 16 are believed to have been sent to Europe before the conquest was concluded, and there is no compelling reason to doubt that 12 of the 16 may not have reached Europe early in the 16th century. Of the remaining four, two first appear in Mexico in the 18th century in the Boturini collection, suggesting a history of successive Mexican collectors. The other two (Codices Becker no. 1 and Colombino, probably fragments of the same original manuscript) appear to derive directly out of Indian possession after 1850.

Spanish Patronage

Ranking only second in importance and content to the preconquest survivals are the manuscripts produced under Spanish patronage of the pictorial manuscript art (see Table 2). Renaissance Europe in the 16th century was vastly curious about the New

TABLE 2—SELECTED LIST OF PICTORIAL MANUSCRIPTS AND ILLUSTRATED TEXTS COPIED OR PRODUCED UNDER SPANISH PATRONAGE

Crónica X Group:
114 DURAN: Historia de las Indias
365 TOVAR: Códice Ramírez
366 TOVAR: Historia de la Benida

Drawings by the informants of Sahagún:
271 SAHAGUN: Primeros Memoriales
274 SAHAGUN: Florentine Codex

Huitzilopochtli Group:
270 Codex Ríos
308 Codex Telleriano-Remensis

Magliabecchiano Group:
171 Codex Ixtlilxochitl, part 1
188 Codex Magliabecchiano
229 Códice del Museo de América

Ceremonies of the 18 months:
205 Kalendario Mexicano, Latino y Castellano
364 The Tovar Calendar

Tribute of the Triple Alliance:
196 Codex Mendoza, part 2
368 Matrícula de Tributos

Calendar wheels:
272 Sahagún Calendar Wheel
388 Veytia Calendar Wheel no. 2

Miscellaneous manuscripts:
85 CRUZ: Libellus de Medicinalibus . . .
172 Codex Ixtlilxochitl, part 2
196 Codex Mendoza, parts 1 and 3
213 Relación de Michoacán
280 Santa Cruz Map of the City and Valley of Mexico

---

[10] A more detailed discussion of dating would require a distinction between manuscripts wholly unaffected by European influence but painted after the conquest and those having an equally pure native style painted before the conquest. Theoretically, a matter of days or a few years might be crucial and certainly removed from the possibilities of available methods of analysis. Whether or not the style of a manuscript exhibits European influence, regardless of its date in these terms, is more subject to analysis even though equally debatable. The latter is as much at issue in the case of Codex Borbonicus as is its date.

The ramifications of preconquest/postconquest and native style/acculturated style possibilities are considerable. The case of Codex Selden is one that we have mentioned; a native style/postconquest example. The Matrícula de Tributos is in native style but its format is European. It is also possible that there are manuscripts whose colonial dating *may* be based on later additions and the base manuscript conceivably painted before the conquest or at least free of European influence. This may be true of the Plano en Papel de Maguey. There are also manuscripts whose date and style have not been determined.

World. Spanish historians responded by producing a long series of works on native history and customs as well as of the history of conquest, exploration, and politics of the new colonial world. Eventually Spain appointed chroniclers of the Indies whose appetite for documentary source material was insatiable.

The Spanish Crown and its organ, the Council of the Indies, through which Charles V and Philip II and later sovereigns governed their far-flung empire, demanded of its distant administrators all manner of statistical and descriptive reports. They were made in response to the widest range of inquiry. The *descripciones* and *relaciones* that were sent to Europe enriched the libraries and archives of Spain.

The Church was faced with problems of converting a whole population and destroying a highly organized religion in New Spain. Faced with the subtle merging of native symbolism into the elaborate paraphernalia of Catholic ritual, it soon realized the necessity for systematic investigation of native customs and religions.

The result was that both the secular and religious authorities were confronted with the need to commission investigations into Indian life. The motivation was intellectual, practical, and administrative. Spanish patronage of such research was thus promoted by the viceregal authority as well as by the Church though the distinction, in practice, is largely technical and frequently inseparable. The broad range of inquiry, covering almost the entire spectrum of Indian life, was explicitly directed toward preconquest rather than colonial patterns. The pictorial manuscripts collected and sought by individual Spanish investigators include copies of preconquest and colonial manuscripts and drawings created *de novo*.

Viceregal patronage of what may be termed ethnographic research produced, through the agency of the first viceroy, Codex Mendoza, named after him, and the

Relación de Michoacan. The former is a manuscript of composite content and an important product of the pictorial art of colonial Tenochtitlan. The Matrícula de Tributos, a copy in European format of the tribute register of Moctezuma's "Empire," may have been sponsored prior to the establishment of viceregal government (1535). The investigations pursued later in the century by Tovar, with whom two extant series of native-based paintings are associated, were also commissioned by a viceroy.

It was the research of the mendicant Orders, particularly the Franciscans, that produced the most patronage of native manuscript painters. The Colegio de la Santa Cruz in Tlatelolco, an academy for Indians founded by Franciscans, is associated with several major manuscripts including the Santa Cruz Map of the City and Valley of Mexico, the Libellus de Medicinalibus Indorum Herbis by Martín de la Cruz, and Códice de Tlatelolco.[11] Sahagún, the foremost of the missionary scholars, assembled a group of native informants whose work produced the illustrations in the Primeros Memoriales and the Florentine Codex.

Two important groups of pictorial manuscripts have yet to be adequately identified as to the source which produced them. These are the Huitzilopochtli and Magliabecchiano Groups.[12] Both sets or their immediate prototypes were evidently painted by Indians for Spaniards who added their comments in the gloss. The Magliabecchiano Group is closely connected with Cervantes de Salazar, commissioned to write a history of New Spain by the Spanish cabildo of Mexico City in 1558. The manuscripts of both groups have a similar outline of content: a ritual-calendrical section, a section

[11] Robertson (1959) defines and discusses the "school" of manuscript painting associated with the Colegio de la Santa Cruz.

[12] "Groups" of manuscripts are defined in the census (Article 23) and will be found there in alphabetical order.

14

devoted to gods and customs, and portrayals of native types. One of the groups also includes a copied native chronicle.

Further examples of pictorial manuscripts made under such direct or indirect Spanish patronage are cited in Table 2. The importance of the manuscripts so produced by the artists, despite possible selection and editing of data to cater to Spanish patronage, is considerable. For the Valley of Mexico, where this patronage was most important, such manuscripts include practically all of the known pictorial depictions of ritual-calendrical material; some are painted in relatively unacculturated style. Another characteristic of these manuscripts is that they almost alone are directly ethnographic in that they contain explicit sections devoted to gods (outside of calendrically structured contexts), customs, and portrayals of native types.

In historiographic terms the manuscripts produced by Spanish patronage present complex problems. Often of composite content, they may derive from synthetic interpretations of divergent native traditions. The understanding of their relationships to the texts of the Spanish historians who utilized or annotated them requires subtle points of comparison and analysis, little of which have been published. Several versions for certain of the manuscripts exist; these were available to successive commentators and passed through the hands of various collectors. For some, sent to Europe in the 16th century, versions remained in Mexico, apparently in conventual archives. Thus the texts of Codex Mendoza, part 1, and the Florentine Codex continued to be accessible to writers in Mexico through unidentified versions long after the known manuscripts had been sent to Europe.

Native Colonial

Most of the 434 pictorial manuscripts in the census were produced during the early colonial period to serve its everyday needs. Pictorial records of all kinds, painted initially in the older tradition, later in a developing colonial style, and finally in a symbolically degenerate form, were produced throughout the 16th century and served all manner of ends. The usefulness of such documents and their production ceased, for practical purposes, sometime toward the end of the century or the beginning of the 17th century when effective literacy spread to local officials. Such documents of colonial origin may be discussed under two headings, those painted by Indians in perpetuation of older patterns (native colonial) and those destined for use as records of the economic and mundane affairs of the colonial world or in relationship with Spaniards (mixed colonial).[13] The distinction is not absolute; the two categories should not be viewed as mutually exclusive. A selected list of native colonial documents is given in Table 3.

The destruction of pagan books was a prime aim of the missionary church in New Spain. Bishop Zumárraga, in the role of inquisitor into idolatrous practices, has been singled out by history as the symbol of such book-burning practices.[14] His counterpart in Yucatan was Bishop Landa. The divinatory almanacs and calendars in native possession were sought and destroyed; their ownership created positive hazards for their Indian owners. It is thus no accident that practically all of the known ritual-calendrical pictorial manuscripts exist only in versions promptly sent to Spain as curiosity pieces or in redactions made under the forgiving and permissive license of Spanish patronage. As a consequence of this situation there are in existence today hardly any ritual or divinatory pictorial manuscripts painted during

[13] Kubler (1961, p. 22) describes the entire corpus of the Mexica-Tenochca pictorial manuscripts as "explants," i.e., organisms surviving in a foreign or artificial environment.

[14] For one of many discussions of this point see García Icazbalceta (1947, 2: 87–162). For Zumárraga as inquisitor, see Greenleaf (1961).

TABLE 3—SELECTED LIST OF NATIVE
COLONIAL PICTORIAL MANUSCRIPTS

Manuscripts whose content in whole or in part
treats preconquest events and institutions and
which exhibit traits of style, format, or composition
painted in perpetuation of traditional patterns.
Some of these are copies of preconquest originals.

Valley of Mexico:

13 Codex Aubin
20 Códice Azcatitlan
30 Boban Calendar Wheel
34 Códice Boturini
84 Códice en Cruz
189 Plano en Papel de Maguey
207 Codex Mexicanus (BNP 23–24)
263 Mapa Quinatzin
290 Mapa Sigüenza
317 Tira de Tepechpan
356 Mapa Tlotzin
412 Códice Xolotl

Central Mexico:

21–22 Códices de Azoyu nos. 1 and 2
94–96 Mapas de Cuauhtinchan nos. 1–3
135 Códice de Huamantla
142 Códice de Huichapan
147 Humboldt Fragment 1
359 Historia Tolteca-Chichimeca
369 Anales de Tula

Northern and Western Oaxaca:

8 Lienzo Antonio de León
28 Codex Becker no. 2
70 Lienzo de Coixtlahuaca no. 1
71 Lienzo de Coixtlahuaca no. 2
119 Códice Fernández Leal
157 Lienzo de Santiago Ihuitlan
232 Lienzo de Santa Maria Nativitas
255 Códice Porfirio Díaz
283 Codex Selden
284 Selden Roll
422 Lienzo de Zacatepec no. 1

the colonial period for Indian use. To a lesser
degree the same is true of calendrical manuscripts since the distinction between idolatrous (forbidden augural and pantheistic)
and calendrical (permitted secular time
count) manuscripts was difficult to maintain.[15]

Ritual manuscripts of the colonial period
—excepting those made under Spanish patronage—may be listed: Codex Borbonicus

and Tonalamatl Aubin (but note that their
date and freedom from Spanish patronage
are debatable points), a section of Códice
Porfirio Díaz, and certain pages of the curious and late Codex Mexicanus (BNP 23–
24).[16]

It is beyond dispute that the Indians of
Central Mexico had a strong sense of tribal
history, which could be expressed through
chronicled records. Throughout the first 50
years of the colonial period the Indians of
the Valley of Mexico continued to develop
this historical consciousness both for the establishment of their own historical legitimacy and claims and for the edification of
the curious Spaniard. As a consequence a
sizable body of pictorial, textual, or combined picture-text chronicles are extant today; no Spanish prohibition existed for their
production and use.[17] Notable copied annals treating preconquest events exist in the
pictorial manuscripts made under Spanish
patronage. A comparable series exists in
manuscripts that were not made under such
influence. Among them are Codices Boturini, Xolotl, and Azcatitlan, whose content
and sometimes style and format as well must
reflect their preconquest models. Also in this
category are histories cast as maps such as
Mapas Sigüenza, Tlotzin, and de Cuauhtinchan nos. 1–3, the latter from Puebla. Annals
of events of the colonial period, sometimes

[15] In a famous passage Sahagún charged another
Franciscan (Motolinía, apparently) with promul-
gating the depiction of a 260-day cycle (see Veytia
Calendar Wheel no. 2) as calendrical, whereas he
contended that it was idolatrous, divinatory, and
noncalendrical.

[16] Since Indian ritual manuscripts seem not to be
forthcoming from Indian possession, it would appear that those secreted from the Inquisition must
have perished. Conceivably Tonalamatl Aubin,
Aubin Manuscript no. 20, and the Codex Paris may
have been in Indian hands throughout the 16th
century, but this is conjectural.

[17] Among wholly textual sources are examples of
17th- and 18th-century native chronicles, some
little more than diaries of religious, secular, and
personal events. The span of these documents is
greater than single lifetimes, indicating different
authors or copying of older annals.

incorporating copied preconquest sections, include Codices Aubin and Mexicanus (BNP 23–24), and Tira de Tepechpan.

Historical manuscripts from other regions of Central Mexico dating from the colonial period but made in perpetuation of older patterns were also painted. The Códices de Azoyu and the Historia Tolteca-Chichimeca, from Guerrero and Puebla respectively, are notable examples of colonial annals that also include significant bodies of copied preconquest data. From the Maya region we have only the Books of Chilam Balam, 18th-century redactions of older material which unfortunately are almost exclusively textual. Their pictorial antecedents are at best conjectural.

Another and significant corpus of native colonial documents are those associated in one way or another with village titles. The most interesting are those of the cartographic-historical type, best known through examples from outside the Valley of Mexico but wholly unrepresented by extant versions from the Maya regions. The nature of these manuscripts, equivalent to village charters, is discussed in the definition of typological categories. They were not produced for Spanish consumption; in Western Oaxaca, especially, extant versions are probably close to preconquest prototypes in both style and composition.

Combining features of both the historical and cartographic-historical types are certain commemorative historical documents. Among them are Lienzo de Tlaxcala, Mapa de Cuauhtlantzinco, and Lienzo de Cuauhquechollan and perhaps such Eastern Oaxaca examples as Lienzo de San Miguel Tiltepec and Lienzo de San Juan Tabaa no. 1. They portray historical events glorifying and commemorating local or regional events such as the Spanish conquest, the first baptism, etc., and were evidently intended for public display.

Pictorial manuscripts in other categories —genealogies, economic records, maps, and miscellaneous drawings—continued to be produced for Indian use in great abundance during the 16th century. Except as they may include copied preconquest data or utilize older patterns of composition, however, they are generally indistinguishable from those discussed under the "mixed colonial" heading below. Manuscripts painted in traditional or acculturated styles may be encountered in any of the three colonial sources of manuscripts under discussion.

The history of manuscripts of native colonial origin is also distinct. Preconquest survivals and those produced under Spanish patronage have descended through secular or religious archives since the 16th century and would have remained there had they not been of interest as works of art to collectors. Those of mixed colonial origin owe their survival in large part to their preservation in administrative and litigative records. The native colonial records, on the other hand, are those that have been "collected" directly from their Indian owners. Many of those listed in Table 3 were in Indian possession as recently as the 19th century. Others, which first appear in the Boturini collection, have probable antecedents in the Sigüenza y Góngora and Ixtlilxochitl collections with subsequent descent through the hands of Veytia, León y Gama, Pichardo, Aubin, and Goupil before coming to rest in the Bibliothèque Nationale. Only the two Selden manuscripts may not have been in Indian hands at the end of the 16th century. These general observations are not absolute; both mixed and native colonial documents have formed part of archives as well as having remained in Indian possession.

Mixed Colonial

Pictorial manuscripts of mixed colonial origin account for the majority of manuscripts in the census. It follows that most are concerned with such colonial institutions as encomienda tribute or the proof of land titles before Spanish courts. Wherever the

Spanish administration treated with Indians on a local level a medium of expression and record was required that was mutually intelligible. Although the interpretation of pictorial materials seems always to have been beyond the competence or interest of Spanish officials, an interpreter served to relate Spaniard, Indian, pictorial document, and written text.[18]

The needs of the viceregal administration (as well as that of the earlier period, 1521–35) and that of the local Indian governments were met by the production of a wide variety of pictorial documents. It was in this context that the manuscripts that we have classed under the broad rubric of economic were prepared. They are the numerous tribute assessments and financial records such as town salaries, registers of tributaries, and cadastral lists of properties (see Table 4). Such manuscripts are most abundant from the Valley of Mexico but are also represented from most other regions of Central Mexico. For the Maya region comparable examples are lacking; there are only several maps forming parts of land titles.

A second context in which pictorial documents were called forth and where the Indian and Spanish worlds met was in litigation. In the uncounted thousands of cases between Indians or between Indian and Spaniard before the Audiencia Real in Mexico City and elsewhere, an untold number of drawings by Indians were submitted as exhibits or in evidence. Their variety includes most known categories of pictorial manu-

[18] The "nahuatlato" or interpreter is a frequent figure in 16th-century documents; not infrequently he was a friar. The need for interpreters of native documents, written or pictorial, continued throughout the colonial period. In the 18th century Rosa y Saldívar was called upon to appraise the Nahuatl texts in the Boturini collection; he is also known for a description of the Lienzo de Yolox. The more ubiquitous Carlos or Manuel Mancio has left 18th-century "interpretations" of the Ordenanza del Señor Cuauhtemoc, the Títulos de Santa Isabel Tola, the Genealogía de la Familia Cano, and the description of a lost pictorial manuscript from Magdalena Mixiuca (*Títulos principales*, 1915).

18

TABLE 4—SELECTED LIST OF MIXED COLONIAL PICTORIAL MANUSCRIPTS

Manuscripts whose content is primarily concerned with colonial events, instituitons, and purposes. In style, composition, or format most of these manuscripts reflect colonial developments out of preconquest traditions. The list is selected for diversity of representation as well as relative importance and artistic interest.

Records of colonial history:
- 89 Lienzo de Cuauhquechollan
- 344 Códice de Tlatelolco
- 350 Lienzo de Tlaxcala

Genealogies:
- 35 Confirmation des Elections de Calpan
- 235 Circular Genealogy . . . Nezahualcoyotl
- 258 Genealogía de los Principes Mexicanos
- 347 Genealogie des Tlatzcantzin
- 427 Genealogía de Zolin

Maps and cartographic-historical documents:
- 41 Lienzo Chalchihuitzin Vásquez
- 68 Mapa de Coatlinchan
- 90 Mapa circular de Cuauhquechollan
- 181 Codex Kingsborough (part)
- 214 Lienzo de Misantla
- 320 Mapa de San Antonio Tepetlan

Economic and land records:
- 11 Códice de Santa Maria Asuncion
- 43 Códice Chavero
- 83 Codex Cozcatzin
- 139 Matrícula de Huexotzingo
- 148, 150 Humboldt Fragments 2 and 6
- 181 Codex Kingsborough (part)
- 193 Códice Mariano Jiménez
- 243 Códice Osuna
- 246 Oztoticpac Lands Map
- 311 Libro de Tributos de San Pablo Teocaltitlan
- 323 Census of Tepoztlan
- 324 Mapa catastral de Tepoztlan, Panhuacan, etc.
- 341 Códice de Tlamapa no. 3
- 386 Codex Vergara
- 407 XOCHIMILCO: Plan de plusiers Propriétés
- 424 Codex Santa Anita Zacatlalmanco

scripts, but the various categories of the economic type were most common.

In the defense of land titles or in other disputes over possessions, the Indians prepared and submitted historical documents and genealogies as well as maps and property plans as proofs of claim for inheritance.

In cases involving grievances over abuses graphic portrayals of the complaints were painted. Documents having such origins, some amounting to pictorial depositions, occasionally contain records of events (history, tribute, genealogy) extending into the preconquest era. Both Codex Cozcatzin and Codex Kingsborough contain such material as well as the litigated subject matter.

An uncertain but significant percentage of all the mixed colonial documents, particularly genealogies, maps, economic documents, and various miscellaneous drawings, have survived through having formed part of the records of colonial litigation and viceregal administration. Yet today most of the more important of these pictorial records are separated from the written texts of the related procedures. In the case of the Archivo General de la Nación, Mexico, the most relevant of all archives of court cases, we may presume—and in some cases it is almost certain—that the pictorial sheets have been removed by collectors who ignored the (to them) less interesting written accompaniment. The removal of such documents, we may speculate, probably began in the 17th century and continued throughout the 18th and 19th centuries. An unknown number may have perished in the fire which destroyed many viceregal records in Mexico in 1692. It was on that occasion during at attempts to save endangered documents that Sigüenza y Góngora acquired parts of his collection. The Boturini and Aubin collections, which were assembled in Mexico 1736–43 and 1830–40, respectively, both have antecedents in the 17th-century collection of Sigüenza y Góngora and probably included many documents formerly in viceregal archives.

The observations concerning the removal of documents from the Archivo General and other viceregal and municipal archives are more than just a matter of bibliographical curiosity. The interpretation of any colonial pictorial manuscript is immeasurably aided and made more significant when it can be placed side by side with contemporary documentation. In a recent case, illustrating the pairing of pictorial documents with related archival material to which we refer, M. E. Smith identified an early 18th-century court case in which Códice Colombino had been submitted in evidence by its Indian owner. The record of the proceedings contains a description, interpretation, and a partial translation of its very difficult glosses. This information led to the decipherment of a major Mixtec place glyph. In this instance, unusual in that the manuscript is a preconquest survival, the document was returned to the owner rather than kept in archival record, but the point remains. In investigations for the present census, relationships between mixed colonial pictorial manuscripts and documentation in the Archivo General are noted for the Genealogía de la Familia Cano, the Códice de los Señores de San Lorenzo Axotlan y San Luís Huexotla, and various equally minor documents from Xochimilco (Census, 403–407).[19] In the latter case the archival documentation served to demonstrate a connection that could be inferred only from the drawings themselves. Further undiscovered examples undoubtedly exist.

RESEARCH AND PUBLICATION

The following overview of the publication and development of research into Meso-

[19] In two of these cases the relationship was discovered by Henry B. Nicholson, possibly with the assistance of Pedro Carrasco. It may also be pointed out that the date of litigation is no clue to the date of documentary evidence; the Lienzos of Zacatepec and Totomixtlahuaca appeared in litigative contexts in 1892 and about 1948, respectively. Public knowledge of the existence of the Lienzos de San Miguel Tequixtepec is owed to the need by the village to prove boundary claims about 1969. These are examples of the still viable legal importance of ancient documents as land titles. We understand that a local district of Mexico City cited the published Codex Santa Anita Zacatlalmanco (now in the Musée de l'Homme) as proving its right over lands wanted by the Distrito Federal for public housing.

american pictorial manuscripts is intended primarily to place selected authors, editions, collections, and events cited in the census into a minimal chronological framework. A review of substantially the same material has been published by Nicholson (1962).

Pictorial manuscripts from Mesoamerica were included by Cortés in his first remission of New World treasures to Spain. Few early accounts of what are now Mexico and Guatemala fail to mention the existence of picture books either as curiosities or as part of the ethnographic picture of Spain's new dominions. The writings of Cortés, Peter Martyr, López de Gómara, Díaz del Castillo, Las Casas, Oviedo, Motolinía, Mendieta, and Acosta, who represent but a sampling of the best-known 16th-century authorities, all describe or refer in passing to pictorial manuscripts. A somewhat later cycle of writers mention such documents from the Maya lowlands.

The 16th century is the period when most of the manuscripts in the census were produced. It would be a tedious and, for the present purpose, a somewhat irrelevant exercise to discuss "research" during that century. Suffice it to say that historians in Mexico during the 16th century both utilized and commissioned pictorial manuscripts in their writings. Sahagún, Durán, Tovar, Valadés, Motolinía, Landa, and de los Ríos as well as the anonymous Franciscan author of the Relación de Michoacan are friars with whom extant drawings based on native originals are associated.

The early years of the 17th century witnessed the first editions of the *Monarchia indiana* by Torquemada (1615) and the *Historia general* by Herrera (1601–15). The former had access to an extensive corpus of native sources, including pictorials, and made use of both (see Article 16). Herrera, writing in Spain, contributed less to the knowledge of native sources but the illustrated title pages to two of his books include details copied from two Central Mexican

20

pictorial manuscripts (see Article 15). Ixtlilxochitl, a contemporary of Torquemada, had an important collection of native manuscripts, some of which, such as Codex Xolotl, were among the sources of his historical writings, unpublished until the 19th century. Later, the manuscript collection owned by Ixtlilxochitl was secured from his heirs by Sigüenza y Góngora, a dominant figure in many fields of Mexican studies in the latter half of the 17th century. It was he who provided the Italian world-traveler, Gemelli Careri, with the illustrations of three different pictorial manuscripts which the latter published in his *Giro del Mondo* in 1700 (Gemelli Careri, 1699–1700; see Census, 172, 290, 390).

The dominant figure of the 18th century is Lorenzo Boturini (fig. 18), an Italian who arrived on the Mexican scene in 1736. He assembled a truly prodigious collection of Indian manuscripts (including part of the Sigüenza y Góngora collection) only to see it confiscated by the viceroy in 1743. He was arrested and deported to Spain for technical reasons in connection with his efforts to crown the Virgin of Guadalupe. In 1746 he published a catalog of his collection. Although absolved of charges against him and appointed a royal chronicler, he was never reunited with his cherished "Museo histórico indiano." His catalog became universally known among all writers on Mexico and was a primary but enigmatic source on Mexican manuscripts for many years. The assembly, inventory, and dispersal of the collection is one of the more significant series of events in the entire history of Mexican ethnohistorical documentation. Further information on his collection is given in Article 29.

The collection itself soon had an impact on the writing of Mexican history. As early as 1750–55 Veytia secured access to it and copied various of its documents, including some of the calendar wheels illustrated in his *Historia del origen . . .* , first published posthumously in 1836 (see Census, 387–393). In 1770 two pictorial documents from the collection were published by Lorenzana (see Census, 368, 391). About 1780 another was copied by Beaumont for his *Crónica de Michoacan*. In 1790 the Viceroy Revillagigedo received orders from Spain calling for copies of various documents, including some from the Boturini collection. The resultant *Colección de memorias de Nueva España* contained little in the way of pictorial manuscripts, but the copying project is nevertheless an important event that is related to the collection formed by the royal historian, Muñoz, and even to the contemporary transfer of selected documents of the Indies from the archive in Simancas to that of Seville.

Possession of some of the more important documents in the Boturini collection was gained by León y Gama, whose heirs, after his death in 1802, further dispersed the collection. His treatise on the Mexican calendar, first published in 1792 and again with extensive added material in 1832, cites and describes some of the documents known to him (see Article 12, Item 97). An important work in its era, it is now mainly of antiquarian interest. Both León y Gama and Pichardo, who also secured documents from the Boturini collection, made copies of many pictorial manuscripts which now, like their originals, are in the Aubin-Goupil collection.

In Italy, Cardinal Borgia commissioned Fábrega, an exiled Jesuit from Mexico, to prepare a commentary on Codex Borgia. Probably written between 1792 and 1797, the work is remarkable primarily for its scholarly restraint and lack of fanciful conjecture; interpretation of Codex Borgia was a major task for Eduard Seler over a hundred years later. In the course of the work (not published until 1899 but widely known in manuscript) Fábrega gives a listing of 11 pictorial manuscripts of which he had notice. All things considered, the listing is a remarkable and pioneer achievement in cataloging.

Other 18th-century scholars deserving mention in this chronological summary are Clavigero and William Robertson. The former, who like Fábrega was an exiled Jesuit from Mexico, is the author of a general history of ancient Mexico first published in Italian in 1780–1781 (see Article 17). Although a consistently overrated secondary source, Clavigero's history circulated widely and his comments and illustrations were often copied. It contained a general section on Indian painting, listed a few manuscript collections, and illustrated details of several pictorial manuscripts from earlier publications. Clavigero's reproductions of calendar wheels, however, are imaginative adaptations of earlier publications. He perhaps deserves credit for having publicized the existence of Codex Cospi.

William Robertson's *History of America* (1777) published a page from Codex Vienna and in a less well known second edition (1778) notified the world of the existence of Codex Borbonicus, then in the Escorial.

By 1814, the approximate publication date of Humboldt's *Vues des Cordillères* (cited as Humboldt, 1810), 14 of the pictorial manuscripts in the present census had been published in whole or in part (see Table 5 and Article 12, Item 99). Humboldt's *Vues*, rare in its own time in the full folio edition, illustrated 10 pictorial manuscripts and details from a number of fragments acquired by him in Mexico in 1803. His collecting activities in Mexico, his rational discussions of the manuscripts, and his international reputation as a scholar probably did much to further interest in Mexican studies.

The years following 1821—three centuries after the fall of Tenochtitlan—were active ones in the field of Mexican pictorial manuscripts. Most fundamental was Mexican independence from Spain, which allowed Europeans other than Spaniards their first free access to Mexico. The first two decades after 1821 saw the founding of the Mexican National Museum, new inventories by the

TABLE 5—PUBLICATION OF PICTORIAL MANUSCRIPTS, 1579–1796

Chronological listing of works in which Middle American pictorial manuscripts were published in whole or in part prior to Humboldt's *Vues des Cordillères* (1810), published about 1814. Second editions and reprintings of these works are not noted.

Editor	Date	Manuscript
Valadés	1579	Veytia Calendar Wheel no. 2, version
Herrera	1601–15	Details from a manuscript of the Magliabecchiano Group and from an unidentified manuscript
Cartari	1615	Codex Ríos, seven details
Purchas	1625	Codex Mendoza
Cartari	1626	Codex Ríos, eight details
Nierembergii	1635	Hernández, Historia natural, selected details
Hernández	1651	Hernández, Historia natural, Italian copies
Kircher	1652–54	Codex Mendoza, selected pages after Purchas
Worm	1655	Codex Vienna, details
Thevenot	1672	Codex Mendoza, after Purchas
Legati	1677	Codex Cospi, details
Lambeck	1679	Codex Vienna, one page
Nessel	1690	Codex Vienna, one page after Lambeck
Gemelli Careri	1699–1700	Mapa Sigüenza; Veytia Calendar Wheel no. 4; Codex Ixtlilxochitl, part 2, selected pages
Warburton	1738–41	Codex Mendoza, one page after Purchas
Boturini	1746	Veytia Calendar Wheel no. 4, after Gemelli
Kollar	1769	Codex Vienna, one page
Lorenzana	1770	Matrícula de Tributos; Veytia Calendar Wheel no. 5
Robertson, W.	1777	Codex Vienna, one page
Granados y Gálvez	1778	Calendar wheel diagrams
Clavigero	1780–81	Details from earlier publications
Racknitz	1796	Codex Dresden, details; details from earlier publications

Mexican government of the now depleted Boturini collection, the loan and subsequent exhibit in London by Bullock of some 17 pictorial manuscripts,[20] and the descent upon Mexico of a number of determined European collectors. Aubin, resident in Mexico between 1830 and 1840, amassed a significant collection of Mexican manuscripts, including many of the more important pictorial items from the Boturini collection and many of the copies made by Veytia, León y Gama, and Pichardo. Other collectors during this early period were Vischer and Waldeck. The acquisition of a small collection of Mexican Indian pictorial manuscripts by

the French National Library received publicity in at least three journals.

The first three volumes of Kingsborough's *Antiquities of Mexico* (1831–48), initially issued with a title page dated 1830 and then with one dated 1831, reproduced 16 major pictorial manuscripts in full and in color in copies by Augustine Aglio. These pictorials constituted most of the then known inventory of such manuscripts available to Kingsborough with the exception of Codex Borbonicus, which he was apparently refused permission to publish. Copies or proofs from his collection of the Maya Codex Paris and of Techialoyan Codex "W" (Article 24, Catalog, 721) suggest that their publication was also planned. The editions in this monumental work remained a basic source until

---

[20] Glass (1964, pp. 21–22) identifies eight of these and gives a brief discussion of Bullock's exhibit of 1824.

the end of the century, when more accurate facsimiles began to appear.

These events of the 1820s and 1830s were, of course, not occurring in isolation. During this same period Champollion deciphered the Egyptian hieroglyphs, interest in Maya archaeology was steadily increasing, and Ternaux-Compans in France and Bustamante in Mexico were initiating the publication of various Mexican ethnohistorical texts.

The middle years of the century were no less active. In 1849 Aubin published his *Mémoire sur la Peinture Figurative* and followed it by a series of lithographs which eventually reproduced seven pictorial documents for the first time. His *Mémoire* and *Notice* (1851) not only put on public record the existence and nature of his collection but included the first scholarly attempts to interpret pictorial materials and hieroglyphs from Central Mexico. The frequency with which they were reprinted or extracted testifies to their influence. In 1857 Aubin and others founded the Société Américaine de France, which under a complex series of changes in names published a bewilderingly complicated series of journals throughout most of the remainder of the century. Their pages contained frequent contributions to the incipient field of Mexican ethnohistoriography and hieroglyphic decipherment by Aubin, Brasseur de Bourbourg, Léon de Rosny, Charency, and others. The present *Journal de la Société des Américanistes* published in Paris is the modern successor to these early journals, of which the *Revue Orientale et Américaine* was the first.

In 1864 Brasseur de Bourbourg published Landa's history of Yucatan, which he had discovered not long before (see Article 18). In 1869 he published Codex Troano with a now discredited interpretation of its hieroglyphic text based on Landa's Maya "alphabet" (Brasseur de Bourbourg, 1869–70). To him are also owed a general history of the ancient civilizations of Mesoamerica (1857–

59) and a catalog of his manuscript collection (1871).

From 1810 to 1870 Mexico was in an almost continuous state of political turmoil, a circumstance that undoubtedly hindered Mexican participation in the developing field of Mexican archaeology and facilitated the export of antiquities. A few figures nevertheless stand out. Most prominent of them is José Fernando Ramírez, politician, historian, bibliographer, and museum director (see Article 21). His influence has always been greater than the bulk of his published historical writings. The distribution of the Aubin-Desportes lithographs is largely owed to him (though Squier, Peñafiel, Goupil, and others also secured copies from Aubin and furthered their distribution). The first edition of Durán's illustrated history is also due to his activity. Much of his collection of books and manuscripts was sold at auction in London in 1880; other parts of his collection remained in the possession of Alfredo Chavero and are now in the Mexican National Museum of Anthropology; other manuscripts and copies from his collection are probably in some unidentified private collection. Closely associated with Ramírez was Faustino Galicia Chimalpopoca, copyist and translator of many Nahuatl texts.

The last quarter of the 19th century witnessed events and the emergence of new personalities that were soon to put research into Mesoamerican pictorial manuscripts on its modern basis. The first International Congress of Americanists was held in Nancy, France, in 1875. At its fourth session in Madrid in 1881 many of the pictorial manuscripts in Spain were exhibited and must have been seen by scholars, who soon utilized them in their writings. The manuscripts included both of Sahagún's *Códices Matritenses*, both parts of Codex Madrid, numerous maps of the *Relaciones geográficas* of 1579–85, a Techialoyan codex, and various others (*Lista*, 1881). In 1877 the Mexican National Museum inaugurated publication of its *Anales*. These events reflect the institutionalization of archaeological research and the shift of research from private endeavor to academic auspices.

In Mexico two historians at first dominated the scene: Orozco y Berra and Chavero (see Article 21). Each wrote a history of ancient Mexico and of its Spanish conquest, appearing respectively in 1880 and about 1887 (Chavero, n.d.). Both works are ambitious attempts to synthesize the entire body of material then available; no comparable attempts have since appeared. It took Mexican scholarship years to escape from their sometimes deadening influence. Perhaps more than anything else their works mark the end and the beginning of eras in Mesoamerican ethnohistory.

Chavero, the more prolific writer, was also a collector and editor of numerous manuscripts. Various editions initiated by Ramírez, whose manuscript collection Chavero acquired, were brought to fruition by him. He made important contributions to Mesoamerican bibliography, but many of his writings are diffuse and digressive, a factor that has detracted materially from his stature. A curious lack of discrimination led him to publish falsified artifacts and manuscripts, some of which he later defended.

In France, Léon de Rosny, a frequent contributor to the developing field of Maya decipherment, began publication of his *Essai sur le Déchiffrement de l'Écriture de l'Amérique Centrale* in 1876. It was soon available in three different illustrated editions (1876a, 1876b, 1881b). To him are also owed the first edition of the Maya Codex Cortesianus (1883) and the second and third photographic editions of the Maya Codex Paris (1887, 1888).

In Germany Förstemann published the first photographic edition of Codex Dresden in 1880, the first in a series of publications that inaugurated a brilliant career in Maya hieroglyphic decipherment. During the 1880s the first publications of Eduard Seler

appeared (see Article 20). By the turn of the century and to his death in 1922 he was the outstanding scholar in Mesoamerican archaeology. His establishment of the Borgia Group of manuscripts as such in 1887 (Seler, 1902b), his first major contribution to the study of the Mexican *tonalamatl* (1890), and his study of the Humboldt Fragments (1893) are some of his early works that foreshadow his later achievements discussed in our survey of the Borgia Group.

In 1889 Goupil purchased the Aubin manuscript collection, somewhat to the consternation of Peñafiel, who seems to have represented the Mexican government in an attempt to regain its possession. The two-volume catalog of the Aubin-Goupil collection, illustrated with 80 photographs, appeared in 1891 under the authorship of Eugène Boban, who like Goupil was an art dealer. A work of unsurpassed scholarship in its field, it appears to have had limited circulation for many years since so little use was made of it in the ensuing generation.

For the quatricentennial of the discovery of America in 1892 the Mexican Government commissioned a distinguished group of men to prepare Mexico's exhibit. The Junta Colombina, under the editorship of Chavero, published the *Antigüedades mexicanas* (1892), which gave the first colored lithographs of five pictorial manuscripts. For the Exposición Histórico-Americana in Madrid the Junta Colombina gathered and made some 40-odd copies of pictorial manuscripts. The collection so assembled was to have an enduring importance for the museum in Mexico.

At the head of the Junta Colombina was Francisco del Paso y Troncoso, who left Mexico for Madrid in 1892 (see Article 21). He remained in Europe until his death in 1916, during which time he wrote a major commentary on Codex Borbonicus (1898b) and an introduction to the first modern edition of Codex Cospi (1898a), prepared the illustrations in the Florentine Codex for pub-

24

lication, and published the photographic facsimiles of Sahagún's Códices Matritenses (1905–07), the *Relaciones geográficas* from the manuscripts in Spain (1905–06), and Codex Kingsborough (1912). He was also responsible for the appearance of the colored edition of the Veytia Calendar Wheels (Veytia, 1907) and the first photographic edition of Codex Mendoza (Galindo y Villa, 1925). Most of his publications, with the exception of limited numbers of advance copies, were not distributed until the 1920s, when the Mexican government obtained his papers. Many of his projects were left unfinished; several editions of pictorial manuscripts which he projected never got beyond printer's proofs.[21] His contribution to the field as editor, interpreter of Nahuatl texts, discoverer and publisher of new manuscripts, and as the author of substantive commentaries, is considerable. His European projects, largely frustrated during his lifetime, are fully chronicled in a detailed biobibliography by Galindo y Villa (1922) and in a publication of his official correspondence and listing of the documents he had copied by Zavala (1938).

Notable contemporaries of Paso y Troncoso whose influence was felt on the Mexican or international scene and whose works figure prominently in the census bibliography are Antonio Peñafiel, Zelia Nuttall, and Nicolás León. Joaquín García Icazbalceta, an editor and publisher of note, was an important collector of Mexican manuscripts; his collection is now in the University of Texas (see Article 21).

An American, the Duc de Loubat, is noted for his patronage of many Americanist ventures around the turn of the century. Between 1896 and 1904 he financed the facsimiles of Codices Vaticanus B, Borgia, Cospi, Telleriano-Remensis, Ríos, Féjérváry-Mayer, Tonalamatl Aubin, and Magliabecchiano. These editions, which were made by a photolithographic process in color, set a new standard in publication. The quality of their binding, in the screenfolds, has yet to be equaled. For introductions or commentaries to these editions he called upon such distinguished scholars as Seler, Ehrle, Paso y Troncoso, and Hamy.

The period between the two World Wars saw a steady but slow increase in the number of new editions and commentaries. William Gates, known for contributions to Maya hieroglyphic writing and for collections of original and photographed manuscripts, published various manuscripts such as the Lienzos Coixtlahuaca no. 1, Córdova-Castellanos, and Meixueiro under the aegis of the Maya Society which he founded, as well as editions of the three Maya screenfolds, the earliest of which appeared in 1909.

The first accurate facsimile of Codex Vienna by Lehmann and Smital appeared in 1929. A translation of the Nahuatl text of the Historia Tolteca-Chichimeca with a reproduction of its drawings and a commentary by Preuss and Mengin was published in 1937–38 and was followed by an excellent monochrome facsimile in 1942, edited by Mengin. A magnificent color photographic edition of Codex Mendoza with a commentary by Clark was published in 1938 in an edition believed to have been partially destroyed during the Battle of Britain. These are but highlights of the inter-war period.

A major figure in Mexican pictorial manuscript studies is Alfonso Caso, whose first commentary on such a manuscript appeared in 1930. His editions and commentaries form one of the largest personal bibliographies in the census. Although his interest has by no means been confined to the Western Oaxaca group, his role in the study of the Mixtec manuscripts has been of unusual importance and is further discussed in our survey of that region.

Robert Barlow, an American resident in

---

[21] Zavala (1938, pp. 589, 592) reports proofs for editions of the Codices Borbonicus, Borgia, and Vaticanus B and the Kalendario Mexicano, Latino y Castellano. None of them was published by Paso y Troncoso.

Mexico, was a founder of the journal *Tlalocan* and a prolific author of studies relevant to this field; his is another of the largest personal bibliographies in the census. Had his career not been cut short by an untimely death his major contributions would have been more numerous.

Since 1945 the number of persons who have contributed new editions and commentaries has increased considerably. Excellent new editions of the Santa Cruz Map of the City and Valley of Mexico by Linné in 1948 and of the Relación de Michoacan by Tudela in 1956 in Sweden and Spain, respectively, and of the Selden Roll by Burland (1955b), an Englishman, who published in Germany, testify to the continuing international character of the field. A resumption of interest in the Central Mexican historical sources was briefly reflected by editions and commentaries by Dibble on the Códices en Cruz (1942a) and Xolotl (1951), by Barlow (1949b) on the Códice Azcatitlan, and Mengin (1952a) on Codex Mexicanus (BNP 23–24).

No single trend characterizes the field today. The beginnings of attempts toward synthesis may be seen in such works as Robertson (1959) and Nowotny (1961b). The recognition of the need for publishing the too frequently neglected minor types of documents and the demonstration of their value when studied in depth characterizes recent publications by Galarza and Kutscher. The demand for new editions of the great manuscripts is being met in part by a new publisher, the Akademische Druck und Verlagsanstalt in Graz, Austria, and in the photographic edition of the manuscripts originally published by Kingsborough now being published by the Secretaría de Hacienda y Crédito Público in Mexico.[22]

The considerable problems faced in organizing scattered information and bibliography and in cataloging the many manuscripts have prompted such specialized surveys as that of certain calendrical sources

in Kubler and Gibson (1951), general guides such as Alcina Franch (1955) and León-Portilla and Mateos Higuera (1957), a catalog of the pictorial manuscripts in the Mexican National Museum of Anthropology by Glass (1964), and various regional surveys by Cline.

A significant body of pictorial manuscripts, both relatively important and relatively minor, remains unpublished and unconsulted. Their publication and critical elucidation appears to be the most important task to be undertaken in this area of ethnohistorical research. Progress has been made over the years only through comparative study. No synthesis worthy of the name can proceed without it. There is little justification today for not utilizing the entire corpus of documents for this purpose. Unlike archaeology, which must proceed by a sampling of its raw data, the number of manuscript sources for ethnohistory, particularly pictorial manuscripts, is not infinite but very limited indeed. The same comment applies to the purely Nahuatl and Spanish texts in the native traditions that form part of the same reservoir of cultural information and that beg translation and editing.

GUIDES AND BIBLIOGRAPHIES

Although the publication of Mesoamerican pictorial manuscripts began in the 17th century, it was not until the early part of the 19th century, with the publications of Humboldt (1810) and Kingsborough (1831–48),

[22] The Akademische Druck und Verlagsanstalt in Graz, Austria, has published facsimile editions of the Codices Becker nos. 1 and 2 (1961), Vienna (1963), Sánchez Solís ("Egerton 2895"; 1965), Laud (1966), Madrid (1967), Cospi (1968), Paris (1968), and Magliabecchiano (1970). They have announced plans to publish Codex Vaticanus B, Codex Féjérváry-Mayer, the Matrícula de Huexotzingo, and various others.

Only vols. 1–4 (Corona Núñez, 1964–67) of the projected five-volume edition of the pictorial manuscripts originally published by Kingsborough (1831–48) have been examined and cited for the present census.

that the foundations were laid for the relatively large literature that has now come into being.

The number of scholarly commentaries and editions that had been published by 1900 was relatively large and listings of them soon appeared. Saville (1901) provided a comprehensive list of reproductions issued between 1885 and 1901. The brief notices by Dalton (1899, 1902a, 1902b), however, are little more than multiple book reviews. The bibliography of Mexican antiquities by Lejeal (1902) specifically included an annotated section on pictorial manuscripts and hieroglyphic writing and cited works already rare in his day.

The bibliographic survey of Borgia Group and Oaxaca pictorials by Lehmann (1905a), still of considerable significance, indicated the depth and scope of the historical literature available for the understanding of manuscript histories. A general account by Galindo y Villa (1950b) is a very derivative publication with notices about the Boturini collection, the publication by Kingsborough, and the Aubin-Goupil collection.

An excellent and extensive bibliography by Noguera (1933a) was for many years a standard reference source, which was not superseded by any more recent work. The mimeographed catalog by Arpee (1937) is of little general significance and is limited to works in the libraries of the University of Chicago and the Field Museum of Natural History. Only an abstract (Ortega Martínez, 1948) was published of a listing and bibliography of pre-Hispanic pictorial manuscripts presented at the 28th International Congress of Americanists.

The *Colección de estudios sumarios* by Mateos Higuera (1944–49), unfortunately discontinued after describing only 15 manuscripts, is one of several sources that together provided the model for the present census.

Two important guides and bibliographies

appeared in 1955. Alcina Franch's annotated listing (1955) provides brief descriptions and bibliographies for the approximately 86 pictorial manuscripts which it treats. Kutscher (1955) gives bibliographies for 69 separate manuscripts. The León-Portilla and Mateos Higuera (1957) catalog, restricted to manuscripts that treat pre-Columbian institutions, provides limited bibliographies for about 61 manuscripts. Another useful bibliography appears in Robertson's (1959) study of pictorial manuscripts from the Valley of Mexico. The recent guide by Azcué y Mancera (1966) depends heavily on the León-Portilla and Mateos Higuera catalog for the 75 manuscripts it lists but is so full of errors that it is utterly useless for scholarly purposes.

The general guide to historical sources for Mesoamerica by Carrera Stampa (1959) draws heavily on its immediate predecessors but contains some new material; its revised versions (Carrera Stampa, 1962–63, 1965) have extensive additions. Galarza's (1960) useful and extensive listing of titles concerning pictorial sources in the Library of the Musée de l'Homme, Paris, should also be mentioned. The alphabetically arranged census by Mateos Higuera (1966) unfortunately extends only through "Cuauhtlantzinco" after listing 98 manuscripts. Its continuation, when published, will be an important addition to the inventory literature.

The nearly exhaustive bibliography of the archaeology and ethnography of Mesoamerica by Bernal (1962) is of fundamental importance. It includes sections on "codices" from within and outside the Maya area. Its scope far exceeds the resources of any limited number of major libraries. The author and subject catalogs of the Peabody Museum Library, published in 1963 and including journal articles, is another useful bibliographical source. The continuing coverage of ethnohistory and archaeology in the *Handbook of Latin American Studies* is an indispensable tool, especially for current titles.

Topical and regional guides and bibliographies are cited in the section "Regional Survey" below; catalogs of institutional collections are cited in the institutional checklist (Article 28).

The pictorial manuscripts of Mesoamerica are primarily a visual record; the reader desiring an introduction to these documents may be referred to the illustrated catalogs of the collections of the Bibliothèque Nationale, Paris, and the Museo Nacional de Antropología, Mexico, by Boban (1891) and Glass (1964), respectively. Together they illustrate the known varieties of pictorial manuscripts and provide 219 photographic plates. Robertson's (1959) excellent study of the pictorials from the Valley of Mexico and Nowotny's (1961b) survey of the Borgia Group and other ritual-calendrical manuscripts are also extensively illustrated. The new edition of the manuscripts published by Kingsborough (1831–48) now being prepared by the Secretaría de Hacienda in Mexico will make at least 16 major

LIST 1—TYPOLOGICAL CLASSIFICATION USED IN THE CENSUS OF TRADITIONAL PICTORIAL MANUSCRIPTS

Ritual-calendrical
   260-day almanacs
   18-month calendars
   Calendar wheels
Historical
Genealogical
Cartographic
Cartographic-historical
Economic
   Cadastral
   Census
   Financial records
   Property plans
   Tribute
Ethnographic
Miscellaneous
   Litigative
   Natural history
Unclassified
Unavailable

pictorial manuscripts available in one set of volumes.

CLASSIFICATION

Only two formal classifications of manuscripts have been employed in the census. These are regional and typological. The former is discussed at the beginning of the regional survey in the following section. The typological classification (see List 1) derives directly from that proposed by Nicholson (1960b, 1961b). It varies only in detail from classifications used in earlier catalogs and surveys such as Hirtzel (1928), Mateos Higuera (1946c), León-Portilla and Mateos Higuera (1957), and others discussed by Alcina Franch (1955, pp. 422–28). Its major novelty is the inclusion of ethnographic and unavailable categories and a greater emphasis on the isolation of the cartographic-historical type. The latter, partially defined by format and composition, frequently includes historical, genealogical, and cartographic material.

The different types are discussed separately below: the regional and typological distribution of the 434 manuscripts in the census is summarized in Table 6 and is presented in detail in Tables 7–26.

Ritual-Calendrical Manuscripts

Under the rubric of ritual-calendrical have been classified those manuscripts primarily devoted to religion, the calendar, and such related topics as divination, religious ceremonies, and the systematic depictions of gods of the native pantheon. The 50 documents so classified (see Table 6) amount to approximately 12 per cent of all manuscripts in the census. The recurrent topics in the calendrical manuscripts are the 260-day almanac, the ceremonies of the 18 months of the 365-day year, and various approaches to the structure of the calendar through the medium of the calendar wheel. Various numerical cycles with associated gods, sequences of deities, miscellaneous religious and funerary rites, and cosmology are less frequently found topics but all have attracted the attention of scholarship.

Among the manuscripts in this division are some of the most famous and well known of all the pictorial manuscripts of ancient Mesoamerica. The three Maya screenfolds, the five manuscripts of the Borgia Group, Codex Borbonicus, and Tonalamatl Aubin are the most prominent examples of the type. Some of these are both the oldest in terms of their being known to the scholarly world and in the date of their composition. Most of those named are preconquest in date. They preserve the native style in a less acculturated fashion than any other group, except for the historical and genealogical screenfolds of Western Oaxaca.

Of all the manuscript types, it was the ritual-calendrical type that was selected for destruction by the ecclesiastical authorities. That most of the manuscripts mentioned above survived the systematic extirpation of native paganism is undoubtedly due to their having been sent back to Europe as curiosity pieces immediately after their discovery. Few surviving ritual-calendrical manuscripts were produced by Indians for use in Indian contexts in the postconquest period. Indeed, the use and ownership of a *tonalamatl* made any Indian liable for prosecution by the Inquisition.

Colonial pictorial manuscripts containing ritual or calendrical information that have survived date from well into the 16th century; most are the product of Spanish patronage in terms of both historical and missionary research. Such manuscripts as those of the Huitzilopochtli and Magliabecchiano Groups already show definite indications of having been produced, and possibly edited, for Spaniards. These manuscripts date from no earlier than the middle of the 16th century. Later in the century a period of retrospective historical research began that produced the illustrations for Durán's his-

tory, the Florentine Codex, and the Tovar Calendar.

The calendrical sections of Codex Mexicanus (BNP 23–24), from the Valley of Mexico, and the calendrical illustrations in the Books of Chilam Balam, from Yucatan, are perhaps the only significant body of ritual-calendrical pictorial documents made after the middle of the 16th century and not intended for Spanish consumption. Unfortunately, the latter are known only through copies of 18th-century versions.

General discussions of particular examples and groupings of ritual-calendrical manuscripts will be found in the section "regional survey" under the state of Mexico and the Distrito Federal, the lowland Maya region and the Borgia Group. Few manuscripts of this type from other regions are now extant.

Two surveys of ritual-calendrical manuscripts are of particular importance. The "Handlist of Sources on the Mexican 365-day Year" by Kubler and Gibson (1951) is a descriptive and bibliographical guide to the pictorial and other manuscripts that deal with the indicated topic. Nowotny (1961b) gives a detailed analytical guide to the content of the early ritual-calendrical manuscripts having mantic and religious content. Although he is largely concerned with the manuscripts of the Borgia Group, he includes Codex Borbonicus, Tonalamatl Aubin, and several other manuscripts as well as ritual scenes in several of the Mixtec historical screenfolds. His coverage omits the later documents of the 16th century, the unpublished Códice del Museo de América, and treats the Maya screenfolds only in passing.

The writings of Eduard Seler are of fundamental and lasting significance for the interpretation of ritual-calendrical manuscripts. His major contributions are discussed in the survey under the Borgia Group. The study of the Aztec and other Central Mexican but non-Mixtec, non-Maya calendars by Caso (1967) is also of importance and contains reprints or revisions of a number of his earlier works in this field.

The main and recurrent topics in the ritual-calendrical pictorial manuscripts are discussed below.

THE DIVINATORY ALMANAC. The *tonalpohualli*, the divinatory aspect of the calendar, is based on the permutation of 20 named days and 13 numbers forming a cycle of 260 days. In more elaborated forms it also has associations with 13 birds, 9 Lords of the Night, and 13 gods. In book form the *tonalpohualli* is known as a *tonalamatl*, which was used for augury, prophesy, the determination of good and bad days, and in the naming of children. It is comparable to the European zodiac combined with the Christian calendar in the form of a horoscope. As a cycle of 260 days the tonalpohualli was a trait of practically all ancient Mesoamerica. Its use continues unbroken to the present time, especially in certain highland Maya villages in Guatemala and in some sections of southern Mexico; no modern ethnographer, however, has reported the use of a tonalamatl.

The tonalpohualli is well represented among surviving manuscripts. Codex Borbonicus and Tonalamatl Aubin from Central Mexico both contain early and relatively full versions. Colonial tonalamatls, in some instances much edited by Spanish patronage, from the Valley of Mexico are contained in the Códices Telleriano-Remensis, Ríos, Museo de América, and Mexicanus (BNP 23–24). The tonalpohualli, both in full and in its more abstruse aspects, is the subject of the Borgia Group manuscripts and of parts of the three Maya screenfolds.

The literature on the interpretation and description of the tonalpohualli is large. Both specific and general references will be found in the bibliographies of Article 23 given for the manuscripts named above. Generalized and simplified accounts are

30

given in most popular books on the archaeology of Middle America.

EIGHTEEN-MONTH FESTIVAL CALENDARS. The representation of the "fixed" ceremonies, those celebrated or connected with each of the 18 months or periods of 20 days forming the 365-day year, was of great interest to missionary authorities. Drawings of these ceremonies are known only from the Valley of Mexico (see Table 8) and in one of the Sahaguntine manuscripts prepared at Tepepulco, Hidalgo. The most extensive treatment of this subject is by Kubler and Gibson (1951), who also provide a comprehensive survey of both pictorial and other sources bearing on the subject.

CALENDAR WHEELS. A large number of manuscript calendar wheels from Mesoamerica are in existence. All are colonial in date. Some may date from the 17th and 18th centuries although the latter may derive from earlier prototypes. Since calendar wheels are known in other media, such as stone, there seems little reason to doubt that manuscript calendar wheels were produced before the conquest. The depiction of the calendar and the zodiac in a circular format, however, was also a European trait during the Renaissance and Middle Ages; the Mesoamerican calendar wheels, as we now know them, are probably influenced by European ideas.

The calendar wheels usually depict particular cycles of the calendar with the appropriate glyphs or names arranged around or within the periphery of the circular format. Some combine two or more cycles, and occasionally other data, such as colors, are also shown. In the calendar wheels from Central Mexico the most common subject is the representation of the permutation of the 13 numbers with the four year-bearer days which define the 52-year cycle. Other calendar wheels depict the 18 months, the 20 days, or the 13 katuns of the Maya calendar.

Of the approximately 25 calendar wheels or manuscripts containing one or more examples specifically identified in the census, nine are from the Valley of Mexico, four from Tlaxcala, one from Hidalgo, one from Michoacan (in Códice Cuara), six from Yucatan, and four are from unclassified Central Mexican proveniences. Aside from the Mayance examples, which have been discussed by Bowditch (1910), no specific study of calendar wheels has appeared although individual examples have been studied.

The calendar wheel diagrams published (and possibly invented) by Granados y Gálvez (1778, pp. 54–57) are not included in the census. The chronological drawing in the Histoyre du Mechique (Article 27B, no. 1049), also not included in the pictorial census, may represent a form of calendar wheel. For further remarks see Veytia Calendar Wheels in Article 23.

MISCELLANEOUS MANTIC AND RELIGIOUS MATERIAL. Associated sequences of gods, days, and numbers not directly part of the 365-day year (*xiuhmolpilli*) or of the 260-day cycle (*tonalpohualli*) or of the 52-year cycle but related to them in various mantic and ritual ways are presented in detail and at length in the manuscripts of the Borgia Group and in the three Maya screenfolds. Comparable material is generally not preserved in manuscripts from the Valley of Mexico although pages 21–22 of Codex Borbonicus are an exception to this statement.

Representations of ritual ceremonies occur in manuscripts of the Borgia Group and in certain Mixtec histories; they are discussed and indexed by Nowotny (1961b). Depictions of religious ceremonies, particularly in ethnographic manuscripts made under European patronage, are common in documents from the Valley of Mexico. The movable ceremonies (those not tied to a specific day or month of the 365-day year) are pictured in the Florentine Codex, books 1 and 3, in manuscripts of the Magliabecchiano Group, in Codex Ríos, and in the Durán history.

Drawings of gods may be found in a wide variety of manuscripts, including the ton-

alamatls mentioned above, in various books of the Florentine Codex (especially book 2), and in other manuscripts listed in Table 8, as well as in manuscripts not here classified as ritual-calendrical.

MYTHOLOGY, COSMOLOGY, AND ASTRONOMY. Few Indian pictorial manuscripts specifically record native beliefs about mythology, cosmology, or astronomy. Cosmographic traditions of the Aztecs, especially the concept of the four eras of mankind, are treated in the opening pages of Codex Ríos; these pages have been the subject of much discussion. Some of the relevant studies are cited in the bibliography of that manuscript. Book 3 of the Florentine Codex treats the origins of the gods. A vertically stratified layering of the universe is pictured in the Fragmento Gómez de Orozco, in the Selden Roll, and in very late drawings in one or more of the Books of Chilam Balam. Mythological and cosmological information may also be contained in some of the more obscure passages of the manuscripts of the Borgia Group and in parts of the Maya screenfolds as well as in the early sections of both Valley of Mexico and Mixtec historical manuscripts.

Astronomical material in the pictorial manuscripts has long been sought by scholars. Seler, Lehmann, and Kreichgauer belonged to a school that sought to discover astronomical significances between dates in the Mixtec histories at a time when the nature—historical and genealogical—of those manuscripts was not fully recognized. Their writings on this subject have not been appraised or evaluated in recent years. The student should be cautioned about the validity of much of the interpretations of Central Mexican pictorial manuscripts that deal with planetary cycles, particularly Venus, and eclipses. In the Maya hieroglyphic manuscripts the subject is more complex; Codex Dresden is believed to contain various astronomical calculations.

The depiction of natural celestial phenomena—comets, eclipses, constellations, etc.—is contained in the Florentine Codex, book 7, and in part of the Primeros Memoriales; these sections are here classified as ethnographic rather than as ritual-calendrical.

THE CORRELATION OF THE CALENDAR. No attempt has been made in the census to single out or to classify those manuscripts bearing on the correlation of the native calendars with the Christian calendar. Suffice it to say that such data derive from many calendrical and historical manuscripts as well as from many here classified under other headings. In the Lowland Maya Region the Maya screenfolds have had little bearing as yet on the correlation of the Maya calendar.

Historical Manuscripts

Under historical manuscripts we have classified those documents that narrate events in sequence through time or depict isolated military, political, or administrative events. The 78 manuscripts so classified represent 18 per cent of the manuscripts in the census. In a perceptive contribution to this subject Robertson (1959) has classified the organizing principles for the pictorial presentation of history in the pictorial manuscripts of Central Mexico and Western Oaxaca. The present discussion depends in part on his exposition.

Most historical manuscripts from Central Mexico are year-to-year chronicles or annals. Many of them are "time-oriented." Such examples as the Tira de Tepechpan, the Codices Aubin, Huichapan, Mendoza (part 1), Mexicanus (BNP 23–24), Saville, and the Anales de Tula are organized about a straight, linearly ordered series of year signs. This mode of composition is particularly suited to the tira or screenfold format. In such manuscripts as Codices Azcatitlan, Azoyu (nos. 1 and 2), Boturini, Ríos, and Telleriano-Remensis[23] the linear organization of year signs is broken into clusters or segments or follows two or more margins of the page, possibly a more efficient use of

space than the linear arrangement.[24] Events in either case are drawn opposite the relevant dates or are attached to them by lines. Códice en Cruz is a complex compositional variant of the time-oriented type.

In the Tenochca Mapa Sigüenza and in the Texcocan Códice Xolotl and Mapas Quinatzin (leaf 1) and Tlotzin a "place-oriented" mode of presentation is followed. Here historical and genealogical events are placed in a cartographic or protolandscape setting; time signs are subordinate or absent. This variety of historical manuscript includes such examples as the Mapas de Cuauhtinchan nos. 1–3 and several of the maps in the Historia Tolteca-Chichimeca from the same provenience, here classified under the cartographic-historical type.

The Mixtec historical screenfolds of Western Oaxaca are seen by Robertson as "event-oriented." Although two examples of this corpus depict political events in one person's life, most are primarily genealogical narratives embracing many generations; dates are but an incidental detail in the composition.

Four examples of historical (and one cartographic-historical) manuscripts in the census are commemorative documents that place history on display on a single-sheet document. Each also organizes its content into discrete segments in separate rectangular compartments. These manuscripts are the Lienzos of Jucutacato, Tabaa (no. 1), San Miguel Tiltepec, Tlaxcala, and the Mapa de Cuauhtlantzinco. The Lienzo de San Miguel Tequixtepec no. 1, in its lower portion only, also has such a composition.

Many of the historical manuscripts are illustrations for written texts in the tradition of European book design (see Durán, His-

[23] Robertson (1959) has shown that Codices Ríos and Telleriano-Remensis derive from a linear tira format or mode of composition.

[24] In the stylistically early Codices de Azoyu from Guerrero the partial framing of each page by the year signs suggests the similar treatment of day signs in the Central Mexican tonalamatls.

toria; Tovar, *Relación*; Sahagún, *Florentine Codex*; *Relación de Michoacan*; *Historia Tolteca-Chichimeca*, etc.). The nature of their native prototypes, when postulated, can only be inferred or reconstructed by analysis.

Further general discussion of historical manuscripts will be found in the regional survey in the sections devoted to the state of Mexico and Western Oaxaca. Pictorial historical manuscripts from the Maya region do not survive, but various early chronicles testify to their existence.

Genealogical Manuscripts

Approximately 12 per cent or 54 of the manuscripts in the census have been classified as genealogies. They present few problems of classification. The number of extant genealogies, however, is greater than this figure as they also occur in the cartographic-historical type. Most of the manuscripts explicitly classified as genealogical are of mixed colonial origin and doubtlessly documented litigants' claims to hereditary rights.

The close relationship between genealogy and history in the surviving Mixtec manuscripts from Western Oaxaca has resulted in a classificatory situation where the "histories" of that region are essentially genealogical in content. There, as in the cartographic-historical manuscripts from the same and other regions, the genealogies are also statements of dynastic succession, a factor that introduces genealogical discontinuities into otherwise uniform sequential listings of persons and their descent.

Synthetic interpretation of genealogical pictorial elements in the Central Mexican genealogies has yet to appear. In such documents relationships are indicated by solid lines, broken lines, footprints, speech scrolls, vertical columns of couples, or other spatial arrangements. Dotted lines and speech scrolls, for instance, may denote concubinage rather than marriage. Monogamous and

incest regulations introduced by European contact may also be reflected in pictorial conventions. Nicholson (1967, p. 95) has noted that genealogies drawn below a house appear to be limited to manuscripts that he considers of Tlaxcalan or Huexotzingo origin.

Cartographic Manuscripts

Maps have been classified in the census under three categories. "Cartographic" manuscripts are maps in the normal sense of the term. "Cartographic-historical" manuscripts are maps that include historical and genealogical information and frequently have a particular mode of composition. The "property plans" subtype of the economic classification are maps and plans of restricted areas or regions such as groups of houses or agricultural fields. In particular instances these distinctions are difficult to maintain in classification. The cartographic-historical and economic (property plans) types are discussed separately.

Mexican Indian maps were one of the categories of manuscripts that most impressed the earliest Spaniards in the New World. References to maps will be found in the letters of relation of Cortés, the writings of Bernal Díaz and Peter Martyr, and in other sources.

The major surviving Mesoamerican maps are from the Valley of Mexico. Such maps as the two in Codex Kingsborough, the Santa Cruz Map of the City and Valley of Mexico, the maps in Codex Xolotl, and the Plano en Papel de Maguey are major documents in Mexican art and ethnohistory. Each of them has been discussed by Robertson (1959), who also treats the related subject and development of landscape painting in the historical manuscripts. He also devotes some attention to two of the maps in the Historia Tolteca-Chichimeca, from Cuauhtinchan, Puebla, here classified under the cartographic-historical type. In this document, as in the related Mapas de

33

Cuauhtinchan, nos. 1–3, the arrangement of place glyphs sometimes accommodates historical narrative perhaps more than it reflects the distribution of places in space. The same is true of the migration itinerary of the Mapa Sigüenza, a major historical source from the Valley of Mexico.

Other major studies of maps from the Valley of Mexico are by Linné (1948) and Toussaint, Gómez de Orozco, and Fernández (1938). The former treats the Santa Cruz Map in considerable detail and devotes a chapter to native cartography. The latter study the Plano en Papel de Maguey, the Santa Cruz Map, and the "Cortés" or "Nuremberg" map of the City and Valley of Mexico, first published in 1524, from three intensive points of view.[25] In the course of their discussions they give general observations on native cartography and lost native maps.

Circular maps have attracted attention for their conceivable independence from European influence in their primary format. Examples of circular Maya maps from colonial Yucatan are discussed in the survey. From Puebla and Western Oaxaca circular maps are represented in the census by the Mapa circular de Cuauhquechollan and the late Plano de San Andres Sinaxtla.[26] Among the maps of the Relaciones geográficas (not treated in this census), the Mapa de Teozacoalco contains a circular map, and the Mapa de Amoltepec has a semicircular arrangement of place glyphs. Both of these examples are from Western Oaxaca. The circular Map of Tabasco by Melchor de Alfaro Santa Cruz, also a Relación geográfica map, is probably of European origin although the issue is in doubt.

Many maps in the census are relatively minor, late, or crude productions; this is less true of the maps classified as cartographic-historical. Such late and peripheral examples as the Mapa de Santa Cruz Xoxocotlan, the Lienzo de Tamazulapan, and the Map of Tzintzuntzan in the Crónica de Michoacan

exhibit extensive Spanish influence. They are as much "views" or landscapes as they are "maps."

Although the 38 maps in the census comprise approximately 9 per cent of all the manuscripts, their number does not reflect the quantity of available, unpublished, and minor maps excluded from the census. Maps, of course, are not as readily replaced by the written word as are other types of pictorial manuscripts. It is in maps (and in the cartographic-historical and property plans types) where one finds elements of the native tradition continuing into the 17th century long after other modes of manuscript painting had ceased to be practiced. In such late examples traditional iconography or symbolism is primarily expressed through the continued use of footprints (also horses' hoofprints) to identify roads, water symbols to indicate rivers and springs, and vestigial place glyphs (particularly the tepetl or hill symbol, frequently without added rebus qualifiers). These three symbolic elements alone, particularly in late contexts where purely stylistic elements (quality of line, proportions, composition, etc.) are missing, are present in innumerable unpublished documents.[27]

Such mixed colonial maps survive in great quantity in the Archivo General de la Na-

[25] The Cortés map, first published in Nuremberg in 1524 with one of Cortés letters, is a document of considerable interest and relative presumptive accuracy; it is based on firsthand acquaintance with Tenochtitlan, but there has been no suggestion as yet that it in any way derives directly from any native map.

[26] "Circular" formats or compositions also occur in other categories of manuscripts. The Circular Genealogy of the Descendants of Nezahualcoyotl arranges generations in concentric circles; a page of the Codex Mexicanus (BNP 23–24) has a comparable arrangement of genealogical relationships in concentric arcs of a circle. The largely effaced obverse side of the Códice de Tlaxcala once contained a circular composition. The Boban Calendar Wheel in its present state is painted on a circular sheet of paper.

[27] In property plans the use of native symbols for units of linear measurements may continue for almost as long a period.

ción, Mexico, particularly in the Ramo de Tierras. Their origin lies in ownership and jurisdictional disputes, in applications for concessions of lands for cattle and other uses, and so forth. Some examples of such documents are in the census, but by far the greater number are unpublished and excluded from the census.[28]

Two great administrative campaigns conducted during the period when most of the documents in the census were painted called forth local maps made either by Indians or by Spaniards. The first was the statistical questionnaire of 1577 which produced the *Relaciones geográficas* of 1579–85 (see Cline, Article 8). The 76 extant maps in this series (16 are known to be lost) include 35 that are wholly European in style and 41 that display either native or mixed native and European traits. The latter, in particular, are essential to any discussion of Indian cartography. Robertson (Article 6) gives a comprehensive catalog, discussion, and bibliography of these important documents.

The second major campaign of map production was occasioned by the specific instructions for the civil congregations of about 1599–1601. A moderately large body of village maps from this activity is preserved in the Archivo General de la Nación, Mexico. Four have been published by Simpson (1934), but none is sufficiently Indian to qualify for the present census although some have minor native elements. Only one map of the civil congregations is in the census—the Mapa de la Visita y Congregación de Amecameca—a relatively minor document exhibiting slight traditional influence. We have not examined any of the unpublished corpus.

Later series of 18th-century *Relaciones geográficas* also called forth local maps. Relatively few have been published but native elements are presumably no longer present. The authorship of these later series may, of course, merely be wholly European rather than Indian. West (Article 10) discusses these 18th-century documents. Examples of 18th-century maps are given in the *Cartografía de Nueva Galicia* (1961).

General and rather popular studies of Mexican Indian cartography, with illustrations of well-known examples, have been published by Burland (1947a, 1960) and Guzmán (1939b). Robertson (1959) has discussed the subject with illustrations of examples from the Valley of Mexico. Linné (1948) gives another general account as does Orozco y Berra (1871). The usefulness of native documents for historical cartography and toponymic information is illustrated by Cline's (1959, 1961a, 1964) study of Veracruz, Chinantec, and Mazatec native maps. In the Chinantec documents he analyzes two interesting instances of variant orientations in the same document. Apenes (1947) and Carrera Stampa (1949b) reproduce, respectively, maps of the Valley and City of Mexico; few of them are native.

Cartographic-historical Manuscripts

As cartographic-historical we have classified those manuscripts that in a single-panel format combine cartographic and historical or genealogical information. These documents are one of the more interesting realizations of the pictorial manuscript art of Mexico. The 87 available examples account for a fifth of all documents in the census. Only the Maya regions are not represented by the type.

Many cartographic-historical manuscripts

[28] Examples of late 16th- and early 17th-century colonial maps showing minor native elements may be consulted in the *Cartografía de Puebla* (1958). Chevalier (1956, pp. 21, 23, 49, 77, 169) also illustrates some maps that to one degree or another are of interest in this connection as does Pérez García (1956) for Northern Oaxaca. Cuevas (1921–28) reproduces the "Pintura del Pueblo de Ocuituco" (Morelos) and the "Mapa primitivo de Tepotzotlan y sus Contornos" (Mexico), both from the AGN and excluded from the present census. He also reproduces the "Mapa del Obispado de Nueva Galicia, 1550" from the AGI, not here considered to be in the native tradition although it shows Indians.

are lienzos and conform to a general pattern. Place glyphs arranged around the periphery or border represent boundaries, usually of a definite village and its outlying lands. The sign for the village in question is frequently depicted near the center; surrounding it will be the genealogy of the ruling cacique or family and historical scenes tending to establish the legitimacy of the existence of the village and its jurisdiction or merely recording notable historical events and disputes with neighboring villages. In effect, such documents are village charters, histories, and land titles. They are thus regarded as having considerable value and are zealously guarded from strangers' eyes. Examples of this particular type come from practically all regions of Central Mexico and Oaxaca; variations of the basic pattern are common.

Other varieties of cartographic-historical manuscripts lack the village charter pattern and simply contain drawings of historical events or genealogies placed in a cartographic setting. Although most of the documents in this category tend to be quite large, size is not a factor in determining the type.

Economic Manuscripts

The 124 economic pictorial manuscripts account for 29 per cent of all documents in the census. They are most numerous from Central Mexico, particularly the Valley of Mexico; Northern and Eastern Oaxaca and the Maya regions are not represented in the census by the type. The economic manuscripts are the civil, fiscal, and secular records of Indian life; only a very few are concerned with preconquest subjects. Their quantity and diversity necessitate a descriptive sub-typology (see List 1).

As cadastral we have classified or described those sections of manuscripts that are listings of land units not organized as maps. The type is best represented in manuscripts of the Ixhuatepec and Vergara

Groups and in certain pages of Codex Kingsborough. In these listings of lands the properties, frequently shown as rectangular or irregular shapes with their measurements and place glyphs, are typically drawn opposite a human figure or head with its personal name glyph. The pictorial modes of composition and forms used in the cadasters comprise a pattern evident in property plans and other colonial documents.

Population counts, tax lists, and other listings of persons (Spanish: *padrón*) have been classified as census documents without reference to the purposes of the listings. Notable examples are the Matrícula de Huexotzingo, the Census of Tepoztlan, the Códice del Tequitlato de Zapotitlan, and the major manuscripts of the Vergara Group.

Financial records of various kinds include records of payments, disbursements, or receipts in kind or money by municipal Indian governments and the pictorial equivalents of accounting ledgers. Códice de Tlamapa no. 3, Financial Accounts of Cuitlahuac, Códice Indígena, Códice Indígena, 1564–65, and the Libro de Tributos de San Pablo Teocaltitlan are among manuscripts falling in this category. They are frequently indistinguishable from tribute records. Códice Sierra is an Indian record of the expenses for the support and maintenance of a colonial church.

Property plans are maps of restricted areas such as agricultural fields, houses, or house precincts. The Humboldt Fragments 2 and 6, the Oztoticpac Lands Map, and Códice de las Posesiones de Don Andrés are published examples that illustrate the type. Property plans are relatively common among economic manuscripts in the census; documents of this minor variety abound among unpublished documents in the Archivo General de la Nación, Mexico.[29]

[29] Cline (1966a, pp. 93–94, fig. 14) reproduces two plans of house precincts showing Indian symbols for units of land measurement that are typical of scores of such documents not in the census.

On a number of single-leaf property plans there are also genealogies drawn to represent the ownership of the lands or houses in question. The three examples from Xochimilco in Table 12 exemplify this class of document.

As tribute manuscripts we have classified those manuscripts whose main pictorial content consists of drawings of goods typical of Mexican Indian tribute during the 16th century, such as foodstuffs, chickens, turkeys, cloth and clothing, loads of wood and fodder, and Spanish money, as well as services and labor. The type includes tribute lists, assessments, and contracts in addition to drawings reflecting litigation over such matters.

Códice de los Alfareros de Cuauhtitlan and the Mizquiahuala Sales Receipts are examples of this type whose content is not concerned with tribute but whose pictorial forms are devoted to goods and services. Codices Chavero, Kingsborough, and Mariano Jiménez are major documents that represent colonial tribute. Codex Mendoza, part 2, the Matrícula de Tributos, certain initial pages of Codex Kingsborough, and perhaps Códice de Azoyu no. 2 (reverse) and Humboldt Fragment 1 treat preconquest tribute.

An inevitable miscellaneous economic subtype includes those manuscripts whose content does not readily fit any of the foregoing categories.

The various parts of Códice Osuna, Códices Indígenas del Marquesado del Valle nos. 1–28, and most of the Humboldt Fragments typify the range of content of the minor colonial economic manuscripts and may be consulted in a limited number of publications.

Ethnographic Manuscripts

The ethnographic pictorial manuscripts are those that explicitly depict Indian customs, behavior, and laws. Parts of 11 manuscripts from the Valley of Mexico are so classified (see Table 13). The only others in this category are parts of the Relación de Michoacan and the Primeros Memoriales from Hidalgo. Practically all the ethnographic manuscripts are products of European patronage and interest. The depictions of the Indian life-cycle from birth to old age in Codex Mendoza, part 3, and in part of the Florentine Codex are probably European in concept and are also invaluable sources for Aztec ethnography.

Miscellaneous and Unclassified Manuscripts

Thirty-two manuscripts in the census fail to qualify for any of the established categories or are too fragmentary to classify. In several instances they are unclassified only because we have not obtained photographs for study or available information is insufficient. Among the miscellaneous manuscripts are some that illustrate personal grievances with drawings of beatings or personal assaults; further unpublished examples of such drawings exist in the Archivo General de la Nación, Mexico. In Table 14 four such documents have been subtyped as "litigative," but it may be noted that drawings of assaults or illegal punishments also occur in various tribute manuscripts such as Humboldt Fragments 9–12, Códice Osuna, and Codex Kingsborough, among others, and the "litigative" type is an unsatisfactory one. Botanical, zoological, and similar drawings as well as herbals are subclassified as "natural history" in Table 14; further sets of such drawings will be found in the census under the names of Gómez de Cervantes and Francisco Hernández.

Unavailable Manuscripts

For 27 manuscripts in the census there are no copies, photographs, or reproductions known to be available. For all there exists some form of modern bibliographical reference; their inclusion serves to record present knowledge concerning them. Ten of the 27 are recorded in such standard catalogs or guides as Paso y Troncoso (1892–93), Lehmann (1905a), Mena (1923), and Gómez de Orozco (1927a). Nine have been reported in village archives in the writings of anthropologists during the present century. Lost documents such as Serna Calendar Wheel no. 1 and Códice de Tlamapa no. 2 are included in order to complete information on groups of manuscripts. In all these cases there is some possibility that the document may become available. The number of pictorial manuscripts mentioned or cataloged in 19th-century and earlier sources and now unknown is, of course, considerably greater than that reflected by the 27 unavailable entries in the census.

REGIONAL SURVEY

The regional classification used in the census is based primarily on the modern political states of Mexico (see fig. 1) organized into four major areas. Western Mexico includes Michoacan and Jalisco, the only states in that region represented by manuscripts in the census. Central Mexico embraces two major divisions: (1) the state and Federal District of Mexico and (2) the peripheral states of Central Mexico comprising Guerrero, Hidalgo, Morelos, Puebla, Queretaro, Tlaxcala, and Veracruz. The state of Oaxaca is divided into Western, Northern, and Eastern regions. Only the state of Yucatan and the Republic of Guatemala in the region designated as Southeastern Mexico and Guatemala are represented in the census.

Alternative regional classifications, such as colonial political jurisdictions, native tribal or linguistic areas, natural areas, or archaeological culture areas, were considered but found impractical for the purposes of the census.

The cultural affiliation of manuscripts, so prevalent in earlier classifications, is thus avoided. Certain ethnic correlations may nevertheless be observed. Most manuscripts from Western Mexico are Tarascan. Mixtec

and Zapotec manuscripts, generally speaking, are from Western and Eastern Oaxaca, respectively. Mazatec, Chinantec, and Cuicatec manuscripts are from Northern Oaxaca. "Aztec" manuscripts are from the Valley of Mexico (comprehended within the state of Mexico and the Federal District). Maya manuscripts originate in Southeastern Mexico and Guatemala. Other such correlations are noted in the survey.

The survey is organized around Tables 7–26, which provide a typologically classified listing of all the manuscripts in the census by regional or state units. Maps for each region locate, when possible, the towns or villages which are the ostensible proveniences of manuscripts described in the census or discussed in the survey. Sections devoted to the regionally unclassified manuscripts from Central Mexico and the manuscripts of the Borgia Group treat items whose provenience is unknown or speculative.

Of the 76 extant maps or *pinturas* of the *Relaciones geográficas* of 1579–85, 41 have been classified by Robertson (Article 6) as exhibiting native or mixed European and native styles. Although not included in the census, these 41 pictorial documents are listed in the regional and typological tables by the place name and catalog number (distinguished by the abbreviation RG) assigned by Robertson. Within parentheses is given the modern identification of the place name according to Cline (Article 8). The ex-districts (Dto.) are added for the examples from Oaxaca. The regional distribution of the native and mixed RG maps is given in List 2.

The spatial and typological distribution of manuscripts in the census is summarized in Table 6. Of the 434 documents in the census, 27 are unavailable, leaving a total of 407 available for study. The addition of the 41 mixed and native RG maps increases this figure to 448. The most numerous grouping is the 133 manuscripts from the state and

List 2—Regional Distribution of
Native and Mixed Relación
Geográfica Maps

Mexico and D.F. (Table 11)	7
Guerrero (Table 15)	2
Hidalgo (Table 16)	4
Morelos (Table 17)	2
Puebla (Table 18)	8
Veracruz (Table 20)	3
Western Oaxaca (Table 23)	5
Northern Oaxaca (Table 24)	2
Eastern Oaxaca (Table 25)	8
Total	41

Federal District of Mexico. Of these, 129 are from the Valley of Mexico region. The 114 examples from the peripheral states of Mexico and the 93 from Oaxaca are the other largest groupings.

Regions of Mesoamerica not represented in the census by manuscripts or by mixed or native RG maps are Western Guerrero, Northern Hidalgo, Queretaro, southern Veracruz, most of Southeastern Mexico and Guatemala, and all of the Central American republics. In Western Mexico only northern Michoacan is represented; the isolated example from Jalisco is a very late and marginal case.

Western Mexico

Most of the 18 pictorial manuscripts from Western Mexico (see Table 7) are Tarascan in subject matter or origin and are associated with proveniences in northern Michoacan more or less near Lake Patzcuaro (see fig. 2). A single example, the Mapa de las Tierras de Chiquilistlan, known only through a 19th-century copy, is from Jalisco.

Table 6—REGIONAL AND TYPOLOGICAL CLASSIFICATION OF THE PICTORIAL MANUSCRIPTS OF MIDDLE AMERICA

Region \ Type	Ritual-calendrical	Historical	Genealogical	Cartographic	Cartographic-historical	Economic	Ethnographic	Miscellaneous & Unclassified	Unavailable	Subregional Totals°	Regional Totals°
Western Mexico		4	2	2	7	2	1	1	1	18	18
Central Mexico:											
Mexico and D.F.	20	34	19	11	6	57	11	13	3	133	133
Peripheral states:											
Guerrero		3	2	1	5	5			1	14	
Hidalgo	3	3		1		8	1	1	1	14	
Morelos		1	1		3	6		1		10	
Puebla		8	6	3	11	8		2		33	
Tlaxcala	5	5	8	1	6	3		2	1	29	
Veracruz				1	12				1	14	114
Unclassified	4	1	9	4	2	31		6	2	59	59
Borgia Group	5									5	5
Oaxaca:											
Western	3	15	3	4	17	4		1	2	47	
Northern		2		3	8				4	17	
Eastern		2	3	3	10			1	11	29	93
Southeast Mexico and Guatemala	9			4					4	13	13
Totals°	50	78	54	38	87	124	13	32	27	435	435

° Totals for each region do not correspond to the sum of numbers for each type as some manuscripts are classified under more than one type. One economic manuscript, the Codex Osuna, is classified under two regions; this accounts for the discrepancy between the 435 manuscripts of this table and the 434 manuscripts of the census.

Table 7—CLASSIFICATION OF THE
PICTORIAL MANUSCRIPTS FROM
WESTERN MEXICO

Historical manuscripts:
25 BEAUMONT: Crónica de Michoacan: nine historical scenes
39 Carapan, Códice de, no. 2
213 Michoacan, Relación de
357 Tocuaro, Títulos de

Genealogical manuscripts:
40 Carapan, Genealogía de los Caciques de
87 Cuara, Códice (part)

Cartographic manuscripts:
26 BEAUMONT: Crónica de Michoacan: Map of Tzintzuntzan
281 Santa Fe o de Patzcuaro, Mapa de

Cartographic-historical manuscripts:
38 Carapan, Códice de, no. 1
56 Chiquilistlan, Mapa de las Tierras de
177 Jucutacato, Lienzo de
231 Nahuatzen, Lienzo de
248 Patzcuaro, Lienzo de
261 Puacuaro, Lienzo de
288 Sevina, Lienzo de

Economic manuscripts:
87 Cuara, Códice (part)
379 Tzintzuntzan and Tlalpujava, Tributes of

Ethnographic manuscripts:
213 Michoacan, Relación de

Miscellaneous manuscripts:
430 Huapean, Códice

Unavailable manuscripts:
10 Arantza, Códice de

No manuscript in the census is classified under Guanajuato but the Tributes of Tzintzuntzan and Tlalpujava bears a Spanish text relating it to the cacique of Acambaro.

At the present time no clear evidence has been noted to demonstrate either the presence or absence of the trait of manuscript picture writing among the Tarascans, the dominant Indian group of Michoacan. If any early relation or chronicle refers to preconquest Tarascan manuscripts, it has not been reported by modern investigators. Indeed, the anonymous author of the Relación de Michoacan, writing ca. 1539–41, says, "these people [the Tarascans] did not have

books" ("esta gente no tenia libros"—Tudela, 1956, p. 3). Since this statement may refer to *screenfold* books and not to manuscripts such as lienzos, its full import is not clear.

In the 18th century, Boturini (1746, 2: 29) understood that the Tarascans used "pinturas" in the preconquest period but he was unable to travel to Michoacan to collect specimens for his collection.

The Tarascan pictorial manuscripts in the census are all colonial in date. There is no compelling suggestion that any of them derive from preconquest prototypes. If the art was practiced in Western Mexico, as it probably was, its colonial examples contain no reflection that the region was characterized by the developed body of pictorial symbols used in Central Mexico and Oaxaca. Only the Tributes of Tzintzuntzan and Tlalpujava, a manuscript that may well have been painted in Mexico City, displays conventional signs or ideographs, the form and style of which are recognizably Central Mexican.

Two bibliographic surveys of Tarascan pictorial manuscripts have appeared: Lehmann (1905b) and Mateos Higuera (1948b). The survey of sources for Tarascan ethno-history and geography by Brand (1944) comments on some of the manuscripts treated herein. The several installments of Nicolás León's incompletely published *Los Tarascos* (1903, 1903–04, 1904a, 1906c), as well as Seler's (1908a) study of Michoacan, utilize or comment on such prominent sources as the Relación de Michoacan and the Lienzo de Jucutacato.

Two lost pictorial manuscripts described in two notable texts from Michoacan are not included in the census. One is the "antigua pintura de los Indios tarascos" described by Moxó (1828; reprinted 1837, 1839, 1888). Brand (1944, p. 98) asserts, without discussion, that it is the title to the Hacienda Bellas Fuentes near Zamora. For this reason it may perhaps be identified with a Lienzo de Bellas

Fuentes mentioned in passing by N. León (1903, p. 453). Códice Plancarte has been published by N. León (1888c) and reprinted by Corona Núñez (1959). It may be related to the three extant pictorial manuscripts from Carapan.

Lehmann's (1905b) survey of Tarascan pictorials lists several items that we have excluded. The Lienzo de Yuririapundaro (Yuriria, Guanajuato) is briefly described in the Boturini collection inventories of 1743 and 1745 (Item 4-32) and in the 1746 catalog (Item 14-2) but is otherwise unknown (see Article 29). Lehmann also cites a description by Granados y Gálvez (1778, pp. 184–86) of another lost pictorial manuscript. The Armas de Patzcuaro cited by Lehmann as being in Seler's personal collection may correspond to the colonial coat of arms of Patzcuaro on stone or to the colonial coats of arms contained in the Crónica de Michoacan. Seler appears to have had copies or versions of the illustrations in the latter document but Lehmann's reference to the Armas de Patzcuaro remains vague.

Among published colonial maps from Western Mexico considered for listing in the census, three have been rejected as not being in the native tradition. They are the Mapa del Obispado de Nueva Galicia, Año de 1550, published by Cuevas (1921–28, 2: facing p. 380) and in the *Cartografía de la Nueva Galicia* (1961, p. 31, no. 10), the Mapa de Huango, 1582, published by N. León (1890), and a map of Tingambato and other localities in Michoacan forming part of a civil congregations document of 1599 published by Simpson (1934, pl. 10).

Central Mexico

Central Mexico as defined here comprises the Federal District of Mexico and the states of Guerrero, Hidalgo, Mexico, Morelos, Puebla, Queretaro, Tlaxcala, and Veracruz. The state and Federal District of Mexico are considered as forming one region centered on the Valley of Mexico. The re-maining states are treated both as individual regions and as a large area peripheral to the Valley of Mexico. One section of the survey, below, treats manuscripts whose provenience cannot confidently be placed except within the large Central Mexican area. A total of 305 of the 434 manuscripts in the census are from Central Mexico.

STATE AND FEDERAL DISTRICT OF MEXICO. The 133 pictorial manuscripts from the state and Federal District of Mexico are classified and listed in Tables 8–14. The localities believed to represent their proveniences are shown in figures 3 and 4. The region may be discussed in terms of eastern and western subregions.

The western and larger part of the state of Mexico is represented in the census by four manuscripts:[30] Anales de San Lorenzo Haucalpan; Carte de la Ville de Temazcaltepec; TEMAZCALTEPEC: Pièces d'un Procès Criminel . . . ; and TLACOTEPEC: Pièce du Procès de Pablo Ocelotl . . . .

The scarcity of surviving manuscripts from the western subregion may perhaps be explained in part by the extensive Otomian (Otomi, Mazahua, Matlatzinca) settlements in the region. The four manuscripts listed, however, are not Otomian.[31] In the late 17th or early 18th century the region around Toluca in the Matlatzinca Valley eastward into the Valley of Mexico was the provenience of

[30] From Tzompahuacan in the western subregion is Pedro Ponce's *Breve relación de los dioses y ritos de la gentilidad* generally known only through a copy in Códice Chimalpopoca. An illustrated manuscript of the *relación* dated 1597 was in the collection of the Condes de la Cortina in 1930 (Sociedad española de Amigos del Arte, 1930, pp. 23, 100). It is also mentioned by Romero and Pereda (1860, p. 262). See Article 27B, no. 1088.

[31] Manuscript picture writing is considered to have been a trait of at least some Otomi groups (Carrasco Pizana, 1950, pp. 22, 219). Códice de Huichapan from Hidalgo contains a written Otomi text. Carrasco Pizana (1950, passim) accepts Códice de Huamantla from Tlaxcala as Otomi. Other Otomi pictorials perhaps may be numbered among manuscripts from the Valley of Mexico, Hidalgo, Tlaxcala, or northern Puebla. Some of the known Testerian manuscripts bear Otomi glosses.

many of the illustrated Nahuatl texts known as the Techialoyan Codices (see Article 24).

All other manuscripts from the state and Federal District of Mexico are from the eastern subregion, a zone generally approximate to the Valley of Mexico. It was the center of the alliance of Aztec tribes that dominated most of Central Mexico at the time of the Spanish conquest; it accounts for 129 pictorial manuscripts. The Valley of Mexico region stands next to the screenfolds of the Borgia Group, the Maya screenfolds, and Western Oaxaca in the number or quality of surviving manuscripts. All known categories of pictorial manuscripts are represented in the Valley of Mexico inventory, but none is of undisputed preconquest date. As the center of church and viceregal administration of New Spain, the Valley of Mexico was the focus for manuscripts produced under European patronage (see Table 2) as well as for those of ethnographic content (see Table 13).

For the purposes of the present survey the Valley of Mexico, encompassing the Federal District and its immediate environs, is treated as a single region together with all of the state of Mexico. Little attention is paid to possible subregional criteria. Such subregions of the Valley could be defined on the basis of colonial jurisdictions of the viceroyalty or on tribal areas (Mexica, Tepaneca, Acolhua, Culhua, Chalca, Xochimilca, etc.). An intensive study of the style of a selected number of pictorials from the Valley of Mexico by Robertson (1959) has successfully defined manuscript painting schools from Mexico-Tenochtitlan, the Colegio de la Santa Cruz in Tlatelolco, and for Texcoco. The study by Robertson may be considered the most important treatment of the Valley of Mexico pictorial manuscripts in practically all aspects other than their content. Other general works are cited below in our survey of the different content-types of documents from the region.

Ritual-calendrical Manuscripts. Ritual-

calendrical parts of 20 manuscripts, all from the Valley of Mexico, are classified in Table 8 as divinatory almanacs, festival calendars, calendar wheels, or as miscellaneous. All but

TABLE 8—THE RITUAL-CALENDRICAL MANUSCRIPTS OF THE STATE, FEDERAL DISTRICT, AND VALLEY OF MEXICO

260-day divinatory almanacs (tonalpohualli):
32 Codex Borbonicus, part 1
207 Codex Mexicanus (BNP 23–24) (part)
229 Códice del Museo de América (part)
270 Codex Ríos (part)
308 Codex Telleriano-Remensis (part)
[See also 15, Tonalamatl Aubin]

18-month festival calendars:
32 Codex Borbonicus, part 3
114 DURAN: Historia de las Indias, Tratado 3 (part)
171 Codex Ixtlilxochitl, part 1
188 Codex Magliabecchiano (part)
205 Kalendario Mexicano, Latino y Castellano
229 Códice del Museo de América (part)
270 Codex Ríos (part)
274 SAHAGUN: Florentine Codex, book 2 (part)
308 Codex Telleriano-Remensis (part)
364 The Tovar Calendar
394 Codex Veytia (part)

Calendar wheels:
13 Codex Aubin (part)
30 Boban Calendar Wheel
114 DURAN: Historia de las Indias, Tratado 3 (part)
207 Codex Mexicanus (BNP 23–24) (part)
272 Sahagún Calendar Wheel
365 TOVAR: Códice Ramírez (part)
366 TOVAR: Historia de la Benida . . . (part)
387 Veytia Calendar Wheel no. 1
390 Veytia Calendar Wheel no. 4

Miscellaneous religious and calendrical documents:
32 Codex Borbonicus, parts 2 and 4
114 DURAN: Historia de las Indias, Tratados 2 and 3 (part)
188 Codex Magliabecchiano (part)
207 Codex Mexicanus (BNP 23–24) (part)
229 Códice del Museo de América (part)
270 Codex Ríos (part)
273 SAHAGUN: Table of day signs . . .
274 SAHAGUN: Florentine Codex, books 1–4 (part)
365 TOVAR: Códice Ramírez (part)
366 TOVAR: Historia de la Benida . . . (part)

two (Códice del Museo de América and Tovar, Historia de la Benida . . .) have been published. The nature and general bibliography of the Central Mexican ritual-calendrical manuscripts has been previously discussed under the definition of the type.

With several exceptions most of the manuscripts in Table 8 are the product of European patronage and are composite manuscripts in that many of them have several parts: calendrical, historical, or ethnographic.[32] It is worthy of note that four of the five 260-day almanacs are accompanied by 18-month calendars, a pattern that may reflect a preconquest mode or be a result of European editing. The exception, the tonalpohualli of Codex Mexicanus (BNP 23–24), is an appendix to a native chronicle. Even it reflects some concern with the 18-month calendar; its first section is a 365-day saints' calendar which is correlated with native months. Extensive effacements and palimpsests preclude accurate statements about its original character. Although no part of the Florentine Codex is classified under the divinatory almanacs, its book 4 contains a section devoted to the auguries of the 20 days (a subject of the tonalpohualli) but its pictorial format is not that of a tonalamatl. The same book also contains a 260-day-sign table. It is perhaps no accident that the 18th-month calendars that are not accompanied by divinatory almanacs are all later than those that are.

The number of independent ritual-calendrical manuscripts from the Valley of Mexico is actually somewhat less than 20 since the Huitzilopochtli, Magliabecchiano, and Crónica X Groups are each represented by two or more manuscripts in Table 8 and the Tovar Calendar is represented twice on the list since the Kalendario Mexicano, Latino y Castellano has been considered a copy of it. The Tonalamatl Aubin has been considered of Valley of Mexico provenience but is here classified and discussed as Tlaxcalan on rather slender evidence.

Only Codex Borbonicus among the ritual-calendrical manuscripts has been considered preconquest in date. Much of it is certainly in an early style; it is the only screenfold in Table 8. The ritual-calendrical parts of Codices Telleriano-Remensis and Museo de América (and, indirectly, their derivatives of the Huitzilopochtli and Magliabecchiano Groups) may conceivably be copied from substantially earlier examples or have been painted by artists trained or influenced by the precolonial tradition. Otherwise, most of these manuscripts, particularly those associated with Durán, Tovar, and Sahagún, are relatively late 16th-century products which reflect their European editing.

Historical Manuscripts. We have classified 35 pictorial manuscripts, or parts thereof, from the state and Federal District of Mexico as historical (see Table 9). Only one, the unavailable Anales de San Lorenzo Haucalpan, is not from the Valley of Mexico. All are colonial in date although the case for so dating Códice Boturini is not compelling and the date of Códice Xolotl has not been determined. Both are certainly relatively early manuscripts in style and composition, if not in date.

For 23 of the manuscripts that may be considered as chronicles we have indicated in Table 9 the approximate span of years that their content embraces. The years are given according to the "Mexica" correlation of 1 Acatl equals A.D. 1519. Dates in parentheses are approximations on a basis as consistent as possible with most of the other manuscripts.

The mechanics of the calendar used throughout most of Mesoamerica, outside of the Maya region, is such that for all correlations any date may be in error by any multiple of 52 years. The resultant uncertainty

[32] Those ritual-calendrical manuscripts in Table 8 not evidently produced under European patronage are the Boban Calendar Wheel, Codices Aubin and Mexicanus (BNP 23–24), and, possibly, Codex Borbonicus and Veytia Calendar Wheels nos. 1 and 4.

TABLE 9—HISTORICAL MANUSCRIPTS OF THE
STATE, FEDERAL DISTRICT, AND
VALLEY OF MEXICO
Dates in parentheses are approximations.

Chronicles:	Period
2 Anales de San Gregorio Acapulco (text)	1520–1606
13 Codex Aubin	1168–1608
18 Historia de Ayotzingo (text)	1519–1590
20 Códice Azcatitlan	1168–1381 & (1376–1521)
34 Códice Boturini	1168–1355
84 Códice en Cruz	1402–1569
114 DURAN: Historia de las Indias, Tratado 1	(1168–1521)
196 Codex Mendoza, part 1	1325–1521
201 Histoire mexicaine depuis 1221 . . .	1168–1573
202 Fragment de l'Histoire des anciens . . .	1196–1405
206 Mexicanos, Anales, 1398–1596	1398–1596
207 Codex Mexicanus (BNP 23–24) (part)	1168–1583
208 Codex Mexicanus (BNP 83)	(not examined)
211 Anales de Mexico y Tlatelolco . . .	1473, 1521–1522
270 Codex Ríos (part)	1195–1549
282 Codex Saville	1407–1535
290 Mapa Sigüenza	(1168–1325)
308 Codex Telleriano-Remensis (part)	1198–1562
317 Tira de Tepechpan	1298–1596
344 Códice de Tlatelolco	1554–1562
365 TOVAR: Códice Ramírez	(1168–1521)
366 TOVAR: Historia de la Benida . . .	(1168–1521)
412 Códice Xolotl	(1224–1427)

Miscellaneous and other historical documents:
30 Boban Calendar Wheel (part)
83 Codex Cozcatzin (part)
92 Ordenanza del Señor Cuauhtemoc (part)
181 Codex Kingsborough (part)
230 Unos Annales históricos de la Nación Mexicana
243 Codex Osuna, part 6
263 Mapa Quinatzin, leaves 1–2
264 Mapa Quinatzin, leaf 3
274 SAHAGUN: Florentine Codex, books 8 (part) and 12
356 Mapa Tlotzin
358 Títulos de Santa Isabel Tola (part)

Unavailable historical manuscripts:
131 Anales de San Lorenzo Haucalpan

about the date of any event substantially preceding the Spanish conquest was as true for the 16th-century Indian historians as it is for the modern investigator. In many sources discrepancies of approximately 52 years exist for the same event even between manuscripts whose narrative may be continuous through the conquest. Such discrepancies may be due to error on the part of the artist-author or may derive from faulty synthesis of antecedent sources.

It has long been evident, furthermore, that the dates of events in Central Mexican ethnohistorical sources (both written and pictorial) often vary from one source to another by amounts less than that of the 52-year cycle, sometimes on an approximately consistent basis. This has led to the postulation that a number of different calendars, each requiring a different correlation, were in use in the Valley of Mexico. Since many of the major colonial sources, particularly written ones, are synthetic compilations, a single narrative may incorporate dates in more than one system. The examination of this problem lies outside the scope of the present survey, but the reader should be cautioned that the dates shown in Table 9 and in the census descriptions represent an arbitrary simplification. This, of course, is less true of the 15th- and 16th-century dates shown; differences of one year in colonial dates may be due to the fact that the European and native calendars did not start on the same day (or month). For somewhat superficial but important discussions of the problem of variant calendars in the Valley of Mexico, see Kirchhoff (1950, 1956a) and Jiménez Moreno (1961).[33]

[33] A typical case that illustrates the difficulty of dating events in the pictorial manuscripts is that of the founding of Tenochtitlan on f. 73v of Codex Ríos. The page has year glyphs for 19 years (1366–84?, 1314–32?) and a drawing representing the event without any indication of which of the 19 years is that of the event. Kirchhoff (1950) somewhat arbitrarily picks the first of these (4 Tochtli), although five of his ten other alternative dates also appear on this page.

A finer regional classification of the historical manuscripts from the Valley of Mexico might sort them according to tribal or other regional divisions of the Valley of Mexico. In the absence, however, of firm knowledge of varying local historical traditions in the Valley and of variant calendrical systems based on both pictorial and written sources, such a classification would be premature and misleading. Suffice it to say, however, that Códices en Cruz and Xolotl, the Mapas Quinatzin and Tlotzin, the Boban Calendar Wheel, and Codex Kingsborough may be considered as Texcocan (Acolhua). On a thematic basis (caves: see Robertson, 1959, p. 141) the first (unnumbered) illustration in Tratado 1 of the Durán atlas might also be attributed to Texcoco. The content of the Tira de Tepechpan (an Acolhua town), with its almost equal emphasis on Acolhua and Mexica history, complicates its classification. Most of the other historical manuscripts are presumably affiliated with western or southern traditions and regions of the Valley.

Certain historical pictorial manuscripts from other regions of Central Mexico contain extensive notices of events in the Valley of Mexico. Most prominent among them are the Anales de Tula, the Otomi Códice de Huichapan, and part of the Primeros memoriales, all from Hidalgo, and Códice Moctezuma from Morelos.

The chronicles believed to be from the western Valley of Mexico typically contain linearly ordered year glyphs with drawings for the first settlement of the Tenochca-Mexica at Chapultepec, the founding of Tenochtitlan, and a subsequent emphasis on the presentation of the Tenochtitlan dynastic succession. Other events shown include successions of rulers of such centers as Tlatelolco, Azcapotzalco, Tacuba, and Texcoco, the wars and conquests of the rulers of Tenochtitlan, incidental political, secular, and religious events, and natural phenomena such as earthquakes, famines, and eclipses. Their colonial sections record scenes of the conquest, the dates of Indian governors, Spanish viceroys and bishops, etc. Dates are almost invariably given according to years; month and day dates are quite rare.

The chronicles that preserve their initial pages usually commence with the date 1 Tecpatl, here presumed equivalent to A.D. 1168 but also possibly equivalent to 1116 or 1220. This is the date of the emigration of the Tenochca–Mexica and certain other Chichimec tribes from the legendary Aztlan (also given as Chicomoztoc, Culhuacan, etc.). Codices Aubin, Azcatitlan, Boturini, Mexicanus (BNP 23–24), and the Histoire mexicaine depuis 1221 jusqu'en 1594 all start with this fundamental and possibly mystical date of Aztec history. The Mapa Sigüenza and the drawings associated with Durán and Tovar, although lacking explicit hieroglyphic or pictorial dates, appear to commence with the same episode.

The synthesizing Codex Ríos, if one accepts its two major historical sections as being continuous and in the same calendrical system, opens with a date equal to A.D. 1195 in the Mexica system (but glossed 1194) coupled with the depiction of the emigration from Chicomoztoc. There may be a parallel here with Codex Mexicanus (BNP 23–24), in which two emigrations are depicted, one in A.D. 1168 and another, from Chicomoztoc, about 1194. A double or repeated emigration from Chicomoztoc is also given in the Historia Tolteca-Chichimeca from Puebla.

There are, unfortunately, few modern published comparative studies of the content of the historical pictorial manuscripts from the Valley of Mexico, a lack that is reflected in the dearth of recent syntheses of Aztec history in general archaeological works on ancient Mexico. A survey of early written and pictorial sources for the history of the Valley of Mexico by Radin (1920) is severely out of date except for its most general observations. Its continuing usefulness lies in its digests, translations, and reprinted illustrations from earlier commentaries. More recent topical studies by other authors in the field of Aztec history are too frequently superficial, undocumented, based on too limited a number of sources, or simply generalizing. The exceptions are on topics of too limited scope to warrant citation here.

It is a curious fact of the ethnohistorical literature on the Valley of Mexico that the most ambitious comparative and interpretive treatments of the historical manuscripts date from the late 19th century. Chavero (n.d. [ca. 1887]) and Orozco y Berra (1880) and other writings of these authors are now outmoded but they are still the main touchstone of popular consultation. The former retains some interest in this respect since its narrative is illustrated by an almost complete reprinting of most of the pictorial historical manuscripts available in the 1880s. Perhaps they may be replaced by the centennials of their first editions.

Robertson (1959) has distinguished various principles of organization in the native colonial historical manuscripts from the Valley of Mexico. He notes that those associated with the western Valley or Mexican School are time-oriented, with events and places subordinate to the linear stream of dates. Those from the Texcoco School such as the Mapas Quinatzin and Tlotzin and Códice Xolotl are place-oriented, with events drawn against a cartographic or landscape background. Some documents, such as Códice Azcatitlan, as might be expected from the variety of surviving manuscripts, do not fit this classification, but the distinction is an important one that contributes to our understanding of subregional traditions and influences. Historical drawings in the manuscripts of Durán, Sahagún, and Tovar, as illustrations to European edited texts, are removed from their compositional contexts.

Among the miscellaneous or non-annalistic historical manuscripts in Table 9 are two documents which are primarily economic in content. They are Codex Cozcatzin and

Títulos de Santa Isabel Tola, both of the Ixhuatepec Group. Each contains a section devoted to a sequential listing of the native rulers of Tenochtitlan–Tlatelolco. Codex Aubin and Códice Azcatitlan have such appended lists of rulers following their annalistic sections; such a list also occurs on the Plano en Papel de Maguey.

As with other categories of pictorial manuscripts, the historical manuscripts contain different component parts. They may be described as the primary pictorial material, added short identifying glosses, and, occasionally, longer written texts in Spanish, Nahuatl, or some other language. In some instances the written component may be in several handwritings. It is generally doubtful that any written surcharge would be by the artist. In other instances the pictorial component is recognizably a synthesis of several antecedent sources or a compilation of copies of several originals. Competent analysis should recognize that each of these parts—text, glosses, pictures, different handwritings or pictorial styles, analyzably different sections—constitutes a discrete human and historical record. Failure to distinguish among these different aspects of a single manuscript and to recognize their interrelationships can lead to deficient interpretation.

The segregation of the written and pictorial sources from the Valley of Mexico in any discussion of Central Mexican ethnohistorical sources creates a false dichotomy. This is particularly true since so many of the latter contain major texts. In Codex Aubin parts of its written text are parallel not only to texts in other pictorial manuscripts (cited in the census) but to various purely textual accounts as well, such as the Crónica Mexicayotl, the historical writings of Chimalpahin, and probably others. Here the text preserves a tradition embodying data only in part communicated by any known drawings. Pictorially, Codex Mendoza, part 1, records the lengths of reigns of the Te-

46

nochca rulers and their conquests; its accompanying text is clearly a separate document with its own bibliographical history. Many of the purely textual primary sources are themselves transliterations of lost pictorial manuscripts (such as the Historia de los Mexicanos por sus Pinturas, various of the documents in the Anales Antiguos de Mexico y sus Contornos, and numerous others). These few remarks should make it clear that the census distinction between pictorial and written sources is based on a criterion that serves only particular ends.[34]

The greatest impediment to research in the interpretation and synthesis of the historical manuscripts is that so much of the known corpus of pictorial and written texts continues unpublished or, in the case of the Nahuatl texts, untranslated. No less of an impediment is that no comprehensive documented research or more than the most preliminary and summary findings have been published on the problem of the conflicts in dates in native sources.

Genealogical Manuscripts. Twenty manuscripts are classified as genealogical in Table 10. Five are primarily concerned with the Tenochtitlan dynasty or with its colonial descendants. Five are similarly associated with Texcoco, but intermarriage between the two centers blurs this distinction. The third city of the Triple Alliance, Tacuba, is represented directly only by an unidentified and unavailable manuscript (no. 297). The others, including all those combined with property plans, are concerned with otherwise undistinguished colonial litigants.

[34] Certain historical texts with minor or nontraditional pictorial elements excluded from the census include the Fragment of Aztec Manuscript (UTX, CDG 556), the Nahuatl text known as Códice Gómez de Orozco (MNA/AH, Col. Gómez de Orozco), the Tratado del Principiado y Nobleza del Pueblo de Teotihuacan (in vol. 3 of CMNE; AAMC 3), the Leyenda de los Soles (MNA/AH), and the Histoyre du Mechique (BNP, MS Français 19031, part). We have not examined the Anales del Siglo 19 "con jeroglíficos" (microfilm copy in MNH/CD). All these documents are described in the prose census (Article 27B).

TABLE 10—GENEALOGICAL MANUSCRIPTS OF THE STATE, FEDERAL DISTRICT, AND VALLEY OF MEXICO

Genealogies:
37 Genealogía de la Familia Cano
44 Colección Chavero no. 4, part 1
81 COYOACAN: The Concubines of Martín Xuchimitl
111 CULHUACAN: Proceso de Marta Petronila y Augustín de Luna . . . (part)
197 Genealogía de la Familia Mendoza Moctezuma
207 Codex Mexicanus (BNP 23–24), pp. 16–17
235 Circular Genealogy of the Descendants of Nezahualcoyotl
258 Genealogía de los Principes Mexicanos
269 Mappe Reinisch
330 TEXCOCO: Stammbaum des königlichen Geschlechtes von Tetzcoco
356 Mapa Tlotzin
404 XOCHIMILCO: Genealogy of Pedronila and Juana
412 Códice Xolotl

Genealogies combined with property plans:
83 Codex Cozcatzin (ff. 15v–16r)
209 MEXICO–TENOCHTITLAN: Procès entre Diego Francisco et Felipe de Santiago (part)
336 TLACOTEPEC: Pièce du Procès de Pablo Ocelotl et ses fils, contre Alonzo Gonzales
402 XOCHIMILCO: Procès entre Francisco de la Cruz Cohuatzincatl, Indio natural de Xochimilco, et Joachim Tecoloatl
405 XOCHIMILCO: Plan et titre d'une propriété sise à Huexocolco
406 XOCHIMILCO: Document relating to the descendants of Don Miguel Damian

Unavailable genealogical manuscripts:
297 Genealogía de los Señores de Tacuba

Only one of the genealogies (no. 336) is not from the Valley of Mexico.

An important genealogical manuscript is Codex García Granados, a Techialoyan manuscript (see Article 24, Catalog, 715), and thus not included in Table 10. In content, iconographic forms, and place and personal name glyphs, it must derive from earlier traditional pictorial sources, either mural or manuscript.

Cartographic and Cartographic-historical Manuscripts. Eleven pictorial manuscripts from the state and Federal District of Mexico are classified as cartographic and six as cartographic-historical in Table 11. Only the

TABLE 11—CARTOGRAPHIC AND CARTOGRAPHIC-HISTORICAL MANUSCRIPTS OF THE STATE, FEDERAL DISTRICT, AND VALLEY OF MEXICO

Cartographic manuscripts:

2 Anales de San Gregorio Acapulco (part)
6 Mapa de la Visita y Congregación de Amecameca
18 Historia de Ayotzingo (part)
68 Mapa de Coatlinchan
109 CUITLAHUAC: Mapa de Santa Marta, Santiago, Cuitlahuac y Ixtapalapa
110 Plan topographique de Cuitlahuac
181 Codex Kingsborough (part)
189 Plano en Papel de Maguey
244 Mapa de Otumba
280 Santa Cruz Map of the City and Valley of Mexico
309 Carte de la Ville de Temascaltepec

Cartographic-historical manuscripts:

12 Lienzo de Atlauhtlan
46 Map of Chichimec History
198 Lienzo de San Andres Metla
254 Mapa de Popotla
424 Codex Santa Anita Zacatlalmanco
429 Lienzo de San Bartolome Coatepec

Maps of the Relaciones Geográficas, 1579–85:

RG 11 Chicoalapa (Chicoloapan de Juarez), Mex.
RG 13 Chimalhuacan Atengo (Santa Maria Chimalhuacan), Mex.
RG 15 Coatepec Chalco (Coatepec, Mun. Ixtapaluca), Mex.
RG 19 Culhuacan, D.F.
RG 29 Ixtapalapa, D.F.
RG 64 Tequizistlan (Tequisistlan, Mun. Tezoyuca), Tepechpan, Acolman, and San Juan Teotihuacan, Mex.
RG 68 Teutenango (Tenango de Arista, Mun. Tenango del Valle), Mex.

document from Temascaltepec is from outside the Valley of Mexico. Few of these manuscripts have attracted scholarly attention.

The Plano en Papel de Maguey, a major document in the urbanization of Mexico-Tenochtitlan, is a detailed plan of a native section of Tenochtitlan-Tlatelolco. The depiction of colonial Indian governors along its right margin has been considered a later addition; it may represent the city at a quite early 16th-century date. The Santa Cruz Map is a mid-16th-century view of the Val-

ley of Mexico and a map of the city. Its scale, cartographic accuracy, ethnographic scenes, and quality as a work of art place it among the most valuable and interesting of the colonial manuscript paintings. These two documents have been studied in detail as have the two maps in Codex Kingsborough. Aside from the Mapa de Coatlinchan, the significance of which has yet to be determined, most of the other documents in the cartographic category are of less interest and further removed from the Indian tradition.

The cartographic-historical is one of the most common types from other regions of Mexico, yet in its usual form of village titles it is the rarest from the Valley of Mexico. Only the lienzos from Atlauhtlan, San Andres Metla, and San Bartolome Coatepec, known through late versions, represent this particular type. The documents from Popotla and Zacatlalmanco both contain cartographic as well as what we have considered historical elements. Both also are concerned with titles of village or barrio property but they lack the typical presentation of boundary locations. Like the Mapa de Coatlinchan, the unpublished Map of Chichimec History awaits proper interpretation.

Mapa Sigüenza and Códice Xolotl, here classified as historical, both present their historical narrative against a cartographic background, but their subject matter is specifically historical and only incidentally cartographic. They deserve attention, however, in any discussion of cartography from the Valley of Mexico. The maps in Códice Xolotl are among the most detailed and perhaps most native of all surviving Indian maps from Central Mexico. The historical Códice Azcatitlan also contains scenes with cartographic or landscape elements.

Maps of more restricted areas, particularly of agricultural fields, are classified herein under the property plans subtype of the economic category. Robertson's (1959) study of cartography and landscape has been

48

discussed above in our treatment of the cartographic type in general.

Economic Manuscripts. Including one lost manuscript, there are 58 pictorial manuscripts classified as economic from the state and Federal District of Mexico. All but one (TLACOTEPEC: Pièce du Procès de Pablo Ocelotl . . .) are from the Valley of Mexico region. Most are colonial in origin and reflect colonial institutions. In addition, many are relatively minor documents with respect to their artistic and substantive content.

Outstanding among the few economic manuscripts whose content concerns preconquest material are the Matrícula de Tributos and the related Codex Mendoza, part 2. These two documents are pictorial records of the tribute paid to the Triple Alliance. They form the basis of the study and map of the Empire of the Culhua-Mexica by Barlow (1949d). The Ordenanza del Señor Cuauhtemoc and parts of some of the manuscripts of the Ixhuatepec Group treat economic matters of the 15th century.

Among the manuscripts listed as tribute and financial documents in Table 12 are records of economic tribute from encomiendas or corregimientos such as Codex Kingsborough and Códice Mariano Jiménez) and financial records of municipal governments (Financial Accounts of Cuitlahuac, Libro de Tributos de San Pablo Teocaltitlan, Códice Indígena, 1564–65, and Códice de Tlamapa no. 3).

Codex Vergara and Códice de Santa Maria Asuncion are notable statistical records of demography and landownership. Their exact provenience is unfortunately conjectural. The several documents forming the Ixhuatepec Group contain related cadastral and village title data; no analysis of this interesting and unique corpus has yet been published.

The large number of property plans, some combined with genealogies, form a body of minor documents that has received little attention. An untold number of further examples exist in the Ramo de Tierras and other branches of the Archivo General de la Nación, Mexico. Most of these property plans form or formed parts of lawsuits over ownership of particular pieces of land; others such as the Teotihuacan Maps, appear to derive from village archives. Various of the documents of this type from Xochimilco may be studied in conjunction with related archival records; they typify the use of manuscript picture-writing by Indians in viceregal courts during the early colonial period. Those from Xochimilco (including two pages of Codex Cozcatzin), the Plano en Papel de Amate, the Oztoticpac Lands Map, and Humboldt Fragments 2 and 6 are the most interesting examples of this class of documents.

Ethnographic Manuscripts. Eleven manuscripts are classified in Table 13 as ethnographic. The actual number of original documents represented is somewhat less since two versions of the common prototype of the Magliabecchiano Group are represented and the two Tovar manuscripts derive from that by Durán. The ethnographic part of Codex Veytia is of interest only because it preserves a page now lost from Codex Ixtlilxochitl, part 2. With the exception of leaf 3 of Mapa Quinatzin all were created under the stimulus of European patronage. This classification includes manuscripts or parts thereof that depict miscellaneous and movable religious ceremonies, mortuary and other customs, laws, Indian types and portraits, and gods out of calendrical or other formal contexts. It may be noted that the Indian types drawn in the Códices Ríos and del Museo de América include Indians from other regions of Mexico.

Miscellaneous and Unclassified Manuscripts. The 13 manuscripts listed in Table 14 represent the miscellaneous and unclassified documents from the state and Federal District of Mexico. All are probably from the Valley of Mexico. Four of the manuscripts form or formed part of civil suits involving personal or similar grievances and are sub-

TABLE 12—ECONOMIC MANUSCRIPTS OF THE STATE, FEDERAL DISTRICT, AND VALLEY OF MEXICO

Tribute manuscripts and other financial documents:

42 CHALCO: Reçus presentes par le Capitaine Jorge Ceron y Carabajal, Alcalde Mayor de Chalco
82 Pintura de los Tributos de Coyoacan
99 Códice de los Alfareros de Cuauhtitlan
107 Financial accounts of Cuitlahuac
145 HUITZILOPOCHCO: Contrat de Commanderie
158 Códice Indígena
159 Códice Indígena, 1564–1565
181 Codex Kingsborough (part)
193 Códice Mariano Jiménez
196 Codex Mendoza, part 2
203 Códices del Cristo de Mexicaltzingo
243 Códice Osuna, parts 1–4, 7
276 Codex San Andres
310 TEMASCALTEPEC: Pièces d'un Procès criminel
311 Libro de Tributos de San Pablo Teocaltitlan
322 TEPOTZOTLAN: Los Naturales de los Pueblos de . . .
341 Códice de Tlamapa no. 3
353–354 TRIBUTES OF TLAXINICAN, TLAYLOTLACAN, TECPANPA, ETC.
368 Matrícula de Tributos

Census and cadastral manuscripts:

11 Códice de Santa Maria Asuncion
83 Codex Cozcatzin (part)
181 Codex Kingsborough (part)
324 Mapa catastral de Tepoztlan, Panhuacan, Ayapango y Tlanahuac
339 Códice de Tlamapa no. 1
386 Codex Vergara

Land titles:

44 Colección Chavero no. 4
83 Codex Cozcatzin
167 Códice de Ixhuatepec
358 Títulos de Santa Isabel Tola

Property plans:

4 Plano en Papel de Amate
17 Códice de los Señores de San Lorenzo Axotlan y San Luis Huexotla
19 Trozo de Azcapotzalco
44 Colección Chavero no. 4, part 2
92 Ordenanza del Señor Cuauhtemoc (part)
100 Títulos de la Casa que está en el Pueblo de Cuauhtitlan
111 CULHUACAN: Proceso de Marta Petronila . . . (part)
148 Humboldt Fragment 2
150 Humboldt Fragment 6
209 MEXICO–TENOCHTITLAN: Procès entre Diego Francisco et Felipe de Santiago (part)

210 MEXICO–TENOCHTITLAN: Titres de Propriété
246 Oztoticpac Lands Map
252 Mapa de San Martin de las Piramides
312 TEOTIHUACAN: Ayer Map of Teotihuacan
313 TEOTIHUACAN: Saville Map of Teotihuacan
314 TEOTIHUACAN: Mapa de San Francisco Mazapan
329 Plan topographique de Texcoco
363 Testamento de Don Antonio Totoquihuaztli
371 Mapa de Santa Maria Nativitas Tultepeque
403 XOCHIMILCO: Document concerning Property of Pedronilla Francisca and Costantino . . . (part)

Property plans combined with genealogies:

83 Codex Cozcatzin (part)
209 MEXICO–TENOCHTITLAN: Procès entre Diego Francisco et Felipe de Santiago (part)
336 TLACOTEPEC: Pièce du Procès de Pablo Ocelotl . . .
402 XOCHIMILCO: Procès entre Francisco de la Cruz Cohuatzincatl, Indio natural . . .
405 XOCHIMILCO: Plan et Titre d'une Propriété sise à Huexocolco
406 XOCHIMILCO: Document relating to the Descendants of Don Miguel Damian

Miscellaneous and unclassified economic manuscripts:

5 AMECAMECA: Cédula de Diligencia
44 Colección Chavero no. 4, parts 3 and 4
108 Los Cuatro Barrios de Cuitlahuac
243 Códice Osuna (part)
260 Pièce d'un Procès (BNP 392)
303 Códice del Tecpan de Santiago Tlatelolco
332 Plan du Tianquiztli
407 XOCHIMILCO: Plan de plusiers Propriétés

Unavailable economic manuscripts:

340 Códice de Santa Cruz Tlamapa no. 2

TABLE 13—ETHNOGRAPHIC MANUSCRIPTS OF THE STATE, FEDERAL DISTRICT, AND VALLEY OF MEXICO

Ethnographic manuscripts:

114 DURAN: Historia de las Indias, parts 2 and 3 (part)
172 Codex Ixtlilxochitl, part 2
188 Codex Magliabecchiano (part)
196 Codex Mendoza, part 3
229 Códice del Museo de América (part)
264 Mapa Quinatzin, leaf 3 (part)
270 Codex Ríos (part)
274 SAHAGUN: Florentine Codex, books 3–10 (part)
365 TOVAR: Códice Ramírez (part)
366 TOVAR: Historia de la Benida . . . (part)
394 Codex Veytia (part)

TABLE 14—MISCELLANEOUS AND UNCLASSIFIED MANUSCRIPTS OF THE STATE, FEDERAL DISTRICT, AND VALLEY OF MEXICO

Miscellaneous (litigative) manuscripts:
- 9 Manuscrito del Aperreamiento
- 98 Codex Procès de Cuauhtitlan
- 106 Códice Cuevas
- 315 Códice de San Juan Teotihuacan

Miscellaneous (natural history) manuscripts:
- 85 CRUZ: Libellus de Medicinalibus Indorum Herbis
- 246 Oztoticpac Lands Map (part)
- 274 SAHAGUN: Florentine Codex, book 11

Miscellaneous (unclassified) manuscripts:
- 16 Portrait of Axayacatl
- 62 Códice de Coacalco
- 133 Los Idolos del Templo de Huitzilopochtli
- 155 HERRERA: Historia general . . ., title-page vignettes
- 176 Las Joyas de Martin Ocelotl
- 325 Miscellaneous pages in Testerian Manuscript BNP 399

classified as litigative. The three natural history manuscripts are a remarkable herbarium produced at the Colegio de la Santa Cruz in Tlatelolco, a set of drawings of tree grafts associated with Oztoticpac near or in Texcoco, and a compilation of drawings of plants and animals in the Florentine Codex. Other drawings of a similar natural historical character are entered in the census under the names of Gómez de Cervantes and Francisco Hernández.

PERIPHERAL STATES OF CENTRAL MEXICO. To north, east, and south of the state and Federal District of Mexico lie the modern states of Guerrero, Hidalgo, Morelos, Puebla, Queretaro, Tlaxcala, and Veracruz (see Map 1). Our classification of pictorial manuscripts assigns 114 examples to these states, surveyed individually below. The region they represent is diverse in language, history, and culture. In linguistic terms, manuscripts from the peripheral states derive from Huastec (northern Veracruz), Otomi (Tlaxcala and Hidalgo), Popoloca (Puebla), Totonac (central Veracruz), Tlapanec (eastern Guerrero), and other communities. Most manuscripts, however, are from ostensible proveniences that were at least nominally Nahuatl during the 16th century. It may be noted that Queretaro, western Guerrero, northern Hidalgo, and southern Veracruz are unrepresented by pictorial manuscripts in the census. These regions are on the peripheries of Central Mexico.

As a broad generalization, the pictorial forms and styles present in most manuscripts from the peripheral states of Central Mexico often appear to be a provincial reflection of developments in the Valley of Mexico. This is perhaps also true of those from the western part of the state of Mexico centered around Toluca, a region represented by remarkably few 16th-century manuscripts. Specific traits of manuscript picture-writing in the peripheral states—the forms and composition of hieroglyphic place names, for instance,—may be compared with traditions in the Valley of Mexico, which was certainly a focus of developments in manuscript painting during the earliest colonial period. In this sense one may perhaps characterize the style of most manuscripts from the peripheral states as belonging to a generalized Central Mexican tradition, distinct, for instance, from the Mixtec style of Western Oaxaca. These remarks are based on the evidence of surviving manuscripts, most of which are colonial in both date and inspiration. Distinct regional styles of painting in other media, such as on ceramics and murals, do exist in late preconquest horizons in Central Mexico. It must be presumed that this was equally true of manuscript painting. Unfortunately, there are few truly early manuscripts in either style or date from the peripheral states. Many regions are represented only by copies or crude renditions by unskilled artists. Although of use in studying iconographic forms and other traits, such examples are poor vehicles for the analysis of style.

There are almost no published attempts to define regional styles of manuscript painting in Central Mexico outside of the Valley of Mexico and Western Oaxaca, but that regional styles and traits will be defined to some extent is certain. Nicholson (1967) has defined an element of costume apparently restricted in occurrence to manuscripts of Tlaxcalan origin. We have used this ethnographic trait to classify certain manuscripts of otherwise uncertain provenience. Studies of regional styles and traits are required to confirm the regional classifications given in the census as well as to determine the provenience of examples which we have not classified. Ordinarily, a regional style is only usefully defined when it can be based on more than one specimen. As possibilities for such analysis we may suggest the groups of manuscripts from Azoyu (Guerrero), Cuauhtinchan (Puebla), Cuernavaca (Morelos), Mizquiahuala (Hidalgo), and, from northern Puebla, the Papers of Itzcuintepec, and the Lienzo de Metlatoyuca. Huexotzingo (Puebla) is the center of another region whence there is a sufficient corpus of manuscripts to permit a comparative study of dated manuscripts from the same provenience.

The possibility that a distinct style of manuscript painting related to the archaeological Mixteca-Puebla style, centered in Tlaxcala and Puebla, survives in extant manuscripts is discussed in connection with the Borgia Group of ritual-calendrical manuscripts.

Guerrero. The 14 pictorial manuscripts from the state of Guerrero are listed and classified in Table 15. All are from northern or eastern proveniences within the state (see fig. 5). Five are from the northern part of the state and the remaining nine are from the eastern part of the state, south of the Rio Mezcala, in the Tlapa region. Some of the latter, the two Códices de Azoyu, the Lienzo de Tlapa, and possibly, the Lienzo de Aztactepec y Citlaltepec and the process from Huamuxtitlan may be considered as Tlapanec in origin. The others are all apparently from Nahuatl-speaking communities.

Códice de Veinte Mazorcas is the only pic-

TABLE 15—CLASSIFICATION OF THE PICTORIAL MANUSCRIPTS OF THE STATE OF GUERRERO

Historical manuscripts:
21 Códice de Azoyu no. 1 (obverse)
22 Códice de Azoyu no. 2 (obverse)
86 Códice de Cualac

Genealogical manuscripts:
21 Códice de Azoyu no. 1 (reverse, part)
342 Lienzo de Tlapa

Cartographic manuscripts:
318 Mapa de Tepecuacuilco

Cartographic manuscripts:
22 Códice de Azoyu no. 1 (reverse, part)
23 Lienzo de Aztactepec y Citlaltepec
238 Lienzo de Noxtepec
362 Lienzo de Totomixtlahuaca
385 Códice de Veinte Mazorcas

Economic manuscripts:
22 Códice de Azoyu no. 2 (reverse)
136 HUAMUXTITLAN: Pièces d'un Procès
147 Humboldt Fragment 1
326 Códice de Tetelcingo
334 Códice de Tlachco

Unavailable manuscripts:
58 Lienzo de Chontalcoatlan

Maps of the Relaciones Geográficas, 1579–85:
RG 41 Muchitan (Mochitlan)
RG 91 Zumpango, Minas (Zumpango del Rio)

torial manuscript from Guerrero that has not been associated with some putative local provenience, but it exhibits place glyphs for localities near Tlapa. Among its later additions are Mixtec glosses; it is the only manuscript from eastern Guerrero that shows the influence of Mixtec settlements in the area. Its pictorial style, however, is not Mixtec.

The two screenfolds from Azoyu are the most important and interesting of the manuscripts from Guerrero. Although they were discovered in Azoyu, together with the genealogical Lienzo de Tlapa, they have been attributed to Tlapa partly on the grounds that the place glyph for Tlapa is prominent in all three manuscripts. The obverse of Códice de Azoyu no. 1 and its copy or related version, the obverse of Códice de Azoyu no. 2, are historical annals embracing a 266-year period, possibly equivalent to A.D. 1300–1565. The reverse of Códice de Azoyu no. 2 and its continuation, Humboldt Fragment 1, together form a remarkable tribute document spanning 36 years, possibly 1487–1522.

The two Códices de Azoyu and Humboldt Fragment 1 are the only manuscripts from the Tlapa region that have calendrical hieroglyphs and, like certain other manuscripts from provenences bordering the Mixtec region of Western Oaxaca, they exhibit a variant calendrical system. As in the Códices Porfirio Díaz and Fernández Leal of Northern Oaxaca and the Mapa de Tecamachalco from Puebla, the year-bearer days, instead of being the standard Calli, Tochtli, Acatl, and Teopatl, are one day earlier—Ehecatl, Mazatl, Malinalli, and Olin. In addition, the Azoyu manuscripts utilize the numbers 2–14 rather than 1–13 as coefficients in year dates.

The dates cited above for the Azoyu manuscripts are based on the preliminary study by Toscano (1943). His correlation of the Tlapanec calendar (3 Ehecatl, Tlapanec, equals 3 Calli, Aztec, or A.D. 1521) must be regarded as tentative pending full publication and study of the manuscripts in question.

The rather large, unpublished, and privately owned Lienzo de Totomixtlahuaca, also from the Tlapa region, is drawn in a crude manner that probably represents unskilled artistry rather than a local or provincial style. Its hieroglyphic forms are in the Central Mexican tradition. As in Códice de Veinte Mazorcas individual Indians are shown holding hafted (copper?) axes and a device resembling a feather, possibly a macana.

From the northern part of the state are a very minor illustrated tribute assessment of Tetelcingo, a tribute document from Taxco,

and a fragmentary native map from the region south of Tepecuacuilco. No data are available at present on the document from Chontalcoatlan although photographs are in private collections. The Lienzo de Noxtepec shows place glyphs for surrounding communities in Guerrero as well as in the neighboring states of Mexico and Morelos. It is closely related to the lienzo or lienzos from Tetlama, Morelos.

Hidalgo. The 14 pictorial manuscripts from the state of Hidalgo (fig. 6) are listed and classified in Table 16. The most notable is the Primeros Memoriales, containing drawings by the informants of Sahagún. It

TABLE 16—CLASSIFICATION OF THE PICTORIAL MANUSCRIPTS OF THE STATE OF HIDALGO

Calendrical manuscripts:
142 Códice de Huichapan (part)
212 Meztitlan Calendar Wheel
271 SAHAGUN: Primeros Memoriales (part)

Historical manuscripts:
142 Códice de Huichapan
271 SAHAGUN: Primeros Memoriales (part)
369 Anales de Tula

Cartographic manuscripts:
3 Mapa de Actopan y sus Alrededores

Economic manuscripts:
MIZQUIAHUALA SALES RECEIPTS:
216 —— Humboldt Fragment 7
217 —— Humboldt Fragment 13
218 —— Poinsett Fragment 1
219 —— Poinsett Fragment 2
220 —— Rechnung über gelieferte Naturalien
221 —— Tira de Tributos
243 Códice Osuna, part 5
304 Pintura del Peublo de Tecpatepec

Ethnographic and miscellaneous manuscripts:
271 SAHAGUN: Primeros Memoriales (part)

Unavailable manuscripts:
222 Tributos de Mizquiahuala

Maps of the Relaciones Geográficas, 1579–85:
RG 10 Cempoala (Zempoala)
RG 22 Epazoyuca (Epazoyucan)
RG 38 Misquiahuala (Mixquiahuala)
RG 67 Tetlistaca (Atliztaca, Mun. Metepec)

is the first product of Sahagún's campaign of work in Tepepulco, Hidalgo, and is the oldest of the surviving Sahaguntine manuscripts related to the Florentine Codex. The drawings in the Primeros Memoriales include a wide range of ritual, calendrical, religious, historical, and miscellaneous subjects, some of which were later copied into the Florentine Codex. It is perhaps uncertain if the artists were natives of the Tepepulco region or if they were from Texcoco, the dominant town of the Acolhua region of which Tepepulco was a part.

The historical annals from Tula—the Otomi Códice de Huichapan and the Anales de Tula—embrace the years 1403–1528 and 1361–1521, respectively. Their historical notices are more extensive for happenings in the Valley of Mexico than for Hidalgo. The specifically historical section of the Primeros Memoriales (Paso y Troncoso, 1905–07, 6: 113–8) has drawings of the native rulers of Tenochtitlan, Texcoco, and Huexotla.

The one manuscript classified as cartographic, the Mapa de Actopan y sus Alrededores, is a late production, marginal to the native artistic tradition. Excluded from the census are three published maps of 1599 from Tlilcuautla, Tornacustla, and Ilamatlan, Hidalgo. They accompany documents of civil congregation in the AGN (Tierras, vol. 64, exps. 1 and 2) and have been published by Simpson (1934, pp. 58, 60, 68). Only the example from Tornacustla exhibits specific native iconographic features, such as a few personal name glyphs and several vestigial place glyphs.

From Mizquiahuala is a remarkable corpus of six drawings of various foodstuffs and other goods and services sold by the Indians to a Spaniard. They are typical of relatively late (1569–73) tribute manuscripts. The Pintura del Pueblo de Tecpatepec may belong to the same series, though its subject matter is somewhat different. Whether or not the lost Tributos de Mizquiahuala belonged to the same series is unknown.

Morelos. Pictorial manuscripts classified under the state of Morelos (fig. 7) are listed in Table 17. Most of them are economic manuscripts which treat colonial tribute, property disputes, or the census of local populations. The Códice de Moctezuma, the only annals from Morelos, concerns the history of Mazatepec and Xochiltepec and includes notices of the Valley of Mexico as well as notable drawings of the Spanish conquest of Tenochtitlan.

The diverse corpus of manuscripts known collectively as the Códices de Tlaquiltenango contain tribute documents, a genealogy, sheets of music, and other fragments.

The Mapa de Coatlan del Rio is typical of 16th-Century colonial cartographic-historical manuscripts and presents the hieroglyphs of boundaries and data on local cacique succession. Another manuscript in this category, the Lienzo de Tetlama, is unstudied and is known through a relatively large number of versions, only one of which has been published.

The 28 Códices Indígenas del Marque-

TABLE 17—CLASSIFICATION OF THE PICTORIAL MANUSCRIPTS OF THE STATE OF MORELOS

Historical manuscripts:
223 Códice Moctezuma

Genealogical manuscripts:
343 Códices de Tlaquiltenango (part)

Cartographic-historical manuscripts:
 65 Mapa de Coatlan del Rio
141 Plan topographique de Hueyapan
327 Lienzo de Tetlama

Economic manuscripts:
  1 Padrón de los Mayeques de Acapixtla
144 HUITZILA: Pintura de las Tierras de Quahunacazco
160 Códices Indígenas de algunos Pueblos del Marquesado del Valle, nos. 1–28
178 Manuscrit Judiciaire de 1534
323 Census of Tepoztlan
343 Códices de Tlaquiltenango (part)

Miscellaneous manuscripts:
343 Códices de Tlaquiltenango (part)

Maps of the Relaciones Geográficas, 1579–85:
RG 2 Acapistla (Yecapistla)
RG 23 Guaxtepec (Oaxtepec, Mun. Yautepec)

TABLE 18—CLASSIFICATION OF THE PICTORIAL
MANUSCRIPTS OF THE STATE OF PUEBLA

Historical manuscripts:

69 Códice de Coetzala
93 Libro de los Guardianes de Cuauhtinchan
101 Mapa de Cuauhtlantzinco
102 —— additional fragments
161 Papers of Itzcuintepec
316 Anales de Tepeaca, 1528–1634
359 Historia Tolteca-Chichimeca (part)
432 Mapa de Chalchihuapan

Genealogical manuscripts:

35 Confirmation des Elections de Calpan
91 Genealogía de Cuauhquechollan-Macuilxochitepec
  (obverse)
139 Matrícula de Huexotzingo (part)
161 Papers of Itzcuintepec (part)
173 Genealogía de Don Felipe Ixtlilxochitl
175 SAN MATEO JOPANAQUE: Property plan and
  genealogy

Cartographic manuscripts:

91 Genealogía de Cuauhquechollan-Macuilxochitepec
  (reverse)
97 Mapa de Cuauhtinchan no. 4
338 Mapa de San Matias Tlalancalco

Cartographic-historical manuscripts:

57 Códice de Cholula
89 Lienzo de Cuauhquechollan
90 Mapa circular de Cuauhquechollan
94 Mapa de Cuauhtinchan no. 1
95 Mapa de Cuauhtinchan no. 2
96 Mapa de Cuauhtinchan no. 3
115 Mapa de Ecatepec y Huitziltepec
199 Lienzo de Metlatoyuca
245 Lienzo de Oyametepec y Huitzilatl
300 Mapa de Tecamachalco
359 Historia Tolteca-Chichimeca (part)

Economic manuscripts:

43 Códice Chavero
139 Matrícula de Huexotzingo
175 SAN MATEO JOPANAQUE: Property plan and
  genealogy
224 Codex Monteleone
321 The Painted Tribute Record of Tepexi de la Seda
400 Plainte . . . de Xalpantepec
408 Codex of Xochitepec
426 Códice del Tequitlato de Zapotitlan

Miscellaneous and unclassified manuscripts:

50 Lienzo de Chicontla
169 Une Emeute parmi les Indigènes d'Ixtacmaxtitlan

Maps of the Relaciones Geográficas, 1579–85:

RG 14 Cholula (Cholula de Rivadabia)

RG 20 Cuzcatlan (Cozcatlan), version 1
RG 21 Cuzcatlan (Cozcatlan), version 2
RG 25 Gueytlalpa (Hueytlalpan)
RG 31 Jujupango, Xuxupango (Jojupango)
RG 34 Matlatlan (Chila)
RG 58 Tenanpulco and Matlactonatico (Tenampulco)
RG 87 Zacatlan (Zacatlan)

sado del Valle, comprehended under one number in the census, come from the Cuernavaca-Xiutepec region. They were exhibits in local disputes with the Cortés estate, about 1549.

A large number of maps from Morelos which are in the Ramo de Tierras of the Archivo General de la Nación, Mexico, have been listed and briefly described by Mazari (1926c). Some are of late 16th- or early 17th-century date. Mazari's descriptions suggest that at least some are partially in the native traditon. One, the "Pintura del Pueblo de Ocuituco" (AGN-T 2782, exp. 7; Mazari, 1926c, pp. 332–33, no. 35), has been published by Cuevas (1921–28, 1: 361). It shows Tlalnepantla, the church of Ocuituco, and a hieroglyph for the volcano of Popocatepetl. Since it is only marginally in the native tradition, it is not included in the census. The only documents listed by Mazari that we have included are the property plan from Huitzila (Mazari, 1926c, no. 12) and the map from Santa Cruz Xoxocotlan (ibid., no. 68), the latter from Eastern Oaxaca and not Morelos.

Puebla. The 33 pictorial manuscripts here classified under the state of Puebla (see Table 18) represent a wide variety of types and proveniences. All are presumably colonial in date; few have been adequately or fully published. Like other regional divisions used in this survey, the state of Puebla (fig. 8) is an arbitrary region, embracing various linguistic groups. The pictorial manuscripts from Puebla have diverse cultural origins and stylistic affiliations. Most of the manuscripts are attributed to Nahuatl communities, but from the northern and southeastern parts of the state there are documents that may be from Totonac, Otomi, Popoloca, or Mixtec proveniences.[35]

We know of no previous attempt to isolate, classify, or to discuss the pictorial manuscripts from Puebla as a whole. The *Cartografía de Puebla* (1958), however, is devoted to a listing of maps from Puebla that are in the Archivo General de la Nación, Mexico. Included among those that are reproduced in the publication are a small number from the late 16th and early 17th centuries that exhibit such details as an occasional place glyph, the use of footprints (as well as horses' hoofprints) to indicate roads, and water signs. None of these items, all of which are relatively peripheral, is included in the census.

The Mixteca-Puebla style, which is recognized in late archaeological horizons and may have centered in the Valley of Puebla, is considered manifest in some of the manuscripts of the Borgia Group of ritual-calendrical manuscripts. Although members of the group have been assigned by some authorities to Cholula, or at least to Puebla, the provenience of the group is both speculative and controversial and is therefore discussed separately. Otherwise, there are no surviving ritual or calendrical manuscripts from Puebla.

An interesting set of pictorial manuscripts comes from Cuauhtinchan in central Puebla. One of them, the Historia Tolteca-Chichimeca, is a major historical and artistic document. Primarily a Nahuatl text treating the migration of the Nonoualca and Tolteca-Chichimeca from Tollan into Puebla and later events, it is a "commentary on a lost pictorial manuscript from which it copies occasional pictures" (Barlow, 1948f, p. 266).

Among them are a number of maps combining toponymic and historical details. The manuscript has been published in an excellent black and white facsimile. Part of a mural in the convent of Cuauhtinchan is comparable to a part of the manuscript (Edwards, 1966, fig. 40; Reyes Valerio, 1967).

Three of the four Mapas de Cuauhtinchan that were discovered in the town in 1891 are handsome and important examples of histories set in cartographic frameworks. In style and content they form part of the series of maps contained in the Historia Tolteca-Chichimeca. Although two of the originals and two copies have been published and studied by Simons (1968), they continue inadequately published and deserve full-scale facsimile editions in color. The fourth map from Cuauhtinchan is in a far more acculturated and later style but forms part of the same series. Cartographically, the maps depict an area that in the most comprehensive example includes Cholula, Cuauhtinchan, Tecamachalco, Nopaluca, and Mount Matlacueyatl (La Malinche). Cuauhtinchan is depicted in all four examples by an eagle in the midst of a range of hills; this pictorial detail persists in a late map of the town of about 1698–1705 (*Cartografía de Puebla*, 1958, pl. 18), not included in the census.

Only extracts and a single illustration from the privately owned colonial annals (1519–1629) from the town, the Libro de los Guardianes de Cuauhtinchan, have been published (Barlow, 1946b; E. Orozco, 1892).

From Huexotzingo comes a unique corpus of economic manuscripts, one of which, Codex Monteleone, is among the earliest of the surely dated colonial tribute manuscripts. The Matrícula de Huexotzingo, in number of pages, is the largest of all known pictorial manuscripts from any region. It contains information on tribute, demography, countless personal name glyphs, and very striking drawings of colonial churches, comparable in their general style to the Franciscan convent murals at Huexotzingo, as well as genealogies. Códice Chavero pre-

[35] The Anales de Puebla, 1638–77 (BNP 377) and the Anales de Puebla y Tlaxcala no. 2 (AAMC 19), which contain some minor pictorial elements, or copies thereof, are described in Art. 27B, nos. 1090 and 1094. We have not examined the documents from Xalpantepec or Tlalancalco (both BNP) or an adequate photograph of the Lienzo de Oyametepec y Huitzilatl (the regional classification of which is provisional).

sents the tribute for various dependencies or barrios of Huexotzingo for the years 1571–79. Unpublished notes by Nicholson suggest the possibility of a Huexotzingo vicinity provenience for the Map of Chichimec History, here classified with documents from the Valley of Mexico.

Several pictorial manuscripts are associated with Cuauhquechollan, the modern Huaquechula. The large Lienzo de Cuauhquechollan is an intricate portrayal of warfare and other events of the early colonial period. Also from Cuauhquechollan are a genealogy and an unpublished map cast in an interesting circular pattern.

The Mapa de Cuauhtlantzinco, like the Lienzo de Tlaxcala, is a commemorative document intended to portray the exploits of the town in events of the early period of Spanish conquest. Similar to this curious series of paintings are the "additional fragments" (no. 102), of uncertain provenience, and the Mapa de Chalchihuapan (no. 432).[36]

The partially published Códice de Cholula is an extraordinarily crude and complex document, drawn on both sides, that combines Nahuatl texts, historical scenes, and cartographic material. Also from Cholula is the "Mapa de Santa Isabel Iztazoatlan Atli-meian," a copy of which is reproduced by de la Maza (1959, p. 74). Although the depiction of roads by footprints may suggest some Indian influence, it is too peripheral for inclusion in the census. Attention may also be drawn to the Confirmation des Elections de Calpan, an important record of town hierarchy of 1578, from the western border of central Puebla.

[36] A. Bandelier (1884, p. 143, and in White and Bernal, 1960, p. 240), who mentioned these manuscripts, also refers to a Mapa de (San Jeronimo) Tecuanipan, otherwise unknown. The possibility that the "additional fragments" of the Mapa de Cuauhtlantzinco are the Mapa de Tecuanipan deserves investigation. The "Plano del pueblo de Cuauhtlantzinco hecho por orden del Virey Velasco" reported by Bandelier (in White and Bernal, 1960, p. 328) has not come to the attention of modern investigators.

From northern Puebla, an area inhabited by Totonac, Otomi, and Nahuatl groups in the 16th century, are two documents that share a very distinctive regional style: the Lienzo de Metlatoyuca and Papers of Itzcuintepec. The latter is of unidentified local provenience, but analysis of place names among its glosses should clarify the question. Like the Lienzo de Metlatoyuca, its content is largely genealogical but it also has ethnographic and historical information. A northern Puebla provenience for the Lienzo de Tzoquitetlan, here listed among the unclassified manuscripts of Central Mexico, is suggested by the occurrence of "Metlateocan" among its glosses and a superficial resemblance to the Lienzo de Chicontla.

Four pictorial manuscripts are from southeastern Puebla, in part a Popoloca region bordering on the Mixtec region of Western Oaxaca. The Zapotitlan shown in figure 8 is the unverified provenience of a local pictorial census which bears glosses in a Mixtec dialect. The Mapa de Tecamachalco has a long genealogy, the origin of part of which may extend into the Mixteca. The provenience of the unpublished Mapa de Ecatepec y Huitziltepec is uncertain. It exhibits the interlaced A–O year symbol and, for persons depicted thereon, calendrical rather than personal name glyphs, as is also true with the Mapa de Tecamachalco. Persons having the same names as some of those appearing on the manuscript also appear in the Anales de Tecamachalco (see Art. 27B, no. 1112). The Huitziltepec shown in figure 8 may or may not correspond to the Huitziltepec of the manuscript. The fourth document from southeastern Puebla is a minor and late tribute manuscript from Tepexi de la Seda.

A possible Tecamachalco region provenience for Códice de la Cueva and Códice Topográfico Fragmentado has been indicated by Nicholson in unpublished notes. These manuscripts are grouped herein with unclassified Central Mexican documents and as Western Oaxacan, respectively. Place glyphs in the Mixtec Códice Sánchez Solís include Acatlan, a community in southern Puebla on the border of the Mixteca Baja region.

Queretaro. The state of Queretaro, lying between the states of Hidalgo and Guanajuato, for the most part falls outside the Mesoamerican culture area. It is not represented by any pictorial manuscripts in the census. From San Juan del Rio, near the southern extremity of the state, however, there is a minor and published property plan of 1590 showing such native elements as water symbols, footprints to indicate roads, and vestigial place glyphs. It has been reproduced by Ayala Echávarri (1940). The original forms part of a document in AGN-T 2782.

Tlaxcala. The state of Tlaxcala, like other states used in the present classification, is an arbitrary region. It is smaller than the preconquest province of Tlaxcala and its neighbors, who together maintained an independent enclave within the Aztec Empire (Barlow, 1949d, end map), and it is considerably smaller than the 16th-century bishopric of Tlaxcala (Gibson, 1952, map, p. 59), with which it should not be confused, centered in Puebla.

An uncertain number of pictorial manuscripts in the Archivo General del Estado, Tlaxcala, have been excluded from the census. Photographic copies of several have been examined; none are major documents, most being genealogies and property plans forming part of late 16th- and early 17th-century lawsuits. A detail from one, the "Genealogy and Properties of Descendants of Iztac Chichimecatl no. 2," has been published by Nicholson, 1967, fig. 4.

In a series of bibliographical appendices to his *Tlaxcala in the Sixteenth Century* Gibson included an annotated listing of Tlaxcalan pictorial manuscripts (Gibson, 1952, pp. 264–69). These and a number of additions are in the census (see Table 19). Under "documents now unknown" Gibson

TABLE 19–CLASSIFICATION OF THE PICTORIAL MANUSCRIPTS OF THE STATE OF TLAXCALA

Ritual-calendrical manuscripts:
15 Tonalamatl Aubin
388 Veytia Calendar Wheel no. 2
391 Veytia Calendar Wheel no. 5
392 Veytia Calendar Wheel no. 6
393 Veytia Calendar Wheel no. 7

Historical manuscripts:
104 Códice de Cuetlaxcohuapan
348 Anales de Tlaxcala no. 2, 1519–1692
350 Lienzo de Tlaxcala
351 —— Códice de la Conquista
352 —— untitled pages

Genealogical manuscripts:
61 Genealogy of Citlalpopoca
103 Genealogía de Cuauhtli
194 Genealogy of Maxixcatzin
227 Das Dokument der Familie Mundanegre aus Chichimecapan
262 Properties of the Descendants of Quauhtliztactzin (part)
319 Genealogía de una Familia de Tepeticpac
347 Genealogie des Tlatzcantzin
427 Genealogía de Zolin

Cartographic manuscripts:
349 Códice de Tlaxcala (reverse)

Cartographic-historical manuscripts:
41 Lienzo Chalchihuitzin Vasquez
45 Lienzo de Don Juan Chichimecatecuhtli
76 Pintura de Contlantzinco
135 Códice de Huamantla
337 Mapa de San Pedro Tlacotepec
411 Pintura de Santo Tomas Xochtlan

Economic manuscripts (property plans):
257 Códice de las Posesiones de Don Andrés
262 Properties of the Descendants of Quauhtliztactzin (part)
298 Mapa de Santa Barbara Tamasolco

Miscellaneous and unclassified manuscripts:
275 Manta de Salamanca
349 Códice de Tlaxcala (obverse)

Unavailable manuscripts:
278 Linderos del Pueblo de San Matias

(ibid., pp. 269–72) discussed a number of lost pictorial manuscripts. Two, the "Calendar of movable and fixed ceremonies" and the Xicotencatl genealogy, have since been identified as the Tonalamatl Aubin and the Genealogía de una Familia de Tepeticpac, respectively. The others, still unidentified, are not listed in the census. Some are genealogies that were in the Boturini collection and may unknowingly be included in Table 19 or be among the regionally unclassified manuscripts of Central Mexico (Table 21), their Boturini antecedents or numbers unidentified.

In a recent study of Tlaxcalan pictorial manuscripts Nicholson (1967) has shown that a twisted bicolor (red and white) headband, frequently with a plume of feathers (*aztaxelli*), appears as an element of costume in 11 (12, if one includes the Veytia Calendar Wheel no. 5) pictorial manuscripts that on other grounds may be classified as Tlaxcalan, as well as in two documents in the Archivo General del Estado, Tlaxcala, not included in the census. Since the element may be diagnostic of Tlaxcalan provenience, we have accordingly classified six manuscripts, of otherwise uncertain origin, as Tlaxcalan: Lienzo de Don Juan Chichimecatecuhtli, Genealogía de Cuauhtli, Das Dokument der Familie Mundanegre aus Chichimecapan, Códice de las Posesiones de Don Andrés, Généalogie des Tlatzcantzin, Genealogía de Zolin. Despite the compelling nature of Nicholson's presentation, the provenience of these manuscripts must be regarded as tentative.

Nicholson (1967) also notes other traits that occur frequently in Tlaxcalan manuscripts: the use of a serrated vertical profile in the depiction of native structures, the representation of coursed masonry (particularly above the lintels of doors), wooden stools rather than the backed seat of authority (*tepotzoicpalli*), the drawing of a house at the head of genealogies, and floral bouquets held by persons of high rank. Since these traits may also occur in non-Tlaxcalan manuscripts (such as the Matrícula de Huexotzingo), however, they have not been used as classificatory devices.[37]

Among the calendrical documents, the Tonalamatl Aubin is a major and possibly preconquest divinatory almanac; its Tlaxcalan provenience, however, has yet to be demonstrated. Various lines of evidence relate Veytia Calendar Wheel no. 2 to Tlaxcala, but in view of its association with European authorship it may be a synthetic product drawing on generalized Central Mexican calendrics. It is known through several versions; the oldest and probable original is associated with Fray Toribio de Benavente or Motolinía.

Veytia Calendar Wheel no. 5 is the only calendrical document reliably attributed to Tlaxcala. First published in 1770, it is known through a copy or copies of a document attributed to Manuel de los Santos y Salazar (1685–1715), a Tlaxcalan religious and cura of Cuapiaxtla.[38] It begins the year with the month Atemoztli, a feature that is considered a Tlaxcalan trait (Caso, 1958a, p. 69, and Table II). Veytia Calendar Wheels nos. 6 and 7 have also been attributed to Santos y Salazar on the basis of statements in the inventories of the Boturini collection.

Of the historical manuscripts, the Lienzo de Tlaxcala is one of the outstanding documents from mid-16th-century Mexico. Details from it have been used to illustrate an untold number of historical works on Mexico. Although the origins of the lienzo are still obscure, its large size and format suggest that it was intended for display by the officialdom of Tlaxcala. It is a commemor-

---

[37] Nicholson (1967) lists 34 Tlaxcalan pictorials as opposed to the 29 given here. The difference lies in his inclusion of four manuscripts in the AGT and five others here listed among the regionally unclassified manuscripts of Central Mexico. We have added Veytia Calendar Wheels 2, 6, and 7 and the Linderos del Pueblo de San Matías.

[38] *Certificados de estudio . . . de Manuel de los Santos y Salazar*, MS 1735, Library of Congress Ac. 1121, III–48-B,2. This manuscript contains a pictorial genealogy of the ascendants of Santos y Salazar extending to Bartolomé Citlalpopoca; it is not in the native tradition and is not included in the census.

ative document that portrays the role of the Tlaxcalans as allies of Cortés in the conquest of Mexico. Its separate scenes depict Tlaxcalans engaged in events that include the first baptism of the Lords of Tlaxcala, the massacre at Cholula, the conquest of Tenochtitlan, and later episodes of the conquest. Although several "originals" and early copies are lost, it may be studied through an 18th-century copy in Mexico and two variant lithographed editions based on another version as well as related manuscripts listed in the census.

The Códice de Cuetlaxcohuapan, possibly drawn in the city of Puebla de los Angeles, depicts an isolated event of Tlaxcalan colonial judicial or administrative procedure. If its date is correctly assigned, it was probably drawn by a Spaniard.

Of the eight genealogies in the inventory, only two—those of Citlalpopoca and Maxixcatzin—are of persons known through other sources. The single manuscript classified as cartographic, the reverse of Códice de Tlaxcala, is a late and very crude map drawn on the back of a now effaced painting in the native tradition.

Among the more complex cartographic-historical manuscripts, the Códice de Huamantla may represent the Sacred War of the Flowers. Its provenience and distinctive style have been associated with the Otomi of eastern Tlaxcala; it is the only Tlaxcalan pictorial not associated with a presumably Nahua origin. Only the inclusion of a few Spaniards and some Christian crosses testify to its colonial date. Also from the same provenience was a large lienzo that was in the Boturini collection. Now lost, it is not included in the census. The Lienzo Chalchihuitzin Vásquez stands out for the achievement of its artist; its style suggests that it is a relatively late document of the 16th century. It has no adequate interpretation or commentary, although good photographs have been· published. Its apparent provenience is in doubt; the Tzompantepec in

figure 9 is based on the reading of several place-name glosses on the lienzo.

The Mapa de San Pedro Tlacotepec, showing the boundaries of the town, is of interest for its depiction of Cortés and Marina. The original shows Cortés' left leg in a very deformed position, a feature not evident in the published copy. A very similar and undoubtedly related portrait of Cortés (with his left leg also deformed) and Marina is contained in a possibly 18th-century oil painting preserved in the nearby village of Ahuazhuatepec. The latter, not included in the census, shows them meeting a group of Tlaxcalan nobles. An oil painting showing the boundaries of Ahuazhuatepec, also preserved in the village, is not in the native tradition.

The paintings from Contlantzinco and Xochtlan are of a late type that would possibly never have been brought to scholarly attention had they not been included in a codex collection. We have not identified the Xochtlan with certainty; it may correspond to the Santo Tomas shown in figure 9 in the ex-district of Zaragoza.

The three manuscripts classed as economic are all property plans. The Códice de las Posesiones de Don Andrés, tentatively assigned to Tlaxcala, shows numerous plots of land with place glyphs and dimensions. The Mapa de Santa Barbara Tamasolco is a late item with Nahuatl glosses only peripherally in the native artistic tradition. The drawing of the Properties of the Descendants of Quauhtliztactzin has place glyphs for localities in eastern Tlaxcala and includes a genealogy in a handsome colonial style.

Veracruz. The 14 pictorial manuscripts here classified under the state of Veracruz (fig. 10) are listed in Table 20. None are from southern Veracruz. The single cartographic document is unpublished and known only through a late copy. No description is available for the Códice de Chumatlan, which has been reported only by title. The 12 cartographic-historical manuscripts

TABLE 20—CLASSIFICATION OF THE
PICTORIAL MANUSCRIPTS OF
THE STATE OF VERACRUZ

Cartographic manuscripts:
292 Mapa jeroglífico de Sintlatetelco

Cartographic-historical manuscripts:
  49 Mapa de Chiconquiaco
  63 Lienzo de Coacoatzintla
214 Lienzo de Misantla
233 Lienzo de San Juan Nayotla
320 Mapa de San Antonio Tepetlan
360 Mapa de Tonayan
373–378 Lienzos de Tuxpan nos. 1–6

Unavailable manuscripts:
  59 Códice de Chumatlan

Maps of the Relaciones Geográficas, 1579–85:
RG 39 Mizantla (Misantla)
RG 44 Papantla (Papantla de Olarte)
RG 53 Tecolutla (Tecolutla)

depict town boundaries and incidental historical detail. All are fully in the native tradition of the 16th century, but, with the possible exception of the unstudied Lienzos de Tuxpan, probably none derive from preconquest prototypes. The three documents associated with Misantla, Tepetlan, and Tonayan are the only ones that have been studied. None, however, have been examined in conjunction with the extensive documentation available in the AGN on jurisdictional disputes in Veracruz which are the apparent origins of most of these documents. Cline (1959) provides a survey of 16th-century cartographic sources for Veracruz toponyms and reproduces the documents from Misantla and Tonayan.

The documents from Chapultepec or Tonayan, Chiconquiaco, Coacoatzintla, Tepetlan, and Misantla are from communities that were Totonac or bilingual (Totonac and Nahuatl) in the 16th century. The six Lienzos de Tuxpan are from the Huastec region of Veracruz. The provenience of the Lienzo de San Juan Nayotla is in doubt; we have not identified any community with this name.

A summary listing of pictorial manuscripts from Veracruz has been published by Melgarejo Vivanco (1953). The bibliographies of two works by Ramírez Lavoignet (1959, 1962), both on the Misantla region, provide additional data. These three sources together list six unpublished "codices" from the Ramo de Tierras of the AGN, most of which we have not examined. Since they are undescribed in the literature and their relevance to the census is uncertain, they have been omitted. They are listed here as a matter of record:

1. Códice Tonayan, 1643. AGN-T 1209
2. Pintura de Chacaltianguis, 1589. AGN-T 2082
3. Pintura de Cosamaloapan, Huaxpaltepec y Rio Alvarado. AGN-T 963
4. Pintura de Ixmatlahuacan, 1587. AGN-T 2687
5. Códice Joaquín de Leguizamo, 1573. AGN-T 2672
6. Códice Rodrigo Cano de Villegas, 1589. AGN-T 2672

Two further documents, also from the AGN and listed by Melgarejo Vivanco (1953, p. 334), have been published by Domínguez (1943, pp. 58–64) but are omitted from the census. They are simple local maps with minor native components related to early 17th-century grants of land. They are probably typical of scores of documents in the AGN that preserve the Indian tradition only in such peripheral details as footprints to indicate roads and rudimentary place glyphs. Their titles are:

7. Códice Teteltzinco. (Pintura mandada a hacer por los naturales, con motivo de la merced concedida de las tierras llamadas Teteltzingo.) AGN-T 2702
8. Códice Tlacotepec. (Pintura mandada a hacer por los naturales con motivo de las mercedes concedidas de Tlacotepeque y Atecaxic). AGN-T 2775

REGIONALLY UNCLASSIFIED MANUSCRIPTS OF CENTRAL MEXICO. The regional provenience of 59 pictorial manuscripts in the census has not been determined. They are

TABLE 21—TYPOLOGICAL CLASSIFICATION OF THE REGIONALLY UNCLASSIFIED PICTORIAL MANUSCRIPTS OF CENTRAL MEXICO

Calendrical manuscripts:

239 Rueda de los Nueve Señores de la Noche
285 SERNA: Drawings of day and month symbols
287 Serna Calendar Wheel no. 2
389 Veytia Calendar Wheel no. 3

Historical manuscripts:

120 Anales de Diego García, 1502–1601

Genealogical manuscripts:

 80 Genealogía de Cotitzin y Zozahuic
121 Genealogie von 33 Personen
146 Genealogy of Huitznahuac Calpulli
200 Genealogía de Metztepetl
226 Fragmento de las Mujeres
234 Genealogía de Nexmoyotla, Ateno, Zoyatitlan y Hueytetla
237 Genealogía de Nopalxochitl
253 Genealogía de Pitzahua
328 Genealogía de Tetlamaca y Tlametzin

Cartographic manuscripts:

268 Mapa de una Región Boscosa
331 Mapa de San Pedro Tezontepec
380 Lienzo de Tzoquitetlan
381 Map of unidentified locality

Cartographic-historical manuscripts:

105 Códice de la Cueva
134 Lienzo of the Heye Foundation

Economic (tribute) manuscripts:

122–127 Gilcrease Fragments 1–6
152 Humboldt Fragments 9–12
153 Humboldt Fragment 14
154 Humboldt Fragment 15
259 Fragment d'un Procès (BNP 86)
345 Rôle des Impôts . . . de Tlatengo
367 Fragmento de Tributos
396 Códice del Volador
428 Códice Lucas Alaman
431 American Manuscript no. 10, part 8

Economic (census and cadastral) manuscripts:

149 Humboldt Fragment 5
151 Humboldt Fragment 8
236 Nómina escrita en geroglífico
267 Cadastral Fragment of the Ramírez Collection
294 Steuerliste von 40 Personen

Economic (property plans) manuscripts:

 55 Die Flurkarte des Chiquatzin Tecuihtli
 64 Mapa de Coatepetl
116 Plano de un Edificio
277 Plano de San Joseph, sujeto a Xilotepeque

382 Plan of unidentified property
383 Códice Valeriano
398 Códice de Xalapa
399 Plan of the houses of Juan de Xalbornoz & Juan Mateo

Economic (miscellaneous) manuscripts:

 75 Códice de Constancia de Gastos
183 Land Transfer Manuscript
256 Códice Porrúa Turanzas

Miscellaneous and unclassified manuscripts:

 36 Fragmento Caltecpaneca
128 GOMEZ DE CERVANTES: Relación de la Grana Cochinilla
132 HERNANDEZ: Historia natural de Nueva España
138 Plano ideográfico del Señorio de Huaxtepec
186 Legal Document in Hieroglyphics
204 Mexican Manuscript no. 2

Unavailable manuscripts:

140 Mapa de los Terrenos de Hueyapan
286 Serna Calendar Wheel no. 1

listed and classified typologically in Table 21. General considerations of style, content, and language of glosses indicate that it is doubtful that any are from Western Mexico or from Oaxaca, the other major regions of Mexico.[39] It is probable that many are from the Valley of Mexico or from adjacent regions—Tlaxcala or Puebla, for instance—but the research or data to classify them regionally are lacking. Most are relatively minor documents, of peripheral interest.

None of the persons shown on the nine genealogies has been identified through other sources. The few place names in these documents are insufficiently distinctive to locate without extensive research. Seven were in the Boturini collection; it is not unlikely that they all were. It may be noted here that the early inventories of the Boturini collection coincidentally list nine Tlaxcalan genealogies that have not been identified (Boturini, 1746, Catalog, Items 17-2 and 17-3; nos. 4-22 and 4-23 of the inventories of 1743 and 1745; see Article 29).

[39] The Plano ideográfico del Señorio de Huaxtepec, however, has been classified as from Oaxaca by Tamayo and Alcorta (1941, p. 23). We have not examined this document.

There is thus a possibility that some of the unclassified genealogies listed here may be Tlaxcalan. In this connection it should be noted that four genealogies, which may also have been in the Boturini collection, are here classified as Tlaxcalan solely on the basis of a headdress type.

Five of the manuscripts in Table 21, including two of the genealogies, have been classified by Nicholson (1967) as Tlaxcalan. These are: Fragmento Caltecpaneca, Genealogía de Nopalxochitl, Genealogie von 33 Personen, Flurkarte des Chiquatzin Tecuihtli, and Fragmento de las Mujeres. Although his classification is inherently probable, it is too tentative to accept in the present context.

The genealogies of Cotitzin y Zozahuic, Tetlamaca y Tlametzin, and Pitzahua, while varying in specific features of style, share certain attributes such as a checkerboard-and-dot decoration of the seats on which some individuals are seated. On this basis a common but unknown provenience might be postulated.

Among the cartographic manuscripts, the Lienzo de Tzoquitetlan is a detailed map showing numerous place names. Careful analysis of them should enable its provenience, possibly northern Puebla, to be determined. Both cartographic-historical manuscripts are of more than usual interest; the Lienzo of the Heye Foundation treats preconquest history and deserves full study.

Most manuscripts in the various economic subtypes are minor and typical documents of the middle and late periods of the 16th century. The six Gilcrease Fragments and the related Códice del Volador are probably from the Valley of Mexico. Humboldt Fragment 8 and the Cadastral Fragment of the Ramírez collection may, like other members of the Vergara Group, also be from the Valley of Mexico.

The Borgia Group

The Borgia Group of ritual-calendrical manuscripts presents the ethnohistorian with a singularly valuable corpus of documents surrounded by important problems of interpretation and provenience. In the context of a regional survey the manuscripts of the group require segregation because their provenience is both unknown and controversial. The group consists of from five to seven manuscripts. The basic five are Codices Borgia, Cospi, Féjérváry-Mayer, Laud, and Vaticanus B. They share certain traits which define their relationship: (1) preconquest date, (2) animal-hide screenfold format, (3) gross similarity of style, (4) intricate symbolism and iconography, and (5) complex religious and calendrical content involving elaborations of the 260-day divinatory cycle or tonalpohualli and associated gods. The histories of these manuscripts, all in Europe, are poorly known (see Tables 1 and 22).

The group as such was first defined by Seler (1902b) in an article initially published in 1887. Since then a sixth manuscript, Aubin Manuscript no. 20, a single panel of animal hide, has usually been considered a member of the group. In recent years a consensus for a Mixtec provenience for it has developed; it has accordingly been

TABLE 22—BORGIA GROUP OF RITUAL-CALENDRICAL MANUSCRIPTS

Dates of major commentaries by Eduard Seler (dates of translations in parentheses) and of the color facsimile editions patronized by the Duc de Loubat are shown as are the number of identifiable sections in each manuscript.

Borgia Group Manuscripts	Commentary by Seler	Facsimile by Loubat	No. of Sections
33 Codex Borgia	1904–09 (1963)	1898	28
79 Codex Cospi	1900	1898	4
118 Codex Féjérváry-Mayer	1901 (1901–02)	1901	17
185 Codex Laud			11
384 Codex Vaticanus B	1902 (1902–03)	1896	28

classified as Western Oaxacan in this survey. The ritual-calendrical passages on the reverse of Códice Porfirio Díaz have frequently been compared with the Borgia Group, but its association therewith is less direct, particularly since it has an ostensible Northern Oaxaca provenience.

No treatment of the Borgia Group can proceed without a discussion of the researches of the German scholar Eduard Seler and the excellent color facsimiles published under the patronage of the Duc de Loubat, who also financed the publication of the commentaries by Seler and other Americanist studies of the time (see Article 20). The dates of the Seler commentaries and of the Loubat facsimile editions are shown in Table 22.

Following the establishment of the group and of his basic methodological approach in 1887, Seler published a short study of Codex Borgia in 1898 (Seler, 1902f, represents a considerable expansion of this exposition). In the same year (Seler, 1902l; English translation, 1904h) his interpretation of parts of Codices Borgia, Cospi, Féjérváry-Mayer, and Vaticanus B as representing a Venus cycle appeared. In 1890 his study of Central Mexican tonalamatls was published; this was subsequently revised and appeared as a commentary on the Tonalamatl Aubin, a ritual-calendrical manuscript from either Tlaxcala or the Valley of Mexico (Seler, 1900; English translation, 1900–01). It accompanied a color facsimile financed by the Duc de Loubat and included treatments of comparable sections of Codices Borgia, Cospi, and Vaticanus B. With these publications as prelude his major commentaries on Féjérváry-Mayer, Vaticanus B, and Borgia soon followed. Although he never devoted a full-scale commentary to Codex Laud and only a short article to Codex Cospi, the latter is also treated in his other commentaries as are certain sections of the former. The last of his commentaries, that on Codex Borgia, is the crowning

achievement of his interpretive campaign; it includes interpretations of comparable passages in other manuscripts of the group as well as in other Central Mexican, Mixtec, and Maya manuscripts. It is a work of fundamental and enduring importance.

A recent appraisal of Seler's commentaries on the Borgia Group manuscripts (Nicholson, 1966b) notes his outstanding achievements in identifying mathematical-calendrical material and the iconographic attributes of gods. His success on an interpretive level, although considerable, is clouded by his speculative structures based in part on an increasing obsession with astronomical, Venus, and lunar theories. Advances in this field since his time, however, have been few. Until 1963, with its first translation (into Spanish), his commentary on Codex Borgia (1904–09) was his only major work untranslated from the German. Its appearance in a language more widely read among Middle Americanists may provide the groundwork for more research into this specialized field.

The five screenfolds of the Borgia Group were first published in color copies by Aglio in 1830 (Kingsborough, 1831–48). Inaccurate in detail and with consistently erroneous paginations, the Aglio-Kingsborough reproductions were the only editions available until the publication of the color facsimiles in screenfold format patronized by the Duc de Loubat. Four of the five manuscripts were so published between 1896 and 1901 with introductory and descriptive pamphlets by himself, Franz Ehrle, or Paso y Troncoso. For other editions and further bibliographic comment see the Borgia Group entry in the census as well as the five individual census entries.

By far the most important publication on the group since the work of Seler is the detailed analytical and annotated survey of their content as well as of other early ritual-calendrical manuscripts by Nowotny (1961b.) This intricate and ambitious work provides an outline (under 66 "catalog" headings) of the content of all these manuscripts, relates each manuscript to the outline, and provides descriptions, commentaries, and interpretations, when possible, of all sections of the manuscripts. It is generously illustrated; the plates and many of the expositions are accompanied by explanatory diagrams. With respect to particular sections of given manuscripts his interpretations differ from those of Seler and may be regarded as more conservative. A work of outstanding importance and utility, it is for the serious student and specialist the modern introduction and guide to the manuscripts of the Borgia Group and other manuscripts having similar content. Spranz (1964) is an ambitious study of the iconographic attributes of gods in the manuscripts of the group with important and revealing statistical studies of their associations and occurrences.

The problem of the provenience of the Borgia Group has attracted increasing attention in recent years. Studies of the problem, by an art historian (Robertson, 1963, 1964, 1966) and by an archaeologist (Nicholson, 1966c), together summarize all aspects of the question. One of the most notable developments in these treatments is the increasing emphasis on a Mixtec provenience for at least some members of the group, an hypothesis first seriously advanced by Robertson. In support for a Mixtec origin for most of the Borgia Group, Robertson has argued that differences in style between members of the group are no greater than between such pairs of Mixtec histories as Codices Nuttall and Vienna on the one hand and Bodley and Selden on the other.

Since the question of the meaning of the terms "Mixtec," "Puebla-Tlaxcala," and "Mixteca-Puebla" in this context are of importance, two articles by Nicholson (1960a, 1961a) on these terminological aspects are cited in the present bibliography.

No known evidence indicates where in Mexico the Borgia Group documents were collected. Since they uniformly lack identifiable historical, genealogical, or circumstantial geographical content, their provenience must be based on stylistic, iconographic, or other comparisons with archaeological remains from known cultures. Such comparisons have been made with painted pottery generally associated with the Mixteca–Puebla sphere, the mural paintings at Tizatlan, Tlaxcala (Caso, 1927), and the Mixtec murals at Mitla, in Eastern Oaxaca (Seler, 1895), and with other artifacts. The closest iconographic and stylistic resemblances, at least to some of the manuscripts of the group, in manuscript painting are to such Western Oaxaca Mixtec screenfold histories as Codices Nuttall and Vienna. As Robertson (1963, p. 154) has pointed out, most theories as to the provenience of the group prior to the recognition of the Mixtec origin of the Western Oaxaca historical screenfolds are of less importance than subsequent theories. Possible alternative proveniences that continue in consideration are central or southern coastal Veracruz, "Puebla-Tlaxcala," Cholula, Western Oaxaca (the "Mixteca"), and the Tehuacan–Cozcatlan–Teotitlan del Camino region on the Puebla-Oaxaca border. The latter region was favored at one time by Seler. Comparison of artifacts, pottery, and ethnographic traits of the Tehuacan Valley with depictions in Codex Borgia have led Chadwick and MacNeish (1967, p. 115) to the conclusion that "it seems probable that the Codex Borgia originated in the Señorio de Teotitlan, with the culture characterized as the Venta Salada [Postclassic] phase, and quite possibly within the Tehuacan Valley itself." This region lies to the north of the Mixteca Baja region of the Contact and early colonial period and was populated by Chocho–Popoloca, Mazatec, Nahuatl, and some Mixtec groups.

No serious consideration has been made

in modern times of a Valley of Mexico provenience. Few students of the question have felt that all five members of the group have the same provenience or even the same cultural affiliation. Alfonso Caso (1927, and personal communication), a prominent authority on Mixtec manuscripts, felt that nothing so much resembles Codex Borgia as the murals of Tizatlan. The similarities include representations of gods, specific iconographic and other forms, and various details, such as blue fingernails and claws. He rejected, on the basis of day-sign forms, a close relationship between the Mitla murals and the Borgia Group manuscripts. On the question of provenience he felt that available evidence does not permit a more precise assignment for Codices Borgia, Cospi, and Vaticanus B than "Puebla-Tlaxcala" and that this area includes the Tehuacan-Teotitlan del Camino region. For Codices Laud and Féjérváry-Mayer he apparently favored an unknown region subject to "Mixteca-Puebla" influence. Three other recent opinions are shown in List 3.

Stylistic and other subdivisions of the group have usually indicated a close relationship between Codices Féjérváry-Mayer and Laud with the others either grouped together or assigned separate status. The presence of what appear to be bar-and-dot numerals in the Maya system in Codices Laud, Féjérváry-Mayer, and Cospi reverse

has frequently attracted attention. Differences between the two sides of Codex Cospi are such that they have been treated as separate documents in comparative studies. A statistical study of the attributes of day signs in the screenfolds of the Borgia Group, the Mixtec histories, and certain other manuscripts by García Granados (1942) supports the pairing of Codices Féjérváry-Mayer and Laud with Codices Vaticanus B, Cospi reverse, Borgia, and Cospi obverse less closely related to the pair in that approximate order. The same study also reveals a closer relationship between Féjérváry-Mayer, Laud, and Vaticanus B than between such pairs of Mixtec screenfolds as Codices Bodley and Selden and Nuttall and Vienna, as well as other interesting but inconclusive relationships based on this single criterion. The same author (García Granados, 1940–41) has studied the occurrence of weapons in the same manuscripts, showing a greater difference among the Mixtec screenfolds than among the screenfolds of the Borgia Group.

State of Oaxaca

The geographical classification of the 93 pictorial manuscripts from Oaxaca utilized herein divides the state into three regions (see fig. 1). The Western region is closely associated with the important corpus of Mixtec manuscripts; the Northern region embraces Cuicatec, Mazatec, and Chinantec proveniences. The dominant linguistic family in Eastern Oaxaca was Zapotec. The regions are defined on the basis of these gross linguistic factors. The individual maps of the three regions (figs. 11–13) include the former political districts of Oaxaca, as defined by Lemoine (1954), for additional cartographic information.

In an important and early pioneer publication, Lehmann (1905a) surveyed the known pictorial manuscripts from Oaxaca. His study continues to be of great utility although it is naturally out of date in specific respects. The listing and bibliography of

LIST 3—PROVENIENCE OF THE BORGIA
GROUP MANUSCRIPTS ACCORDING TO
THREE AUTHORITIES

Manuscript	Nowotny (1961b)	Robertson (1964, 1966)	Nicholson (1966c)
Borgia	Cholula–Tlaxcala	Mixtec	Puebla–Tlaxcala
Cospi	Mixtec	Non-Mixtec?	Puebla–Tlaxcala
Féjérváry	Unclassified	Mixtec	Mixtec
Laud	Unclassified	Mixtec	Mixtec
Vaticanus B	Mixtec	Non-Mixtec?	Puebla–Tlaxcala

TABLE 23—CLASSIFICATION OF THE PICTORIAL
MANUSCRIPTS OF WESTERN OAXACA

Ritual-calendrical manuscripts:

14 Aubin Manuscript no. 20
112 Códice Dehesa (part)
395 Codex Vienna (obverse)

Historical manuscripts:

24 Códice Baranda
27 Codex Becker no. 1
28 Codex Becker no. 2
29 — additional fragment
31 Codex Bodley
72 Códice Colombino
112 Códice Dehesa
129 Fragmento Gómez de Orozco
228 Códice Muro
240 Codex Nuttall
279 Códice Sánchez Solís
283 Codex Selden
284 Selden Roll
370 Codex Tulane
395 Codex Vienna

Genealogical manuscripts:

156 Genealogy of the Cacique of Igualtepec
355 Genealogy of Tlazultepec
421 Mapa de San Pedro Yucunama

Cartographic manuscripts:

164 Plano topográfico de Santa Maria Ixcatlan (1870)
165 Plan topographique de Santa Maria Ixcatlan (1508)
291 Plano de San Andres Sinaxtla (1730)
299 Lienzo de Tamazulapan (1733)

Cartographic-historical manuscripts:

8 Lienzo Antonio de León
70 Lienzo de Coixtlahuaca no. 1
71 Lienzo de Coixtlahuaca no. 2
77 Lienzo Córdova-Castellanos
157 Lienzo de Santiago Ihuitlan
174 Lienzo de San Pedro Jicayan
195 Lienzo Meixueiro
215 Códice Mixteco Post-cortesiano no. 36
232 Lienzo de Santa Maria Nativitas
242 Lienzo de Santo Tomas Ocotepec
251 Lienzo of Philadelphia
409 Mapa de Xochitepec
419 Lienzo de Yolotepec
422 Lienzo de Zacatepec no. 1
423 Lienzo de Zacatepec no. 2
433 Lienzo de San Miguel Tequixtepec no. 1
434 Lienzo de San Miguel Tequixtepec no. 2

Economic manuscripts:

289 Códice Sierra
302 Códice de Tecomaxtlahuaca

361 Códice Topográfico Fragmentado
415 Códice de Yanhuitlan

Miscellaneous and unclassified manuscripts:

397 Waldeck Judgment Scene

Unavailable manuscripts:

163 Mapa de Santa Maria Ixcatlan
372 Códice de Tututepec

Maps of the Relaciones Geográficas, 1579–85:

RG 4 Amoltepec (Santiago Amoltepec, Dto. Nochistlan)
RG 18 Cuahuitlan (Cahuitan, Mun. Santiago Tepextla, Dto. Jamiltepec)
RG 43 Nochiztlan (Asuncion Nochixtlan, Dto. Nochistlan)
RG 60 Teozacoalco (San Pedro Teozcoalco, Dto. Nochistlan)
RG 69 Texupa (Santiago Tejupan, Dto. Teposcolula)

pictorial manuscripts from Oaxaca given by Martínez Ríos (1961, pp. 135–40) is fully comprehended in the present census. Other general works on pictorial manuscripts from Oaxaca are discussed below.

WESTERN OAXACA. The region here defined as Western Oaxaca comprises the former districts of Oaxaca shown in figure 11 with the ex-district of Teotitlan divided between the Northern and Western regions of the state. The eastern boundary is arbitrary. The region approximates the somewhat larger area known as the Mixteca, a geographic and linguistic region not readily adaptable to the present classification. In the 16th century the region was inhabited primarily by Mixtec Indians; it is the known provenience of most Mixtec manuscripts for which such data are available. The region, however, also includes other linguistic or ethnic groups, such as the Chocho-Popoloca, whose potential involvement with some of the "Mixtec" manuscripts from the region has yet to be investigated. Mixtec groups were also to be found in neighboring areas of Guerrero, Puebla, and Eastern Oaxaca.

The 47 pictorial manuscripts from Western Oaxaca (see Table 23) may be considered Mixtec on the basis either of style or of known provenience. The listing, however, does not include all documents sometimes

67

cited in connection with Mixtec studies. Códices Fernández Leal and Porfirio Díaz, both of which have the interlaced A–O year sign, sometimes considered a distinctive Mixtec and Popoloca trait, have been attributed to the Cuicatecs on slender evidence and are here classified under Northern Oaxaca. The same motif is present on the Mapa de Ecatepec y Huitziltepec, which we attribute to Puebla, as well as on the Mapa de Santa Cruz Xoxocotlan from Eastern Oaxaca. Two other manuscripts from Puebla, the Mapa de Tecamachalco and the Códice del Tequitlato de Zapotitlan, also have "Mixtec" features.

Recent years have seen a renewed interest in the provenience of the manuscripts of the Borgia Group. Robertson (1963, 1964, 1966) has argued on the basis of style that at least some of the group are Mixtec. Otherwise, ritual-calendrical manuscripts are poorly represented from Western Oaxaca. The question is discussed herein under the separate treatment of the Borgia Group.

An extensive and very specialized literature exists for the Mixtec manuscripts of Western Oaxaca, but there are few general works. A partial listing by Caso (1958e) as well as standard bibliographies of pictorial manuscripts supplement the basic survey by Lehmann (1905a). His survey, which covers 20 of the 47 pictorial manuscripts from Western Oaxaca, will continue to be of value although it was written before the Mixtec group of manuscripts and their provenience had been defined. A general survey of Mixtec writing and calendar is given by Caso (1965c).

Editions of four of the most important Mixtec manuscripts (Codices Bodley, Selden, Vienna, and the Selden Roll) were published by Kingsborough (1831–48) in the early 19th century, but their nature and significance were not determined until the early years of the 20th century. Around the turn of the century, Eduard Seler, engrossed in the interpretation of the ritual-calendri-

cal manuscripts of Central Mexico and of the Borgia Group, frequently utilized the Mixtec manuscripts (especially Codices Nuttall and Vienna) in his identification of the iconographic attributes of gods. He was also prominent in attempts to determine calendrical or astronomical significance in the intervals between dates in the Mixtec screenfolds (Seler, 1908c, for example)—dates now accepted as having at least a primary genealogical or historical character. Researches of this nature were also pursued by Lehmann, Kreichgauer, and others.

The calendrical-astronomical approach to the Mixtec histories has now largely been discredited and abandoned although its validity has yet to be determined. Further investigations along these lines, particularly in ritual passages (Codex Vienna, obverse, for example) or in the early or mythical parts of Mixtec history may still prove rewarding.

The realization that the Mixtec screenfolds were primarily historical in nature is generally credited to Zelia Nuttall. In her commentary on Codex Nuttall (Nuttall, 1902) she determined that historical sequences involving specific persons could be isolated. She is also credited with identifying the nature of the personal name glyph (as distinguished from the calendrical name glyph). She was followed in this approach by Clark (1912), who showed that the life of 8 Deer, a famous Mixtec ruler of the 11th century, could be studied in Codices Becker no. 1, Bodley, Colombino, Nuttall, Selden, and Vienna—the so-called Nuttall Group of manuscripts. In 1926 Long analyzed the dates in Codex Nuttall (obverse) and noted that they were more compatible with genealogical-historical events than with calendrical or ritual interpretations.

The study by H. J. Spinden (1935) continued this line of approach and further defined the historical character of such manuscripts as Codices Bodley and Selden. He also established the interpretive method so successfully pursued in more recent years by Alfonso Caso. The Spinden study, though out of date in some respects, particularly in chronology, remains a useful introduction in English to the Mixtec histories.

The foundation for the successful interpretation of the Mixtec pictorial manuscripts, however, was laid in a study by Alfonso Caso published in 1949 but apparently presented in preliminary form in a lecture before the Sociedad Mexicana de Antropología in November of 1942.[40] In it he showed that the two genealogies on the Mapa de Teozacoalco (a *Relación geográfica* map of 1580) were those of the interrelated dynasties of Tilantongo and Teozacoalco and that the same persons appeared with essentially the same personal name and place glyphs in Codices Nuttall, Bodley, Selden, and Vienna. This study established the Western Oaxaca provenience of the Nuttall Group of Mixtec screenfolds beyond doubt. In subsequent studies of the dates in Codices Bodley, Selden, and Vienna Caso (1951, 1952) established a chronology for the Mixtec genealogies extending from the 16th century back to the mythological beginnings of recorded Mixtec history in the 7th century. The correlation between Mixtec and Christian dates utilized by Caso and in the present census is that proposed by Jiménez Moreno (in Jiménez Moreno and Mateos Higuera, 1940).

Since 1949 Caso has prepared commentaries on practically all the known Mixtec historical and cartographic-historical manuscripts. Twelve of them have been published. Together they constitute the groundwork for his planned comprehensive interpretation of Mixtec history and genealogy, *Reyes y Reinos de la Mixteca*.[41] Other scholars who have been associated with similar research are Burland, Dark, Nowotny, and M. E. Smith.

The surviving corpus of pictorial manuscripts from Western Oaxaca displays a more uniform and native style than those from any other region of Oaxaca or Central Mexico. It also includes a relatively higher percentage of traditional documents made exclusively for Indian rather than Spanish purposes. This may be explained in part by two factors. One is the fortunate preservation of a number of early documents, including perhaps five preconquest examples. Another factor is the relative isolation of Western Oaxaca from the administrative centers of New Spain. Acculturative influences were thus less intensive and undoubtedly slower in reaching the native artists than was the case in the Valley of Mexico. Viceregal and missionary patronage, such as produced the Mendoza and Florentine Codices, were apparently a negligible stimulant in Western Oaxaca. Códice de Yanhuitlan and Códice Sierra survive as lone examples of the fusion of Mixtec and European modes of manuscript art in major manuscripts from Western Oaxaca.

The uniformity of style among the Mixtec manuscripts has led to the concept of a Mixtec pictorial style, but few attempts have been made to define it. Robertson (1959) has carefully defined the style and ways of depicting forms in Codex Nuttall and, in connection with studies of the Borgia Group (1963, 1964, 1966), has amplified his analysis to include other Mixtec manuscripts. Although the style of Mixtec manuscripts is relatively homogeneous and distinct from that of other regions, there is nevertheless considerable diversity within the corpus. To what extent this may be a matter of date or peripheral provenience is not known at this time.

A marked conservatism is evident in the surviving pictorial manuscripts from West-

---

[40] Adelhofer (1963, p. 35) cites Caso, "The caciques of Tilantongo, Mexico, 1944", a work that we have not seen. It may be a preliminary version of the 1949 paper.

[41] An announcement for this work appears in the *Boletín* of the Instituto Nacional de Antropología e Historia, Mexico, no. 38, pp. 50–51, 1 plate (cover dated December, 1969, but with colophon dated May, 1970).

ern Oaxaca. Traditional style, forms, and format were retained into the late 16th century. Codex Selden, for instance, is contemporary with or later than strongly acculturated manuscripts from the Valley of Mexico but shows no signs of European influence. The Genealogy of Tlazultepec, painted in 1597, is markedly conservative in its depictions of persons and costume although a written gloss replaces what traditionally would have been hieroglyphic names. Even manuscripts believed to date from as late as the 17th century, such as Codices Baranda and Muro, cling to the tira or screenfold format although degenerate in other respects. They lack, however, the distinctive meander pattern of guidelines used to organize the content of early colonial and preconquest Mixtec screenfolds.

A distinctive feature of the more traditional Mixtec manuscripts is their emphasis upon genealogy. This is particularly true of such "historical" manuscripts as Codices Bodley and Selden, whose content is as much genealogical as historical. The recital of political and other secular events, common in annals from the Valley of Mexico, is not a trait of the surviving Mixtec manuscripts. A further trait of these documents is that they are of two main types of format: screenfold and lienzo. Thus the historical and cartographic-historical types in Table 23 are segregated as much by format as by historical or cartographic considerations. Both types contain extensive genealogical material.

Most Mixtec manuscripts here classified as historical are skin screenfolds. The only other types of format represented are the tira and the roll. Of the 15 historical manuscripts only the Selden Roll is not made of animal skin, suggesting that native paper may have been rare in Western Oaxaca. The best-known and most studied historical screenfolds—Codices Bodley, Nuttall (obverse), Selden, and Vienna (reverse)—form a group whose content is closely re-

lated and clearly Mixtec. Their content concerns the origin and history of the various royal Mixtec lineages or dynasties.

Few of the numerous place glyphs shown in the genealogies of these manuscripts have been identified, but enough is known to permit certain generalizations. As established both by Caso (1952) and by Dark (1958b), the dates connected with the genealogies may be traced from historical personages in the 16th century back to the 7th and 8th centuries. Codex Bodley presents the genealogies of the dynasties of Tilantongo, a principal Mixtec center, and Teozacoalco as well as other localities related to them by marriage. Its record, extending from A.D. 692 to about 1521, is the most detailed of all the screenfolds. Codex Vienna (reverse) records the genealogy of Tilantongo; a part of Codex Nuttall (obverse) portrays the genealogy of Teozacoalco and its Tilantongo antecedents. The narrative in both Nuttall and Vienna ends at about the same time in the middle of the 14th century, a date that is not necessarily that of their manufacture. Codex Selden treats an as yet unidentified locality the glyph for which is read as Belching Mountain; its record extends into the 16th century and includes persons shown in the other manuscripts. The genealogy in the late Códice Muro, which extends into the 17th century, also appears to be related to those of Tilantongo and Teozacoalco. Place glyphs for Acatlan (southern Puebla), Tequixtepec, and Tilantongo have been identified in Códice Sánchez Solís, the genealogies of which may be of persons from localities in the Mixteca Baja region.

The interpretation of genealogies of the Nuttall Group of Mixtec screenfolds has been greatly aided by the fact that many of the events and persons depicted occur in two or more manuscripts and by the record of the Mapa de Teozacoalco, previously discussed. The interpretation of the other Mixtec histories that are primarily gene-

70

alogical, Codices Sánchez Solís, Becker no. 2, Dehesa, Tulane, and Baranda, is far less advanced. They also lack the explicit chronological organization and meander guidelines of the other manuscripts. Persons portrayed in them, with the exception of two members of the Tilantongo dynasty in Códice Sánchez Solís, have not been identified in other sources.

The reverse of the Codex Nuttall and the manuscript known through its two fragments, Codices Colombino and Becker no. 1, depict the life and history of 8 Deer, a prominent Mixtec ruler of the second dynasty of Tilantongo in the 11th century. They are thus practically the only Mixtec historical manuscripts not primarily concerned with genealogy.

The earliest passages in the Mixtec histories treat the origins of the various dynasties. The first ancestors are shown as descending from the skies, being born from trees, or emerging from the earth. Some of them have the attributes of known gods. Thus the early sections of the Mixtec histories are considered mythological and concerned with theogony. Such passages occur in the genealogies of the Nuttall Group (especially in Codices Nuttall and Vienna), in Códice Baranda, and are almost the exclusive concern of Fragmento Gómez de Orozco and the closely related Selden Roll. They also occur in certain manuscripts here classified as cartographic-historical, such as Lienzo Antonio de León.

The interpretation of mythological passages presents numerous problems. It has long been evident that the Mixtec screenfolds, like other categories of Mesoamerican pictorial sources, are not self-sufficient or independent documents but required an oral commentary that drew upon knowledge only suggested by the pictures on the manuscripts. The mythological passages that are best comprehended are those for which the corresponding myths were recorded by Reyes, García, and Burgoa. Continued success in the interpretation of the Mixtec histories will undoubtedly require the discovery of further sources, either other pictorial manuscripts or related textual material, in the archives of Spain, Mexico, or Indian villages.

The close interrelationship of manuscripts of the Nuttall Group has necessitated a somewhat arbitrary treatment of individual manuscript bibliographies in the census. It should be pointed out that important observations on one manuscript may be contained in works listed only under another manuscript of the group. Certain general studies of Mixtec manuscripts not cited specifically in the individual bibliographies but containing interpretative data are Caso (1955b, 1959a, 1960a, 1960d, 1964c, 1966b), Burland (1951b, 1962b), Dark (1958b), and Chadwick (1967).

As with the historical manuscripts, the cartographic-historical manuscripts from Western Oaxaca listed in Table 23 form a remarkably traditional or conservative corpus. All but two of the 17 manuscripts listed are lienzos. The two that are not on cloth have the composition usually associated with the cartographic-historical type of village titles on cloth. All but six or seven of the 17, in addition to historical or genealogical content, have a peripheral boundary of place glyphs which usually represents the boundary of the jurisdiction responsible for the map. Those not having this trait, such as Lienzo Antonio de León and Lienzos of Ihuitlan, Philadelphia, and Coixtlahuaca no. 2, are primarily large-format genealogies. The related place glyphs shown do not appear to have any cartographic arrangement. In the case of the Lienzo de Yolotepec, the content is apparently almost exclusively historical rather than either cartographic or genealogical.

With the exception of Lienzo of Philadelphia and Códice Mixteco Post-cortesiano no. 36, all of the cartographic-historical documents have a known or presumed provenience or can be associated with some other document from a known region. Six of the 15 lienzos are from the Coixtlahuaca region and have been defined as forming the Coixtlahuaca Basin Group (Parmenter, 1961a, p. 2). These are: Lienzo Meixueiro, Lienzo Antonio de León, and Lienzos de Coixtlahuaca nos. 1 and 2, Ihuitlan, and Nativitas. The first four are very closely related and probably share a common history of prototypes.

Much remains to be learned concerning the modern history of the Mixtec lienzos. The earliest date associated with any of them is 1889, the date of a copy of Lienzo de Yolotepec. Details concerning ownership are obscure with respect to the collection of Manuel Martínez Gracida (who appears to have been involved with Lienzo de Coixtlahuaca no. 2, Lienzo de Yolotepec, and the lost Mapa de Santa Maria Ixcatlan among others), the copies associated with Nicolás León and successively owned by Wilkinson, Gates, and Garrett (Lienzo Córdova-Castellanos, Lienzo Meixueiro, and Lienzo de Coixtlahuaca no. 1), and those sold by Hearst (Lienzos of Philadelphia and Ihuitlan). The destruction of much of the Seler collection in World War II may have resulted in the loss of important data in this regard, but remnants of his collection in the Ibero-Amerikanisches Institut have not been studied with a view to establishing what manuscripts were known to him or the dates of various copies which he made. Further data on the subject are required to clarify obscure references such as those to lienzos from Coixtlahuaca and Zacatepec cited in the census. Such information might provide clues to the present location of several lost originals now known only through copies. The identity of five manuscripts owned by Belmar, possibly the Mixtec lienzos, mentioned by N. León (1905a, p. 182), is also unknown.

The ownership history of the historical screenfolds is quite different. Five of them

(Codices Bodley, Nuttall, Vienna, and both Selden manuscripts) probably survived through having reached Europe during the 16th century. They thus escaped the hazards and vicissitudes of 19th-century Mexican collections. The circumstances under which they were sent to Europe are unknown except for the quite probable theory concerning Codices Nuttall and Vienna. Most of the other screenfolds appear to have remained in Indian hands until after the middle of the 19th century. After that time their histories are shrouded by the usual vagaries of rumor.

Where the Western Oaxaca corpus is strong in native-oriented or traditional documents—most of which are classified under the two historical categories—it is surprisingly weak in documents produced to meet the exigencies of the early colonial world. The tribute registers, property plans, fiscal documents, and maps so well represented from the Central Mexican regions are barely represented in the Western Oaxaca inventory. Again, the relative isolation of Oaxaca may have played a part in this but it is also true that whether or not fewer such documents were produced in Western Oaxaca, there may also have been fewer early collectors of manuscripts, such as Boturini and his predecessors, in the region. The inacessibility and lack of research into such potentially relevant archives as the Archivo de Justicia in Puebla and the colonial archives of Oaxaca may be another factor. There are, of course, further unpublished minor documents in the Archivo General de la Nación, Mexico, not entered in the census.

Most documents of the genealogical, cartographic, and economic types are less traditional; they exhibit acculturation in style or format , having been made under indirect Spanish patronage or influence. Two genealogies in Table 23 are late 16th-century drawings made in connection with affairs of the Spanish world. The Genealogy of Tlazultepec, notable for its conservative rendering of human forms, was made for use in a suit before a Spanish court. The genealogy from Igualtepec illustrates a petition in Spanish and strangely lacks specific traits of Mixtec style.

Among the cartographic documents, the maps from Ixcatlan (1870) and Sinaxtla (1730) are peripheral to native style but are included in the census as examples of the retention of native influence in wholly colonial or modern documents. The Ixcatlan map of 1580 exhibits calendrical and place glyphs and other native forms in a traditional but acculturated style. The Lienzo de Tamazulapan is included largely because it is part of a codex collection; it exhibits only traces of native influence.

It should be noted that other pictorial cartographic manuscripts from Western Oaxaca are included among the maps of the *Relaciones geográficas* of 1579–85, not treated in this census. The most notable is the Mapa de Teozacoalco, whose genealogies have already been mentioned. It contains, in addition, a remarkable circular map with place glyphs. The maps of Texupan and Amoltepec also exhibit native features.

The economic documents are a pictorial accounting ledger from Texupan (Códice Sierra), a tribute document from Tecomaxtlahuaca, and fragments from a large property plan. Códice de Yanhuitlan is a handsomely drawn and incomplete colonial compilation of economic and historical matters.

NORTHERN OAXACA. The Northern Oaxaca region, as here defined, consists of the former districts of Tuxtepec and Cuicatlan, the eastern part of the district of Teotitlan, and the northern parts of the districts of Etla, Ixtlan, and Choapan (see fig. 12). The region was inhabited in the 16th century by Cuicatecs, Mazatecs and Chinantecs, the headings under which the pictorial manuscripts from the region are discussed below.

Most of the 17 pictorial manuscripts of

the region (see Table 24) have been classified and listed by Cline (1966c), together with documents here classified under Eastern Oaxaca. He provides extensive data on geographic and ethnic classification.

Cuicatec Pictorial Manuscripts. Two early, important, and closely related manuscripts, Códices Fernández Leal and Porfirio Díaz, have been attributed to the Cuicatec subregion, largely on the grounds that one and possibly both were owned by Benjamin Ladrón de Guevara, a descendant of Francisco Monjaraz y Cortés. The latter was one of the early caciques of Quiotepec or Cuicatlan, and is shown on Códice de Quiotepec y Cuicatlan. Although both manu-

TABLE 24—CLASSIFICATION OF THE PICTORIAL MANUSCRIPTS OF NORTHERN OAXACA

	Ethnic Affiliation
Ritual-calendrical manuscripts:	
255 Códice Porfirio Díaz	Cuicatec
Historical manuscripts:	
119 Códice Fernández Leal	Cuicatec
255 Códice Porfirio Díaz	Cuicatec
Cartographic manuscripts:	
137 Mapa de Huautla	Mazatec
346 Mapa de San Pedro Tlatepusco	Chinantec
418 Mapa de Yetla	Chinantec
Cartographic-historical manuscripts:	
51 Lienzo de Santa Maria Chilchotla	Mazatec
53 Lienzo de la Chinantla	Chinantec
54 Lienzo de la Gran Chinantla	Chinantec
162 Lienzo de San Pedro Ixcatlan	Mazatec
265 Lienzo de Quiotepec y Ayauhtla	Cuicatec(?)
266 Códice de Quiotepec y Cuicatlan	Cuicatec
335 Lienzo de Tlacoatzintepec	Chinantec
420 Lienzo de Yolox	Chinantec
Unavailable manuscripts:	
74 Lienzo de Santiago Comaltepec	Chinantec
190 Mapa de Malinaltepec	Chinantec
225 Plan cadastral de Muaguia	Chinantec(?)
410 Plan cadastral de Xochitepec	Chinantec(?)

Maps of the Relaciones Geográficas, 1579–85:

RG 6 Atlatlauca (San Juan Bautista Atatlahuca, Dto. Etla) and Malinaltepec (Maninaltepec, Mun. San Juan Quiotepec, Dto. Ixtlan)

RG 59 Teotitlan del Camino (Teotitlan del Camino, Dto. Teotitlan)

scripts have been published, neither has been adequately interpreted. Codex Porfirio Díaz bears glosses in an as yet unidentified language and both use a variant set of year-bearer days in their calendrical dates. The year symbol used is the interlaced A–O, generally found only in Mixtec or Popoloca sources.

The ethnic affiliation of the late but still traditional Lienzo de Quiotepec y Ayauhtla is in doubt. It may be affiliated with the Cuicatecs or the Mazatecs or both. Its native gloss may be in one or the other of these related languages. The place names Quiotepec, Teopa, and Ayauhtla in glosses suggest that the document relates to Santiago Quiotepec in Cuicatec territory and San Bartolome Ayauhtla in the Mazatec subregion. The San Juan Quiotepec in the Chinantla is presumably not at issue.

Mazatec Pictorial Manuscripts. The three manuscripts from the Mazatec subregion, the Lienzos of Chilchotla and San Pedro Ixcatlan and the Mapa de Huautla, are all late and quite removed from whatever native tradition may have existed among the Mazatecs. The three are reproduced, two for the first time, by Cline (1964, 1966b), with descriptive and interpretive material. The lost Mapa de Santa Maria Ixcatlan or Lienzo Seler no. 1, formerly classified as Mazatec (Lehmann, 1905a, p. 278), bore glosses believed to be in Chocho–Popoloca or Ixcatec and is here classified under Western Oaxaca.

Chinantec Pictorial Manuscripts. The Chinantec manuscripts have been described at length and their cartographic content analyzed by Cline (1961a). More recent data are cited in the census. Since the date of his basic survey the Genealogías de los Señores de Etla have been reclassified as Zapotec and are here listed among the manuscripts from Eastern Oaxaca. Cline (1957) has discussed ethnohistorical documentation of the Chinantla.

Of the eight pictorial manuscripts se-

curely identified with the Chinantla, two are unavailable and few are of more than local interest. The Lienzo de la Chinantla is a painted map in acculturated or nontraditional style with ethnographic scenes which unfortunately cannot be studied in the published photographs; its circular orientations, however, may well reflect earlier usages. Together with the related Lienzo de la Gran Chinantla and the Mapa de Yetla, it forms an important cartographic source for the eastern colonial Chinantla. The Mapa de Yolox is notable for a migration legend and its trilingual glosses. The Lienzo de Tlacoatzintepec is a typical document of the cartographic-historical type, showing hieroglyphic boundaries and historical scenes.

Two documents, probably misattributed to the Chinantla, the cadastral plans of Muaguia and Xochitepec, are wholly unavailable and their copies considered lost.

EASTERN OAXACA. The 29 pictorial manuscripts from Eastern Oaxaca (fig. 13) are listed and classified in Table 25. Most of them have been listed in the survey of pictorial manuscripts from Eastern and Northern Oaxaca by Cline (1966c). Four manuscripts have been added to his listing: the Lienzos de Tecciztlan y Tequatepec, Yatao, Yatini, and the Mapa de Santa Cruz Xoxocotlan. The Saville Fragment, listed by Cline, has since been identified by him and Alfonso Caso as a falsification.

Aside from the Cline survey, which is primarily devoted to problems of verification and ethnic and regional provenience, there is no general study of the content or styles of the pictorial manuscripts from Eastern Oaxaca. The Lehmann (1905a) survey listed only seven of the manuscripts on our list. Only one, the Lienzo de Guevea, has been studied in detail. Pérez García (1956) and Schmieder (1930), both of whom have published pictorial documents from Eastern Oaxaca, provide examples of later cycles of cartography from the region.

All but four of the pictorial manuscripts

TABLE 25—CLASSIFICATION OF THE PICTORIAL MANUSCRIPTS OF EASTERN OAXACA

Historical manuscripts:
295 Lienzo de San Juan Tabaa no. 1
333 Lienzo de San Miguel Tiltepec

Genealogical manuscripts:
117 Genealogías de los Señores de Etla
425 Arbol genealógico de los Reyes Zapotecos

Cartographic manuscripts:
182 Mapa de Lachiyoo
306 Mapa de Tehuantepec
413 Mapa de Santa Cruz Xoxocotlan

Cartographic-historical manuscripts:
  7 Lienzo de Analco
 47 Lienzo de San Juan Chicomesuchil (no. 1)
 66 Lienzo de San Jeronimo Coatlan (no. 1)
 88 Mapa de San Pablo Cuatro Venados
130 Lienzo de Guevea
143 Lienzo de Huilotepec
241 Genealogía Oaxaqueña
301 Lienzo de Tecciztlan y Tequatepec
416 Lienzo de San Lucas Yatao
417 Lienzo de Yatini

Miscellaneous manuscripts:
307 Querella criminal contra Don Juan, cacique de
       Tehuantepec

Unavailable manuscripts:
 48 Mapa de San Juan Chicomesuchil (no. 2)
 52 Lienzo de Santa Maria Chimalapa
 67 Mapa de San Jeronimo Coatlan (no. 2)
 73 Códice de San Juan Comaltepec
 78 Descendientes de Cosijoeza, Rey de Zaachila
166 Mapa de Ixhuatan
170 Códice de Santa Catarina Ixtepeji
250 Lienzo de Petapa
296 Lienzo de San Juan Tabaa no. 2
305 Fragmento del Mapa del Istmo de Tehuantepec
414 Lienzo de Santa Maria Yahuiche

Maps of the Relaciones Geográficas, 1579–85:
RG 30 Ixtepexic (Sta. Catarina Ixtepeji, Dto. Ixtlan)
RG 32 Macuilsuchil (S. Mateo Macuilxochitl, Mun.
       Tlacochahuaya, Dto. Tlacolula)
RG 33 Macupilco, San Miguel (near Sta. Maria Xadan,
       Mun. San Miguel del Puerto, Dto. Pochutla)
RG 49 Suchitepec (Sta. Maria Xadan, as above)
RG 51 Temagastepec (Tlamacazcatepec), San
       Bartolome (near Sta. Maria Xadan, as above)
RG 55 Tehuantepec, Pintura 1 (Santo Domingo
       Tehuantepec, Dto. Tehuantepec)
RG 74 Tlacotepec, San Sebastian (near Sta. Maria
       Xadan, as above)
RG 90 Zozopastepec, Sta. Maria (near Sta. Maria
       Xadan, as above)

from Eastern Oaxaca are of certain or probable Zapotec origin. The Lienzo de Analco is from a community known to have been founded in the 16th century by Tlaxcalan Indians. The Mapa de San Francisco Ixhuatan, known only through prerevolutionary rumor, is from a Huave provenience and the Mapa de Santa Cruz Xoxocotlan is Mixtec in origin. The Lienzo de Tecciztlan y Tequatepec is believed to be from Astata in the Chontal region. The Mixe, Zoque, and other groups of Eastern Oaxaca are unrepresented by extant pictorial manuscripts in the census.[42]

Few generalizations may be made about the manuscripts from the region. The historical or genealogical lienzos from Tabaa and Tiltepec share a common format, a division of the cloth into horizontal rows of rectangular compartments, a feature also true of the Lienzo de Tlaxcala and the Mapa de Cuauhtlantzinco from Puebla. The Lienzo de Guevea and the Lienzo de Tecciztlan y Tequatepec both exhibit the traits of depicting boundaries by the peripheral placement of place glyphs and the use of personal name glyphs. They are among the few surviving documents from Eastern Oaxaca clearly in the native tradition. The early and unpublished Lienzo de Analco, from a non-Zapotec provenience, is probably colonial in inspiration and shows native features only in an indirect manner.

Aside from the examples mentioned, all the other available documents are known

[42] From a Mixtec village in Eastern Oaxaca, the Mapa de Cuilapam (ex-district of Centro) is a late and acculturated map not included in the census. It has been published by Steininger and Van de Velde (1935, facing p. 106). A probably 17th-century map in a crude style forming part of a suit between San Juan Chapultepec and San Martin Mexicapan (also in or near the ex-district of Centro) in AGN-T 236 has been published by Vásquez (1931, p. 22bis). It shows Indians, bows and arrows, buildings, etc., and has a genealogy but is too removed from the native tradition for inclusion in the census. Both Alfonso Caso and Peter Tschol (personal communications) informed us of this relatively rare publication.

only through late versions or copies and are peripheral to the native tradition. The Mapa de Lachiyoo and the Mapa de Tehuantepec, which are included only in perpetuation of prior listings, are wholly European in origin.

Four textual documents from Eastern Oaxaca, published by de la Fuente (1949, pp. 185–97) and Pérez García (1956, 2: 339–43), contain claims by Zapotec caciques to hereditary rights, particularly to lands. Their descriptions of boundaries, history, and genealogy indicate that they are probably written transcriptions of oral commentaries on cartographic-historical lienzos. These "verbal lienzos" are of interest as examples of informed interpretations of such documents.

Southeastern Mexico and Guatemala

The Southeastern Mexico and Guatemala region encompasses Guatemala, British Honduras, and the Mexican states of Campeche, Chiapas, Quintana Roo, Tabasco, and Yucatan. The predominant population of the region in pre-Contact and colonial times spoke various mutually unintelligible Maya languages. This Maya region of Mesoamerica is usually considered in two divisions: lowland and highland. The lowland region corresponds approximately to Campeche, Quintana Roo, Yucatan, Tabasco, the Guatemalan Department of the Peten, and British Honduras. The highland region comprises Chiapas and the mountainous and Pacific coastal areas of Guatemala.

The 13 pictorial manuscripts in the census from the region are listed in Table 26, classified into five descriptive categories. Only one, the Map from a Kekchi Suit of 1611, is from the highland subregion. Nine are from known proveniences in Yucatan (see fig. 14) and the three screenfolds are believed to have originated in the lowland subregion.

In Central Mexico the simple pictographic writing of that region endured or was modified as a vehicle of expression throughout the 16th century. In the Maya region, however, the complex hieratic hieroglyphs and symbols of Maya writing appear not to have been adaptable for continued use in colonial contexts. No known colonial manuscript exhibits any meaningful use of Maya hieroglyphs or other pictorial usages. Maya hieroglyphs in the 18th-century Books of Chilam Balam (see below) are but vestigial devices decorating written texts; their early colonial antecedents are unknown. The common pictorial tribute registers and place glyphs of colonial Central Mexican pictorial manuscripts have no counterpart in lowland colonial Maya manuscripts. Whether this is a function of the scarcity of early colonial Maya documents, of the character of Maya-Spanish relationships, or of the nature of Maya hieroglyphic writing is a subject for further investigation. For a review of a large number of colonial descriptions of both lowland and highland Maya pictorial manu-

TABLE 26–CLASSIFICATION OF THE PICTORIAL MANUSCRIPTS OF SOUTHEASTERN MEXICO AND GUATEMALA

Preconquest ritual-calendrical screenfolds:
113 Codex Dresden
187 Codex Madrid
247 Codex Paris

Colonial calendar wheels:
 60 The Book of Chilam Balam of Chumayel (part)
168 The Book of Chilam Balam of Ixil (part)
179 The Book of Chilam Balam of Kaua (part)
184 LANDA: Relación de las cosas de Yucatan (part)
191 Katun Wheel of Mani
249 Codex Pérez (part)

Genealogical manuscripts:
401 Genealogical Tree of the Xiu Family

Cartographic manuscripts:
 60 The Book of Chilam Balam of Chumayel (part)
180 Map from a Kekchi Suit of 1611
192 Map of the Province of Mani
293 Map of the Province of Sotuta

Miscellaneous calendrical illustrations and hieroglyphs:
 60 The Book of Chilam Balam of Chumayel (part)
179 The Book of Chilam Balam of Kaua (part)
184 LANDA: Relación de las cosas de Yucatan (part)
249 Codex Pérez (part)

scripts in the writings of the early chroniclers and in other accounts, see Genet (1934a). Most are quoted at length.

The three preconquest screenfolds—Codices Dresden, Madrid, and Paris—are among the most important of all surviving Mesoamerican pictorial manuscripts.[43] They complement the far more extensive corpus of Maya hieroglyphic inscriptions on stone and other monuments; their study forms a specialized branch of Maya hieroglyphic writing.

The content of the three screenfolds is largely divinatory and, like the manuscripts of the Borgia Group, each is primarily a tonalamatl. Mathematical computations relating to eclipses and the Venus cycle, ceremonies, and much undeciphered material are also found. For general bibliography and a statement of the limited treatment afforded these documents in the present work see the entry "Maya Screenfolds" in the census. J. E. S. Thompson (1965) and Satterthwaite (1965), both in volume 3 of this *Handbook*, give general descriptions of Maya hieroglyphic writing and calendrics.

The Yucatec Maya texts known as the Books of Chilam Balam form another major corpus of native documents from the lowland Maya region. Of the approximately 10 available examples, four contain drawings. Each has one or more calendar wheels. Other drawings are simplified maps (as in the Chumayel manuscript), Maya hieroglyphs (in three of the examples), and depictions of various calendrical and cosmological subjects. Illustrations for passages concerning the zodiac and a European romance (as in the Ixil and Kaua manuscripts) are not in the native tradition. As now known, the Books of Chilam Balam derive from 18th-century redactions; their drawings are consequently late, acculturated, and marginal to the study of colonial Maya art (see "Books of Chilam Balam," Article 27B, nos. 1145–58 for general bibliography).

Under "colonial calendar wheels" in Table 26 are six manuscripts produced in Yucatan. Seven calendar wheels are represented as the Ixil manuscript contains two examples. The wheel drawn in Bishop Landa's 16th-century *Relación de las cosas de Yucatan* is comparable in all respects to those in the much later Books of Chilam Balam, an indication that the versions in the latter may not be greatly changed from their earlier prototypes. Bowditch (1910, pp. 324–31) reproduces five of the wheels (mostly after Berendt's copies) and provides an incomplete discussion. As with the Central Mexican calendar wheels, no full-scale inquiry into the origin of the colonial Maya calendar wheels has yet been made.

Not included in the census are two calendar wheels from the highland Maya region. One has been published with Ordóñez y Aguiar's *Historia de la creación y de la tierra* by N. León (1907, facing p. 264). It is uncertain if the wheel originates with Ordóñez y Aguiar or if it is from a lost Tzeltal calendrical manuscript known to Bishop Núñez de la Vega in the late 17th century in Chiapas or from some other source. In two of its concentric circles are written Tzeltal or Tzotzil day names. The arms of a cross at the center reach to the year-bearer days of the first day-name circle, and the four directions are written in an outer circle. Aside from the cross and the concentric circles there are no other pictorial elements.

The second highland Maya calendar wheel, in the unpublished Quiche Calendar of 1722, similarly has no pictorial symbols.[44]

[43] Since the two parts of Codex Madrid—Codices Troano and Cortesianus—were discovered separately in the 19th century, the literature of that period occasionally refers to four Maya manuscripts.

[44] "Calendario de los Indios de Guatemala, 1722, Kiche." Copy of 1877 in Berendt Linguistic Collection, University Museum, Philadelphia (Brinton, 1900, no. 58). Photographic copies by Gates of the Berendt copy are in LC, TU/LAL, PML, BYU, and NLA 1546 (see Gates, 1924, no. 1006; 1937a, no. 310; 1940, section A, p. 14). Acuña (1968, p. 39) provides some information on the original of this document. Several calendar wheels, without hieroglyphic elements, are contained in the Kalendario . . . (de) Ixtlavacan, a manuscript formerly

It presents Arabic-numbered day names written in Quiche within the 20 radii of a circle.

Three colonial maps from Yucatan, the Maps of the Provinces of Mani and Sotuta, and a simplified diagram in the Book of Chilam Balam of Chumayel share the traits of a circular composition and an orientation of east at the top. These features may be derived from the native tradition. Roys (1943, p. 184) discusses these maps and the possible independence of their circular format and orientation from European influence. The Melchor de Alfaro Santa Cruz *Relación geográfica* Map of the Province of Tabasco of 1579 (not treated in this census) is another circular map that is possibly influenced by Maya cartography.[45]

The only highland Maya manuscript in this census is the Map from a Kekchi Suit of 1611 from near Coban, Guatemala. A marginal example, it indicates roads by the use of footprints, also a Central Mexican trait. Very few highland Maya manuscripts of 16th- or 17th-century origin with drawings of any kind have come to our attention. The Quiche and Tzeltal or Tzotzil calendar wheels, described above, are certainly poor reflections of highland Maya pictorial art.

The Anales de los Cakchiqueles (also known as the Memorial de Tecpan-Atitlan, Memorial de Solola, and Anales de los Xahil [see Article 27B, no. 1172]), a Cakchiquel text known through a mid-17th-century copy, contains a single drawing (not in the census) showing bows and arrows, shields, and various symbols of uncertain meaning. It symbolizes a late 15th-century rebellion among the Cakchiquel Indians.[46]

A notable discussion of highland Maya picture writing (possibly including Pipil sources) is given by Fuentes y Guzmán (1932–33, 2: 107–12; 1933), writing in the 17th century. He clearly describes a Quiche lienzo of the cartographic-historical type and two "pergaminos" (Indian paintings on animal skin), apparently tribute lists. From the latter and from a sculptured monument he gives and describes various symbols. They are recognizable as numbers (digits, 20, 400, 8000), a rebus place glyph, a day sign, day-sign coefficients, the symbol for the binding of the years at the end of a 52-year period, and drawing of items of tribute. These symbols are intelligible, despite Fuentes y Guzmán's own confusion, in terms of about Central Mexican picture writing; they bear no relationship to the hieroglyphs of lowland Maya inscriptions.[47]

---

in the Brasseur de Bourbourg and Pinart collections, now in the Brinton collection at UP/UM.

[45] Scholes and Roys (1948, p. 16 and facing plate) reproduce a copy of the Alfaro de Santa Cruz map and comment briefly on the question of circular Maya maps. For a full bibliography of the Alfaro map see Robertson's catalog of maps of the *Relaciones geográficas* (Article 6, no. 50). See *Título de los Señores de Sacapulas* (Article 27B, no. 1182) for comment on a circular map which exists in both Quiche and Spanish versions.

[46] A photographic reproduction is given by Mengin (1952b, second pagination, p. 49). Other reproductions of the drawing are given by Villacorta (1934a, p. 65), Recinos (1950a, frontispiece), Recinos (1953, facing p. 118) and in other editions of the document. Fuentes y Guzmán (1932–33, 2: 178) gives a drawing apparently copied from the Cakchiquel manuscript. Genet (1934b) discusses its symbolism.

[47] Genet (1934c) attempts a partial interpretation of the more complex symbolic device illustrated by Fuentes y Guzmán.

REFERENCES (compiled by Mary W. Cline)

Acuña, 1968
Adelhofer, 1963
Alcina Franch, 1955
Anders, 1965
Anonymous, 1829, 1830a

Apenes, 1947
Arpee, 1937
Arreola, 1920
Aubin, 1849, 1851
Ayala Echávarri, 1940

Azcué y Mancera, 1966
Bandelier, A., 1884
Barlow, 1946b, 1948f, 1949b, 1949d, 1949f
—— and McAfee, 1949
Barthelemy, 1798
Bernal, 1962
Boban, 1891
Borson, 1796
Boturini Benaduci, 1746
Bowditch, 1910
Brand, 1944
Brasseur de Bourbourg, 1857–59, 1864, 1869–70, 1871
Brinton, 1900
British Museum, 1833, 1933
Burland, 1947a, 1951b, 1955b, 1960, 1962b
Carrasco Pizana, 1950
Carrera Stampa, 1949b, 1959, 1962–63, 1965
Cartari (Reggiano), 1615, 1626
Cartografía de la Nueva Galicia, 1961
Cartografía de Puebla, 1958
Caso, 1927, 1930, 1949, 1951, 1952, 1955b, 1958a, 1958e, 1959a, 1960a, 1960d, 1964c, 1965c, 1966b, 1967
Chadwick, 1967
—— and MacNeish, 1967
Chavero, n.d., 1892, 1901c
Chevalier, 1956
Clark, 1912, 1938
Clavigero, 1780–81
Cline, 1957, 1959, 1961a, 1964, 1966a, 1966b, 1966c, 1969b, 1972
Corona Núñez, 1959, 1964–67
Cuevas, 1921–28
Dalton, 1899, 1902a, 1902b
Dark, 1958b
Dibble, 1940a, 1942a, 1951, 1955
Domínguez, 1943
Edwards, 1966
Fábrega, 1899
Förstemann, 1880
Fuente, 1949
Fuentes y Guzmán, 1932–33, 1933
Galarza, 1960, 1964, 1966, 1967
Galindo y Villa, 1905b, 1922, 1925
García Granados, 1940–41, 1942
García Icazbalceta, 1947, 1954
Gates, 1909, 1924, 1929, 1937a, 1940
Gemelli Careri, 1699–1700
Genet, 1934a, 1934b, 1934c
Gibson, 1952
Glass, 1964
Gómez de Orozco, 1927a, 1939a
Gonçalves de Lima, 1956
Götze, 1743–44
Granados y Gálvez, 1778
Greenleaf, 1961

Guzmán, 1939b
Hernández, 1651
Herrera, 1601–15
Hirtzel, 1928
Hoerschelmann, 1922
Humboldt, 1810
Jiménez Moreno, 1961
—— and Mateos Higuera, 1940
Junta Colombina, 1892
Kelemen, 1943
Kingsborough, 1831–48
Kircher, 1652–54
Kirchhoff, 1950, 1956a
Kollar, 1769
Kubler, 1961, 1962
—— and Gibson, 1951
Kutscher, 1955
Lambeck, 1679
Legati, 1677
Lehmann, 1905a, 1905b
—— and Smital, 1929
Lejeal, 1902
Lemoine V., 1954
León, N., 1888c, 1890, 1903, 1903–04, 1904a, 1905a, 1906c, 1907
León-Portilla and Mateos Higuera, 1957
León y Gama, 1832
Linné, 1948
Lista, 1881
Long, 1926
López, P., 1925
Lorenzana, 1770
Margáin Araujo, 1943
Martínez Ríos, 1961
Mateos Higuera, 1944–49, 1946c, 1948b, 1966
Maza, 1959
Mazari, 1926c
Melgarejo Vivanco, 1953
Mena, 1923
Mengin, 1942, 1952a, 1952b
Mercati, 1589
Moxó, 1828, 1837, 1839, 1888
Nessel, 1690
Nicholson, 1960a, 1960b, 1961a, 1961b, 1962, 1966b, 1966c, 1967
Nierembergii, 1635
Noguera, 1933a
Nowotny, 1959, 1961b
Núñez y Domínguez, 1947a
Nuttall, 1902
Orozco, E., 1892
Orozco y Berra, 1871, 1880
Ortega Martínez, 1948
Palomera, 1962
Parmenter, 1961a
Paso y Troncoso, 1892–93, 1898a, 1898b, 1905–06, 1905–07, 1912

Peabody Museum, 1963
Peñafiel, 1885, 1897c, 1903b
Pérez García, 1956
Preuss and Mengin, 1937–38
Purchas, 1625
Racknitz, 1796
Radin, 1920
Ramírez, J. F., 1855
Ramírez Lavoignet, 1959, 1962
Ramusio, 1556
Recinos, 1950a, 1953
Reyes Valerio, 1967
Robertson, D., 1959, 1963, 1964, 1966
Robertson, W., 1777, 1778
Romero and Pereda, 1860
Rosny, Léon de, 1876a, 1876b, 1881b, 1883, 1887, 1888
Roys, 1943
Satterthwaite, 1965
Saville, 1901
Schmeider, 1930
Scholes and Roys, 1948
Seler, 1890, 1893, 1895, 1900, 1900–01, 1902b, 1902e, 1902f, 1902j, 1902l, 1902–03, 1902–23, 1904b, 1904c, 1904f, 1904h, 1904–09, 1908a, 1908c, 1915, 1923, 1963
Simons, 1968
Simpson, 1934
Smith, M. E., 1963, 1966a

Sociedad Española de Amigos del Arte, 1930
Spinden, H. J., 1935
Spranz, 1964
Steininger and Van de Velde, 1935
Sydow, 1941
Tamayo and Alcorta, 1941
Tentori, 1961
Thevenot, 1672
Thevet, 1584
Thompson, J. E. S., 1965
Títulos principales, 1915
Torquemada, 1615
Toscano, 1943, 1944
Toussaint, Gómez de Orozco, and Fernández, 1938
Tozzer and Allen, 1910
Tudela, 1956
Valadés, 1579
Vásquez, 1931
Veytia, 1836, 1907
Villacorta C., 1934a
Warburton, 1738–41
Waterman, 1916
Weiditz, 1927
Weitlaner de Johnson, 1959
White and Bernal, 1960
Worm, 1655
Zarco Cuevas, 1924–29
Zavala, 1938

23. A Census of Native Middle American Pictorial Manuscripts

JOHN B. GLASS
in collaboration with
DONALD ROBERTSON[1]

ENTRIES IN THE CENSUS take two forms.[2] Unnumbered "group" entries treat manuscripts having a common origin, bibliography, or other unusual relationship

[1] Preliminary development of the census, particularly the gathering of inventory material and bibliography as well as the solution of numerous problems of identification, was a collaborative endeavor by Nicholson, Glass, and Robertson. Classified checklists by Nicholson (1960b, 1961b) were of particular importance as were numerous notes by him on particular manuscripts, collections, and related problems. Nicholson withdrew from the project in August, 1967. The final organization, the descriptive material, and the actual writing of the census are by Glass. Major assistance was received from Howard F. Cline, Alfonso Caso, and Charles Gibson. Financial support was given by the Hispanic and Ford Foundations.

Many persons have aided in the compilation of the data presented here. Zita Basich de Canessi, Margaret Currier, Jorge Enciso, Eulalia Guzmán, Salvador Mateos Higuera, Antonio Pompa y Pompa, David Warren, and the late Roberto J. Weitlaner were particularly helpful.

It is Glass's intention to prepare a supplement to this census which will incorporate bibliography through about 1975. Suggestions concerning omissions, errors, revisions, and additions may be sent to him at Box 282, Lincoln, Mass. 01773.

[2] The nature and scope of this census are discussed in the introduction to the survey (Article 22).

(see Table 1). The individual manuscripts of the group may be entered consecutively following the group entry, or the entry may provide a cross-reference to their separately entered descriptions. Most groups are of relatively long standing; a few have been devised for the present census.

All other entries are numbered and describe individual documents. Except for those that follow a group entry, they are in alphabetical order by a leading or principal name in the title, frequently a place name. Each entry has the following outline, discussed in detail below:

1. Main entry: (a) title, (b) synonyms, (c) location, (d) history, (e) publication status, (f) typological classification, (g) regional classification, (h) date, (i) physical description
2. Description
3. Bibliographical essay
4. List of copies
5. Classified bibliography

MAIN ENTRY. Each main entry describes an "original" manuscript even if the "original" is lost and is known only through one

TABLE 1—"GROUP" ENTRIES IN THE
CENSUS OF TRADITIONAL PICTORIAL
MANUSCRIPTS

BEAUMONT: Crónica de Michoacan: copied illustrations
Borgia Group
Carapan, Códices de
Chavero, Colección
Coixtlahuaca Basin Group

Cuauhtinchan, Mapas de
Gilcrease Fragments
Huitzilopochtli Group
Humboldt Fragments
Indígenas de algunos pueblos del Marquesado del
    Valle, Códices

Ixhuatepec Group
Ixtlilxochitl, Codex
Magliabecchiano Group
Maya screenfolds
Mizquiahuala Sales Receipts

Nuttall Group
SAHAGUN: Drawings by the informants of
SERNA: Manual de Ministros de Indios: illustrations
Teotihuacan Maps
Tlamapa, Códices de

Tlaxinican, Tlaylotlacan, Tecpanpa, etc., Tributes
    of
TOVAR: Relación del Origen de los Yndios . . .
Tuxpan, Lienzos de
Vergara Group
Veytia Calendar Wheels
X, Crónica, Group

XOCHIMILCO: Pedronilla Francisca vs. Juliana
    Tlaco
XOCHIMILCO: Damian Family vs. Pedronilla
    Francisca

See Article 27B for following groups:
    Chilam Balam, Books of (nos. 1145–58)
    Memorias de Nueva España, Colección de
      (no. 1051)
    Mexico y sus Contornos, Anales Antiguos de
      (no. 1066)

See also: Codex Mendoza
       Códice Osuna
       Lienzo de Tlaxcala

---

or more copies. This does not imply, however, that a given manuscript represented by a main entry may not derive from some older prototype nor does it mean that a given "original" in the census may not be related in some way as original and copy to another manuscript in the census. Generally, however, no 19th-century or more recent copy is described by a main entry. By "original" we refer to a 16th-century or comparably old manuscript that is either extant or, if unknown, may be postulated directly as the source of a known copy. Some 16th-century "copies" have been entered in the census as "originals." In certain cases (such as the Lienzo de Tetlama and the Mapa de Santa Cruz Xoxocotlan) there exist several closely related manuscripts or versions of essentially the same composition whose exact interrelationship is unknown. For these we have postulated a single unknown original for the main entry and listed the known versions thereunder. In other cases the mechanics of description and bibliography have favored separate entries for related manuscripts. We hope that cross-references within the census descriptions will clarify such relationships.

Title. Main titles have been selected among synonyms on the basis of common usage. A certain amount of revision and editing of titles has nevertheless been undertaken and a few titles have been created for the census. In the case of lesser documents we have occasionally substituted such words as "Genealogía de . . . ," "Mapa de . . . ," "Anales de . . . ," or "Lienzo de . . ." for the term "Códice de . . ." that is so common in pictorial manuscript nomenclature. The term "lienzo" is used only for originals on cloth; "mapa" is used generally only for maps and single-sheet cartographic-historical documents on paper or unknown material.

Entries for illustrations in manuscripts associated with known authors are made under the author's name (Beaumont, Durán, Sahagún) rather than under the titles of their works, which may be found in the index of titles and synonyms (Article 31).

Many unpublished manuscripts have been

listed in catalogs of collections under such descriptive headings as "Pièce d'un Procès." Some of these designations have been perpetuated herein, but when a document with such a name can be associated with a known or putative provenience, it is entered in the census alphabetically under the name of a town (HUITZILOPOCHCO: *Contrat de Commanderie*, for instance). Unnecessarily long descriptive catalog headings have been shortened.

Synonyms. The listing of synonyms is not exhaustive but does include the more common names and unusual titles that have been used to describe the document in the literature. Slight variations in titles have not been noted. Descriptive headings in institutional catalogs and the titles of published commentaries have not been entered as synonyms except when such listing aids in identifying the document.

Location. The location of the manuscript described by the main entry is designated by the name or abbreviation of the institution or library where it is located. "Private collection" may refer to an individual or to a dealer. Names of private collectors are given when the datum is a matter of public record. "Pueblo" indicates that the manuscript was last reported in local Mexican possession or village archive. Catalog numbers are given for manuscripts forming parts of large collections such as the MNA or BNP. Some catalog numbers not given in the census entries may be found in the institutional checklist (Article 28). Abbreviations of collections are given at the front of this volume.

History. The history or pedigree of a manuscript is expressed by a listing of former owners (and some dealers) following the "ex–" prefix. No attempt has been made to name every person through whose possession the manuscript may have passed. Antonio de León y Gama and José Pichardo have generally been excluded from these listings when their ownership can only be inferred from their having made copies;

most of the latter are in the BNP. The Boturini collection inventory numbers for manuscripts identified in the census as having been in that collection are given in Article 29.

Publication status. The designations "published," "partially published," or "unpublished" do not distinguish between the publication of a document through a copy or through the original.

Typological classification. The typological classification is given in Article 22. Some manuscripts are classified under more than one type, but the entire range of subject matter of a given manuscript is not necessarily reflected by its classifications, which are intended only to classify its most salient features.

Regional classification. Whenever possible, the town and state of Mexico that may be associated with the content of a manuscript is stated as the regional classification. In most cases this will correspond to the actual or putative provenience of the document, but in other instances it may reflect only the locality mentioned or treated in the document. The regional classification thus should not be viewed as synonymous with actual place of origin. The designations "Central Mexico," "Valley of Mexico," and "Borgia Group" have been discussed under the regional survey in Article 22.

Date. Actual dates are given for manuscripts when there is evidence that the date is approximately correct or when the style of a manuscript is believed to be consistent with the most recent date appearing in it. Unsubstantiated estimates have been avoided. We have dated most of the manuscripts in the census only as 16thC, by which we refer exclusively to the postconquest period (ca. 1521 in the Valley of Mexico). This general designation includes manuscripts definitely produced between 1521 and 1600 as well as manuscripts of unknown date that exhibit traits of native style compatible with that date. Most "17thC" or "18thC" dates are

83

approximations that reflect later styles of painting, extensive degeneration of native symbolism, or the absence of native or European style traits.

Physical description. In most cases the physical description is limited to the identification of the material, the number of leaves (if more than one), and the dimensions. Paper is identified as European (including modern and all non-native paper), native paper, amatl paper, and maguey paper. Practically all identifications of native paper made herein as either amatl or maguey fiber derive from the publications by Schwede (1912, 1916) or Lenz (1949, 1950). Other materials include cloth (few fiber identifications exist), skin or animal hide (presumably deer hide), and parchment.

In stating the number of leaves for most of the documents in the census we have had to rely on published statements. The number of leaves stated is always intended to include blank leaves falling within the document. Few publications have distinguished consistently between leaves and pages and some published descriptions omit blank leaves and pages from their counts.[3] This is particularly true of the catalog of the Goupil collection (Boban, 1891) as may be seen by comparing his descriptions with those by Omont (1899) for the same manuscripts.

When the format of a manuscript is a screenfold, that fact is so stated. The tira format is also identified as such or is implied by its dimensions (see discussion of nomenclature in Article 22). Most other manuscripts consist of leaves or signatures gathered in the European (i.e., codex) manner. All dimensions are stated in centimeters and expressed in terms of height × width. Where inches have been converted to centimeters we have used a conversion factor of 1 inch equals 2.54 centimeters. Many published

and unpublished measurements for the same manuscript vary considerably or are not in accord with proportions visible in photographs. Since sizes of pages may vary within a single manuscript, published dimensions may be of the largest page, the smallest page, an average of page sizes, or of a single page (or other dimension) chosen at random. Most measurements, like the number of leaves, should therefore be viewed as approximations.

Since most manuscripts described in the census have been examined only through photographs or publications, it has proved impossible to indicate on a consistent basis whether or not the reverse side of a document is blank or not. Such statements would in any case be subject to qualification; the subject has therefore generally been ignored. Consideration was also given to indicating whether or not manuscripts were complete or incomplete. This subject cannot be treated accurately by any single statement that could be encompassed within the space limits and purpose of the census. It, too, has had to be ignored. In general, practically all manuscripts in the census are incomplete or removed from the context of other documents with which they may once have been associated.

DESCRIPTION. The descriptions are intended to provide a general and, sometimes, a specific indication of the content of each manuscript. In the case of unpublished or less accessible manuscripts an attempt has been made to indicate their general appearance and the extent to which they contain elements of native iconography. The intended (but not the actual) limit of these descriptions is between 25 and 75 words.

BIBLIOGRAPHICAL ESSAY. The bibliographical essay comments briefly on the more important publications concerning each manuscript and indicates its editions, commentaries, and other studies. It constitutes a guide to the classified bibliography.

COPIES. The somewhat selective listing of copies includes all copies listed in the insti-

---

[3] One of the most common errors in the literature is that of describing a manuscript foliated 20–100 (for example) as having 80 leaves; the true number in this case is 81 and not the difference between the two inclusive figures.

tutional checklist (Article 28). It does not include all copies that have been mentioned in the literature and it generally excludes copies prepared for an engraver or lithographer and subsequently published. Copies are of importance for the history of manuscripts as well as for the study of details that have disappeared on deteriorated originals. The listing of copies in the census and the repository list also serves to identify their originals, particularly in those cases where original and copy are in different collections.

CLASSIFIED BIBLIOGRAPHY. Extensive bibliographies are provided for each manuscript. The major classifications used are publication (editions, including editions with commentaries), partial publication, studies, "other" (miscellaneous topical studies including references cited in the bibliographical essay), brief descriptions, and brief mentions (for manuscripts having little other bibliography). This classification is modified to suit particular circumstances.

Partial publications or the illustration of details from manuscripts that have readily available editions are listed only on a selected basis. In those instances where the bibliography given for a particular manuscript is more than usually selected that fact is clearly stated.

Institutional and sale catalogs are usually cited only in Article 28. The latter should in all cases be checked (both as to originals and copies) for supplementary data and bibliography, even in those cases where the bibliography in the census is given as "none."

Practically all entries in certain previous catalogs and handlists are cited in the present census under "brief description" (or other appropriate category). They are: Alcina Franch (1955), Boban (1891), Gibson (1952), Glass (1964), Kubler and Gibson (1951), Lehmann (1905a), and Paso y Troncoso (1892–93). The census thus provides an index to these publications.

CENSUS OF NATIVE MIDDLE AMERICAN PICTORIAL MANUSCRIPTS

1

Acapixtla, Padrón de los Mayeques de. AGN-HJ 276, exp. 78. Published. Economic (census). Yecapixtla, Morelos. 1564. Physical description not determined.

Simple drawings of human heads and of a few place glyphs illustrate a list of *mayeques* of various localities of Yecapixtla. The document forms part of a visita and tasación of the town.

Text, figures, and photographs of two pages are published in *Nuevos Documentos* ... (1946).

Publication: Nuevos Documentos, 1946, pp. 185–203, 2 plates.

2

Acapulco, San Gregorio, Anales de. Guillermo Cabrera collection. Published. Historical and cartographic. San Gregorio Atlapulco, D.F. ca. 1606. Physical description not determined.

Nahuatl annals (1520–1606) and land documents accompanied by two local maps showing churches, boundaries, and fields and a drawing of three Indians, one of whom is identified as Cuauhtemoc. Style of pictorial material is late but may derive from older originals.

McAfee and Barlow (1952) provide palaeography, translation, and reproduction of the three illustrations. They do not reproduce or describe the vertical columns of year glyphs present in the original.

Publication: McAfee and Barlow, 1952.
Other: Chapa, 1957, p. 87 ff.

3

Actopan y sus Alrededores, Mapa de. Un-

known. Published. Cartographic. Actopan, Hidalgo. 17th–18thC. Physical description not determined.

Map of the Actopan-Ixmiquilpan region
with the convent of Actopan at the center.
Spanish glosses include a reference to a
17thC viceroy. Style is late and peripheral
to the Indian tradition.

Reproduction (of a copy?) is given without comment by Roquet (1938).

Publication: Roquet, 1938, folding plate
following p. 13.

4

Amate, Plano en Papel de. MNA 35-94. Ex–
Godofredo del Castillo Velasco collection.
Published. Economic (property plans).
Mexico City–Tlatelolco region, D. F., 16thC.
Amatl paper. 40.5 × 34 cm.

Obverse is a map of an unidentified region
showing parallel strips of land with glossed
place glyphs and the colonial symbols for the
four major barrios of Mexico City, as well as
a stream, a road, and, possibly, a stone dike.
The reverse is a similar but more simple
map. All the legible place names on the map
also appear in documents of the Ixhuatepec
Group (q.v.).

Both Caso (1956) and Glass (1964) give
photoreproductions of both sides of the
manuscript. The former has discussed its
major features. The place glyphs published
by Peñafiel (1897c) and attributed to a
"Pleito de Tierras" derive from the Códice
de Ixhuatepec and, apparently, from this
manuscript or from another version thereof.

Publication: Caso, 1956, pp. 59–61, 2
plates; Glass, 1964, p. 148, pls. 100–01.

Other: Peñafiel, 1897c, passim.

5

AMECAMECA: *Cédula de Diligencia.*
BNP 26. Ex–Aubin collection. Published.
Economic (miscellaneous). Amecameca
region, Mexico. ca. 1532–39. Native paper. 45 × 45 cm.

Drawings of Indians and place glyphs
with dated Spanish texts. The document ap-

parently concerns a property settlement with
lands or settlements (referred to as pueblos)
assigned to one or the other of two male
Indians depicted. The regional provenience
indicated here is tentative.

Boban (1891) reproduces and describes
the manuscript.

Publication: Boban, 1891, 1: 383–85, pl.
26.

6

*Amecameca, Mapa de la Visita y Congrega-
ción de.* AGN-T 2783, exp. 5. Published.
Cartographic. Amecameca, Mexico. 1599.
European paper. 61 × 51 cm.

Map of the Amecameca region shows
Amecameca and 13 small dependencies.
Spanish glosses give locality names and
other data. Limited native influence.

The map and accompanying text of this
civil congregations document of the 1598–
1606 series is published and interpreted by
Lemoine Villicaña (1961). Cook de Leonard and Lemoine Villicaña (1956) also reproduce the map with a brief description.

Publication: Cook de Leonard and Lemoine Villicaña, 1956, pp. 290–91, fig. 3;
Lemoine Villicaña, 1961.

7 (figs. 19, 20)

Analco, Lienzo de. MNA Codex collection.
Partially published. Cartographic-historical. Analco (now a barrio of San Ilde-
fonso Villa Alta), ex-district of Villa Alta,
Eastern Oaxaca. 16thC. Cloth. 245 ×
180 cm.

The lienzo is a detailed map of a large region. Numerous roads and rivers wind between depictions of mountains and houses.
Scattered across this intricate geographic
setting are drawings of innumerable Spanish soldiers (with cannon, crossbows, horses,
etc.), usually in battle with Indians. Near
the center is a town plan with further scenes
of warfare. The almost complete absence of
any glosses, dates, place names, or glyphs
of any description complicates its interpretation.

Blom (1945) gives description, illustrates several details, and suggests alternative interpretations.

Copies: Photographs in LC/HF.

Partial publication: Blom, 1945.

8

Antonio de León, Lienzo. Codex Rickards. Lienzo of Chicomostoc. Lienzo de Tlapiltepec, Papalutla y Miltepec. Royal Ontario Museum, Toronto. Ex–Abraham Castellanos and Constantine G. Rickards collections. Published. Cartographic-historical. Western Oaxaca. 16thC. Cloth. 432 × 165 cm.

Very large lienzo covered with a profusion of persons, place glyphs, and dates including two long genealogies, one of which is related to the dynasty of Coixtlahuaca as presented on Lienzo de Ihuitlan and Lienzo Meixueiro. At the lower left are historical scenes pertaining to early Mixtec mythology having parallels in various other Mixtec histories. The manuscript is closely related to Lienzo de Coixtlahuaca no. 2.

Caso (1961) provides commentary and photographic reproduction. The history of the lienzo is treated by Parmenter (1961a), who advances evidence that the document may have come from Tlapiltepec (ex-district of Coixtlahuaca). He also reviews most of the peripheral literature listed below. Rickards (1913) comments on the document and gives partial reproduction. The mythico-historical section is also reproduced in Caso's (1954) study of the Fragmento Gómez de Orozco.

Copies: Seler collection copy ("Lienzo de Tlacotepec"; for Tlacotepec Plumas?), IAI. Location of copy owned by Paul Henning unknown. The negative blueprint in the BM is presumably from the copy presented to the 18th International Congress of Americanists (ICA 18, 1: xlii, lxxix, 1913). Partial copies by Saldaña made about 1912 (*Boletin del Museo Nacional,* ep. 3, 1: 205, 262, Mexico, 1912) may correspond in part to copies listed in an unpublished inventory of copies in the MNA in 1934 and now unknown.

Publication: Caso, 1961, pp. 251–74, with 7 plates.

Studies: Caso, 1954, fig. 7; Parmenter, 1961a; Rickards, 1913.

Other: Burland, 1962a; Castellanos, 1912a, 1912b, 1917, pp. 10–11, 41–44, figs. 1, 6; Henning, 1912.

Brief description: Alcina Franch, 1955, p. 489.

9

Aperreamiento, Manuscrito del. Aperreamiento o Suplicio Ejecutado por Medio de Perros de Presa. Supplice des Caciques. BNP 374. Ex–Boturini, Mexican National Museum, and Reinisch (?) collections. Published. Miscellaneous. Coyoacan, D. F. 16thC. European paper. 43 × 31 cm.

Shows Cortés, Marina, Andrés de Tapia, six Indians chained together, and another Indian being attacked by a dog. A place glyph is identified as Coyoacan and the Nahuatl gloss includes a reference to Cholula.

The stylistically inaccurate handcolored lithograph and the translation of the Nahuatl text provided by J. F. Ramírez (1847) is largely reprinted in Madier de Montjau (1875). Wagner (1944) gives a b/w reproduction of the Ramírez illustration and a detail is given by Mayer (1844).

Copies: Interpretation made in 1867 for Simon León Reinisch, BNP 419–7. The location of a copy in a miscellaneous volume in the Fischer and Phillipps collections is unknown (*Bibliotheca mejicana,* 1869; Phillipps no. 21288; Sotheby, Wilkinson, and Hodge, 1919a).

Publication: Madier de Montjau, 1875, pp. 230–41, pl. 1; J. F. Ramírez, 1847, pp. 290–99, pl. 4; Wagner, 1944, pp. 76–78, pl. 4.

Other: *Bibliotheca mejicana,* 1869, no.

1925; Mayer, 1844, pp. 99–100; Sotheby, Wilkinson, and Hodge, 1919a, no. 489.

10

Arantza, Códice de. Unknown. Ex–García Abarca collection (?). Unpublished. Unavailable (cartographic-historical). Arantza, Michoacan. Date and physical description unknown.

The document is said to have depicted events of Tarascan history and to have shown 15 towns, 13 of them as dependencies of Tzintzuntzan. The content of the manuscript is described by Mena (1913) and repeated by Mateos Higuera (1948a).

Copies: García Abarca copy reportedly given to SMGE could not be located in July, 1964.

Brief descriptions: Mateos Higuera, 1948a; Mena, 1913.

11

Asunción, Santa María, Códice de. Apeo y Deslinde de Tierras (de los terrenos) de Santa María de la Asunción. MS de Olaguibel. BNMex. Ex–Olaguibel collection. Partially published. Economic (census and cadastral). Valley of Mexico (Santa Maria Magdalena Tepetlaoxtoc?). 16thC. Watermarked European paper. 80 leaves. 31 × 21 cm. Incomplete.

Contains pictorial registers of persons and properties for a number of named localities, probably located in the Atenco-Chiautla-Tepetlaoxtoc region of the eastern Valley of Mexico. Dates mentioned in several Nahuatl texts include 1550, 1571, and 1579. Final leaf bears signature of Pedro Vásquez de Vergara.

The codex closely resembles the Codex Vergara but differs slightly in organization. A manuscript translation of the Nahuatl texts by Francisco Rosales is in MNA/AH. This includes introductory text on initial page now missing from the original. Carreño (1950) gives a brief description and reproduces a sample page as does R. Moreno

(1966). Gibson (1964a) has commented on it briefly. The document is one of the sources, cited under the name "MS de Olaguibel," used by Peñafiel (1897c) for his study of place glyphs.

Partial publication: Carreño, 1950, pp. 12–15, 17; R. Moreno, 1966, pp. 112–14.

Other: Gibson, 1964a, p. 269, note 74, p. 300; Peñafiel, 1897c, pp. 66, 78, 84, 97, 285, 286, 289, 303.

12

Atlauhtlan, Lienzo de. Unknown. Published. Cartographic-historical. Atlautla, Mexico. 1639. Physical description unknown.

The lienzo, known through a copy (cloth, 142 × 195 cm.) preserved in the town, exhibits strong European influence, particularly in its perspective view of mountains, and is of peripheral interest. Cook de Leonard and Lemoine Villicaña (1956) give brief description, inadequate photographic reproduction, and list the towns shown on the copy as boundaries of Atlautla.

Publication: Cook de Leonard and Lemoine Villicaña, 1956, pp. 292–93, fig. 5.

13

Aubin, Codex. Codex de 1576. Histoire de la Nation Mexicaine depuis le départ d'Aztlan jusqu'à l'arrivée des Conquérants Espagnols. Anales Mexicanos no. 1. British Museum, Add. MSS 31219. Ex–Boturini, Aubin, and Desportes collections. Published. Historical and calendrical. Mexico City, D.F. ca. 1576–96 and 1597–1608. European paper codex. 81 leaves. 15 × 11 cm.

Pictorial and Nahuatl chronicle (pp. 3–135), covering the years 1168–1591 and 1595–96 with an addition for 1597–1608, begins with the departure from Aztlan and includes the dynastic history of Tenochtitlan and colonial events. The early part of the text has parallels to various other sources including Fragment de l'Histoire des anciens Mexicains (no. 202) and Histoire mexicaine depuis 1221 jusqu'en 1594 (no. 201). The content through 1355 is very similar to Codex Boturini (no. 34) but the dates for the rulers of Tenochtitlan beginning with Acamapichtli vary slightly from comparable sources. Translations of the important calendrical passage on p. 82 (including that in Caso, 1967) omit the values of the glyphs for Panquetzaliztli and Acatl that are part of the text and omit altogether the transcription and translation of the text on p. 48.

An appendix (pp. 139–57), the so-called "Códice de 1607," lists rulers of preconquest and colonial Tenochtitlan from Tenoch through 1607. Its chronology was originally in agreement with the first part of the codex, but changes (not all of which are evident in the editions) convert it to another tradition.

A 52-year calendar "wheel" in a rectangular format occupies the reverse of p. 1 and p. 2 but is omitted in the edition of 1963, as is the facsimile of the title page on p. 1.

The handcolored lithograph editions (Aubin, n.d.*a*, 1893) are inadequate for serious study of the codex. They fail to convey the pictorial style of the original, changes in handwritings and styles, changes and alterations of the drawings, and are inaccurate or misleading with respect to innumerable details. The second of these (Aubin, 1893) includes a defective French translation of the text. Dibble (1963) reprints most of the 1893 lithographs in color and gives a transcript and new Spanish translation of the text based on the original. Partial editions and translations are Peñafiel (1902) and McAfee and Barlow (1947). An edition with German translation by Walter Lehmann has long been in preparation by the Ibero-Amerikanisches Institut, Berlin. Guzmán (1949) describes the physical aspect of the manuscript. The mistitled publication, *Anales Mexicanos no. 1* (1948), is not of this manuscript. The bibliography given here is selected.

Copies and translations: The following list, offered with some misgivings, may be inaccurate in certain details. The importance of these copies is bibliographical and historical rather than scholarly.

1. Partial copy by León y Gama, BNP 35-36, described and partially published by Boban (1891).

2. Partial copy (by Pichardo?), ex–Aubin collection, SSPK, MS Amer. no. 5. The Peñafiel (1902) edition is based on this copy.

3. Late 18thC or early 19thC copy, described by Siméon (1889b), PUL.

4. Copy with French translation by Rémi Siméon, HSA.

5. Partial copy by Peñafiel (of the SSPK MS), HSA.

6. Partial copy by Peñafiel (of SSPK MS?), MHP.

7. Photographs of the original by Gates; see Article 28, Appendix A, for location of copies.

8. Copy of Nahuatl text and Spanish translation by Galicia Chimalpopoca, *Anales Mexicanos no. 1* (MNA/AH, Col. Antig. 273, AAMC 7). This copy of the Nahuatl text appears to be that published in *Anales Mexicanos no. 3* (1948, pp. 77–98) and continued in *Anales Mexicanos no. 4* (1948).

9. Spanish translation by Galicia Chimalpopoca in J. F. Ramírez, *Opúsculos históricos*, MSS, 13: 315–76 (MNA/AH, Col. Antig. 202). This translation, or possibly that in the preceding copy, has been published as *Anales Mexicanos Uno Pedernal* (1949) and as *Códice de 1576* (1950).

10. Incomplete transcript of text and partial Spanish translation, possibly by León y Gama, BNP 332.

11. French translation by Aubin, BNP 333. This and the previous item were photographed by Gates; see Article 28, Appendix A, for location of copies.

12. Notes by Aubin, BNP 346.

13. A manuscript translation, location unstated, has been cited by Galarza (1962, p. 32; 1964, p. 223).

14. Chavero (1886) cites a copy which had two pages of the original copied on each page; location unknown.

Editions: Aubin, n.d.*a*, 1893; Dibble, 1963.

Partial editions: McAfee and Barlow, 1947; Peñafiel, 1902.

Editions of text not recommended: *Anales Mexicanos no. 3*, 1948, pp. 77–98; *Anales Mexicanos no. 4*, 1948; *Anales Mexicanos Uno Pedernal*, 1949; *Códice de 1576*, 1950.

Other: Caso, 1967, pp. 88–90; Chavero, 1886, pp. 244–45; García Granados, 1937; Guzmán, 1949; Siméon, 1889b.

Brief descriptions: Alcina Franch, 1955, pp. 448–49; Boban, 1891, 1: 413–19, 2: 474–75, 486, pls. 35–36; Chavero, n.d., pp. xi–xii, xxiii; Kubler and Gibson, 1951, p. 55; Radin, 1920, pp. 13–14, 26–27.

14

Aubin Manuscript no. 20. Le Culte Rendu au Soleil. Códice del Culto a Tonatiuh. Fonds Mexicains 20. Códice de Teozoneas. BNP 20. Ex–Boturini and Aubin collections. Published. Ritual-calendrical. Western Oaxaca. Preconquest. Skin. 51 × 91 cm.

Complex composition featuring five gods of the West and five of the South with calendrical names, place glyphs, and other iconographic symbols, in pairs at the four corners and at the center of the document. Subject concerns the fivefold division of the tonalpohualli and the five cosmic directions. Although frequently classified with the Borgia Group, a Western Oaxaca or Mixtec provenience is now accepted on the basis of the style and form of place glyphs.

The central details of the original are now lost but are either preserved or restored in the León y Gama, Pichardo, and MNA copies. In the 19thC the improbable idea that the document represented the colored reliefs on a buried stone monument near the Cathedral in Mexico City was promoted by Gondra (in Mayer, 1844, with reproduc-

tion of central detail) and is reflected in the captions ("Relieves en la Piedra de los Gladiadores," "Piedra policroma del Sacrificio Gladiatorio," etc.) of various early reproductions.

The original and the León y Gama copy are photographically reproduced by Boban (1891). Lehmann (1905c) gives tracings, based on Boban's plates, and a detailed commentary and interpretation. A Spanish translation of Lehmann's study (Lehmann, 1966) is accompanied by a modern commentary by Caso (1966a), in which the original manuscript and the MNA copy are photographically reproduced in color. Seler (1904–09; Spanish translation, 1963) also gives drawings and summary of content. Nowotny (1961b) reproduces the von den Steinen copy of the original, a copy of the central detail from the León y Gama copy, and gives an annotated presentation of its content. See Borgia Group for further comment.

The MNA copy is photographically reproduced and described by Glass (1964) and is the apparent source of the reproductions in Prescott (1844), Chavero (n.d., 1882–1903), and Peñafiel (1910). The illustrations by Chavero are in color.

Copies: León y Gama copy, BNP 21. Pichardo copy, BNP 88-4. Anonymous copy (by León y Gama?) MNA 35-12. Von den Steinen copy, IAI. Modern copy of MNA 35-12, MNA 35-12A.

Publication with modern commentary: Caso, 1966a; Lehmann, 1905c, 1966; Nowotny, 1961b, pp. 46–47, 202, 227–28, fig. 6, pl. 51; Seler, 1904–09, 2: 102–03, figs. 70a-f; 1963, 2: 82–83, figs. 70a-f.

Other reproductions: Boban, 1891, 1: 329–52, pls. 20, 21; Chavero, n.d., p. 748, plate facing p. 749; 1882–1903, in *Anales*, 2: 117, plate facing p. 233; Glass, 1964, pp. 51–52, pl. 14; Peñafiel, 1910, pp. 44–45, pl. 103; Prescott, 1844, 1: 85.

Other: Mayer, 1844, pp. 123–24; Orozco y Berra, 1880, 3: 348–49 in note.

Brief descriptions: Alcina Franch, 1955, pp. 473–74; Lehmann, 1905a, pp. 258–59.

15

Aubin, Tonalamatl. Kalendario Ydolatrico. Códice Gama (rare). BNP 18–19. Ex–Boturini, Nebel (ff. 9–20), Waldeck (ff. 9–20), and Aubin collections. Published. Ritual-calendrical. Tlaxcala (?). Early 16thC. Native paper screenfold painted on one side. 18 leaves plus additional leaf with title in Spanish; 2 leaves missing. 24 × 27 cm.

Possibly preconquest tonalamatl (divinatory almanac) in early unacculturated style. Each page depicts patron deities, 13 birds, 13 gods, and the Nine Lords of the Night associated with each 13-day period of the 260-day divinatory cycle. The tentative Tlaxcalan provenience is based on a statement in the 1745 inventory of the Boturini collection.

A lithograph edition, with two pages in color and with the missing pages supplied on the basis of the León y Gama reconstruction, was printed for Aubin about 1851 (Aubin, n.d.g). It had limited circulation until it was issued with a study by Orozco y Berra (1897). Commentary by Seler (1900; English translation, 1900–01) is accompanied by a color lithograph facsimile. Two pages are photographically reproduced by Boban (1891).

Copies: León y Gama copy, BNP 19bis. Pichardo copies, BNP 88-2 and 88-6 (b). Ramírez copy of four pages (pp. 11, 13, 19, 20), mentioned by Chavero (1903b) and partially published by Chavero (1906).

Publication: Aubin, n.d.g; Librería Echániz, 1938b; Orozco y Berra, 1897; Seler, 1900, 1900–01.

Other: Chavero, 1903b, pp. 289–90, 298; 1906, pp. 199, 206; Léon de Rosny, 1876a, pl. 18; Seler, 1890.

Brief descriptions: Alcina Franch, 1955, pp. 430–31; Boban, 1891, 1: 293–318, pls. 18, 19.

16 (fig. 21)

Axayacatl, Portrait of. Nationalbibliothek, Vienna. CVM 12. Ex–Bilimek collection. Published. Miscellaneous. Valley of Mexico. 17th–18thC (?). Oil painting on cloth. Dimensions not determined.

The painting portrays Axayacatl, one of the 15thC rulers of Tenochtitlan. He is dressed in a flayed human skin, holds a shield, and bears a feather banner supported on his back. Although the style is not in the native tradition, the composition and iconographic details are reminiscent of a similar portrayal of this individual in Codex Cozcatzin and the two depictions may be related.

The painting has been described and reproduced in color by both Hochstetter (1884) and by Nuttall (1888). Seler (1904a, 1904e) interprets it, criticizes Nuttall's interpretation, and reproduces its major features.

Publication: Hochstetter, 1884, p. 15, pl. 2; Nuttall, 1888, pp. 10–22, pl. 2, fig. 7; Seler, 1904a, 1904e.

17

Axotlan, San Lorenzo, y San Luis Huexotla, Códice de los Señores de. MNA 35-64. Ex–Boturini collection. Published. Economic (property plans). San Luis Obispo Huexotla, Mexico. ca. 1672. Tira of European and native paper. 29 × 111.5 cm.

The strip is divided into rectangular sections, representing plots of land, separated by roads. In most of the divisions are a drawing of a house or an Indian and Nahuatl texts. Substantially the same texts and a contemporary translation occur in AGN-T 1520, exp. 6, and allow the identification of the document as a statement of land titles and boundaries of properties in San Lorenzo Acxotlan, a barrio of San Luis Obispo Huexotla. The text is dated 1531 but in the AGN accompanies 17thC documents.

A brief description and a photograph of the drawing are given by Glass (1964). Arreola (1922) has published the related texts and translation from AGN-T 1520.

Publication: Glass, 1964, pp. 116–17, pl. 67.

Brief description: Mena, 1923, p. 60, no. 15.

Other: Arreola, 1922, pp. 582 (lines 31–46), 583 (lines 1–33 and 43–47), 585–86.

18

Ayotzingo, Historia de. BNP 84. Ex-Aubin collection. Unpublished. Historical and cartographic. Ayotzingo, Mexico. ca. 1607–1635. European paper. 8 pages of Spanish text and 10 leaves (pages?) of drawings. 30 × 21 cm.

Not examined. As described by Boban (1891) the document has historical notices in Spanish encompassing the years 1519–90 and two detailed maps of the Ayotzingo region. The final pages have drawings of Indians, some of whom are identified as the first Christians of Ayotzingo; others are identified as paying tribute, 1592–93.

Brief description: Boban, 1891, 2: 215–18.

19 (fig. 22)

Azcapotzalco, Trozo de. Archivo General de Indias, Seville. Unpublished. Economic (property plans). Azcapotzalco, D.F. 1543. Native paper. 45 × 49 cm.

Simple property plan showing the glyph for Azcapotzalco, a house, adjacent fields, a maguey plant, and Spanish money. It is related to a visita by Tello de Sandoval, the text of which may also be in the AGI.

A printed reproduction was prepared for Paso y Troncoso before 1916 but not published; it has had little circulation. Zavala (1938) erroneously refers to this reproduction as the "Mapa de Xaltocan."

Brief references: Torres Lanzas, 1900, 1: 20, no. 7; Zavala, 1938, p. 604.

20

Azcatitlan, Códice. Histoire mexicaine.

BNP 59-64. Ex–Boturini and Aubin collections. Published. Historical. Valley of Mexico. 16thC. European paper. 25 leaves. 21 × 28 cm.

Annals of Mexican history, commencing with the departure from Aztlan (here given as Azcatitlan) and Culhuacan A.D. 1168 and continuing with the migration and the beginnings of the dynastic history of Tenochtitlan through A.D. 1381, followed by pages devoted to individual rulers of Tenochtitlan from Acamapichtli through Moctezuma II. Final pages present drawings of the Spanish conquest and of the earliest colonial period.

For commentary and photographic edition see Barlow (1949b). Some pages are reproduced in Boban (1891) and in Robertson (1959). Three pages of one of the copies are reproduced in color in Athearn (1963) and two in Blacker (1965).

Copies: León y Gama copy, BNP 90-1. Pichardo copy, BNP 89-3.

Publication: Barlow, 1949b

Partial publication: Athearn, 1963, pp. 29, 31, 38; Blacker, 1965, pp. 58, 136–37; Boban, 1891, 2: 103–13, pls. 59–64; Robertson, 1959, pp. 184–85, pls. 78–79.

Brief description: Alcina Franch, 1955, pp. 447–48.

21

Azoyu, Códice de, no. 1. Códice Rodríguez-Ortega. MNA 35-108. Partially published. Historical, genealogical, and cartographic-historical. Tlapa, Guerrero. 1565 (?). Amatl paper screenfold painted on both sides. 38 leaves. 20.5 × 23 cm. approx.

The manuscript, together with Códice de Azoyu no. 2 and Lienzo de Tlapa, were discovered in Azoyu in 1940. The individual leaves of the document are composed of thin sheets of laminated amatl paper. In either this manuscript or in Códice de Azoyu no. 2 there is a painting on at least one such internal leaf, now covered by the overlying lamination.

On each of the 38 pages of the obverse are

drawings of historical episodes and seven year dates. The total number of years so represented is 266, possibly equivalent to A.D. 1300–1565 on a correlation that equates 3 Ehecatl, on p. 32, the first in which Spaniards appear, with 3 Calli (Aztec) or A.D. 1521. The year-bearer days used in the dates are one day earlier than those used in the normal or Aztec calendar and the accompanying numbers are 2–14 rather than 1–13.

At one end of the reverse side is a genealogy on six pages in the style of the obverse. Five pages at the other extremity of the reverse are in a much later and possibly 17thC style and contain a sort of map showing persons and boundaries with explanatory Nahuatl texts. The style of this addition is reminiscent of the additions to Códice de Veinte Mazorcas. The 27 intermediate pages of the reverse are blank.

A brief preliminary study of the manuscript by Toscano (1943) reproduces two pages of the obverse and one page of the genealogy on the reverse. Glass (1964) briefly describes the manuscript and reproduces one page from each of the three sections. Caso (1943b) gives color reproductions of two pages of the obverse; one of them is reprinted in b/w by Vivó (1946).

Copy: Modern copy, MNA 35-108A.

Partial publication: Caso, 1943b; Glass, 1964, pp. 163–64, pls. 115–17; Toscano, 1943, pp. 128–33, 3 plates.

Other: Vivó, 1946, pl. 53.

22

Azoyu, Códice de, no. 2. Códice Ortega. MNA 35-109. Partially published. Historical and economic (tribute). Tlapa, Guerrero. ca. 1565(?). Amatl paper screenfold painted on both sides. 15 leaves. 22 × 27 cm. approx.

The obverse is similar in content, style, and format to the obverse of Códice de Azoyu no. 1 but has eight rather than seven dates per page. It has been considered a version of pp. 19–38 of the latter manuscript; it spans the period believed equivalent to 1429–1564. Two leaves, corresponding to pp. 10 and 11 of the obverse, are missing.

The paintings on the reverse ("Nómina de Tributos de Tlapa y su Señorío al Imperio Mexicano"; "Códice Humboldt") which begin on the back of p. 8 of the obverse are concerned with tribute. Humboldt Fragment 1 (q.v.) is a continuation of this side of the manuscript.

Toscano (1943) gives preliminary interpretation and reproduces a page from each side of the manuscript. Two different pages, also from opposite sides of the manuscript, are published by Glass (1964) together with a brief description. The latter's statement that the manuscript has 17 leaves misleadingly includes the two lost leaves. See Humboldt Fragment 1 for additional bibliography on the reverse side.

Partial publication: Glass, 1964, p. 165, pls. 118–19; Toscano, 1943, pp. 133–36, 2 plates.

23 (fig. 23)

Aztactepec y Citlaltepec, Lienzo de. Códice de las Vejaciones. Lienzo de Tlapa no. 2. Casa del Alfeñique, Puebla. Published. Cartographic-historical. Citlaltepec, Guerrero. 1572. Cloth. 107 × 135 cm.

Around the periphery of the lienzo are glossed place glyphs including Aztactepec and Atlimeaxac. In the center, which is traversed by a river, are drawings of native rulers, Spaniards, Indians fighting, a large snake, and two women, and the glyph for Citlaltepec. Nahuatl glosses mention Tlapa and the date 1572 (1574?).

Glass (1964) reproduces the MNA copy, describes it briefly, and cites an unpublished translation of the Nahuatl glosses.

Copies: Copy by Rodolfo Barthez made in 1933, MNA 35-126. Photograph of unidentified copy, apparently on paper, in INAH/AF.

Publication: Glass, 1964, p. 184, pl. 137.

24

Baranda, Códice. Codex Alvarado. Códice de las Conquistas de Alvarado. MNA 35-4. Ex–Boturini and BNMex collections. Published. Historical. Western Oaxaca. 17thC. Skin tira painted on one side. 37 × 228 cm.

The tira opens with historical scenes having parallels in the early or mythical sections of several Mixtec manuscripts. It continues with drawings of 26 houses with as many pairs of persons with calendrical names and several further historical scenes. In one of the latter are a Spaniard and a horse.

The commentary by Caso (1958b) includes photographic reproduction in both color and b/w. Colored lithographs were published by the Junta Colombina (Chavero, 1892) with an unacceptable commentary. A colored reproduction of a copy by J. S. León appears in Mendieta y Núñez (1949). The synonym, Codex Alvarado, derived from a brief reference by Chavero (1899), is sometimes mistaken for a distinct document. Chavero (1906) explains the confusion.

Copy: Modern copy by Saldaña, MNA 35-4A.

Publication: Caso, 1958b; Chavero, 1892, pp. xix–xxii, with 4 double plates in atlas; Mendieta y Núñez, 1949, folding plate facing p. 62.

Other: Chavero, 1899, p. 402, note 1; 1906, pp. 203–04, note 2; Ruz Lhuillier, 1944.

Brief descriptions: Alcina Franch, 1955, pp. 479, 482; Glass, 1964, pp. 41–42, pl. 6; Lehmann, 1905a, pp. 274–76; Paso y Troncoso, 1892–93, 1: 263–67.

❖❖❖

BEAUMONT, FRAY PABLO. *Crónica de Michoacan.* The Beaumont chronicle, written ca. 1776–80, contains copies of the three pictorial items listed separately below. The only one of several editions of the *Crónica* to reproduce the illustrations is Beaumont (1932). Part of the original Beaumont manuscript is in JCBL. The three CMNE copies of ca. 1792 are in RAH (two copies) and AGN-H. Other copies, presumably from the CMNE, are in NYPL (two copies, one incomplete), BAN, and UTX. A copy from the Kingsborough and Phillipps collections (Phillipps 11692–94; Sotheby, Wilkinson, and Hodge, 1919a, no. 345; Sotheby and Co., 1948, no. 4857) is unknown. Copies of the illustrations were in the Gómez de Orozco collection (Gómez de Orozco, 1927a, p. 160); these may have been the copies of 1892 made for the Exposición Histórico-Americana of Madrid (Paso y Troncoso, 1892–93, 1: 10).

25

—— Nine historical scenes in the *Crónica de Michoacan* (see above). Originals lost. Published. Historical. Tzintzuntzan, Michoacan. 16thC (?). Physical description uncertain.

The nine copies, with identifying Spanish glosses, depict events of the conquest of Michoacan and the history of the religious establishment before 1550. Some ethnological data are included. Cristóbal de Olid, the Tarascan chieftain, Caltzontzin, Fr. Martín de Jesús, and Vasco de Quiroga are shown. References to the originals by Beaumont are unclear but suggest that more than one original was copied.

The drawings were first published by Riva Palacio (n.d.) and later, with slight commentary, by N. León (1903, 1903–04, 1904a). All are reproduced in color in Beaumont (1932). Josephy and Brandon (1961) reproduce one scene in color from a NYPL copy. Five details are photographically reproduced in color by López Sarrelangue (1965). Seler (1908a) reproduces and comments on three of the drawings from copies in his collection.

Copies: See above for copies of the Beaumont chronicle. An uncolored copy ("Códice de la Conquista de Michoacan") of the nine scenes on a long strip (75 × 308 cm.) is in the MNA (uncataloged; no. 32 of the inventory of 1934). It presumably derives from the copy in AGN-H.

Publication: Beaumont, 1932, 2: 25, 36, 124, 366–68, 380; plates in vols. 2 and 3; N. León, 1903, pls. 6, 25bis; 1903–04 (reprinted, 1904a), pls. 29–34, 37–38; Riva Palacio, n.d., pp. 27–33, 297–98.

Partial publication: Josephy and Brandon, 1961; pp. 132–33; López Sarrelangue, 1965, following pp. 38, 50, 150, 158, 170; Seler, 1908a, figs. 33, 42, 56.

26

—— Map of Tzintzuntzan in the *Crónica de Michoacan* (see above). Original unknown. Published. Cartographic. Tzintzuntzan, Michoacan. 16thC. Physical description unknown.

Glossed map of Lake Patzcuaro and surrounding towns with Tzintzuntzan, its church and atrium, and other buildings prominent near the center. Historical detail relates to transfer of episcopal see from Tzintzuntzan to Patzcuaro about 1540.

Reproduced in color in Beaumont (1932), B. Smith (1968), and in López Sarrelangue (1965). Other reproductions are given by N. León (1903, 1906b). Seler (1908a) reproduces one of the Beaumont copies as well as a variant copy in his collection. The latter indicates that the original was glossed in Tarascan. McAndrew (1965) also illustrates and comments on the Beaumont and Seler versions. Yet another version is published by Cuevas (1921–28).

Publication: Beaumont, 1932, 2: 36–37, 366–69; vol. 3, plate facing p. 410; Cuevas, 1921–28, 1: 313; I. Espinosa, 1945, pl. 10; N. León, 1903, pl. 7; 1906b, fig. 6; López Sarrelangue, 1965, following p. 70; McAndrew, 1965, pp. 508, 633; Seler, 1908a, figs. 17, 18; B. Smith, 1968, p. 191.

❖❖❖

—— *See* Tributes of Tzintzuntzan and Tlalpujava.

27

Becker, Codex, no. 1. Manuscrit du Cacique. Codex Saussure. Codex Tzapoteque. Codex Franz Josefino. Museum für Völkerkunde, Vienna. Ex–Pascual Almazan and Philip J. Becker collections. Published. Historical. Tututepec, ex-district of Juquila, Western Oaxaca. Preconquest. Skin screenfold painted on one side. 16 leaves in 3 fragments (pp. 1–4, 5–14, 15–16). 18.7 × 396.4 cm. (total length).

The manuscript consists of fragments of a larger document of which Códice Colombino (q.v.) also forms a part. It treats the life and history of the 11thC Mixtec ruler, 8 Deer. Codex Becker no. 1 has dates embracing the years A.D. 1047–68.

Color lithographs of the copy made by Saussure shortly after 1852 were published in 1891 (Saussure, 1891). A commentary and photographic facsimile were published by Nowotny (1961a). Caso (in Caso and Smith, 1966) also interprets its content and discusses its relationship to Códice Colombino. Partial interpretations of the content appear in Clark (1912) and Caso (1955b).

Copy: The location of the Saussure copy is unknown.

Publication: Nowotny, 1961a; Saussure, 1891.

Studies: Caso, 1955b; Caso and Smith, 1966; Clark, 1912; Nowotny and Strebinger, 1958.

Other: Hamy, 1897; Nowotny, 1964.

Brief descriptions: Alcina Franch, 1955, pp. 487–88. Lehmann, 1905a, pp. 259–60.

28

Becker, Codex, no. 2. Museum für Völkerkunde, Vienna. Ex–Philip J. Becker collection. Published. Historical. Western Oaxaca. Early 16thC. Skin screenfold painted on one side. 4 leaves. 26.5 × 115.6 cm. (total length).

The manuscript is divided into two horizontal bands. In the lower are nine Indian couples with calendrical and personal name glyphs. In the upper are six couples by a different or later hand, also responsible for the addition of place glyphs to the lower division. Both sets of drawings are in the traditional Mixtec style. None of the persons shown have been identified in other Mixtec genealogies. What may be another fragment of this manuscript is described in the following entry.

Nowotny (1961a) provides commentary and photographic color reproduction. He also gives line drawings of the manuscript first published by him in 1957.

Copies: An unpublished 19thC copy, MNA 35-8, may include details now illegible on the original. MNA 35-77 (partially published by Glass, 1964) is a modern copy based on photographs of the original. The location of the Seler collection copy is unknown. A copy by Becker is owned by C. A. Burland.

Publication: Nowotny, 1957, 1961a.

Other: Glass, 1964, pp. 46, 130, pl. 82; Nowotny, 1964.

Brief descriptions: Alcina Franch, 1955, p. 491; Lehmann, 1905a, p. 261.

29 (fig. 24)

——, additional fragment. Fragmento Mixteco de Nochistlan. Museum für Völkerkunde, Hamburg. Unpublished. Historical. Western Oaxaca. Early 16thC. Skin, painted on one side. 26 × 50 cm. approx.

Like Codex Becker no. 2, the fragment is divided into two horizontal bands. Each band has a hieroglyphic place symbol and date as well as two pairs of Indian couples depicted in much the same manner and style as those in the lower half of Codex Becker no. 2, of which the fragment is believed to form a part. Mixtec (?) glosses are in two different handwritings.

The existence of the document was communicated by G. Zimmermann, who courteously supplied a photograph to LC/HF for description. The history of the manuscript and the reason for the word Nochistlan in the title are unknown to us.

Bibliography: None.

30

Boban Calendar Wheel. John Carter Brown Library, Providence. Ex–Boban, Pinart, C. F. Gunther, and Chicago Historical Society collections. Published. Calendrical and historical. Texcoco, Mexico. ca. 1538. Circular leaf of native paper. 38 cm. diameter.

Calendar wheel with symbols for the 18 months in the outer circle with the 20 day signs clustered at the top. In the center are two sets of drawings and Nahuatl texts of an historical nature. One, with the date 7 Rabbit (1538), concerns the Texcocan town officers, Hernando de Chávez and Antonio Pimentel. The text of the other includes references to Netzahualcoyotl, Itzcoatl, and Totoquihuatzin, 15thC rulers of Texcoco, Tenochtitlan, and Tlacopan.

The Nahuatl texts have not been fully translated. Color lithographs have been published by Doutrelaine (1867) and in Veytia (1907). Color photographs of the original and the 1867 edition are given by Caso (1967). Calendrical interpretations are provided by Paso y Troncoso (1898b), Jonghe (1906a) and by Caso (1959b; reprinted in Caso, 1967). The month symbols are reproduced by Orozco y Berra (1880) and Robertson (1959) gives a general analysis of the document. B/w reproductions of one or the other of the color lithographs appear in some of the publications cited.

Publication without comment: Peñafiel, 1910, pl. 110; Veytia, 1907, pl. 8.

Publication with partial study: Caso, 1959b, pp. 23–25, fig. 4; 1967, pp. 71–73, fig. 22; Doutrelaine, 1867; Jonghe, 1906a, pp. 495–96, fig. 3; Kubler and Gibson, 1951, p.

56, fig. 12; Robertson, 1959, pp. 146–49, pl. 51.

Other: Boban, 1891, 1: 360, note 1; 2: 100; Orozco y Berra, 1880, atlas, pl. 18, figs. 67–84; Paso y Troncoso, 1898b, pp. 295–302.

31

Bodley, Codex. Codex Bodleianus. Códice Bodleiano. Bodleian Library, Oxford. Ex–Sir Thomas Bodley collection. Historical. Western Oaxaca. ca. 1521. Skin screenfold painted on both sides. 23 leaves with 20 painted pages on each side. 26 × 29 cm.

The obverse contains a detailed presentation of the genealogies of the dynasties of Tilantongo and Teozacoalco and the mythological origins of the former. Its first date is believed equivalent to A.D. 692, and the last event shown is the marriage of the rulers of Tilantongo who were ruling at the time of the Spanish conquest. The reverse contains related genealogies for various localities, most of which have not been identified. This codex is one of the most replete and important of the Mixtec histories.

The detailed interpretation and commentary by Caso (1960b, 1960c), is accompanied by a photographic color facsimile. The first edition was published by Kingsborough (1831–48). Another edition (Corona Núñez, 1964–67) has a commentary, possibly based on that by Caso, with the pages of the manuscript reproduced by color photography. Its quality is inferior to that of the Caso edition. The genealogies on the obverse have also been studied by Dark (1958a).

Publication: Caso, 1960b, 1960c; Corona Núñez, 1964–67, 2: 33–75; Librería Echániz, 1947a; Kingsborough, 1831–48, vol. 1.

Studies: Caso, 1952, 1958f, 1964c, 1966b; Dark, 1958a, 1958b, 1959.

Brief descriptions: Alcina Franch, 1955, p. 488; Lehmann, 1905a, p. 271; Nowotny, 1961b, pp. 51, 271, pl. 60.

32

Borbonicus, Codex. Codex du Corps Legislatif. Codex Legislatif. Codex Hamy. Calendario de Paris. Bibliothèque de l'Assemblée Nationale Française, Paris. Published. Ritual-calendrical. Mexico City–Tenochtitlan, D.F. Preconquest or early 16thC. Native paper screenfold painted on one side. 36 leaves (pp. 3–38). ca. 39 × 39.5 cm.

The manuscript was first described by Waddilove (in W. Robertson, 1778) when it was in the Escorial in Spain and before its pp. 1–2 and 39–40 were lost. It was purchased by the library of the French Chamber of Deputies in 1826. Kingsborough (1831–48) reported its presence in Paris but was apparently refused permission to publish it (Anonymous, 1829).

The date of this major and early calendrical source is controversial. Caso (1939a, 1962) has argued for a preconquest dating whereas D. Robertson (1959) has argued for an early colonial date, possibly before 1541. Caso (1967, pp. 103–12) again discusses its dating and attempts a refutation of Robertson's arguments.

The manuscript has four major sections. Part 1 (pp. 3–20) is a tonalpohualli or 260-day divinatory almanac. The first and second of the 20 periods, presumably depicted on the missing pp. 1 and 2, are lacking. The presiding deities and other symbols of each period are shown in a main panel on each page. The day signs, the 13 Lords of the Day, the 9 Lords of the Night, and the 13 birds are drawn in compartments below and to the right of each main panel. The pictorial detail is greater than that in any other central Mexican tonalamatl or than those in the Borgia Group manuscripts. As in other parts of the document there are later Spanish glosses.

Part 2 (pp. 21–22) shows the association of the 9 Lords of the Night with the year–bearer days for a 52-year period. Part 3 (pp.

23–36) is an 18-month festival calendar for a New Fire ceremony year. Part 4 (pp. 37–38 and the missing pp. 39–40) repeats one of the month ceremonies and continues with year dates for a 52-year period.

Hamy (1899a) gives descriptive commentary and color lithograph facsimile. A photographic edition of part 1 only was issued by Vaillant (1940). Paso y Troncoso (1898b) is a detailed but unillustrated commentary on the entire manuscript. An edition and commentary by Caso has long been in press.

The correlation of the Aztec and Christian calendars by Caso (1939a; 1967, pp. 41–64) depends heavily on an analysis of part 3 of this manuscript. Part 2 has been the subject of a number of technical studies and is also treated in some of the other calendrical studies of the document listed below. Chavero (n.d.) illustrated several details from the manuscript under the name "Calendario de Paris," presumably from a copy by J. F. Ramírez in his collection. A single page was first reproduced by Léon de Rosny (1876a, 1881b) and a detail was reproduced by Lucien de Rosny (1877). Eleven of its pages are reproduced (nine in color) in Caso (1967).

Copies: An incomplete copy from the Ramírez and Chavero collections is in MNA/AH. An unpublished commentary by Ramírez (cited by Paso y Troncoso, 1898b) may also be in that collection. Full-size photographs were given limited distribution in the late 19thC. Examples of these are in NYPL, MHP, and elsewhere but are not listed in the institutional checklist. A set of photographs is BNP 80.

Editions: Hamy, 1899a; Librería Echániz, 1938a.

Partial edition: Vaillant, 1940.

Commentary: Paso y Troncoso, 1898b.

Studies of Part 2: Apenes, 1953; Bowditch, 1900; Burland, 1957b; Caso, 1953; 1967, pp. 112–29; Lizardi Ramos, 1953a.

Other calendrical studies: Caso, 1939a;

1940; 1967, chaps. 1 and 3 (includes revision of his 1939a and 1940); Jonghe, 1906a, 1906b; Kreichgauer, 1917–18; Margáin Araujo, 1945; Nowotny, 1961b, passim, pls. 63–65; Seler, 1904–09, chap. 23; 1963, chap. 23.

General study: Robertson, 1959, pp. 86–93, pls. 9, 21.

Other: André-Bonnet, 1950; Anonymous, 1829; Boban, 1891, 2: 202–07, pl. 80; Caso, 1962; Chavero, n.d., pp. xvi, 707–11; Collin, 1952; Galindo y Villa, 1923; Kingsborough, 1831–48, 6: 95; Léon de Rosny, 1876a, pl. 10; 1881b, pl. 10; Lucien de Rosny, 1877, pl. 12.

Brief descriptions: Alcina Franch, 1955, pp. 429–30; Aubin, 1859; Kubler and Gibson, 1951, p. 56; W. Robertson, 1778, 2: 477–78.

33

Borgia, Codex. Codex Borgianus. Códice Borgiano. Manuscrit de Veletri. Biblioteca Apostolica Vaticana, Rome. Ex-Palazzo Giustiniani (?), Cardinal Stefano Borgia and Sacra Congregatione de Propaganda Fide collections. Published. Ritual–calendrical. Borgia Group. Preconquest. Skin screenfold. 39 leaves (38 painted pages on each side; initial and terminal pages formerly attached to covers, blank). 27 × 26.5 cm. (total length ca. 1027–34 cm.).

Generally conceded to be among the finest specimens of pre-Columbian art, the manuscript is the most important, detailed, and complex pictorial source extant for the study of Central Mexican gods, ritual, divination, calendar, religion, and iconography. Most of its 28 sections are devoted to different aspects of the tonalpohualli, the Mesoamerican 260-day divinatory period. Other sections depict complex rituals whose significance remains obscure.

The Fábrega (1899) commentary, commissioned by Cardinal Borgia before the former's death in 1797, is of historical interest

98

only. Details were first published by Humboldt (1810); the first edition is in Kingsborough (1831–48). A color screenfold facsimile with history of the manuscript was published by the Duc de Loubat (Ehrle, 1898). The copiously illustrated and comprehensive commentary by Seler (1904–09) includes annotated drawings of all pages. Its Spanish translation (Seler, 1963) is also accompanied by a photographic color reproduction. Nowotny (1961b) provides comparative summary and interpretations of all its sections, differing from those by Seler in some instances. He also reproduces 38 of its 76 pages. The color in the editions of 1898 and 1963 may be compared with color photographs of selected pages in *Flor y Canto* (1964) and in various other art books. See annotation in bibliography under Corona Núñez (1964–67) for an edition now in press. Studies of particular passages of the manuscript are listed below. See Borgia Group, below, for further bibliography and comment.

Copies: Ramón Rodríguez Arangoiti, whose name appears on the manuscript as having made a copy in 1856, has been identified (Chavero, 1899, p. 321) as having been retained by J. F. Ramírez to color an uncolored version of the Kingsborough edition from the original.

Publication: Librería Echániz, 1937a; Ehrle, 1898; Kingsborough, 1831–48, vol. 3; Seler, 1904–09, 1963.

Studies: Beyer, 1912a, 1912b; Nowotny, 1961b, passim; Seler, 1902f, 1902l; J. E. S. Thompson, 1934, pp. 217–19, 223–25, pls. 1–2; 1966.

Historical references: Barthelemy, 1798; Borson, 1796, p. 39; Paulinus de Sancto Bartholomaeo, 1805; Zoega, 1797, pp. 530–31.

Other: Caso, 1927; Chadwick and MacNeish, 1967; Chavero, 1899, pp. 319–24 and passim; Fábrega, 1899; *Flor y Canto*, 1964, pls. 4, 361, 363; Humboldt, 1810, pp. 89–101,

212, 235–37, pls. 15, 27, 37; Márquez, 1911, 1912; Seler, 1895, 1904g.

Brief descriptions: Alcina Franch, 1955, pp. 471–73; Lehmann, 1905a, pp. 251–53.

❖❖❖

BORGIA GROUP. Five pictorial manuscripts—the screenfold Codices Borgia, Cospi, Féjérváry-Mayer, Laud, and Vaticanus B—entered separately in the census but linked together by preconquest date, intricate symbolism, a largely common religious content related to the divinatory tonalpohualli 260-day cycle, and unknown and probably different proveniences. The group was first defined by Seler (1902b) in 1887. Part of the reverse side of Códice Porfirio Díaz (pp. 33–42) has a similar content and is sometimes considered a member of the group. Aubin Manuscript no. 20, also considered a member of the group, has been classified herein as Western Oaxacan or Mixtec.

Unsatisfactory color reproductions of the five screenfolds were published by Kingsborough (1831–48); more adequate editions are cited in the census entries. The commentaries by Seler on Tonalamatl Aubin (1900) and Codices Féjérváry-Mayer (1901a), Vaticanus B (1902a), and especially Borgia (1904–09) constitute the fundamental body of interpretation; each of these commentaries also treats comparable passages in other members of the group, excepting the greater part of Codex Laud. Most earlier 19thC studies, such as those in Chavero (n.d.) and elsewhere, are now either only of historical interest or superseded.

Only Nowotny (1961b) is an important, elaborate, and illustrated presentation of the content of all members of the group. His revision of the numeration of sections of some manuscripts as used by Seler will probably be accepted as a new standard for citations. As there are numerous cases where a section of one manuscript is parallel in content to one or more of the other members of the group, his indexes to their content facilitate study of these similarities. Spranz (1964) is a detailed analysis of the iconography of deities depicted in the five screenfolds.

The provenience of the group is treated in detail in three recent studies (Robertson, 1963, 1964; Nicholson, 1966c) and in more general terms by Martínez Marín (1961). Modern opinion has limited the probable provenience of the five screenfolds to the Mixteca-Puebla, Puebla-Tlaxcala, Western Oaxaca, or Gulf Coast regions.

Brief descriptions of the group as a whole and of its five basic members are cited below.

Single publication of the five screenfolds: Kingsborough, 1831–48, vols. 2 and 3.

Commentaries: Nowotny, 1961b; Seler, 1900, 1901a, 1902a, 1904–09 (and English or Spanish translations cited in the bibliography); Spranz, 1964.

Provenience (modern works only): Martínez Marín, 1961, pp. 6–10; Nicholson, 1966c; Robertson, 1963, 1964.

Other: Chavero, n.d., passim; Nowotny, 1955; Seler, 1902b.

Brief description: Alcina Franch, 1955, pp. 471–78; Lehmann, 1905a, pp. 251–59; Toscano, 1944, pp. 370–77.

34

Boturini, Códice. Tira de la Peregrinación. Tira del Museo. MNA 35-38. Ex-Boturini collection. Exhibited in London by Bullock in 1824. Published. Historical. Mexico City, D.F. 16thC. Amatl paper screenfold painted on one side only. 21 and one-half leaves. 19.8 × 549 cm. (total length).

Early pictorial chronicle (1168–1355), in native or slightly acculturated style, gives the history of the Tenochca-Mexica beginning with the emigration from Aztlan through the arrival at Chapultepec to the period of their subjugation to Coxcox, ruler of Culhuacan. The sole color is in the red lines that connect the dates.

The only photographic edition (Corona Núñez, 1964–67) is in color. Early lithograph editions are Bullock (n.d.), Kingsborough (1831–48), Delafield (1839), and J. F. Ramírez (1858), by Chavero (n.d.), Librería Echániz (1944c,d,e), Mendizábal (1946), and inferior versions in Gondra (1846) and Schoolcraft (1851–57). References to an edition by Aubin are probably in error. Robertson (1959) and Glass (1964) reproduce photographs of individual pages.

The manuscript has been interpreted by J. F. Ramírez (1858), by Chavero (n.d.), with full reproduction of the tira as text figures, by Orozco y Berra (1880) with unorthodox chronology, in Librería Echániz (1944c), and by Corona Núñez (1964–67). Radin (1920) reproduces Kingsborough's plates and gives a digest of the Orozco y Berra commentary. The comparative studies by García Conde (1926) and García Cubas (1912), both of which include reproductions, depend on J. F. Ramírez and Orozco y Berra. Barlow (1949b) indicates the basis for a colonial dating; Robertson (1959) comments on the style and dating. The few glosses have been transcribed (incompletely) only on the Bullock and Delafield lithographs. No commentary provides a full treatment and the bibliography given here for this major source is selective.

Copies: Among the very large number of copies that have been reported in the literature are: BNP 93, BNP 96, and MNA 35-38A. See also the Mapa Monclova (Article 26, no. 963).

Publication with commentary: Corona Núñez, 1964–67, 2: 7–29; Librería Echániz, 1944c; García Conde, 1926, pp. 312–27, pl. 33; García Cubas, 1912, pp. 411–18, pl. 71; Radin, 1920, pp. 11–12, 33–35, pls. 1–11; J. F. Ramírez, 1858.

Publication without significant comment: Bullock, n.d.; Delafield, 1839, pp. 95–101, folding plate; Librería Echániz, 1944d,

1944e; Gondra, 1846, pp. 10–36, pls. 2–5; Kingsborough, 1831–48, vol. 1; Mendizábal, 1946, folding plate; Schoolcraft, 1851–57, vol. 1, pls. 1–2.

Studies: Chavero, n.d., pp. vii, 459–507; Orozco y Berra, 1880, 3: 67–87; J. F. Ramírez, 1945a, 1952, 1953, 1956; Robertson, 1959, pp. 83–86, pl. 20.

Other: Barlow, 1949b, p. 104; Bullock, 1824c, no. 48.

Brief descriptions: Alcina Franch, 1955, pp. 444–45; Glass, 1964, pp. 83–84, pl. 40.

35

Calpan, Confirmation des élections de. BNP 73. Ex–Boturini (?) and Aubin collections. Partially published. Genealogical. Calpan, Puebla. 1578. European paper. 9 leaves. 30 × 21 cm.

Seven drawings, each on two facing pages, and two pages of text in Nahuatl and Spanish. The drawings, glossed in Nahuatl, are genealogies and apparently pertain to the following localities: Ayapanco, Santa Maria Tepetipan, San Juan Tlaxichco, San Miguel Tlalnauac, San Juan Tianquizmanalco, San Baltasar Atlimeyaya, and Santiago Tenayocan. The abundant genealogical detail extends before the conquest; the glosses are notable for their inclusion of numerous Indian titles. The text identifies the document as a viceregal confirmation of barrio elections of the town of Calpan.

The first and most elaborate of the drawings and part of the final text have been published by Boban (1891).

Partial publication: Boban, 1891, 2: 156–59, pl. 73.

36

Caltecpaneca, Fragmento. MNA 35-79. Ex–Boturini collection. Published. Unclassified. Central Mexico. 16thC. Maguey paper. 18 × 55 cm.

The drawing, which is but a fragment of a lost larger drawing, shows an Indian man and woman inside a doorway that has floral decorations. One of the glosses reads "Caltecpaneca."

Glass (1964) gives photoreproduction and brief description. It has also been described by Mateos Higuera (1949c) and by Mena (1923).

Publication: Glass, 1964, p. 133, pl. 84.

Brief descriptions: Mateos Higuera, 1949c; Mena, 1923, pp. 62–63, pl. 6, no. 21.

37

Cano, Genealogía de la Familia. BNP 388. Unpublished. Genealogical. Valley of Mexico. 17thC (?). Parchment. 31 × 43 cm.

Not examined. A description of the document by Carlos Mancio, dated 1715, is contained in AGN-V 110 and has been published by Fernández de Recas (1961). According to this the genealogy depicts Chimalpopoca, Huitzilihuitzin, Acamapichtli, Moctezuma, and various colonial persons having the surnames Cano and Moctezuma. It also contains native numerals for the sum of 285, ostensibly the date of the manuscript in years elapsed since the founding of Tenochtitlan.

Brief description: Fernández de Recas, 1961, pp. 77–81; J. F. Ramírez, 1855, no. 5.

❖❖❖

CARAPAN, CÓDICES DE. Three pictorial documents listed below. A fourth and lost pictorial manuscript associated with Carapan is known through Códice Plancarte (see Article 27B, no. 1007). The first two are in the Museo Michoacano, Morelia, which also holds other (nonpictorial) documents relating to Carapan. Notes and transcripts of related documents for an unpublished study by R. H. Barlow are in the library of the University of the Americas, Mexico.

38 (fig. 25)

—— *Carapan, Códice de, no. 1.* Museo Michoacan, Morelia. Unpublished. Cartographic-historical. Carapan, Michoacan. 1589 or later. Cloth. Dimensions not reported.

The lienzo depicts roads, various groups of Indians, friars, and Spaniards. Some of the latter are on horseback and appear to be receiving tribute. A coat of arms surmounted by an eagle is drawn near the lower left. Glosses refer to place names and to colonial Tarascan Indians, such as Antonio Huitzmengari. The style and content appear wholly colonial. The Lienzo de Patzcuaro (q.v.) is a later version of this document.

Mateos Higuera (1948b) gives brief description and transcribes some of the glosses.

Copy: Modern copy, without glosses, in Hotel Virrey de Mendoza, Morelia, Michoacan.

Brief description: Mateos Higuera, 1948b, pp. 169–72.

39

—— *Carapan, Códice de, no. 2.* Museo Michoacano, Morelia. Unpublished. Historical. Carapan, Michoacan. 16thC. Native (?) paper. 1 leaf. Dimensions not determined.

Not examined. Mateos Higuera (1948b) describes it as showing various Tarascan Indians (six of whom are at the upper left), a temple, other details, and as having Tarascan glosses which refer to the Indian rulers of Carapan. In citing a publication of this document Mateos Higuera confuses it with the Genealogía de los Caciques de Carapan.

Brief description: Mateos Higuera, 1948b, pp. 172–74.

40

—— *Carapan, Genealogía de los Caciques de.* Unknown. Ex–León collection. Published. Genealogical. Carapan, Michoacan. Date unknown. Physical description unreported except as 1 fragmentary leaf.

Glossed "Irecha Uacus Trongo Real," the document shows eight persons, some identi-

fiable as Tarascan rulers, a double-headed eagle, and lesser detail.

Known data derive from the brief description and tracing in N. León (1903–04; 1904a). Corona Núñez has reproduced the León tracing several times (1946, 1957, 1959) with brief comment and has interpreted the symbolism of the two eagle heads (1942b; 1957). He considers it a part of the lost Códice Plancarte, also associated with Carapan.

Publication: N. León, 1903–04, pp. 318–19, pl. 41; 1904a, 142–43, pl. 41.

Other: Corona Núñez, 1942b, pp. 87–88; 1946, pp. 26–27, pl. 9; 1957, pp. 62–63, fig. 11; 1959, frontispiece.

41

Chalchihuitzin Vásquez, Lienzo. American Museum of Natural History, New York. Ex–Mrs. John Hay collection. Published. Cartographic-historical. San Salvador Tzompantepec (?), Tlaxcala. 16thC. Cloth. 165.10 × 127 cm.

Two individuals, one of whom is identified as Chalchihuitzin Vásquez, are shown seated in a house at the center of the lienzo. Surrounding this are other houses and numerous portraits of Indian men and women, most of whom are identified by the Nahuatl glosses. Place names appear to include Tlaquatzinco, Quaxumolco, Xaltianguisco, and San Salvador Tzonpa . . . (Tzonpanco?, Tzompantepec?, Tzompantzinco?). These localities may be identified in the ex-districts of Cuauhtemoc and Juarez, Tlaxcala.

Photoreproduction and a very superficial commentary are provided by Vaillant (1939). A photograph also appears in Vaillant's *Aztecs of Mexico* (1941, and other editions).

Publication: Vaillant, 1939; 1941, pl. 44.

Brief description: Gibson, 1952, p. 264.

42

CHALCO: *Reçus presentes par le Capitaine Jorge Ceron y Carabajal, Alcalde Mayor de*

Chalco. BNP 30. Ex–León y Gama and Aubin collections. Partially published. Economic (tribute). Chalco, Mexico. 1564. Native paper, 1 leaf, 53 × 41 cm., and 12 or 13 leaves of European paper (ff. 93–105?), dimensions not determined.

Only one page of the document has been published; it contains pictorial representations of tribute and nine place glyphs. Accompanying this pictorial sheet are a Nahuatl text, a Spanish translation, and further drawings. The whole is said to concern litigation over the payment for goods and services.

Boban (1891) reproduces one page, describes the document, and reprints the description by León y Gama (1832).

Copies: Pichardo Copy, BNP 296.

Partial publication: Boban, 1891, 1: 400–02, pl. 30.

Brief description: León y Gama, 1832, 2: 137–42.

43

Chavero, Códice. Códice de Tributos de Huexotzingo. MNA/AH Col. Antig. 259 (also cataloged as MNA 35-25). Ex–Boturini and Chavero collections. Partially published. Economic (tribute). Huexotzingo, Puebla. ca. 1579. European paper. 139 leaves of text (ff. 86–220, 222–25), 32 × 22 cm., and 18 drawings (ff. 221, 229–45), 72 × 32 cm.

Drawings of the tribute for the years 1571–79 for 17 localities, including Huexotzingo, Almoyahuacan, Tezmelucan, Tianguistengo, and Atlisco, all located between Tezmelucan and Atlixco or in the vicinity of Huexotzingo. The same places figure in the Matrícula de Huexotzingo. The accompanying text is in Spanish. The inventories of the Boturini collection describe it as having had 301 leaves and 22 "mapas."

Glass (1964) briefly describes the manuscript and reproduces one of its pictorial pages. García Granados and MacGregor (1934) also describe it and publish three of

its pages. Chavero (1901a) refers to his ownership of the volume.

Partial publication: Glass, 1964, pp. 67–68, pl. 26; García Granados and MacGregor, 1934, pp. 23–24, 77–81.

Other: Chavero, 1901a, pp. 10–11.

❖❖❖

CHAVERO, COLECCIÓN. Under this title Chavero (1901a,b,c) published five pictorial documents. Nos. 1–3 are falsifications; nos. 4 and 5 comprise the AMNH volume known as Codex Chavero, also known as Códice de Ixhuatepec. Parts listed individually below.

❖❖❖

—— *no. 1.* Mapa de Tlaxcallan. *See* Article 26, no. 902.

❖❖❖

—— *no. 2.* Códice Ciclográfico. *See* Article 26, no. 903.

❖❖❖

—— *no. 3.* Calendario o Rueda del Año. *See* Article 26, no. 904.

44

—— *no. 4.* Códice de Ixhuatepec (part). Codex Chavero (part). American Museum of Natural History, New York. Ex–J. F. Ramírez and Chavero collections. Published. Economic (land titles, property plans, and miscellaneous) and genealogical. San Juan Ixhuatepec, Mexico, or Mexico City–Tlatelolco region, D.F. 18thC (?). European paper. 8 leaves (ff. 34–39, 41–42). 30 × 21 cm.

The AMNH document, "Codex Chavero," contains old copies of five different manuscripts defectively published by Chavero (1901c) as Colección Chavero no. 4, parts 1–4, and Colección Chavero no. 5. The latter (ff. 25–33) is described in the census under the title Códice de Ixhuatepec, a term by which Chavero (n.d.) also referred to the entire document. The five manuscripts together may represent the titles of San Juan Ixhuatepec.

Part 1 (ff. 41v–42r) has glossed drawings, with personal name glyphs, of seven preconquest rulers of Tenochtitlan as well as of numerous other 14th and 15thC persons including Ilancueitl of Culhuacan (wife of Acamapichtli), Netzahualcoyotl of Texcoco, Tezozomoc of Azcapotzalco, Acolmiztli of Coatlinchan, and Cuacuapitzahuac of Tlatelolco. Various genealogical relationships among these persons are indicated. Near the center is a simple plan of Tenochtitlan showing the four major barrios.

Part 2 (ff. 38v–39r) is a simple plan of two native houses with the names of two Indians (Andrés and Magdalena Ramírez y Nemac).

Part 3 (ff. 36v–37r) is divided into nine vertical columns in which there are place glyphs (most of which also appear in part 4), numerical signs, and symbols for the four barrios of Tenochtitlan.

Part 4 (ff. 34v–35r) is divided into six vertical columns and 10 horizontal rows. In 50 of the 60 compartments thus formed are glossed place glyphs. These appear to represent all the place names in Códice de Ixhuatepec other than those also listed in the Títulos de Santa Isabel Tola as well as certain additional place names.

The only edition of the manuscript consists of the probably inaccurate tracings published by Chavero (1901c) with a superficial commentary. Chavero (n.d.) refers to the manuscript and illustrates several details from parts 1 and 2. More than half the place glyphs from part 4 of the manuscript were published by Peñafiel (1897c) under the title "Pleito de Tierras." See Ixhuatepec Group for related manuscripts.

Publication: Chavero, 1901c, pp. 15–23, pls. 1–4.

104

Other: Chavero, n.d., pp. xxvi, 620, 638, 642; Peñafiel, 1897c, passim.

❖❖❖

—— *no. 5. See* Códice de Ixhuatepec.

45

Chichimecatecuhtli, Don Juan, Lienzo de. Lienzo Vischer no. 2. Museum für Völkerkunde, Basle. Ex–Vischer collection. Published. Cartographic-historical. Tlaxcala (?). 16thC. Cloth. ca. 91 × 123 cm. Incomplete.

The lienzo shows numerous seated Indians in genealogical relationships as well as native houses, the sides of which have serrated profiles. The central house is glossed "Ychan Quauhtliztac." A prominent Indian figure with spear and shield next to a European sword is named Don Juan Chichimecatecuhtli. A European building appears near the bottom. There are no place glyphs or dates and only a few personal name glyphs and glosses.

The manuscript is classified as Tlaxcalan, following Nicholson (1967); a provenience in the Texcoco region of the Valley of Mexico is also conceivable. A description and poor reproduction are given by Caso (1965a).

Publication: Caso, 1965a.

Brief mention: Dietschy, 1960, p. 71; Nicholson, 1967.

46 (figs. 26, 27)

Chichimec History, Map of. Unknown. Unpublished. Cartographic-historical. Valley of Mexico. 16thC. Physical description unknown.

Map of 17 localities, denoted by glossed calli symbols, with roads and a church glossed "Santa Maria de la Me." Adjacent to an historical scene is a Nahuatl gloss with the date 1466. The two known copies vary in proportions and details.

Vaillant (MS*b*) describes the AMNH

copy and suggests a provenience in the Amecameca-Chalco region of the Valley of Mexico.

Copies: Certified copy, 1854, AMNH. Photograph of unidentified copy, possibly by Nebel, BYU.

Bibliography: Vaillant, MSb.

47

Chicomesuchil, San Juan, Lienzo de (no. 1). Pueblo. Partially published. Cartographic-historical. San Juan Chicomesuchil, ex-district of Ixtlan, Eastern Oaxaca. 17thC. Cloth. ca. 150 × 150 cm.

The lienzo is very briefly described by Schmieder (1930) as representing the Upper Rio Grande Valley and as bearing Zapotec glosses. The detail published by him shows mounted Spaniards attacking a village. The style of the document is apparently not in the native tradition.

Partial publication: Schmieder, 1930, pp. 51–52, fig. 6.

48

Chicomesuchil, San Juan, Mapa de (no. 2). Pueblo. Unpublished. Unavailable. San Juan Chicomesuchil, ex-district of Ixtlan, Eastern Oaxaca. 17thC. European paper. Dimensions not reported.

The map is mentioned by Schmieder (1930) as being similar to the Lienzo de San Juan Chicomesuchil and as having illegible Zapotec glosses.

Brief mention: Schmieder, 1930, p. 52, note 60.

49

Chiconquiaco, Mapa de. Unknown. Published. Cartographic-historical. Chiconquiaco, Veracruz. 1542 (?). Physical description unreported except as 1 sheet.

The published copy of the document exhibits a peripheral border of numbered, glossed, and very rudimentary place glyphs. In the center are crude drawings of place glyphs, numerous Indians without personal name glyphs, at least one Spaniard, a friar (Alonso de Santiago), three churches (including San Pedro Chiconquiaco and Miahuatlan), and the native date 11 Rabbit (1542). Most of the many Nahuatl glosses are illegible in the reproduction. A long Nahuatl text in two parts refers to the distribution of lands in a year 10 House (1541) and mentions the names of Indians (whose heads are among the drawings) from Naolingo, San Antonio, Chiconquiaco, Colipa, and Misantla.

A palaeography and translation of the long Nahuatl text by Barlow (MSb) are unpublished. A poor reproduction of a copy is given without significant comment by Melgarejo Vivanco (1949). Ramírez Lavoignet (1959, 1962) refers to the document.

Copies: Copies are reported in the Archivo Municipal of Chiconquiaco and in the Departamento de Antropología of the state of Veracruz.

Publication: Melgarejo Vivanco, 1949, plate facing p. 286.

Brief mention: Melgarejo Vivanco, 1953, p. 333; Ramírez Lavoignet, 1959, pp. 37–40, 96, 168; 1962, pp. 25, 143.

Other: Barlow, MSb.

50

Chicontla, Lienzo de. Pueblo. Unpublished. Unclassified. Chicontla (municipio de Jopala?), Puebla. Date unknown. Cloth. Dimensions unknown.

The lienzo is known only through an extremely poor photograph in the INAH/AF in which practically no details are legible. Visible in the photo are roads depicted by parallel lines with footprints and a few tepetl symbols. The original appears to be in poor condition and of secondary interest.

Bibliography: None.

51

Chilchotla, Santa Maria, Lienzo de. Pueblo (?). Published. Cartographic-historical. Santa Maria Chilchotla, ex-district of Teotitlan, Northern Oaxaca. 1751 (?). Cloth. ca. 230 × 60 cm.

Drawn in a very crude style, the lienzo depicts the boundaries of Chilchotla and includes schematic drawings of two churches, several place glyphs, native rulers, etc., in the center. The date 1751 appears among the Spanish glosses.

The document is known only through three photographs (copies in LC/HF) taken in the Mazatec region by Bernard Bevan in 1937. One is of half of the lienzo; the other two are of a copy on paper dated 1924. Cline (1964, 1966b) reproduces the first of the photographs and gives a drawing of the lienzo based on all three. He also identifies the area covered by the document but fails to indicate that the photos are of two manuscripts rather than of one.

Publication: Cline, 1964, pp. 408–10, 420–21, figs. 9–12; 1966b, pp. 279–85, figs. 3–5, map 7.

52

Chimalapa, Santa Maria, Lienzo de. Pueblo. Unpublished. Unavailable. Santa Maria Chimalapa, ex-district of Juchitan, Eastern Oaxaca. Physical description unknown.

Seler (1908b) reports the alleged existence of a pictorial manuscript in Santa Maria Chimalapa. Further data unavailable.

Brief mention: Alcina Franch, 1955, p. 456; Lehmann, 1905a, p. 276; Seler, 1908b, p. 158.

53

Chinantla, Lienzo de la. Lienzo de Tuxtepec. MNA 35-112. Published. Cartographic-historical. San Juan Bautista Valle Nacional, ex-district of Tuxtepec, Northern Oaxaca. 17thC (?). Oil on canvas. 110 × 130 cm. Palimpsest.

Glossed map of about 27 colonial Chinantec communities around present Valle Nacional depicts rivers, mountains, and other features of terrain. Small ethnographic

scenes are barely visible in available reproductions. Similar in coverage and composition to the Lienzo de la Gran Chinantla and the Mapa de Yetla.

Cline (1961a) provides reproduction and study of cartographic content with diagrams. Cline (1961b) also reproduces the document but gives less detailed discussion. A larger reproduction is in the MNA catalog (Glass, 1964).

Publication: Cline, 1961a, pp. 50–57, pls. 1, 3; 1961b, pls. 3, 6; Glass, 1964, p. 168, pl. 122.

Brief description: Cline, 1957, pp. 289–92.

54 (fig. 28)

Chinantla, la Gran, Lienzo de. Mapa de la Chinantla. Princeton University Library. Ex–Mariano Espinosa and C. C. James collections. Inadequately published. Cartographic-historical. San Juan Bautista Valle Nacional, ex-district of Tuxtepec, Northern Oaxaca. 16thC. Cloth. 128 × 188 cm.

The lienzo depicts communities, rivers, and surrounding mountains in the region around Valle Nacional and is similar in cartographic respects to the Lienzo de la Chinantla (see previous entry). Also shown are numerous Indians seated on small stools. There are 44 glosses on sewn-on slips of paper.

A poor photograph was wretchedly published by M. Espinosa (1910). A copy of the photograph has served as the basis for Cline's (1961a, 1961b) study, reproduction, and reconstruction of the original, the whereabouts of which was unknown until late 1967.

Publication: Cline, 1961a, pp. 57–60, pl. 4; 1961b; M. Espinosa, 1910, plate facing p. 24.

55

Chiquatzin Tecuihtli, Die Flurkarte des. Museum für Völkerkunde, Berlin. Published. Economic (property plans). Central Mexico. 16thC. Native paper. 93.5 × 60.5 cm.

Plan of an unidentified locality shows fields, roads, houses, an Indian pyramid, and various Indians, one of whom has the hieroglyph of an owl (Chiquatli). There are Nahuatl and Spanish glosses. Kutscher suggests Tlaxcala or Puebla as a probable provenience.

Photoreproduction and commentary by Kutscher (1962).

Publication: Kutscher, 1962.

56

Chiquilistlan, Mapa de las Tierras de. Unknown. Published. Cartographic-historical. Chiquilistlan (near Sayula), Jalisco. 1563 (?). Physical description unknown. 1 sheet.

Ramírez Flores (1959) reproduces a crude copy of 1884 (location unreported, 58×82 cm.), which may derive from a 16thC original, and publishes related documents. The subject of the map is the boundaries of Chiquilistlan, established in 1563. Persons, houses, crosses, crude symbols, and geographical details are depicted.

Publication: Ramírez Flores, 1959.

57

Cholula, Códice de. Mapa de Cholula. MNA 35-56. Ex–Boturini collection. Partially published. Cartographic-historical. Cholula, Puebla. 1586 (?). Amatl paper. 1 sheet drawn on both sides. 112 × 166 cm.

Obverse is a map of a territory in Puebla around Cholula comprehended within the region bounded by Tlatenango and La Malinche on the north and Totomihuacan and Atlixco on the south. Drawings are of mountains, rivers, roads, villages, churches, pyramids, persons, battles, and historical scenes.

Reverse is a map of a more restricted area, perhaps of Cholula itself. Drawings are on a larger scale than those of the obverse and are of buildings, persons, and pyramids. Numerous short Nahuatl texts on both sides

include references to the founding of churches, tribute, land grants, and provide historical references from legendary period to 1586.

Glass (1964) reproduces a detail from the reverse of the original and the entirety of the two copies of the obverse and describes each briefly. One of the two copies (MNA 35-57) has been studied in detail by Simons (1962) with a translation of its texts. A condensation of this study, with a photoreproduction, has been published (Simons, 1967–68). Ceballos Novelo (1934) and Maza (1959) reproduce some details with minimal comment.

Copies: Two copies, both of the obverse and both from the Boturini collection, are in the MNA (MNA 35-10; 35-57). Sketches of the reverse of the original and of the second copy (MNA 35-57) with palaeography of the texts by Gómez de Orozco are also in the MNA codex collection.

Partial publication: Glass, 1964, pp. 48, 106–07, pls. 12, 59–60; Simons, 1967–68.

Partial commentary: Simons, 1962, 1967.

Brief description: Mena, 1923, p. 59, no. 13.

Other: Ceballos Novelo, 1934, pp. 259–60, pl. 1; Maza, 1959, p. 42–44; Olivera and Reyes, 1969, figs. 2–3.

58

Chontalcoatlan, Lienzo de. Pueblo. Unpublished. Unavailable. Chontalcoatlan, Guerrero. Further data unavailable.

Not examined. The existence of the document has been mentioned by Guzmán (1958), who owns a small photograph taken by Alexander von Wuthenau; attempts to secure a copy of the photograph for description have been fruitless.

Brief mention: Guzmán, 1958, pp. lxxviii–lxxix.

59

Chumatlan, Códice de. Pueblo. Unpublished. Unavailable. Chumatlan, Veracruz. Further data unavailable.

Knowledge of the document is limited to the reference by Melgarejo Vivanco (1953): "Simple noticia y descripción del General Herrero; dice lo conservan los nativos de Chumatlan, Ver."

Brief mention: Melgarejo Vivanco, 1953, p. 333.

60

Chumayel, The Book of Chilam Balam of. Códice de Chumayel. Princeton University Library. Ex–Carrillo y Ancona, Cepeda Library (Merida), and Julio Berzunza collections. Published. Historical, calendrical, and miscellaneous. Chumayel, Yucatan. 1782. European paper. 58 leaves (ff. 1, 50, and 55 missing). Quarto.

The drawings in this Yucatecan text include symbols for months (20-day periods or uinals), diagrams of eclipses, representations of the Lords of the Katuns, a calendar wheel, a simple circular map of northern Yucatan, and lesser or miscellaneous drawings.

Reproductions of the drawings are given in the photographic edition of the manuscript by Gordon (1913) and through line drawings in the edition by Roys (1933). A comparative discussion of the calendar wheel with a reproduction of the Berendt copy is given by Bowditch (1910, pp. 329–30, fig. 63). Carrillo y Ancona (1882) discusses and reproduces the circular map and a coat of arms from the manuscript, which he also interprets as a map.

See prose census for general comment on the Books of Chilam Balam and for further data on this manuscript (Article 27B, no. 1146).

61

Citlalpopoca, Genealogy of. Généalogie de l'un des Quatre Gouverneurs de la République de Tlaxcala. BNP 104. Ex–Aubin collection. Unpublished. Genealogical.

Quiahuixtlan, Tlaxcala. 1570. European paper. 2 leaves. Folio.

Simple genealogy of six persons beginning with Citlalpopoca and ending with the name Diego Sánchez. It includes a written list of 17 place names and it forms an integral part of a separately cataloged and unpublished lawsuit preserved in the same repository (BNP 117).

Copy: BNP 104bis (unverified).

Brief descriptions: Boban, 1891, 2: 280, 303–04; Gibson, 1952, pp. 92, 266–67.

62

Coacalco, Códice de. Códice de Cohuacalco. Unknown. Unpublished. Miscellaneous. Coacalco, Mexico. Date and physical description unknown.

The TU/MARI copy of the Techialoyan Codex of Coacalco includes three pages (ff. 1v, 2r, 2v) that are not Techialoyan. See Article 24, Catalog, 743, for further information, copies, and bibliography.

63 (fig. 29)

Coacoatzintla, Lienzo de. AGN-T 685, exp. 3. Unpublished. Cartographic-historical. Coacoatzintla, Veracruz. 1555. Cloth. 124 × 91 cm.

The lienzo apparently shows the boundaries of Coacoatzintla. Mojoneras (boundary markers) at the top, together with the glyph for Chapultepec, may coincide with those on one side of the Lienzo de Misantla. Prominently shown are Miguel Arias, encomendero, Juan García Galleja (?), corregidor of Jalapa, and various Indian officials. The accompanying early 18thC lawsuit between Coacoatzintla and Santa Maria Magdalena on the one hand and San Pedro Tonayan and San Pablo Coapan on the other has not been examined.

The document is briefly mentioned by Ramírez Lavoignet (1959, 1962) and is erroneously reported as being in AGN-T 556 by Melgarejo Vivanco (1953).

Brief mention: Melgarejo Vivanco, 1953,

p. 334; Ramírez Lavoignet, 1959, pp. 123–24, 133; 1962, p. 106.

64

Coatepetl, Mapa de. MNA 35–19. Published. Economic (property plans). Central Mexico. Late 16thC. Maguey paper. 56 × 42 cm.

The manuscript is a map of a limited region in which appear Christian churches, rows of native houses, roads, and agricultural plots. One of several place glyphs is glossed "Cohuatepetl."

Glass (1964) gives photoreproduction and brief description.

Publication: Glass, 1964, p. 61, pl. 21.

65

Coatlan del Rio, Mapa de. BNP 102 (part). Unpublished. Ex–Aubin collection. Cartographic-historical. Coatlan del Rio, Morelos. 16thC. European paper. 60 × 62 cm.

Around the periphery of the document are hieroglyphic place names with Nahuatl glosses. At the center are the glyph for Coatlan, a church, and six Indians with personal name glyphs and numerical symbols.

Very brief description in Boban (1891). Cataloged with the document are the Réédification de la Ville de Cuernavaca and the Títulos del Pueblo de Quauhxomulco. The former appears to be related to the Document sur la Fondation de Cuernavaca (BNP 291–92), also known as the Códice Municipal de Cuernavaca. The relationship of the pictorial to these documents, not treated here, is uncertain. Charles Gibson provided us with data on these texts.

Brief description: Boban, 1891, 2: 276–77.

66

Coatlan, San Jeronimo, Lienzo de (no. 1). Pueblo. Published. Cartographic-historical. San Jeronimo Coatlan, ex-district of Miahuatlan, Eastern Oaxaca. 16thC (?). Cloth. 100 × 90 cm. approx.

The lienzo depicts a church, mountains, and historic personages at the center; around the periphery are boundary symbols. There are Zapotec glosses.

An inadequate photograph and a description of the document are published by Cicco (1963).

Publication: Cicco, 1963.

67

Coatlan, San Jeronimo, Mapa de (no. 2). Pueblo. Unpublished. Unavailable (cartographic-historical). San Jeronimo Coatlan, ex-district of Miahuatlan, Eastern Oaxaca. 1690. European paper. Dimensions unreported.

The map is related to the lienzo from the same locality and depicts the same boundaries. Cicco (1963) comments briefly on the manuscript and transcribes its Spanish text.

Brief description: Cicco, 1963.

68

Coatlinchan, Mapa de. Plano topográfico del Señorío de Coatlinchan. MNA 35-16. Ex–Chavero collection. Published. Cartographic. Coatlinchan, Mexico. 16thC. Amatl Paper. 45 × 42 cm.

Map has glossed place glyphs showing 68 cabeceras, barrios, and estancias. Coatlinchan is at the center and the more prominently depicted localities are Mexicapan, Culhuacan, and Tlalnahuac. The cartographic significance of the document has not been interpreted.

A brief description and photoreproduction are in the MNA catalog (Glass, 1964). A copy is reproduced by Chavero (n.d.) with an inaccurate transcript of the glosses.

Copies: Saldaña copy, MNA 35-16A. The location of the copy made in 1892 is unknown.

Publication: Chavero, n.d., plate facing p. 517; Glass, 1964, pp. 57–58, pl. 18.

Brief descriptions: García Cubas, 1892, pp. 6–7, figure facing p. 6; Mateos Higuera,

1945; Paso y Troncoso, 1892–93, 1: 52; Tamayo and Alcorta, 1941, pp. 17–18.

69

Coetzala, Códice de. Códices indígenas del Marquesado del Valle no. 32. AGN-T 689. Partially published. Historical. Coetzala, Puebla. 16thC (?). Native paper. 2 leaves (ff. 45–46). Dimensions not determined.

Incomplete Nahuatl text with drawings of four year-bearer day symbols beginning with 3 Acatl.

Colored reproductions of the four drawings are in *Códices indígenas* (1933). Barlow (1949c) comments briefly on the document and reproduces the drawings. The accompanying 18thC lawsuit is unpublished.

Publication: Barlow, 1949c; *Códices indígenas*, 1933, Item 32.

❖❖❖

COIXTLAHUACA BASIN GROUP. Entered separately in the census, the following Mixtec lienzos share a common subregional provenience: Lienzos Antonio de León, de Coixtlahuaca nos. 1 and 2, de Ihuitlan, Meixueiro, and de Santa Maria Nativitas. The relationship was defined by Parmenter (1961a).

70 (fig. 30)

Coixtlahuaca, Lienzo de, no. 1. Codex Ixtlan. MNA 35-113. Published. Cartographic-historical. Coixtlahuaca, ex-district of Coixtlahuaca, Western Oaxaca. 16thC. Cloth. 425 × 300 cm.

The lienzo was found in Coixtlahuaca in 1940 and obtained for the MNA in 1941 or 1942; it was temporarily in the Regional Museum of Oaxaca (on the latter point see Monroy, 1946). At its center is a composition of two distinct place glyphs with temples, what appears to be a wall, and a large serpent (the principal element of the Coixtlahuaca place glyph). Adjacent to this are seven Indians, one of whom is partially

obliterated by a hole in the cloth, with calendrical name glyphs. Around the periphery are a large number of place glyphs, dates, and persons including Spaniards mounted on horseback. The lienzo is closely related to the Lienzo Meixueiro and to the Lienzo de Coixtlahuaca no. 2.

The Nicolás León copy, purchased by Gates from Wilkinson in 1912 and later in the Garrett collection, was redrawn and published in 1931 (*Codex Ixtlan*, 1931). A brief description and a photograph of the original as well as of the central detail are given by Glass (1964). The comments by Bunting (1931) are of little value. There is no published commentary on the document.

Copies: The León-Gates copy may possibly be the copy in TU/LAL. A modern copy by Saldaña is MNA 35-113A. A copy of a lienzo from Coixtlahuaca exhibited by Peñafiel in 1895 (Anonymous, 1897) remains unidentified and unlocated.

Publication: Codex Ixtlan, 1931; Glass, 1964, pp. 169–70, pls. 123–24.

Other: Anonymous, 1897, p. 38; Bunting, 1931; Gates, MS; Monroy, 1946, p. 31; Parmenter, 1961b, 1961c.

71

Coixtlahuaca, Lienzo de, no. 2. Lienzo Seler no. 2., Lienzo de Cohaixtlahuaca. Museum für Völkerkunde, Berlin. Ex–Martínez Gracida and Seler collections. Unpublished. Cartographic-historical. Coixtlahuaca, ex-district of Coixtlahuaca, Western Oaxaca. 16thC. Cloth. 375 × 425 cm.

Brief examination of photographs of the IAI copy of the lienzo indicates that its content appears to include both that of Lienzo de Coixtlahuaca no. 1 and Lienzo Antonio de León. Its importance is thus considerable.

A very brief description of the lienzo is given by Lehmann (1905a). Seler-Sachs (1900) refers to the Selers' acquisition of a lienzo from Coixtlahuaca.

Copy: Seler collection copy, IAI.

Brief description: Lehmann, 1905a, pp. 278–79.

Other: Seler-Sachs, 1900, p. 90.

72

Colombino, Códice. Codex Dorenberg. MNA 35-30. Ex–Manuel Cardoso and Josef Dorenberg collections. Published. Historical. Tututepec, ex-district of Juquila, Western Oaxaca. Preconquest. Skin screenfold painted on one side. 24 leaves in 4 fragments (pp. 1–15, 17–19, 20–24, 16). 18.5 × 25.5 cm. (total length 606 cm.).

The manuscript, in traditional Mixtec style, treats the life and history of 8 Deer, Tiger Claw (A.D. 1011–63), from A.D. 1028 to 1048. Códice Colombino and Codex Becker no. 1 are believed to be parts of the same original manuscript; the parts of the two fit together in a complex sequence with missing initial, intermediate, and terminal pages. A reconstruction of this sequence is presented by Caso (in Caso and Smith, 1966).

A study of the Mixtec glosses on the manuscript by M. E. Smith (in Caso and Smith, 1966) indicates that they were written in 1541 and list the boundaries of various towns on the south coast of Western Oaxaca in the Tututepec region. The glosses do not specifically describe the pictorial content. The manuscript was utilized in a land suit between Tututepec and San Miguel Sola in 1717. Documents (in AGN-V 272) pertaining to the suit have been published by Berlin (1947) and studied by M. E. Smith, who gives a partial and preliminary study of the glosses (1963).

A photographic color facsimile has been published by Caso and Smith (1966) with a detailed and comparative commentary by Caso and a study of the glosses by Smith. Color lithographs of the document, without the glosses, were published by the Junta Colombina (Chavero, 1892). A study of the life of 8 Deer in the Códice Colombino and other Mixtec histories is Clark (1912). The first publication of any page of the manuscript was by Batres (1888, 1889). Photographs of individual pages have been published by Glass (1964), Toscano (1944), and Rubín de la Borbolla (1953). Chavero (1901c) gives data on the 19thC ownership history.

Copies: The location of the Seler copy made in 1888 is unknown. Lehmann (1905a) reports a copy in the Leipzig Museum. A copy attributed to Mateo A. Saldaña is MNA 35-30A. Mounted 19thC photographs are in MNA/BNA and in the MNA codex collection.

Publication: Caso and Smith, 1966; Chavero, 1892, pp. x–xi, 12 plates in the atlas.

Partial publication: Batres, 1888, pl. 20; 1889, pl. 20; Glass, 1964, pp. 73–74, pl. 31; Rubín de la Borbolla, 1953, vol. 1, pl. 223; Toscano, 1944, p. 368.

Studies: Clark, 1912; M. E. Smith, 1963.

Other: Berlin, 1947, pp. 43–44, 54–57; Castellanos, 1910, passim; Chavero, 1901c, pp. 4–5; Clark, 1913a.

Brief descriptions: Alcina Franch, 1955, pp. 485–87; Lehmann, 1905a, pp. 260–61; Paso y Troncoso, 1892–93, 1: 57–59.

73

Comaltepec, San Juan, Códice de. Pueblo. Unpublished. Unavailable. San Juan Comaltepec, ex-district of Choapan, Eastern Oaxaca. Physical description not reported.

The existence of the document, presumably a lienzo, is mentioned by Fuente (1949) and is listed as an unverified Zapotec pictorial by Cline (1966c). Further data unavailable.

Brief mention: Cline, 1966c, app. 2, no. 44; Fuente, 1949, p. 176.

74

Comaltepec, Santiago, Lienzo de. Pueblo. Unpublished. Unavailable. Santiago Comaltepec, ex-district of Ixtlan, Northern Oaxaca. 1816. Oil on cloth. Dimensions not reported.

The document is reported, but not described, by Pérez García (1956) and is listed as an unverified Chinantec pictorial by Cline (1966c). It may relate to litigation between Comaltepec and Yolox over disputed territory. Whether or not the manuscript is in the native tradition is unknown.

Brief mention: Cline, 1966c, app. 2, no. 45; Pérez García, 1956, 2: 176.

75

Constancia de Gastos, Códice de. MNA 35-13. Published. Economic (miscellaneous). Central Mexico. 16thC. Amatl paper. 104 × 32 cm.

The drawings of the manuscript depict several buildings surmounted by crosses and adjacent to a course of water. Lesser drawings and Nahuatl glosses concern construction expenses.

Photograph and brief description in the MNA catalog (Glass, 1964).

Publication: Glass, 1964, p. 53, pl. 15.

76

Contlantzinco, Pintura de. Linderos del Pueblo de Contlantzinco. MNA 35-34. Published. Cartographic-historical. Contlantzinco, Tlaxcala. 18thC. Oil on cloth. 74 × 53.5 cm.

Painting of the region around Contlantzinco, including Mount Matlacueyetl (La Malinche) and eight standing Indian figures. Nahuatl texts mention Chimalpopocatzin, Pablo Xicotencatl, and Pedro Maxixcatzin.

Photograph and brief description are in MNA catalog (Glass, 1964). Other brief descriptions are listed below. The Nahuatl texts have not been translated.

Copies: Two copies made in 1892 are now unknown.

Publication: Glass, 1964, p. 79, pl. 36.

Brief descriptions: Gibson, 1952, p. 265; Mateos Higuera, 1944b; Paso y Troncoso, 1892–93, 1: 59.

77 (fig. 31)

Córdova-Castellanos, Lienzo. Codex Abraham Castellanos. Códice Mixteco Precortesiano Javier Córdova. Códice de San Esteban Atlatlauhca. Mapa Regional de Atlatlauhca. Mapa del Distrito de Tlaxiaco. Unknown. Ex-Javier Córdova collection. Published. Cartographic-historical. San Esteban Atlatlauhca, ex-district of Tlaxiaco, Western Oaxaca. 16thC. Cloth. 117 × 138 cm.

Around the periphery of the lienzo are 30 place glyphs glossed in Nahuatl, presumably boundaries. In the center are three large unidentified place glyphs, a hieroglyphic date with the Mixtec year sign, and other detail. The lienzo is said to have come from San Esteban Atlatlauhca.

A copy of the document and an analysis of the place glyphs is given by Peñafiel (1914); his earlier study of 1907 is believed not to be illustrated. A slightly variant copy owned by Nicolás León and purchased by Gates from Wilkinson in 1912 was published as *Codex Abraham Castellanos* (1931).

Copies: The León-Gates copy is in the Garrett collection in the Princeton University Library. Another copy is in IAI.

Publication: *Codex Abraham Castellanos*, 1931; Peñafiel, 1914, pp. 29–34, pls. 24–32.

Other: Gates, MS; Parmenter, 1961d; 1966, p. 21, fig. 9; Peñafiel, 1907.

78

Cosijoeza, Rey de Zaachila, Descendientes de. Unknown. Unpublished. Unavailable. Santa Maria Teozapotlan Zaachila, ex-district of Zaachila, Eastern Oaxaca. Further data unknown.

The exhibit catalog of the Mexican section of the Exposición Histórico-Americana of 1892 (Paso y Troncoso, 1892–93) describes three photographs showing persons named Velasco. The persons in two of the photographs were identified as descendants of Cosijoeza. Lehmann (1905a) lists the photographs as representing a Zapotec document although it is probable that they were of living people and not of a manuscript.

Bibliography: Lehmann, 1905a, p. 276; Paso y Troncoso, 1892–93, 2: 58–59.

79

Cospi, Codex. Codex Cospianus. Códice Cospiano. Codice di Bologna. Códice de Bolonia. Libro della China. Biblioteca Universitaria, Bologna. Ex–Valerio Zani, Ferdinando Cospi, and Istituto delle Scienze e dell'Arti, Bologna, collections. Published. Ritual-calendrical. Borgia Group. Preconquest. Skin screenfold. 20 leaves (24 painted pages, 13 on obverse, 11 on reverse; pp. 14–20 and 32–38, blank; initial and terminal pages of reverse attached to modern covers). ca. 18 × 18 cm. (total length ca. 364 cm.).

One of the five divinatory screenfold almanacs of the Borgia Group, its first three sections on the obverse each present a different aspect of the 260-day tonalamatl. The fourth section on the reverse is in a different style and its interpretation is uncertain. It includes deities, what may be offerings, and sets of bar-and-dot numerals.

Details were first published by Legati (1677). The first edition was by Kingsborough (1831–48), the second (facsimile) by Paso y Troncoso (1898a). The third (Corona Núñez, 1964–67) is by color photography and includes a page-by-page commentary. The fourth (Nowotny, 1968) is a photographic color facsimile. In this edition one leaf (two blank pages) is omitted and the back cover placed on the wrong side. There is a short commentary by Seler (1902g), and Nowotny (1961b) gives an analysis of all its sections, differing from those by Seler, particularly in the case of the second and fourth sections. The history of the manuscript is given by Paso y Troncoso (1898b) and by Lehmann (1905a). See Borgia Group for further comment and bibliography.

Copies: 18thC (?) copy by Antonio Ba-soli, Biblioteca Apostolica Vaticana, Rome (unverified). Partial copy and notes by Mezzofanti, Biblioteca Comunales del'-Archiginnasio, Bologna.

Editions: Corona Núñez, 1964–67, 4: 5–49; Kingsborough, 1831–48, vol. 2; Nowotny, 1968; Paso y Troncoso, 1898a.

Commentaries, studies: Caso, 1967, pp. 79–80; García Granados, 1939a; Nowotny, 1961b, passim, pls. 43–44; Seler, 1902g, 1902l; J. E. S. Thompson, 1934, pp. 231–33, pl. 5.

Historical references: Clavigero, 1958–59 (first published 1780–81), 2: 288, 291; Fábrega, 1899, pp. 7–8; Humboldt, 1810, p. 75; Legati, 1677, pp. 191–92.

Brief descriptions: Alcina Franch, 1955, pp. 474–75; Lehmann, 1905a, pp. 254–56; Paso y Troncoso, 1898b, pp. 54–55, 330.

80

Cotitzin y Zozahuic, Genealogía de. Códice Genealógico. Dos Fragmentos (part). MNA 35-84. Ex–Boturini collection. Published. Genealogical. Central Mexico. 16thC. European paper. 32.5 × 27 cm.

Fragmentary and incomplete genealogy of 12 persons in Indian costume, some of whom are women. Personal names are given in the gloss. There are no hieroglyphs.

Glass (1964) gives brief description and photographic reproduction. The document is believed to have been included in the Mena (1923) catalog as one of the two fragments cataloged therein as no. 28.

Publication: Glass, 1964, p. 138, pl. 89.

Other: Mena, 1923, p. 64, no. 28 (b).

81

COYOACAN: *The Concubines of Martín Xuchimitl.* AGN-I 36, exp. 6. Published. Genealogical. Coyoacan, D.F. 1539. Native (?) paper. Dimensions not determined.

Simple genealogy of 11 Indians, including four sisters with whom Martín Xuchimitl was accused of concubinage. The drawing is reproduced and briefly mentioned by Greenleaf (1961). The accompanying process is unpublished.

Publication: Greenleaf, 1961, p. 108, note 35, and facing plate.

82 (fig. 32)

Coyoacan, Pintura de los Tributos [que pagaban los Indios] *de* [según la Moderación que hizo el Doctor Gómez de Santillan]. Archivo General de Simancas. Unpublished. Economic (tribute). Coyoacan, D.F. ca. 1555. Physical description not determined.

Photographs (in LC/HF) show a single sheet divided by lines into three vertical columns and four horizontal rows. The drawings are of Indians, Spaniards, items of tribute, and money. Spanish texts identify the document as representing the tribute paid by Coyoacan for 27 years, the tribute paid in each of two subsequent three-year periods (according to the moderation by the Oidor Quesada in one case), and a final and reduced annual tribute assessment by the Oidor Dr. Gómez de Santillan. There are no personal, place, or calendrical glyphs.

Brief mention: Rodríguez Marín, 1916–25, 1: 265.

83

Cozcatzin, Codex. BNP 41-45. Ex–Boturini and Aubin collections. Partially published. Economic (land titles, property plans, and cadastral), historical, and genealogical. Mexico City–Tlatelolco region, D.F. 1572. European paper. 17 leaves (ff. 2–10, 10bis, 11, 13–18). 20 × 22 cm. Incomplete.

The manuscript is a diverse but handsomely executed compilation of various economic and historical matters. Fifteen pages (ff. 3r, 4r–10v) constitute a listing of 55 parcels of land and the Indians to whom they were given by Itzcoatl in 1439 with accompanying Spanish texts. These pages reflect litigation of ca. 1572 over their ownership. A possibly 18thC copy of these pages (or of

a common prototype) is represented by the Códice de Ixhuatepec (q.v.). For other manuscripts related to this section see Ixhuatepec Group.

Seven pages of the manuscript (ff. 10bis, r–14r) are devoted to drawings of the preconquest and early colonial rulers of Tenochtitlan and Tlatelolco, some with short Nahuatl texts. A similar and related series occurs in the Títulos de Santa Isabel Tola (q.v.). Three pages (ff. 14v–15r, 18r) contain a famous drawing of the conquest of Tlatelolco by Tenochtitlan in 1473 with a long historical Nahuatl text. Two pages (ff. 15v–16r) are a plan of properties with drawings and a genealogy of Indians associated with Xochimilco. Three pages (ff. 16v–17v) contain a repetitive listing of place glyphs for Tenochtitlan, Culhuacan, Istapalapa, Mexicaltzinco, and Ixtacalco and are probably cadastral in nature. Other pages contain miscellaneous historical notices. The final page has a text in Spanish seemingly descriptive of the planets and stars.

Boban (1891) describes the codex, illustrates 10 of its pages, and publishes some of its Spanish texts. Barlow (1946a) reproduces and gives an incomplete commentary on the seven pages devoted to the rulers of Tenochtitlan and Tlatelolco. McAfee and Barlow (1946a) transcribe and translate the text concerning the conquest of Tlatelolco in 1473. A color photograph of f. 15r is given by Caso (1967).

Copies: León y Gama copy, BNP 45bis. Pichardo copy, BNP 89-5.

Partial publication: Barlow, 1946a; Boban, 1891, 2: 39–50, pls. 41–45; Caso, 1967, pp. 97–98; McAfee and Barlow, 1946a.

Other: Barlow, 1946d; Caso, 1945b; 1958c, p. 28, fig. 2; Robertson, 1959, pp. 184–85, pl. 80.

Brief description: Alcina Franch, 1955, p. 448.

84

Cruz, Códice en. Codex en Croix. Annales de Cuauhtitlan, de Texcoco, et de Mexico. Anales de San Andres Chiautla. BNP 15-17. Ex–Boturini and Aubin collections. Published. Historical. Texcoco region, Mexico. 1553–69. Native paper screenfold or tira. 3 leaves. 57 × 166 cm. (total length).

Chronicle cast in unique framework of yearly events from 1402 through 1553 with additions through 1569. A later gloss refers to an event in 1603. The emphasis is on the dynastic successions at Texcoco, Tenochtitlan, Chiautla, and Tepetlaoxtoc. Notices of famines, rains, wars, conquests, etc., are included.

The fundamental study is that by Dibble (1942a); it includes a useful redrawing of the document. Boban (1891) gives photographic reproduction of its three pages.

Copies: León y Gama copy, BNP 90-2. Pichardo copy, BNP 88-5.

Publication: Boban, 1891, 1: 279–91, pls. 15–17; Dibble, 1942a.

Studies: Robertson, 1959, pp. 144–46, pl. 50.

Brief description: Alcina Franch, 1955, pp. 452–53.

85

CRUZ, MARTÍN DE LA. *Libellus de Medicinalibus Indorum Herbis.* The Badianus Manuscript. Códice Badiano. The Badianus (–de la Cruz) Herbal. Codex Barberini. Códice Cruz. Biblioteca Apostolica Vaticana, Rome. Codex Barberini Latin 241. Ex–Francisco Barberini and Diego de Cortavila collections. Published. Miscellaneous. Colegio de Santa Cruz, Tlatelolco, D.F. 1552. European paper. 63 leaves plus preliminary and end flyleaves. 20.6 × 15.2 cm.

The manuscript was discovered almost simultaneously by Charles Upson Clark and Thorndike in 1929. It contains ca. 184 exquisitely rendered colored drawings by an Indian artist of Mexican plants and herbs, some incorporating elements of native sym-

bolism. The Latin text is a translation by Juan Badiano (an Indian from Xochimilco, a reader at the Colegio de Santa Cruz) of a Nahuatl text (not given) by Martín de la Cruz, a native physician at the same college. The text and glosses give medical and pharmacological remedies for the treatment of diseases. Dedicated to Francisco de Mendoza, son of the Viceroy Diego de Mendoza, it was intended for presentation to Charles V.

There are three editions (Gates, 1939a,b; Emmart, 1940; M. de la Cruz, 1964). Those of 1940 and 1964 are in color. The 1939 and 1940 editions are based on an accurate copy, best reproduced by Emmart (1940). The third edition is by direct color photography and contains contributions by various specialists. It also gives an extensive bibliography of minor publications relating to the codex. A single but representative page is reproduced by Robertson (1959).

Copies: Late 16th or 17thC copy, described by Gabrieli (1929), Royal Library of Windsor Castle. The copy used for the Gates and Emmart editions appears to be cataloged in Gates (1940); unverified information reports it in the Bliss collection at Dumbarton Oaks, Washington, D.C.

Editions: M. de la Cruz, 1964; Emmart, 1940; Gates, 1939a, 1939b.

Studies and brief descriptions: Emmart, 1935a, 1935b, 1935c; Gabrieli, 1929; Guerra, 1952; Leicht, 1938; Robertson, 1959, pp. 156–58, pl. 54; Thorndike, 1929–30.

Other: Gates, 1940, sec. C, p. 9; Noguera, 1933b; Pruneda, 1953.

Propagandists: Acevedo López y de la Cruz, 1958; Aragón Leyva, 1945; Cordero Mendoza, 1954.

86

Cualac, Códice de. Pueblo. Published. Historical. Cualac or Cototolapan, Guerrero. 17th or 18thC. European paper. Four fragments: 39 × 59, 39 × 39, 39 × 39, and 39 × 58 cm.

The four fragments probably represent remnants of the local titles and history of Cototolapan and have late drawings of a miscellaneous character, including baptisms and marriages. Two of the fragments with historical scenes have peripheral borders of rudimentary place glyphs. Nahuatl glosses allow their identification with localities near Cualac and Olinala.

Commentary and reproduction of copies are given by Muller (1958).

Publication: Muller, 1958.

87

Cuara, Códice.   Códice (Genealogía) de la Familia Cuara.   Genealogía de los caciques Cuara Irecha de Patzcuaro.   Princeton University Library (16 leaves); lost (2 pages). Ex–Nicolás León and Museo Michoacano collections.   Partially published.   Economic (property plans) and genealogical. Patzcuaro, Michoacan.   17thC (?).   European paper.   17 or 18 leaves.   30 × 20 cm.

Land titles of the Cuara family containing drawings of the family genealogy, various property plans, and a fragmentary calendar wheel with glossed European month names. The many drawings of persons are much acculturated. The PUL manuscript includes six pages of Tarascan and Spanish text and six blank pages not previously mentioned in the literature. Two of the pages with drawings are lost.

The MNA copy is reproduced and its content described by Mateos Higuera (1948b). Glass (1964) describes the same copy briefly and reproduces two of its pages. A reproduction of the calendar wheel is given by N. León (1903).

Copy: 1892 copy, MNA 35-98.

Publication: Mateos Higuera, 1948b, pp. 167–69, pls. 38–48.

Other: N. León, 1903, p. 490; 1903–04, p. 333, note 44; 1904a, p. 157, note 44.

Brief descriptions: Alcina Franch, 1955, pp. 497–98; Glass, 1964, p. 152, pl. 106; N.

León, 1906c, pp. 401–05; Mateos Higuera, 1944f; Paso y Troncoso, 1892–93, 1: 252–55.

88 (fig. 33)

Cuatro Venados, San Pablo, Mapa de. Mapa de San Miguel de las Peras.   Pueblo. Published.   Cartographic-historical.   San Pablo Cuatro Venados, ex-district of Zaachila, Eastern Oaxaca, 1806.   Paper.   Dimensions not reported.

The document is an 1806 copy of a lost 1588 pictorial. Its pictorial component is slight and not recognizably in any native tradition. The placement of written Spanish texts describing boundaries around the periphery, however, indicates its traditional origin and composition. Texts at the center record the founding of San Pablo in 1588 by persons from San Miguel.

Steininger and Van de Velde (1935) give description and photograph of the manuscript and an English translation of its texts.

Publication: Steininger and Van de Velde, 1935, pp. 24–27, 100–03.

89

Cuauhquechollan, Lienzo de.   Lienzo de la Academia de Puebla.   Casa del Alfeñique, Puebla.   Ex–José Manso collection.   Published.   Cartographic-historical.   Huaquechula, Puebla.   16thC.   Cloth.   235 × 320 cm.

Complex and detailed painting of a landscape covered with trees, roads, rivers, etc., with numerous scenes showing warfare between Indians as well as between Indians and Spaniards. On the left is a large two-headed eagle, which forms part of a place glyph that has been identified as that for Cuauhquechollan. The subject matter of the lienzo may represent episodes in the Spanish conquest of central Mexico.

One of the two copies in the MNA has been published and briefly described by Glass (1964).

Copies: In the MNA are copies of 1892 (MNA 35-44) and of 1933 (MNA 35-44A).

Publication: Glass, 1964, p. 90, pls. 44–45.

Brief description: Paso y Troncoso, 1892–93, 1: 71–74.

90 (fig. 34)

Cuauhquechollan, Mapa circular de. Codex Becker no. 3. Nationalbibliothek, Vienna. CVM 5. Ex–Becker collection. Unpublished. Cartographic-historical. Cuauhquechollan, Puebla. 1546. Skin. 87.5 × 89.5 cm.

A church glossed "Sanct Martyn," an eagle glossed "Quauhquechollan," 16 Indians seated on thrones, five house symbols, and an individual in European dress identified as Don Martín Cortés appear at the center of the document. Surrounding them is a circle with 47 calli symbols, with place glyphs drawn around its circumference. A second and outer concentric circle, further place glyphs, and other details encompass the central details. There are numerous glosses and a long Nahuatl text with the date 1546.

Bibliography: None.

91

Cuauhquechollan-Macuilxochitepec, Genealogía de. Códice de Guaquechula. Casa del Alfeñique, Puebla. Ex–José Manso collection. Published. Genealogical and cartographic. Huaquechula, Puebla. 16thC. Skin. 83 × 80 cm.

The obverse is a genealogy of more than 60 Indian men, women, and children, most of whom have both written and hieroglyphic names. The glyph for Cuauhquechollan-Macuilxochitepec appears at the top. On the reverse is a crude map.

Both sides of the MNA copy are reproduced by Glass (1964). Peñafiel (1914) gives a tracing of the obverse.

Copies: Modern copy on skin, MNA 35-101. Separate copies of the obverse and reverse, both on leather, in AMNH. Glass (1964) mentions two further copies, now unknown.

Publication: Glass, 1964, p. 155, pls. 108–09; Peñafiel, 1914, p. 86, pl. 2 of the series devoted to Atlixco.

92

Cuauhtemoc, Ordenanza del Señor. Plano de Tlatelolco. Plano de Derechos de Pesca, 1430. TU/MARI. Ex–Gates collection. Published. Historical and economic (property plans). Tlatelolco, D.F. 1523 (?). Native paper. 3 leaves (2 of 6 pages are blank). 28 × 36 cm.

The manuscript is a Nahuatl text with a map of properties in Tenochtitlan-Tlatelolco and several miscellaneous historical drawings. As a whole it is a reaffirmation made by Cuauhtemoc in 1523 of certain land and fishing rights that date from about 1430. The map is described as a copy of an ancient original. The text contains notices of historical relationships between Tlatelolco and Tenochtitlan for such dates as 1361, 1392, and 1431.

Rendón (1952) gives photographic reproduction of the four utilized pages, commentary, and palaeography and translation of the Nahuatl text. Barrios (1954) criticizes details of this translation. Studies with photographic reproductions of the map are Espejo and Barlow (1944) and Caso (1956). Barlow (1947a) also treats the map. An uncaptioned and apparently 19thC heliographic reproduction of the map is in TU/LAL. Individual pages, other than the map, are reproduced by Hagen (1944), Gropp (1933), Caso (1956), and Gates (1924).

The document was translated by Manuel Mancio, an interpreter of the Audiencia Real, in 1704. A copy of his translation and of the drawings by León y Gama is in the BNP and is briefly described by Boban (1891). This translation has been published (*Cédula dada . . .*, 1943) with three photographs of the copy (including the map). Barlow (1944f) has commented on this publication.

A possibly related document, also concerning an early concession of land by Cuauhtemoc and accompanied by a translation of 1714 has been briefly described by Anonymous (1888) and by Siméon (1888). The latter reproduces one original page of its Nahuatl text. This document, also described in a sale catalog of ca. 1888 (Dufosse, n.d.*a*), is now unknown.

Copy: León y Gama copy of 1704 copy, BNP 105.

Publication: Rendón, 1952.

Studies: Barlow, 1947a, pp. 152–53, pl. D; Caso, 1956, pp. 42–43, planos 4 and 5; Espejo and Barlow, 1944.

Brief descriptions and partial reproductions: Boban, 1891, 2: 281–82; Gates, 1924, Item 758, with 1 plate; Gropp, 1933, pp. 271–73, fig. 5; Hagen, 1944, pls. 5b, 37.

Other: Barlow, 1944f; Barrios, 1954; *Cédula dada*, 1943.

Related document: Anonymous, 1888; Dufosse, n.d.*a*, Item 9497; Siméon, 1888, pp. 86–91, 1 pl.

93

Cuauhtinchan, Libro de los Guardianes de. Codex of the Derrumbe del Templo Mayor. Andrés Serra Rojas collection. Partially published. Historical. Cuauhtinchan, Puebla. 1629. Physical description unavailable.

Nahuatl and Spanish historical notices from 1519 to 1629 with drawings of year symbols. The single published page shows armed and mounted Spaniards engaged in blowing up the tecpan or government house of Tenochtitlan; a Nahuatl text refers to the arrival of the Spaniards in 1519.

E. Orozco (1892) described the manuscript while it was still in Cuauhtinchan and published extracts from its Spanish texts, including those for 1522 and 1629. A tracing of one page and a translation of its Nahuatl text have been published by Barlow (1946b). Berlin and Rendón (1947) note that the manuscript is no longer in the

118

town. Accounts of its present ownership have appeared in Mexican newspapers.

Partial publication: Barlow, 1946b; E. Orozco, 1892.

Other: Berlin and Rendón, 1947, p. 147.

❖❖❖

CUAUHTINCHAN, MAPAS DE. The four maps from Cuauhtinchan, Puebla, listed separately below, form an important and related corpus of historical and cartographic sources. Further maps of the same series are contained in the Historia Tolteca-Chimeca, from the same provenience. Cartographically, the area represented by the maps includes Cholula, Puebla, Totomihuacan, Tecali, Tecamachalco, Acatzinco, Nopaluca, Mount Metlacueyetl, and part of the Atoyac River. Some of the maps depict a somewhat larger or smaller region.

The existence of the first three was first communicated by E. Orozco (1892) when they were still in Cuauhtinchan. They were copied in that year for the Exposición Histórico-Americana of Madrid (Paso y Troncoso, 1892–93). Since the foregoing description of the group and of the four maps, below, was written (in 1965), an important and detailed commentary on the four maps has been published (Simons, 1968). It includes photographic reproductions of the 1892 copies of Maps 1 and 2 and of the originals of Maps 3 and 4.

General references: E. Orozco, 1892; Paso y Troncoso, 1892–93, 1: 9–10; Simons, 1968; Velasco, 1903.

94

—— *no. 1*. Mappe Baur-Goupil. BNP 375. Ex–Charles Baur and Eugène Goupil collections. Published. Cartographic-historical. Cuauhtinchan, Puebla. 16thC. Native paper. 113 × 167 cm.

The map shows three temples and a place glyph on the left representing Cholula. As in each of the other three maps from Cuauhtinchan, the Atoyac River and a central range of hills with an eagle in a stone enclosure (Cuauhtinchan: house of the eagle) are prominent features. Scattered across the map are numerous roads, Indian caciques, and place glyphs, many of the latter with the arrow symbol denoting war or conquest. Near the center is an assemblage of more than 34 Indians and the Atl-tlachinolli symbol for warfare.

The MNA copy is reproduced and briefly described by Glass (1964). A poor photo of the copy is given by Tamayo (1949). Boban (1899) provides the datum concerning its ownership by Charles Baur. See group entry, above, for important additional bibliography.

Copy: 1892 copy, MNA 35-32.

Publication: Glass, 1964, pp. 76–77, pl. 34; Tamayo, 1949, 1: 46–47.

Brief descriptions: Mateos Higuera, 1946a; Paso y Troncoso, 1892–93, 1: 261; Tamayo and Alcorta, 1941, pp. 13–14.

Other: Boban, 1899, pp. viii–ix.

95 (fig. 35)

—— *no. 2.* Peregrinación de los Totomihuacas. Obregón Santacilia collection. Published. Cartographic-historical. Cuauhtinchan, Puebla. 16thC. Native paper. 109 × 204 cm., approx.

Chicomoztoc, legendary point of departure of Nahua migrations, appears in the upper left corner. A meandering road marks two itineraries from there to Cholula. Along the road are paintings of place glyphs, day signs, and historical episodes. Part of the content of this half of the map is also presented in the text of the Historia Tolteca-Chichimeca (pars. 166–267), according to which some of the events shown occurred in A.D. 1173. The right half of the document is a map of the Cuauhtinchan-Tecali-Tepeaca region with historical scenes, surrounded by a twisting road that leads to and from Cholula.

Published photographs of the original in color (Martínez Marín, 1963) and in b/w (Quintana, 1960) are of poor quality. The MNA copy is reproduced by Glass (1964) and was first published by Miyar (1928). According to E. Spinden (1933), the original was formerly in the Regional Museum of Puebla. See group entry, above, for important additional bibliography.

Copy: 1892 copy, MNA 35-24. Photographs in INAH/AF.

Publication: Glass, 1964, p. 66, pl. 25; Martínez Marín, 1963; Miyar, 1928, pl. 57; Quintana, 1960, pl. 1.

Brief descriptions: Mateos Higuera, 1946b; Paso y Troncoso, 1892–93, 1: 255–57; Tamayo and Alcorta, 1941, pp. 15–16.

Other: E. Spinden, 1933, p. 236.

96

—— *no. 3.* MNA 35-70. Ex–Aristides Martel collection. Published. Cartographic-historical. Cuauhtinchan, Puebla. 16thC. Amatl paper. 92 × 112 cm.

The smallest of the four maps from Cuauhtinchan, it exhibits such typical features as Cholula, the Atoyac River, the mountains with the Cuauhtinchan place glyph, etc.

A photograph of the original is published in the MNA catalog (Glass, 1964). See group entry, above, for important additional bibliography.

Copy: 1892 copy, formerly in the MNA, is unknown.

Publication: Glass, 1964, p. 123, pl. 73.

Brief descriptions: Alcina Franch, 1955, p. 462; Mateos Higuera, 1947a; Paso y Troncoso, 1892–93, 1: 262.

97

—— *no. 4.* Mapa de Puebla. MNA 35-31. Ex–Boturini collection. Published. Cartographic. Cuauhtinchan, Puebla. ca. 1563. Amatl paper. 113 × 158 cm.

The fourth map from Cuauhtinchan is the least native and probably the most recent of the four; nevertheless it includes place glyphs and hieroglyphic dates. Grid-iron plans for Tlaxcala, Puebla, Tepeaca, Tecamachalco, and other towns are shown and are connected by numerous roads. The 1563 date appears in a Nahuatl gloss. It is the only one of the four that does not include Cholula. Straight lines and place glyphs denote boundaries, some of which also appear on the second map from the town. Jurisdictions appear to be indicated by different colors in the background.

Glass (1964) gives a photograph of the original. The brief description by Mena (1923) includes an incomplete transcript of the glosses. See group entry, above, for important additional bibliography.

Publication: Glass, 1964, p. 75, pls. 32–33.

Brief descriptions: Alcina Franch, 1955, pp. 462–63; Mateos Higuera, 1947b; Mena, 1923, pp. 43–47, no. 3.

98

Cuauhtitlan, Codex Procès de. BNP 31. Ex–Aubin collection. Published. Miscellaneous. Cuauhtitlan, Mexico. 1568. Native paper. 42 × 37 cm.

Drawings of 13 Indians with personal name glyphs, circles representing days of the week of the Christian calendar, a bench, and a jail. Spanish text concerns accusation and complaint by the Indians relating to nonpayment for the construction of the bench.

Galarza (1964) gives photoreproduction and highly detailed commentary. It is also published and superficially described by Boban (1891).

Publication: Boban, 1891, 1: 404–05, pl. 31; Galarza, 1964.

99

Cuauhtitlan, Códice de los Alfareros de. BNP 109. Ex–Aubin collection. Published. Economic (tribute). Cuauhtitlan, Mexico. 1564. European paper tira. 190 × 32 cm.

Drawings of numerous and varied kinds

of colonial pottery vessels as well as of other detail—jails, persons, porters, money—with Spanish glosses. The manuscript is a bill of complaint over payment for the pottery depicted.

The very brief study by Barlow (1951a) includes somewhat deficient photographs of the manuscript.

Publication: Barlow, 1951a.

Brief description: Boban, 1891, 2: 291–93.

100

Cuauhtitlan, Títulos de la casa que esta en el pueblo de. MNA/AH Col. Antig. T-2-57 (first 9 leaves of the volume). Unpublished. Economic (property plans). Cuauhtitlan, Mexico. 16thC. European paper. 9 leaves. Dimensions not determined.

Drawings are of roads with horse and human footprints, plots of land with heads of persons and personal name glyphs, a stream of water, a bridge, and a house. One of the persons is identified as Alonso Vejarano, possibly one of the informants of Sahagún. The single drawing is accompanied by eight leaves of Nahuatl text.

Bibliography: None.

101

Cuauhtlantzinco, Mapa de. Códice Campos. Codex Chalco. Codex Tepozteco. Unknown. Partially published. Historical. San Juan Cuauhtlantzinco, Puebla. 17th–18thC. Oil paintings on European paper. 44 leaves. 30 × 40 cm.

The manuscript was photographed in the pueblo by Starr in 1895 and in 1898; between his two visits some of the paintings were destroyed by fireworks. According to his description, the manuscript consisted of 44 paintings mounted on two stretchers. The first contained 27 painted scenes, arranged in three horizontal rows, with 29 numbered Nahuatl texts. The second frame contained 17 paintings, 11 of which are copies or variants of paintings on the first frame. Around the border of each of these frames was a written Spanish translation of the Nahuatl texts by José Vicente Campos, 1855–56.

The paintings, in a primitive style with few traditional elements, commemorate the experiences of an Indian cacique named Tepoztecatzin in the Spanish conquest of Mexico. One of the paintings shows him meeting Cortés in Jalapa; another shows him in alliance with the Spaniards fighting other Indians. Others show baptisms, battles, tribute, a coat of arms, and Cortés departing for Spain.

Starr (1898) published photographs of 43 of the 44 scenes, together with a transcript of the Campos translation. Another transcript of the Campos translation is in MNA/AH. Four scenes from the MNA copy are reproduced by Glass (1964), and Seler (1902h) has commented on the Starr publication. See next entry and the Mapa de Chalchihuapan (Census, 432) for related and similar documents.

Copies: A copy probably made about 1855 was in the J. F. Ramírez collection (*Bibliotheca mexicana*, 1880). It was acquired by the London bookdealer Quaritch, who advertised it in two later catalogs (Quaritch, 1880, 1885). This copy was acquired by Gates in 1912; its present location is uncertain.

A copy of the larger frame was described and partially illustrated in the Gates sale catalog of 1924 (Gates, 1924) and is presumably the copy now in TU/LAL (not examined). A copy of the smaller frame from the Gates collection is at PUL. These two copies may be the ex–Ramírez copy or copies thereof.

A complete watercolor copy, also ex–Gates, is in PML and is presumably a copy of the ex–Ramírez copy. Photostats of the smaller part of the PML copy are in the Gates collection at BYU (Gates, 1940).

A colored copy of 24 scenes from the 27-scene original and the Nahuatl texts, made by Basilio Argil in the pueblo in May of 1892, is owned by Jorge Enciso. This copy (with recent additions based on the MNA copy) was formerly owned by Demetrio García; photographs of it are in the MNA Fototeca. Another copy by the same artist, containing about 28 or 30 scenes but lacking the Nahuatl texts, is MNA 35-102. It has been briefly described by Paso y Troncoso (1892–93) and by Glass (1964).

Another copy, apparently by Velasco, was in the possession of Alfonso Caso in 1964, and the late Salvador Toscano is believed to have owned a copy. Galarza (1965) reviews an edition (not examined) of an unidentified copy published by Echániz under the name "Códice Manuel de Velasco y Amendaro"; this may be based on the copy in the possession of Caso.

Publication: Starr, 1898.

Brief descriptions: Glass, 1964, pp. 156–57, pl. 110; Paso y Troncoso, 1892–93, 1: 52; Seler, 1902h.

Brief mention: A. Bandelier, 1884, p. 123; Peñafiel, 1914, pp. 9–10; White and Bernal, 1960, pp. 236, 238, 240.

Sale Catalogs: *Bibliotheca mexicana*, 1880, no. 540; Gates, 1924, frontispiece and no. 557; Quaritch, 1880, no. 176; 1885, no. 29045.

Other: Galarza, 1965; Gates, 1937a, nos. 468–69; 1940, sec. F, p. 17, nos. 3 and 4.

102

——, additional fragments. SMGE. Partially published. Historical. San Juan Cuauhtlantzinco (?), Puebla. 17th–18thC. European paper. 21 leaves. 30 × 40 cm.

Twenty-one further leaves of the Mapa de Cuauhtlantzinco (or from a similar document) were reported in an article published in a Mexican periodical (Anonymous, 1942). These leaves are mounted on two panels, one containing 10 scenes and the other containing 11 scenes. The 10-scene panel, reproduced in the article, contains only one scene that is duplicated in the versions published by Starr (see previous entry). A small portion of this panel is also reproduced by López Beltrán (1966). Only four of the scenes from the second panel were published; they duplicate the content of four scenes in the versions published by Starr but lack the Nahuatl texts although there are short glosses. None of this material could be located in the SMGE in 1964.

León-Portilla and Mateos Higuera (1957) mention "originals" of the Mapa de Cuauhtlantzinco in the SMGE, in the possession of the heirs of Demetrio García (a bookdealer), in the possession of Antonio Pompa y Pompa (librarian of the SMGE in 1942), and in the Bancroft Library. They imply that the portions owned by Demetrio García and the Bancroft Library were published by Starr. These two items probably correspond, respectively, to the Enciso collection copy and the copy from the Ramírez sale mentioned in the previous entry. Pompa y Pompa has personally informed us that he does not own any part of the manuscript. Photographs of what are presumably the SMGE fragments and notes for an unpublished study by Barlow are in the library of the University of the Americas, Mexico.

Partial publication: Anonymous, 1942; López Beltrán, 1966, p. 58.

Brief mention: León-Portilla and Mateos Higuera, 1957, p. 23.

103

Cuauhtli, Genealogía de. Otra Genealogía. MNA 35-128. Ex–Boturini and BNMex collections. Published. Genealogical. Tlaxcala (?). 16thC. European paper. 21.4 × 30.2 cm.

Unglossed genealogy of nine Indians with personal name glyphs. Individual at top has a glyph showing an eagle's head (Cuauhtli).

Reproduced with short description by Glass (1964). Gurría LaCroix (1964) gives a somewhat inaccurate color photograph.

It is briefly mentioned in the Mena (1923) catalog.

Publication: Glass, 1964, p. 186, pl. 139; Gurría Lacroix, 1964.

Brief mention: Mena, 1923, p. 63, no. 25.

104

Cuetlaxcohuapan, Códice de. Introducción de la Justicia Española en Tlaxcala. Códice Valencia. Códice Xochitecatl. MNA 35-17. Ex–Boturini collection. Published. Historical. Cuetlaxcohuapan (Puebla de los Angeles), Puebla (but classified as Tlaxcalan). ca. 1531–33. European paper. 50.7 × 35.8 cm.

Drawing in acculturated style or perhaps by a Spaniard shows Fr. Martín de Valencia, Hernando de Saavedra (corregidor of Puebla), and a group of Tlaxcalan nobles. A Nahuatl text treats an agreement concerning the payment of painters and scribes.

The document is described and its Nahuatl text transcribed and translated by Paso y Troncoso (1892–93). Gómez de Orozco's (1937) study includes a reprint of the Paso y Troncoso translation. Glass (1964) also describes it and publishes a photograph of the manuscript. Toussaint (1936, 1948, 1965) and Gibson (1952) reproduce a copy (the 1892 copy?).

Copy: Location of 1892 copy unknown; probably reproduced by Toussaint (1936) and Gibson (1952).

Publication: Glass, 1964, p. 59, pl. 19; Gibson, 1952, pp. 93, 264–65, fig. 3; Toussaint, 1936, fig. 32; 1948, fig. 40; 1965, pl. 22.

Studies: Gómez de Orozco, 1937; Paso y Troncoso, 1892–93, 1: 257–60.

105

Cueva, Códice de la. MNA 35-7. Ex–Boturini collection. Published. Cartographic-historical. Central Mexico. 16th C. Skin. 77.5 × 160 cm. Incomplete.

The document depicts a mountainous region crossed by rivers. Along the lower border are place glyphs. Near the center is a

European building and five Indian caciques with personal name glyphs seated on native thrones. Elsewhere armed Indians are shown attacking other Indians in the mountains.

Glass (1964) gives photoreproduction and a brief description. The manuscript was exhibited in London by Bullock in 1824 and is registered in his catalog (Bullock, 1824c). The Boturini collection inventory descriptions of 1743 and 1746 associate the document with the "Provincia de Tlaxcala" and the "pueblo de Amatla," respectively. On the basis of place glyphs Nicholson (unpublished notes) suggests a provenience in the Tecamachalco-Cuauhtepec region of Puebla.

Publication: Glass, 1964, p. 45, pls. 9–10.
Other: Bullock, 1824c, no. 51.

106

Cuevas, Códice. Archivo General de Indias, Seville. Partially (?) published. Miscellaneous. Tenayuca-Tlalnepantla, Mexico-Tacuba, D.F., region. 1551–67. Physical data not determined; apparently 4 or 6 leaves of drawings.

Notes on the original taken by Donald Robertson appear to indicate that the description, palaeography of Spanish texts, and the six negative photostats published by Cuevas (1913) do not represent the entirety of the original pictorial manuscript. The published drawings have Spanish glosses and illustrate complaints against Francisco Rodríguez Magariño, corregidor of Tacuba. The complaints and the drawings concern beatings, the holding of Indians in stocks, and various failures to pay for goods and services, etc.

In addition to the publication by Cuevas (1913), a single detail is reproduced by Cuevas (1921–28); Gibson (1964a) has commented on its content. The accompanying text, also in the AGI, has not been published.

Partial (?) *publication*: Cuevas, 1913, pp. 129–35, 6 plates.
Other: Cuevas, 1921–28, 2: 240; Gibson, 1964a, pp. 92, 275.

107 (fig. 36)

Cuitlahuac, Financial accounts of. NLA 1476 (part). Unpublished. Economic (tribute). Tlahuac, D.F. 1573–78. European paper. 9 leaves. Dimensions not determined.

Fourteen of the 18 pages have pictorial symbols for the sum of 115 pesos, 5 tomines, and dated monthly Nahuatl texts for the years 1573–78. The encomendero, Alonso de Cuevas, and the names of native officials of Cuitlahuac are mentioned. The documents are "cartas de pago" and may be records of tribute payment. The other four pages have drawings of objects, foodstuffs, Spanish money, and Nahuatl texts. The relationship between these and other documents bound with them has not been determined.

Bibliography: None.

108

Cuitlahuac, Los Cuatro Barrios de. Unknown. Unpublished. Economic (miscellaneous). Cuitlahuac (Tlahuac), D.F. 16thC. Physical description unknown.

The document is known through a copy in BNMex. It is a single-leaf drawing divided into four horizontal divisions. In each is a place symbol, Nahuatl glosses, numerical symbols, and drawings of a man's and a woman's head. The numbers may refer to population or to tribute. The four barrios are Ixcic Tlaxillacalli, Teopancalcan, Atenchical, and Tecpan Tlaxilacalli.

Copy: F. Galicia Chimalpopoca copy, 1857, in BNMex MS, "Origen de Cuitlahuac y otros documentos," f. 6bis, r.
Bibliography: None.

109

CUITLAHUAC. *Mapa de Sta. Marta, Santiago, Cuitlahuac y Ixtapalapa.* Unknown.

Published. Cartographic. Cuitlahuac (Tlahuac), D.F. 1579. Physical description unknown.

Known only through the two copies listed below, the map shows four churches representing the localities named in the title, several roads, several tepetl signs, two milpas, a boundary line, and lesser detail with Spanish glosses. The copies are accompanied by a related "merced de un sitio" by the Viceroy Martín Enríquez.

The BNMex copy has been published by Apenes (1947).

Copies: Galicia Chimalpopoca copy, 1862, in BNMex MS, "Origen de Cuitlahuac y otros documentos," ff. 34r–43r. The map (27 × 35.5 cm.) is copied on f. 43r. Another copy, also by Galicia Chimalpopoca, 1853, is MNA/AH Documentos Sueltos, ser. 2, leg. 88, no. 12; no. 11 is the related text.

Bibliography: Apenes, 1947, p. 18, pl. 4.

110

Cuitlahuac, Plan topographique de. Unknown. Unpublished. Cartographic. Tlahuac, D.F. Date unknown. Cloth. ca. 200 × 200 cm.

Not examined. The 19thC (?) Aubin collection copy is cataloged but not described by Boban (1891). Donald Robertson informs us that it may derive from a native tradition original and that its details include standing "kings" and water signs.

Copy: BNP 152.

Brief mention: Boban, 1891, 2: 324.

111

CULHUACAN: *Proceso de Marta Petronila y Augustín de Luna, Indios, contra Juan Francisco, María, y Juana*. BNP 110. Ex–Aubin collection. Unpublished. Economic (property plans) and genealogical. Culhuacan, D.F. 1590. European paper, 45 or 75 leaves (dimensions not reported) and native paper, 1 leaf, 60 × 38 cm.

The process, said to be complete, concerns litigation over a house and other properties.

One leaf of the volume contains a simple drawing showing the plan of a native house, the heads of two persons, a metate, and a chest. Also with this material is a six-generation genealogy on native paper showing more than 75 Indians, some with personal name glyphs.

The document is classified under Culhuacan following information supplied by H. B. Nicholson (personal communication); Boban (1891) reports it as Coyoacan.

Brief description: Boban, 1891, 2: 293–94.

112

Dehesa, Códice. MNA 35-51. Ex–Manuel Cardoso, Melgar y Serrano, and Teodoro A. Dehesa collections. Partially published. Historical and calendrical. Western Oaxaca. 16th and 17thC. Skin screenfold painted on both sides. 23 leaves. 17.5 × 498 cm. (total length).

The first nine pages contain historical or mythical scenes. Fourteen pages of the obverse and 10 of the reverse present a long series of pairs of Indians with calendrical name glyphs. Hieroglyphic dates with the Mixtec year sign and Nahuatl glosses, most of which are place names, appear. The latter apparently include localities in Puebla and Veracruz as well as Western Oaxaca. The 13 remaining pages of the reverse are occupied by a calendrical table, without drawings, for the years 1506–1692 except 1643–72, with correlations and Nahuatl annals.

A b/w lithograph facsimile, without the glosses and the calendrical table, was published by Melgar y Serrano (1875). Colored lithographs of the painted pages of the manuscript, excluding three illegible pages, were published by the Junta Colombina (Chavero, 1892) with a commentary of uncertain validity. Photographs of a page from the calendrical section and one from the genealogical section are given by Glass (1964). A photo of a page from the historical section is in Galindo y Villa (1905a). Caso (1928) notes the variant day signs used in this document and claims that the year-bearer days are not the usual ones; the latter observation is disputable.

Publication: Chavero, 1892, pp. xxii–xxvii and 30 plates in atlas; Melgar y Serrano, 1875.

Other: Caso, 1928, pp. 11, 55–57.

Brief descriptions: Alcina Franch, 1955, p. 492; Galindo y Villa, 1905a, p. 220, pl. 7; Glass, 1964, p. 98, pls. 53–54; Lehmann, 1905a, p. 274; Paso y Troncoso, 1892–93, 1: 55–56.

113

Dresden, Codex. Codex Dresdensis. Sächsische Landesbibliothek, Dresden. Published. Ritual-calendrical. Lowland Maya region, Southeastern Mexico and Guatemala. Preconquest. Amatl paper screenfold. 39 leaves painted on both sides (4 pages blank). 9 × 20.5 cm. (total length 356 cm.).

The manuscript was purchased in 1739 from an unidentified person in Vienna by Johann Christian Götze, librarian of the Königlichen Bibliothek zu Dresden, and acquired by that library in 1740 (Götze, 1743–44). Some details from the manuscript were published in a somewhat exotic context by Racknitz (1796), a curiosity recently reported and reprinted by Coe (1963). Humboldt (1810) published five of its pages in color after having learned of its existence from an account by Böttiger (1811). The known history of the manuscript is given by Förstemann (1880) and by Deckert (in Lips and Deckert, 1962).

One of the most important of the surviving preconquest Mesoamerican pictorial manuscripts, the Codex Dresden contains divinatory almanacs, multiplication tables for synodical revolutions of the planet Venus, representations (with explanatory glyphic texts) of various ceremonies and deities, eclipse and Venus tables, multiplication tables of various numbers (presumably astronomical, divinatory, or calendrical

in nature), and other matters, including disease and agriculture. J. E. S. Thompson (1950), from whose brief description the foregoing is adapted, notes that it is almost certainly a copy, that it exhibits Mexican influence, and that it may date from the 12thC.

Eleven complete editions of the manuscript have appeared. The first, by Kingsborough (1831–48), is still considered to be of use because of the deterioration of the original. The first and "second" editions by Förstemann (1880, 1892) are photographic and in color, but the color is inaccurate in detail. The Förstemann edition dated 1882 may be only a publisher's variant of the 1880 edition. The editions by Villacorta and Villacorta (1930, 1930–33), Evreinov, Kosarev, and Ustinov (1961), and Knorozov (1963) derive from earlier editions as does that by Librería Echániz (1947b). The Gates (1932) edition has the glyphs set in type, a much criticized feature. The color photographic edition by Lips (Lips and Deckert, 1962) is similar to those by Förstemann but differs from them in detail. It contains an excellent historical and bibliographical review of the manuscript and studies thereof superseding that by Förstemann (1880). It also gives a bibliography of over 800 titles in which the manuscript has been mentioned, studied, or reproduced in whole or in part. Krusche (1966) gives direct color photographs of 24 pages of the manuscript showing its present (post–World War II) state. An edition with commentary by J. E. S. Thompson is in preparation. See annotation in bibliography under Corona Núñez (1964–67) for an edition now in press.

See Maya Screenfolds for comment on the scope and nature of the selected bibliography given below.

Copy: The copy made by Aglio for Kingsborough ca. 1825–30 is in the British Museum.

Editions: Librería Echániz, 1947b; Evreinov, Kosarev, and Ustinov, 1961, 2: 5–250;

Förstemann, 1880, 1882, 1892; Gates, 1932; Kingsborough, 1831–48, vol. 3; Knorozov, 1963, pp. 424–97; Lips and Deckert, 1962; Villacorta and Villacorta, 1930, pp. 11–159; 1930–33 (various paginations).

Other: Krusche, 1966.

Historical references: Böttiger, 1811, 1, pp. 20–21; Coe, 1963; Götze, 1743–44, 1: 1–5; Humboldt, 1810, pp. 266–67, pl. 45; Racknitz, 1796, pl. 34.

Brief description: J. E. S. Thompson, 1950, pp. 23–25.

114

DURÁN, FRAY DIEGO. *Historia de las Indias de Nueva España y Islas de Tierra Firme.* Códice Durán. Durán Atlas. Biblioteca Nacional, Madrid. Published. Ritual-calendrical, historical, and ethnographic. Valley of Mexico. 1579–81. European paper. 344 leaves. Dimensions not determined.

Manuscript in Spanish with three sections, each illustrated by drawings having diverse origins and remote inspiration in native traditions. Robertson (1968) reports that, beginning with Tratado 2, the drawings are pasted in and that some have a written text on their reverse sides. These drawings were cut out of an earlier manuscript.

Tratado 1, with 63 illustrations, is a history of the Tenochca-Mexica from their departure from Aztlan-Chicomoztoc through the Spanish conquest, with emphasis on the dynastic history of Tenochtitlan. Part of the text of Tratado 1 derives from a lost manuscript (see Crónica X) also believed to have been utilized by Alvarado Tezozomoc.

Tratado 2 treats gods, ceremonies, and various customs and has 34 illustrations. Tratado 3, with 21 illustrations, is a calendrical treatise with drawings of a calendar wheel, day signs, and the ceremonies of the 18 months of the 365-day year.

The text and many of the drawings of Tratados 1 and 2 are parallel to those in Tovar's *Historia del Origen* (q.v.), most of the text and drawings of which are believed to derive from the Durán manuscript. The festival calendar of Tratado 3 is not copied in the Tovar manuscripts.

The first edition (Durán, 1867–80; second edition, 1951) is based on a copy made for Ramírez in 1854 and now in MNA/AH. This edition contains the text, reproductions (sometimes handcolored) by Aubin's lithographer (Jules Desportes) of the illustrations and those of the unrelated Codex Ixtlilxochitl, a preface by Ramírez, and a very digressive appendix by Chavero. The plates are frequently gathered in a separate atlas. A recent edition edited by Garibay (Durán, 1967) and based on the Madrid manuscript, reproduces the illustrations by color photography (except for two, now lost from the manuscript, and reproduced after the 1867–80 edition), changes the sequence of the tratados (and the numeration of some of the chapters), and adds a useful index, glossary, and vocabulary. An abridged and partial English translation (Durán, 1964) has few of the illustrations.

Photoreproductions of six Durán drawings from the Madrid manuscript are in Horcasitas (1959) and seven (with five in color) are given by Blacker (1965). Glass (1964) reproduces a page from the MNA/AH copy. Most of the plates of the 1867–80 edition are reprinted in Chavero (n.d.). Kubler and Gibson (1951) provide a study of the festival calendar illustrations in Tratado 3. For further comment and bibliography see Crónica X and Tovar, *Relación del Origen.*...

Copies: LC, NYPL, MNA/AH, BAN, BNMA. The location of a copy successively in the Kingsborough, Phillipps (no. 11639), and Stetson collections (*Bibliotheca inlustris*, 1842; Sotheby, Wilkinson, and Hodge, 1919a; Parke-Bernet, 1953) has not been determined.

Editions: Durán, 1867–80, 1951, 1967; Librería Echániz, n.d.*a.*

Partial publications: Blacker, 1965, pp.

10–11, 32–33, 35, 36–37, 94–95, 106–07, 126–27; Chavero, n.d., passim; Durán, 1964; Glass, 1964, p. 143, pl. 95; Horcasitas, 1959; Velásquez Chávez, 1939, color pl. 1; Yáñez, 1942, pp. 103–200.

Other: Barlow and Smisor, 1943a; *Bibliotheca inlustris*, 1842, no. 536 (part); Fernández del Castillo, 1925a; Hagar, 1912c; Kubler and Gibson, 1951, pp. 56–57, fig. 7 and passim; Parke-Bernet, 1953, 1: no. 214; Robertson, 1968; Sandoval, 1945; Sotheby, Wilkinson, and Hodge, 1919a, no. 330.

Brief descriptions: Alcina Franch, 1955, p. 451; Garibay, 1953–54, 2: 50–56, 293–99; Radin, 1920, pp. 14–15, 20–24.

115

Ecatepec y Huitziltepec, Mapa de. Codex Charles Ratton. Codex Quetzalecatzin. Charles Ratton collection (Paris). Ex–William Randolph Hearst collection. Unpublished. Cartographic-historical. Todos Santos Ehecatepec (?), Puebla. ca. 1575–90. European paper. ca. 90 × 74 cm.

The right half of the manuscript is a map of numerous small localities indicated by glossed place glyphs between two mountain ranges. A place glyph above a European building is that for Ehecatepec and is glossed "Ecatepec" and "Todos Santos"; a less prominent glyph is Huitziltepec.

The left half includes a vertical column of Indians with calendrical name glyphs whose names are given in the gloss as Cozcaquauhtzin, Ollintzin, Xochitzin, Pedro de León, etc. Short Nahuatl texts refer to Quetzalecatzin, Ecatepec, Huitziltepec, and to lands. Hieroglyphic dates have the interlaced A-O form. Nicholson (in unpublished notes) suggests an association with Santa Cruz Huitziltepec and Todos Santos Xochitlan in the Tecamachalco region of Puebla.

Caso (1958e) lists it among Mixtec documents and erroneously states that it is in the BNP. Guzmán (1939c) notes that some of the personal names on the manuscript are the same as, or homonymous with, those of some persons who appear in the *Anales de Tecamachalco*.

There is a possibility that this document may correspond to the "Mapa jeroglífico del Señorío de Quetzala" of the Chavero collection mentioned by Chavero (1901a) and N. León (1905a). Chavero also owned a "pintura de un cacicazgo popoloca que llegaba hasta Tetela, de la Sierra de Puebla . . ." (Chavero, 1906) and a genealogy "que traía la descendencia de un cacique hasta cerca del fin del siglo pasado" (Chavero, n.d.). All these references may be to the same manuscript. The suggestion is based partially on the fact that at least one Chavero collection manuscript (the falsified Colección Chavero no. 1) was owned by Hearst; the Ecatepec document, also owned by Hearst (see Sotheby and Co., 1939), may thus also have come from the Chavero collection.

Copies: Photographs are in the BM, LC/HF, and other collections.

Brief mention: Caso, 1958e, p. 460.

Other: Guzmán, 1939c, pp. 53–55; Sotheby and Co., 1939, no. 399.

Loc. cit.: Chavero, 1901a, p. 11; 1906, p. 227, note; n.d., p. v; N. León, 1905a, p. 182.

116

Edificio, Plano de un. DGMH 1171. Unpublished. Economic (property plans). Central Mexico. 16thC. European paper. 52 × 39 cm.

Plan of a precinct showing a church and a cross, surrounded by 39 calli (house) symbols, and lesser detail.

Bibliography: None.

117

Etla, Genealogías de los Señores de. Genealogías de Yetla. Genealogía de Ixtlan. MNA 35-85. Ex–Boturini collection. Partially published. Genealogical. Villa de Etla, ex-district of Etla, Eastern Oaxaca. 17thC. European paper. 6 sheets. Dimensions vary between 51× 43 and 92 × 83 cm.

Six related genealogies in wholly Europeanized style show between six and eleven generations. All the persons have written Zapotec or Spanish names, the latter usually beginning in the fifth generation. There are no hieroglyphic symbols. The inventories of the Boturini collection ascribe the documents to both Yetla (a Chinantec community) and to the Villa de Etla, a more probable provenience.

Two of the genealogies have been reproduced by Cline (1961a, 1961b). Glass (1964) provides a brief description and reproduces one of the fragments.

Partial publication: Cline, 1961a, pl. 2a; 1961b, pl. 7; Glass, 1964, p. 139, pl. 90.

Brief description: Mena, 1923, p. 64, no. 29.

118

Féjérváry-Mayer, Codex. Códice Mayer. Codex de Pesth. Free Public Museums, Liverpool. Ex–Féjérváry, Pulszky, and Mayer collections. Published. Ritual-calendrical. Borgia Group. Preconquest. Skin screenfold. 23 leaves (22 painted pages on each side; initial and terminal pages, formerly attached to covers, blank). 16.2 × 17.2 or 17.5 × 17.5 cm. (total length ca. 385 or 400 cm.).

Divinatory almanac in 17 sections. Most sections concern specific aspects of the tonalpohualli, the 260-day Mesoamerican augural cycle. Some sections of the obverse with bar-and-dot numerals may relate to unidentified ceremonies or offerings. Stylistic resemblance to Codex Laud has led to their classification as the Féjérváry-Laud subgroup within the Borgia Group of manuscripts.

The first edition (Kingsborough, 1831–48) is superseded by the facsimile edition by Loubat (1901) and the photographic color edition by Corona Núñez (1964–67); the latter is accompanied by a page-by-page

commentary. The commentary by Seler (1901a; English translation, 1901–02) is accompanied by annotated drawings of all pages. Nowotny (1961b) gives comparative exposition of all sections. The history of the manuscript prior to about 1829 has not been studied. See Borgia Group for further bibliography and comment.

Editions: Corona Núñez, 1964–67, 4: 185–275; Librería Echánez, 1945; Kingsborough, 1831–48, vol. 3; Loubat, 1901.

Commentaries: Seler, 1901a, 1901–02; Nowotny, 1961b, passim.

Studies: Beyer, 1911; Burland, 1950a, 1951a; Caso, 1967, pp. 80–81; Hagar, 1911, 1912a; Seler, 1902l; Thomas, 1884, pp. 31–36, pl. 3, fig. 6; J. E. S. Thompson, 1934, pp. 225–26, 233–34; 1966.

Other: Forty-fourth annual report, 1897, pp. 50–51.

Brief descriptions: Alcina Franch, 1955, pp. 475–76; Lehmann, 1905a, pp. 256–57; Paso y Troncoso, 1898b, pp. 55–59, 330–32.

119

Fernández Leal, Códice. Bancroft Library, Berkeley. Ex–Benjamín Ladrón de Guevara, Martínez Gracida, E. J. Molera, and W. H. Crocker collections. Published. Historical. Santiago Quiotepec–San Juan Bautista Cuicatlan region, ex-district of Cuicatlan, Northern Oaxaca. 16thC. Native paper tira painted on one side. ca. 36 × 580 cm. An additional fragment, ca. 36 × 28 cm., is now lost.

Pictorial and historical narrative has drawings of Indians with personal name glyphs, over 25 elaborate place signs, warfare and conquests, roads, etc. The Volador and arrow-sacrifice ceremonies are each shown twice. Calendrical year dates have variant year-bearer days. The content parallels a portion of Códice Porfirio Díaz.

A photographic edition, handcolored in most examples, was published by Peñafiel (1895); small photographs of all but the missing fragment have been published by Tompkins (1942). The commentaries by these authors have been severely criticized by Barlow (1944e). Details have been illustrated by Galindo y Villa (1905a) and by Hagen (1944).

Publication: Peñafiel, 1895; Tompkins, 1942.

Other: Barlow, 1944e; Galindo y Villa, 1905a, pls. 9–10; Hagen, 1944, pl. 6; Lizardi Ramos, 1955.

Brief descriptions: Alcina Franch, 1955, p. 499; Lehmann, 1905a, pp. 277–78.

120

García, Diego, Anales de, 1502–1601. Anales Antiguos de Mexico y sus Contornos no. 24. Unknown. Ex–Boturini collection. Unpublished. Historical. Central Mexico. After 1620. European paper. 13 leaves. Quarto.

The Galicia Chimalpopoca copy contains the Nahuatl text, his Spanish translation, and a very few minor copied drawings, including year signs for the years 1500–02. The text contains annalistic entries for events in the Valley of Mexico and elsewhere.

Copy: Galicia Chimalpopoca copy and translation, MNA/AH Col. Antig. 274, no. 24 (AAMC 24).

Bibliography: None.

121

Genealogie von 33 Personen. Lost. Formerly DSB MS Amer. 10 (part). Published. Genealogical. Central Mexico. 16thC. Native paper. 45 × 64 cm.

Thirty-three Indians, all in Indian costume and all identified by personal name glyphs and Nahuatl glosses, are shown in genealogical relationships through six generations. Also depicted are five native houses.

The document has been studied and reproduced photographically by Lehmann (1906a). An inaccurate copy is given by Gondra (1846) and by Chavero (n.d.).

Publication: Lehmann, 1906a, pp. 331–37, pl. 3.

Other: Chavero, n.d., p. 655; Gondra, 1846, pp. 113–14, pl. 24.

122–127 (fig. 37)

Gilcrease Fragments 1–6. Gilcrease Institute, Tulsa. Unpublished. Economic (tribute). Central Mexico. 16thC. Native paper. 32 fragments of varying dimensions.

The "Gilcrease Fragments" consist of approximately 32 fragments representing about six different manuscripts. Only the largest (ca. 152 × 46 cm.) is drawn on both sides. All exhibit various adhesions of glue, cane, and pith and all have been crumpled, suggesting that they derive from the stuffing of a cane statue of Christ in the manner of the Códices del Cristo de Mexicaltzingo. Two of the manuscripts are vertical tiras, each about 12.7 cm. wide. One is represented by 13 fragments, the other by 14; none of them fit together. The overall lengths of the two tiras (ignoring the fact that their component fragments do not fit together) are about 417 and 716 cm. The Códice del Volador (q.v.) is most probably a further fragment of one of these tiras. The history of the manuscripts is unknown. It is possible that they may correspond to the pictorial manuscripts found in a cane Christ near Mixtepec (state of Mexico) and reportedly sold to Ignacio Bernal after having been moved to Tlaxcala (see Carrillo y Gariel, 1949).

The manuscripts all fall within the type, content, and style of middle to late 16thC pictorial tribute, fiscal, and accounting documents from the Valley of Mexico. One, with short Nahuatl texts, is a register of payments with Christian month and day dates by or for the regidores of an unstated locality. Place glyphs include two that may represent Tenochtitlan and Culhuacan. There are no year dates.

129

Loc. cit.: Carrillo y Gariel, 1949, note following p. 81.

128

GÓMEZ DE CERVANTES, GONZALO. *Relación de* [lo que toca a] *la Grana Cochinilla.* British Museum in Add. MSS 13964. Published. Miscellaneous. Central Mexico. ca. 1599 (?). European paper. Drawings on 4 leaves. Dimensions not determined.

The relación concerning cochineal ("a dye made from the dried bodies of insects cultivated on the tuna or nopal cactus" [Gibson, 1964a, p. 354]) is one of the final sections of the Gómez de Cervantes *Memorial*, a work on the social and economic life of New Spain at the end of the 16thC. At the end of the manuscript are seven pages of drawings illustrating the care and cultivation of the cactus (*Nopalea cochenillifera*) on which the insect (*Coccus cacti*) is grown and its enemies (birds, other insects). The style of the drawings is suggestive of an earlier period of native style than the date of the Gómez MS (1599). Whether or not the gloss on the drawings is in Gómez' hand, or if the drawings are originals or copies or an integral part of the MS is unknown. The drawings may be European in origin.

An illustrated relación on cochineal by Muñoz Camargo is now lost (Gibson, 1952, pp. 238–39) but may have some relationship to the drawings in the Gómez MS. It may be noted that, coupled with an account of his lost relación, Muñoz Camargo (1947b) refers to a botanical treatise by Alonso de la Mota (y Escobar), one of whose works is bound with the Gómez MS.[4]

The drawings are reproduced in Gómez de Cervantes (1944) and in Dahlgren de

Jordán (1963). One of the drawings from the Toledo copy appears in Esteve Barba (1942). The ownership history of the manuscript is the same as that of the Codex Kingsborough, at least since the time that it was owned by Renouard.

Copy: 18thC copy, drawings only, Biblioteca Publica de Toledo.

Publication: Dahlgren de Jordán, 1963 (page citations not determined); Gómez de Cervantes, 1944, pp. 163–82, plates at end of vol.

Other: Esteve Barba, 1942, p. 142, pl. 8; Gibson, 1952a, pp. 238–39; González de Barcia, 1737–38, 2: 766; Muñoz Camargo, 1947b, p. 293.

129

Gómez de Orozco, Fragmento. Códice Gómez de Orozco. Fragment Dorenberg. Gómez de Orozco collection (present location uncertain; not MNA). Ex–Dorenberg and Francisco León Calderón collections. Published. Historical. Western Oaxaca. 16thC. Skin tira painted on both sides. 21.4×69.5 cm. Folded to form 3 leaves.

The manuscript is a fragment with two painted pages on the obverse and one on the reverse. The obverse depicts the descent of a god whose image has been effaced (probably 9 Wind, Quetzalcoatl) from the eight skies to the earth and related detail. This forms a very close parallel to the opening scene in the Selden Roll. The reverse shows a number of persons and place glyphs that also appear on the Lienzo Antonio de León.

Caso (1954) gives commentary, comparison with other sources, and good photographic color facsimile. Kelley (1955) adds alternative interpretation of one symbol. Lehmann (1905a) describes the Seler collection copy (location now unknown) made in 1894.

Publication: Caso, 1954.

Other: Kelley, 1955; Lehmann, 1905a, pp. 273–74.

---

[4] An interesting drawing of cochineal harvest, evidently marginal to the native stylistic traditional and not included in this census, is reproduced by West and Augelli (1966, p. 285). They give its date as 18th century and its location as AGI. It may correspond to the document cataloged by Torres Lanzas (1900, 2: 150, no. 515).

Brief description: Alcina Franch, 1955, pp. 491–92.

130

Guevea, Lienzo de. Genealogía de los Señores Zapotecos. Códice Petela. Lienzo de Petapa. Mapa de Santiago Guevea. Lienzo de Zaachila. Unknown. Published. Cartographic-historical. Santiago Guevea (Guevea de Humboldt), ex-district of Tehuantepec, Eastern Oaxaca. 1540. Cloth (?). Dimensions unknown (MNA copy is 309 × 98.5 cm.).

The upper half of the lienzo depicts 18 place glyphs, glossed in both Zapotec and Spanish, surrounding several central details such as a seated Indian cacique in the representation of a house and two churches. Seler has suggested that the peripheral place glyphs, ostensibly representing boundaries established in 1540, may also have a calendrical significance. The lower part of the lienzo shows 16 persons with personal name glyphs, including Cosiobi and Cosijoeza, arranged in two columns. These probably represent a dynastic succession list. Place glyphs include Zaachila and Tehuantepec.

Seler (1908b) gives commentary and reproduction of the variant copies A and B. Both Glass (1964) and Galindo y Villa (1905a) provide photographs of copy A, as does Caso (1965b). A colored copy of copy A is reproduced in color by Mendieta y Núñez (1949) and a copy of the upper half of copy A is reproduced in color by Lenz (1950). The Zapotec place names have been studied by Reko (1945). See Lienzo de Petapa for the use of that name as a synonym.

Copies: Copy A, made in 1892 from a now unknown copy apparently dated 1820 and owned by Porfirio Díaz, is MNA 35-1. Copy B is known only through Seler's publication. Glass (1964) mentions another version, also unknown, published in a Mexican newspaper in 1928.

Publication: Caso, 1965b, fig. 19; Galindo y Villa, 1905a, p. 200, pls. 11–13; Glass, 1964, pp. 35–36, pls. 1–2; Mendieta y Núñez, 1949, folding plate between pp. 38 and 39; Seler, 1908b.

Other: Lenz, 1950, p. 158, pl. 3; Reko, 1945, pp. 143–54.

Brief descriptions: Alcina Franch, 1955, p. 480; Lehmann, 1905a, p. 275; Paso y Troncoso, 1892–93, 1: 39–40.

131

Haucalpan, San Lorenzo, Anales de. Unknown. Ex–Auguste Lesouef collection. Unpublished. Unavailable. San Lorenzo Haucalpan (now San Lorenzo Tepealtitlan, pueblo in municipio Toluca), Mexico. 1604. European (?) paper. 14 leaves. 21.5 × 15.5 cm.

The manuscript has been briefly described by Anonymous (1888), by Siméon (1888), and in a sale catalog (Dufosse, n.d.*a*) as a Nahuatl historical text with some pictorial figures embracing the years 1382–1604. Siméon comments on its chronological disorder and its references to Aztec rulers.

Brief descriptions: Anonymous, 1888, p. 39; Dufosse, n.d.*a*, Item 9495; Siméon, 1888, pp. 85–86.

132 (fig. 38)

HERNÁNDEZ, FRANCISCO. *Historia natural de Nueva España* (and other titles). Lost. Miscellaneous. Central Mexico. 1571–1577. Physical description omitted.

The "protomédico" Hernández, one of the great figures in the history of science, medicine, botany, and herbals, was on a scientific mission to Mexico, 1571–77. During his stay he compiled a massive series of works of which the *Natural History* (plants, animals, birds, reptiles, insects) is the best known. Hundreds of drawings, many by Indian artists (whose names he gives), illustrated the work. The original manuscripts and all the drawings were almost certainly destroyed by the Escorial fire of 1671. The text is known through various publications based on extracts, a severely edited summary, and a contemporary copy, the latter lacking the drawings. Nierembergii (1635) described the character of the drawings and published some copies which together indicate their traditional native origin (such as the use of glyphs for water and stone in conjunction with the drawings of plants). The edition of 1651 (some copies bear dates of 1630, 1648, or 1649) reproduced hundreds of the drawings (mostly of plants) through Italian copies in which all elements of native style and iconography have been removed.

The Hernández bibliography and studies relating thereto are too extensive to present here, and therefore only selected illustrated editions of the *Historia natural* will be cited. The modern critical edition of the works of Hernández (Hernández, 1959–60) gives the text of the *Historia natural* (including the *Historia de las plantas de Nueva España*) from the editions of 1651 and 1790. It reproduces the illustrations of the edition of 1651 and some of those given by Nierembergii in 1635. It also includes a comprehensive scholarly apparatus and a revision of the annotated bibliography of the writings of Hernández published by Somolinos d'Ardois (1957). The copied drawings of plants from the 1651 edition also appear in Hernández (1942–46). A study of the original iconography of the drawings is given by Somolinos d'Ardois (1954) with selected illustrations from the 1635 edition.

Manuscripts of the works of Hernández, none of which appear to include any of the drawings, are not cited in the repository checklist. The drawings in Hernández, *De Antiquitatibus Novae Hispaniae*, are copies of calendrical illustrations in Sahagún's *Manuscrito de Tlatelolco* (or some other manuscript of that work). See Sahagún Calendar Wheel (no. 272) and table of day signs in the Manuscrito de Tlatelolco (no. 273) for description of these copies.

Selected bibliography: Hernández, 1651,

1942–46, 1959–60; Nierembergii, 1635; Somolinos d'Ardois, 1954, 1957.

133

HERRERA, ANTONIO DE. *Historia general de los Hechos de los Castellanos. . .*: title-page vignettes. Published. Unclassified. Valley of Mexico. 1601.

Two of the illustrated title pages of parts of Herrera's *Historia* have a total of 14 vignettes copied from Mexican pictorial manuscripts. Six of those on the *Descripción de las Indias occidentales* title page depicting Aztec gods are copied from the Codex Magliabecchiano, the *Códice del Museo de América*, or from a lost manuscript of the Magliabecchiano Group (q.v.). Two of those on the *Decada segunda* title page may have the same origin.

The remaining six drawings represent copies or adaptations from one or more unknown manuscripts. It is this unknown source that is represented by the present census number and entry. One of these six (*Descripción*, lower left) shows Acamapichtli and place glyphs for four towns that he conquered (compare Codex Mendoza, f. 2*v*).

The two title pages in question were first published in 1601 (Herrera, 1601–15); there are numerous later editions. The relationship between the vignettes and Codex Magliabecchiano was noted by Nuttall (1903).

Bibliography: Herrera, 1601–15, loc. cit.; Nuttall, 1903, p. vii.

134

Heye Foundation, Lienzo of the. Museum of the American Indian, Heye Foundation, New York. Ex–W. W. Blake and T. Philip Terry collections. Published. Cartographic-historical. Central Mexico. 16thC. Cloth. ca. 117 × 150 cm.

The historical content of this interesting lienzo has not been interpreted nor has its provenience been determined. On the right are two rows of place glyphs and Indians with personal name glyphs. Accompanying Nahuatl glosses are almost illegible. On the left are drawings of several historical scenes, native temples, and further place glyphs connected by lines of footprints indicative of migrations or historical narrative.

An inadequate photograph has been published without comment by Hagen (1944).

Publication: Hagen, 1944, pl. 1.

135

Huamantla, Códice de. Nine fragments: 7 in MNA and 2 in DSB. (1) MNA 35-22, (2) MNA 35-40, (3) MNA 35-37, (4) MNA 35-41, (5) MNA 35-2, (6) MNA 35-55, (7–8) Humboldt Fragments 3–4, in DSB MS Amer. 1, and (9) in Techialoyan Codex of Ixtapalapa, MNA 35-107. Ex–Boturini and Humboldt (2 fragments only) collections. Published. Cartographic-historical. Huamantla, Tlaxcala. 16thC. Amatl paper. 9 sheets. (1) 47 × 114, (2) 154 × 92, (3) 187 × 95, (4) 189 × 91, (5) 242 × 95, (6) 50 × 178 cm.; the dimensions of the two Humboldt Fragments are unpublished; the ninth fragment is very small.

The fragments are part of a single large painting, some of which is believed to have been lost since it was first described by Boturini in the 18thC. Three of the fragments fit together; two others may.

Drawn and painted in a distinctive style, the principal theme is warfare. Indians armed with bows, arrows, macanas, and shields with the atltlachinolli symbol for war between them form a frequent motif. The taking of prisoners and sacrifices are shown as are clusters of native houses, place glyphs, Indians, and other symbols. One scene depicts tribute being offered to a Spaniard; adjacent to this two mounted Spaniards thrust lances into bleeding Indians. Although there are both place and personal name glyphs, no native dates appear. Faded glosses in Nahuatl include

place names, some of which are at least homonymous with localities in the ex-districts of Juarez and Morelos in Tlaxcala.

Photographs and brief descriptions of the MNA Fragments 1–6 have been published by Glass (1964), who cites an unpublished and relatively detailed description of the MNA fragments by Caso and Gómez de Orozco. Fragments 2–5 are very briefly described by Paso y Troncoso (1892–93). They were exhibited in London in 1824 by Bullock and are listed in his catalog (Bullock, 1824c). A superficial study of Fragments 3 and 4 by Barlow (MS*a*) is unpublished. Fragment 6 ("Fragmento de Fiesta Ciclica"; "El Fuego Nuevo") is described twice by Mena (1923) and is included in Seler's study of the two Humboldt Fragments. Carrasco Pizana (1950) utilizes the manuscripts as a source for data on Otomi ethnography, and Gibson (1952) mentions them in his listing of Tlaxcalan pictorials.

The unpublished ninth fragment, discovered by Donald Robertson in 1967, has been used to repair f. 1 of the Codex of Ixtapalapa (Article 24B, no. 706). It shows parts of three footprints only.

Humboldt Fragment 3 was first published, in color, by Humboldt (1810). Both of the Humboldt Fragments were published photographically in *Historische Hieroglyphen* (1892). A commentary by Seler (1893) on the latter publication includes an exhaustive treatment of the two fragments. There is an English translation of the 1893 commentary (Seler, 1904f), with reproductions of copies of the two fragments, and a slight revision (Seler, 1902e) which lacks full reproductions. Veytia (1848) reports on his visit to the place of their discovery in Huamantla. See Humboldt Fragments for further data.

Copies: Copies of 1892 of Fragments 2–5 are MNA 35-40A, 35-37A, 35-41A, and 35-2A. Copies of Fragments 1–5 were made by Mateo A. Saldaña about 1933; the first two of these are MNA 35-22B and 35-40B. The

Saldaña copies are so accurate that they may be mistaken for the originals.

Publication: Glass, 1964, pp. 37–38, 64, 82, 86, 87, 105, pls. 3, 4, 23, 39, 58; *Historische Hieroglyphen*, 1892, pls. 3, 4; Seler, 1904f, pp. 176–87, pls. 8–9.

Commentaries: Seler, 1893, pp. 61–73; 1902e, pp. 227–42.

Brief descriptions: Barlow, MS*a*; Gibson, 1952, p. 265; Mena, 1923, pp. 39–41, 56–57, nos. 1, 12; Paso y Troncoso, 1892–93, 1: 60–62.

Other: Bullock, 1824c, nos. 4, 15, 20, 41; Carrasco Pizana, 1950, passim; Humboldt, 1810, pp. 237–38, pl. 38; Veytia, 1848, p. 163.

136

HUAMUXTITLAN: *Pièces d'un Procès.* BNP 116. Ex–Aubin collection. Unpublished. Economic (tribute). Huamuxtitlan, Guerrero. 1580. European paper. "12 pages in-fol." (6 leaves?).

Not examined. Boban (1891) describes the manuscript as concerning complaints by the Indians of Huamuxtitlan against town officials. The drawings are of persons and sums of money.

Brief description: Boban, 1891, 2: 303.

137

Huautla, Mapa de. Mapa de San Juan Evangelista Huautla de Jimenez. Pueblo. Published. Cartographic. Huautla de Jimenez, ex-district of Teotitlan, Northern Oaxaca. 18thC. Cloth. 117 × 213 cm.

Landscape painting, not in native tradition, showing Huautla, Ayautla, Tenango, and other localities as well as details of the countryside.

The map was first published by Starr (n.d.). Cline (1964, 1966b) reproduces the Starr photograph and analyzes its cartographic content.

Publication: Cline, 1964, pp. 410–13, figs. 13–15; 1966b, pp. 285–89, figs. 6–7, Map 8; Starr, n.d., Item 4.

Brief mention: Starr, 1900, p. 77; 1908, pp. ix, 236.

138

Huaxtepec, Plano ideográfico del Señorío de, Año 1376. Location uncertain. Unpublished. Unclassified. Central Mexico. Date and physical description not determined.

The document is briefly described by Tamayo and Alcorta (1941) on the basis of a heliographic copy (DGMH 2763) as a composition (or copy) of 1907 which includes aboriginal elements. The original appears to be listed in a catalog of maps in the SMGE (Mirabal Lausan, 1937) but neither original nor copy has been examined for the present census.

References: Mirabal Lausan, 1937, p. 167; Tamayo and Alcorta, 1941, p. 23, no. 14.

139

Huexotzingo, Matrícula de. MS de 1560. BNP 387. Ex–Boturini collection. Partially published. Economic (census) and genealogical. Huexotzingo, Puebla. 1559–60. European paper. ca. 562 leaves (ff. 464–1032 with 6, 7, or 8 leaves missing internally). 31.5 × 21.5 cm.

The Matrícula is a census, conducted by Diego de Madrid, *Juez de Comisión*, of about 18 localities in the Huexotzingo region and four or five localities farther south (Atlisco, Cuauhquechollan, Tianguismanalco, etc.). For each of most of these localities there are two separate pictorial sections. One gives a classified listing (by barrio, civil status, profession, etc.) of individuals, usually identified by personal name glyphs and glossed Nahuatl names. The total number of Indians so depicted is enormous. The other section lists *principales* by families or houses of each locality; these sections frequently include genealogies. Numerous pages of text include procedural matter in Spanish related to the census.

The pictorial sections (referred to as

"quadernos" in the text) represent discrete documents compiled for the census by the Indians. Different individual styles are recognizable. The place glyphs for the major localities are carefully executed and include depictions of churches and patron saints of the towns. Their general style is reminiscent of the colonial murals at Huexotzingo.

Only one page of the document has been reproduced (by Kubler, 1961). Many of the place glyphs, including those for barrios of the major localities, are included in the compilation by Peñafiel (1897c). Some name glyphs and numerical symbols from the manuscript are reproduced by Orozco y Berra (1880); others are used to illustrate Seler's study of the Humboldt Fragments (q.v.). Hanns J. Prem has made a study of the personal name glyphs (citation not available), and a facsimile edition has been announced by the Akademische Druck und Verlagsanstalt, Graz, Austria. David Warren (1971) has summarized the demographic content.

Copies: Photographic copy by Gates in PML and BYU. A partial copy of ff. 482–583, perhaps made by Aglio for Kingsborough, was in the Phillipps collection (Phillipps no. 14262; Sotheby, Wilkinson, and Hodge, 1919a, no. 357; Sotheby and Co., 1935, no. 300).

Partial publication: Kubler, 1961, fig. 4.

Brief descriptions: García Granados and MacGregor, 1934, pp. 77–81; Núñez y Domínguez, 1947a, pp. 357–58; J. F. Ramírez, 1855, nos. 3–4.

Other: Nicholson, 1967, figs. 8–9; Orozco y Berra, 1880, atlas, pls. 3–10, 13, 15; Peñafiel, 1897c, passim; 1903c, pl. 106, figs. a, b; D. Warren, 1971.

140

Hueyapan, Mapa de los Terrenos de. Unknown. Ex–García Icazbalceta collection. Unpublished. Unavailable. Central Mexico. Date and material unknown. 58 × 43 cm.

The document is known only through its listing in the published catalog of the García Icazbalceta collection (Gómez de Orozco, 1927a). There is no record of its accession by UTX, which acquired most of that collection.

Brief mention: Gómez de Orozco, 1927a, Item XXVI-22.

141

Hueyapan, Plan topographique de. BNP 25. Ex–Aubin collection. Published. Cartographic-historical. Hueyapan, Morelos. 1574. Native paper. 42 × 38 cm.

Map shows several rivers, numerous trees, and place glyphs, some of which are glossed in Nahuatl. That for Hueyapan appears near the lower center below drawings of six Indian caciques. A glyph at the top probably represents Mount Popocatepetl. A dated Spanish text on the reverse suggests that the map formed part of a lawsuit.

Boban (1891) gives photoreproduction and brief description.

Brief description and publication: Boban, 1891, 1: 381–82, pl. 25.

142

Huichapan, Códice de. Códice del Monasterio de San Mateo Huichapan. Códice de Ueychiapan. Códice Otomí. MNA 35-60. Partially published. Historical and calendrical. San Mateo Huichapan, Hidalgo. 16th and 17thC. European paper. 34 leaves. 29 × 21 cm.

The manuscript was removed from the museum sometime after about 1901 but was recovered in 1930 from C. C. James.

Seven pages of the codex are textual annals in Otomi of the convent of Huichapan for the years 1539–1618 and 1629–32. Two pages contain hieroglyphs of Otomi towns and another two contain a written calendar with Otomi month and day names. Fifty-five pages contain pictorial annals with Otomi texts from 1403 to 1528; pages for 18 years are missing. The annals treat the rulers of

Tenochtitlan, events in Cuauhtitlan and in villages near Jilotepec, the arrival of Spaniards, etc.

The codex has been described by Caso (1930), who published three of its pages and two details, and by Soustelle (1937). A brief description and a reproduction of one page are given by Glass (1964). The calendrical pages have been studied by Caso (1930), Soustelle (1937), and by Carrasco Pizana (1950). Caso (1967) gives a reprint of his earlier study with added material and reproduces nine pages (four in color).

Copies: MHP and in the possession of Alfonso Caso.

Partial publication: Caso, 1930; 1967, pp. 211–25; Glass, 1964, pp. 111–12, pl. 63.

Studies: Carrasco Pizana, 1950, pp. 169–84; Ecker, 1966; Soustelle, 1937, pp. 213–14, 521–28.

Brief mention: Alcina Franch, 1955, p. 498; Chavero, 1901a, p. 9; Kubler and Gibson, 1951, p. 61.

143

Huilotepec, Lienzo de. Mapa de Huilotepec. Pueblo. Published. Cartographic-historical. San Pedro Huilotepec, ex-district of Tehuantepec, Eastern Oaxaca. 18thC (?). Cloth. 155.5 × 54 cm.

Shows a river, several place glyphs (including that for Tehuantepec), a number of Indians, and lesser detail with glosses, presumably in Zapotec. Barlow (1943b) gives brief commentary and two different photo-reproductions, both apparently from the earlier edition by Starr (n.d.).

Publication: Barlow, 1943b; Starr, n.d., Item 3.

Brief description: Alcina Franch, 1955, pp. 479–80, fig. 18; Gadow, 1908, p. 173; Lehmann, 1905a, p. 275; Seler-Sachs, 1900, pp. 90–91; Starr, 1908, pp. 330–31; MS, p. 50.

144

HUITZILA: *Pintura de las Tierras de Qua-*

hunacazco. AGN-T 1535, exp. 4. Published. Economic (property plans). Huitzila, Morelos. 1592. European paper. 42 × 30 cm.

Painting of plots of land, four persons, a church, and lesser detail. The document forms part of a petition for a land title.

Copy in color reproduced in *Códices indígenas* (1933). It is described in detail, with translation of Nahuatl glosses, by Mazari (1926c).

Publication: Códices indígenas, 1933, no. 30.

Commentary: Mazari, 1926c, pp. 315–20, no. 12.

145

HUITZILOPOCHCO: *Contrat de Commanderie.* BNP 27. Ex–Aubin collection. Published. Economic (tribute). Huitzilopochco (Churubusco), D.F. 1554. European paper. 42 × 31 cm.

Drawings of items of tribute (corn, wood, pesos, etc.) with a Spanish text, signed by town officials, stating the details of tribute payment to the encomendero, Bernardino Vásquez de Tapia.

The document has been published and described by Boban (1891).

Publication: Boban, 1891, 1: 387–89, pl. 27.

❖❖❖

HUITZILOPOCHTLI GROUP. The relationship between the twin Codices Telleriano-Remensis and Ríos (described separately in this census) has been discussed many times. One school of thought common in the 19thC held that the latter was copied from the former before the presumably missing pages of the Parisian manuscript were lost. The reverse relationship is admitted as impossible since the Telleriano-Remensis is clearly the product of several Indian artists, whereas Codex Ríos is in the uniform style of its presumably Italian (?) copyist. J. E. S. Thompson (1941b) has advanced iconographic reasons to show that Ríos cannot be a copy of Telleriano-Remensis and that the two therefore derive from a common original. Barlow (in unpublished lecture notes) has named this hypothetical lost manuscript Codex Huitzilopochtli after the god who appears at the beginning of the migration history in both manuscripts "as a traveller guiding his people."

The theory of a single common prototype may oversimplify a very complex historiographic problem that has been inadequately studied. It fails, for instance, to explain the remarkable coincidence of a change in artists and style in Codex Telleriano-Remensis at precisely the point where its page composition changes from one format to another. As Robertson (1959) has pointed out, the Telleriano-Remensis appears more as a synthesis of several sources than a copy of a single original. He admits, nevertheless, the possibility of an original comprised of several component parts.

The concordance of the two copies, presented in Table 2, constitutes an outline of the content of Codex Huitzilopochtli and indicates a variety of topics, typical in outline to pictorial manuscripts produced under European patronage. It is probable that the origins of the different sections of this composite manuscript are as diverse as its content. It may well have embodied copies derived from various native originals as well as drawings originally created for this manuscript, both from different regions of the Valley of Mexico and possibly elsewhere. In its cosmological, mythological, and ethnographic sections (represented only in Codex Ríos), this diverse origin may apply to individual pages. In its two copies the glosses may not always refer to the subject which the original artist intended to represent.

The history of Codex Huitzilopochtli must of necessity depend on data from the two copies. In both manuscripts the most recent pictorial entry is the death of Zumárraga, which occurred in 1548; this entry may approximate the earliest date for the completion of the historical part of Codex Huitzilopochtli. The most recent dates in the gloss of Codex Telleriano-Remensis are 1562 and 1563 and are in the handwriting believed to be that of Pedro de los Ríos.

The Italian gloss on Codex Ríos associates Pedro de los Ríos with the compilation of its paintings, identifies him as a Dominican friar, links him with an episode in Mexico in 1566, indicates that he supplied the data for the glossed commentary, and provides incidental biographical data, such as his firsthand knowledge of Oaxaca. Aside from this gloss and similar statements in the glosses on Codex Telleriano-Remensis, only one further datum has been reported about this elusive monk. An apparent report of his death by 1565 (cited in Jiménez Moreno and Mateos Higuera, 1940) conflicts with the 1566 date in Codex Ríos and the presumption that he was present when the codex was painted and annotated in Rome ca. 1570.

If the 1566 date in the codex is correct and Ríos died in 1565, then it may appear that the original of Codex Ríos (i.e., Codex Huitzilopochtli) was taken to Rome by someone else. Whether this original was glossed is uncertain; possibly it was not, and there may have existed a separate written text by Ríos, now unknown, from which the Codex Ríos annotator gleaned his information.

The watermarked paper of Codex Ríos has been reported as having been first made ca. 1569–70. The date of the death of Cardinal Amulio, 1570, with whom a copy of Codex Ríos details is associated, establishes the *terminus ante quem* date for Codex Huitzilopochtli. Mercati (1589) refers to two Vatican Mexican manuscripts in such terms that it may not include Codex Vaticanus B, the only other Mexican pictorial manuscript definitely known to have been in the Vatican in the 16thC. The 1589 refer-

137

TABLE 2—HUITZILOPOCHTLI GROUP

Simplified concordance of the content of the Codices Ríos and Telleriano-Remensis. Foliation cited is that of the editions of 1900 and 1899, respectively. Blank pages are indicated only between sections.

Subject	Codex Ríos	Codex Telleriano-Remensis
1. Cosmological and mythological traditions:		
blank	1r	
The skies and the four suns	1v–7r	
Quetzalcoatl, Toltecs, etc.	7v–11v	
blank	12r	
2. Tonalpohualli:		
Gods, day signs, Nine Lords of the Night	12v–33r	8r–24r*
later gloss		24v
blank	33v–34r	
3. Calendrical tables:		
1558–1619, without drawings	34v–36r	
blank	36v–42r	
4. 18-month calendar:		
Gods for each period	42v–51r	1r–6v*
Nemontemi symbol		7r
later gloss		7v
blank	51v–53v	
5. Ethnographic section:		
Day signs attributed to body parts	54r	
Sacrificial and mortuary customs	54v–57r	
Portraits of Indian types	57v–61r	
Miscellaneous drawing	61v	
blank	62r–66r	
6. Pictorial annals, 1195–1549:		
First major style, 1195–1294	66v–71r	25r–28v*
Second major style, 1295–1549	71v–94r	29r–47r*
blank	94v–95r	
7. Continuation of the annals, 1550–1562:		
1550–1555, without pictorial entries		47v–48r
1556–1562, without pictorial entries	95v–96v	48v–49r
Written historical notices, 1519–1557		49v–50r
later gloss		50v
blank	97r–101v	

* Pages missing in Codex Telleriano-Remensis can be reconstructed from Codex Ríos in all cases.

ence definitely seems to describe a scene present in Codex Ríos, but whether the second manuscript is Codex Huitzilopochtli, Codex Telleriano-Remensis (the history of which is unknown before 1700), Codex Vaticanus B, or some other manuscript is unknown.

The first unequivocal reference to Codex Ríos is of 1596–1600, the date of an inventory (cited by Ehrle, 1900) which gives the Vatican number 3738 and a circumstantial description.

A reference by Acosta (1962; first published in 1590) to an "Anales Mexicanos" in the Vatican only complicates the situation. He seemingly describes a drawing therein which corresponds better to one in the Tovar *Relación* than to any scene in Codex Ríos and he proceeds to state that it was explained to the Vatican librarian by a Jesuit (which Tovar was). Acosta was in Rome in 1588; that his reference published only two years later should be so enigmatic may perhaps be explained by his ownership of the Tovar manuscript at that time.

The foregoing review of the salient historical record concerning Codex Huitzilopochtli indicates that it was a pictorial manuscript containing various originals or copies, that it was probably painted by 1549, that it had additions through 1562, and that it was taken to Rome by 1570. It is associated with an otherwise unknown Dominican friar, who provided the information in the gloss on its most complete copy, Codex Ríos, and who is responsible for one of the handwritings on its now incomplete copy, Codex Telleriano-Remensis. All aspects of this theory require critical review, but the fact that Codex Ríos is a copy of a lost pictorial manuscript related to the copies in Codex Telleriano-Remensis is inescapable.

Bibliographic and other data bearing on the relationship between the two copies have been summarized by Ehrle (1900) in the introduction to his edition of Codex Ríos. The stylistic analysis of Codex Telleriano-Remensis by Robertson (1959) and the postulation by J. E. S. Thompson (1941b) are the most pertinent modern contributions to the subject. The discussion by Paso y Troncoso (1898b) embodies important observations and treats the history of Codex Telleriano-Remensis in detail. Other sources treating both manuscripts and their interrelationships are listed below.

The two calendrical sections common to both manuscripts are treated in many general calendrical studies. The comparative studies by Seler (1899a, 1899b) on the 18-

month calendar and his commentaries on Tonalamatl Aubin (1900; English translation, 1900–01) and Codex Borgia (1904–09; Spanish translation, 1963) which include detailed treatments of the tonalpohualli section of both manuscripts are the most important of these.

Loc. cit.: Ehrle, 1900; Jiménez Moreno and Mateos Higuera, 1940, p. 72; Robertson, 1959, pp. 107–15, pls. 10, 27–29.

Comparative studies: Beauvois, 1886; Charency, 1859; Chavero, 1903a, pp. 5–12; Paso y Troncoso, 1898b, pp. 60–61, 332–59; Reina, 1924–27; J. E. S. Thompson, 1941b.

Other: Acosta, 1962, p. 354 (1590, bk. 7, chap. 19); Mercati, 1589, p. 96; J. F. Ramírez, 1945b.

Calendrical sections: Seler, 1899a; 1899b; 1900; 1900–01; 1904–09, chap. 23; 1963, chap. 23.

146

Huitznahuac Calpulli, Genealogy of. Genealogía de un noble Azteca. British Museum Ethnological Document 1386. Ex–Christy collection. Unpublished. Genealogical. Central Mexico. 16th or 17th C. European paper. Dimensions not determined.

Late style, simple genealogy of about 40 persons in eight generations. The Nahuatl gloss mentions Acolman, Tlacopan, and Tlaqualtzinco. Huitznahuac is a common designation of wards or barrios in the Valley of Mexico and perhaps elsewhere as well.

Unpublished notes on the document by C. A. Burland are in the Ethnological Documents file of the BM. Except for brief citations in the catalog literature there is no bibliography.

Bibliography: None.

❖❖❖

HUMBOLDT FRAGMENTS. Some, if not all, of the 16 manuscripts, representing 12 different documents, described separately below, were purchased by Baron Alexander von Humboldt at a sale of manuscripts from the León y Gama collection in Mexico in 1803 and presented to the Royal Library of Berlin in 1806. All are believed to have been in the Boturini collection. Fragments 2–16 comprise MS Amer. 1 in the Deutsche Staatsbibliothek in East Berlin. Fragment 1 (MS Amer. 2) is on deposit in the Staatsbibliothek Stiftung Preussischer Kulturbesitz in West Berlin. Photographs of all the fragments have been beautifully published in a heliogravure atlas (*Historische Hieroglyphen*, 1892). There is a separate commentary by Seler (1893). The 1893 commentary has been translated into English (Seler, 1904f) and illustrated by copies, apparently by von den Steinen. The revision of the 1893 commentary (Seler, 1902e; reprinted 1960–61) does not reproduce all the fragments. Details, in color, of Fragments 1, 2, 8, and 10–14 and the entirety of Fragments 3, 6, and 16 were published by Humboldt (1810). The paper of the manuscripts is analyzed by Schwede (1916). Additional bibliography is given under the individual entries.

Publication: *Historische Hieroglyphen*, 1892; Seler, 1893, 1902e, 1904f.

Other: Humboldt, 1810, pp. 51–56, 234–38, 283, pls. 12, 36, 38, 57; Schwede, 1916; Valentini, 1893, 1895.

147

—— *Humboldt Fragment 1.* Codex Humboldt. Codex Berlin. SSPK MS Amer. 2. See above for history. Published. Economic (tribute). Tlapa, Guerrero. 16th C. Amatl paper screenfold painted on one side. 15 leaves. 28.5 × 24.5 cm., approx. (published width of 8 cm. is an error).

The screenfold, which reads vertically, records the tribute in gold, cloth, and other items for a 19-year period. The tribute for each year is divided into four parts corresponding to each of four months of the native year. Occasional drawings of Indian

rulers and place glyphs are included. The year-bearer days and their numbers used in year dates vary from the normal or Aztec system.

The manuscript is a continuation of the reverse side of Códice de Azoyu no. 2 (q.v.) but the (four?) pages that would connect the two manuscripts are lost. Códice de Azoyu no. 2 contains the beginning of the document, with the place glyph for Tlapa, and apparently presents 12 years of the tribute. The two manuscripts, together with the missing pages, embrace a period of 36 years, a period that has been tentatively equated with the years 1487–1522.

The commentary by Seler on the excellent photographic reproduction of 1892 (see above) does not treat the related Códice de Azoyu no. 2 which was not discovered until 1940. A colored reproduction of the manuscript is given by Kingsborough (1831–48). Barlow (1943d) comments on the month glyphs, and Beyer (1910) discusses the identification of one of the personal name glyphs. Kubler and Gibson (1951) treat chronological implications of both manuscripts. See Códice de Azoyu no. 2 for further comment.

Additional publication: Kingsborough, 1831–48, 15 pls. in vol. 2.

Other: Barlow, 1943d; Beyer, 1910.

Brief descriptions: Alcina Franch, 1955, p. 431; Kubler and Gibson, 1951, pp. 63–64.

148

—— *Humboldt Fragment 2.* Généalogie des Princes d'Azcapotzalco. DSB in MS Amer. 1. See above for history. Published. Economic (property plans). Valley of Mexico. After 1565. Amatl paper. 68 × 40 cm.

Plan of property divided into parallel strips in which are drawings of heads of individuals identified by Nahuatl glosses and personal name glyphs. Identified persons appear to include Cuauhtemoc, Moctezuma, and Tehuetzquititzin. A gloss refers to the year 1565. The significance of the document has not been determined.

In addition to the bibliography common to the Humboldt Fragments as a whole (see above), Kingsborough (1831–48) gives a version in color, and Schmieder (1930) provides an interpretive tracing.

Additional publication: Kingsborough, 1831–48, 3 plates in vol. 2.

Other: Schmieder, 1930, pp. 28–29, 84, plan 2.

❖❖❖

—— *Humboldt Fragments 3 and 4. See* Códice de Huamantla, Fragments 7 and 8.

149

—— *Humboldt Fragment 5.* DSB in MS Amer. 1. See above for history. Published. Economic (census). Central Mexico. 16thC. Amatl paper. 42 × 15.5 cm.

Simple and incomplete fragment divided into horizontal divisions in which are drawings of human heads and name glyphs. One place glyph is identified as Tezontepec by the gloss. See Humboldt Fragments, above, for bibliography.

150

—— *Humboldt Fragment 6.* DSB in MS Amer. 1. See above for history. Published. Economic (property plans). Texcoco, Mexico. ca. 1546. Amatl paper. 20 × 21 cm.

Plan of buildings within a precinct with native measurements (misinterpreted by Seler as population figures) is surrounded by drawings of seven Indians and Spaniards. Above the plan is the place glyph for Oxtoticpac and the plan is glossed "Ciudad de Tetzcuco." An almost identical plan, representing the same property, appears on the Oztoticpac Lands Map (q.v.).

For bibliography, see Humboldt Fragments, above. An excellent photograph is given by Robertson (1959). Cline (1966a)

compares the document with the Oztoticpac Lands Map and also provides a reproduction. Further commentary and interpretation are given in Cline (1968).

Additional publication: Cline, 1966a, 1968; Robertson, 1959, pl. 68.

❖❖❖

—— *Humboldt Fragment 7. See* MIZQUIAHUALA SALES RECEIPTS: Humboldt Fragment 7.

151

—— *Humboldt Fragment 8.* DSB in MS Amer. 1. See above for history. Published. Economic (cadastral). Central Mexico. 16thC. Amatl paper. 22 × 33 cm.

Plan of measured units of property drawn opposite heads of Indians with personal name glyphs. Content and organization of pictorial elements are comparable to other manuscripts of the Vergara Group (q.v.).

For bibliography see Humboldt Fragments, above. A detail from the drawing is given by Gibson (1964a).

Additional partial publication: Gibson, 1964a, pl. 10, top.

152

—— *Humboldt Fragments 9–12.* DSB in MS Amer. 1. See above for history. Published. Economic (tribute). Central Mexico. 16thC. Amatl paper. 4 fragments originally in 2 parts: 98 × 17 and 146.5 × 17 cm.

Drawings of items of tribute and Indians on two vertical strips believed originally to have formed part of a single document but now incomplete.

Bibliography: See Humboldt Fragments, above.

❖❖❖

—— *Humboldt Fragment 13. See* MIZ-

QUIAHUALA SALES RECEIPTS: Humboldt Fragment 13.

153

—— *Humboldt Fragment 14.* DSB in MS Amer. 1. See above for history. Published. Economic (tribute). Central Mexico. ca. 1562. Amatl paper. 34 × 15 cm.

Drawings of cacao beans, turkeys, and other goods and foodstuffs with numerical signs. The single gloss reads "Estancia de Tlatonpan." The manuscript is a fragment of the Rôle des Impôts de Tlatengo (q.v.).

Bibliography: See Humboldt Fragments, above.

154

—— *Humboldt Fragment 15.* DSB in MS Amer. 1. See above for history. Published. Economic (tribute). Central Mexico. 16thC. Amatl paper. 34 × 52 cm.

The heads of 324 turkeys are drawn opposite the heads of six Indians. A missing corner of the fragment may have had 102 further turkeys.

Bibliography: See Humboldt Fragments, above.

❖❖❖

—— *Humboldt Fragment 16.* See Testerian MS of the Deutsche Staatsbibliothek, Census of Testerian MSS (Article 25, no. 817).

155

Idolos del Templo de Huitzilopochtli, Los. Los principales idolos del templo mayor de Mexico. AGN-I 37, exp. 3. Published. Miscellaneous. Mexico City, D.F. 1539. Native paper. Dimensions not determined.

The drawing is part of an inquisitorial process concerning charges of idolatry and shows ceremonial objects, individuals named in the process, and five bundles wrapped in cloth representing the idols removed from the main temple of Tenochtitlan at the time of the conquest.

An inadequate photograph and a discussion of the process have been published on two occasions by Nuttall (1911a, 1911b); her article in French (1911a) is more detailed. Greenleaf (1961) gives a better reproduction of the drawing and comments on the trial. The text of the process, but not the drawing, is published in *Procesos de Indios* (1912).

Publication: Greenleaf, 1961, pp. 58–60, plate facing p. 52; Nuttall, 1911a, 1911b.

Other: *Procesos de Indios*, 1912, pp. 115–40.

156

Igualtepec, Genealogy of the Cacique of. Unknown. Unpublished. Genealogical. San Juan Igualtepec, ex-district of Silcayoapan, Western Oaxaca. 16thC. European paper. Dimensions unknown.

The document is known only through a single photograph in the Gates collection at BYU. The upper half is a three-generation genealogy showing the two wives and descendants of Don Diego, cacique of Igualtepec (also called Yoaltepec in the text). There are no hieroglyphs or calendrical names. A Spanish text at the bottom reveals that the manuscript concerns a petition for a dispensation for two cousins to marry. Both are shown in the genealogy; one is the cacique of Sochiquilazala.

Bibliography: None.

157

Ihuitlan, Santiago, Lienzo de. Brooklyn Museum. Ex–William Randolph Hearst collection. Published. Cartographic-historical. Santiago Ihuitlan (Plumas), ex-district of Coixtlahuaca, Western Oaxaca. 16thC. Cloth. 244 × 152 cm.

The content is almost entirely genealogical; it has 171 drawings of men and women, including a few gods or idols. Two of the longest genealogies are those of the dynasties of Coixtlahuaca and Ihuitlan. Most of the place glyphs are identified by Nahuatl inscriptions. Many persons depicted also appear on Lienzo Antonio de León.

Caso (1961) gives commentary and photographic reproduction. It is also reproduced in Caso (1965c).

Copy: 19thC copy on cloth in Ihuitlan.

Publication: Caso, 1961, pp. 238–49 and 5 plates; 1965c, fig. 1.

158

Indígena, Códice. Libro de Tributos. UTX, CDG 560. Ex–Genaro García collection. Unpublished. Economic (tribute). Mexico City, D.F. ca. 1550. European paper. 10 leaves. 32 × 21 cm.

Pictorial register, with Spanish glosses, of payments in goods and services by various barrios of Mexico City. Gibson (personal communication) interprets it as charges against the governor, Don Diego de San Francisco Tehuetzquititzin.

Bibliography: None.

159

Indígena, Códice, 1564–65. UTX, CDG 561. Ex–Genaro García collection. Unpublished. Economic (tribute). Mexico City, D.F. 1564–65. European and native paper. 23 leaves. 31 × 21 cm.

Pictorial and Nahuatl receipts for salary and other payments to Indian officials of the native government of Mexico-Tenochtitlan, 1564–65. Drawings are almost entirely of numerical and monetary symbols.

Bibliography: None.

160

Indígenas de algunos pueblos del Marquesado del Valle, Códices, nos. 1–28. AGN-HJ 276, exp. 79, pt. 2. Published. Economic (property plans and tribute). Cuernavaca region, Morelos. 1549. Native paper. 28 separate single-leaf documents. Dimensions vary from 21 × 24 to 48 × 122 cm.

Drawings of lands and tribute from estancias, barrios, and pueblos in the vicinity of Cuernavaca and Jiutepec. The documents are part of litigation between Martín Cortés and Indian principals over the restitution of lands and rents.

Colored copies and transcripts of Spanish glosses are published in *Códices indígenas* (1933), and each document is assigned a number and title. Cline (1963a) provides a general comment and further inventory data. Caso (1963) interprets the pictorial content of drawing no. 27, and Burland (1960) reproduces and comments on a detail of drawing no. 11. The text of the lawsuit itself has not been published.

Publication: *Códices indígenas*, 1933, nos. 1–28.

Other: Burland, 1960, p. 14, fig. 3; Caso, 1963, pp. 27–29, fig. 1; Cline, 1963a.

Brief description: Alcina Franch, 1955, pp. 495–97.

❖❖❖

—— no. 29. *See* Querella criminal contra Don Juan, Cacique de Tehuantepec.

❖❖❖

—— no. 30. *See* HUITZILA: Pintura de las Tierras de Quahunacazco.

❖❖❖

—— no. 31. *See* TEPOTZOTLAN: Los Naturales de los Pueblos de Cuautlalpan, Tepujaco y Xoloc, de la Jurisdicción de Tepotzotlan, Mex., contra su Gobernador, por malos Tratamientos y pago de Tributos (1552).

❖❖❖

—— no. 32. *See* Códice de Coetzala.

161

Itzcuintepec, Papers of. Papers of Itzcuintlan. Códice de Tulantzinco. Códice de Julancingo. British Museum, Egerton MSS 2896 (3 sheets) and 2897 (11 sheets). Partially published. Historical and genealogical. Northern Puebla. 16thC. Native paper. 14 sheets. Dimensions vary between 85 × 39 and 43 × 22 cm.

The 14 fragments, all of which share aspects of the crude and distinctive style (forms) of the Lienzo de Metlatoyuca, are named after the place sign for Itzcuintepec, which is prominent in a number of the fragments. Most fragments depict parts of long genealogies of Indians with both personal and calendrical name glyphs. Historical scenes with native dates also appear; in one fragment (Egerton MS 2896, B) four Indians are shooting arrows at a target suspended between two poles. One of several Nahuatl glosses is a long list of place names. Some of the fragments fit together (Egerton MSS 2896, B and C; 2897, Fragments 3, 5, 6, 8, 9, and 10) so that perhaps eight manuscripts are represented by the collection. Drawings also appear on the reverse of Egerton MS 2897, Fragment 7.

One fragment (Egerton MS 2897, Fragment 1), typical of the style but not of the content of the collection, has been published and described by Burland (1960). Two of the fragments (Egerton MS 2897, Fragments 2 and 4) are published by Nicholson (1966d).

An incomplete set of photographs of the Papers (together with photographs of the Lienzo de Tecciztlan y Tequatepec), attributed to T. Maler, was listed in the Wilkinson sale catalog of 1915 (American Art Association, 1915) under the title "Códice de Julancingo." These photographs are now in the Peabody Museum Library, Cambridge, cataloged as the "Códice de Tulantzinco." A complete set of excellent photostats is in the Manuscripts Division, Library of Congress.

Partial publication: Burland, 1960, pp. 12–13, fig. 2; Nicholson, 1966d, figs. 14, 15.

Brief mention: Burland, 1955b, p. 37, note 4; p. 42, note 23.

144

Other: American Art Association, 1915, no. 167.

162 (fig. 39)

Ixcatlan, San Pedro, Lienzo de. Lienzo de San Pedro Ixcatlan–San Miguel Soyaltepec. Lienzo de Tuxtepec. Princeton University Library. Ex–Mariano Espinosa and C. C. James collections. Published. Cartographic-historical. San Pedro Ixcatlan, ex-district of Tuxtepec, Northern Oaxaca. 18thC (?). Cloth. 128 × 138 cm.

The lienzo, a map of a region around San Pedro Ixcatlan, shows rivers and trees and has a peripheral border of glossed and crudely drawn place signs. A scene at the center with a Nahuatl text depicts Juan Marqués (one of the first Spanish conquerors of the region), the baptism of an Indian, and a 16thC encomendero.

The PML copy is reproduced with a study of its cartographic and historical content by Cline (1964, 1966b). The document was utilized in a study of the Mazatecs by M. Espinosa (1910, 1961). The copy is briefly mentioned in two publications of the Escuela Internacional de Arqueología y Etnología Americanas (Escuela Internacional, 1913a, 1913b).

Copy: Copy of 1912, PML.

Publication: Cline, 1964, pp. 403–08, 418–20, figs. 6–8; 1966b, pp. 273–79, 293–94, figs. 1–2.

Other: Escuela Internacional, 1913a, p. 5; 1913b, p. xix; M. Espinosa, 1910, pp. 49–58; 1961, pp. 93–107.

163

Ixcatlan, Santa Maria, Mapa de. Lienzo de Santa Maria Ichcatla. Lienzo Seler no. 1. Seler collection; believed lost. Ex–Martínez Gracida collection. Unpublished. Unavailable. Santa Maria Ixcatlan, ex-district of Teotitlan, Western Oaxaca. 16thC (?). European paper. 170 × 310 cm.

The document is known only through Lehmann's (1905a) brief description, which allows its provenience to be identified although Lehmann erroneously classified it as Mazatec. It is said to have depicted numerous villages and historical scenes. Caso (personal communication) suggests that the glosses described by Lehmann are in Chocho-Popoloca or Ixcatec.

Brief descriptions: Alcina Franch, 1955, p. 500; Lehmann, 1905a, p. 278.

164 (fig. 40)

Ixcatlan, Santa Maria, Plano topográfico de, Año de 1870. Pueblo. Unpublished. Cartographic. Santa Maria Ixcatlan, exdistrict of Teotitlan, Western Oaxaca. 1870. Modern paper (?). Dimensions unknown.

The map is a modern drawing showing the church of Ixcatlan within a rectangle around which are conventional symbols and names for the boundaries of the town. Surrounding this are conventionalized representations of the churches of neighboring localities, including Coixtlahuaca, Huautla, and Quiotepec. Although the map does not exhibit any traditional symbols, it is included in the census for its possible dependence on a native prototype for its composition.

The map, together with another unpublished map from the town, is apparently mentioned by Cook (1958). A photocopy is in the LC/HF collection.

Brief mention: Cook, 1958, p. 3.

165 (fig. 41)

Ixcatlan, Santa Maria, Plan topographique de. BNP 103. Ex–Aubin collection. Unpublished. Cartographic. Santa Maria Ixcatlan, ex-district of Teotitlan, Western Oaxaca. 1580. European paper. 60 × 43 cm.

Map showing Ixcatlan and its boundaries (with place glyphs) between Coixtlahuaca and Huautla. Other pictorial detail and Spanish glosses refer to disputed settlement in a locality named Axumulco. Two Indians with hieroglyphic calendrical names are shown.

Boban (1891) gives brief description and partial palaeography. A long Spanish text of 1580 on the reverse is unpublished.

Brief description: Boban, 1891, 2, pp. 277–79.

166

Ixhuatan, Mapa de. Unknown. Unpublished. Unavailable. San Francisco Ixhuatan, ex-district of Juchitan, Eastern Oaxaca. Date and physical description unknown.

The existence of the manuscript is known only through an entry in an unpublished diary kept by Frederick Starr during a trip through southern Mexico in 1901 (Starr, MS). It is described through hearsay as "an interesting map of all the Huave lands at Ixhuatan" that may have been taken to Oaxaca by a Manuel Gómez. It is listed as an unverified Huave pictorial by Cline (1966c).

Brief mention: Cline, 1966c, app. 2, no. 47; Starr, MS, p. 50.

167

Ixhuatepec, Códice de. Colección Chavero no. 5. Pleito de Tierras. American Museum of Natural History, N.Y., in Codex Chavero ff. 25v–33r. Ex–J. F. Ramírez (?) and Chavero collections. Published. Economic (land titles). Mexico City–Tlatelolco, D.F., region or San Juan Ixhuatepec, Mexico. 18thC (?). Watermarked European paper. 9 leaves. 30 × 21 cm.

Fifteen of the 16 utilized pages of the manuscript are a page-by-page version of ff. 3r and 4r–10v of Codex Cozcatzin (q.v.), with only minor variations. Page 1 of the manuscript probably corresponds to a lost page of Codex Cozcatzin. For related manuscripts see Colección Chavero no. 4 and Ixhuatepec Group.

The document is a pictorial and hieroglyphic listing of 60 place names and persons with accompanying Spanish texts. The 60 places represent lands awarded by Itzcoatl in 1439. The document reflects

16thC and later litigation over their ownership.

The only edition, in unjustified tira format, omits the Spanish texts and is only superficially described by its editor (Chavero, 1901c). Chavero (n.d.) briefly refers to it and illustrates two details. All of its place glyphs were published by Peñafiel (1897c) under the title "Pleito de Tierras."

Copies: A transcript of the texts is apparently contained in MNA/AH Col. Ant. MS 201 under the title "Pleito sobre Tierras."

Publication: Chavero, 1901c, pp. 15–16, 34–36, folded plate.

Other: Chavero, n.d., pp. xxvi, 638; Peñafiel, 1897c, passim.

❖❖❖

IXHUATEPEC GROUP. Five manuscripts described separately in the census: Plano en Papel de Amate, Colección Chavero no. 4 (especially its parts 3 and 4), Codex Cozcatzin, Códice de Ixhuatepec, and Títulos de Santa Isabel Tola. Their common features concern lands which were awarded by Itzcoatl ca. 1438–39 and which in the 16thC and later were the subject of litigation. The lands appear to be located in the Tlatelolco–Santa Isabel Tola–San Juan Ixhuatepec region of the Valley of Mexico. Future investigations should include an attempt to locate further documentation which might exist in the AGN.

168

Ixil, The Book of Chilam Balam of. Códice de Ixil. MNA 35-67. Ex–Carrillo y Ancona, Cepeda Library (Merida), and Laura Temple collections. Partially published. Miscellaneous and calendrical. Ixil, Yucatan. 18thC. European paper. 44 leaves. 21.5 × 14.6 cm.

The drawings are of Maya glyphs, calendar wheels, and nontraditional illustrations for each sign of the zodiac. Two of the calendar wheels have been published a number of times, most recently by Glass (1964), who gives the only photographic reproduction from the original. Other reproductions, from copies, include those by Chavero (n.d.) and by Bowditch (1910). A copy of the same two wheels is in Codex Pérez (no. 249) and appears in the 1949 edition of that work.

See Article 27B, no. 1147, for general comment on the Books of Chilam Balam and for further data on this manuscript.

Publication of two of the calendar wheels: Bowditch, 1910, pp. 327–28, fig. 62; Chavero, n.d., p. 440; Glass, 1964, p. 120, pl. 70.

169

Ixtacmaxtitlan, Une Émeute parmi les Indigènes d'. BNP 75. Ex–Aubin collection. Partially published. Miscellaneous. Ixtacmaxtitlan, Puebla. ca. 1564. European paper. 31 × 22 cm. and 53 leaves of Spanish text.

The drawing shows Indians fighting and being punished. These events, related to problems of civil congregation, are shown as occurring within and outside the walls of a Franciscan convent, a plan of which is part of the drawing.

Boban (1891) gives a photoreproduction of the drawing and an extract from the accompanying text. A much reduced photograph of the drawing is given by Kubler (1948).

Partial publication: Kubler, 1948, p. 138, fig. 34; Boban, 1891, 2: 169–70, pl. 75.

170

Ixtepeji, Santa Catarina, Códice de. Unknown. Unpublished. Unavailable. Santa Catarina Ixtepeji, ex-district of Ixtlan, Eastern Oaxaca. Date unknown. Skin. 6–8 m. long.

Pérez García (1956) reports a local tradition about a manuscript on skin, formerly in the village but sold about 1908–11 to a German consul through a lawyer named José Ruíz Jiménez. Cline (1966c) lists it as an unverified Zapotec pictorial.

Bibliography: Cline, 1966c, app. 2, no. 48; Pérez García, 1956, 1: 140.

❖❖❖

IXTLILXOCHITL, CODEX. (BNP 65-71.) The codex consists of three unrelated parts, two of which are pictorial and are listed below. The present foliation on the manuscript continues the numeration on the manuscript of the *Historia de Tlaxcala* (BNP 210) by Muñoz Camargo, with which it was bound when owned by Boturini. Part 3 of the codex is described in Article 27B, no. 1101.

171

Ixtlilxochitl, Codex, part 1. Aubin'schen Handschrift. Códice geroglífico de Mr. Aubin. Códice Goupil. BNP 65-71 (ff. 94–104). Ex–Sigüenza y Góngora, Boturini, and Aubin collections. Published. Ritual-calendrical. Valley of Mexico. 16th C. European paper. 11 leaves. 31 × 21 cm.

Contains Spanish texts and drawings illustrative of the gods and ceremonies of 17 of the 18 months of the 365-day year (omitted text and drawing are not of the same ceremony), two drawings and texts of gods, and two of mortuary customs. This material is probably a copy of corresponding texts and drawings in Codex Magliabecchiano (ff. 28v–46r, 60v–62r, 66v–68r). There are minor differences in the two texts, and the drawings in Codex Ixtlilxochitl are more acculturated. Some month names are given in Otomi and in an unidentified language as well as in Nahuatl. Attributions of the codex to Ixtlilxochitl (León y Gama, 1832) or to Sigüenza y Góngora (Robertson, 1959) are speculative. For further relationships see Magliabecchiano Group.

Lithographed copies of the drawings by Desportes have been published in two versions (Aubin, n.d.*b*, and Durán, 1867–80), each without the texts. Photographs of two pages and transcripts of all the texts are given by Boban (1891). Seler (1899a) discusses and reproduces the 17 monthly ceremony drawings (after the Desportes lithographs). Folio 94v has not been described but is presumably blank. See Magliabecchiano Group for further bibliography.

Copies: See Codex Veytia. A 19thC transcript of the text from the J. F. Ramírez collection is in MNA/AH.

Publication: Aubin, n.d.*b*; Durán, 1867–80, atlas, appendix, pls. 1–14.

Descriptions and studies: Boban, 1891, 2: 114–31, pl. 65; Robertson, 1959, pp. 131–33; Seler, 1899a.

Other: Carrasco Pizana, 1950, pp. 179–83; Chavero, 1880, pp. 163–69 and passim; León y Gama, 1832, 2: 78; Soustelle, 1937, pp. 524–25.

Brief description: Kubler and Gibson, 1951, pp. 58–59.

172 (figs. 42, 43)

Ixtlilxochitl, Codex, part 2. Illustrations for the Relación de Texcoco by Juan Bautista Pomar. BNP 65-71 (ff. 105–112, with 2 leaves missing). Ex–Sigüenza y Góngora, Boturini, and Aubin collections. Published. Ethnographic. Texcoco, Mexico. 1582(?). European paper. 6 leaves. 31 × 21 cm.

Six drawings: four full-length portraits of Indians, including Nezahualcoyotl and Nezahualpilli, rulers of Texcoco; a similarly executed drawing of the god Tlaloc; and a drawing of the double pyramid-temple at Texcoco. The latter two have on their reverse sides descriptive texts which are less corrupt versions of substantially identical passages in the Relación de Texcoco by Pomar. The drawings may be leaves from a lost Pomar manuscript or from a manuscript utilized by him. Attributions of the drawings and texts to Ixtlilxochitl are unfounded.

Two further drawings, now lost from the manuscript, survive through copies. The copy of the drawing of the god Huitzilopochtli is in Codex Veytia (q.v.). A drawing of Nezahualpilli, seated on a throne, was copied by Gemelli Careri in 1697 and published by him in 1700. Here he misidentified Nezahualpilli as Moctezuma. Another drawing published by Gemelli ("Soldato Mexicano") may also derive from this manuscript. The Pomar Relación refers to at least six and possibly eight drawings, of which only three (Huitzilopochtli, Tlaloc, and the Texcoco pyramid) may be identified securely with extant versions.

The six drawings and the two texts in the BNP manuscript have been published and described by Boban (1891). The drawing of Tlaloc, misidentified as Huitzilopochtli, was published by Moxó (1828). The drawings of Tlaloc and the Texcoco pyramid are reproduced by Moxó (1837, 1839), by Aubin (n.d.*b*), and in Durán (1867–80). Copies of the four portraits in the BNP manuscript, the Tlaloc drawing, and the two further drawings mentioned above were published with erroneous captions by Gemelli Careri (1699–1700). Kingsborough (1831–48) reprints some of the Gemelli plates. Peñafiel (1903c) reprints most of the Boban and Gemelli plates. For reproductions of the Huitzilopochtli drawing see Codex Veytia. The drawing of the Texcoco pyramid has been published many times, usually identified as depicting the pyramid of Tenochtitlan.

The connection between the drawings and the Pomar text was first noted by Chavero (1903b); the subject is discussed by J. E. S. Thompson (1941a) and by Robertson (1959). The latter also discusses the subject of full-figure portraiture. The seated portrait of Nezahualpilli is described by Boturini (1746). A copy of the Pomar Relación was first published by García Icazbalceta (1886–92).

Copies: See Codex Veytia. Present location of a copy or partial copy by León y Gama is unknown. Partial copies made before 1790 are in Diego García Panes, *Teatro de la Nueva España*, vol. 6, MS, BNMex.

148

Whether these are based on the Gemelli reproductions or on the original has not been determined.

Publication: Boban, 1891, 2: 114–39, pls. 66–71.

Partial publication: Aubin, n.d.*b*; Durán, 1867–80, atlas, appendix, pls. 15–16; Gemelli Careri, 1699–1700, 6: 68–80; Kingsborough, 1831–48, vol. 4; Moxó, 1828, vol. 1, facing p. 158; 1837, facing pp. 70 and 108; 1839, facing pp. 86 and 132; Peñafiel, 1903c, pls. 186–91.

Studies: Robertson, 1959, pp. 130–33, 149–51, 201–02, pl. 52; J. E. S. Thompson, 1941a.

Other: Boturini, 1746, 1: 12, 76, 84; Chavero, 1903b, pp. 285–86; García Icazbalceta, 1886–92, 3: 1–69.

173

Ixtlilxochitl, Don Felipe, Genealogía de. BNMex. Ex–Boturini collection. Published. Genealogical. Tepeaca (?), Puebla. 16thC. European paper. 34.5 × 23.5 cm.

The drawing shows an Indian seated on a throne, a woman seated on a mat, and three persons above a building (in unusual perspective) in the background. A gloss on the mount reads "Arbol genealógico del cacicasgo de D. Felipe Ixtlilsochil en el pueblo de Tepecapa."

R. Moreno (1966) provides photoreproduction, description, and transcript of Nahuatl glosses.

Publication: R. Moreno, 1966, pp. 70–72.

Brief descriptions: Carreño, 1950, p. 15; Mena, 1923: 60, no. 17.

174

Jicayan, San Pedro, Lienzo de. Pueblo. Unpublished. Cartographic-historical. San Pedro Jicayan, ex-district of Jamiltepec, Western Oaxaca. 16thC. Cloth. Dimensions unknown but photographs suggest about 150 × 110 cm.

The lienzo depicts the boundaries of Jicayan and over 40 place glyphs, at least

30 of which are glossed in Mixtec. These form an irregular circle around a central detail composed of a temple and place glyph, a date, and a seated Indian with a calendrical name.

Although the lienzo has not previously been described, the Mixtec glosses have been published by M. E. Smith (1963). Poor color transparencies are in INAH/AF.

Bibliography: M. E. Smith, 1963, pp. 281–83; 1966a.

175

JOPANAQUE, SAN MATEO: Property plan and genealogy. MNA/AH Col. Ant. 757-A. Unpublished. Economic (property plans) and genealogical. San Mateo Jopanque (also Hopanac or Xopanac, northwest of Huexotzingo), Puebla. ca. 1567. European paper, 20 × 31 cm. (property plan), and native paper, 20 × 66 cm. (genealogy), being ff. 82v and 147, respectively, of a larger written document of 518 leaves.

The two pictorial sheets are a plan of properties with a Nahuatl text dated 1567, place glyphs, and numerical symbols. The name Andrés de Quesada appears frequently. The other is a genealogy of approximately 33 Indians with personal name glyphs.

The two drawings are contained in a larger compilation containing 16thC through 18thC Nahuatl and Spanish documents relating to the Hacienda of San Mateo Jopanaque owned by Gabriel de Alvarado and, later, his son Bartolomé Alvarado.

Bibliography: None.

176

Joyas de Martín Ocelotl, Las. AGN-I 37, exp. 4. Published. Miscellaneous. Tlatelolco, D.F. ca. 1540. Native paper. Number of leaves and dimensions not determined.

The possessions of Martín Ocelotl, convicted of witchcraft in 1536–37, were confiscated by the Inquisition in 1540. Included in the process of the trial are drawings of gold jewelry, cloth, and pottery.

The drawings are reproduced and discussed in Barlow (1954b). The text of the process, but not the drawings, is published in *Procesos de Indios* (1912).

Publication: Barlow, 1954b.

Other: *Procesos de Indios*, 1912, pp. 17–51.

177

Jucutacato, Lienzo de (also Cucutacato, Tucutacato, and Xucutacato). Lienzo de Tiripetio. Lienzo de Xiuhquilan. Lienzo del Reino de Michoacan. Sociedad Mexicana de Geografía y Estadística. Ex-García Abarca collection. Published. Cartographic-historical. Jucutacato or Xiuhquilan, Michoacan. 16thC. Cloth. 203 × 263 cm.

Depicts a migration itinerary from Chalchihuitlapazco through numerous localities, including Tenochtitlan to Xiuhquilan from whence four routes continue, one to Tzintzuntzan-Patzcuaro. Each locality on the route is represented by a hill or church drawn within adjoining rectangular compartments of varying sizes. Drawings of persons, symbols, and Nahuatl glosses are among lesser details.

The lienzo was first reported by Rea (1643). Interpretations vary considerably. Jiménez Moreno (1948), who does not give a reproduction, maps most of the localities and interprets it as representing the migration of a Nahua metallurgical guild in search of mines. Mendizábal (1926) has interpreted it as referring to the arrival of Spanish friars. Corona Núñez (1951) interprets it as the ancient history of the inhabitants of Jiquilpan. Other detailed studies are by Seler (1908a) and two different ones by N. León (1889b; 1903–04, reprinted 1904a). Many of the works listed below reproduce copies in black and red, the only colors on the original. A selected bibliography is given here.

Copies: Late 19thC copy, MNA 35-5. Modern copy, MNA 35-5A (the latter reproduced by Glass, 1964).

Selected studies: Corona Núñez, 1951; Jiménez Moreno, 1948, pp. 151–55, map at end of volume; N. León, 1889b; 1903–04, passim, pl. 2; 1904a, passim, pl. 2; Mendizábal, 1926, 1946; Seler, 1908a, pp. 42–61.

Lesser references: Chavero, n.d., p. 892; Corona Núñez, 1942a; 1942b, pp. 90–95; Rea, lib. 1, cap. 5; Rojas González, 1940, pp. 16–19.

Brief descriptions: Alcina Franch, 1955, pp. 455–56; Glass, 1964, p. 43, pl. 7; Mateos Higuera, 1948b, pp. 160–63; Paso y Troncoso, 1892–93, 1: 245–49; Tamayo and Alcorta, 1941, pp. 18–19, no. 5.

178

Judiciaire de 1534, Manuscrit. Mappe inédite de 1534. Royal Ontario Museum, Toronto. Ex–Kalt and Capitan collections. Published. Economic (tribute). Totolapa, Morelos. 1534. Native paper. 75 × 23 cm.

Drawings of typical items of tribute, with a Spanish text concerning a grievance between Totolapa and Atlatlauca, Morelos.

Both sides of the document are studied and reproduced photographically by Capitan (1923), a work that supersedes his earlier publications.

Publication: Capitan, 1923.

Other: Capitan, 1911, 1912.

179

Kaua, The Book of Chilam Balam of. Códice de Kaua. Tratado de las 7 Planetas y otro de Medicinarum . . . , 1789. Princeton University Library (19 leaves, ex–Gates) and unknown (122 leaves). Ex–Carlos María Pacheco (of Hocaba, Yucatan), Carrillo y Ancona, and Cepeda Library (Merida) collections. Partially published. Ritual-calendrical and miscellaneous. Kaua, Yucatan. 18thC. European paper. 141 leaves. 20 × 15 cm.

Illustrations include cosmological subjects (heavens, skies, planets, sun, moon, eclipses), various calendar wheels, drawings depicting European months and the zodiac, and a Maya version of a Spanish romance. Most of these illustrations are in no recognizable native traditional style. Roys (1965) reproduces and interprets one drawing of a disease from the manuscript. One of the zodiacal drawings is reproduced in the second Wilkinson sale catalog (American Art Association, 1915).

More relevant to this census are a calendar wheel and drawings depicting the 13 Lords of the Katuns, the latter illustrating a Maya prophetic-historical text. Both of them are in the portion of the manuscript now in PUL and both are published by Gates (1931). The calendar wheel has been published from an inaccurate copy by Bowditch (1910).

See Article 27B, no. 1148, for general comment on the Books of Chilam Balam and for further data on this manuscript.

Works cited: American Art Association, 1915, no. 156; Bowditch, 1910, pp. 330–31, fig. 64; Gates, 1931; Roys, 1965, p. xi, plate facing p. 66.

180

Kekchi Suit of 1611, Map from a. Local archive of San Pedro Carcha, Guatemala (in 1897). Published. Cartographic. Coban region, Guatemala. 1611. Physical description unpublished.

One of two maps in a lawsuit of 1611 between the towns of San Pedro Carcha and San Juan Chameleco, both near Coban, over the possession of lands, shows Indian tradition only in the use of footprints to indicate roads. See *Libro antiguo de Carcha* (Article 27B, no. 1173) for comment on associated text.

Sapper (1897) describes the lawsuit document and publishes a copy of one of the two maps. His illustration is reprinted by Miles (1957).

Publication: Sapper, 1897; Miles, 1957, fig. 4.

181

Kingsborough, Codex. Memorial de los Indios de Tepetlaoztoc. Códice de Tepetlaoxtoc. British Museum, Add. MSS 13964 (part). Ex–"Biblioteca del Rey" (Spain), Renouard, and Kingsborough collections. Published. Historical, economic (tribute), and cartographic. Tepetlaoztoc, Mexico. ca. 1555. European paper. 72 leaves. 29.8 × 21.5 cm.

The codex is related to a lawsuit held before the Council of Indies between the Indians of Tepetlaoztoc and the encomendero, Juan Velásquez de Salazar. Part 1 (ff. 1–7) contains two maps of the Tepetlaoztoc region and introductory material relating to preconquest history, tribute, genealogy, and social organization. Part 2 (ff. 8–39) presents a yearly record of the tribute and other goods and services provided to various encomenderos by the Indians from 1522/23 through 1550/51. Part 3 (ff. 40–46r) contains a summary of selected items in part 2 and a presentation of the tribute and other matters for the years 1551/52 through 1553/54. Part 4 (ff. 46v–72r) recapitulates the *servicio cotidiano* part of the tribute for the years 1527/28 through 1550/51. Folio 72v has a textual conclusion to the document and a petition. The Spanish text is contemporary with the drawings. Discontinuities in two of the three foliations on the codex do not reflect missing pages.

Most copies of the photographic edition (Paso y Troncoso, 1912) are defective and lack 16 leaves of the reproduction. Both maps from the codex are reproduced by Guzmán (1939b), who interprets the place glyphs, and by Robertson (1959). Reproductions of one of the maps are contained in Burland (1947a), Paso y Troncoso (1913), and, from the Madrid copy, in Léon de Rosny (1881a) and Keleman (1943). Paso y Troncoso (1913) and Seler (1915)

comment on general aspects of the codex. Breton (1919) analyzes place glyphs from the codex. Gibson (1964a) treats the history of the Tepetlaoztoc encomienda.

Copies: A copy of at least two pages of the manuscript was in the now-defunct Museum of Artillery, Madrid, in 1880. Watercolor copy in PML. Photographed by Gates (see Article 28, Appendix A, for location of copies).

Publication: Paso y Troncoso, 1912.

Publications relating to the maps: Burland, 1947a; Guzmán, 1939b; Keleman, 1943, 2: pl. 276c; Robertson, 1959, pp. 185–86, pls. 83–84; Léon de Rosny, 1881a, pp. 69–70, pl. 2.

General descriptions: Paso y Troncoso, 1913; Seler, 1915, pp. 155–67, figs. 3–15, 18–19.

Other: Breton, 1919; Gibson, 1964a, pp. 78–80, 429; González de Barcia, 1737–38, 2: 700; Hunter, 1917; *Noticias relativas*, 1944, pp. 8–24.

Brief description: Alcina Franch, 1955, p. 455.

182

Lachiyoo, Mapa de. MNA 35-95. Published. Cartographic. Eastern Oaxaca. 18thC (?). European paper. 107 × 85 cm.

The map is a painting of a landscape showing two churches, 12 chapels, cattle, trees, roads, a river with aquatic birds, and mountains. Neither the style nor the artistic forms are in the native tradition; it is listed here only because it forms part of a codex collection and has been included in previous listings.

Glass (1964) gives brief description and a photoreproduction.

Publication: Glass, 1964, p. 149, pl. 102.

183

Land Transfer Manuscript. Unknown. Unpublished. Economic (miscellaneous).

Central Mexico. 16thC. Single sheet of unidentified paper.

A photograph, with the indicated title, is in TU/MARI. Only briefly seen, its general appearance is reminiscent of the type of pictorial manuscript represented by the Códices indígenas del Marquesado del Valle, nos. 1–28. Further examination of the photograph would yield more classificatory and descriptive data.

Bibliography: None.

184

LANDA, FRAY DIEGO DE. *Relación de las Cosas de Yucatan.* Unknown. Published. Calendrical, ethnographic, and miscellaneous. Yucatan. 1566. Physical description unknown.

Landa's *Relación* is known only through a copy in the RAH first published (incompletely) by Brasseur de Bourbourg in 1864. The text contains important data on the history of Yucatan and on most phases of Maya life, including the calendar and hieroglyphic writing. Illustrations in the native tradition are of: glyphs for the 20 days, glyphs for the four year-bearer days, glyphs for the 18 months, a calendar wheel, examples of Maya phonetic writing, and a Maya "alphabet" in hieroglyphs. Other illustrations, not relevant to the present census, are of an artifact, Maya buildings, and two maps.

The glyphs of days and months given by Landa have proved of value in deciphering Maya hieroglyphic writing. His calendar wheel is comparable to other colonial wheels in the Books of Chilam Balam. The examples of phonetic writing and the Landa "alphabet," which have formed the basis for various frustrated attempts to decipher Maya hieroglyphs, are now considered to rest on a misunderstanding between Landa and his informant as to what the former was attempting to accomplish in eliciting an "alphabet."

There have been 10 editions of Landa's

Relación. They include two translations in French, two in English, and one in Russian (1955; not cited in the Annotated Bibliography, Article 32). The second English translation (Tozzer, 1941) omits the "Kalendario Romano y Yucatanense" and its day and month glyphs but gives extensive notes and topical bibliographies.

The literature concerning the glyphs and the "alphabet" given by Landa is quite large and, as with other works concerning Maya hieroglyphic writing (see Maya Screenfolds), is not cited here. For a denunciation of the "alphabet" see Valentini (1880); for a more restrained critique, see J. E. S. Thompson (1950). A linguistic study is given by Durbin (1969).

Copy: RAH.

Publication: Brasseur de Bourbourg, 1864 (Spanish-French, incomplete); Garibay, 1959b (Spanish, reprinted 1966); Gates, 1937b (English); Pérez Martínez, 1938 (Spanish); Rada y Delgado *in* Léon de Rosny, 1881b, pp. 69–114, pl. 19 (Spanish, lacks maps); *Relaciones de Yucatan*, 1898–1900, 2: 265–411 (Spanish, incomplete); Rosado Escalante and Ontiveros, 1938 (Spanish); Tozzer, 1941 (English, incomplete).

Other: Durbin, 1969; J. E. S. Thompson, 1950, pp. 28, 46; Valentini, 1880.

185

Laud, Codex. Liber *hieroglyphicorum* Aegyptorum. Bodleian Library, Oxford. Ex–William Laud collection. Published. Ritual-calendrical. Borgia Group. Preconquest. Skin screenfold. 24 leaves (22 painted pages on obverse, 24 on reverse; first and last pages of obverse are unpainted and attached to skin covers). 15.7 × 16.5 cm. (total length 398.4 cm.).

One of the five screenfold divinatory almanacs of the Borgia Group. Most of its 11 sections develop particular aspects of the tonalpohualli, the Mesoamerican 260-day augural cycle. Other sections, including two with bar-and-dot numerals, may pertain to rituals or offerings. Stylistic resemblance to Codex Féjérváry-Mayer (q.v.).

The first edition (Kingsborough, 1831–48) is superseded by the photographic color facsimile published by the Akademische Druck- und Verlagsanstalt, Graz, Austria (Burland, 1966a) and by the photographic color edition by Corona Núñez (1964–67). The latter is accompanied by a page-by-page commentary. The b/w photographic edition by Martínez Marín (1961) contains a general introduction and reprints selected earlier descriptions and studies. The commentary by Seler on Codex Féjérváry-Mayer (q.v.) includes interpretation of parts of Codex Laud. Nowotny (1961b) gives comparative interpretation of all its sections. See Borgia Group for further bibliography and comment.

Copies: Handcolored copy by A. G. Hunter in PML.

Editions: Burland, 1966a; Códice Laud, n.d.; Corona Núñez, 1964–67, 3: 315–409; Librería Echániz, 1937b; Kingsborough, 1831–48, vol. 2; Martínez Marín, 1961.

Commentaries: Nowotny, 1961b, passim, pls. 47–50a.

Studies: Beyer, 1912b; Burland, 1947c, 1948; Caso, 1967, p. 81; J. E. S. Thompson, 1966.

Brief descriptions: Alcina Franch, 1955, pp. 476–77; Lehmann, 1905a, pp. 257–58; Paso y Troncoso, 1898b, pp. 57–59, 330–32.

186

Legal Document in Hieroglyphics. Private collection (Switzerland). Partially published. Miscellaneous. Central Mexico. 16thC. European paper. 42 × 89 cm.

A detail of the manuscript, published in a sale catalog (Sotheby and Co., 1936b), shows two Indians being attacked or killed by other Indians. Short Spanish glosses concern confessions to the crimes illustrated.

Partial publication: Sotheby and Co.,

1936b, Item 242 and plate captioned "lot 242."

187

Madrid, Codex. Codex Tro-Cortesianus. Codex Cortesianus (21 leaves: pp. 1–21, 57–76, 78 of Codex Madrid). Codex Troano (35 leaves: pp. 22–56, 77, 79–112 of Codex Madrid). Museo de América, Madrid. See below for former owners. Published. Ritual-calendrical. Lowland Maya region, Southeastern Mexico and Guatemala. Preconquest. Amatl paper screenfold. 56 leaves painted on both sides. ca. 22.6 × 12.2 cm. (total length ca. 682 cm.).

Codex Madrid was arbitrarily divided or fell into two parts at an unknown date. The two parts (Troano and Cortesianus) have somewhat different ownership and publication histories during the 19thC.

Codex Troano was shown to Brasseur de Bourbourg in the Real Academia de la Historia in Madrid in 1866. At that time it was owned by Juan de Tro y Ortolano, who is said to have purchased it from descendants of Cortés (Rada y Delgado in Léon de Rosny, 1881b, p. 11). In that same year or shortly thereafter several announcements of the existence of the manuscript appeared (such as Anonymous, 1865). The proofs for the first edition of 1869 were exhibited in 1867 at the Ministry of Public Education in Paris (Brasseur de Bourbourg, 1869–70, 1: vi) and possibly at the Paris Exposition of that year as well (Exposition Universelle, 1867). In 1881 the manuscript was exhibited at the Fourth International Congress of Americanists by Luis María de Tro y Moxó (*Lista*, 1881, no. 1109). It was acquired by the Museo Arqueológico, Madrid, in 1888.

Codex Cortesianus was offered in sale to the Bibliothèque Imperiale, Paris, in 1867 by a Juan Palacios of Madrid, and it may also have been offered to the British Museum. The correspondence related to this offer with photographs of two pages of the manuscript are still in the BNP. The photographs appear to have been known to Brasseur de Bourbourg (1869–70, 1: 5). Léon de Rosny first learned of the photographs about 1876 and published one of them in the first and second editions of his *Essai sur le déchiffrement de l'écriture hiératique de l'Amérique Centrale* (Léon de Rosny, 1876a, 1876b). The Palacios correspondence and the photographs have been described by Núñez y Domínguez (1947a) and, in less detail, by Zimmermann (1954).

In 1871 one page of Codex Cortesianus was published in a Spanish periodical in Madrid and this reproduction was reprinted in Mexico by Melgar y Serrano (1873). The manuscript was acquired by the Museo Arqueológico, Madrid, in 1872 (also reported as 1875) from José Ignacio Miró, a noted bibliophile, who is said to have bought it in Extremadura, Spain (Rada y Delgado in Léon de Rosny, 1881b, p. iii). Like Codex Troano, Codex Cortesianus was also exhibited at the Fourth International Congress of Americanists (*Lista*, 1881, no. 130).

Léon de Rosny learned that the Spanish government had acquired Codex Cortesianus in 1879. In 1880 he examined both parts of Codex Madrid. Shortly thereafter he published photographs of one page of Codex Troano and three of Codex Cortesianus and demonstrated that they were parts of the same manuscript (Léon de Rosny, 1881a). Two pages of Codex Cortesianus and several from Codex Troano were published by him in the Spanish edition of his *Essai* (Léon de Rosny, 1881b).

The content of Codex Madrid appears to be primarily concerned with divination; the divinatory almanacs which it contains cover various subjects including hunting, beekeeping, weaving, rain-making, crops, and diseases. It exhibits much attention to world directions and world colors but lacks the astronomy, multiplication tables, prophecies, and other mathematical reckonings of Codex Dresden, one of the other three

surviving Maya screenfolds. J. E. S. Thompson (1950), from whose description these remarks are adapted, notes that it may date from the late 15thC.

Codex Troano and Codex Cortesianus have each had three separate editions, listed below. The first edition of the Troano (Brasseur de Bourbourg, 1869–70), in color, was published with a now wholly discredited "translation." The first edition of the Cortesianus (Léon de Rosny, 1883), in b/w, was based on a photographic process; its second edition (Rada y Delgado and López de Ayala y del Hierro, 1892) is in color.

Seven editions of Codex Madrid as a whole have appeared. Both of the editions by Gates (1911, 1933) reportedly consist of photographs mounted in screenfold format. Anders (1967a), the only edition in color, is a photographic screenfold facsimile. The other four are based on the earlier editions of the Troano and Cortesianus.

See Maya Screenfolds for comment on the scope and nature of the selected bibliography given below.

Copies: Photographs of 2 pages of Codex Cortesianus with Palacios correspondence of 1867, BNP 395.

Editions (Codex Troano): Brasseur de Bourbourg, 1869–70, vol. 1; *Códice Troano*, 1930; Librería Echániz, 1939b.

Editions (Codex Cortesianus): Librería Echániz, 1949; Rada y Delgado and López de Ayala y del Hierro, 1892; Léon de Rosny, 1883.

Editions (Codex Madrid): Anders, 1967a; Evreinov, Kosarev, and Ustinov, 1961, vol. 1; Gates, 1911, 1933; Knorozov, 1963, pp. 520–631; Villacorta and Villacorta, 1930, pp. 225–449; 1930–33, various paginations.

Historical references (loc. cit.): Anonymous, 1865; Brasseur de Bourbourg, 1869–70, 1: vi. 5; *Exposition Universelle*, 1867; *Lista*, 1881, Items 130, 1109; Melgar y Serrano, 1873; Núñez y Domínguez, 1947a, pp. 360–61; Léon de Rosny, 1876a, pl. 11; 1876b, pl. 25; 1881a, pp. 78–83, pls. 5–6, 8–9; 1881b, pp. iii, 11, pls. 11, 17; Zimmermann, 1954, p. 64.

Brief description: J. E. S. Thompson, 1950, pp. 25–26.

188

Magliabecchiano, Codex. The Book of Life of the Ancient Mexicans. Libro de la Vida que los Yndios antiguamente hazian y Supersticiones y malos Ritos que tenian y guardavan. Codex Nuttall (rare). Biblioteca Nazionale Centrale, Florence. MS Magl. XIII-3. Ex–Antonio Magliabecchi collection. Published. Ritual-calendrical and ethnographic. Valley of Mexico. Before ca. 1566 (?). European paper codex. 92 leaves. 15.5 × 21.5 cm.

Native drawings and facing Spanish texts illustrative of festival designs on blankets (ff. 2v–8v), day signs (11r–13v), year signs (14v–28r), ceremonies of the 18 months (28v–46r), and a long section on movable ceremonies, gods, and mortuary, sacrificial, and other customs (46v–92r). For other versions of this material in related manuscripts see Magliabecchiano Group.

There are three major editions. Nuttall (1903) and *Codex Magliabecchiano* (1904) are by color lithography. That by Nuttall omits preliminary and blank leaves, repetitious year signs, and one text considered unfit for publication. Both are superseded by Anders (1970), by color photography with detailed description and introduction. There is no published transcript or translation of the texts. For literature on relationships to other manuscripts see Magliabecchiano Group.

Statements of correlation contained in the codex have been cited and discussed throughout most of the modern calendrical literature. Utilizing a copy obtained from Nuttall prior to her edition, Seler published and commented on many figures from the codex in numerous works. Of particular relevance are his comparisons of blanket designs (Seler, 1904c), his study of pictorial representations of the 18 monthly ceremonies based on the related Codex Ixtlilxochitl, part 1 (Seler, 1899a), and iconographic identifications made throughout his study of Codex Borgia (Seler, 1904–09, 1963). Three pages from the codex are reproduced in Robertson (1959).

Copies: See, in this census, Codex Ixtlilxochitl, part 1, and Antonio de Herrera, *Historia general.*

Editions: Anders, 1970; *Codex Magliabecchiano*, 1904; Librería Echániz, 1947c; Nuttall, 1903.

Selected studies by Seler: Seler, 1899a; 1904c, pp. 530–33; 1904–09, passim; 1963, passim.

Other: Paso y Troncoso, 1898b, p. 68, passim; Schuller, 1919–20; Waterman, 1931.

Brief descriptions: Alcina Franch, 1955, pp. 431–34; Kubler and Gibson, 1951, p. 58; Robertson, 1959, pp. 125–33, pls. 40, 42, 44.

❖❖❖

MAGLIABECCHIANO GROUP. See Codices Ixtlilxochitl, part 1, Magliabecchiano, and del Museo de América, entered separately in the census. Pictorial content of these manuscripts is such that they must be related as original and copies or share a common prototype. Codex Magliabecchiano may be a partial copy of the drawings in Códice del Museo de América but with a different Spanish text (or different Spanish translation of a common original Nahuatl text) and calendrical correlation. Codex Ixtlilxochitl, part 1, appears to be a partial copy of the drawings and text of Codex Magliabecchiano although there are slight variations in the two texts. Codex Veytia includes an 18thC copy of Codex Ixtlilxochitl, part 1. The Costumbres de Nueva España is considered an old copy of part of the text of Códice del Museo de América. See Table 3 for a concordance of most of these manuscripts.

TABLE 3—MAGLIABECCHIANO GROUP

Simplified concordance of the content of the Codices del Museo de América, Magliabecchiano, Ixtlilxochitl (part 1), and the Costumbres de Nueva España (a copy of the text of the Códice del Museo de América). Both of the Codices del Museo de América and Magliabecchiano have drawings not in the other. The texts of the Codices Magliabecchiano and Ixtlilxochitl are close and different from the text of the Códice del Museo de América. Blank pages are indicated only between sections.

Subject	Códice del Museo de América	Costumbres de Nueva España	Códice Maglia-becchiano	Códice Ixtlil-xochitl
1. Portraits	7 pages	331r–338v		
later gloss	1 page			
2. 20-day calendar			11r–13v	
3. 18-month festival calendar	11r–28v	339r–353r	28v–46r	94r–102v
4. Gods, movable ceremonies				
and customs	29r–77r	353v–381v	46v–88r	103r–104v
blank			88v	
Additional gods			89r–92r	
5. 52-year calendar	77v–83v	382r–386v	14r–27v	
Text (in re 52 years)	84r–84v	387r–387v	28r	
blank	85r			
6. Blanket designs	85v–88v		2v–8v	
blank	89r–89v		9r–10v	
7. Calendrical text	90r–96v			
8. 260-day calendar	97r–125r			

Cervantes de Salazar, in Mexico, and Herrera, in Spain, appear to have had access to a manuscript of the group. Various passages in Cervantes' *Crónica* (bk. 1, caps. 19, 21, 26, 28, 30, 31) written in Mexico after 1551 and before 1567 are very close to sections of Codex Magliabecchiano. A calendrical chapter of the *Crónica* (bk. 1, cap. 29) is comparable to otherwise unique material in the last part of Códice del Museo de América but does not derive from it or from Codex Magliabecchiano. Cervantes planned or finished an unknown work on Indian ceremonies (*Crónica*, bk. 1, caps. 28, 31).

Herrera, who also had access to Cervantes' *Crónica*, includes details copied from a pictorial manuscript of the group on two of the illustrated title pages of his *Historia general* published in 1601. See Antonio de Herrera (no. 133) for comment on these copies.

The relationship between the manuscripts of the Magliabecchiano Group has been dis-

cussed by Robertson (1959). An earlier discussion by Nuttall (1903) antedates the discovery of the Códice del Museo de América. The connection with Cervantes de Salazar was noted by Nuttall (1913) and elsewhere (Nuttall, 1921) she gives data bearing on the possible history of these manuscripts. Paso y Troncoso (in Cervantes de Salazar, 1914–36) has compared parallel passages in the *Crónica*, Codex Magliabecchiano, and Codex Ixtlilxochitl, part 1. See individual entries for the manuscripts of the group for further bibliography.

Group relationships: Nuttall, 1903; 1913; 1921, pp. 88–90; Paso y Troncoso *in* Cervantes de Salazar, 1914–36, 3: 395–401; Robertson, 1959, pp. 125–33, 201–02.

Related works: Cervantes de Salazar, 1914, 1914–36; Herrera, 1601–15.

189

Maguey, Plano en Papel de. Plano (parcial) de la Ciudad de Mexico. Plano en

Papel Indígena. Plano de Tenoxtitlan. Plano antiguo de México. MNA 35-3. Ex–Boturini collection. Exhibited in London in 1824 by Bullock. Published. Cartographic. Mexico City–Tlatelolco, D.F. ca. 1557–62. Amatl paper. 238 × 168 cm.

The Plano is a detailed map of a part of the native city of Mexico-Tenochtitlan-Tlatelolco, possibly of a ward located to the east of Tlatelolco and north of the center of Mexico City. It shows over 400 house and property locations with approximately as many personal name glyphs. The plan is a gridiron layout crossed by roads and canals. Along the right margin is a column of human figures representing the preconquest and early colonial rulers of Tenochtitlan from Itzcoatl through Cristóbal de Guzmán (1557–62).

The document has been studied in some detail, particularly with regard to what area of Mexico-Tenochtitlan it represents, by Toussaint, Gómez de Orozco, and Fernández (1938). They give photoreproduction of the original and details. An earlier study by Maudslay (1908–16) includes an excellent large-scale retouched photograph (the only reproduction adequate for study), a lithographed copy in color by Adela Breton, and superficial identification of 404 glyphs by Seler. Robertson (1959) gives photograph and details, analyzes its styles, and suggests a date as early as 1540 for the map before later additions. Barlow (1947a) suggests reasons for a provenience further north than that suggested by Toussaint et al.

The first reproduction was by Bullock (1824a, 1824b); this is reprinted in Fernández (1956) and is similar to a lithograph in Prescott (1844).

Copies: An old copy on cloth, with the missing sections of the original either copied before their loss or reconstructed, was, until recently, in the MNA but its present location is unknown. It has been reproduced by Gamio (1917), Toussaint et al. (1938), and Marquina (1960) in inadequate photographs. Toussaint et al. date it as 18thC; it may be the same as that attributed to Sigüenza y Góngora by Gondra (1846) and mentioned by Orozco y Berra (1867, 1871). It may also have been in the Boturini collection. A copy of 1892 is MNA 35-3A.

Publication with commentary: Maudslay, 1908–16, vol. 3; Robertson, 1959, pp. 77–83, pls. 17–19; Toussaint et al., 1938, pp. 55–84, figs. 5–12.

Bullock lithograph: Bullock, 1824a, pp. 297–300, plate following p. 532; 1824b, atlas, pl. 19; Fernández, 1956, fig. 19; Prescott, 1844, 2: 157.

Other: Barlow, 1947a, pp. 153–54, pl. E; Bullock, 1824c, no. 3 or 45; Carrera Stampa, 1949b, pp. 325–28, pl. 3; Eriksson, 1919; García Cubas, 1909–10; Maudslay, 1909–10.

Old copy: Gamio, 1917, pp. 130–31, pl. 8; Marquina, 1960, foto 2.

Brief descriptions: Glass, 1964, pp. 39–40, pl. 5.

Brief mention: Gondra, 1846, p. 10; Orozco y Berra, 1867, pp. 1–2; 1871, no. 2159; Paso y Troncoso, 1892–93, 1: 53–54.

190

Malinaltepec, Mapa de. Pueblo. Unpublished. Unavailable. San Miguel Malinaltepec (also Maninaltepec), ex-district of Ixtlan, Northern Oaxaca. Data and physical description unknown.

The document is mentioned by Cline (1961a) and is listed as an unverified Chinantec pictorial by Cline (1966c). Pérez García (1956) reports a map of 1870, apparently not preserving native elements, in Malinaltepec. Whether these references are to the same document is uncertain, and further investigation is required to determine the nature, loss, or existence of the original.

Bibliography: Cline, 1961a, p. 75; 1966c, app. 2, no. 49; Pérez García, 1956, 1: 121.

191

Mani, Katun Wheel of. Katun Wheel of López Cogolludo. Lienzo de Mani. Unknown. Published. Calendrical. Mani, Yucatan. 1536 (?). Painting on cloth. Dimensions unknown.

The painting shows 13 human heads, each identified by a Maya name, surrounding a shield within which is a tree. Although both Cogolludo and Stephens were led to believe that it had an historical meaning—the Otzmal massacre of 1536—modern scholars interpret it as an esoteric calendar wheel.

The painting is known only through the López Cogolludo reproduction first published in 1688. It is also described by Stephens (1843), who saw the original. The fullest commentary is by Morley (1920). It is discussed by Martínez Hernández (1927, 1940) and by Gates (1931). Other authors who have contributed to its understanding are listed below; this is a selected bibliography.

Publication: Blom, 1928, pl. 1; Gates, 1931, pp. 1–4; López Cogolludo, 1688, pp. 132–33; Martínez Hernández, 1927, pp. 31–34; 1940, pp. 30–33; Morley, 1920, pp. 472–73, 480–83, fig. 73.

Other: Morley *in* Morley and Roys, 1941, 1 (part 1): 104–07; Roys, 1954, p. 6; Stephens, 1843, 2: 260–62; J. E. S. Thompson, 1950, p. 202; Tozzer, 1941, p. 55.

192

Mani, Map of the Province of. Unknown. Published. Cartographic. Mani, Yucatan. 1557. Physical description unknown.

The boundaries of the Tutul Xiu province of Mani were defined by the 1557 Land Treaty of Mani. Manuscripts of the treaty and the map are in the Crónica de Mani and in the Xiu Chronicles. Codex Pérez (q.v.) contains a text of the treaty but not the map. The 1596 copy of the map in the Crónica de Mani is a circular composition with boundary towns evenly spaced around its periphery, east at the top. They are its only native features. A similar version was obtained in Mani and published by Stephens (1843). The version of the map in the Xiu Chronicles

is not circular and is even more Europeanized.

Roys (1943) presents a study of the land treaty documents and reproduces the copies of the map in the Crónica de Mani and the Xiu Chronicles. The commentary by Roys (in Morley and Roys, 1941) is unpublished. The version in the Xiu Chronicles is reproduced and discussed by Gates (1937b). See Genealogical Tree of the Xiu Family in this census for further data on the Xiu Chronicles. The version in the Crónica de Mani is reproduced by Morley (1946) and by Gropp (1933). Roys (1957) discusses the Maya province of Mani.

Copies: The Crónica de Mani is in TU/-LAL. The Xiu Chronicles are in PML. The Stephens copy may be in the New-York Historical Society (not entered in Article 28). A copy described as similar to that published by Stephens is cataloged by Orozco y Berra (1871) and may be in DGMH.

Publication: Gates, 1937b, pp. 132–34; Gropp, 1933, pp. 260–63, fig. 4; Morley, 1946, pp. 165–66, pl. 20; Roys, 1943, pp. 175–94, Maps 5–6, figs. 1–3; Stephens, 1843, 2: 263–73, plate facing p. 265.

Commentary: Morley and Roys, 1941, 2: 622–31, 773–77.

Other: Orozco y Berra, 1871, p. 309, no. 3041; Roys, 1957, pp. 61–77.

193

Mariano Jiménez, Códice. Códice de Otlazpan. Nómina de los Tributos de los Pueblos Otlazpan y Tepexic. HSA HC 378/222. Published. Economic (tribute). Utlaspa, Mexico. 1549–50. European paper. 8 leaves. 31 × 21 cm.

Pictorial and Spanish assessment of salaries for native officials of Utlaspa (Otlaxpan, Mexico, south of Tepeji del Rio, Hidalgo) and other tribute on 11 painted pages. Final pages in Nahuatl list witnesses to an agreement (not given) between Otlaxpan and Tepeji del Rio. Old foliations on the manuscript are 17–24 and 130–137.

Lithograph edition in color (N. León, n.d. [ca. 1904]) includes translation of Nahuatl text and incomplete commentary. A very detailed commentary on pp. 1–11 of the codex (only) is given by Leander (1967) together with a color reproduction of the plates of the earlier edition. One page of the codex is reproduced in a sale catalog (Hiersemann, 1910).

Copy: Small photographs of original in AMNH.

Publication: Leander, 1967; N. León, n.d.

Other: Brinton, 1899; Gibson, 1964a, pp. 260–61, 269; Hiersemann, 1910, Item 222; Leander, 1966a, 1966b.

194

Maxixcatzin, Genealogy of. AGN-T 20, part 1, exp. 1, fol. 63v. Published. Genealogical. Ocotelulco, Tlaxcala. 1562. Probably European paper. Dimensions not determined.

Simple genealogy of 13 persons showing 12 heads and two personal name glyphs. Included are Tlacomihuatzin and his grandson, Maxixcatzin (died 1520). The document forms part of the dispute over the cabecera succession at Ocotelulco.

Gibson (1952) interprets and reproduces a tracing of the manuscript.

Publication: Gibson, 1952, p. 267, fig. 5, Table 3.

❖❖❖

MAYA SCREENFOLDS. Only three Maya hieroglyphic manuscripts survive: the screenfold Codices Dresden, Madrid, and Paris. A very large literature of hieroglyphic interpretation surrounds these manuscripts. Much of it concerns the nature and decipherment of Maya writing, the identification of particular glyphs and deities, astronomical and mathematical subjects, the survey of particular topics, or (particularly in Codex Dresden) the interpretation of specific passages. Most of it is highly technical.

None of this literature is cited in the present work. Excellent bibliographies of the subject will be found in J. E. S. Thompson (1950), Bernal (1962), Lips and Deckert (1962) and in the continuing coverage of Mesoamerican ethnohistory in the *Handbook of Latin American Studies*.

Under the census entries for each of the three manuscripts we have listed only editions, selected works bearing on their history, and the brief descriptions and concise outlines of content given by J. E. S. Thompson in his *Maya Hieroglyphic Writing* (1950).

Commentaries on the entirety of each manuscript are singularly rare. Those by Förstemann on each of the manuscripts, cited below, were written at the end of an era of research into Maya writing, and although significant advances have occurred since then, they appear to be of continuing usefulness. The edition of all three manuscripts by Villacorta and Villacorta (1930, 1930–33) provides explanatory comment facing each reproduced page. Nowotny's (1961b) study of Central Mexican and Borgia Group ritual-calendrical manuscripts notes parallels in content between the Mayan and Mexican pictorial sources. The history of research into Codex Dresden by Deckert (in Lips and Deckert, 1962) is also of relevance for the other manuscripts. Schwede (1912) reports on a technical analysis of the manuscripts and their paper fiber.

Commentaries: Förstemann, 1886, 1901, 1902, 1903a, 1903b, 1906; Villacorta and Villacorta, 1930, 1930–33.

Bibliography: Bernal, 1962, pp. 317–47; Lips and Deckert, 1962; J. E. S. Thompson, 1950.

Other: Nowotny, 1961b, passim; Schwede, 1912.

Brief descriptions: J. E. S. Thompson, 1950, pp. 23–26; Toscano, 1944, 350–54.

195 (fig. 44)

Meixueiro, Lienzo. Codex Meixueiro. Un-

159

known. Published. Cartographic-historical. Coixtlahuaca region, Western Oaxaca. 16thC. Cloth. Dimensions unknown (TU/LAL copy is 380 × 360 cm.).

The document duplicates the content and composition of Lienzo de Coixtlahuaca no. 1 with some rearrangement of details; it may be considered a version of the latter manuscript. Variations include additional place glyphs within the peripheral boundary and six additional persons in the dynastic list at the center, some of whom appear in the Coixtlahuaca dynasty on the Lienzo de Santiago Ihuitlan. The lienzo was named after Guillermo Meixueiro, a Jefe Político of Ixtlan, a fact presumed not to bear on the history of the manuscript.

The León copy, purchased by Gates from Wilkinson in 1912 and later in the Garrett collection, was copied and the copy was published in 1931 (Codex Meixueiro, 1931). The comments by Bunting (1931) are of little value.

Copies: The León-Gates copy may possibly be the tracing in TU/LAL.

Publication: *Codex Meixueiro*, 1931.

Other: Bunting, 1931; Gates, MS; Parmenter, 1961c.

196

Mendoza, Codex. The Collection of Mendoza. Códice Mendocino. Bodleian Library, Oxford. Ex–Thevet, Hakluyt, Purchas, and Selden collections. Published. Historical, economic (tribute), and ethnographic. Mexico City, D.F. ca. 1541–42. European paper. 71 numbered leaves plus added title leaf. 32.7 × 22.9 cm.

The codex is believed to have been commissioned by the Viceroy Mendoza for presentation to Charles V and is said to have been seized by French pirates. It was in the possession of André Thevet, the French cosmographer, by 1553. It contains 72 pages of drawings with Spanish glosses, 63 pages of Spanish commentary, 1 text figure, and 7 blank pages. Its three sections, although in

a uniform style of drawing and annotation, have different subject matters and origins.

The drawings of part 1 (ff. 1–16) present a history of the Tenochca-Mexica from the founding of Tenochtitlan (apparently given here as A.D. 1325) through 1521 in terms of the lengths of the reigns of the rulers and of the towns they conquered. The Spanish text adds some supplementary data. A version of the same text is given by Mendieta (1870). See Article 27B, no. 1099, for comment on alleged relationships between Codex Mendoza and glosses by Sahagún in book 8, chaps. 1–2, of the Manuscrito de Tlatelolco.

Part 2 (ff. 17–55) is a pictorial record of the tribute paid by the different provinces of the Aztec Empire with a Spanish interpretation. It closely resembles the Matrícula de Tributos (no. 368), of which it has long been considered a copy but preserving five pages now lost from the Matrícula. In a recent study of a third related source, the Información sobre los tributos que los Indios pagaban a Moctezuma (Article 27B, no. 1136), Borah and Cook (1963) advance reasons to indicate that part 2 and the Matrícula derive from a common lost prototype.

Part 3 (ff. 56–71) is a graphic portrayal of Aztec life probably drawn especially for the codex. It includes a year-to-year history of an Aztec from birth onward. Other pages depict warriors, priests, and other professions, the palace of Moctezuma, and the laws and punishments of the latter's rule. It is an almost unique ethnographic account, comparable only to parts of the later Florentine Codex.

The first edition (Purchas, 1625) is of historical interest only. It gives an incomplete and inaccurate series of woodcuts of the drawings and an English translation of the text. The second edition (Thevenot, 1672; reissued 1696) is based on that by Purchas. The third edition (Kingsborough, 1831–48) reproduces the drawings and gives the Spanish text and an English translation. The useful and most accessible edition (Galindo y Villa, 1925), in b/w photography, has a brief introduction. The rare edition by Clark (1938) is a superb color photofacsimile and is accompanied by a good commentary and an English translation of the text. Another edition in color photography (Corona Núñez, 1964–67) has a transcript of the text and a page-by-page commentary but reproduces the illustrated pages only.

Gómez de Orozco (1941) and Robertson (1959) present detailed analyses of the authorship and style of the codex, respectively. A general but incompletely published commentary is Orozco y Berra (1877–82). Other specialized studies of the codex are listed below and classified as to parts 1, 2, or 3 of the codex and studies of its place glyphs. Part 1, with its data on the founding of Tenochtitlan, the chronology of the rulers of Tenochtitlan, and its town conquest lists, has often been utilized in comparative and general studies, but we have cited only an appraisal of its value (Barlow, 1946f) and a study of the Aztec conquests (Kelly and Palerm, 1952). For the bibliography of part 2, that of the Matrícula de Tributos should also be consulted; Barlow (1949d) and Borah and Cook (1963) are basic sources.

Although drawings or extracts from part 3 have illustrated countless studies on Mexico, no important critique of its content appears to have been published. The bibliography of this important and well-known codex could easily be expanded greatly beyond that given here.

The location of the codex was generally unknown between its first edition in 1625 and the edition by Kingsborough in 1830 (Kingsborough, 1831–48). During that interval it was frequently discussed in print, and numerous reproductions of individual pages (after one of the three 17thC editions) appeared. Many works gave its location as the Bibliothèque du Roi, Paris, reflecting a confusion with Codex Telleriano-Remensis.

Some of them are cited under historical references below.

Early editions: Kingsborough, 1831–48, vols. 1, 5: 37–126, 6: 3–94; Purchas, 1625, 3: 1065–117; Thevenot, 1672, 1696.

Modern editions: Clark, 1938; Corona Núñez, 1964–67, 1: 1–149, 2: 119–49; Librería Echániz, n.d.*b*; Galindo y Villa, 1925.

General: Gómez de Orozco, 1941; Orozco y Berra, 1877–82; Robertson, 1959, pp. 95–107, pls. 22–26.

Part 1: Barlow, 1946f, p. 212; Kelly and Palerm, 1952, pp. 264–317.

Part 2: Anderson and Barlow, 1943; Barlow, 1945f, 1949d; Borah and Cook, 1963, pp. 29–33, 36–37; Gibson, 1964a, pp. 194–95, note 4, p. 516; Long, 1942; Molins Fábrega, 1956a, 1956b; Nuttall, 1901; Zantwijk, 1967.

Part 3: Esteve Barba, 1952; Mendieta y Núñez, 1961; Orozco y Berra, 1880, 1: book 2, passim.

Place glyphs: Barlow and McAfee, 1949; Clark, 1938, 2: 1–55; Nowotny, 1959; Orozco y Berra, 1880, 1: book 3, passim; Peñafiel, 1885.

Historical references: Barthelemy, 1798; Fábrega, 1899, pp. 5–6; Humboldt, 1810, pp. 284–91, pls. 58–59; Kircher, 1652–54, 3: 28–36; Papillon, 1766, 1: 364; Spineto, 1829, pp. 240–48; Warburton, 1738–41, 2: 67–70; 1744, p. 18.

Other: Mendieta, 1870, pp. 148–53; Paleografía, 1951.

Brief descriptions: Alcina Franch, 1955, pp. 441–43; Kubler and Gibson, 1951, pp. 64–65; Radin, 1920, pp. 25–26, 50–56.

197

Mendoza Moctezuma, Genealogía de la Familia. Arbol genealógico de la Casa de Moctezuma. Cacicazgo de Tetepango. Known versions listed below. Published. Genealogical. Valley of Mexico. 17th–18thC.

Three different and possibly 17th or 18thC versions of the painting have been published. Each depicts six standing figures identified in genealogical succession as Tezozomoc (15thC ruler of Azcapotzalco), Quaquapitzauac (15thC ruler of Tlatelolco), Moctezuma (identified in one version as Nezahualcoyotl), Fernando Cortés Moctezuma (Cuauhtemoc), Diego de Mendoza de Austria y Moctezuma (governor of Tlatelolco, 1549–62), and Baltasar de Mendoza Moctezuma, Señor de Tezontepec (governor of Tlatelolco, ca. 1583?).

The two versions in the AGN are associated with a supposedly falsified or possibly misdated cédula of 1523 granting certain rights and privileges to Diego de Mendoza. Also in question is the authenticity of his descent from Cuauhtemoc. Although we have classified the painting according to its content under the Valley of Mexico, it may have originated with descendants of the Mendoza Moctezuma family in Tezontepec or Tetepango, Hidalgo.

Riva Palacio (n.d.) gives a color lithograph of a copy of the version in AGN-T 1586; Fernández de Recas (1961) reproduces a color photo of the version in AGN-T 2692. Both publications and documents include the cédula of 1523. Glass (1964) reproduces the MNA 35-11 version; Blacker (1965) gives a detail of it in color. Velázquez Chávez (1939) reprints the Riva Palacio reproduction in b/w.

The authenticity of the related cédula of 1523 has been discussed by Pérez Martínez (n.d.), I. B. del Castillo (1906), and Barlow (1945b). Barlow (1944h, 1945b, 1947e) has commented briefly on the depictions of Quaquapitzauac, Diego de Mendoza, and Baltasar de Mendoza. Details, presumably from the MNA version, are reproduced in the early Mexican editions of Prescott (Prescott, 1844; Gondra, 1846).

Published versions: (1) AGN-T 1586, exp. 1. (2) AGN-T 2692, exp. not determined. (3) MNA 35-11.

Other versions: (1) On two sheets of parchment, HSA 397/497. (2) Photograph, probably of one of the known versions, BM.

162

(3) Unidentified probable version may have been in the Poole collection (Leonard and Co., 1871; Bangs and Co., 1893).

Publication: Fernández de Recas, 1961, pp. 269–84, color pls. 2–3; Glass, 1964, pp. 49–50, pl. 13; Riva Palacio, n.d., pp. 110–14, color plate facing p. 113; Velázquez Chávez, 1939, pl. 7.

Other: Barlow, 1944h, 235, pl. 2; 1945b, pp. 476–77, pl. E; 1947e, p. 190, pl. J; Blacker, 1965, p. 36; Carbajal Espinosa, 1862, 1: 318, 376, 408; I. B. del Castillo, 1906; Gondra, 1846, p. 152, pl. 65; Pérez Martínez, n.d., pp. 261–64, 272–73; Prescott, 1844, 3 plates in vol. 2.

Sale catalog references: Bangs and Co., 1893, p. 150, no. 1740; Leonard and Co., 1871, p. 58, no. 970.

198

Metla, San Andres, Lienzo de. Unknown. Published. Cartographic-historical. San Andres Metla, Mexico. 1674. Physical data unknown.

The lienzo is known through a 19thC copy (cloth, 160 × 145 cm.) preserved in the town. It depicts the pueblo of San Andres Metla, its boundaries, its 15thC foundation, and a 16thC friar.

Cook de Leonard and Lemoine Villicaña (1956) give brief description and a tracing of the copy.

Publication: Cook de Leonard and Lemoine Villicaña, 1956, pp. 291–92, fig. 4.

199

Metlatoyuca, Lienzo de. Codex of Huachinango. Plano mixto de un Pueblo en el Distrito de Huachinango. British Museum Add. MSS 30, 088. Ex–Colonel Juan Bautista Campos, Porter C. Bliss, and Simon Stevens collections. Published. Cartographic-historical. Metlatoyuca, Puebla. 16thC. Cloth. 180 × 105 cm.

The lienzo is said to have been found in archaeological ruins near Metlatoyuca in 1865 or 1866. It shows 79 Indians in genealogical relationships with personal as well as calendrical name glyphs, several rivers and roads, and place glyphs. Its style is similar to that of the Papers of Itzcuintepec.

The copy made by Hunter is reproduced and described by Breton (1920a). Guzmán (1939b) also reproduces the lienzo and gives a study of its place glyphs. A partial reproduction is given by Burland (1947a).

Copies: The Annie G. Hunter copy is in the library of the late A. M. Tozzer. A copy by Valentini was owned by Saville and may now be in the library of the Museum of the American Indian, N.Y. Another copy is DGMH 1183.

Publication: Breton, 1920a; Burland, 1947a; Guzmán, 1939b.

Other: Breton, 1920b.

200

Metztepetl, Genealogía de. Códice del Señorío de Tenochtitlan. Genealogía de Huitzitzilitzin y Axayacatzin. MNA 35-62. Ex–Boturini collection. Partially published. Genealogical. Central Mexico. 16th or 17thC. European paper. Four fragments from a single sheet; the largest is 72 × 42 cm. approximately.

The four fragments form an incomplete genealogy of more than 22 persons, all of whom are in native costume. On the largest fragment are 18 Indians without hieroglyphs but whose names are given by Nahuatl glosses. Among these are Axayacatzin and Atzotzomoctzin. On the reverse are two further figures, one of whom is glossed Quactemoc (Cuauhtemoc), and various glosses including "Metztepetl." Huitzilihuitzin appears on one of the smaller fragments. The presence of the Aztec rulers' names on the genealogy may be coincidental.

Glass (1964) gives a brief description and a photoreproduction of the obverse of three of the fragments.

Partial publication: Glass, 1964, p. 114, pl. 65.

201

Mexicaine, Histoire, depuis 1221 jusqu'en 1594. BNP 40. Ex–Aubin collection. Partially published. Historical. Mexico City, D.F. 1573. European paper codex. 17 leaves plus added title leaf and 4 leaves of notes and copies by Aubin and Pichardo. 21 × 16 cm.

Pictorial and Nahuatl chronicle of Tenochca history from 1168 through 1573. Leaves representing the years 1312–63 and 1559–64 are missing. A later gloss provides an erroneous correlation equivalent to 1221–1569 and 1594. The first part of the Nahuatl text parallels that at the beginning of Codex Aubin.

Boban (1891) gives a brief description and reproduces two pages.

Copy: Pichardo copy, BNP 89-1.

Brief description: Boban, 1891, 2: 34–38, 228–32, pl. 40.

202

Mexicains, L'Histoire des anciens, Fragment de. BNP 85. Ex–Boturini and Aubin collections. Partially published. Historical. Valley of Mexico. 16thC (?). European paper. 8 leaves. 20 × 15 cm.

Historical Nahuatl text embracing the period 1196–1405, with notices concerning the Aztec emigration from Tula, the migration itinerary to Chapultepec, and episodes of later history to the death of Acamapichtli and the installation of Huitzilihuitl. The unpublished drawings (not examined) "appear to derive out of the later colonial period" (Zimmermann, loc. cit.).

Zimmermann (1963–65) gives palaeography of the text, indicates the subject of the drawings, and suggests a relationship to the writings of Chimalpahin and Crónica X. His translation of the text into German or Spanish is in preparation. Gibson (personal communication) notes a possible relationship to the text of Codex Aubin, and Aubin (in BNP 85bis) notes a parallel with the writings of Tezozomoc.

Copies: The Anales Mexicanos no. 3, 1196–1396 (MNA/AH-CA 273; AAMC 9; Anónimo núm. 6) is a Spanish translation of the text by Aubin. It has been published as *Anales Mexicanos no. 2* [*sic*] in *Anales Mexicanos no. 2* (1948), continued in *Anales Mexicanos no. 3* (1948). A copy by Aubin, with a French translation, is BNP 85bis.

Publication: *Anales Mexicanos no. 2*, 1948, pp. 55–67; *Anales Mexicanos no. 3*, 1948, pp. 69–74; Zimmermann, 1963–65, 2: 161–66, 204–05.

Brief description: Boban, 1891, 2: 219–21.

203

Mexicaltzingo, Códices del Cristo de. MNA 35-127. Published. Economic (tribute). Mexicaltzingo, D.F. 16thC. European (?) paper. 7 fragments of varying dimensions.

Seven fragments from three original Indian pictorial manuscripts, together with paintings and Nahuatl texts of a Christian religious content, were found within the structure of a cane sculpture of Christ in 1946. Most of the native pictorial fragments contain drawings of the heads of Indians with personal name glyphs, units of Spanish money, and various objects (including cattle and a spinning wheel) arranged in horizontal rows. The documents may be tribute registers or an accounting of the payments for services performed by Indians.

All the fragments are described and reproduced by Carrillo y Gariel (1949). One fragment is reproduced in the MNA catalog (Glass, 1964).

Publication: Carrillo y Gariel, 1949, pp. 37–48, 73–74, pls. 4–14 of the accompanying atlas.

Brief description: Glass, 1964, p. 185, pl. 138.

204

Mexican Manuscript no. 2. Códice Fisher. John Rylands Library, Manchester. Ex–Agustín Fischer and Sir Thomas Phillipps collections. Unpublished. Unclassified.

Central Mexico. Date unknown. Native paper. 3 leaves. 25.5 × 16.5 cm.

Nahuatl text with crude drawings. Documents of 1867 believed to bear on the history of this manuscript have been published by Lemoine Villicaña (1960). On the basis of a Phillipps sale catalog description (Sotheby, Wilkinson, and Hodge, 1919a), Gómez de Orozco (1948) mistakenly suspected that it was a Techialoyan codex.

Bibliography: *Bibliotheca mejicana*, 1869, p. 215, no. 1929; Gómez de Orozco, 1948, p. 67; Lemoine Villicaña, 1960; Sotheby, Wilkinson, and Hodge, 1919a, p. 36, no. 178.

205

Mexicano, Latino y Castellano, Kalendario. BNMex, MS 1628bis, ff. 86–100. Published. Calendrical. Tlatelolco, D.F. ca. 1585. European paper. 15 (16?) leaves. 20.5 × 15 cm.

The document is bound with the *Cantares Mexicanos* (Article 27B, no. 1019) and the *Arte Adivinatoria* (Article 27B, no. 1107). The *Kalendario* consists of: a title and prologue, a calendar in Spanish arranged according to the 12 European months but describing the 18 native monthly ceremonies similar to book 2, chaps. 1–18, of the Florentine Codex, and a passage entitled "Al lector" treating the calendar and idolatry. These texts (ff. 86–94) are by Sahagún although not all authorities (Kubler and Gibson, Toro) agree with this attribution. See Article 27B, no. 1106.

The second and only pictorial section on six leaves (ff. 95r–100r) has drawings for 10 of the 18 monthly ceremonies and an eleventh drawing of the *nemontemi*. This section may be a copy of the Tovar Calendar (no. 364) but lacks the texts of the latter and has added day signs and other variations.

The manuscript has been published by Iguíniz (1918) with photographs of the illustrated pages. Kubler and Gibson (1951) have described the compilation, published one of its drawings, and attributed the "Al lector" to Martín de León whose *Camino del Cielo* (1611) contains some resemblance to it. The "Al lector" has also been published by García Icazbalceta (1954). Carreño (1950), Toro (1923, 1928), and R. Moreno (1966) have each published two pages from the document.

Copies: (1) BNMA. (2) in MNA/AH Col. Antig. 210. (3) in MNA/AH Col. Antig. 254. (4) HSA 397/464.

Publication: Iguíniz, 1918.

Partial publication: Carreño, 1950, pp. 8–13; Kubler and Gibson, 1951, pp. 66–67, fig. 18; R. Moreno, 1966, pp. 38–45; Toro, 1923, pl. 5; 1928, fig. 25.

Other: García Icazbalceta, 1954, pp. 368–69, 380–82; M. de León, 1611, ff. 95r–100v; Nicolau d'Olwer, 1952, pp. 113–15.

206

Mexicanos, Anales, 1398–1596. Two parts: (A) *Anales Mexicanos no. 4, 1589–1595.* AAMC 10. Unknown. Ex–Boturini collection. Partially published. Number of leaves uncertain. (B) *Fragment d'une histoire du Mexique en langue Nahuatl* (1398–1589, 1595–96). BNP 217. Ex–Boturini and Aubin collections. Partially published. European paper. 11 leaves. Quarto. Historical. Valley of Mexico. 1596.

The document is known through a partial copy (AAMC 10) of a lost fragment and another fragment of the original (BNP 217). The two parts represent most of the 26 or 28 leaves of the original; available evidence suggests that two leaves are missing at the beginning and some additional notices for 1595 and to June 13, 1596, are missing at the end. The original and the drawings copied in AAMC 10 are described in relative detail in the Boturini collection inventory of 1791 (see Article 29).

AAMC 10 is a copy by Galicia Chimalpopoca that includes the Nahuatl text, his Spanish translation, and a copy of two drawings by J. F. Ramírez. The text records events in Mexico-Tenochtitlan from Decem-

ber 30, 1589, through February 13, 1595. The text and translation have been published as *Anales Mexicanos, 1589–1596* (1949). The publication *Anales Mexicanos no. 4* (1948) is not of this document.

The drawings depict events opposite year signs for the years 1573–81 in a style and composition similar to Codex Aubin. The copy does not include all the drawings once with the original (see Ramírez's preface to the copy), and their relationship to the text is uncertain. One of the two drawings is reproduced without comment by Chavero (n.d.), who quotes a passage from the text describing the death of Fray Bernardino de Sahagún.

The Nahuatl text of BNP 217 begins with 1398 and continues through December 26, 1589 (old ff. 3–12); an additional torn leaf has notices from December 1595 through April 1596. One unpublished drawing (old f. 6v) has a symbol for warfare and chronological signs representing the siege of Tenochtitlan-Tlatelolco by the Spaniards in 1521. With the manuscript are 36 pages of notes, transcripts, and translations, in part by Aubin, that at least in part pertain to Codex Aubin and not to this manuscript. A transcript of the Nahuatl text of BNP 217 has been published by Zimmermann (1963–65); his translation will presumably be published at a later date.

Copies: AAMC 10, described above. BNP 217 was photographed by Gates and copies are in PML, LC, NLA, TU/LAL, and BYU.

Publication of text: *Anales Mexicanos 1589–1596*, 1949; Zimmermann, 1963–65, 2: 166–75, 204–05.

Brief description: (BNP 217), Boban, 1891, 2: 240.

Other (loc. cit.): Chavero, n.d., pp. xxv, upper figure, xliv.

207

Mexicanus, Codex. BNP 23-24. Ex–Aubin collection. Published. Calendrical, historical, and genealogical. Valley of Mexico.

1571–90. Native paper codex. 51 leaves. 10 × 20 cm.

The calendrical sections of the codex (pp. 1–15, 89–102) exhibit extensive and deliberate effacements of native symbols as well as palimpsests. They contain an incomplete Christian saints' calendar for 1570, based on dominical letters, and a tonalamatl (each correlated with two or more native years), Christian and native calendar wheels, and various tables. In the latter, emphasis is on the zodiac as well as on paschal and lunar cycles. One diagram relates illegible signs to parts of the body. A Nahuatl text inserted into the annals section (pp. 23–24) also treats the zodiac.

A genealogy of the descendants of Tezozomoc, Acamapichtli, Itzcoatl, and others occupies two pages (pp. 16–17).

The bulk of the codex (pp. 18–85) contains pictorial annals from 1168 through 1571, with some emphasis on the Tenochca-Mexica. These are continued (pp. 86–87) by two different artists to 1590, but the last entry is for 1583. Christian scenes occupy page 88.

Mengin (1952a) provides a facsimile edition and a commentary. Selected pages are reproduced in Boban (1891), Kubler and Gibson (1951), and Robertson (1959). The latter analyzes variant styles in the manuscript and discusses (1954) certain aspects of the tonalamatl. Galarza (1966) gives a study of Christian and phonetic symbolism in the first part of the codex.

Copy: Pichardo copy, BNP 89-9.

Publication: Mengin, 1952a.

Other: Galarza, 1966; Robertson, 1954.

Brief descriptions: Boban, 1891, 1: 373–79, pls. 23–24; Kubler and Gibson, 1951, pp. 70–71, fig. 1; Robertson, 1959, pp. 122–25, pls. 37–38.

208

Mexicanus, Codex. BNP 83. Ex–Laine Villevigue and Aubin collections. Unpublished. Historical. Valley of Mexico.

16thC (?). Native paper tira in 2 fragments. 18 × 220 cm.

Not examined. The brief description by Boban (1891) indicates that the tira has native-year dates, drawings of Indians and Spaniards, and Nahuatl glosses. Both preconquest and colonial events and persons are depicted.

Copy: Aubin copy, BNP 83bis.

Brief description: Boban, 1891, 2: 213–14.

209

MEXICO-TENOCHTITLAN: *Procès entre Diego Francisco et Felipe de Santiago.* BNP 112. Ex–Aubin collection. Unpublished. Genealogical and economic (property plans). Mexico City (Tecpancaltitlan, barrio of San Juan Moyotlan), D.F. 1593. European paper. 33 (?) leaves. Dimensions not determined.

Only partially examined. Lawsuit in Spanish and Nahuatl over properties and houses. Includes three simple drawings showing plans of houses with measurements given in native pictorial conventions. One of the drawings includes a genealogy.

Brief description: Boban, 1891, 2: 296.

210

MEXICO-TENOCHTITLAN: *Titres de Propriété.* BNP 114. Ex–Aubin collection. Unpublished. Economic (property plans). Santa Maria Copolco (a barrio of the parcialidad of Santa Maria Redonda Cuepopan of Mexico City), D.F. 1574. 3 drawings, one on native paper, included in a document of 43 leaves. Dimensions not determined.

Not examined. The brief description by Boban (1891) indicates that the drawings are plans of houses and properties; one also depicts Huanitzin and Tehuetzquititzin, early Indian governors of Mexico City. The accompanying text, in Spanish and Nahuatl, contains land titles with dates from 1574 to 1709.

Brief description: Boban, 1891, 2: 298–301.

211

Mexico y Tlatelolco, Anales de, 1473, 1521–22. Anales Antiguos de Mexico y sus Contornos (AAMC) no. 11. Anónimo núm. 7. Anales de la Conquista de Tlatelolco en 1473 y en 1521. Unknown. Ex–Boturini collection. Published. Historical. Tlatelolco, D.F. 16thC. European paper. 6 leaves. Quarto.

Nahuatl text treating conquest of Tlatelolco by Tenochtitlan in 1473 and by the Spaniards in 1521 (given in the document as 1522). A single and simple drawing in the Chimalpopoca copies shows the glyphs for Tlatelolco and Tenochtitlan with the symbol for warfare.

McAfee and Barlow (1945) publish and translate the Chimalpopoca copy (AAMC 11) of the Nahuatl text with commentary and reproduction of the drawing. Chavero (n.d.) also reproduces the drawing, as does Alcina Franch (1955). *Qualli Amatl* (1950) gives Nahuatl text from MNA/AH Col. Antig. 254 copy with Spanish translation by Porfirio Aguirre.

Copies: Chimalpopoca copy and translation, MNA/AH Col. Ant. 274, Item 11 (AAMC 11). Chimalpopoca copy of Nahuatl text and drawing, MNA/AH Col. Ant. 254, ff. 49r–51r (old ff. 246r–48r).

Publication: McAfee and Barlow, 1945; *Qualli Amatl*, 1950.

Other: Alcina Franch, 1955, pp. 508–09, fig. 8; Chavero, n.d., p. xxv, lower figure.

212

Meztitlan Calendar Wheel. In Gabriel de Chávez, *Relación* (Descripción) *de la Provincia de Meztitlan.* UTX. CDG 1285. Ex–García Icazbalceta collection. Published. Calendrical. Meztitlan, Hidalgo. 1579. Physical data not determined.

Appended to the *Relación geográfica* of Meztitlan is a description of the native calendar illustrated by a drawing of the four year-bearer days. They are drawn at each end of a Maltese cross–like device and labeled according to the four directions. The description indicates that the drawing is intended to represent a calendar wheel.

The drawing has been published at least twice but only from the Muñoz collection copy. The first (Chávez, 1865) is inaccurate; the second (Chávez, 1925) is presumably adequate. An edition of the relación of 1840 appears not to have included the drawing. Carrasco Pizana (1950) has discussed the day and month names in the text. See Robertson (Article 6, Appendix, 2) for further information and comment.

Copies: Muñoz collection copy, RAH. Numerous copies of this copy are not included in Article 28.

Publication: Chávez, 1865, 1925.

Other: Carrasco Pizana, 1950, pp. 193–95; Robertson, loc. cit.

Brief mention: Kubler and Gibson, 1951, p. 71.

213

Michoacan, Relación de. Códice de El Escorial. Biblioteca del Monasterio de El Escorial, Madrid. Ex–Diego González collection. Published. Historical and ethnographic. Tzintzuntzan, Michoacan. ca. 1539–41. European paper. 140 leaves. 20 × 15 cm.

Manuscript in Spanish by anonymous Franciscan, illustrated by 44 colored drawings. Treats preconquest and very early colonial Tarascan history. Text and drawings contain wealth of historical, ethnographic, and genealogical information. All but one leaf of part 1, descriptive of gods and ceremonies, is lost. Bound with the manuscript is the unrelated "Calendario de toda la índica gente," a text describing the Veytia Calendar Wheel no. 2 (q.v.).

Attribution of the document to Fray Maturino Gilberti has been shown by Glass (1958b) to rest on false premises. Fray Martín de Jesús (de la Coruña), reported by Beristáin de Souza (1883–97) to be the author of an otherwise unknown manuscript history of Michoacan in the Escorial, is a logical candidate for the authorship but is not accepted by most students of the question. J. B. Warren (1971) advances evidence to show that the author is the Franciscan friar Jerónimo de Alcalá.

Some copies of the photographic edition and commentary by Tudela (1956) are handcolored. This edition includes a study by Kirchhoff. The first edition (*Relación de Michoacan*, 1869) did not include the illustrations, which are poorly reproduced from a copy of those in the LC copy in the second edition (*Relación de Michoacan*, 1903). All but one of the illustrations are given, in poor copies, in parts 1 and 2 of N. León's study of the Tarascans (N. León, 1903, 1903–04, reprinted, 1904a). Selected illustrations are reproduced, some in color, from the copy owned by Gómez de Orozco in N. León (1927), I. Espinosa (1945), and Toussaint (1937).

Critical bibliographical commentaries are given by N. León (1927) and Bravo Ugarte (1962). The bibliography given below is selected.

Copies: LC, NYPL, RAH, BNMA. The Gómez de Orozco collection copy, mentioned above, was probably made for Paso y Troncoso. Two copies were owned by Kingsborough (*Bibliotheca inlustris*, 1842, nos. 535-1, 536-11). The first appears to be listed in Rich (n.d.) and may correspond to the copy now in LC or NYPL. The location of the second, Phillipps 11642, is unknown but is described in Sotheby, Wilkinson, and Hodge (1919a) and in Sotheby and Co. (1948). Further copies are mentioned in the literature.

Editions: *Relación de Michoacan*, 1869, 1903; Tudela, 1956.

Partial publication of drawings: N. León, 1903, pls. 1–3, 13–25; 1903–04, pls. 3–28, 40; 1904a, pls. 3–28, 40.

Studies: Bravo Ugarte, 1962; N. León, 1927; F. Ramírez, 1956; J. B. Warren, 1971.

Other: Beristáin de Souza, 1883–97, 1: 354; *Bibliotheca inlustris*, 1842, nos. 535-1, 536-11; Caso, 1943a; 1967, pp. 241–52; I. Espinosa, 1945, pls. 4–6; Glass, 1958b; Gómez de Orozco, 1940, pp. 9–29; N. León, 1888b, 1889a; A. López, 1920; Paso y Troncoso, 1888; Rich, n.d., no. 51; Seler, 1908a; Sotheby and Co., 1948, no. 4858, plate facing p. 44; Sotheby, Wilkinson, and Hodge, 1919a, no. 346.

Brief description: Brand, 1944, pp. 95–96.

214

Misantla, Lienzo de. Códice Misantla. Location uncertain but variously reported as Ayuntamiento, Misantla, and as Archivo Municipal, Tonayan, Veracruz. Published. Cartographic-historical. Misantla, Veracruz. After 1564. Cloth. 160 × 100 cm.

Map of the Misantla region shows numerous place glyphs and Indian principales with name glyphs, the landing of Cortés, and boundaries between Coacoatzintla and Chapultepec.

Photograph of original or copy poorly published with brief commentary by Mena (1911a). Cline (1959) reprints the Mena photograph; Ramírez Lavoignet (1959, 1962) makes considerable use of the lienzo in studies of the Misantla region.

Copies: Reported copies are an old copy in the Vicente Lombardo Toledano collection, a recent copy in the Departamento de Antropología of the state of Veracruz, and a copy made for the Secretaría de Gobierno, Xalapa, about 1911.

Publication: Cline, 1959, pp. 654–55, figs. 8, 9; Mena, 1911a.

Other: Ramírez Lavoignet, 1953, pp. 321–22; 1959, passim; 1962, pp. 27–28, passim.

Brief descriptions: Alcina Franch, 1955, p. 455; Melgarejo Vivanco, 1953, p. 333.

215

Mixteco Post-Cortesiano no. 36, Códice. MNA 35-36. Published. Cartographic-historical. Western Oaxaca. 16thC. European paper. 85 × 87 cm.

The manuscript is bordered on all four sides by place glyphs identified by written Mixtec glosses, representing the boundaries of an as yet unidentified place. In the center is a church, two buildings with seated persons, three hieroglyphic dates, and drawings of plots of land.

Incomplete commentary, palaeography, and photographic reproduction are given by Rosado Ojeda (1945). A brief description and photograph are in the MNA catalog (Glass, 1964).

Copy: Copy of selected details, MNA 35-20.

Publication: Glass, 1964, p. 81, pl. 38; Rosado Ojeda, 1945.

Brief description: Alcina Franch, 1955, pp. 492–93.

❖❖❖

MIZQUIAHUALA SALES RECEIPTS. Six pictorial documents, listed individually below, most or all of which are receipts for the payments of goods and services provided by the Indians to Manuel de Olvera, corregidor of Mizquiahuala. All are probably ex–Boturini collection.

216

—— *Humboldt Fragment 7.* DSB. MS Amer. 1, f. 6, upper. Ex–Boturini, León y Gama, and Humboldt collections. Published. Economic (tribute.) Mizquiahuala, Hidalgo. 1571. Amatl paper. 25 × 18 cm.

Simple drawings of zacate, fish, and other goods sold to Manuel de Olvera. Spanish gloss on reverse.

Seler (1893, 1902e, 1904f) interprets and describes the document. It is photographically reproduced in *Historische Hieroglyphen* (1892); a copy is reproduced by Seler (1904f). See Humboldt Fragments for further data.

Publication: *Historische Hieroglyphen*, 1892, pl. 6; Seler, 1904f, pp. 196–200, pl. 12.

Commentary: Seler, 1893, pp. 85–90; 1902e, pp. 252–59.

217

—— *Humboldt Fragment 13.* DSB. MS Amer. 1, f. 3, upper. Ex–Boturini, León y Gama, and Humboldt collections. Published. Economic (tribute). Mizquiahuala, Hidalgo. 1569. Amatl paper. 31 × 49 cm.

Drawings of the heads of women, numerals, and circles representing day signs. A Spanish gloss on the reverse identifies the document as a receipt for the services of Indian women for the manufacture of tortillas.

Seler (1893, 1902e, 1904f) interprets and describes the manuscript. It is photographically reproduced in *Historische Hieroglyphen* (1892); a copy is reproduced by Seler (1904f). A detail in color is given by Humboldt (1810). See Humboldt Fragments for further data.

Publication: *Historische Hieroglyphen*, 1892, pl. 9; Seler, 1904f, pp. 212–17, pl. 18.

Commentary: Seler, 1893, pp. 105–10; 1902e, pp. 276–83.

Other: Humboldt, 1810, pl. 36, fig. 2.

218

—— *Poinsett Fragment 1.* MNA 35-117. Ex–Poinsett and American Philosophical Society collections. Published. Economic (tribute). Mizquiahuala, Hidalgo. ca. 1570. Native paper. 105 × 20 cm.

Similar to Humboldt Fragment 13 but with further detail. Reverse, which might bear a text, is covered by the mount.

Reproduced photographically in color by Brinton, Phillips, and Morris (1892) without significant comment. Photographic detail and brief description are given in the MNA catalog (Glass, 1964).

Publication: Brinton et al., 1892, folding plate captioned, "Tribute Roll 4 (Calendar 1)."

Brief description: Glass, 1964, pp. 174–75, pl. 128.

219

—— *Poinsett Fragment 2.* MNA 35-118. Ex–Poinsett and American Philosophical Society collections. Published. Economic (tribute). Mizquiahuala, Hidalgo. ca. 1570. Native paper. 80 × 19 cm.

Vertical tira divided into horizontal divisions in which are drawn various goods such as zacate, fish, and turkeys as well as monetary units. The reverse is covered by the mount.

Reproduced photographically in color by Brinton et al. (1892) without significant comment. Brief description and photographic reproduction by Glass (1964).

Publication: Brinton et al., 1892, folding plate captioned, "Tribute Roll (Calendar 2)"; Glass, 1964, p. 176, pl. 129.

220

—— *Rechnung über gelieferte Naturalien.* Lost. Formerly DSB. MS Amer. 10 (part). Ex–Boturini collection. Published. Economic (tribute). Mizquiahuala, Hidalgo. 1573 (?). Native paper. 25 × 20 cm.

Drawings of zacate, fish, turkeys, etc., similar to Humboldt Fragment 7 and Poinsett Fragment 2. Spanish text on reverse side.

Described, interpreted, and reproduced photographically by Lehmann (1906a).

Publication: Lehmann, 1906a, pp. 322–26, pl. 1.

221

—— *Tira de Tributos.* TU/MARI. Ex–Boturini and BNMex collections. Published. Economic (tribute). Mizquiahuala, Hidalgo. 1569. Native paper. 39 × 19 cm.

Drawings of zacate, circles indicating days, and pesos. Spanish text on reverse side.

Both sides are reproduced photographically, without comment, by Wauchope

170

(1946). The description by Mena (1923) includes a transcript of the text.

Publication: Wauchope, 1946, p. 30.

Brief description: Mena, 1923, p. 52, no. 5.

222

Mizquiahuala, Tributos de. Lost. Ex–Boturini and BNMex collections. Unpublished. Unavailable. Mizquiahuala, Hidalgo. 16thC. Native paper. 79 × 49 cm.

The document, briefly described by Mena (1923) is lost, and no photograph or other reproduction is known. It is said to have had drawings of articles of tribute, 15 men, 60 days, and a written text. It is remarkable how closely Mena's description corresponds to the Tributes of Tzintzuntzan and Tlalpujava (no. 379).

Brief description: Mena, 1923, p. 54, no. 8.

223

Moctezuma, Códice. MNA 35-26. Partially published. Historical. Mazatepec or Xochitepec, Morelos. 16thC. Amatl paper tira. 250 × 20 cm.

The two surviving fragments of the tira are composed vertically and read upward. Along the left border are year glyphs and to the right are drawings and Nahuatl texts. Much of the manuscript is in very poor condition; many dates and some text are wholly illegible. The reverse is completely blank; its prior history is unknown. The lower and most poorly preserved fragment apparently represents about 15 years, possibly ca. 1419–35. One drawing is of Maxtla (a ruler of Azcapotzalco); the texts mention Tecpanecatzin, Cuatotzin, Quetzaltototzin, Tezozomoc, and Chimalpopoca.

The longer fragment embraces about 30 years, the most recent glyph being that for 1523. Opposite the year glyphs for 1519–23 are drawings of Moctezuma held prisoner by a Spaniard, a pyramid of Tenochtitlan in flames, and Cortés on a horse near a glyph believed to represent Coyoacan. In the lower section of this fragment, opposite what may have been the year glyph for 1495, is a drawing of Itzcoatl; the text contains a reference to Chimalpopoca. Here and elsewhere the manuscript has a chronological error of at least 52 years from the standard calendar.

According to an unpublished study of the tira by Barlow and Mateos Higuera (MS), of which we have consulted only a very incomplete copy, the manuscript also contains references to Xochitepec and Mazatepec. They believed that the document may have been painted in Morelos, but a Coyoacan, D.F., or Valley of Mexico provenience appears equally likely. A superficial description and a photographic detail are given by Glass (1964). A detail in color is given by B. Smith (1968).

Partial publication: Glass, 1964, p. 69, pl. 27; B. Smith, 1968, p. 166.

Other: Barlow and Mateos Higuera, MS.

224 (fig. 45)

Monteleone, Codex. Códice del Archivo de los Duques de Monteleone y Marqueses del Valle. Library of Congress, Washington. Ex–Archivo del Hospital de Jesús, Mexico, and Edward S. Harkness collections. Partially published. Economic (tribute). Huexotzingo, Puebla. ca. 1531–32. Native paper. 8 leaves. Dimensions vary between 19.7 × 48.3 and 44.5 × 45.7 cm.

The eight pictorial sheets illustrate a 79-leaf lawsuit brought by Hernando Cortés against Nuño de Guzmán, Juan de Ortiz Matienzo, and Diego Delgadillo, president and oidores of the First Audiencia (1528–30), to recover incomes claimed by Cortés from the pueblo and province of Huexotzingo. The paintings are of various kinds of foodstuffs, clothing, and other items. One published painting also shows slaves and a primitive Indian painting of a Madonna and Child.

Toro and Fernández del Castillo (1925) reproduce two of the paintings and give a transcript of a part of the accompanying lawsuit. Zavala (1952, 1967) reproduces a detail from one of the paintings reproduced by Toro and Fernández del Castillo. Three further paintings are reproduced in Cline (1966a). Descriptive memoranda by Stella Clemence and Silvio Zavala are in LC/HF files.

Partial publication: Cline, 1966a, fig. 2; Toro and Fernández del Castillo, 1925.

Other: García Granados and MacGregor, 1934, pp. 81–91; Zavala, 1952, p. 421; 1967, plate facing p. 24.

225

Muaguia, Plan cadastral de. Unknown. Unpublished. Unavailable. Northern Oaxaca. 1550. Physical description unknown.

Lehmann (1905a) reported upon a copy in the Seler collection of a pictorial document, which he classified as Chinantec, with topographic indications, the date 1550, the name Juan de Mendoza, and Chinantec and Zapotec glosses. Both original and copy are now unknown. Cline (1957) has commented on the Lehmann reference.

Bibliography: Cline, 1957, p. 293; Lehmann, 1905a, p. 280.

226 (fig. 46)

Mujeres, Fragmento de las. Genealogy and properties of descendants of Ixtletletzin and Chachatzin. Brooklyn Museum. Ex–Boturini, BNMex, MNA (?), and Emilio Valton collections. Unpublished. Genealogical. Central Mexico (Tlaxcala ?). 16thC. European paper. 43 × 31 cm.

Genealogy of 12 Indians (including five women), all with names glossed in Nahuatl or Spanish, showing descent from two bearded male Indians, Yxtletletzin and Chachatzin.

Very brief description by Mena (1923).

Brief description: Mena, 1923, p. 63, no. 23.

227

Mundanegre aus Chichimecapan, Das Dokument der Familie. Museum für Völkerkunde, Berlin. Published. Genealogical.

171

Tlaxcala (?). Late 16thC or early 17thC. European paper. 58 × 40 cm.

Glossed five-generation genealogy of 11 persons, two of whom are in Spanish dress. Except for an Indian at the head of the genealogy, all the persons have the surname Mundanegre. No glyphs.

Kutscher (1963a) gives commentary and photographic reproduction.

Publication: Kutscher, 1963a.

228 (fig. 47)

Muro, Códice. Códice de Ñunahá. Códice de San Pedro Cantaros. MNA 35-68. Ex–Felix Muro collection. Partially published. Historical. San Pedro Cantaros (Cuzcatepeque), ex-district of Nochistlan, Western Oaxaca. 17thC. Skin screenfold. 11 and one half leaves painted on one side. 14.8 × 223 cm.

The screenfold is in a crude but traditional Mixtec style and has later degenerate additions. There are hieroglyphic dates, place glyphs, and pairs of persons with both calendrical and personal names. The last eight couples of the genealogy have Spanish names only. Several 17thC dates appear in the long written Mixtec text. One or more persons and place glyphs (Teozacoalco, for instance) are believed to be recognizable in other Mixtec histories.

No translation of the text, edition, or commentary on this important screenfold has yet appeared. A brief description and photograph of one page has been published by Glass (1964). Anonymous (1935a) reports the discovery of the manuscript and a notice of its accession by the MNA appeared in the *Boletin del Museo Nacional* (ep. 6, 1: 229, 1934).

Copy: Palaeographic copy by Gómez de Orozco owned by Alfonso Caso.

Partial publication: Glass, 1964, p. 121, pl. 71.

Other: Anonymous, 1935a.

229

Museo de América, Códice del. Codex Tu-

dela. Costumbres, Fiestas, Enterramientos y diversas Formas de Proceder de los Indios de la Nueva España. Museo de América, Madrid. Partially published. Ritual-calendrical and ethnographic. Valley of Mexico. ca. 1553 (?). European paper. 119 leaves (4 ff. and ff. 11–125). 18 or 21 × 15 cm. approx.

The discovery of this major manuscript was announced at the 28th International Congress of Americanists in Paris in 1947 by Tudela (Tudela, 1948a). Part of its pictorial content is a version of material in other manuscripts of the Magliabecchiano Group (q.v.).

The first four leaves have six full-figure portraits of various Indian types (Mexican woman, Tarascan Indian, Yope Indian, etc.) and a drawing of a maguey plant. They have been published and described by Tudela (1960). Two are reproduced by Trimborn (1959). Five or six missing leaves had similar drawings, to judge from copied captions in the Escorial copy of the text.

The next four parts of the codex contain: (1) drawings and Spanish texts illustrative of the gods and ceremonies of the 18 months of the 365-day year (ff. 11r–28v); (2) drawings and texts of other ceremonies, gods, sacrifices, and customs (ff. 29r–77r); (3) year symbols for a 52-year period (ff. 77v–84v); and (4) drawings of ritual symbols on blankets (ff. 85v–88v). The drawings of the four parts just described parallel those in Codex Magliabecchiano, but the Spanish texts in the two manuscripts are different and each manuscript has drawings not in the other. Five pages from the sections cognate with Codex Magliabecchiano have been published (Robertson, 1959; Trimborn, 1959; Tudela, 1960).

The final section of the codex contains: (1) a Spanish text describing the native calendar in terms of the 20-day periods subdivided into periods of 13 and 7 days (ff. 90r–96v) and (2) drawings and Spanish texts depicting and describing the 260-day divinatory almanac (ff. 97r–125r). The highly detailed latter section contains almost unique data relating to a four-way division of the tonalpohualli (four direction trees), pairs of gods for 13-day periods, as well as data on the 13 birds and the Nine Lords of the Night. The final page (f. 125r) has a drawing of a spread deerskin with day signs attributed to different parts of the body. This drawing, which has been published by Robertson (1959, pl. 45), is the only part of this section of the codex that has been published. A transcript of the text of this section has been prepared by García Abrines and Robertson (MS). Rauh (1970) has tabulated much of its calendrical information.

Descriptions of the codex have been published by Tudela (1948a) and by Ballesteros Gaibrois (1948a, 1951). Robertson (1959) has reproduced four pages from the manuscript and studied its style and relationship to other sources. Tudela (1960) has published the drawings from the initial section. For further comment see Magliabecchiano Group.

Copies: The "Costumbres . . . de Nueva España" (see first paragraph of entry for full title), an old copy of the text through f. 84v, is in the Escorial. It has been published by Gómez de Orozco (1945a). An unlocated copy of this copy was in the Kingsborough collection (*Bibliotheca inlustris*, 1842). Another copy, also ex-Kingsborough and also unlocated, was in the Phillipps collection (no. 11797; Sotheby, Wilkinson, and Hodge, 1919a).

Description and studies: Ballesteros Gaibrois, 1948a, 1951; Rauh, 1970; Robertson, 1959, pp. 125–33, pls. 39, 41, 45; Tudela, 1948a, 1960.

Partial publication of text: Gómez de Orozco, 1945a.

Other: *Bibliotheca inlustris*, 1842, no. 582; García Abrines and Robertson, MS; Sotheby, Wilkinson, and Hodge, 1919a, no. 338; Trimborn, 1959, pls. 2 (bottom) and 3.

Brief descriptions: Alcina Franch, 1955, pp. 434–35; Kubler and Gibson, 1951, p. 56.

230

Nación Mexicana, Unos Annales Históricos de la. Manuscrit de 1528. Anales de Tlatelolco. Two closely related manuscripts: (A) BNP 22 and (B) BNP 22bis. Both ex–Boturini and Aubin collections. Published. Historical. Tlatelolco, D.F. (A) ca. 1528. Native paper. 21 leaves (19 utilized). 41 × 23 cm. (B) 17thC (?). European paper. 23 leaves (excluding 4 later added leaves). 30 × 21 cm.

Major Nahuatl historical text comprising five separate documents: (1) Lista de los Reyes de Tlatelolco, (2) Lista de los Reyes de Tenochtitlan, (3) Genealogía de los Reyes de Azcapotzalco, (4) Suplemento de la Genealogía de los Reyes de Azcapotzalco, and (5) Historia de Tlatelolco desde los Tiempos mas remotos.

The text is known through two manuscripts, BNP 22 and BNP 22bis. Missing parts of BNP 22 can be supplied from BNP 22bis. This latter, once considered a copy of BNP 22, is now thought to be related to it through a common original. BNP 22 has one minor drawing; BNP 22bis has a number of minor illustrations including place glyphs, symbols, and miscellaneous historical drawings.

Mengin (1939–40) gives Nahuatl text based on both MSS, German translation, redrawing of illustrations, and commentary. Berlin and Barlow (1948) provide a Spanish translation but do not give the drawings. There is a facsimile photoreproduction of both manuscripts (Mengin, 1945). Garibay (1956) translates the Spanish conquest part of Document 5.

Copies: Aubin copy and French translation, BNP 22ter.

Facsimile edition: Mengin, 1945.

Editions and commentaries: Berlin and Barlow, 1948; Mengin, 1939–40.

Extended descriptions: Jiménez Moreno, 1938b, pp. 555–63; Seler, 1913.

Brief descriptions: Boban, 1891, 1: 365–

70, pl. 22; Garibay, 1953–54, 1: 34–35, 452–54; 2: 285–88; Toscano, 1948.

Other: Garibay, 1956, 4: 167–85.

231

Nahuatzen, Lienzo de. MNA 35-42. Ex-Pulido and Museo Michoacano, Morelia, collections. Published. Cartographic-historical. Nahuatzen, Michoacan. 16thC. Cloth. 72 × 102 cm.

Near the center of the lienzo are drawings of Spanish soldiers and the date July 20, 1521, a date that precedes by one year Spanish penetration into Michoacan. Other pictorial elements are Tarascan Indians, roads, and buildings. Tarascan glosses refer to place names and such persons as Tzintzicha or Caltzontzin and Huitziméngari.

A brief description and photograph are given by Glass (1964). N. León (1903–04; reprinted 1904a) reproduces a tracing, gives an interpretive description, and translates the Tarascan glosses.

Copy: 1892 copy, unknown.

Publication: Glass, 1964, p. 88, pl. 42; N. León, 1903–04, pp. 305–08, pl. 36; 1904a, pp. 129–32, pl. 36.

Brief descriptions: Mateos Higuera, 1948b, pp. 165–66; Paso y Troncoso, 1892–93, 1: 250–52.

232 (fig. 48)

Nativitas, Santa Maria, Lienzo de. Pueblo. Unpublished. Cartographic-historical. Santa Maria Nativitas, ex-district of Coixtlahuaca, Western Oaxaca. 16thC. Cloth. 173 × 175 cm.

Around the periphery of the lienzo are 26 place glyphs glossed in Mixtec, representing the boundaries of the town. Within the center is a two-column genealogy of 24 couples with calendrical glyphs, also glossed in Mixtec, and other detail, including two year-and-day dates.

The calendrical names on the lienzo have been studied by Dahlgren de Jordán (1954a).

Copies: The copy made by Dahlgren de Jordán in 1941 is in the possession of Alfonso Caso. Photographs of a copy said to have been made by a schoolteacher of the town are in INAH/AF. The latter is incomplete with respect to the glosses.

Bibliography: Dahlgren de Jordán, 1954a, pp. 366–70.

233

Nayotla, San Juan, Lienzo de. Códice Actopan. MNA 35-97. Published. Cartographic-historical. San Juan Nayotla (?), Veracruz(?). 1950(?). Cloth. 194 × 236 cm

Map of unidentified region showing roads, historical episodes, Indians, and approximately eight Christian churches, etc., surrounded by boundary of place glyphs. The date 1519 appears at least twice among the Nahuatl glosses, one of which reads "San Juan Nayotla (?), Visorrey Antonio de Mendoza, Año de 1534." Another legend states that the document was made in 1590, but both the date and provenience of the lienzo are in doubt.

A variant version of the document is known through a photograph and a copy made in 1956. In this version the word "Achtopa" is added to the legend quoted above, and the place name reads San Juan Mojotlan.

The MNA original and the 1956 copy are briefly described and reproduced by Glass (1964). Reports that the document, under the name Códice Actopan, was in the Biblioteca del Pueblo (Biblioteca Venustiano Carranza), Veracruz, Ver. (Melgarejo Vivanco, 1953; Ramírez Lavoignet, 1962), may refer to loan of the MNA original or to the original of the 1956 copy.

Copies: (1) Villagra copy, 1956, from unidentified variant, MNA 35-97A. (2) Photograph of original of 1956 copy, MNA codex collection files. (3) Copy, apparently also by Villagra and similar to MNA 35-97A, "on deposit" (1964) in MNA/BNA.

Publication: Glass, 1964, p. 151, pls. 104–05.

Brief mention: Melgarejo Vivanco, 1953, p. 334; Ramírez Lavoignet, 1962, p. 186.

234

Nexmoyotla, Ateno, Zoyatitlan y Hueytetla, Genealogía de. Genealogía de Ateno. MNA 35-82. Ex–Boturini collection. Published. Genealogical. Central Mexico. 17thC. European paper. 31.5 × 86.5 cm.

Drawings in unusual style of 72 Indians, some of whose names are given hieroglyphically or by Nahuatl glosses, arranged in four horizontal rows. Pyramidally shaped place signs are glossed with the place names indicated in the title.

Glass (1964) gives brief description and photographic reproduction. It has also been described by Mateos Higuera (1944d) and, very briefly, by Mena (1923).

Publications Glass, 1964, p. 136, pl. 87.

Brief descriptions: Alcina Franch, 1955, p. 459; Mateos Higuera, 1944d; Mena, 1923, pp. 63–64, no. 26.

235

Nezahualcoyotl, Circular Genealogy of the Descendants of. UTX. Ex–Boturini and Stendahl collections. Unpublished. Genealogical. Valley of Mexico. 16thC. European paper. 85 × 58 cm.

The lower part of the manuscript is a genealogy of 47 Indians: the eight wives and descendants of (?) Ixtecatzin. Each of five generations forms one of a series of concentric circles. Christian names appear in the second generation. At the top is a related and antecedent genealogy of 21 further Indians including Itzcoatl, Nezahualcoyotl, and Nezahualpilli. Two of the women in the upper part appear to be daughters of rulers of Otumba and Chimalhuacan.

Brief description: Präkolumbische Kunst, 1958, p. 93, no. 747.

236

Nómina Escrita en Geroglífico. Unknown: Gómez de Orozco collection about 1927. Partially (?) published. Economic (census). Central Mexico. 16thC. Native paper. Number of leaves and dimensions unknown.

The single published photograph shows one page on which are drawn eight horizontal rows of Indian heads with what may be a personal name glyph at the end of most of the rows. The drawings bear a remarkable similarity to those on a small fragment included in the Testerian manuscript BNP/FM 399 (no. 325).

The photograph is published by Gómez de Orozco (1927a) with a brief comment.

Publication: Gómez de Orozco, 1927a, pp. 157–58, plate facing p. 156.

237

Nopalxochitl, Genealogía de. "Genealogía." MNA 35-81. Ex–Boturini collection. Published. Genealogical. Central Mexico. 16th or 17thC. European paper. 22 × 31 cm.

Fragmentary and incomplete genealogy showing two Indians with personal name glyphs (Nopalxochitl and Teuhhuexoloa) and portions of three native houses. An additional gloss gives the place name Ixaiotepetl.

Glass (1964) gives brief description and photographic reproduction. The manuscript is no. 24 of the Mena (1923) catalog.

Publication: Glass, 1964, p. 135, pl. 86.

Other: Mena, 1923, p. 63, no. 24.

238

Noxtepec, Lienzo de. Códice de Nochtepec. Códice Spratling. Pueblo (?). Published. Cartographic-historical. Noxtepec, Guerrero. 16thC. Cloth. Dimensions not determined.

The published copy shows a row of glossed place glyphs across the top. Below is a group of native rulers with personal name glyphs and two place glyphs, one of which is glossed Nochtepec. Other details include glyphs for Tetipac and Cacalotenango and numerous rivers. The glyphs, glosses, and composition show numerous specific and general similarities to the Lienzo de Tetlama (q.v.).

Barlow (1948a) mentions and reproduces the copy in the Ayuntamiento of Taxco.

Copies: Copy by Spratling dated 1929 in Ayuntamiento, Taxco. A large colored tracing, also by Spratling, in TU/LAL.

Publication: Barlow, 1948a, p. 186, 1 plate.

Brief mention: Rubín de la Borbolla and Spratling, 1964, p. 35.

239

Nueve Señores de la Noche, Rueda de los. Lost. Published. Calendrical. Central Mexico. Date and physical description unknown.

A copy on European paper of a calendar wheel said to depict the Nine Lords of the Night is listed in the 1746 catalog of the Boturini collection. A drawing by Boturini, made after he was separated from his collection and so presumably from memory, is in the AGI and is reproduced in his *Historia general* (Boturini, 1948). It is divided into nine numbered sections and has an owl in the center but lacks symbols for the Nine Lords.

Publication: Boturini, 1948, p. 120, pl. 20.

240

Nuttall, Codex. Codex Zouche. British Museum Add. MSS 39671. Published. Historical. Western Oaxaca. Preconquest. Skin screenfold painted on both sides. 47 leaves. ca. 19 × 25.5 cm.

The manuscript is believed to have been sent, together with Codex Vienna, to Charles V in 1519 by Cortés. It was in the Dominican monastery of San Marco, Florence, Italy, in 1859, when it was sold to John Temple Leader. It was subsequently owned

by Robert Curzon, 14th Baron Zouche, and was acquired by the British Museum in 1917.

In the 1902 edition two pages are reproduced on the wrong side. The correct sequence is: cover + pp. 1–41 + 4 blank pages and (reverse) pp. 42–84 + 2 blank pages + cover. Page 42 is on the reverse of the first cover. The 1902 pagination, which is cited, assigned the numbers 19 and 76 to facing pairs of pages so that there are 42 painted pages on the obverse and 44 on the reverse. Neither cover has the decorative calendrical signs reproduced on one of them in the 1902 edition.

The obverse (pp. 1–41) presents a genealogical and historical narrative divided into six or more sections. Pages 23–32 contain a genealogy of the first and second dynasties of Tilantongo through the marriage of 8 Deer and the genealogy of the rulers of Teozacoalco through the children of the third rulers of the third dynasty. The Cuilapan genealogy on pp. 33–35 shows two marriages with the Teozacoalco dynasty. These pages (pp. 23–35) cover the period from the 9th through the middle of the 14thC. Other pages of the obverse contain less well studied but related genealogies, some antedating the first Tilantongo dynasty or involved with the divine origin of the Mixtec lineages. The emphasis on Teozacoalco suggests that town as a probable provenience.

The reverse of the manuscript (pp. 42–84) presents an incomplete history of the life and exploits of 8 Deer from the marriage of his parents in 1009 and his birth in 1011 to the year 1050.

The colored facsimile edition (Nuttall, 1902) is based on a copy. Some errors of this edition are treated by Burland (1957c) and by Caso (in Caso and Smith, 1966). The historical nature of the manuscript and its emphasis on the history of 8 Deer was recognized and discussed by Nuttall (1902). Long's (1926) study of the obverse treats the historical and genealogical content in a preliminary fashion through the analysis of the dates. The artistic forms and style are studied by Robertson (1959), who also gives photographs of seven pages of the obverse. Robertson (1966) and Caso (1966b) each reproduce three pages photographically and give three details in color. Three pages are reproduced and briefly interpreted by Caso (1965c). An illustrated exposition of a passage on the reverse is given in Leonard (1967).

Selected pages are reproduced in color in *Flor y Canto* (1964). The astronomical studies of Kreichgauer (1915–16) and Seler (1908c) may be outmoded by advances in the knowledge of the Mixtec histories. No modern commentary has been published. Further references to the manuscript will be found in the bibliographies of Codices Colombino, Becker 1, Bodley, and Vienna (reverse), whose content is frequently parallel. See also Nuttall Group.

Publication: Librería Echániz, 1939a; Nuttall, 1902.

Studies: Burland, 1957c, 1958a; Caso, 1955a, 1964c, 1966b; Kreichgauer, 1915–16; Long, 1926; Robertson, 1959, pp. 14–23, pls. 1–7; Seler, 1908c.

Other: Caso, 1965c, pp. 959–61, figs. 10, 11; Caso and Smith, 1966, pp. 15, 115, Table 2; Chadwick, 1967; *Flor y Canto*, 1964, pp. 7, 186, 358–59, 362; Leonard, 1967, pp. 69–77; Robertson, 1966, figs. 1–3, pls. 10–12; Wicke, 1966, fig. 11.

Brief descriptions: Alcina Franch, 1955, pp. 484–85; Lehmann, 1905a, pp. 269–70; Nowotny, 1961b, pp. 51, 202, 271, pl. 59.

❖❖❖

NUTTALL GROUP. *See* Codices Colombino, Becker no. 1, Bodley, Nuttall, Selden, and Vienna, entered separately in the census. All are skin screenfolds; their common content concerns the genealogies of the Mixtec dynasties of Teozacoalco and Tilantongo, Western Oaxaca. Five of the six (all but Codex Selden) are considered preconquest. The group relationship was first noted in specific terms by Clark (1912). See also Códice Muro, Códice Sánchez Solís, and the *relación geográfica* Mapa de Teozacoalco (not in this census) for related manuscripts not usually considered part of the group.

241

Oaxaqueña, Genealogía. Unknown. Ex–Porfirio Díaz collection. Published. Cartographic-historical. Eastern Oaxaca. 18thC. Oil on cloth. MNA copy is 54 × 64 cm.

The painting shows roads, a building glossed "Se'de de Sn. Antonino," and numerous persons with Zapotec names. Two persons with the surname Toledo are painted near a coat of arms at the center. There are several Zapotec texts.

The MNA copy has been published by Galindo y Villa (1905a), who reprints the Paso y Troncoso (1892–93) description, and by Glass (1964).

Copy: 1892 copy, MNA 35-104.

Publication: Galindo y Villa, 1905a, pp. 222–23, note 36, pl. 14; Glass, 1964, p. 159, pl. 111.

Brief description: Paso y Troncoso, 1892–93, 2: 16.

242

Ocotepec, Santo Tomas, Lienzo de. Mapa de Santo Tomas Ocotepeque. Lienzo de Santa Maria Cuquila. Pueblo. Published. Cartographic-historical. Santo Tomas Ocotepec, ex-district of Tlaxiaco, Western Oaxaca. 16thC. Cloth. 104 × 134 cm.

Map with European and native elements showing rivers, roads, and mountains around Ocotepec. A large place glyph represents Cuquila; 24 place glyphs around the margin represent boundary locations. Numerous Mixtec glosses.

Commentary by Caso (1966c) includes color, b/w, and ultraviolet photographic reproductions. Weitlaner de Johnson (1966) gives a technical analysis of the cloth.

Publication: Caso, 1966c.
Other: Weitlaner de Johnson, 1966.

243

Osuna, Códice. Pintura del Gobernador, Alcaldes y Regidores de Mexico. Biblioteca Nacional, Madrid. Ex–Duque de Osuna collection. Published. Economic (tribute and miscellaneous) (Documents 1–5 and 7) and historical (Document 6). Mexico City, Tlatelolco, and Tacuba, D.F., and Tula, Hidalgo. 1565. European paper. 40 leaves. Dimensions not determined.

The codex consists of seven discrete documents forming part of an inquiry into the conduct of the Indian and Spanish governments of Mexico City by the visitador Valderrama in 1565. Document 1 (ff. 1–13) concerns grievances over unpaid deliveries of lime used in construction by the colonial government, the services of Indian troops in the Florida expedition, and personal grievances against the Oider Puga. Documents 2–4 (ff. 14–19, 20–25, 26–29) concern unpaid accounts for services and fodder supplied to the viceroy and oidores. Document 5 (ff. 30–33) presents unpaid accounts for service and food incurred by the Oidor Puga. Document 6 (ff. 34–36) is a listing of place glyphs of towns formerly tributary to Tacuba. Document 7 (ff. 37–39) treats various matters, including labor in public constructions. Documents 1–4 and 7 are from Mexico City and Tlatelolco; Document 5 is from Tula, Hidalgo, and Document 6 is from Tacuba.

The handcolored lithograph edition (*Pintura del Gobernador . . .*, 1878) is reprinted in b/w with added palaeography and translation of the Nahuatl texts in Chávez Orozco (1947). Individual pages are photographically reproduced in Robertson (1959) and in Pérez Bustamante (1928). Barlow (1948e) defines the seven component documents. Robertson (1959) analyzes aspects of pictorial style. Some ar-

chitectural details from the codex are given in Kubler (1948). The study by Gibson (1964b) of the Tepanec zone maps the places listed in Document 6.

Publication: Chávez Orozco, 1947, pp. 171–342; Librería Echániz, n.d.c; *Pintura del Gobernador*, 1878.

Studies: Barlow, 1948e; Gibson, 1964b; Robertson, 1959, pp. 115–22, pls. 30–36.

Other: Kubler, 1948, figs. 41, 43, 53, 81, 106; Pérez Bustamante, 1928, 6 plates.

Brief description: Alcina Franch, 1955, p. 452.

244

Otumba, Mapa de. Mapa de Tlaquitenanco. MNA 35-75. Ex–Boturini collection. Published. Cartographic. Otumba, Mexico. 17thC (?). Amatl paper. 106 × 61.5 cm.

The map shows roads, watercourses, and numerous localities, the latter indicated by simple place glyphs, calli symbols, and circles. A church at the lower left is identified as Santa María Concepción de Otumba. Glosses include place and personal names.

Glass (1964) gives brief description and photograph. Some of the glosses are transcribed in the brief description by Mena (1923).

Publication: Glass, 1964, p. 128, pl. 80.

Brief description: Mena, 1923, p. 55, note on p. 69, no. 10.

245

Oyamatepec y Huitzilatl, Lienzo de. Códice de las Romerías. Casa del Alfeñique, Puebla. Unpublished. Cartographic-historical. State of Puebla (?). 16thC (?). Cloth. 142 × 206 cm.

Not examined. Glass (1964) refers to the existence of the lienzo and to a copy made in 1933 by Rodolfo Barthez, formerly in the Palacio de Bellas Artes, Mexico, but now unknown.

Brief mention: Glass, 1964, p. 193.

246

Oztoticpac Lands Map. Library of Congress, Washington. Published. Economic (property plans) and miscellaneous. Texcoco, Mexico. ca. 1540. Native paper. 75 × 84 cm.

Most of the drawings on the document are plans of fields with native measurements and place glyphs. Near the upper left is the plan of several houses within a precinct almost identical to that in Humboldt Fragment 6 (q.v.) and representing the same property. On the upper right is a map showing approximately 75 plots of land. Further fields are drawn at the lower right. Nahuatl and Spanish glosses as well as three long Nahuatl texts include mention of Tollancingo, Oztoticpac, Tezcuco, Don Carlos, and Don Hernando.

At the lower left are unique depictions of fruit-tree grafts, showing branches grafted to tree trunks. Twenty trees, identified by glosses as pomegranates, quinces, apples, pears, etc., are shown. Four place glyphs (including Oztoticpac and Cuauhyacac) and various numerical symbols accompany these drawings.

Cline (1966a) reproduces the entirety and details of the manuscript, with detailed commentary and comparison with other documents. An amplification of this commentary, with translation of the glosses, is given in Cline (1968).

Publication: Cline, 1966a, 1968, 1972.

247

Paris, Codex. Codex Peresianus. Codex Pérez. BNP 386. Published. Ritual-calendrical. Lowland Maya region, Southeastern Mexico and Guatemala. Preconquest. Amatl paper screenfold painted on both sides. 11 leaves. Height reported as 20.2–25 cm.; width usually reported as 12.5 cm. (total length between 137.5 and 145 cm.).

The date and source of the acquisition of the manuscript by the BNP are unknown although J. F. Ramírez (1855) states that its acquisition was verified by purchase in 1832. Its discovery is widely credited to Léon de Rosny, who reported (1875, 1876a, 1876b, etc.) finding it in a basket in the BNP in 1859 together with other Mexican manuscripts. Attached to it was a slip of paper with the name Pérez, from which one of its synonyms derives.

Perhaps the earliest reference to the manuscript is by Aubin (1849). His brief reference is mentioned by Brasseur de Bourbourg (1852) and quoted in Brasseur de Bourbourg (1857–59). One of two editions of a description written in 1858 by J. Pérez (1859a) reproduces a page of the manuscript. Pérez knew of the then unpublished description by J. F. Ramírez (1855) and refers to a complete edition as being in preparation for Léon de Rosny's *Collection d'anciennes Peintures mexicaines*. We have not seen this presumably ephemeral edition, cited herein as Léon de Rosny (1856). Its plates were perhaps the same as, or similar to, those in Léon de Rosny (1869).

Also bearing on the history of the manuscript is the existence (in NLA) of a copy (or proofs?) attributed to Augustine Aglio from the Kingsborough (and Phillipps?) collections. Zimmermann (1954) discusses the history of the manuscript and prints the J. F. Ramírez description.

The description by J. E. S. Thompson (1950) indicates that each page of the obverse depicts deities ruling over a katun, that little progress has been made in elucidating the hieroglyphic texts, and that "it is a fair assumption that ritual, prophecies, and perhaps historical events" are given. "The reverse is in poor condition. Remains of some divinatory almanacs, new year ceremonies . . . , what is probably a kind of Maya zodiac with divisions of the 364-day years associated with it . . . and miscellaneous scenes can be recognized" (Thompson, 1950, p. 25). The content of two pages has been lost through deterioration of the original.

Thompson (1950) thinks that the manuscript may be a copy, with alterations, of a Classic ("Initial Series") Period document. The pagination utilized by most authorities includes the lost hypothetical pages 13 and 14.

A limited number of sets of photographs of the manuscript were distributed by the Commission Scientifique du Mexique (1864); these are usually recognized as the first edition. A reproduction of the 1864 photographs accompanies the editions by Gates (1909) and Anders (1968). An incomplete and inferior edition is given by Léon de Rosny (1869). Eleven editions, excluding the possible edition of 1856 mentioned above, have appeared and are cited below. An edition planned by Gates as Maya Society Pub. No. 20 was not published.

See Maya Screenfolds in this census for data on the nature and scope of the selected bibliography given below. Commentaries on the Maya screenfolds are not cited in this census except for those by Förstemann (cited under "Maya Screenfolds"); that by Gates (1910), giving a detailed description of the physical state of Codex Paris, is cited as it complements his edition of the manuscript (Gates, 1909).

Copy: Copy (or proofs?) attributed to Augustine Aglio, NLA.

Editions: Anders, 1968; Azcué y Mancera, 1967; Commission Scientifique du Mexique, 1864; Gates, 1909; Knorozov, 1963, pp. 498–519; Léon de Rosny, 1869, pls. 117–32; 1887; 1888; Villacorta and Villacorta, 1930, pp. 161–223; 1930–33, various paginations; Willard, 1933.

Commentary (selected): Gates, 1910.

Historical references: Aubin, 1849 (and other editions); Brasseur de Bourbourg, 1852; 1857–59, 1: lxxi, lxxiii; J. Pérez, 1859a, 1859b; J. F. Ramírez, 1855, no. 2; Léon de Rosny, 1856, 1875, 1876a, 1876b; Zimmermann, 1954.

180

Brief description: J. E. S. Thompson, 1950, p. 25.

248 (fig. 49)

Patzcuaro, Lienzo de. Unknown. Ex-Orozco y Jiménez collection. Published. Cartographic-historical. Patzcuaro, Michoacan. 18thC(?). Cloth. ca. 86 × 150 cm.

Across the top of the lienzo are Indians, friars, and Spaniards on horseback. The latter appear to be receiving tribute. Further groups of Indians appear along the bottom, and a coat of arms surmounted by an eagle is drawn at the lower right. Glosses are illegible in the published photograph. The document is a late version of the subject matter of Codice de Carapan no. 1 (q.v.).

Cuevas (1921–28) gives a photograph with little comment. Another photograph and a typed description of the original were sent from Chicago in 1936 to the Peabody Museum, Harvard University, where they are preserved.

Publication: Cuevas, 1921–28, vol. 1, facing p. 176.

249

Pérez, Codex. MNA/AH. Ex–Carlos Peón Carrillo y Ancona (temporarily), Nicolasa Peón, Eusebio Escalante y Bates, and Josefa Escalante (all of Merida) collections. Published. Ritual-calendrical, historical, and miscellaneous. Mani and other localities, Yucatan. 1837 and later. European paper. ca. 100 leaves. Dimensions not determined.

Drawings copied in Codex Pérez include the 13 Lords of the Katuns, Ahau glyphs, day glyphs, a katun calender wheel with Ahau glyphs, and a copy of two of the calendar wheels in the Book of Chilam Balam of Ixil (no. 168). Line drawings of them are reproduced in Solís Alcalá (1949).

See Article 27B for general comment on the Books of Chilam Balam and for further data on this manuscript (no. 1152).

250

Petapa, Lienzo de. Unknown. Unpublished. Unavailable. Santa Maria Petapa (?), ex-district of Juchitan, Eastern Oaxaca. Further data unavailable.

Sometime before 1905 Martínez Gracida sold the MNA a collection of watercolor drawings, including one showing the hieroglyph of Zaachila taken from the "Lienzo de Petapa" (Galindo y Villa, 1905a). The lienzo is otherwise unknown. The drawings were in the MNA library at one time but we have made no attempt to locate them. An MNA exhibit label of about 1939 for the Lienzo de Guevea (in which the Zaachila hieroglyph appears) lists it as a synonym for that manuscript. Since Galindo y Villa also refers to the Lienzo de Guevea, the two are presumed to be distinct documents. Lehmann (1905a) lists the lienzo as a Zapotec manuscript on the strength of the Galindo y Villa reference.

Bibliography: Galindo y Villa, 1905a, p. 200; Lehmann, 1905a, p. 276.

251

Philadelphia, Lienzo of. Lienzo de Filadelfia. Lienzo de Coatepec. University Museum, University of Pennsylvania. Ex–William Randolph Hearst collection. Cartographic-historical. Western Oaxaca. 16thC. Cloth. 108 × 118 cm.

One part of the lienzo contains a traditional-style genealogy or dynastic succession list of 24 couples with calendrical name glyphs. The locale of this dynasty is unidentified but may be in the Coixtlahuaca–Tlaxiaco–Texupan region. Other drawings represent the origin of the dynasty as well as of others, for which only the founding couples are drawn. Some of the place glyphs and persons occur in other Mixtec manuscripts.

Caso (1964b) provides summary interpretation, description, and photoreproduction. A photograph has also been published by Mason (1943) and by Dockstader (1964) without comment.

Publication: Caso, 1964b; Dockstader, 1964, pl. 30; Mason, 1943, fig. 15; Parmenter, 1966.

252

Piramides, San Martin de las, Mapa de. Pueblo. Published. Economic (property plans). San Martin de las Piramides, Mexico. 17thC. European paper. 43 × 60 cm.

The map depicts the church and atrium of San Martin (on the site of Teotihuacan), roads, houses, and other detail. Prominent is a well-drawn Chichimec warrior in traditional style.

Arreola (1922) gives description, color reproduction, and identifies its cartographic content.

Publication: Arreola, 1922, pp. 558–59, pl. 149.

253

Pitzahua, Genealogía de. Códice de la Descendencia de Pitzahua. Fragmento de dos Guerreros. Dos Fragmentos (part). MNA 35-80. Ex–Boturini collection. Published. Genealogical. Central Mexico. 16th or 17thC. Amatl and European paper. 1 sheet. 77 × 31 cm. approximately.

Incomplete and fragmentary genealogy of approximately 13 Indians, whose names are given in the gloss and, in several instances, by rudimentary personal name glyphs. Several of the Indians hold bows and arrows.

A brief description and a photographic reproduction are given in the MNA catalog (Glass, 1964). It has also been described by Mateos Higuera (1949b) and, very briefly, by Mena (1923).

Publication: Glass, 1964, p. 134, pl. 85.

Brief descriptions: Mateos Higuera, 1949b; Mena, 1923, pp. 63–64, nos. 22 and 28 (a).

254 (fig. 50)

Popotla, Mapa de. Unknown. Published. Cartographic-historical. San Estevan Popotlan, D.F. 16thC (?). Physical data unknown.

The document is known through several copies, listed below. It is a town plan showing roads, canals, bridges, and native houses. A Christian church next to a tzompantli or skull rack is at the center. Historical details include 18 Indians in warriors' costumes, some with name glyphs, and 22 Indians seated on thrones. One of the two copies in Vienna (CVM 2) has glosses and a Spanish text identifying it as a copy of 1720. These glosses are also on the tracing owned by Gómez de Orozco.

The MNA copy has been reproduced photographically by Caso (1947) and by Glass (1964). The study by the former includes the glosses from the Gómez de Orozco collection tracing.

Copies: CVM 2, ex–Bilimek collection, parchment, 70 × 85.5 cm., has glosses and may be the original copy of 1720. CVM 6 (also ex–Bilimek) and MNA 35-88, both also on parchment, lack the glosses and are more deteriorated than CVM 2. A tracing, with the glosses, was in the Gómez de Orozco collection.

Publication: Caso, 1947; Glass, 1964, p. 142, pl. 94.

Brief descriptions: Alcina Franch, 1955, p. 463; Mateos Higuera, 1944a.

255

Porfirio Díaz, Códice. MNA 35-50. Published. Ritual-calendrical and historical. Cuicatlan, ex-district of Cuicatlan, Northern Oaxaca. 16th–17thC. Skin screenfold painted on both sides. 21 leaves. 15.5 × 421 cm. (total length).

Pages 1–29 are historical in content and treat conquests and warfare with place glyphs, drawings of Indians with personal and calendrical name glyphs, roads, historical scenes, etc. Calendrical year dates have a variant set of year-bearer days. Pages 6–25 are parallel to most of Códice Fernández Leal. Short glosses are in an unidentified language. Written texts in a different style on pp. 30–32 are also unidentified but possibly Cuicatec.

The final 10 pages are calendrical and ritual in content with drawings of gods and calendrical signs and have frequently been compared with the Borgia Group manuscripts.

The colored lithographs by Genaro López (in Chavero, 1892) are accompanied by a short unacceptable and undocumented commentary. There is no modern commentary on the historical section. Nowotny (1961b) provides a brief study of the calendrical section. Seler (1904–09; Spanish translation, 1963) and Beyer (1912a) analyze specific sections of the calendrical section. Photographs of two pages are in the MNA catalog (Glass, 1964).

Copy: MNA 35-50A.

Publication: Chavero, 1892, 1: xi–xix, 21 plates in the atlas.

Studies: Beyer, 1912a; Nowotny, 1961b, passim and pl. 50B; Seler, 1904–09, 3: 1–4, figs. 1–5; 1963, 2: 146–48, figs. 152–56; Villacorta, 1934b.

Brief descriptions: Alcina Franch, 1955, pp. 499–500; Glass, 1964, pp. 96–97, pls. 51–52; Paso y Troncoso, 1892–93, 1: 50–52.

256

Porrúa Turanzas, Códice. MNA 35-119. Partially published. Economic (miscellaneous). Central Mexico. 16thC. Native paper. 9 fragments of varying dimensions.

The fragments, which were found in the binding of a 16thC book, are in a poor state of preservation. Drawings are of Indians, streams of water, and various objects. A Spanish gloss refers to measurements of land.

The fragments have been very briefly described and two of them published by Glass (1964).

Partial publication: Glass, 1964, p. 177, pl. 130.

257

Posesiones de Don Andrés, Códice de las. Repartición de Tierras Testamentarias (Fragment 2). Codex Book of Tribute (Fragment 3). Three fragments: (1) MNA 35-87A, (2) MNA 35-87B, (3) UTX, CDG 559. Ex–Boturini (Fragments 1–3), BN-Mex (Fragments 1–2), and Genaro García (Fragment 3) collections. Partially published. Economic (property plans). Tlaxcala (?). 16thC. European paper. (1) 42 × 22 cm., (2) 15.7 × 86.6 cm., (3) 42 × 22 cm.

Drawings of rectangular plots of land with place glyphs and glosses giving dimensions. A seated Indian is glossed "Don Andrés"; on the basis of his headdress type the document is tentatively classified as Tlaxcalan.

Fragments 1 and 2 are published and briefly described by Glass (1964). Mena (1923) describes Fragment 2 and illustrates details from both fragments. Fragment 3, which adjoins the left side of Fragment 1, is unpublished.

Partial publication: Glass, 1964, p. 141, pls. 92–93.

Brief description: Mena, 1923, p. 65, pl. 1, no. 31.

258

Principes Mexicanos, Genealogía de los. BNP 72. Ex–Aubin collection. Published. Genealogical. San Cristobal Ecatepec, Mexico, or Mexico City, D.F. After 1554. European paper. 30 × 20 cm.

Genealogy, with Nahuatl and later Spanish glosses, of 13 persons from Itzcoatl and Moctezuma Ilhuicamina through a son of Don Diego Tehuetzquititzin, a colonial governor of Mexico City.

The drawing has been reproduced and described by Boban (1891). A color reproduction accompanies the commentary by Caso (1958c).

Publication: Boban, 1891, 2: 151–55, pl. 72; Caso, 1958c.

259

Procès, Fragment d'un. BNP 86. Ex–Boturini and Aubin collections. Unpublished. Economic (tribute). Central Mexico. 1567. European paper. 6 leaves. 31 × 21 cm.

Not examined. The brief description by Boban (1891) indicates that most of the document depicts the tribute, in money, for numerous Indians, who are drawn at the left of each of the horizontal rows into which the pages are divided.

Brief description: Boban, 1891, 2: 222–23.

260 (fig. 51)

Procès, Pièce d'un. BNP 392. Ex–Boturini collection. Unpublished. Economic (miscellaneous). Valley of Mexico. 16thC. Native paper. 48 × 81 cm.

On the left side of the document are drawings of items of tribute. Near the center are various groups of Indians, a friar, a Spaniard, place glyphs, short Nahuatl texts, and other detail. On the right is what appears to be the representation of an island. Persons identified by personal name glyphs or glosses include the "Marqués," Doña Isabel Ixtlilxochitzin (?), Itzcoatl, Nezahualcoyotl, and Nezahualpilli.

Brief description: J. F. Ramírez, 1855, no. 9.

261

Puacuaro, Lienzo de. Lienzo de Patzcuaro. Museo Michoacano, Morelia. Ex–Nicolás León collection. Published. Cartographic-historical. Puacuaro, Michoacan. 16thC. Cloth. ca. 84.5 × 75.5 cm.

Shows Indians, Spaniards, churches, pyramids, trees, and other detail, including four vertical rows of skulls. Short Tarascan texts have not been published.

The MNA copy has been published and very briefly described by Glass (1964).

Mateos Higuera (1948b) gives a somewhat longer description.

Copy: 1892 copy, MNA 35-33.

Publication: Glass, 1964, p. 78, pl. 35.

Brief descriptions: Mateos Higuera, 1948b, pp. 163–65; Paso y Troncoso, 1892–93, 1: 244.

262

Quauhtliztactzin, Properties of the Descendants of. UTX. Ex–Stendahl collection. Unpublished. Economic (property plans) and genealogical. Tlaxcala. 16thC. Native paper. 72 × 67.5 cm.

In the upper right corner are elegant drawings of two native houses and six seated Indians, whose names are given both by personal name glyphs and Nahuatl glosses. The latter includes Don Pedro Chichimecatecuhtli, shown as the son of Quauhtliztactzin. The lower half is occupied by drawings of plots of land, houses, and place glyphs. Place names such as Altzayancan, Xalaxco, and Tecopilco indicate a provenience in the ex-district of Juarez, Tlaxcala. On the reverse there are a single house and human figure, without gloss or glyphs.

Brief description: *Präkolumbische Kunst*, 1958, p. 93, no. 746.

263

Quinatzin, Mapa, leaves 1 and 2. Cour Chichimeque et Histoire de Tezcuco. BNP 11–12. Ex–Ixtlilxochitl, Boturini, and Aubin collections. Published. Historical. Texcoco, Mexico. ca. 1542–48. Native paper tira folded to form two leaves. 77 × 44 cm. (each leaf ca. 38 × 44 cm.).

Leaf 1 of the manuscript depicts historical events in the time of Quinatzin and Techotlalatzin. Leaf 2 depicts the palace of Nezahualcoyotl with various details, including a partially effaced series of place glyphs of towns subject to Texcoco and their rulers as of some date in the latter half of the 15thC. A third leaf attributed to the manuscript is described in the next entry.

The early lithograph by Desportes (Au-

bin, n.d.d) was apparently printed to illustrate the commentary by Aubin (1849). The Aubin commentary is illustrated by color lithographs in its reprint of 1885 (Aubin, 1885) and by photoreproductions in its reprinting in Boban (1891). The Spanish translation of the commentary (Aubin, 1886a) is illustrated by the Desportes lithograph. Radin (1920) digests the Aubin commentary and reproduces the 1885 lithographs in b/w. Robertson (1959) reproduces both leaves and discusses their style and date. Ixtlilxochitl (1891–92) describes a source very similar to leaf 2, and Gibson (1956) analyzes the town list of leaf 2.

Copies: Pichardo copy, BNP 89-8.

Publication: Aubin, n.d.d; 1885, pp. 74–106, pls. 4–5; 1886a; Boban, 1891, 1: 219–42, pls. 11–12; Radin, 1920, pp. 19, 38–41, pls. 16–17; Robertson, 1959, pp. 135–40, pls. 13, 46–47.

Commentary: Aubin, 1849 (and other editions).

Other: Chavero, n.d., pp. xiii–xiv, 509–36, 565–75; Gibson, 1956, pp. 3–5; Ixtlilxochitl, 1891–92, 2: 173–81; Léon de Rosny, 1863.

Brief description: Alcina Franch, 1955, pp. 457–58.

264

Quinatzin, Mapa, leaf 3. Códice de Delitos y Castigos. BNP 396. Ex–Marqués de Moncada and Cabinet des Medailles collections. Published. Historical and ethnographic. Texcoco, Mexico. ca. 1542–48. Native paper. 34.5 × 43.5 cm.

The drawing is a fragment believed to have formed part of the Mapa Quinatzin. Across the top are seven place glyphs representing towns conquered by Nezahualcoyotl and his allies during the Tepanec War, 1428–33. Most of the other drawings are of crimes and their punishments and presumably illustrate the laws of Nezahualcoyotl and their enforcement by his son Nezahualpilli.

Barlow (1950b) reproduces the manuscript and provides an adequate commentary. Núñez y Domínguez (1947a) publishes a letter of 1770 describing the manuscript.

Publication: Barlow, 1950b.

Other: Núñez y Domínguez, 1947a, pp. 361–63.

265 (fig. 52)

Quiotepec y Ayauhtla, Lienzo de. Private collection in 1936. Unpublished. Cartographic-historical. San Bartolome Ayautla, ex-district of Teotitlan (or Santiago Quiotepec, ex-district of Cuicatlan, or San Juan Quiotepec, ex-district of Ixtlan), Northern Oaxaca. 1677. Cloth. Dimensions unknown.

Around most of the periphery of the lienzo are drawings of Indian men and women, many of whose names are given by calendrical or personal name glyphs. Also shown are trees and roads; a church on the right appears to represent San Bartolome Ayautla. Near the center is a long list of personal names in Nahuatl, Spanish, and possibly Cuicatec or Mazatec.

Glosses also mention Fray Alo. Valeojo (a Fray Luis de Valeojo or Vallejo is mentioned on the Lienzo de San Pedro Ixcatlan), Fernando Cortés, the baptism of a Miguel de Mendoza, the election of alcaldes, various place names, and the date 1677.

Jiménez Moreno (MS) gives description, incomplete palaeography, and translation of the Nahuatl glosses. Cline (personal communication) believes that the area and some of the cartographic details of the lienzo overlap with the Mazatec Mapa de Huautla. In 1937 the municipal authorities of Ayautla inquired of the MNA as to the whereabouts of their "códice" (administrative archive, MNA); whether this relates to this lienzo is unknown.

Copy: A photograph accompanies the Jiménez Moreno (MS) description in the MNA codex collection files; copies of both are in LC/HF.

Description: Jiménez Moreno, MS.

266

Quiotepec y Cuicatlan, Códice de. Códice Martínez Gracida. MNA 35-29. Ex–Martínez Gracida collection. Published. Cartographic-historical. Santiago Quiotepec, ex-district of Cuicatlan, Northern Oaxaca. 16thC (?). European paper. 61 × 102 cm.

Map in late, acculturated, or merely crude style showing Quiotepec, roads to Cuicatlan and Ixcatlan, as well as Hernan Cortés and other persons. Glosses appear to be in several languages. Unpublished descriptions in MNA inventories interpret the document as representing the arrival of Cortés in Quiotepec in 1527.

Glass (1964) provides brief description and photograph.

Publication: Glass, 1964, p. 72, pl. 30.

267

Ramírez Collection, Cadastral Fragment of the. MNA/AH Col. Antig. 213 (José Fernando Ramírez, *Opusculos históricos*, MS, vol. 25), pp. 499–500. Ex–José Fernando Ramírez collection. Unpublished. Economic (cadastral). Central Mexico. 16th-C. Native paper. Fragment. 11 × 21 cm.

The fragment exhibits drawings of small plots of land with measurements and place glyphs opposite the heads of Indians with personal name glyphs and Nahuatl glosses. Its style and composition are comparable to Humboldt Fragment 8 and, to a lesser degree, to other manuscripts of the Vergara Group.

Bibliography: None.

268

Región Boscosa, Mapa de una. "Copia de Boturini?" MNA 35-74. Ex–Boturini collection. Published. Cartographic. Central Mexico. 16thC. European paper pasted on amatl paper. 35.7 × 28.6 cm. and a small fragment 7.5 × 4.5 cm.

The manuscript is a fragment of a larger document. It shows trees, a road with numerical symbols, place glyphs, and other detail. What region is represented by this map is unknown.

Glass (1964) gives photoreproduction and brief description. Mena (1923) attempts to identify the place glyphs.

Publication: Glass, 1964, p. 127, pl. 79.

Brief description: Mena, 1923, pp. 54–55, 58, figs. 1–8, no. 9.

269

Reinisch, Mappe. BNP 400. Ex–Charency collection. Published. Genealogical. Oxtoticpac-Texcoco region, Mexico. 1586. Native paper. 83.5 × 39.5 cm.

The document presents two separate sets of genealogies on the obverse, both glossed in Nahuatl. Each partially duplicates the content of the other. The upper represents persons by the drawings of human heads, the lower by small circles. Place glyphs include Tenochtitlan, Oxtoticpac, and possibly Huexotla (but glossed Tezcapoctli). The numerous persons have names at least homonymous with Indians of the royal families of Texcoco, of its subsidiaries, and their Tenochca relatives (Nezahualcoyotl, Techotlalatzin, Cuauhtlecohuatzin, Huitzilihuitl, Matlacihuatzin, etc.).

On the reverse are several Nahuatl glosses giving personal names, the dates 1545 and 1586, and two sets of native numerals.

The only published reproduction consists of two heliogravure sheets issued about 1886 (*Mappa Reinisch*, n.d.). Boban (1891) comments briefly on this reproduction.

Copy: Small modern copy, BNP 419-9. BNP 99 is a set of the heliogravure sheets.

Publication: *Mappa Reinisch*, n.d.

Brief description: Boban, 1891, 2: 17–18, 273.

270

Ríos, Codex. Codex Vaticanus A. Codex Vaticanus 3738. Copia Vaticana. Biblioteca Apostolica Vaticana, Rome. Codex Vat. Lat. 3738. Published. Ritual-calen-

drical, historical, and ethnographic. Valley of Mexico. ca. 1566–89. European paper. 101 leaves. 46 × 29 cm.

Codex Ríos and Codex Telleriano-Remensis (q.v.) are currently believed to be copies of a common original, the lost Codex Huitzilopochtli (see Huitzilopochtli Group, where the relationship is discussed).

Codex Ríos is believed to have been copied by a non-Indian (?) artist in Italy and its long Italian texts to be based on a commentary by Fr. Pedro de los Ríos. The date 1566 occurs in the text as a reference to a past event; the paper appears not to have been made until 1569–70. The *terminus ante quem*—1570 or 1589—is discussed herein under the Huitzilopochtli Group (q.v.).

The manuscript has seven major sections: (1) cosmogenic and mythological traditions with some emphasis on the four epochs and including notices about Quetzalcoatl and the Toltecs, (2) a 260-day divinatory almanac, (3) calendrical tables without drawings for the years 1558–1619, (4) an 18-month festival calendar with drawings of the gods of each period, (5) sacrificial and other customs including portraits of Indian types, (6) pictorial annals for the years 1195–1549 beginning with the migration from Chicomoztoc and covering later events in the Valley of Mexico, and (7) year glyphs for the years 1556–62 without written or pictorial entries. Most of the codex has a long written commentary in Italian, but only three pages of the historical section are annotated. For a concordance of these sections with Codex Telleriano-Remensis see Table 2 of this census.

Details from four pages were published in Cartari (1615). These were obtained by the editor, Pignoria, from Octavio Malipiero and had formerly been owned by Cardinal Amulio (died 1570), the Vatican librarian. A detail from a fifth page which appears in a later edition (Cartari, 1626) was obtained from Filippo Winghernio (Filippo de Winghe, died 1592). Paso y Troncoso (1898b,

p. 354) identifies these details as copied from Codex Ríos and not from Codex Telleriano-Remensis or, presumably, from Codex Huitzilopochtli.

Twelve pages were reproduced by Humboldt (1810). The first edition was by Kingsborough (1831–48) with palaeography and English translation of the Italian text. The color facsimile by Ehrle (1900) has a palaeography of the text and a detailed bibliographic introduction. Another detailed description is by Paso y Troncoso (1898b). The first edition by color photography, with blank pages omitted, is given by Corona Núñez (1964–67) together with a Spanish translation of the text and a page-by-page commentary.

Innumerable studies of Mexican Indian religion have commented on the cosmological section of the manuscript, particularly its drawings of the four world eras. Among these studies are Chavero (1877a; 1882–1903; n.d., pp. 77–90), Paso y Troncoso (1882), and Imbelloni (1943), which are perhaps no more distinguished than many not cited here.

The month glyphs on ff. 89r and 89v have been reproduced and identified by Seler (1899a) and by Kubler and Gibson (1951). Two scenes from the historical section have been discussed by J. F. Ramírez (1847) and Madier de Montjau (1875). One scene, the death of Alvarado, is also treated by Riva Palacio (n.d.) and by Mendoza (1869). For further bibliography common to both Codex Ríos and Codex Telleriano-Remensis, for studies of their calendrical sections, and further comment see Huitzilopochtli Group.

Copy: A copy (ca. 1592) of a drawing of a god from the codex is in the Biblioteca Angelica, Rome, MS 1564, f. 58/57r. Whether this is the copy by Filippo de Winghe published in 1626 (see above) has not been determined.

Editions: Corona Núñez, 1964–67, 3: 7–313, 411–49; Ehrle, 1900; Kingsborough, 1831–48, reproduction in vol. 2, text in vol.

5, pp. 159–206, translation in vol. 6, pp. 155–232.

Early partial publications: Cartari, 1615, pp. iv–xxiii: 1626, pp. 548–61: Humboldt, 1810, pp. 56–89, 202–11, pls. 14, 26.

Description: Paso y Troncoso, 1898b, pp. 60–61, 340–59.

Miscellaneous studies: Chavero, 1877a; 1882–1903; 1903a, pp. 5–14; n.d., pp. x–xi, xxii, 77–104, and passim; Imbelloni, 1943; Madier de Montjau, 1875, pp. 241–56, pls. 2, 3; Mendoza, 1869, pp. 901–04; Paso y Troncoso, 1882; J. F. Ramírez, 1847, pp. 278–87, pls. 3, 4; Riva Palacio, n.d., p. 269; Seler, 1899a, figs. 20, 21.

Historical references: Barthelemy, 1798, p. 199; Fábrega, 1899, pp. 13–14; Hornius, 1652, pp. 267–76; Mercati, 1589, p. 96; Warburton, 1744, 1: 16; Zoega, 1797, pp. 530–31.

Brief descriptions: Alcina Franch, 1955, p. 437–39; Kubler and Gibson, 1951, pp. 71–72.

271–274

SAHAGUN, FRAY BERNARDINO DE, DRAWINGS BY THE INFORMANTS OF. The Franciscan friar, Bernardino de Sahagún, 1499–1590, ranks as the foremost ethnographer of the 16thC in Mexico. The work for which he is best known is the *Historia general [universal] de las cosas de [la] Nueva España*, an encyclopedic compendium of the religion, customs, and natural history of the Aztecs. A number of different manuscripts, representing successive stages in the writing of the *Historia*, survive. They are in Nahuatl, Spanish, or both, and some are illustrated. The Nahuatl texts and the drawings are considered to be the work of Sahagún's native informants. Only the manuscripts having drawings are treated in the census entries below. See Article 27B, nos. 1097–1108, for a survey of all extant manuscripts related to the *Historia*.

The main manuscripts of the *Historia* are the two *Códices Matritenses*, one in BPN and the other in RAH, and the Florentine Codex (no. 274). The former contain various early manuscripts of the *Historia*. Only two are illustrated: the *Primeros memoriales* of 1559–61 (no. 271, below) and the *Manuscrito de Tlatelolco* of 1561–65, which contains two drawings (nos. 272–73). For a pictorial calendar bound with a Sahaguntine text, see the *Kalendario Mexicano, Latino y Castellano* (no. 205).

For the early bibliography it should be borne in mind that the two *Códices Matritenses* and the Florentine Codex were almost wholly unknown until after 1881 and that no significant part of these manuscripts was published until about 1889. The Spanish text of the *Historia*, however, was published from the Tolosa copy in 1829–30 by Bustamante and in 1830 by Kingsborough (1831–48).

A full bibliography of the *Historia* that would include the numerous partial publications, translations, extracts, and commentaries has yet to be published. The citations given in the following census entries are selected; generally they exclude works primarily related to the partial publication or translation of the texts and not the drawings. The excellent bibliography given by Nicolau d'Olwer (1952) is not complete. Cline (Article 14A) provides a review of the bibliography surrounding the publication of the *Historia*.

A summary history of the Sahagún manuscripts with a study of the nature and significance of the drawings is given by Robertson (1959, pp. 167–78, pls. 11, 60–77).

[271]

—— *Primeros memoriales.* Manuscrito de Tepepulco. BPN *in* Códice Matritense del Real Palacio, ff. 250–303, and RAH *in* Códice Matritense de la Academia de la Historia, ff. 51–85. Published. Ritual-calendrical, historical, ethnographic, and miscellaneous. Tepepulco, Hidalgo. ca. 1559–61. European paper. Folio.

The *Primeros memoriales*, an illustrated Nahuatl text divided into four *capítulos*, is

the oldest of the surviving preliminary manuscripts for the *Historia general*. It is now bound with the *Códices Matritenses* (see preceding entry). Part of its text and some of its drawings were later copied into the Florentine Codex (no. 274).

The major sections of the manuscript having illustrations are a calendar of the 18 monthly ceremonies, a section devoted to the services and offerings to the gods, the costumes and adornments of the gods, as well as one on constellations and other celestial phenomena. Another calendrical section has drawings of day signs; an historical section has drawings of the rulers of Tenochtitlan, Texcoco, and Huexotla. The final pictorial section is devoted to the insignia and accoutrements of the nobility. Among the miscellaneous drawings is the plan of a sacred precinct showing a double temple, a ball court, and other buildings. This drawing has been reproduced innumerable times, usually identified as representing the main center and temple of Tenochtitlan despite the Tepepulco origin of the manuscript.

The entirety of the *Primeros memoriales* was reproduced in photographic facsimile with the drawings also reproduced in color lithographs by Paso y Troncoso (1905–07). Poor color photographs of all the drawings are given in Ballesteros Gaibrois (1964). There are numerous partial translations but not all the illustrated sections have been translated. A selected list of those that are of illustrated passages is given below. Each of them gives copies of most or all of the corresponding drawings. Those by Seler include commentaries and iconographic studies of the drawings. A detailed outline, concordance with the *Historia*, and bibliography are given by Nicholson in Article 14B. See also Article 27B, no. 1098.

Copies: A privately owned copy or falsification of the first 18 drawings and accompanying texts of the *Primeros memoriales* (the festival calendar) on a 10-leaf amatl paper screenfold is described in Article 26 (no. 939). It is not the same copy from which two details are reproduced by Gómez de Orozco (1939a).

Publication: Paso y Troncoso, 1905–07, vol. 6.

Publication of the drawings: Ballesteros Gaibrois, 1964.

Partial translations (selected, illustrated): Aguirre, 1950–51; Fewkes, 1893; Garibay, 1948; León-Portilla, 1958; Seler, 1899b; 1904b; 1904c; 1904d; 1927, pp. 33–53, 54 ff.

Other: Gómez de Orozco, 1939a, pls. 2–3.

Partial brief description: Kubler and Gibson, 1951, p. 72.

[272]

—— *Sahagún Calendar Wheel.* Calendar Wheel in the Manuscrito de Tlatelolco. BPN, Códice Matritense del Real Palacio, f. 189r. Published. Calendrical. Tlatelolco, D.F. ca. 1563–65. European paper. Folio.

The *Manuscrito de Tlatelolco* (see Article 27B, no. 1099) is primarily a Nahuatl text compiled in Tlateloco, ca. 1561–65. It forms the bulk of the *Códices Matritenses* (see above). Much of its text was later copied into the *Florentine Codex* (no. 274) as were its only two drawings, the Sahagún Calendar Wheel, and the table of day signs (treated in the next entry). Both drawings fall in the section of the manuscript known as the *Memoriales en tres columnas*; in the Florentine Codex both illustrate the Spanish rather than the Nahuatl text.

The calendar wheel depicts the 52-year cycle with glyphs for the four year-bearer days, 13 concentric circles with the numbers 1–13 repeated four times, and several Nahuatl glosses. It appears to be an addition to the manuscript page on which it is drawn; it is not mentioned in the Nahuatl text. In the tradition of the spiral calendar wheel, it may be related historiographically to the wheel associated with Motolinía or Francisco de las Navas (see Veytia Calendar Wheel no. 2, no. 388).

A b/w photograph and a color lithograph

are given by Paso y Troncoso (1905–07, vol. 7). The lithograph is reproduced in color in Clark (1938). A poor color photograph is given by Ballesteros Gaibrois (1964).

Copies: A copy appears in the Florentine Codex (bk. 7, fig. 20) together with a description in Spanish at the end of book 7, a description that does not appear in the Nahuatl text. See the Spanish and Nahuatl texts of book 7, chapter 7 (mistakenly numbered 8 in some editions). A color lithograph of this version is given by Paso y Troncoso (1905–07, vol. 5); a b/w reproduction of the lithograph is given in Dibble and Anderson (1950–69) with the Spanish description and an English translation.

Another 16thC copy is in the *Manuscrito de Tolosa* (Article 27B, no. 1105). This copy is reproduced in the Bustamante (1829–30) edition of this manuscript of the *Historia* from a copy; further reproductions, all from copies, appear in most other editions of Sahagún's *Historia general* (see *Florentine Codex*, no. 274, below).

A copy of ca. 1571–77 is in Francisco Hernández, *De Antiquitatibus Novae Hispaniae* (MS in RAH), of which there is a photofacsimile edition (Hernández, 1926) and a Spanish translation (Hernández, 1945). J. F. Ramírez (1898) reproduces and comments on this version of the calendar wheel.

Bibliography (selected): Ballesteros Gaibrois, 1964, pl. 1, fig. 1; Bustamante, 1829–30, 1: p. 345; Clark, 1938, 1: pl. 5; Dibble and Anderson, 1950–69, part 8, fig. 20 and facing text on unnumbered page; Hernández, 1926, f. 118v; 1945, pl. 1; Paso y Troncoso, 1905–07, vol. 5, pl. 45; vol. 7, p. 279 and unnumbered color plate; J. F. Ramírez, 1898, pp. 362–80, fig. on p. 372.

[273]

—— Table of Day Signs in the *Manuscrito de Tlatelolco.* Biblioteca del Palacio Nacional, Madrid, *in* Códice Matritense del Real Palacio, f. 242v. Published. Calendrical. Tlatelolco, D.F. 1564. European paper. Folio.

The second of the two illustrations in the *Manuscrito de Tlatelolco* (see previous entry for comment) is a table of day signs, organized to present the structure of the 260-day cycle of the divinatory almanac. In the left margin are the names of the years in a cycle of 52 years. A Nahuatl text above the table (partially translated by Jiménez Moreno, 1938a, p. 48, note 14) mentions the Colegio de Santa Cruz and the date 1564. This text appears not to have been copied or translated into the Florentine Codex.

A b/w photograph and a color lithograph are given by Paso y Troncoso (1905–07, vol. 7). A color photograph is given by Ballesteros Gaibrois (1964).

Copies: A description and a copy of the table appear in the Florentine Codex in the appendix to book 4, a section that has no equivalent in the Nahuatl text. Reproductions of this copy appear in all editions of the *Historia general* based on the Florentine Codex (see next entry) but not in those editions based on the *Manuscrito de Tolosa*, which lacks the table although it contains the description. Dibble and Anderson (1950–69) give an English translation of the appendix to book 4.

A copy of ca. 1571–77 is in Francisco Hernández, *De Antiquitatibus Novae Hispaniae*, of which there is a photofacsimile edition (Hernández, 1926) and a Spanish translation (Hernández, 1945). J. F. Ramírez (1898) comments on this version of the table.

Bibliography (selected): Ballesteros Gaibrois, 1964, pl. 1, fig. 2; Dibble and Anderson, 1950–69, parts 4 and 5, pp. 135–46, fig. 102; Hernández, 1926, ff. 119v–120r; 1945, pl. 2; Paso y Troncoso, 1905–07, 7: 386; J. F. Ramírez, 1898, pp. 372–75.

[274]

—— *Florentine Codex*. Códice Florentino. Historia general de las cosas de Nueva

España. Biblioteca Medicea Laurenziana, Florence. Partially published. Ritual-calendrical, historical, ethnographic, and miscellaneous. Tlatelolco, D.F. About 1575–77 or 1578–80. European paper. 3 vols. (345, 372, and 493 leaves). Folio.

The Florentine Codex is a final and complete manuscript of the 12 books of the *Historia general*. It contains the Nahuatl text (derived largely from the earlier *Códices Matritenses*) and a parallel Spanish text (part translation, part paraphrase). Each text contains material not in the other. It is illustrated by 1,846 drawings, not counting decorative tailpieces and ornamental designs.

The codex was generally unknown until about 1883 (see Nicolau d'Olwer, 1952, p. 194), although a good catalog description was published by Bandini (1791–93), and Civezza (1879) had confirmed its existence in Florence. A reprint of the description by Bandini in García Icazbalceta (1886), the reproduction of some of its drawings by Brinton (1890b) and Peñafiel (1890) after copies obtained from Eduard Seler, and a description of the manuscript by Paso y Troncoso (1896) are among the first modern publications on the codex. See also Article 27B, no. 1104.

The content of the 12 books of the codex and the distribution of its drawings are as follows:

1. Gods (33 illus.). The first 26 drawings (illustrating the entirety of the book) occupy three leaves preceding the text of this book; all but two derive from the *Primeros memoriales*. Appendix: refutation of idolatry by Sahagún (10 illus.). In general, most of the drawings in the codex occupy the Spanish or translation column (the decorative drawings are found in either column), but in this appendix they are in the Nahuatl column, which in this instance may be a version of the Spanish text.

2. Ceremonies of the 18 months (49 illus.). Appendix: religious customs, temples, songs

(17 illus.). The dominical letter and numerical calendar which frame chapters 1–18 and part of chapter 19 of this book are referred to as "pintado" in the appendix to book 4 but can hardly be considered drawings.

3. Origins of the gods and mythology (14 illus.). Appendix: afterworld and education (5 illus.).

4. The divinatory almanac and various customs (101 illus.). Appendix: treatise on the calendar in Spanish only by Sahagún (3 calendrical tables). The first table derives from the *Manuscrito de Tlatelolco* (no. 273, above).

5. Omens (7 illus.). Appendix: superstitions (2 illus.).

6. Moral philosophy: prayers to the gods, lords' discourses, moral exhortations, marriage and childbirth, adages, riddles, and metaphors (52 illus.).

7. Natural philosophy: celestial phenomena (the sun, the moon, the stars, etc.) and the count and binding of the years (20 illus.). The final illustration is a calendar wheel, derived from the *Manuscrito de Tlatelolco* (no. 272, above), described in a Spanish addition to this book.

8. The lords of Mexico, Tlatelolco, Texcoco, and Huexotla; customs (adornments, costumes, foods, government, etc.) of the lords; education (100 illus.). The drawings of the lords of Mexico, Texcoco, and Huexotla derive from the *Primeros memoriales*.

9. Merchants (39 illus.) and craftsmen (fine arts; 71 illus.).

10. People: vices, virtues, occupations; sicknesses of the body; the nations of Mexico (197 illus.).

11. Natural history (with over half of all the drawings): animals, birds, trees, herbs, etc. (965 illus.).

12. The conquest of Mexico City and Tlatelolco by the Spaniards (161 illus.). Some of the drawings in books 11 and 12 have not been completed or colored.

There have been six editions of the Spanish text of the *Historia*, one French transla-

tion, and one incomplete English translation. They are cited under the names of their editors below. The 19thC editions derive from the Tolosa text; the 20thC editions bear a complex relationship to previous editions, copies of the Tolosa manuscript, partial copies of the Florentine Codex, and, in the case of the edition of 1956, a microfilm or photographic copy for one or more of the books was also consulted. The editions of 1938 and 1956 contain various supplementary material and translations of other texts.

The only complete translation of the Nahuatl text is that published by Dibble and Anderson (1950–69).

The drawings of the Florentine Codex were copied for Paso y Troncoso by Genaro López in 1893–94 and were lithographed in Florence about 1903–09. Sets of the 158 color lithographs form volume 5 of Paso y Troncoso (1905–07). These lithographs are the source of most reproductions of drawings that illustrate numerous works on Mexico. A few are reproduced in the editions of the Spanish text of 1938, 1946, and 1956. B/w photographs of all these lithographs are reproduced in Dibble and Anderson (1950–69).

Photographic reproductions of the original drawings are less numerous. Selected illustrated pages of the Florentine Codex are photographically reproduced in Dibble and Anderson (1950–69). A few are so reproduced by Robertson (1959) and by Blacker (1965). The latter introduces the novelty of giving three in color. Other photographic reproductions of selected drawings have illustrated various recent general works on Mexico and its art. A photofacsimile of the entirety of the codex has been contemplated by the University of Utah Press.

The only specific study of the style of the drawings in the Florentine Codex *per se* is that by Robertson (1959). For a minor critique of his presentation see Glass (1960).

Copies: The López copies (tracings?) of the Florentine drawings, now incomplete, are MNA 35-103. The Paso y Troncoso copy of the Florentine Codex (Spanish, Nahuatl, and drawings, the latter probably by López), books 1–9 only, is in MNA/AH. 25 pages of this copy are reproduced by Acosta Saignes (1946, vol. 3). Jiménez Moreno (1938a, p. 40) expresses a doubt whether the Spanish in this copy is from the Florentine or Tolosa MSS. A copy of book 12 owned by Zelia Nuttall is in MNA/AH, Colección Gómez de Orozco no. 6. Photographs of the codex were exhibited by Nuttall in 1892 (Exposición, 1892). Copies of the drawings by J. Cooper Clark, seemingly made for an edition once contemplated by Peabody Museum, Harvard University, are in PML. A copy of the Nahuatl text and drawings of book 1 made by Daniel G. Brinton in 1889 are in UP/UM.

In HSA is an Italian translation of books 1–5 of the Florentine Codex formerly in the Phillipps collection. Possibly of mid-17thC date, the binding bears the coat of arms of the Medici family and the hat and mantle of a bishop or archbishop. See Article 27B, no. 1105, for comment on the *Manuscrito de Tolosa*, a copy of the Spanish text of the *Historia*.

Editions of the Spanish text: Acosta Saignes, 1946; F. Bandelier, 1932 (English translation, bks. 1–4); Bustamante, 1829 (bk. 12); 1829–30 (bks. 1–11); 1890–96 (reprint of his 1829 and 1829–30); Garibay, 1956 (reprinted 1969); Jourdanet and Siméon, 1880 (French translation of the Bustamante edition); Kingsborough, 1831–48, vols. 5 and 7; Ramírez Cabañas, 1938.

Edition and translation of the Nahuatl text: Dibble and Anderson, 1950–69.

Editions of the drawings: Dibble and Anderson, 1950–69; Paso y Troncoso, 1905–07, vol. 5.

Historical references: Bandini, 1791–93; Civezza, 1879, p. 525; García Icazbalceta, 1886, pp. 289–90; Paso y Troncoso, 1896.

Other: Blacker, 1965, pp. 62, 79, 102, passim; Brinton, 1890b; Exposición, 1892, pp.

125–26; Glass, 1960; Peñafiel, 1890, pls. 90–100; Robertson, 1959, 173–78; Seler, 1927.

275

Salamanca, Manta de. Manta de Tlaxcala. Unknown. Ex–Eufemio de la Cruz Zamora (of Salamanca, Guanajuato) collection. Published. Miscellaneous. Tlaxcala, Tlaxcala. 16thC (?). Cloth. 87 × 63 cm.

The painting, in much-acculturated style, illustrates the four lords of Tlaxcala (Tlehuexolotzin, Maxixcatzin, Citlalpopoca, and Xicotencatl) and associates each with an hieroglyphic coat of arms. At the top is the coat of arms of the kings of Spain.

The document is described in detail by Rivera (1892). Peñafiel (1909) reproduces a photograph and reprints part of the Rivera description. Gibson (1952) describes it briefly; a poor reproduction (after Peñafiel) appears in Muñoz Camargo (1947b). Angulo (1958) reports an unsuccessful search for the document.

Publication: Muñoz Camargo, 1947b, p. 206; Peñafiel, 1909, pp. 4, 16–19, pl. 25.

Descriptions: Gibson, 1952, p. 267; Rivera, 1892.

Other: Angulo, 1958.

276

San Andres, Codex. Musée de l'Homme, Paris. Ex–Doutrelaine collection. Published. Economic (tribute). San Andres (possibly Xaltenco, Xaltocan, or a third locality, all northeast of Cuauhtitlan), Mexico. 16thC. Native paper. 40 × 46.5 cm.

Fragmentary leaf with drawings of heads of Indians with numerical signs, items of tribute, and a place glyph interpreted as representing a San Andres. Glosses include Cuauhtitlan, San Andres, Tenochtitlan, and a reference to calpixque. Galarza (loc. cit.) suggests that the document may be concerned with tribute or repartimiento labor.

A detailed study and photoreproduction are given by Galarza (1963).

Publication: Galarza, 1963.

277

San Joseph, sujeto a Xilotepeque, Plano de. Unknown. Published. Economic (property plans). Central Mexico. 1547 (?) or 1572 (?). Amatl paper. Dimensions not determined.

Plan of part of a town showing houses, a church ("San Joseph"), and native symbols for three currents of water flowing from a spring. The drawing is published by Lenz (1950) without description or indication of its location.

Publication: Lenz, 1950, pp. 108–10, 160, figs. 146–48, 241.

278

San Matias (Tlaxcala), Linderos del Pueblo de. Linderos del Pueblo de Santa Maria Belen, Tlaxcala. Unknown. Unpublished. Unavailable (cartographic-historical). Tlaxcala. 1536 (?). Physical data unknown.

A copy of the document, copied from another copy owned by Cahuantzi, is described by Paso y Troncoso (1892–93). He described it as showing boundaries, human figures, and the date 1536. He also referred to the place as San Martin. Glass (1964) suggests that the copy described by Paso y Troncoso may correspond to the "Linderos del Pueblo de Santa Maria Belen," also a copy of 1892 and bearing the 1536 date. The latter was in the MNA codex collection in 1934, but the present whereabouts of these copies and their originals is now unknown.

Bibliography: Glass, 1964, pp. 24, 28; Paso y Troncoso, 1892–93, 1: 54.

279

Sánchez Solís, Códice. Codex Egerton 2895. Codex Waecker-Götter. Códice Zapoteco. British Museum, Egerton MS 2895. Ex–Felipe Sánchez Solís and Ernst Ludwig Karl, Baron von Waecker-Götter, collections. Published. Historical. Western Oaxaca. 16thC. Skin screenfold. 16 leaves. 21.5 × 27.7 cm. (16 painted pages on obverse; 13 on reverse; initial and terminal pages of reverse serve as covers and are blank). Total length 441 cm.

In traditional but rather large scale Mixtec style, the first three pages open with a place glyph and two dates followed by a procession of figures. Most of the remaining utilized pages present a couple (male and female) with personal and calendrical name glyphs and a place glyph, apparently representing a 26-generation genealogy. Some pages show subsidiary genealogies. Both short and long glosses in at least two handwritings are in Mixtec; most are illegible and have not been studied. Much of the painting is deteriorated; there are also deliberate effacements.

M. E. Smith (MS) has identified two persons of the Tilantongo dynasty in the manuscript and the place glyphs for Acatlan (southern Puebla) and Tequixtepec (ex–Dto. of Huajuapan, Western Oaxaca) as well as that for Tilantongo. She suggests that the manuscript is concerned with genealogies of the Mixteca Baja region.

Burland (1965) gives photographic color facsimile and a detailed physical description. The Peñafiel (1890) edition is based on a copy by Carral of the MNA copy, which lacks the glosses. Burland (1947b) reproduces an ultraviolet photograph of one page and comments on its content. The brief description by Paso y Troncoso (1886) is reprinted by Peñafiel (1890) and by Galindo y Villa (1905a).

Copies: The José María Velasco copy of 1882–83 is in the MNA/BNA. Two other copies by Velasco, the first of 1869, the Seler collection copy, and the Carral copy are unknown.

Publication: Burland, 1965; Peñafiel, 1890, pp. 101–02, pls. 260–88.

Other: Burland, 1947b; Galindo y Villa, 1905a, pp. 224–27; Peñafiel, 1887, p. xvi; M. E. Smith, MS.

Brief descriptions: Alcina Franch, 1955, pp. 480–81; Lehmann, 1905a, pp. 272–73; Paso y Troncoso, 1886.

280 (fig. 53)

Santa Cruz Map of the City and Valley of Mexico. Map attributed to Alonso de Santa Cruz. Mapa de Santa Cruz. Mapa de Uppsala. Plano de la Ciudad de Mexico. La Ciudad Tenuxtitan Mexico. University Library, Uppsala, Sweden. Ex–Carl Gustaf Nordin collection. Published. Cartographic. Tlatelolco, D. F. ca. 1555. Skin (apparently *not* parchment). 78 (75?) × 114 cm.

The map is an extraordinarily handsome and accurate depiction of the City and Valley of Mexico, with great detail. It embodies both native and European artistic and cartographic traditions. The plan of the city, in which Tlatelolco figures most prominently, is at the center. The surrounding view of the valley, in a different scale, is concentrated with detail and genre scenes, such as Indians catching birds with nets in Lake Texcoco. Some of the numerous communities shown in the landscape are identified both by glosses and by place glyphs. The modern attribution of the map is to the Indian Colegio de Santa Cruz in Tlatelolco and certainly not to the Spanish cosmographer, Alonso de Santa Cruz.

The map bears a badly effaced added inscription which mentions Charles V (abdicated 1556) and his Royal Cosmographer, Alonso de Santa Cruz (died 1567). A copied detail of the map appears in the latter's *Islario general*, believed to have been completed by 1556 (Schuller, 1913). Despite this evident *terminus ante quem* of 1556, Toussaint (in Toussaint et al., 1938) adduces cartographic evidence to support an *ante quem* date as late as 1562, in which he is supported by Kubler (1951).

The history of the map between the date of the partial copy by Alonso de Santa Cruz and its reported presence in the Nordin collection in Stockholm by 1792 is uncertain. It *may* have been given by Charles V to Ferdinand I (died 1604) of Germany; it *may* be registered in the posthumous inventory of the Santa Cruz papers of 1572 published by Gómez de Orozco (1927b); a vaguely worded inventory of 1635 suggests that it *may* have been in the Hradschin Palace in Prague, in which case it *may* have been acquired by the Swedish army during the sacking of Prague in 1648. These and other theories are discussed by Linné (1948).

The first publication of the map was a reduced, lithographed line drawing issued simultaneously by Nordenskiöld (1889) and Dahlgren (1889). This lithograph is reprinted in Apenes (1947) and Carrera Stampa (1949b). Another lithograph, apparently based on the 1892 copy now in the MNA/BNA, was issued by Peñafiel (1901).

The first color edition, a natural-size lithograph of a copy by Adela Breton, was published in Maudslay (1908–16). The first important commentary, with a b/w photo of the Breton lithograph, was published by Toussaint, Gómez de Orozco, and Fernández (1938). The major commentary by Linné (1948) has a slightly reduced color photoreproduction, selected b/w photo details, and a b/w reproduction of the Breton lithograph in sections. A color reproduction in six sections (photographic) and one b/w photograph was printed for a commentary planned by Nuttall but not published and has had very limited circulation (Nuttall, n.d.); the sheets of this reproduction are in the Lowie Museum, University of California, Berkeley.

A small photograph of the original and details accompany the illuminating discussion of the style and other aspects of the map by Robertson (1959). Both Linné (1948) and Carrera Stampa (1949b) provide bibliography far exceeding that cited below.

Copies: A watercolor copy of 1892 is in MNA/BNA. Two of the four known manuscripts of the *Islario general* by Alonso de Santa Cruz contain a detail copied from the map. The NBV copy is reproduced in Wieser (1908), Toussaint et al. (1938), and

194

Linné (1948). These vary slightly from the BNMA copy reproduced in Santa Cruz (1918–19).

Publication (selected): Linné, 1948; Maudslay, 1908–16, vol. 3; Nuttall, n.d.; Peñafiel, 1901; Robertson, 1959, pp. 159–63, pls. 55–57; Toussaint, Gómez de Orozco, and Fernández, 1938, pp. 135–66, figs. 21–25.

Other publications (selected): Apenes, 1947, pl. 2; Carrera Stampa, 1949b, pp. 342–46, 407–08, pl. 6; Dahlgren, 1889 (page citation not determined); Nordenskiöld, 1889 (page citation not determined).

Publication, Islario copy: Linné, 1948, fig. 54; Santa Cruz, 1918–19, 61: 695–710, pl. 116; Toussaint, Gómez de Orozco, and Fernández, 1938, fig. 23; Wieser, 1908, pl. 11.

Other: Barlow, 1947a; Gómez de Orozco, 1927b, p. 361; Kubler, 1951; Schuller, 1913.

Miscellaneous studies and references: Baz, 1899; Burland, 1950b; García Cubas, 1897; Linné, 1942; Toussaint, 1938.

281

Santa Fe o de Patzcuaro, Mapa de. Mapa de Santa Fe de la Laguna. Unknown. Published. Cartographic. Santa Fe de la Laguna, Michoacan. ca. 1552. Parchment. Dimensions unreported.

Simple map showing agricultural fields, trees, a boundary line marked by crosses, various buildings, including churches, and roads. Preserved copy exhibits few if any traditional or Indian elements.

The MNA copy is briefly described and reproduced by Glass (1964). Paso y Troncoso (1892–93) transcribes a Spanish text on the face of the map treating land boundaries.

Copy: 1892 copy, MNA 35–105 (131 × 97 cm.).

Publication: Glass, 1964, p. 160, pl. 112.

Brief description: Paso y Troncoso, 1892–93, 1: 241–43.

282

Saville, Codex. Códice Protohistórico. Co-dex Tetlapalco. Codex Telapalco. Museum of the American Indian, Heye Foundation, New York. Published. Historical. Valley of Mexico. 16thC. Native paper tira. 145 × 26 cm.

Vertical tira with pictorial annals, 1407–1535, with succession of the rulers of Tenochtitlan from Huitzilihuitl through Moctezuma Xocoyotzin and the Spanish conquest. A Christian cross, saint, Madonna, and bell with Spanish monetary symbols are drawn opposite the years 1531–35.

Commentary and full reproduction by Cuevas (1929) reprinted with partial reproduction (Cuevas, 1956). The glosses have not been studied. Cuevas (1930) gives controversial interpretation of final details (reproduced in color) as representing the apparition of the Virgin of Guadalupe. A detail is published by Hagen (1944).

Publication: Cuevas, 1929.

Other: Cuevas, 1930, pp. 51–53, colored plate facing p. 50; 1956; Hagen, 1944, pl. 5 (a); Taylor, 1956.

283

Selden, Codex. Codex Selden 1. Codex Selden 2. Códice Selden B. Lienzo de Retapa. MS pictórico de Petapa. Bodleian Library, Oxford. Ex–John Selden collection. Published. Historical. Western Oaxaca. ca. 1556–60. Skin screenfold originally painted on both sides but one side later covered with a white ground so that only one side has a legible content. 20 leaves. ca. 27.5 × 27.5 cm.

Traditional-style Mixtec history; presents the genealogies and origin of the dynasties of an unidentified locality known as Belching Mountain, after the form of its place glyph. The first date is A.D. 783 or 794 and the last legible date is equivalent to 1556. The genealogies include relationships to numerous persons from other localities, including Teozacoalco and Tilantongo, known through other Mixtec manuscripts of the Nuttall Group (q.v.).

The first edition was published by Kingsborough (1831–48). The detailed interpretation and commentary by Caso (1964a) are accompanied by a photographic color facsimile. Another photographic edition in color has a commentary by Corona Núñez (1964–67). The genealogies have also been interpreted by Dark (1958a). Caso (1964a) criticizes the suggestions as to provenience advanced by Dark (1959).

Publication: Caso, 1964a; Corona Núñez, 1964–67, 2: 77–99; Librería Echániz, 1946b; Kingsborough, 1831–48, vol. 1.

Studies: Burland, 1958b; Caso, 1952; Dark, 1958a, 1958b, 1959; Dark and Plesters, 1959; H. J. Spinden, 1935.

Brief descriptions: Alcina Franch, 1955, p. 489; Lehmann, 1905a, p. 271; Nowotny, 1961b, pp. 51–52, 271, pl. 61; Paso y Troncoso, 1898b, pp. 204–05, 364.

284

Selden Roll. Codex Selden 1. Codex Selden 2. Códice Selden A. Bodleian Library, Oxford. Ex–John Selden collection. Published. Historical. Western Oaxaca. 16th-C. Native paper tira, painted on one side. 38 × 350 cm.

The roll begins with a scene, closely paralleled in the Fragmento Gómez de Orozco, showing 9 Wind (Quetzalcoatl), the eight skies, and the earth. It continues with a mythical or historical narrative, which includes some ritual elements. The whole possibly relates to the origin of the dynasty of an as yet unidentified locality in Western Oaxaca.

Burland (1955b) gives commentary and b/w photofacsimile and one colored detail. The only modern edition in color is that by Corona Núñez (1964–67), also with commentary. The manuscript was first published by Kingsborough (1831–48). Caso (1954) and Nowotny (1958) compare some passages of the Selden Roll with other Mixtec manuscripts.

Publication: Burland, 1955b; Corona

196

Núñez, 1964–67, 2: 101–13; Librería Echániz, 1946a; Kingsborough, 1831–48, vol. 1.

Studies: Caso, 1954; Nowotny, 1958.

Brief descriptions: Alcina Franch, 1955, pp. 489–90; Lehmann, 1905a, p. 273.

❖❖❖

SERNA, JACINTO DE LA. *Manual de Ministros de Indios.* Calendrical illustrations in the de la Serna treatise on Indian idolatry, calendar, and superstitions are listed below. The work may be dated between 1646 and 1656. The relationship between the illustrations and possible Indian prototypes is problematical. The Mexican edition (Serna, 1892a), based on a manuscript owned by Paso y Troncoso and now in MNA/AH, includes the illustrations. They are omitted from the Madrid edition (Serna, 1892b), based on a copy owned by Nicolás León. The copy utilized by Boturini in Spain (and perhaps taken there by him from Mexico) is probably the RAH manuscript. Other manuscripts are in BNMA and HSA.

Edition of illustrations: Serna, 1892a.

Other: Serna, 1892b.

Brief description: Paso y Troncoso, 1897c, pp. 268–69.

285

—— Drawings of day and month symbols. See above. Published. Calendrical. Central Mexico. 1646–56.

Descriptions and drawings of symbols for the 20 days and 18 months as well as calendrical tables of day signs occur in the de la Serna text. The drawings are among the sources of calendrical illustrations in Boturini's *Historia general* (Boturini, 1948). Kubler and Gibson (1951) reproduce the month symbols after the Mexican edition of the de la Serna manuscript (Serna, 1892a).

Publication: Serna, 1892a, pp. 314–43, unnumbered plate "Meses del ano mexicano."

Other: Boturini, 1948, pls. 1–3, 5–19, 21–22; Kubler and Gibson, 1951, p. 68, fig. 14.

286

—— *Serna Calendar Wheel no. 1.* Unknown. Unpublished. Unavailable (calendrical). Central Mexico. 1646–56.

The first of two calendar wheels formerly in the de la Serna manuscript is now apparently missing from all known versions of the manuscript. De la Serna referred to it as the "Demostración y pintura de los siglos," thus implying that it depicted the 52-year cycle. The wheel is not mentioned by Boturini in the 1746 catalog of his collection, indicating that it was unknown to him; elsewhere (Boturini, 1948) he attempts to identify it with a spiral wheel similar to Veytia Calendar Wheel no. 2. Whether or not it may be identified with any of the calendars copied by Veytia, one of which is dated 1654, is unknown (see Veytia Calendar Wheels).

Bibliography: Boturini, 1948, pp. 362–63, pl. 21; Serna, 1892a, pp. 313–14, 328–29.

287

—— *Serna Calendar Wheel no. 2.* See main entry, above. Published. Calendrical. Central Mexico. 1646–56.

The second de la Serna wheel depicts the 20 day signs around the periphery of a circle. Glosses associate each year-bearer day with a direction. A lithographic reproduction of the wheel, from the MNA/AH manuscript, is given in de la Serna (1892a). Boturini (1948) gives a copy.

Publication: Serna, 1892a, pp. 329–30, unnumbered plate "Días del mes mexicano."

Other: Boturini, 1948, p. 98, pl. 6.

288

Sevina, Lienzo de. MNA 35-18. Ex–Pulido and Museo Michoacano, Morelia, collections. Published. Cartographic-historical. Sevina, Michoacan. 16thC. Cloth. 125 × 97.5 cm.

Principal pictorial elements are 10 schematic town plans within small squares. Drawings of friars and priests, shown in some form of altercation, appear in the largest square. Other details include Indians holding bows and arrows, Spaniards on horseback, circular temple platforms, trees, roads, and fields.

Glass (1964) gives brief description and photograph of the original.

Copy: 1892 copy, MNA 35-99. Modern copy, MNA 35-99A.

Publication: Glass, 1964, pp. 60, 153, pl. 20.

Brief descriptions: Mateos Higuera, 1948b, pp. 166–67; Paso y Troncoso, 1892–93, 1: 240–41.

289

Sierra, Códice. Códice de Santa Catarina Texupan. Codex Popoloca. Academia de Bellas Artes, Puebla. Ex–José Manso collection (?). Published. Economic. Santa Catarina Texupan, ex-district of Teposcolula, Western Oaxaca. 1550–64. European paper. 31 leaves. Folio (dimensions not determined).

Pictorial accounting ledger, with Nahuatl text, listing the community expenses for the support of the church of the reportedly extinct community of Santa Catarina Texupan (located near Santiago Texupan) for the years 1550–64.

A color facsimile of a copy was given limited distribution in 1906 (N. León, 1906a); the same plates were later issued with a description and a translation of the Nahuatl text (N. León, 1933). The latter reprints most of the Paso y Troncoso (1892–93) description.

Publication: N. León, 1906a, 1933.

Other: Ibarra de Anda, 1937; M. G. de la Rosa, 1907.

Brief descriptions: Alcina Franch, 1955, pp. 500–01; Lehmann, 1905a, p. 279; N. León, 1905b, pp. 25-26; Paso y Troncoso, 1892–93, 2: 346–58.

290

Sigüenza, Mapa. Códice de Sigüenza. Jeroglífico de Sigüenza. Mapa de la Peregrinación de los Aztecas. Pintura del Museo. Códice Ramírez. MNA 35-14. Ex-Sigüenza y Góngora and Boturini collections. Published. Historical. Valley of Mexico. 16thC. Amatl paper. 54.5 × 77.5 cm.

Migration itinerary and history of the Culhua–Mexica in the form of a map from Aztlan-Culhuacan through the settlement at Chapultepec to the founding of Tenochtitlan. The place names on the route vary from other sources, and no satisfactory interpretation has yet been offered.

The copy published in 1700 (Gemelli Careri, 1699–1700) is the source of the reproductions in Kingsborough (1831–48), Humboldt (1810), and Radin (1920), among many others. Most commentators before 1858 sought a biblical interpretation. The standard commentary (J. F. Ramírez, 1858) was accompanied by a color lithograph, the source of many subsequent reproductions. Orozco y Berra (1880) and Chavero (n.d.) also discuss and interpret the document. The only photographic reproductions (Batres, n.d.; Glass, 1964) are inadequate. The comparative studies by García Conde (1926) and García Cubas (1912), both of which have colored lithographs, follow Orozco y Berra and Ramírez. Orozco y Berra (1877–82) interprets some of the personal name glyphs; Chavero (1903a) discusses the history of the manuscript. García Cubas and Galindo y Villa (1904) and Lejeal (1904) treat the recovery of the document by the museum after its loss many years before. Gondra (1846) is of historical interest only.

Copies: Mateo A. Saldaña copy (almost indistinguishable from the original), MNA 35-14A; Pichardo copy, BNP 89-6; León y Gama copy, BNP 91; BNP 91bis; BNP 347; Waldeck copy, NLA 1269 (part). Other copies are reported by Mateos Higuera (1944e) and elsewhere.

Publication (selected): Batres, n.d., pp. 19–22, plate facing p. 22; Gemelli Careri, 1699–1700, vol. 6, facing p. 38; Glass, 1964, pp. 54–55, pl. 16; Humboldt, 1810, pp. 223–30, pl. 32; Kingsborough, 1831–48, vol. 4; J. F. Ramírez, 1858.

Commentaries: Chavero, n.d., pp. vii, 460–507, plate facing p. 462; García Conde, 1926, pp. 329–52, pl. 16; García Cubas, 1912, pp. 418–26, pl. 72; Orozco y Berra, 1880, 3: 131–53.

Other: Chavero, 1903a, pp. 15–17; Fernández del Castillo, 1907, p. 74, note 4; García Cubas and Galindo y Villa, 1904; Gondra, 1846, pp. 1–10, pl. 1; Lejeal, 1904; Orozco y Berra, 1877–82, 2: 67–70.

Brief descriptions: Alcina Franch, 1955, pp. 445–46; Mateos Higuera, 1944e; Radin, 1920, pp. 12–13, pl. 12.

291

Sinaxtla, San Andres, Plano de. AGN-T 308, exp. 1, cua. 3, f. 28bis. Published. Cartographic. San Andres Sinaxtla, ex-district of Nochistlan, Western Oaxaca. 18thC. Physical description not determined.

The map lacks specific Indian iconographic forms but is of interest for its circular depiction of the boundaries of Sinaxtla. These and other nontraditional conventions are glossed in Mixtec. The circular composition may derive from traditional modes of cartography.

Jiménez Moreno and Mateos Higuera (1940) reproduce the map without comment.

Publication: Jiménez Moreno and Mateos Higuera, 1940, p. 4, fig. 1.

292

Sintlatetelco, Mapa jeroglífico de. Códice Cintlatetelco. Unknown. Unpublished. Cartographic. San Francisco Tenampa, Veracruz. 17thC. Physical description not determined.

The map, apparently a very minor item with hieroglyphic place names and a drawing of a pyramid, is known only through a copy of 1687 in the municipal archives of Huatusco, Veracruz. It forms part of a claim by San Francisco Tenampa, a barrio of Tu-

tutla, for lands named Sintlatetelco. The copy is described by Aguirre Beltrán (1940).

Description: Aguirre Beltrán, 1940, pp. 55–56, 91, 220.

Brief mention: Melgarejo Vivanco, 1953, p. 334.

293

Sotuta, Map of the Province of. Mapa Antiguo del Partido de Yaxcaba según existia en 1600. Unknown. Published. Cartographic. Sotuta, Yucatan. 1600 (?) Physical description unknown.

Highly conventionalized circular map of the Maya province of Sotuta with written place names arranged radially within a circle. Yaxcaba and Yaxhaa as well as other place names appear at the center. The map is believed to be related to the Nachi Cocom survey of 1545 known only through the "Documentos de Tierras de Sotuta" copied in Codex Pérez (q.v.).

Roys (1939) reproduces a sketch of an old manuscript of the map in TU/LAL and gives the Maya text and English translation of the Sotuta land documents of 1545 from Codex Pérez. The map is utilized in mapping the province by Roys (1957).

Copies: Old copy (European paper, 33 × 44 cm.) of the map is in TU/LAL. Another copy appears to be cataloged (as "Plano del Reino o Señorio de Yaxhaa") by Orozco y Berra (1871) and may be in DGMH.

Publication: Roys, 1939, pp. 6–11, 87–89, 421–33, fig. 2.

Other: Orozco y Berra, 1871, p. 309, no. 3042; Roys, 1957, pp. 93–101.

294

Steuerliste von 40 Personen. Lost. Formerly DSB MS Amer. 10 (part). Published. Economic (census). Central Mexico. 16thC. Native paper. 21 × 46 cm.

The manuscript consists of a single sheet, drawn on both sides, from a larger assessment register. There are drawings of 40 heads, each with name glyph and name in Nahuatl. Opposite each is the symbol for two reales.

Commentary and photoreproduction, Lehmann (1906a).

Publication: Lehmann, 1906a, pp. 326–31, pls. 2, 2a.

295 (fig. 54)

Tabaa, San Juan, Lienzo de, no. 1. Pueblo. Published. Historical. San Juan Tabaa, ex-district of Villa Alta, Eastern Oaxaca. 16thC (?). Cloth. (MNA copy is 176 × 320 cm.)

The lienzo is divided into 36 rectangular compartments, 12 of which are in each of three horizontal rows. In most of the compartments are drawings of two Indians and a written Zapotec text. The date 1521 appears in one of the latter. The composition of the lienzo is similar to that of the Lienzo de San Miguel Tiltepec.

A brief description and photograph of the MNA copy are given by Glass (1964). De la Fuente (1949) mentions the existence of the lienzo.

Copies: Modern copy on cloth, MNA 35-114. A photograph of a slightly variant copy (the order of the compartments may merely be different) is in the MNA Fototeca. Colored tracings of the drawings and texts on separate sheets of paper are in the MNA codex collection (uncataloged).

Publication: Glass, 1964, p. 171, pl. 125.

Brief mention: Fuente, 1949, p. 176.

296

Tabaa, San Juan, Lienzo de, no. 2. Pueblo. Unpublished. Unavailable. San Juan Tabaa, ex-district of Villa Alta, Eastern Oaxaca. Further data unavailable.

The existence of a second lienzo from Tabaa, similar to the first (see previous entry), is mentioned by de la Fuente (1949).

Brief mention: Fuente, 1949, p. 176.

297

Tacuba, Genealogía de los Señores de. Unknown. Ex–Plancarte collection. Unpublished. Unavailable. Tacuba, D.F. Date and physical description unknown.

Mentioned by Paso y Troncoso (1892–93) as having been copied from a manuscript owned by Plancarte for exhibit at the Exposición Histórico-Americana de Madrid. The copy, however, was not exhibited. Both original and copy are now unknown. Glass (1964) speculates that the original may be the Techialoyan Códice García Granados, the history of which is unknown prior to about 1891.

Bibliography: Glass, 1964, p. 25; Paso y Troncoso, 1892–93, 1: 9.

298 (fig. 55)

Tamasolco, Santa Barbara, Mapa de. British Museum, Add. MSS 22070 (c). Unpublished. Economic (property plans). Santa Barbara Tamasolco, Tlaxcala. Late 16thC. Native paper. Dimensions not determined.

Map of numerous plots of land with Nahuatl texts, showing two churches, four human figures, and several place glyphs, all in crude style. The untranslated texts mention Santa Barbara, Santa Ana, Don Antonio de Mendoza, and Diego Muñoz, governor. Several dates in arabic numerals are illegible in photographs. Two of the place glyphs are glossed Tamasolco and Acolco.

The document has been briefly described by Gibson (1952); he also discusses the location of Santa Barbara Tamasolco.

Brief description: Gibson, 1952, pp. 43, 268.

299

Tamazulapan, Lienzo de. Lienzo Vischer no. 3. Museum für Völkerkunde, Basel. Ex–Lukas Vischer collection. Unpublished. Cartographic. Tamazulapan, ex-district of Teposcolula, Western Oaxaca. 1733. Cloth. About 183 × 122 cm.

Map showing the plan, houses, church, and plaza of Tamazulapan. Surrounding the plan are perspective renderings of hills with boundaries indicated by crosses and what may be some vestigial place glyphs. Glosses are in both Chocho and Mixtec (personal communication, M. E. Smith). The document is not in the native tradition although its composition is comparable to late 16thC native maps.

Brief description: Dietschy, 1960.

300

Tecamachalco, Mapa de. Lienzo de Tecamachalco. Dorfbuch von Tecamachalco. Lienzo Vischer no. 1. Museum für Völkerkunde, Basel. Ex–Lukas Vischer collection. Published. Cartographic-historical. Tecamachalco, Puebla. 16thC. Skin. 242 × 145 cm.

Along the left and upper margins are 26 Indian couples; numerous other couples, some in genealogical relationships, occur elsewhere on the manuscript. Personal name glyphs are expressed calendrically. Other major details are place glyphs and a chain of hills or mountains forming a map at the center. Glosses, some illegible, are in both Spanish and Nahuatl.

A partial commentary and an inadequate photoreproduction are given by Dietschy (1944). He notes its variant calendrical system, comments on persons also mentioned in the *Anales de Tecamachalco* (a text not treated in this census), and dates the document at 1557. A good photograph and a brief description appear in Burland (1960). According to Caso (1961) two of the persons depicted on the document also appear in the Lienzo Antonio de León.

Publication: Burland, 1960, pp. 11–12, 17–18, fig. 1; Dietschy, 1944.

Brief descriptions: Alcina Franch, 1955, p. 493; Dietschy, 1960; Lehmann, 1905a, pp. 263–65.

Other: Caso, 1961, p. 273.

301

Tecciztlan y Tequatepec, Lienzo de. Lienzo de Astata. Lienzo de Putla. MNA

200

35-115. Ex–Ignacio Larrazabal, Oaxaca, collection. Published. Cartographic-historical. Santiago Astata, ex-district of Tehuantepec, Eastern Oaxaca. 16thC. Cloth. ca. 280 × 170 cm.

Along three sides of the lienzo are place glyphs identified by glosses written on pasted-on slips of paper. One of them reads Tecciztlan (possibly for Magdalena Tequisistlan) and another, showing a heron on a hill, is glossed Tequatepec (i.e., Tehuantepec?) although the glyph is better read as Aztatepec (heron-hill) and may represent Santiago Astata, the presumed provenience of the manuscript.

At the bottom of the lienzo are water symbols, fish, and other aquatic animals. Several rivers and roads are shown crossing the document. Near the center is a drawing of a native house and a number of Indians without name glyphs. Glosses identify one of them as Chimeomemaçatecuhtli (sic).

A brief description and a photograph of the lienzo are in the MNA catalog (Glass, 1964). An anonymous and undated description of the lienzo (Anonymous, MS) states that the document was preserved in Astata. In preliminary papers for this census the lienzo was erroneously identified as the "Lienzo de Putla."

Copies: In PML are photographs of the lienzo attributed to Teobart Maler, apparently purchased at the Wilkinson sale of 1915 (American Art Association, 1915).

Publication: Glass, 1964, p. 172, pl. 126.

Description: Anonymous, MS.

Other: American Art Association, 1915, no. 167.

302

Tecomaxtlahuaca, Códice de. AGN-T, 2692, exp. 16. Published. Economic (tribute). San Sebastian Tecomaxtlahuaca, ex-district of Juxtlahuaca, Western Oaxaca. ca. 1578. Native paper tira. 140 × 40 cm.

Drawings of the tribute and services provided to eight successive caciques of Tecomaxtlahuaca, with written Spanish texts. Lacks calendrical and personal name glyphs.

Riva Palacio (n.d.) reproduces a tracing of the document, without comment. Another tracing is given by Schmieder (1930), who also publishes a translation of the Spanish texts and a questionnaire from the accompanying suit.

Publication: Riva Palacio, n.d., p. 77; Schmieder, 1930, pp. 78–80, 83–84, folded sheet facing p. 78.

303

Tecpan de Santiago Tlatelolco, Códice del. MNA/AH, Colección Gómez de Orozco, no. 12. Ex–Boturini and Gómez de Orozco collections. Published. Economic (miscellaneous). Tlatelolco, D.F. 1576–81. European paper. 8 leaves. 32 × 21 cm.

Nahuatl text treating expenses of the construction of the tecpan (native government building) of Tlatelolco, with a single drawing of the building.

Fernández (1939) reproduces the drawing and describes and translates the document. Kubler (1948) also reproduces the drawing.

Publication: Fernández, 1939.

Partial publication: Kubler, 1948, 1: 147, fig. 91.

304

Tecpatepec, Pintura del Pueblo de. UTX, CDG 563. Ex–Boturini and Genaro García collections. Unpublished. Economic (tribute). Tecpatepec, Hidalgo. About 1570. European paper. 31.5 × 80 cm.

Drawings of persons, money, sheep, buildings, and foodstuffs, illustrating financial complaints against Manuel de Olvera (corregidor of Tecpatepec?) with text in Spanish. The document is probably related to the Mizquiahuala Sales Receipts (q.v.).

Bibliography: None.

305

Tehuantepec, Istmo de, Fragmento del Mapa del. Uncertain. Ex–Hans Lenz collection. Unpublished. Unavailable. Tehuantepec region, Eastern Oaxaca. 18thC (?). European paper. Dimensions unreported.

The document is included in a listing of Mexican Indian pictorial manuscripts under the title "Fragmento del Mapa de la Zona correspondiente al Istmo de Tehuantepec y recorrido del Rio Coatzacoalcos" by Lenz (1950). He indicates only that it is possibly an 18thC copy of historical and geographical character on European paper, presented by him to the INAH. Cline (1966c) lists it as an unverified Zapotec pictorial. We have not located or examined the document.

Bibliography: Cline, 1966c, app. 2, no. 53; Lenz, 1950, table, p. 160, fig. 242.

306

Tehuantepec, Mapa de. Unknown. Ex-President Porfirio Díaz collection. Published. Cartographic. Tehuantepec region, ex-districts of Tehuantepec and Juchitan, Eastern Oaxaca. 18thC (?). Dimensions not determined.

A copy of the map figured in the catalog of the Madrid Exposition of 1892 (Paso y Troncoso, 1892–93). Its title has been perpetuated in subsequent listings of native documents (Lehmann, 1905a; Alcina Franch, 1955; Cline, 1966c), although it is not in the native tradition. A fairly detailed description of the copy by Galindo y Villa (1895) allows it to be identified with a map published by Covarrubias (1946). It shows the lagoons between Ixhuatan and Tehuantepec in fair detail; the Pacific Ocean is labeled "Mar Mediterraneo."

Copy: 1892 copy (oil, 90 × 107 cm.), Museo Nacional de Historia, Mexico (unverified).

Publication: Covarrubias, 1946, pl. 40.

Brief descriptions: Galindo y Villa, 1895,

pp. 102–03, no. 134; Paso y Troncoso, 1892–93, 2: 210–11.

Listings: Alcina Franch, 1955, pp. 481–82; Cline, 1966c, app. 2, no. 54; Lehmann, 1905a, p. 275.

307

Tehuantepec, Querella criminal contra Don Juan, Cacique de. AGN-HJ 450, exp. 1. Published. Miscellaneous. Tehuantepec, ex-district of Tehuantepec, Eastern Oaxaca. 1553. Unreported material. 21 × 31 cm.

The drawing shows several bleeding Indians being flogged by other Indians. A seated figure with speech scrolls represents the Indian governor of Tehuantepec. The drawing lacks hieroglyphic symbols.

A colored reproduction and an extract from the accompanying suit is published in *Códices Indígenas* (1933). Covarrubias (1946) also illustrates it.

Publication: *Códices Indígenas*, 1933, Item 29; Covarrubias, 1946, p. 204.

308

Telleriano-Remensis, Codex. Codex Tellerianus. Códice Le Tellier. BNP 385. Ex-Le Tellier collection. Published. Ritual-calendrical and historical. Valley of Mexico. ca. 1562–63. European paper. 50 leaves. 32 × 22 cm.

This manuscript and Codex Ríos (q.v.) are currently believed to be copies of a common original, the lost Codex Huitzilopochtli (see Huitzilopochtli Group, where the relationship is discussed).

Codex Telleriano-Remensis, glossed "Geroglíficos de que usauan los . . ." on the cover, has three major pictorial sections in several native styles. Each is annotated in Spanish, in several handwritings. One of the latter is believed to be by Fray Pedro de los Ríos. The first section is an 18-month calendar with drawings of the gods of each period and a symbol for the nemontemi. The second is a tonalpohualli (260-day divinatory almanac). The third is a pictorial annal for the period 1198–1562 in two major styles.

Two final pages contain historical notices in Spanish, without drawings, for the years 1519–57. There are leaves missing from each pictorial section but in every case they are preserved in the cognate Codex Ríos. See Table 2 for a concordance of the two manuscripts.

Details from the codex were first published by Humboldt (1810). The first edition was issued by Kingsborough (1831–48) with an inaccurate palaeography and translation of the glosses. A second edition, based on that by Kingsborough, was issued by Léon de Rosny (1869). The third edition, by Hamy (1899b) in color lithography, includes a very brief commentary and a careful palaeography of the texts. The Hamy plates are reproduced by color photography in Corona Núñez (1964–67) with uncritical palaeography and a page-by-page commentary.

Six pages of the original are photographically reproduced by Robertson (1959), who provides an analysis of its styles and dating. He also demonstrates that it derives from a screenfold or tira-format prototype. Chavero (n.d.) has commented, perhaps erroneously, on the nemontemi symbol in the codex, possibly the only pictorial element not also in Codex Ríos.

Studies which describe this manuscript and Codex Ríos, comment on their interrelationship, or treat their common content are cited herein under our discussion of the Huitzilopochtli Group (q.v.).

Copies: A statement by Madier de Montjau (1875) suggests that de Rosny owned an old copy of the codex; presumably it is a copy from the Kingsborough edition used for the 1869 edition and not of further significance. Its present location is unknown. An unidentified copy was offered at a Hotel Drouot sale in Paris in February 1965.

Editions: Corona Núñez, 1964–67, 1: 151–337, 2: 151–80; Librería Echániz, n.d.d; Hamy, 1899b; Kingsborough, 1831–48, vols. 1 and 5: 127–58, and 6: 95–153; Léon de Rosny, 1869, pp. 190–232, pls. 24–97.

Other: Anderson and Barlow, 1943, p. 414, note 5; Carrasco Pizana, 1944; Chavero, n.d., p. 156; Humboldt, 1810, pp. 279–83, pls. 55–56; Jourdain, 1889; Madier de Montjau, 1875, p. 242, note 1; Paso y Troncoso, 1898b, pp. 60–61, 332–40; Radin, 1920, pp. 26, 45–50.

Study: Robertson, 1959, pp. 107–15, pls. 10, 27–29.

Brief mention: Gallatin, 1845, passim; Wilson, 1859 (page reference not determined).

Brief descriptions: Alcina Franch, 1955, pp. 435–36; Kubler and Gibson, 1951, p. 71; J. F. Ramírez, 1855, no. 1.

309 (fig. 56)

Temascaltepec, Carte de la Ville de. NLA 1271 (a). Unpublished. Cartographic. Temascaltepec, Mexico. 16thC. Native paper. 77.2 × 59.8 cm.

The map shows several rivers and roads, calli symbols, and churches. The latter are identified as subjects of Temascaltepec. The phrase "sitio que pide Luis Álvarez Azevedo" is typical of other glosses.

Bibliography: None.

310

TEMASCALTEPEC: *Pièces d'un Procès criminel*. BNP 111. Ex–Aubin collection. Unpublished. Economic (tribute). Temascaltepec, Mexico. 1566. 12 leaves of drawings on native paper of varying dimensions and 72 leaves of text.

Not explained. The brief description by Boban (1891) indicates that the drawings illustrate a long criminal process between the towns of Temascaltepec and Malacatepec, Mexico, and depict stolen objects, their values, and other details.

Brief description: Boban, 1891, 2: 294–95.

311

Teocaltitlan, San Pablo, Libro de Tributos de. Códice Valeriano. BNP 376. Ex–Boturini and Goupil collections. Partially published. Economic (tribute). San Pablo

Teocaltitlan (a part of Mexico City), D.F. 1574. European paper. 28 leaves. Dimensions not determined.

Pictorial register of persons and tribute with different sections classified as to categories of persons. Drawings are of personal name glyphs, Indian heads, and monetary units. Short Nahuatl texts occur as does the signature of Don Antonio Valeriano, a late 16thC Indian governor of Mexico City.

Gibson (1964a) gives a brief description of the manuscript and reproduces one of its pages.

Copies: Photographic copies by Gates are in LC, NLA, TU/LAL, PML, and BYU.

Partial publication: Gibson, 1964a, pp. 203, 391, pl. 8.

❖❖❖

TEOTIHUACAN MAPS. The three late pictorial representations of lands listed separately below vary only in relatively minor details and must have a common history or prototype. They depict lands of San Francisco Mazapan and have attracted attention as the Pyramids of the Sun and Moon, the Way of the Dead, and the Ciudadela; prominent features of the archaeological site of Teotihuacan are included. The style of each version is crude; rudimentary place glyphs and Nahuatl glosses are substantially the same on all versions. Above the Pyramid of the Moon is the drawing of a crescent moon with a human face. The "celestial" interpretation given by Hagar (cited below) is groundless.

312 (fig. 57)

—— *Ayer Map of Teotihuacan*. NLA. Ex–Leopoldo Batres, W. W. Blake, and Edward E. Ayer collections. Published. Economic (property plans). San Francisco Mazapan, Mexico. 17thC (?). Amatl paper. ca. 63.5 × 99 cm.

See above for description. Hagar (1912b) gives description, inadequate photoreproduction, and transcribes some of the glosses.

Publication: Hagar, 1912b.

Brief description: Alcina Franch, 1955, pp. 461–62.

313 (fig. 58)

—— *Saville Map of Teotihuacan*. AMNH. Ex–Leopoldo Batres and M. H. Saville collections. Published. Economic (property plans). San Francisco Mazapan, Mexico. 17thC (?). Native paper. ca. 33 × 63 cm.

See above for description. Hagar (1912b) gives description, photoreproduction, and transcribes some of the glosses. A relatively long Nahuatl text that occurs only on this version is unstudied.

Publication: Hagar, 1912b.

Brief description: Alcina Franch, 1955, pp. 461–62.

314

—— *Mapa de San Francisco Mazapan*. Pueblo. Published. Economic (property plans). San Francisco Mazapan, Mexico. 19thC. (?). Parchment. 38 × 62 cm.

See above for description. Arreola (1922) gives description, color reproduction, transcript and translation of Nahuatl glosses, and identification of some of the place names.

Publication: Arreola, 1922, pp. 553–58, pl. 148.

315

Teotihuacan, San Juan, Códice de. Códice Texcoco-Acolman. MNA 35-69. Ex–Boturini collection. Published. Miscellaneous. San Juan Teotihuacan, Mexico. ca. 1557. Amatl paper. ca. 139 × 75 cm., now mounted with 5 small unrelated fragments.

The manuscript relates to a 1557 Indian revolt against the establishment of an Augustinian monastery in Teotihuacan. The drawings, with occasional Nahuatl glosses, depict Indians tied together, an escape from a jail, friars, articles of tribute, and a map depicting Acolman, Texcoco, and, presumably, Teotihuacan. The five small fragments ("Otros Fragmentos") showing heads of Indians pertain to some otherwise unknown document, not separately recorded in this census.

An interpretation of the manuscript with a colored reproduction of a copy is given by Arreola (1922). It has been described and reproduced by Gómez de Orozco (1927a) and Glass (1964). Gibson (1964a), I. B. del Castillo (1922), and Kubler (1948) summarize the revolt of 1557 and cite sources bearing on it.

Publication: Arreola, 1922, pp. 560–65, pl. 150; Glass, 1964, p. 122, pl. 72; Gómez de Orozco, 1927a, pp. 53, 161–62, pl. facing p. 158.

Brief description: Mena, 1923, pp. 65–68, pl. 5 (detail), no. 32.

Other: I. B. del Castillo, 1922, pp. 440–46; Gibson, 1964a, p. 111; Kubler, 1948, 2: 473.

316

Tepeaca, Anales de, 1528–1634. Anales Antiguos de Mexico y sus Contornos (AAMC), no. 21. Anales Mexicanos, Puebla, Tepeaca, Cholula, 1524–1645. Anales Geroglíficos e históricos indianos, desde el ano de 1524 hasta el de 1677. Unknown. Ex–DuPaix collection. Unpublished. Historical. Tepeaca, Puebla. 17thC. Physical description unknown.

The J. F. Ramírez copy (MNA/AH Col. Antig. 229) was made from an original then in the DuPaix collection of the Mexican National Museum in 1847. The original bore a title (see above) indicating the years spanned as 1524–1677, but Ramírez noted that it was apparently incomplete, reaching only to 1645. The Ramírez copy has an introduction by Ramírez (ff. 2r–2v), a copy of the drawings and Nahuatl texts (ff. 3–23), and a translation of the texts (ff. 24–29). Another manuscript translation is AAMC 21.

The pages of the Ramírez copy have vertical columns of native-year dates on the left and historical drawings and Nahuatl texts on the right. The AAMC translation contains political and ecclesiastical notices of Tepeaca and adjacent communities. Only the introduction to the Ramírez copy, which describes the original, has been published (Chavero, 1901a).

Copies: Ramírez copy, with translation, MNA/AH Col. Antig. 229. Translation only, MNA/AH Col. Antig. 274, Item 21 (AAMC 21).

Brief description: Chavero, 1901a, p. 10.

317

Tepechpan, Tira de. Mapa de Tepechpan. Histoire Synchronique et Seigneuriale de Tepechpan et de Mexico. Cronologia Mexicana, 1298–1596. BNP 13-14. Ex–Boturini, Pichardo, Waldeck, and Aubin collections. Published. Historical. Tepechpan, Mexico. 1596. Native paper. 21 × 625 cm. (total length).

Screenfold chronicle originally in 23 leaves covering the years 1298–1596. Portions of the initial and terminal leaves are missing; the extant portion spans the years 1300–1590. The document has been refolded so that it is described by Boban in 20 sections. It depicts the settlement at Chapultepec, the founding of Tepechpan, and continues with the dynasties of Tepechpan and Tenochtitlan. The colonial section is devoted to the occurrence of plagues, the dates of viceroys, and other events. The drawings appear above and below a line of native-year glyphs that divides the tira into two horizontal divisions.

The Desportes lithograph, printed for Aubin about 1849–51 (Aubin, n.d.*f*), was also published (perhaps with slight variation in the printing) by the Mexican National Museum (Aubin, 1886c). Boban (1891) comments on the manuscript at length and reproduces two sections photographically. The same two sections are reproduced by Robertson (1959). Paso y Troncoso (1905–06) comments briefly on the Tepechpan dynasty. Humboldt (1810) mentions a scene in the document.

Copies: Pichardo copy, BNP 88-6 (a). Waldeck copy, NLA 1269 (part). Aubin copy, BNP 14bis. Boturini collection copy on parchment, apparently in the Mexican National Museum in the 19thC, now unknown.

Publication: Aubin, n.d.*f*, 1886c; Librería Echániz, 1944b; Peñafiel, 1889.

Commentary: Boban, 1891, 1: 243–77, pls. 13–14.

Other: Chavero, n.d., pp. xiii and passim; Humboldt, 1810, p. 54; Paso y Troncoso, 1905–06, 6: 233, note 1; Robertson, 1959, pl. 12.

Brief description: Alcina Franch, 1955, pp. 456–57.

318

Tepecuacuilco, Mapa de. "Fragmento." MNA 35-76 and DSB MS Amer. 10 (part) (lost). Ex–Boturini collection. Partially published. Cartographic. Tepecuacuilco region, Guerrero. 16thC. Amatl paper. MNA fragment 113 × 102 cm.; DSB fragments 30 × 52 and 45 × 40 cm.

The MNA fragment is an incomplete native map showing the Rio Balsas and its tributaries, the Zopilote and the Tepecuacuilco, within a restricted region of Guerrero between Iguala and Zumpango. Glossed place glyphs include Chichihualco, Xochipala, and Mexcala. This fragment has been published with commentary by Simons (1969) and with a brief description by Glass (1964).

Two further fragments formed part of the lost DSB MS Amer. 10, described by Guzmán (1936). They have been identified by Bankmann (1970) on the basis of fragmentary tracings by Walter Lehmann in IAI.

Partial publication: Glass, 1964, p. 129, pl. 81; Simons, 1969.

Brief descriptions: Bankmann, 1970, pp. 134–35; Guzmán, 1936, no. 10, parts 2 and 8; Mena, 1923, p. 56, no. 11.

319

Tepeticpac, Genealogía de una Familia de. Genealogía Tlascalteca. Genealogía de Xicotencatl. MNA 35-27. Ex–Ayuntamiento de Tlaxcala. Published. Genealogical. Tepeticpac, Tlaxcala. 16thC. Cloth. 119.5 × 58.8 cm.

Genealogy of 30 individuals in Indian costume but without personal name glyphs. Although the persons are glossed, they appear to be unknown from other sources. A partially effaced text at the top may include the word "Tepeticpac."

A short description and a reproduction of the original and a copy are given by Glass (1964). Other short descriptions are by Paso y Troncoso (1892–93) and Gibson (1952). The latter also reproduces the copy. An illegible photograph of the original with the presumably unjustified title "Genealogía de Xicotencatl" was published by Peñafiel (1909).

Copy: 1892 copy, MNA 35-28.

Publication: Glass, 1964, pp. 70–71, pls. 28–29.

Other: Peñafiel, 1909, pl. 4.

Brief descriptions: Gibson, 1952, pp. 266, 272, fig. IV; Paso y Troncoso, 1892–93, I: 255.

320 (fig. 59)

Tepetlan, San Antonio, Mapa de. Códice Tepetlan. Lienzo de Veracruz. Location uncertain. Published. Cartographic-historical. San Antonio Tepetlan, Veracruz. 16thC. Physical description of original unknown. (AMNH copy is cloth, 108 × 122 cm.)

At the center of the manuscript are drawings of churches representing Tepetlan and four subject localities, Indian caciques, Cortés and Marina with tribute, a Spanish ship in the sea near Quiahuiztlan, the date 1519, a friar (Fray Buenaventura), and a priest (Alonso Muñoz). The word "congregación" appears in one of the Nahuatl glosses. Around the periphery are the hieroglyphic boundaries of Tepetlan.

The 1881 copy, copied from an unidentified original then in the AGN, is reproduced and studied by Mena (1914). The New York and Berlin copies are reproduced and studied by Kutscher (1964).

Copies: (1) Certified copy of 1881 reportedly owned by Tepetlan examined by Mena in the Secretaría de Gobierno, Jalapa, about 1913. (2) 19thC copy, ex–Strebel, MVBE. (3) 18th–19thC copy (possibly the 16thC original or the original of one of the preceding copies?), ex–M. H. Saville, AMNH.

Publication: Kutscher, 1964; Mena, 1914.

321

Tepexi de la Seda, The Painted Tribute Record of, Códice de Tepexic de la Seda. Museum of the American Indian, Heye Foundation, New York. Published. Economic (tribute). Tepexi de la Seda, Puebla. 19thC. Parchment. 41.9 × 58.4 cm.

Detailed drawings of a wide variety of tribute paid by Tepexi and its *sujetos* before the arrival of the Spaniards. Persons shown include Don Gonzalo Mazatzin, Don Juan Moctezuma, and Cortés. The manuscript appears to be a copy of a 16thC original.

Commentary and photographic reproduction by Cook de Leonard (1961) and by Torre and Sandoval (1967).

Publication: Cook de Leonard, 1961; Torre and Sandoval, 1967.

322

TEPOTZOTLAN: *Los Naturales de los Pueblos de Cuautlalpan, Tepujaco y Xoloc de la Jurisdicción de Tepotzotlan, Mex., contra su Gobernador, por malos Tratamientos y Pago de Tributos (1552).* AGN (ramo and volume numbers not determined). Published. Economic (tribute). Tepotzotlan, Mexico. 1552. Unidentified paper. 69 × 65 cm.

The drawing forms part of a complaint against a native judge and depicts various goods and services as well as several Indians.

A color reproduction of the drawing and an extract from the related Spanish text are given in *Códices Indígenas* (1933).

Publication: *Códices Indígenas*, 1933, Item 31.

323

Tepoztlan, Census of. TU/MARI. Partially published. Economic (census). Tepoztlan, Morelos. 16thC. European paper. 6 leaves (ff. 816–821). 31.5 × 21.5 cm.

Each of 11 pages of the document presents a place glyph (the first is Tlalnepantla, a barrio of Tepoztlan) and a pictorial census of persons and houses. The final page contains a summary in Spanish.

Cornyn (1946) reproduces a tracing of the first page, most of the place glyphs, and the Spanish text. This census may be studied in conjunction with the textual census of the Tepoztlan region discussed by Carrasco Pizana (1964).

Publication (partial): Cornyn, 1946.
Others: Carrasco Pizana, 1964.

324 (fig. 60)

Tepoztlan, Panhuacan, Ayapango y Tlanahuac, Mapa catastral de. Nationalbibliothek, Vienna. CVM 4. Ex–Boturini and Bilimek collections. Unpublished. Economic (census and cadastral). Amecameca region, Mexico. 16thC. Native paper. 77.5 × 71.5 cm.

The document is divided into four vertical columns each headed by a glossed place glyph—the localities named in the title. Below each glyph are Indians drawn opposite house symbols and plots of land with numerical signs denoting numbers of persons and land measurements. One of the 32 Indians represented is a Don Diego de Mendoza.

A small detail from the manuscript was reproduced in color and briefly discussed by Nuttall (1888).

Brief mention: Nuttall, 1888, p. 17, note 2, pl. 2, fig. 11.

325

Testerian Manuscript of the Bibliothèque Nationale, Fonds Mexicains 399, Miscellaneous pages in the. BNP 399. Unpublished. Miscellaneous. Valley of Mexico. 16thC. European paper. Further details not determined.

The Testerian MS, BNP 399, contains various texts and drawings unrelated to its Testerian content. They include a history of the missionary effort in Nahuatl and what appear to be fragments from several pictorial manuscripts. The latter exhibit drawings of Indians (including Icxicuauhtli and a Don Pedro . . . Cano), symbolic devices, and glyphs for Tenochtitlan and Tlatelolco. One of the fragments bears a remarkable similarity to the Nómina escrita en Geroglífico (no. 236).

Copies: Photographic copies by William Gates are in LC, TU/LAL, and, possibly, BYU.

Bibliography: None.

326

Tetelcingo, Códice de. Private collection. Ex–Echániz collection. Published. Economic (tribute). Tetelcingo, Guerrero. 1557. European paper. 2 leaves. Dimensions not reported.

A fragment of a tribute register, the document has one page of Spanish text with the tribute assessment of Tetelcingo and one page with a few simple drawings of human heads and monetary symbols.

Described and reproduced by Barlow (1954a).

Publication: Barlow, 1954a.

327 (figs. 61, 62)

Tetlama, Lienzo de. Lienzo de Miacatlan. Códice de Xochicalco. Known versions listed below. Partially published. Cartographic-historical. Tetlama-Miacatlan region, Morelos. 16thC.

The document is known through one "original" and seven copies. Five of the ver-

sions examined vary slightly in content, style, proportions, and arrangement of details. These differences may relate to different related originals from Tetlama and Miacatlan. The subject matter is essentially the same in all, with numerous hieroglyphs, roads, churches, Indian principals, historical scenes, and a peripherally located series of place glyphs. Most details bear glosses in either Spanish or Nahuatl; recognizable among them are place names in the Tetlama-Miacatlan region including Coatlan del Rio. See Lienzo de Noxtepec (Guerrero) for another closely related document.

The Waldeck copy has been published without comment by Fortier and Ficklen (1907). The existence of a pictorial manuscript in Tetlama is mentioned by Humboldt (1810) with sufficient circumstantial comment to identify with the Lienzo de Tetlama. The copies in the BNP are described by Boban (1891). Known manuscripts are:

1. "Original" (but not of all the copies listed below). Cloth, in excess of 100 × 200 cm. Reportedly in Tetlama. Poor photographs are in MNA/BNA and INAH/AF.

2. "Copia del Mapa formado en el año de 1590 del Pueblo de San Agustin Tetlama y Pueblitos aneçsos, sacada por Disposición de D. Francisco Rosales para los Naturales de dicho Pueblo." Photostat (21.5 × 43.5 cm.) in INAH/AF believed to be of a small watercolor copy known as the "Códice de Xochicalco" in the Gómez de Orozco collection from an original in the Bishop Plancarte collection mentioned by Barlow (MSc).

3. Copy with same title as previous item with additional words "en 20 de Abril de 1851." Photograph in INAH/AF.

4. León y Gama copy, BNP 10bis (b).

5. Nebel copy, BNP 98.

6. Anonymous colored copy, BNP 101.

7. Copy, BNP 101bis.

8. Waldeck copy, ca. 1829, from original in Miacatlan. NLA 1269 (part).

Publication: Fortier and Ficklen, 1907, plate facing p. 64.

Other: Barlow, MSc; Boban, 1891, 1: 208; 2: 272, 274–75; Humboldt, 1810, p. 40.

328

Tetlamaca y Tlametzin, Genealogía de. Genealogía de Xochilquexolot. MNA 35-83. Ex–Boturini collection. Published. Genealogical. Central Mexico. 16thC. European paper. 111 × 60 cm.

Incomplete genealogy of 48 Indians drawn in eight horizontal rows. There are no hieroglyphs; personal names are given by Nahuatl glosses. The earliest couple in the genealogy are Tetlamaca and Tlametzin. Males in the earlier generations hold bows and arrows or carry quivers.

Glass (1964) gives brief description and photographic reproduction.

Publication: Glass, 1964, p. 137, pl. 88.
Other: Mena, 1923, p. 64, no. 27.

329

Texcoco, Plan topographique [provenant d'un document judiciaire ayant trait à des terrains en litige situés dans les faubourgs] *de.* BNP 107. Ex–Aubin collection. Unpublished. Economic (property plans). Valley of Mexico (?). Late 16thC. European paper. 59 × 63 cm.

Map showing parcels of land, houses, roads, a stream of water, and various place glyphs in a late style. Spanish glosses refer to the barrios of Tlaxinican and Tlaquechpan. Boban's attribution of the document to Texcoco may be conjectural.

An incomplete description is given by Boban (1891).

Brief description: Boban, 1891, 2: 284–85.

330

TEXCOCO: *Stammbaum des Königlichen Geschlechtes von Tetzcoco.* Museum für Völkerkunde, Berlin. Published. Genealogical. Texcoco, Mexico. 18thC. Parchment. 73 × 48 cm.

Ten-generation genealogical tree cast in European format, depicting descendants of Nezahualcoyotl, most of whom are shown in European or colonial dress. The document, not in the native tradition, is of slight interest for early 16thC or preconquest genealogy. A Spanish text refers to the zoological park at Tetzcotzingo, the glyph for which is given.

Kutscher (1961) gives detailed comparative study and photoreproduction.

Publication: Kutscher, 1961.

331

Tezontepec, San Pedro, Mapa de. Unknown. Unpublished. Cartographic. Central Mexico. 1570. Physical data unknown.

BNP copy not examined (data received in personal communication from Charles Gibson and Donald Robertson). BNP copy, from original that may have been dated 1570, shows lands, roads, and the town of Tezontepec at the center. Presence of native pictorial elements not determined.

Copy: Copy by Manuel Ma. de la Barrera f. Valenzuela dated 1854, BNP 419–8.

Bibliography: None.

332

Tianguiztli, Plan du. Unknown. Ex–Boturini collection. Published. Economic (miscellaneous). Valley of Mexico. 16thC. Native paper. Single sheet.

The document, now unknown, was copied (by Aubin?) from the original then in the MNA. It shows the plan of a colonial town square and market with vendors' stalls indicated by small rectangles. Drawings, glossed in Nahuatl, depict both Indian and Spanish wares. The Boturini collection inventories identify the market as that of Mexico City and one of the inventories gives the date 1531.

Durand-Forest (1971) gives a redrawing of the Aubin collection copy and a transcript and translation of the glosses.

Copy: Aubin collection copy, BNP 106.

Publication: Durand-Forest, 1971, pp. 121–24.

Other: Boban, 1891, 2: 282–83, 520; Durand-Forest, 1962; Gibson, 1964a, p. 353, note 132.

333

Tiltepec, San Miguel, Lienzo de. Codex Pérez García. Pueblo. Poorly published. Historical. San Miguel Tiltepec, ex-district of Ixtlan, Eastern Oaxaca. 16thC (?). Cloth. ca. 150 × 300 cm.

A brief description and photograph of the lienzo, in which no details are legible, have been published by Pérez García (1956). From this it is evident that the lienzo is divided into 36 compartments arranged in three horizontal rows, a composition similar to the Lienzo de San Juan Tabaa no. 1 (q.v.). Both manuscripts have Zapotec texts, the date 1521, and paintings of Indians and Spaniards. The subject matter apparently concerns the Spanish conquest and the conversion of the town to Christianity. Paddock (1959) states that photographs were made in Oaxaca City in 1955.

Publication: Pérez García, 1956, pp. 59–61.

Brief mention: Paddock, 1959, pp. 1–2.

334 (fig. 63)

Tlachco, Códice de. Private collection, Santa Barbara, California. Unpublished. Economic (tribute). Taxco, Guerrero. 16th-C. Native paper. 113 × 44 cm.

Drawings of two houses, Indians, cloth, maize, and turkeys supplied to the corregidor of Tasco. One detail shows the wives of the corregidor and the alguacil being carried in slings. One of several Spanish glosses appears to begin "Proceso hecho ante la justicia de las minas de Tasco entre los Indios de . . . ."

A description of the manuscript by Echániz (1954) is unpublished; photograph in INAH/AF.

Brief description: Echániz, 1954.

335

Tlacoatzintepec, Lienzo de. Pueblo. Published. Cartographic-historical. San Juan Tlacoatzintepec, ex-district of Cuicatlan, Northern Oaxaca. 16thC. Cloth. 222 × 190 cm.

The lienzo shows roads, rivers, historical scenes (including an Indian battle), a peripheral series of place glyphs, and drawings of native houses representing colonial communities. Tlacoatzintepec is at the center.

The Weitlaner and Castro study, illustrated by the modern MNA copy of the 1892 copy, has appeared twice (1953, 1954). The MNA copy is also reproduced by Glass (1964) and by Cline (1961a). The latter comments on its cartographic content.

Copies: Modern copy, MNA 35-111. Copy of 1892, Pueblo.

Publication: Cline, 1961a, pp. 71–74, pl. 6a; Glass, 1964, p. 167, pl. 121; Weitlaner and Castro, 1953; 1954, pp. 188–199, fig. 42.

336

TLACOTEPEC: *Pièce du Procès de Pablo Ocelotl et ses Fils, contre Alonzo Gonzáles*. BNP 32. Ex–Aubin collection. Partially published. Economic (property plans) and genealogical. Tlacotepec (south of Toluca), Mexico. 1565. European paper. 2 leaves of drawings (one is 44 × 32 cm.) and 15 leaves of Spanish text.

Only one of the two drawings in the document has been published. It gives the plan of two maguey fields, in each of which there is a house and a genealogy of individuals with personal name glyphs. Surrounding these and other details are 47 year glyphs for unspecified years. A place glyph, Mitepec, may represent Tlacotepec. The second drawing is said to be similar.

Boban (1891) reproduces one of the two drawings and gives an extract from the first page of the accompanying text.

Partial publication: Boban, 1891, 1: 406–07, pl. 32.

337

Tlacotepec, San Pedro, Mapa de. Pueblo. Published. Cartographic-historical. San Pedro Tlacotepec, Tlaxcala. 18thC (?). Oil (?) on native (maguey fiber?) cloth. Dimensions not determined. (MNA copy is 81 × 122 cm.)

Painting of the boundaries of Tlacotepec also showing the church, a coat of arms, a native building, the date 1535, a statue of St. Peter, Cortés and Marina, and an Indian cacique.

Glass (1964) describes and reproduces the MNA copy; the original was seen by him in 1964. It is also reproduced by Gibson (1952) and described by Paso y Troncoso (1892–93). Peñafiel (1909) reproduces the coat of arms that appears on the map.

Copy: 1892 copy, MNA 35-6.

Publication: Glass, 1964, p. 44, pl. 8; Gibson, 1952, p. 266, fig. 6.

Brief description: Paso y Troncoso, 1892–93, 1: 262–63.

Other: Peñafiel, 1909, pl. 27.

338

Tlalancalco, San Matias, Mapa de. Unknown. Unpublished. Cartographic. San Matias Tlalancalo (also, Tlalancaleca), Puebla. 16th or early 17thC. Native paper. Dimensions unknown.

BNP 419-4 is an 1864–65 copy of a much earlier map of the jurisdiction of San Matias Tlalancalco, with emphasis on boundary markers and distances between them plus houses of certain native nobles and Nahuatl glosses. Copy is stylistically quite Hispanicized, but a few native symbols are present. The copy includes a detailed description as well as a palaeography and Spanish translation of the Nahuatl glosses. (Data communicated by H. B. Nicholson.)

Bibliography: None.

❖❖❖

TLAMAPA, SANTA CRUZ, CODICES

DE. Three pictorial manuscripts, each of which is listed in the Boturini collection inventories of 1743, 1745, and 1804 as well as in the catalog of 1746. They are entered below in the order in which they are described in the inventories of 1743 and 1745.

339

—— *no. 1.* Manuscrito [Códice] Azteca del Museo del Ejercito de Madrid. Museo del Ejercito, Madrid. Ex–Boturini, José Gómez de la Cortina (Conde de la Cortina), and Museo de Artillería, Madrid, collections. Published. Economic (census). Santa Cruz Tlamapa, Mexico. 16thC. Native paper tira. 74 × 17.5 cm.

Vertical tira headed by drawings of a Christian Church and place glyph. Below are eight horizontal rows of Indians identified by Nahuatl glosses as assistants of the church, officials of the town, etc.

The first edition is an excellent natural size photoreproduction by Dios de la Rada y Delgado (in Léon de Rosny, 1881b). It is accompanied by a description and translation of the Nahuatl texts taken from the published catalog of the Museo de Artillería (1856). A second reproduction is given by Estrada (1937), with little comment. The third edition (Alcina Franch, 1960) also describes it and translates the Nahuatl texts.

Publication: Alcina Franch, 1960; Estrada, 1937, p. 53, fig. 64; Léon de Rosny, 1881b, app. 2, pp. 115–16, pl. 20.

Description: Museo de Artillería, 1856, pp. 324–26, no. 3138.

340

—— *no. 2.* Unknown. Ex–Boturini collection. Unpublished. Unavailable. Santa Cruz Tlamapa, Mexico. 16thC. European paper. 1 large tira or leaf.

The manuscript is lost; no reproduction is known. It may someday be identified on the basis of the descriptions in the Boturini collection inventories. It apparently concerned the tributes of Tlamapa and mentioned a

Bernardino del Castillo. Glass (1964) presumes (erroneously?) that the Boturini collection inventory label 1823-2-5 found, in 1930, attached to Fragment 1 of the Códice de las Posesiones de Don Andrés originally belonged to this document.

Work cited: Glass, 1964, pp. 109, 141.

341 (fig. 64)

—— *no. 3.* Códice de Tributos de Santa Cruz Tlamapa. MNA 35-58. Ex–Boturini collection. Partially published. Economic (tribute). Santa Cruz Tlamapa, Mexico. ca. 1577. European paper tira. 383.5 × 31 cm.

Incomplete vertical tira divided into 14 sections corresponding to the years 1564–77. In the first or lowest section is a Christian church surmounted by an Indian building, a place glyph, and a drawing of the gobernador and other officials. The remaining sections each contain a drawing of the escribano and mayordomo, moon symbols for the months of the Christian year, and numerical signs. The latter may refer to tribute or to other financial expenses of the town. Names of town officers are given by Spanish glosses.

The manuscript has been briefly described by Mena (1923) and by Glass (1964); a detail is reproduced by the latter.

Partial publication: Glass, 1964, pp. 108–09, pl. 61.

Brief description: Mena, 1923, p. 62, no. 20.

342

Tlapa, Lienzo de. MNA 35-110. Partially published. Genealogical. Tlapa, Guerrero. 16thC. Cloth. 285 × 76 cm.

Drawings of about 97 Indians and four place glyphs (Tlapa, Tototepec?, Acatepec, and Iguala). The 37 couples in the lower part of the lienzo are arranged in vertical columns and have hieroglyphic or Nahuatl names; those in the upper portion have Spanish names.

The lienzo has been very briefly described by both Toscano (1943) and Glass (1964); the latter illustrates a detail from the upper portion.

Partial publication: Glass, 1964, p. 166, pl. 120.

Brief description: Toscano, 1943, pp. 132–33.

343

Tlaquiltenango, Códices de. Códice Mauricio de la Arena. MNA 35-21 and AMNH. Partially published. Economic (tribute), genealogical, and miscellaneous. Tlaquiltenango, Morelos. 16thC. Native paper. 6 fragments in MNA; over 100 fragments in AMNH. Dimensions vary.

The six fragments in the MNA were discovered pasted face down on the convent walls at Tlaquiltenango about 1909. The fragments in the AMNH were acquired in 1911. Most fragments are from pictorial tribute documents. One is a genealogy; others are of a miscellaneous character and some are sheets of music.

The fragments in the MNA are described and published by Mazari (1926a, 1926b) and by Glass (1964). The Vaillant (MSa) description of the AMNH fragments is unpublished. Only the genealogy of the latter collection has been published (H. Spinden, 1913, 1928). Barlow (1943d) comments on the month glyphs on the MNA fragments.

Publication: Glass, 1964, p. 63, pl. 22; Mazari, 1926a, 1926b; H. Spinden, 1913, plate facing p. 33; 1928, pl. 47b.

Brief descriptions: Alcina Franch, 1955, pp. 443–44; Kubler and Gibson, 1951, p. 65.

Other: Anonymous, 1944; Barlow, 1943d; Vaillant, MSa.

344

Tlatelolco, Códice de. Manuscrito [Pintura] de Xochipilla. MNA 35-39. Ex–Boturini (?) collection. Published. Historical. Tlatelolco, D.F. ca. 1565. Amatl paper tira. 40 × 325 cm.

Pictorial chronicle from before 1554 to after 1562, with notable drawings of colonial events and personages but without explicit chronological framework. Initial scenes refer to participation of Tenochtitlan and Tlatelolco in the Mixton War (ca. 1542). If this document is correctly identified as having been in the Boturini collection (see Article 29), a long section at the beginning is lost.

The manuscript has been studied and reproduced in full on two occasions by Barlow (1944a, 1948b); the more recent study is more detailed. Some details are reproduced in color from a copy in Peñafiel (1903c). Robertson (1959) has discussed its style.

Copies: Copy made for Madrid exposition of 1892, unknown. M. A. Saldaña copy, MNA 35-39A.

Publication: Barlow, 1944a, 1948b.

Other: Peñafiel, 1903c, p. 1, pls. 76, 77, 124, 132; Robertson, 1959, pp. 163–66, pls. 58–59.

Brief descriptions: Alcina Franch, 1955, p. 460; Glass, 1964, p. 85, pl. 41; Paso y Troncoso, 1892–93, 1: 267–69.

345

Tlatengo, Rôle des Impôts [perçus sur les habitants du Canton] *de,* [en 1562]. BNP 390. Unpublished. Ex–Boturini collection (?). Economic (tribute). Central Mexico. ca. 1562. Native paper tira. 175 × 20 cm.

The tira is divided into approximately 10 horizontal divisions marked with year devices and Spanish glosses. The years represented may be 1552–61. In most divisions there are drawings of turkeys, cacao beans, and other goods and foodstuffs with numerical signs. Henry Nicholson (personal communication) has noted that Humboldt Fragment 14 (q.v.) is a fragment of this manuscript. A gloss on the reverse identifies it as assessments of the estancia of Tlatengo.

The 1823 inventory of the Boturini collection (see Article 29) describes it as representing the tribute of the nine wards of Santa Maria Tlatempan.

Brief description: J. F. Ramírez, 1855, no. 7.

346 (fig. 65)

Tlatepusco, San Pedro, Mapa de. Pueblo. Unpublished. Cartographic. San Pedro Tlatepusco, ex-district of Tuxtepec, Northern Oaxaca. 1803. European paper. Dimensions not determined.

The document has been described by Cline (1961a) as showing the church and limits of San Pedro Tlatepusco and the area around San Felipe de Leon. Details include stylized stars and a moon, several human figures, and miscellaneous geographical detail. It is crudely drawn, peripheral to the native tradition, and primarily of local interest only. It may derive from an older original.

Copy: Copy of copy owned by Weitlaner and H. F. Cline, in LC, Manuscripts Division. A photograph of this copy is in LC/HF.

Brief description: Cline, 1961a, pp. 65–66.

347 (fig. 66)

Tlatzcantzin, Genealogie des. Genealogie von 50 Personen. Museum für Völkerkunde, Berlin. Ex–Uhde collection. Published. Genealogical. Tlaxcala (?). 16th-C. European paper. 81 × 56 cm.

Glossed genealogy of 49 descendents of Tlatzcantzin Chichimecatlaque. Names of persons in first four of eight generations given in Nahuatl only. Some personal name glyphs.

Lehmann (1906a) provides commentary and reproduction of a tracing; Kutscher (1963b) gives more detailed comment and photographic reproduction.

Publication: Kutscher, 1963b; Lehmann, 1906a, pp. 337–42, pl. 4.

348

Tlaxcala, Anales de, no. 2, 1519–1692. Anales Antiguos de Mexico y sus Contornos (AAMC) no. 17. Unknown. Ex-Boturini collection. Unpublished. Historical. Tlaxcala. ca. 1692. European paper. 13 leaves. Quarto.

The Galicia Chimalpopoca copy contains the Nahuatl text, his Spanish translation, and nine samples of symbols (including four year signs) copied from the original. The text has historical notices, 1519–1692, of events in Tlaxcala and elsewhere.

Gibson (1952) discusses the history of the manuscript and related documents.

Copy: Chimalpopoca copy and translation, MNA/AH-CA 274, Item 17 (AAMC 17).

Brief description: Gibson, 1952, pp. 254–55.

349

Tlaxcala, Códice de. Toponimia de Tlaxcala. Tlaxcalan Topographic Chart. Códice de San Agustin Tlaxco, Tlaxcala. MNA 35-71. Ex–Boturini collection. Published. Unclassified (obverse) and cartographic (reverse). San Agustin Tlaxco, Tlaxcala. 16thC. Skin. 97.5 × 83 cm.

Most of the painting on the obverse has disappeared; descriptions in inventories of the Boturini collection indicate that it presented a coat of arms, portraits of individuals, and place glyphs and other symbols in concentric circles. A crude map on the reverse, probably a later addition, is not in the native tradition. Apparently it represents a region near San Agustin Tlaxco.

A brief description, together with photographs of the obverse and reverse, is in the MNA catalog (Glass, 1964). Mena (1923) has also described it, and Gibson (1952) has commented on it. It was exhibited in London in 1824 by Bullock and is listed in his catalog (Bullock, 1824c).

Publication: Glass, 1964, p. 124, pls. 74–76.

Brief descriptions: Gibson, 1952, pp. 268–69; Mena, 1923, pp. 47–52, no. 4.

Other: Bullock, 1824c, no. 29.

350

Tlaxcala, Lienzo de. Known versions described below. Published. Historical. Tlaxcala, Tlaxcala. ca. 1550.

The history of the Lienzo de Tlaxcala and the relationship between three "originals" and 11 copies, listed below, are complex and incomplete. A 16thC reference (Cervantes de Salazar, 1914–36) suggests that there may have been a similar mural painting in Tlaxcala. A variant copy and a 16thC manuscript in book form are described seperately in this census (nos. 351, 352). See also *Informe de los méritos de la ciudad de Tlaxcala* (Article 27B, no. 1127).

The 1773 copy and the 1892 and 1939 editions of a lost but similar version depict an original single sheet, which had a large main scene at the top followed by 87 much smaller scenes arranged in 13 horizontal rows. The main scene shows a European coat of arms, the lords and devices of the four quarters of Tlaxcala, Spanish officials (including Cortés, Antonio de Mendoza, and Luis de Velasco), the erection of a Christian cross, and numerous lesser Indian nobles.

The 87 smaller scenes depict the arrival of the Spaniards in Tlaxcala and the participation of the Tlaxcalans as allies in the Spanish conquest of Mexico City and other places. Most of the scenes are of battles. They show Indian warriors and Spanish soldiers, frequently with the place glyph for the town being conquered.

Originals: The three "originals" listed below are reported by Mazihcatzin (1927), writing in 1787 or before.

1. An original kept in the Ayuntamiento of Tlaxcala and described in detail (except whether it was made of cloth or paper) by Mazihcatzin (1927). This version may be the one which Chavero (n.d., 1892) states

was taken to Mexico City to be copied by the French Scientific Commission in the time of Maximilian. The Indian painting on cotton seen by Beltrami in Tlaxcala in 1825 (Beltrami, 1830) may be this original. It is now unknown. Gondra (1846) refers to an original on native paper in the Tlaxcalan Ayuntamiento.

2. An original sent to Spain, presumably to Charles V. It is conceivably the subject of a very brief and enigmatic description by Felipe de Guevara, who died in 1563 (Guevara, 1788). The Guevara description is quoted in full by both Chavero (1892) and Gibson (1952). This version is now unknown.

3. An original which stayed in Mexico. This version may correspond to the "original" on cloth in the Boturini collection, which is described in the inventories of 1743, 1745, and 1804 (where its dimensions are given as 5 × 2 *varas*) as well as in the catalog of 1746. It is not included in the inventory of 1823 and is now unknown.

Copies: 1. MNA 35-45/48 is a copy on four sheets of cloth by Juan Manuel Yllañes and is dated 1773. It includes the main scene and the 87 smaller scenes as described above. It has been described by Glass (1964), but only details from it have been published, as in Gurría LaCroix (1966), Velázquez Chávez (1939), and other works not cited here. It is probably copied from the Ayuntamiento original. Gondra (1846) refers to the Yllañes copy but dates it at 1779. A copy of the Yllañes copy, made by Mateo A. Saldaña about 1933, is MNA 35-45/48A and is poorly reproduced in Glass (1964).

2. An incomplete copy (38 of the final 49 scenes plus the explanatory legend) of the Yllañes copy is in TU/LAL. The possible identification of this copy with one of those listed below has not been investigated.

3. Seven lienzo scenes and four details from the main scene are published by Gondra (1846, pls. 37–43, 59–62). They are said

to be from the Ayuntamiento original; in composition they resemble the Yllañes copy. Two further scenes published by Alaman in Prescott (1844) may be from the same source.

4. Chavero (1892) reports that a copy of the 1773 copy was exhibited at an unspecified exposition in Paris. This copy is now unknown.

5. The copiously illustrated *Teatro de la Nueva España* by Diego García Panes (MS in BNMex) contains scenes either copied from, or inspired by, a version of the Lienzo de Tlaxcala. Four of them are published by Gurría LaCroix (1966). Three or four of Panes' drawings of this nature are reproduced through redrawn and considerably romanticized copies by Gondra (1846, pls. 30–33); one of the latter is reprinted by Gurría LaCroix (1966).

6. An apparently complete copy was made (or owned?) by Diego Panes in the 18thC (Gibson, 1952, p. 250). It is now unknown but may correspond to the lienzo given to the Mexican congress in 1822 (Felix Osores *in* Beristáin y Souza, 1833–97) and/or to the Museo Nacional about 1827 (J. F. Ramírez, 1862). Panes borrowed or secured documents from the Boturini collection (Nuevos datos, 1952). This version might be the Boturini "original," the Yllañes copy, or his own copy.

7. Chavero (n.d., 1892) reported that an inaccurate copy of the Ayuntamiento original was made by the French Scientific Commission. It is now unknown.

8. An oil-on-cloth copy or version of the right third of the main scene is in the Museo Nacional de Historia, Chapultepec, Mexico. Fully glossed, it varies in detail from other versions. A small photo appears in Gurría Lacroix (1967) without comment. It has been briefly described by Gibson (1952).

9. Bullock's description of a painting exhibited by him in London in 1824 certainly suggests another version of the upper part of the lienzo. We quote it in full: "An Oil

Painting, formerly in the collection of the Chevalier Boturini, for whom it was copied. On the top, in a compartment, are the portraits of the Kings of Mexico, arranged in succession, each having his name, in hieroglyphics, placed near him, and a translation below: and underneath each compartment is a Spanish poetical description. At the bottom of the picture is Cortés seated beside the King of Zampoola, several Ladies of his Court, and near them an assemblage of the Warriors of that nation, the first friends of Cortés. In the centre of the lower compartment is Cortés, at the head of his cavalry, preceded by the guide of Zampoola, and the Ambassadors of Tlascalla. The four next compartments are subjects from History, but much defaced" (Bullock, 1824c, pp. 40–41, no. 12). Numbers 21, 42, and 46 of Bullock's catalog should be taken into account in a full discussion.

10. A copy in book form made by Diodoro Serrano and owned by J. F. Ramírez and later by Chavero is the source of the color lithographs made by Genaro López and published by the Junta Colombina with a commentary by Chavero (1892). The Serrano copy, which is now unknown, has been described by Chavero (n.d., 1892), Peñafiel (1909), and by Paso y Troncoso (1892–93). Peñafiel reports that it contained decorative devices by Serrano not on the original; they have been published by Peñafiel (1903c, 1909). The Serrano copy is also the source of the illustrations in Chavero's *Historia antigua* (n.d.), in which the first 48 scenes of the lienzo are reproduced in order together with details from the main scene. The 1892 edition contains the main scene and 80 of the 87 smaller scenes; the presence of the missing seven scenes is indicated, however, by their titles. There is a reprint of the Chavero edition and commentary (Chavero, 1964) but with most of the plates in b/w rather than in color.

11. The color lithographs associated with Cahuantzi "Códice Cahuantzi") appar-

ently correspond to the edition which Starr (1898)—and not Bandelier as reported by Glass (1964)—mentioned as being in preparation by the state of Tlaxcala. These lithographs, which originally measured 50 × 35 cm., presented two of the smaller scenes on each sheet. Sets of the lithographs were secured by Echániz, cut in half or folded, and published in 1939 (Cahuantzi, 1939) together with a reprint of the Mazihcatzin description. This edition lacks the plates corresponding to scenes 2, 3, 4, 6, and 7 of the 1892 edition and places two other scenes in a different order. It also lacks the final seven scenes. Most copies of this edition are incomplete or have missing pages supplied with photostats. Pictorially, the Cahuantzi lithographs are close to those of the 1892 edition; they probably derive from the same ultimate original. Their glosses, however, are occasionally very different. Angulo (1959) reports some of the vicissitudes suffered by this edition.

A concordance of the various published partial versions and copies of the lienzo with the Yllañes copy is given in Table 4.

Most of the relevant publications concerning the lienzo are cited above. The Chavero (1892) and Cahuantzi (1939) editions are adequate for most purposes and, except for the final seven scenes, are probably more important than the 1773 copy. Chavero's commentary on the final 39 scenes has been criticized by Gibson (1952). It may also be noted that Chavero's commentary does not include the glosses and variations in other versions. Gibson (1952) provides a detailed review of most known data concerning the lienzo. The 1787 description by Mazihcatzin (1927) is a basic source. It was probably written at the request of Diego Panes (given as Diego Pérez in the 1927 edition). Falsified versions of the lienzo are listed in Article 26.

Publication: Cahuantzi, 1939; Chavero, 1892, 1964; Glass, 1964, pp. 91–93, pls. 46–49.

TABLE 4—LIENZO DE TLAXCALA (Census, 350)

Concordance of published partial versions of lienzo scenes with the Yllañes copy of 1773.

Yllañes copy of 1773	Chavero 1892 edition plate nos.	Cahuantzi 1939 edition plate nos.	Copies by Gondra, published 1846, plate nos.	Copies published in Prescott, 1844	Panes copies published by Gurría, Panes nos.	Panes copies published by Gondra, 1846, plate nos.	Códice de la Conquista (Census, 351)	UTX manuscript (Census, 352)
main	main	main	details	----	----	----	----	----
A	1	1	----	----	----	----	----	----
B	2	----	----	----	----	----	1	----
C	3	----	----	----	83	31	2	----
D	4	----	----	----	----	----	----	1
E	5	2	----	----	94	----	3	2
F	6	----	----	----	----	----	----	3
G	7	----	----	----	79	30	4	4
H	8	3	----	----	----	32	----	----
J	10	5	37	----	----	----	----	----
K	11	6	----	X	----	----	----	----
P	16	12	----	X	----	----	----	----
S	19	14	40	----	----	----	----	----
X	22	17	41	----	----	----	----	----
F	30	25	----	----	----	33?	----	----
J	34	29	38	----	----	----	----	----
M	37	32	42	----	----	----	----	----
Q	41	36	39	----	----	----	----	----
Y	47	42	43	----	----	----	----	----
----	----	----	----	----	23	----	5	----

Commentaries: Gibson, 1952, pp. 247–53; Mazihcatzin, 1927.

Other: Angulo, 1958, 1959; Beltrami, 1830, 2: 308–09; Beristáin de Souza, 1883–97, 4: 134; Boturini, 1746, 1: 152; Bullock, 1824c, pp. 40–41, no. 12; Cervantes de Salazar, 1914–36, 1: 296; Chavero, n.d., pp. xvi-xvii, 843–911; Gondra, 1846, pp. 122–28, 132–42, 151, pls. 30–33, 37–43, 59–62; Guevara, 1788, p. 236; Gurría LaCroix, 1966, pls. 8, 13, 15, 16, 21, 23, 26, 28, 31; 1967; *Nuevos datos*, 1952, p. 20; Peñafiel, 1903c, pls. 13, 54; 1909, pp. 15–16, pls. 19, 20; Prescott, 1844, 2: 216, 241; J. F. Ramírez, 1862, p. 404, no. 18; Starr, 1898, p. 7; Velázquez Chávez, 1939, pl. 5.

Brief description: Paso y Troncoso, 1892–93, 1: 38–39, 68–70.

351

—— *Códice de la Conquista*. Códice con escenas de la conquista. Historia de la conquista. Códice entrada de los Españoles en Tlaxcala. MNA 35-78. Ex-Boturini collection. Published. Historical. Tlaxcala, Tlaxcala. 17th–18thC. European paper. 56 × 116 cm.

The manuscript is a late and Hispanicized drawing of five scenes from the Lienzo de Tlaxcala, with Spanish glosses, corresponding to plates 2, 3, 5, and 7 of the 1892 edition (see previous entry) together with a scene comparable only to one of Panes' drawings. With this manuscript the inventories of the Boturini collection of 1743 and 1745 also list a separate and sixth scene now lost and unpublished. The latter is also described in the catalog of 1746 and apparently corresponded to plate 1 of the 1892 edition of the lienzo.

A fully illustrated description and comparative study is given by Gurría LaCroix (1966). It has been briefly described and

217

reproduced by Glass (1964). It has also been described by Mena (1923), who illustrates and misrepresents several details, and by Mateos Higuera (1949a). A partial reproduction is given by Cuevas (1921–28). It has been briefly treated by Gibson (1952).

Copies: Modern copy in PML. A modern tracing by Canessi is reproduced by Gurría LaCroix (1966).

Publication: Glass, 1964, pp. 131–32, pl. 83; Gurría LaCroix, 1966.

Partial publication: Cuevas, 1921–28, 1: 124.

Brief descriptions: Gibson, 1952, p. 249; Mateos Higuera, 1949a; Mena, 1923, pp. 61–62, pls. 2 and 3, no. 19.

352

—— Untitled pages of the Lienzo de Tlaxcala. UTX. Ex–Stendahl collection. Published. Historical. Tlaxcala, Tlaxcala. 16th-C. Native paper. 2 leaves painted on both sides, each 55.5 × 43.5 cm.

This version of the Lienzo de Tlaxcala scenes (see Census, 350, above) consists of a large sheet of native paper on which are drawn four scenes so arranged that they constitute two leaves or four pages of a manuscript in the form of a large European book. The four scenes are comparable in subject matter to plates 4–7 of the 1892 edition of the Lienzo de Tlaxcala but present far more detail and include Nahuatl glosses unknown on any other extant version. The manuscript is presumably incomplete but does not exhibit pagination marks.

The manuscript is reproduced without comment on the end papers of Anton (1965).

Copy: A photostat of a copy of one of the four scenes, without the glosses, is among the Barlow papers in the University of the Americas library, Mexico. A photograph of the photostat is in LC/HF.

Publication: Anton, 1965, end papers.

Brief description: *Präkolumbische Kunst*, 1958, p. 93, no. 745.

❖❖❖

TLAXINICAN, TLAYLOTLACAN, TECPANPA, ETC., TRIBUTES OF. Two pictorial tribute manuscripts pertaining to various barrios of an unidentified locality, probably in the eastern Valley of Mexico.

353

—— *Contributions ou Tributs* [que payaient en argent et en nature les indigènes des villages] *de Tlaxinican, Tlaylotlacan, Tecpanpa, Tenanco, Quecholac, Ayocalco, et San Nicolas*. BNP 28. Ex–Aubin collection. Published. Economic (tribute). Valley of Mexico. 16thC. Native paper. 40 × 38 cm.

Drawings of items of tribute—pesos, fish, canoes (?), pottery, turkeys—from each of seven localities identified by place glyphs and glosses (see title).

Boban (1891) gives description and photoreproduction.

Publication: Boban, 1891, 1: 391–95, pl. 28.

354

—— *Contributions ou Tributs* [en argent et en nature] *imposés aux indigènes par* [le chef (caudillo) ou commandeur (encomendero)] *Don Joseph Jorgen*. BNP 108. Ex–Aubin collection. Unpublished. Economic (tribute). Valley of Mexico. 16thC. European paper. 140 × 31 cm.

Drawings of items of tribute—pesos, fish, pottery, turkeys—paid by each of 10 localities. The first seven are the same as those listed in the title of the preceding document. The total of the items is drawn at the bottom of the tira. Also shown are the Indians —merinos—in charge of collecting the tribute. A Spanish gloss identifies Joseph Jorgen as "caudillo."

A detailed description is given by Boban (1891).

Description: Boban, 1891, 2: 287–90.

355

Tlazultepec, Genealogy of. AGN-T 59, exp. 2. Published. Genealogical. Tlazultepec (now San Augustin Tlacotepec), ex-district of Tlaxiaco, Western Oaxaca. 1597. European paper. 42.5 × 31.5 cm.

Drawings of the descendants of a cacique of Tlazultepec and other persons in traditional poses and costume in a conservative Mixtec style. There are no calendrical or personal name glyphs; place glyphs are identified by Spanish glosses.

Spores (1964) reproduces a copy, gives an interpretation of the document, and summarizes the related litigation.

Publication: Spores, 1964.

356

Tlotzin, Mapa. Histoire du Royaume d'-Acolhuacan ou de Tezcuco. Genealogía de los Reyes Chichimecas. BNP 373. Ex-Diego Pimentel, Ixtlilxochitl, Boturini, and Aubin collections. Published. Historical and genealogical. Texcoco, Mexico. 16th-C (before 1550). Skin tira. 31.5 × 127.5 cm.

The document treats the establishment of the Chichimecs of Xolotl in the eastern Valley of Mexico in the time of Nopaltzin and Tlotzin. Genealogies relating to six localities are shown, including Huexotla, Coatlinchan, and Oztoticpac (Texcoco); the latter extends into the colonial period. The Nahuatl texts have been translated by Aubin.

The early Desportes lithograph (Aubin, n.d.*e*) was apparently printed to illustrate the commentary by Aubin (1849). The Aubin commentary is illustrated by color lithographs in its reprint of 1885 (Aubin, 1885) and by b/w lithographs in other reprintings (Aubin, 1859–61, 1875). The Spanish translation of the commentary (Aubin, 1886b) is illustrated by the Desportes lithograph. Radin (1920) digests the commentary and reproduces the 1885 lithographs in b/w. Chavero (n.d.) reproduces most of the figures of the manuscript in his history of ancient Mexico and Orozco y Berra (1880) comments on some of its content.

Alcina Franch (1955) and others mis-takenly list the "Genealogía de los Reyes Chichimecas" as a distinct and lost document.

Copies: Boturini collection copy, BNP 95; Pichardo copy, BNP 89-4.

Publication: Aubin, 1859–61; 1875; 1885, pp. 51–74, pls. 1–3; 1886b; n.d.*e*; Radin, 1920, pp. 18–19, 35–38, pls. 13–15.

Commentary: Aubin, 1849.

Other: Chavero, n.d., pp. xiii–xiv, 509–36; León-Portilla, 1967a, p. 72; Orozco y Berra, 1880, vol. 3, book 2, chaps. 5 and 6.

Brief descriptions: Alcina Franch, 1955, pp. 457, 460; Robertson, 1959, pp. 140–41.

357

Tocuaro, Títulos de. MNA 35-116. Partially published. Historical. Tocuaro, Michoacan. 17thC. European paper. 9 leaves. 31 × 21 cm.

Spanish and Tarascan texts related to history and land titles of Tocuaro. One page has a simple drawing of two Indians holding bows and arrows.

Glass (1964) gives brief description and photograph of the drawing.

Partial publication: Glass, 1964, p. 173, pl. 127.

358

Tola, Santa Isabel, Títulos de [tierras pertenecientes al pueblo de]. Cadastre de Terres conquisés à Izhuatepec. Manuscrito Americano numero 4. Unknown. Published. Economic (land titles) and historical. Santa Isabel Tola, D.F., or San Juan Ixhuatepec, Mexico. ca. 1616. European (?) paper. 13 leaves. "Medio pliego."

The document is known through a copy of its drawings and Nahuatl texts and a detailed description and translation thereof made in 1701 and copied in 1714. From the 1701 description it is evident that the Berlin and Paris copies are incomplete.

The *Títulos* were preserved in Santa Isabel Tola in the late 18thC together with a map of the Villa de Nuestra Señora de

Guadalupe. A brief comment of 1797 by Francisco Sedano on both the map and the titles is quoted by García Gutiérrez (1939, p. 137). Copies of the map, not relevant to this census but containing references to the titles in their legends, are reproduced by Boban (1891, 2: 197–201, pl. 79) and by Pompa y Pompa (1938, p. 15).

The first four pages of the original had Nahuatl texts and drawings of 16 Indians and place glyphs representing lands distributed by Itzcoatl. The same lands are also depicted in Códice de Ixhuatepec and in Codex Cozcatzin. Other pages presented drawings of the nine preconquest rulers of Tenochtitlan from Acamapichtli through Moctezuma, similar to those in Codex Cozcatzin. The remaining sections are concerned with church expenses, 1539 and 1598–1616, and the sale of lands to a Spaniard in 1573.

Two or three final pages, missing from the copies, concerned the Indian rulers of Tenochtitlan from Moctezuma through Cristóbal de Guzmán. The translation of their texts in the 1701 description indicates that they were similar to the series in Codex Cozcatzin.

The Berlin copy, together with the copied description of 1701, was defectively published, in color, by Peñafiel (1897b). Eight of the nine drawings of the preconquest rulers of Tenochtitlan were first published in Prescott (1844) and are also published in Peñafiel (1903c). Drawings of 11 rulers (Acamapichtli through Cuauhtemoc) reproduced by Carbajal Espinosa (1862) are similar to those given in Prescott but with some of the personal name glyphs taken from Clavigero. The source of his glyphs for Cuitlahuac and Cuanuhtemoc is uncertain since they are not present in the copies or in Prescott. López Sarrelangue (1957) cites possibly related litigation in the Archivo Municipal de Mexico. See Ixhuatepec Group for further comment.

Copies: (1) DSB MS Amer. 4, now lost.

(2) Peñafiel copy of the DSB copy, HSA. (3) Aubin collection copy, BNP 94 and 222 (described by Boban, 1891). (4) Location of Galicia Chimalpopoca copy, formerly in the Conway collection, is unknown (mentioned by Barlow, 1946a).

Publication: Peñafiel, 1897b.

Partial publication: Carbajal Espinosa, 1862, 1: pls. facing 316, 322, 334, 356, 382, 396, 415, 419; 2: 6, 449, 466; Peñafiel, 1903c, pls. 128–30; Prescott, 1844, 1: two pls. labeled "Reyes Aztecas."

Other: Barlow, 1946a, p. 416; Boban, 1891, 2: 265–66, 406; García Gutiérrez, 1939, p. 137; López Sarrelangue, 1957, pp. 17–18.

359

Tolteca-Chichimeca, Historia. Historia Tulteca. Anales de Quauhtinchan. Annales Tolteco-Chichimeques. Codex Gondra. BNP 46-58. Ex–Boturini and Aubin collections. Published. Historical and cartographic-historical. Cuauhtinchan, Puebla. After 1544. European paper. 52 leaves. 30 × 22 cm.

The document is in three parts (BNP 46-50, 51-53, and 54-58). The first two contain 22 leaves of the original and copies by Aubin from BNP 54-58. Modern editions combine the three parts, arrange the pages in logical sequence, and omit the redundant Aubin copies.

The manuscript contains 37 pages of Nahuatl text, 35 pages of Nahuatl text with drawings, 25 full-page drawings (including six double-page maps) and seven blank pages.

The manuscript is one of the major sources for the study of the early post-Toltec and subsequent history of the Chichimec migrations from Chicomoztoc to the central Puebla region. It treats the emigration of the Nonohualca and Tolteca-Chichimeca from Tula, the conquest of the Olmeca-Xicalanca at Cholula by the latter, emigrations from Chicomoztoc, the founding of Cuauhtinchan, and the later history and wars of the inhabitants of Cuauhtin-chan. The period embraced by this history is A.D. 1116 through 1544.

The drawings, none of which depict colonial events, are probably copies from the pictorial manuscript or manuscripts on which the Nahuatl text is based. Some of the mans are clearly part of the series repre-sented by the Mapas de Cuauhtinchan nos. 1–3 (q.v., especially no. 2, for further com-ment).

A part of the manuscript was lithographed for Aubin (n.d.c) about 1849–51 or later. This ephemeral edition, which we have not seen, the extracts and translation (partial) in the AAMC (see below), and a copy of a translation supplied to Brasseur de Bour-bourg by Gondra about 1851 made the con-tent of the manuscript known in the 19thC. It is cited or utilized in the major historical writings of Brasseur de Bourbourg, Cha-vero, and Orozco y Berra.

Boban (1891) described the manuscript in considerable detail and reproduced 21 pages of the original and five pages of the Aubin copy catalogued with it. The first complete edition (Preuss and Mengin, 1937–38) was issued in two parts. The first (1937) gives a transcript of the text, a parallel Ger-man translation, and reproduces all of the illustrations (most in line drawings, some by photography). The second (1938) provides an extended commentary. The second full edition (Mengin, 1942) is a b/w photofac-simile of the entirety of the original with a brief introduction.

Berlin and Rendón (1947) give a Spanish translation of the text (based both on the Nahuatl and the German translations) and reproduce the drawings after the 1937 edi-tion. They also provide a chronological essay by Berlin (incorporating a revision of that given in 1937) and an historical study by Kirchhoff.

Kirchhoff (1940) maps and studies the migration itineraries of the Nonohualca and Tolteca-Chichimeca and considers some as-pects of their relationship to the Olmeca-Xicalanca. His study is partially revised in Kirchhoff (1958). Robertson (1959) dis-cusses and reproduces two of the maps. Jiménez Moreno (1961) makes important observations on the chronology and corre-lation of dates in the manuscript. Some of the studies by Preuss (cited below) may be incorporated in the 1938 commentary. Preuss and Mengin (1937–38, 1: 8) cite translations of selected paragraphs by Seler and Krickeberg excluded from the present bibliography.

Copies: (1) Extract in Spanish transla-tion by Aubin, "Anales Toltecas," "Anónimo Número 1," MNA/AH Col. Antig. 273, Item 2 (AAMC 2). Published as *Anales Toltecas* (1949). (2) Partial translation by Galicia Chimalpopoca, apparently from early litho-graph edition, "Anales Tolteca-Chichi-mecas," "Anónimo número 2." MNA/AH Col. Antig. 273, Item 5 (AAMC 5). Pub-lished as *Anales Tolteca-Chichimeca* (1949) and also as *Anales Número Cinco* (1954). (3) Partial copy of Nahuatl text and drawings by Galicia Chimalpopoca, "Venida de los Tultecas," MNA/AH Col. Antig. 254, ff. 21r–28r. (4) Partial copy by Aubin of BNP 54-58 in BNP 46-50 and BNP 51-53. (5) Old (Aubin?) partial copy, BNP 58bis. (6) Aubin copy with French translation, BNP 338. (7) Brasseur de Bourbourg collection copy of incomplete translation made by or-der of Gondra from original ("Codex Gondra"), unknown. (8) León y Gama copy, unknown.

Editions: Berlin and Rendón, 1947; Men-gin, 1942; Preuss and Mengin, 1937–38.

Partial publications and translations (se-lected): *Anales Número Cinco*, 1954; *Anales Toltecas*, 1949; *Anales Tolteca-Chichimeca*, 1949; Aubin, n.d.c; Boban, 1891, 2: 51–102, pls. 46–58; Garibay, 1957; Whorf, 1930.

Studies: Barlow, 1948c; Kirchhoff, 1940, 1958; Preuss, 1936, 1937, 1938, 1948; Robert-son, 1959, pp. 179–80, pls. 81, 82.

Other: Jiménez Moreno, 1961; Nowotny, 1961b, p. 34, pls. 23, 24.

Historical references (selected): Brasseur de Bourbourg, 1851, pp. 26–28; León y Gama, 1832, 1: 29; 2: 31, 34.

Brief descriptions: Alcina Franch, 1955, p. 504; Barlow, 1948f.

360

Tonayan, Mapa de. Códice Tonayan. Códice Chapultepec. Plano de San Juan Chapultepec. Unknown. Published. Cartographic-historical. San Juan Chapultepec or San Pedro Tonayan, Veracruz. 1665. Physical description of original is unknown.

Map of the Tonayan, Chapultepec, and Coacoatzintla region with drawings of roads, mountains, place glyphs, and 16thC personages. The document is related to continuing litigation between named communities over municipal jurisdictions.

Mena (1911b) reproduces and comments on the 1852 copy. Barlow (1947b) gives photographs of the 1849 copy, the tracing of the 1849 copy, and the 1852 copy. Cline (1959) reproduces the 1849 copy and interprets its cartographic aspects.

Copies: Reported copies include: (1) 1849 watercolor, DGMH. (2) Tracing of the 1849 copy, DGMH. (3) 1852 oil on cloth, 137 × 163 cm., in Secretaría de Gobierno, Jalapa, about 1911 and now possibly in the Departamento de Antropología of the state of Veracruz. (4) "Archivo particular," Chapultepec, Veracruz.

Publication: Barlow, 1947b; Cline, 1959, pp. 655–57, figs. 13, 14; Mena, 1911b; Tamayo, 1949, pp. 54–55.

Brief descriptions: Alcina Franch, 1955, pp. 463–64; Melgarejo Vivanco, 1953, p. 334; Tamayo and Alcorta, 1941, pp. 19–20, no. 6.

361

Topográfico Fragmentado, Códice. MNA 35-61. Published. Economic (property plans). Western Oaxaca. 16thC. Amatl paper. 10 to 12 fragments of varying dimensions.

The surviving fragments of the now very incomplete document exhibit drawings of plots of land, native houses, Indians with calendrical name glyphs, and hieroglyphic dates in the "Mixtec" style. One of the glosses reads "tierras de Don Francisco." Caso (personal communication) reports that one of the Indian couples also appears in the Codex Selden.

A brief description and a photograph appear in the MNA catalog (Glass, 1964). Nicholson (unpublished notes) suggests a provenience in the Cuauhtepec-Tecamachalco region of Puebla.

Publication: Glass, 1964, p. 113, pl. 64.

362 (fig. 67)

Totomixtlahuaca, Lienzo de. Private collection. Partially published. Cartographic-historical. Totomixtlahuaca, Guerrero. ca. 1570. Cloth. ca. 189 × 168 cm. or 221 × 188 cm.

The lienzo, with about 75 hieroglyphic place names glossed in Nahuatl, depicts Totomixtlahuaca and surrounding dependencies such as Tlaxcalixtlahuaca, Pazcala, and Tlacoapan. There is a peripheral frame of place glyphs. Two rivers are prominent. Numerous persons, some in warlike attitudes, and the caciques of Totomixtlahuaca are shown. A Nahuatl text dated 1564 indicates that the lienzo concerns a land dispute between Totomixtlahuaca, Ocoapan, and Xochitonala.

A detail is reproduced in a recent catalog (Parke-Bernet, 1967) in which the original, a modern copy on cloth, and related documentary material are described. A detail of the original is reproduced. The documentary material may correspond to an unfinished commentary by R. H. Barlow and an anonymous collaborator; similar material is also in the Southwest Museum, where there is a modern copy on cloth, probably one of four believed to have been made after about 1948, when the lienzo is believed to have appeared in connection with land litigation in Guerrero.

Copies: loc. cit.   Photograph of original in LC/HF.

Bibliography: Parke-Bernet, 1967, p. 29, no. 117, frontispiece.

363

Totoquihuaztli, Don Antonio, Testamento de. BNP 115. Ex–Aubin collection. Unpublished. Economic (property plans). Tacuba, D.F. 1574. European paper. 2 drawings with accompanying text on approximately 10 leaves. Dimensions not determined.

The document contains the Nahuatl text and Spanish translation of the will of Don Antonio Totoquihuaztli, cacique of Tacuba. The two drawings are simple property plans with various hieroglyphic place names and lesser detail. Nicholson (1966a) reproduces a single place glyph from the document.

Brief description: Boban, 1891, 2: 301–02.

Other: Nicholson, 1966a.

364

Tovar Calendar, The. John Carter Brown Library, Providence. Ex–José de Acosta, Richard Heber, and Sir Thomas Phillipps collections. Published. Calendrical. Valley of Mexico. ca. 1585. European paper. 11 leaves. 21.2 × 15.3 cm.

The document is bound at the end of the JCBL MS of Tovar's *Relación del Origen . . .* (q.v.) and has had the same history since it came into the possession of Acosta. Unlike the *Relación*, however, its illustrations do not derive from Durán's *Historia* although its text has some slight relationship to it.

The manuscript is an 18-month festival calendar with drawings and descriptive texts in Spanish for each of the 18 ceremonies and one for the final five-day period.

Kubler and Gibson (1951) give complete photofacsimile and detailed comparative commentary. They consider the pictorial part of the Kalendario Mexicano, Latino y Castellano (q.v.) to be copied from the Tovar Calendar. A single page is reproduced in Robertson (1959).

Publication: Kubler and Gibson, 1951, pp. 18–54, 73–74, pls. 4 (right) and 5–14.

Other: Robertson, 1959, pl. 43.

❖❖❖

TOVAR, FRAY JUAN DE. *Relación del Origen de los Yndios que havitan en esta Nueva España según sus Historias.* This work, considered the second and only surviving historical writing by Tovar, is known through two variant 16thC manuscripts, entered separately below. Current opinion holds that the two Tovar texts are close and that they represent an abridgement by Tovar of Durán's *Historia de las Indias*, with some added material.

The drawings in the two Tovar manuscripts differ notably in style and major details but their essential dependence on those in Durán is evident, complex, and unstudied. Those in the JCBL Tovar MS are ambitious executions in color, perhaps more "native" than those in Durán, whereas those in the MNA MS are crude linear sketches, generally without color. The parallel drawings in Durán are in his Tratados 1 and 2 and those represented in the Tovar MSS are depictions of events of Aztec history and of gods, ceremonies, and customs. Only the calendar wheel and day signs from Durán's Tratado 3 are represented in both Tovar manuscripts.

The JCBL Tovar MS was available to Acosta, who copied numerous passages in his *Historia natural*, first published in 1590 (Acosta, 1962). The MNA or some similar MS was available to Torquemada, who utilized it to criticize Acosta. The bibliography concerning the relationships between Acosta, Tovar, and Durán is extensive. Only a selection is given here. Kubler and Gibson (1951) give a clear analysis of the problem and cite the earlier bibliography. O'Gorman (*in* Acosta, 1962) is another modern treatment with an annotated chronological review of the bibliography and related events. No source adequately treats the problem of the drawings since most of those in the JCBL manuscript are unpublished and those in the Durán manuscript were not adequately published until 1967. For further data and bibliography see the entries below, the Durán *Historia*, and the Crónica X Group in this census.

Selected bibliography on the Acosta-Tovar-Durán relationship: Beauvois, 1885; Kubler and Gibson, 1951, pp. 9–12 and passim; O'Gorman *in* Acosta, 1962, pp. xi–xxiii, lxxvii–xcv.

365

—— *Códice Ramírez*. Códice Anónimo. MNA/AH Col. Antig. 166 (also cataloged as MNA 35-100). Ex–Convento de San Francisco (Mexico City), J. F. Ramírez, and Chavero collections. Published. Calendrical, historical, and ethnographic. Valley of Mexico. 1583–87 or late 16thC. European paper. 169 leaves. 22 × 16 cm.

The manuscript, discovered by J. F. Ramírez in 1856, contains the text of the *Relación* (see previous entry), further fragments of text, and 32 drawings. The first 28 are parallel to those in Tratados 1 and 2 of Durán's *Historia*; drawings 29 and 30 are of calendar wheels and tables of day signs comparable to drawings at the beginning of Tratado 3 of Durán. The final two drawings are symbolic depictions of the Spanish conquest, not in Durán.

The text and the drawings were first published by Orozco y Berra (Alvarado Tezozomoc, 1878; reprinted, Tovar, 1944) with preface by J. F. Ramírez and partial commentary by Chavero and Orozco y Berra, presenting now outdated opinions. There are a French translation with 30 of the drawings (Charnay, 1903) and a partial English translation, without the drawings (Radin,

1920). There are also a recent study by Leal (1953) and a suggested concordance between the drawings and those of Durán (Barlow, 1944b). Glass (1964) reproduces two pages of the manuscript photographically. See previous and following entries in this census for further comment.

Copies: Orozco y Berra collection, now unknown.

Editions: Alvarado Tezozomoc, 1878; Librería Echániz, 1947d; Tovar, 1944.

Translations: Charnay, 1903; Radin, 1920, pp. 14–15, 24, 29–30, 67–123.

Other: Barlow, 1944b, pp. 534–36; Caso, 1945a; 1967, pp. 96–97; Leal, 1953; Yáñez, 1942, pp. 37–100.

Brief description: Glass, 1964, p. 154, pl. 107.

366

—— *Historia de la Benida de los Yndios apoblar a Mexico*. John Carter Brown Library, Providence. Ex–José de Acosta, Richard Heber, and Sir Thomas Phillipps collections. Partially published. Calendrical, historical, and ethnographic. Valley of Mexico. 1583–87. European paper. 81 leaves of text plus drawings and other material. 21.2 × 15.3 cm.

The manuscript, a Tovar holograph in Spanish, contains: added title page ("Historia de la Benida . . ."), correspondence between Tovar and Acosta (3 ff.), the text of the *Relación* (81 ff.), 28 drawings comparable to certain of those in Tratados 1 and 2 of Durán's *Historia*, a drawing of a calendar wheel and miscellaneous calendrical drawings parallel to those in Tratado 3 of Durán, a page in Nahuatl, and a festival calendar now known as the Tovar Calendar (described separately in this census).

The Tovar-Acosta correspondence has been published numerous times, most recently by Kubler and Gibson (1951) in English translation and photofacsimile. Other editions of the correspondence include García Icazbalceta (1881) and Sandoval

(1945). For the text of the *Relación* there is only a partial, inaccurate, and rare publication (Tovar, 1860). Only four of the drawings have been published (see below). Kubler and Gibson (1951) give excellent historiographic commentary, incomplete description, and inaccurate concordance between the drawings and those of the Durán *Historia*. An edition is in preparation. See previous entries for further comment.

Publication of drawings: Kubler and Gibson, 1951, pl. 4 (left); *Mirror of the Indian*, 1958, pl. 1; Sotheby and Co., 1946, p. 17, pl. 6; Wroth, 1949, pl. 8.

Partial publication of text: Tovar, 1860.

Other: García Icazbalceta, 1881 (volume and page references not determined); Sandoval, 1945, pp. 80–82.

Commentary: Burrus, 1957 (biographical data on Tovar); Kubler and Gibson, 1951, pp. 5, 9–18, pls. 1–3, 4 (left).

367

Tributos, Fragmento de. Gilcrease Institute, Tulsa. Ex–Boturini and MNA (no. 35-72) collections. Published. Economic (tribute). Central Mexico. 16thC. Native paper. 38 × 18.9 cm.

Drawings of numerical signs, fish, and other goods arranged in horizontal rows. The document may be a receipt for the payment of goods or for the delivery of tribute.

A photograph and a brief description are given by Glass (1964).

Publication: Glass, 1964, p. 125, pl. 77.

Brief description: Mena, 1923, p. 53, no. 6.

368 (fig. 68)

Tributos, Matrícula de. Tribute Roll of Montezuma. Códice de Moctezuma. Codex Poinsett (part). MNA 35-52. Ex-Boturini collection. Defectively published. Economic (tribute). Mexico City, D.F. 16thC. Amatl paper codex. 16 leaves. 42 × 29 cm.

Itemized pictorial list of tribute paid to the ruling cities of the Valley of Mexico before the conquest by the different provinces of the Aztec Empire. Major source for the study of tribute, place glyphs, and political economy and geography of the Aztecs. Closely related to Codex Mendoza, part 2, and to the *Información sobre los Tributos que los Indios pagaban a Moctezuma* of 1554 (see Article 27B, no. 1136).

The editions of Lorenzana (1770) and Peñafiel (1890) are inadequate for serious research. The two leaves taken to Philadelphia in the 1820s by Poinsett and returned to Mexico in 1942 are reproduced in color by Brinton et al. (1892). Isolated pages are photographically reproduced by Glass (1964), Keleman (1943), Hagen (1944), Lenz (1950), Robertson (1959), and, in color, in *Twenty Centuries* ... (1940). This is not a complete list.

Barlow (1949d) describes the manuscript, analyzes much of its political and economic content, and maps the towns and provinces shown in the document. Robertson (1959) discusses its style, date, and prototype. See Codex Mendoza for further comment. The *Información* of 1554 has been published by Scholes and Adams (1957) and studied by Borah and Cook (1963).

Copies: The Boturini collection copy, MNA 35-52 (part), is also published (defectively) by Peñafiel (1890).

Publication: Lorenzana, 1770, pp. 171–76, pls. 2–32; Peñafiel, 1890, chaps. 13–15, pls. 228–59.

Partial publication: Brinton et al., 1892; Glass, 1964, pp. 99–100, pl. 55; Gondra, 1846, pp. 109–13, pl. 23; Hagen, 1944, pl. 34b; Keleman, 1943, pl. 269; Lenz, 1950, figs. 46, 47; *Twenty Centuries*, 1940, color pl. D.

Commentary: Barlow, 1949d.

Studies: Anderson and Barlow, 1943; Barlow, 1945f; Borah and Cook, 1963, pp. 25–37; Robertson, 1959, pp. 72–77, pls. 15, 16.

Other: Scholes and Adams, 1957.

Brief descriptions: Alcina Franch, 1955,

pp. 439–40; Kubler and Gibson, 1951, pp. 64–65; Glass, 1964, pp. 99–100, pl. 55.

369

Tula, Anales de. Anales Aztecas. Anales Mexicanos del Pueblo de Tezontepec. Anales de Tezontepec. MNA 35-9. Partially published. Historical. Tula, Hidalgo. 16thC. Amatl paper tira. 17 × 487 cm.

The entire length of the tira is divided in half by drawings of the hieroglyphs for the years 1361 through 1521. Above and below them are occasional simple drawings and short Nahuatl texts that refer to historical events in Tenochtitlan, Texcoco, Tula, and other localities.

Two details are reproduced by Barlow (1949a), who gives a transcript and translation of the Nahuatl texts. Another detail and a brief description are given by Glass (1964).

Copies: A modern copy is in MNA/BNA. This copy may or may not be the one made in 1892 for the Exposición Histórico-Americana.

Partial publication: Barlow, 1949a; Glass, 1964, p. 47, pl. 11.

Brief mention: Paso y Troncoso, 1892–93, 1: 56–57.

370 (fig. 69)

Tulane, Codex. Códice de Huamelulpan. TU/MARI. Ex–Samuel Daza of Tlaxiaco and Felix Muro collections. Partially published. Historical. San Juan Ñumi, ex-district of Tlaxiaco, Western Oaxaca. 16thC. Skin roll painted on one side. 22.9 × 378.5 cm.

The roll, composed vertically, has drawings of place glyphs, Mixtec year and day dates, Mixtec glosses, and genealogies of persons with calendrical name glyphs. Some aspects of style and form are occasionally divergent from other Mixtec manuscripts. but there are a few similarities to Códice

226

Dehesa. Its content is genealogical and historical.

Only brief descriptions and notices of its acquisition by Tulane University have appeared. Those by Gropp (1932, 1933) reproduce two different details from the manuscript. Robertson, M. E. Smith, Parmenter, and Chadwick have a work on this manuscript in preparation.

Partial publication: Gropp, 1932, p. 12; 1933, pp. 231–33, fig. 1.

Brief descriptions: Alcina Franch, 1955, pp. 490–91; Blom, n.d., 1936; Rivet, 1932.

371

Tultepeque, Santa Maria Nativitas, Mapa de. MNA 35-90. Published. Economic (property plans). Santa Maria Tultepec, Mexico. ca. 1578. European paper. 72 × 64 cm. Incomplete.

The surviving fragment of the map shows maguey fields and houses in the vicinity of Tultepec. Three Christian churches represent Tultepec and two other localities. A long Spanish gloss concerns a judicial decision by the Audiencia Real relating to lands and mentions Xaltocan and Tultepec.

Photograph and brief description in MNA catalog (Glass, 1964).

Publication: Glass, 1964, p. 144, pl. 96.

372

Tututepec, Códice de. Unknown. Unpublished. Unavailable. Western Oaxaca. Further data unavailable.

A privately owned manuscript history of Tututepec, written by Martínez Gracida about 1907, contains a description of a Mixtec pictorial manuscript. Unfortunately, the two plates that illustrated the document are not preserved with the history, and neither the plates nor the document are otherwise known. The description is published by Berlin (1947), who cautiously compares it with the Códice de Yanhuitlan.

Bibliography: Berlin, 1947, pp. 13–14, 45–49.

373–378

Tuxpan, Lienzos de, nos. 1–6. Tamiahua Codices. Museo Veracruzano de Antropología. Partially published. Cartographic-historical. Tihuatlan-Tuxpan-Tamiahua region, Veracruz. 16thC. Cloth. Six sheets, dimensions not determined.

Six lienzos, each a map with numerous place glyphs and evidently forming part of a related series, were discovered about 1957 or before in the Tihuatlan-Tuxpan region of Veracruz. A very brief examination of color transparencies of the originals suggest that they correspond, at least in part, to three undated and handcolored lithographs reprinted by Barlow (1946e). One of the latter, possibly representing a seventh document, shows Tamiahua, Tihuatlan, Tepetzintla, and Huachinango. A small detail from one of the originals has been published by Medellín Zenil (1957).

Related publication: Barlow, 1946e.
Brief mention: Medellín Zenil, 1957, p. 48, fig. 9; Melgarejo Vivanco, 1953, p. 333.

379 (fig. 70)

Tzintzuntzan and Tlalpujava, Tributes of. Princeton University Library. Ex–Boturini and Garrett collections. Partially published. Economic (tribute). Tzintzuntzan and Tlalpujahua, Michoacan, or Acambaro, Guanajuato. ca. 1542–52. Native paper. 92 × 43 cm.

Obverse bears drawings of Indian heads, cloth, containers of food, turkeys, and other items of tribute. A Spanish text on the obverse and reverse concerns tribute, Tarascan and Otomi Indians, the mines of Tzintzuntzan and Tlalpujava, and the cacique of Acambaro.

An incomplete 18thC copy and transcript of the text appears in Beaumont's *Crónica de Michoacan* (q.v. for manuscripts thereof). This copy and part of the transcript were first published by Riva Palacio (n.d.). Beaumont (1932) gives his copy and transcript of the text.

Partial publication: Beaumont, 1932, 3: 63–67; Riva Palacio, n.d., p. 75.

380

Tzoquitetlan, Lienzo de. Lienzo de Xochimilco. Unknown. Published. Cartographic. Central Mexico. Date unknown. (MNA copy is cloth, 242 × 300 cm.)

The lienzo is covered with drawings of a large number of roads, streams, and rudimentary place glyphs. The latter are identified by more than 100 glossed Nahuatl place names. Among the more prominent are Metlateocan, Tzoquitetlan, Xuchimilco, and Tzicohuac. Place glyphs are drawn around the border. Further research is required to identify the region represented, possibly northern Puebla.

A brief description and a photograph of the copy are given by Glass (1964).
Copy: MNA 35-96.
Publication: Glass, 1964, p. 150, pl. 103.

381 (fig. 71)

Unidentified locality, Map of. NLA 1271 (d). Ex–Latroupelignire and Waldeck collections. Unpublished. Cartographic. Central Mexico. 16thC. Native paper. 39.3 × 41 cm.

Map showing a river, five tepetl symbols, and six native houses. Identifying glosses are illegible.
Bibliography: None.

382

Unidentified property, Plan of. NLA 1477 (part). Unpublished. Economic (property plans). Central Mexico. 16thC (?). European paper. ca. 31 × 22 cm.

Plan of a house and adjacent property, with measurements given by native pictorial conventions. The drawing is on the first leaf of a volume of deeds (not examined), 1678–1751.
Bibliography: None.

383

Valeriano, Códice. MNA 35-121. Ex–González Obregon collection. Published. Economic (property plans). Central Mexico. 1574. European paper. 22 × 31.8 cm.

Fragment showing several plots of land and drawings of a number of Indians (some in genealogical relationships) with personal and other name glyphs. A short Nahuatl text mentions a Pedro Valeriano. The hats worn by the Indians are unusual.

The drawing has been studied by Mateos Higuera (1949d) and briefly described by Glass (1964). Both give a photographic reproduction.

Publication: Glass, 1964, p. 179, pl. 132; Mateos Higuera, 1949d.

384

Vaticanus B, Codex. Codex Vaticanus 3773. Codice Vaticano Rituale. Códice Fábrega. Biblioteca Apostolica Vaticana, Rome. Published. Ritual-calendrical. Borgia Group. Preconquest. Skin screenfold. 49 leaves (48 painted pages on each side; initial and terminal pages attached to original wooden covers). 13 × 15 cm. (total length ca. 735 cm.).

The history of the manuscript prior to 1596–1600, the date of a Vatican catalog which describes the number 3773, is unknown. A reference by Mercati (1589) to two Mexican manuscripts in the Vatican refers to Codex Ríos (Vaticanus 3738 or A) but may not include Codex Vaticanus B.

Like other screenfolds of the Borgia Group, Codex Vaticanus B contains a complex presentation of the tonalpohualli, the 260-day Mesoamerican divinatory calendar. The 28 identifiable sections of the manuscript treat specific aspects of the tonalpohualli such as the 5 × 52 and 20 × 13 days and their associated deities as well as various series of gods, world directions, and so forth.

The first partial publication was by Humboldt (1810), the first edition by Kingsborough (1831–48). The screenfold facsimile in color published by the Duc de Loubat (Ehrle, 1896) is accompanied by pamphlets describing the manuscript (by Paso y Troncoso) and giving its history (by Ehrle). Seler (1902a; English translation, 1902–03) gives detailed commentary and annotated line drawings of each page. Nowotny (1961b) provides comparative interpretation of all sections. A new edition is in preparation by the Akademische Druck- und Verlagsanstalt, Graz, Austria. See annotation under Corona Núñez (1964–67) in bibliography for another edition now in press. See Borgia Group for further bibliography and comment.

Editions: Librería Echániz, 1939c; Ehrle, 1896; Kingsborough, 1831–48, vol. 3.

Commentaries: Nowotny, 1961b, passim, pls. 37–42; Seler, 1902a, 1902–03.

Studies: Seler, 1902l; J. E. S. Thompson, 1934, pp. 217–19, 223–25, pls. 3, 4.

Other: Dorez, 1896; Hagar, 1913; Haro y Cadena, 1940; Humboldt, 1810, pls. 13, 60.

Historical references: Fábrega, 1899, p. 7, passim; Hornius, 1652, pp. 267–76; Kircher, 1652–54 (unverified; page references not determined; not examined); Mercati, 1589, p. 96.

Brief descriptions: Alcina Franch, 1955, pp. 477–78; Lehmann, 1905a, pp. 253–54; Paso y Troncoso, 1897b.

385 (fig. 72)

Veinte Mazorcas, Códice de. BNP 391. Published. Cartographic-historical. Tlapa region, Guerrero. 16thC. Native paper. 76 × 51 cm.

The document has drawings of native caciques and place glyphs of towns in the Tlapa region of Guerrero. The town represented by a central place glyph ("Veinte Mazorcas") has not been identified; Barlow's reading of the glyph may be imaginative. Another glyph has been interpreted as representing Tlaxiaco, Oaxaca. Later additions in a different style (reminiscent of the later style on Códice de Azoyu no. 1, reverse) include drawings of Spaniards, glosses in Mixtec and Nahuatl, and alterations to the content of the earlier drawings.

The document is reproduced with the incomplete and posthumous study by Barlow (1961).

Publication: Barlow, 1961.

Brief description: J. F. Ramírez, 1855, no. 8.

386

Vergara, Codex. BNP 37-39. Ex–Boturini and Aubin collections. Partially published. Economic (census and cadastral). Valley of Mexico. 16thC (1539?). European paper. 55 leaves. 31 × 22 cm. Initial leaf missing.

The codex contains a pictorial census and two cadasters for each of five named localities, possibly in the Chiautla-Tepetlaoxtoc region of the eastern Valley of Mexico. Two different Nahuatl and Spanish glosses each refer to Don Agustín de Rojas and Tepetlaoxtoc. The final leaf bears the signature of Pedro Vásquez de Vergara, as does the Códice de Santa Maria Asuncion, which this manuscript closely resembles.

Boban (1891) describes the codex and reproduces three of its pages. A study of the place and personal name hieroglyphs in the codex was included in Aubin's *Mémoire* (see bibliography for editions); this is reprinted by Boban. Gibson (1964a) comments briefly on the document.

Partial publication: Boban, 1891, 2: 11–33, pls. 37–39.

Other: Aubin, loc. cit.; Gibson, 1964a, p. 269, note 74 (p. 300).

❖❖❖

VERGARA GROUP. Four pictorial manuscripts having both specific and superficial resemblances in page composition, style, and content: Códice de Santa Maria Asuncion, Humboldt Fragment 8, Cadastral Fragment of the Ramírez Collection, and Codex Vergara.

❖❖❖

VEYTIA CALENDAR WHEELS NOS. 1–7. Seven calendar wheels, listed separately below, were copied and numbered for the *Historia del Origen de las Gentes que poblaron la América septentrional* by Mariano Fernández de Echeverría y Veytia, a work unfinished at his death February 25, 1780. An original Veytia manuscript, in the RAH (Muñoz collection, vol. 4), contains the first 11 chapters, which treat the calendar in duplicate, copies of the seven calendars, and variant copies (?) of calendars nos. 1, 2, 5, and 7. These copies and their variants (which we have not examined) are unpublished. Copies, presumably of the Madrid manuscript, are in LC, NYPL, and Yale University Library but appear not to include the four variants. Another manuscript of the first 11 chapters, with six of the calendars (no. 2 is now missing), is MNA 35–54. This manuscript, briefly described by Paso y Troncoso (1897c, 1892–93) and Glass (1964), is the source of the excellent color lithographs published in 1907 (Veytia, 1907). Another copy of the Veytia history, without the illustrations, is in MNA/AH.

The first edition of the Veytia history (Veytia, 1836; republished 1944) was based on a manuscript that lacked the preface,[5] the "Kalendario Tulteco,"[6] the "Tablas chronológicas,"[7] and the calendar wheels.

[5] The author's preface, omitted from the editions of 1836, 1944, and 1907, has been published in the otherwise incomplete edition of 1848, in volume 1 of the Mexican magazine *La Castalia* in 1849, and in Gómez de Orozco (1927a). A variant and shorter preface (together with the published version) is in BNP 215 and may also be represented by manuscripts in UTX (CDG 692 and 1215).

[6] This is a calendrical table for the correlation of the months and days of a leap year 7 Acatl, adapted from Codex Ixtlilxochitl, part 3. The editor of the 1836 edition supplied it according to Veytia's descriptions; it is published in the 1907 edition.

[7] Shows the correlation of years from the creation of the world to the year 5876 (A.D. 1843). It was

Some of the latter (nos. 1–2, 5–7) were supplied by the editor from now unidentified versions then in the MNA. The versions of this edition vary in detail from the 1907 edition and are untrustworthy with respect to nos. 3 and 4, which were drawn by the editor after Veytia's descriptions.

With exception of calendar no. 4, which was copied from a publication, none of the originals copied by Veytia can be located. Veytia states that he copied nos. 5 and 7 from manuscripts in the Boturini collection. It is possible that nos. 1, 3, and 6 also derive from that collection.

Bustamante illustrated a few copies of his edition of the Chimalpahin manuscript of López de Gómara's history with a lithograph of two calendar wheels. We have not examined any copy that contains them. In that work Bustamante stated that he owned three calendars (Bustamante *in* López de Gómara, 1826, 1: 315). It seems probable that the two are the same as the lithograph of the Veytia Calendar Wheels nos. 5 and 6, which he published in 1835 (Bustamante, 1835–36, 1: plate facing p. 94). His description of the two wheels published in 1826 (Bustamante, 1829–30, 1: 340–41, note a) supports this possibility as does the fact that he published extracts from Veytia's history on several occasions.

The three calendar wheels published by Clavigero in 1780 are adaptations of published versions of nos. 2, 4, and 5. Two are reprinted without credit by Chavero (n.d.) and all three by Jourdanet and Siméon (1880). Comparable variations are given by Visino (1864).

In his *Historia general* Boturini (1948) illustrates a number of calendar wheels. This work was written when he no longer had access to his collection; with the exception of the Rueda de los Nueve Señores de la Noche (q.v.), they derive from the de

la Serna manuscript (q.v.), from published versions then available, and, possibly, from his memory of the wheels (including that in the Codex Aubin) that had been in his collection.

It should be noted that only one (no. 2) of the seven calendars of the group is known through a 16thC manuscript. There is no compelling reason to attribute any of the seven to Indian authorship or to date any of the other six before 1654 although any of the seven may ultimately have had Indian prototypes. The iconography of the month symbols in calendar 4 certainly suggests a 16thC origin, however. Seler (1899b) makes the interesting observation that these calendars may have pertained to a work by Sigüenza y Góngora. An unpublished calendar wheel (not examined) in Codex Veytia (q.v.) presumably is a further copy of one of the seven calendar wheels and is not entered separately in this census.

Editions: Veytia, 1836, 1944, 1907, chaps. 5–9; see also editor's notice, 1836, 3: 213 ff., 1944, 2: 191 ff.

Brief descriptions: Glass, 1964, pp. 102–04; Paso y Troncoso, 1892–93, 1: 66–68; 1897c, pp. 269–71.

Other: Boturini, 1948, pls. 2–5, 21–22; Bustamante, 1829–30; 1: 340–41, note a; 1835–36, 1: plate facing p. 94; Chavero, n.d., pp. 726–27; Clavigero, 1958–59, 2: plates facing pp. 128 and 136; Gómez de Orozco, 1927a, pp. 221–56; Jourdanet and Siméon, 1880, pp. lxx–lxxii; López de Gómara, 1826, 1: 315; Seler, 1899b, p. 122; Veytia, 1848; Visino, 1864, pls. 35–37.

387

——— *no. 1*. Unknown. Published. Calendrical. Valley of Mexico. 1654. Physical data unknown.

The first of the calendar wheels copied by Veytia depicts the 52-year cycle correlated with the years 1649–1700, with drawings of the four year-bearer day signs at the center. A Nahuatl gloss reads "now, in this year

---

supplied by the editor of the 1836 edition according to Veytia's references; it is present in the Madrid manuscript but has not been published.

1654." Above the circle, in a rectangular frame, are the glyphs for the places where the Aztecs celebrated New Fire ceremonies in the 2 Reed years 1195, 1247, 1299, and 1351.

See above for manuscripts of the Veytia copies and comment on the editions thereof. León y Gama (1832) claims to have had the original of this wheel in his possession. The date 1654 is contemporaneous with the writing of de la Serna's *Manual de Ministros de Indios* (q.v.).

Publication: Veytia, 1836, 1: 47–48, 55–56, 97–98, pl. 1; 1907, pp. 25, 27, 46, pl. 1; 1944, 1: 32, 37–38, 66–67, pl. 1.

Brief description: León y Gama, 1832, 1: 22–23, note.

388 (figs. 73, 74)

—— *no. 2*. Motolinía Calendar Wheel. Calendario en Caracol. Valadés Calendar Wheel. Known versions listed below. Calendrical. Various publications. Tlaxcala (?). 16thC.

Several closely related calendar wheels and three descriptive texts are subsumed under this entry. The calendar wheel has signs for the 20 days in the inner circle. The numbers 1 to 13 are repeated 20 times and arranged in a spiral to represent the 260-day tonalpohualli cycle. On the periphery are drawings of the four year-bearer days each repeated 13 times to represent the 52-year cycle. The descriptive text records rules for the operation of the calendar. The original may have been illustrated by more than one wheel.

References to this calendar occur in the writings of Zorita (1909), Mendieta (1870), E. Martínez (1606), and Torquemada (1723). Its authorship has been attributed to Motolinía, to Olmos, and to Francisco de las Navas. A version of the text was quoted and denounced as divinatory and not calendrical by Sahagún (*Historia general . . .* appendix to bk. 4; *Arte adivinatoria*, prologue). Nicolau d'Olwer (1952) has com-

mented on this attack but misdated it at 1566 rather than about 1574–76.

A. Motolinía Calendar Wheel. (UTX, in CDG 1363. Ex–Bartolomé José Gallardo, José María Andrade, and García Icazbalceta collections. 1549. European paper. 45 × 30 cm.). The folded drawing and accompanying Spanish text ("Calendario de toda la yndica gente"; "Motolinía Insert no. 2") are bound in the manuscript of Motolinía's *Memoriales* (Article 27B, no. 1071). A color lithograph is published in Motolinía (1903) and is reprinted in b/w in Steck (1951). The manuscript is described by García Icazbalceta (*in* Mendieta, 1870) and Kubler and Gibson (1951) have commented on the calendrical content of the gloss. The January 1st year-beginning is probably illustrative of the two calendars rather than correlative.

B. A version of the descriptive text ("Calendario de toda la índica gente") without the drawing is bound in the Escorial manuscript of the Relación de Michoacan (no. 213) and copies thereof. This text has been published, from the LC copy, by N. León (1888a). Paso y Troncoso (1888) corrects León's attribution of this calendar to the Tarascans. The Relación de Michoacan is among the sources of Motolinía's *Memoriales*.

C. Another version of the text, apparently written by Fray Francisco de las Navas about 1551, is contained in a calendrical treatise of 1584, which also includes an incompletely published description of the 18 months by Antonio de Guevara (an Indian governor of Tlaxcala). A copy, lacking the wheel, is included in J. F. Ramírez, *Opúcculos históricos*, vol. 21, ff. 93–202 (MS, MNA/AH-CA 210) and the relevant section has been published by Chavero (1901a). J. F. Ramírez (1898), Kubler and Gibson (1951), and Gibson (1952) have commented on this text. A version of the section by Guevara underlies Torquemada's (1723, 2: 295–300) statements about the Tlaxcalan calendar and was known to Ixtlilxochitl. See Article 27B, no. 1074.

D. Valadés Calendar Wheel. A version of the wheel, published in Italy by Valadés (1579), includes signs of the European zodiac and a correlation of the 18 months with the Julian calendar. The 1 Tlacaxipe-hualiztli = March 1 correlation which it records is in the tradition established by Motolinía. Reproductions of the Valadés engraving are cited below. De Jonghe (1906a, 1906b), Paso y Troncoso (1882), and Kubler and Gibson (1951) have commented on the Valadés wheel. A copy by Pichardo is BNP 89-7.

E. An unpublished 18th or 19thC version with a drawing of a snake around the periphery is BNP 92.

F. See above for editions and manuscripts of the version associated with Veytia. It is uncertain from what original Veytia secured his copy.

Publication (Motolinía Wheel): Motolinía, 1903, pp. 48–53, colored plate; Steck, 1951, pp. 54–56, plate facing p. 59.

Publication (Veytia 2): Veytia, 1836, 1: 47, 97, 100–02, pl. 2; 1907, pp. 25, 46–48, pl. 2; 1944, 1: 32, 66–69, pl. 2.

Publication (Valadés Wheel): Jonghe, 1906a, pp. 508–11, fig. 4; Maza, 1945, fig. 18; Palomera, 1962, pp. 48, 306, fig. 28; 1963, fig. 14; Valadés, 1579, p. 100.

Historical references: E. Martínez, 1606, Trat. 2, cap. 10; Mendieta, 1870, pp. xxviii, 98–99; Sahagún (loc. cit.); Torquemada, 1723, 2: 301; Zorita, 1909, pp. 8–9, 301–03, passim.

Brief descriptions and other references: Chavero, 1901a, pp. 33–36; n.d., pp. xv–xvi, xxxi–xxxii; Gibson, 1952, pp. 256–57; Jonghe, 1906b, page references not determined; Kubler and Gibson, 1951, pp. 57–58, 68–69; N. León, 1888a; Nicolau d'Olwer, 1952, pp. 67–71; Paso y Troncoso, 1882, p. 379 ff.; 1888; J. F. Ramírez, 1898, pp. 23–26, 467–470.

—— *no. 3.* Unknown. Published. Calendrical. Central Mexico. Date and physical description unknown.

This calendar, known only through the Veytia copies, is the only one of the group that is rectangular rather than circular. Each of its four sides represents a quarter of the 52-year cycle. Spanish glosses associate each of the four year-bearer days with a direction and with one of the four elements (fire, earth, wind, water). Each may also be associated with a color.

The editor of the 1836 edition of Veytia's history was unable to locate a drawing of this calendar so he prepared it from Veytia's description. This version (Veytia, 1836; reprinted, 1944) is thus of little interest. See above for manuscripts of the Veytia copies and comment on the 1907 edition.

Publication: Veytia, 1907, pp. 25–26, 46, pl. 3.

Other: Veytia, 1836, 1: 47, 97–99, pl. 3; 1944, 1: 33, 66, pl. 3.

390

—— *no. 4.* Gemelli Careri Calendar Wheel. Unknown. Ex–Sigüenza y Góngora collection. Published. Calendrical. Valley of Mexico. Date and physical description unknown.

Either the original or a copy of this calendar wheel was acquired from Sigüenza y Góngora by Gemelli Careri in Mexico in 1697 and published by him in Italy in 1700. The original has not been reported since that time. As published, the calendar has symbols for the 18 months and drawings of the phases of the moon in two inner concentric circles. In the center are four glyphs of historical significance. The outer circle represents the 52-year cycle, and the whole is surrounded by a snake. Tlacaxipehualiztli is indicated as the first month; the spelling of the glosses reflects Italian influence. Some of the month symbols resemble those on leaf 89r of the Codex Ríos.

Gemelli Careri's *Giro del Mondo* (1699–1700), which contains the first edition of the calendar, was reprinted numerous times. There are editions in French and English as well as three Mexican editions in Spanish of the Mexican section of the work. An inaccurate copy of the Gemelli wheel with a curious caption appears in Kingsborough (1831–48). A published portrait of Boturini, made in Spain, shows him holding a copy of the calendar (Boturini, 1746).

The Veytia copies derive from the Gemelli engraving but omit the moon phases and alter the sequence of the month symbols. The inaccurate 1836 and 1944 editions of the wheel are based directly on the Gemelli print and not on the Veytia copy. See above for manuscripts of the Veytia copies and comment on the 1907 edition. The Veytia copy in the MNA has been published by Glass (1964); Kubler and Gibson (1951) reproduce the 1907 lithograph. Copies from an unidentified Veytia manuscript are given by Gondra (1846) and Chavero (n.d.).

Other copies: Pichardo copy, BNP 89-2. There may be a copy by Waldeck in NLA.[8]

Publication (Gemelli wheel): Gemelli Careri, 1699–1700, vol. 6, facing p. 68; Kingsborough, 1831–48, vol. 4; Picart, 1733–37, vol. 3, facing p. 159; Vevtia, 1836, 1: 47, 56, 59–60, 68, 72–73, 98, pl. 4; 1944, 1: 33, 38, 40, 46, 48–49, 66–67, pl. 4.

Publication (Veytia 4): Chavero, n.d., p. 343; Glass, 1964, pl. 57; Gondra, 1846: 45–47, pl. 7; Kubler and Gibson, 1951, fig. 15; Veytia, 1907, pp. 28, 33–34, 46, pl. 4.

Brief descriptions: Kubler and Gibson, 1951, p. 60; León y Gama, 1832, 1: 47–48.

Other: Boturini, 1746, second engraving; Sotheby, Wilkinson, and Hodge, 1919a, no. 348 (part).

391 (fig. 75)

—— *no. 5*. Manuel de los Santos y Salazar: Copy of a Calendar Wheel. Unknown. Ex–Boturini collection. Pub-

lished. Calendrical. Tlaxcala. Date and physical description unknown.

The fifth Veytia calendar depicts symbols for the 18 months, with explanatory glosses in Spanish, and the five intercalary days. The first month is Atemoztli, a feature that is considered a Tlaxcalan trait (Seler, 1899b; Caso, 1958a).

The original of this calendar may be identified as Item 28-3 of the Boturini catalog of 1746. Both Kubler and Gibson (1951) and Gibson (1952), however, identify it with Item 27-4, a copy by Santos y Salazar (died 1715). We identify the latter item with Veytia Calendar no. 7 (q.v.). Both, of course, may be by him. All known versions derive from the lost Boturini collection copy.

The wheel was first published by Lorenzana (1770). The unpublished copies made for the CMNE in 1790–92 are substantially the same as the Lorenzana copy. The copies associated with Veytia vary slightly in their glosses from the Lorenzana and CMNE copies. The glosses are omitted in the 1836 and 1944 editions of the Veytia history but are included in the 1907 edition. An anonymous copy (MNA 35-125) is published by Glass (1964). The 1907 lithograph is reproduced by Kubler and Gibson (1951) and by Jiménez Moreno and Mateos Higuera (1940). A possible relationship exists between the glosses on the wheel and month lists given by Torquemada (1723) and in the Guevara Calendar of 1584 (see Kubler and Gibson, 1951).

Copies: See above for the Veytia manuscripts. The CMNE copies are in RAH and AGN-H 1. A copy of the CMNE copy is in the Clements Library, University of Michigan. An anonymous copy made after 1770 is MNA 35-125.

Publication (non-Veytia copies): Glass,

---

[8] Described in a letter from Clara Smith to H. J. Spinden, July 8, 1920 (MS in NLA files), but was not seen by Cline, whose notes on the NLA collection have been used in this census.

1964, p. 183, pl. 136; Lorenzana, 1770, vol. 2, pl. 1.

Publication (Veytia 5): Bustamante, 1835–36, vol. 1, plate facing p. 94; Jiménez Moreno and Mateos Higuera, 1940, p. 71, fig. 14; Kubler and Gibson, 1951, p. 60, fig. 16; Veytia, 1836, 1: 63–69, 98, pl. 5; 1907, pp. 31–33, 46, pl. 5; 1944, 1: 43–46, 66–67, pl. 5.

Other: Caso, 1958a, p. 69 and Table 2; Gibson, 1952, p. 268; Kubler and Gibson, 1951, pp. 57–58; Seler, 1899b, p. 122; Torquemada, 1723, 2: 295 ff.

392

—— *no. 6*. Unknown. Ex–Veytia collection. Published. Calendrical. Tlaxcala. Date and physical description uncertain.

The sixth Veytia calendar, copied from an original in his possession, appears merely to be a copy of the inner portion of Veytia Calendar Wheel no. 7 (q.v.). It depicts the symbols for the 20 days and has drawings of the sun, moon, and stars in the center.

See above for manuscripts of the Veytia copies and comment on the editions thereof.

Publication: Bustamante, 1835–36, vol. 1, plate facing p. 94; Veytia, 1836, 1: 76, 80–81, 98, 104, pl. 6; 1907, pp. 35–36, 46, 48, pl. 6; 1944, 1: 51, 54, 66–67, 70, pl. 6.

393

—— *no. 7*. Unknown. Published. Calendrical. Tlaxcala. Early 18thC. Physical description unknown.

The inner portions represent the symbols for the 20 days and the sun, moon, and stars. This section corresponds to Veytia Calendar Wheel no. 6 (q.v.). One of several outer sections associates the four year-bearer days with summer, fall, winter, and spring in an alternating sequence. Glosses on the MNA variant add the years 1701–20 and the four directions.

The original of the Veytia copies was in the Boturini collection and is probably the copy described by Boturini as having been

copied from older originals by Manuel de los Santos y Salazar (died 1715) (Paso y Troncoso, 1897c). This identification is disputed by Kubler and Gibson (see Veytia Calendar Wheel no. 5). Santos y Salazar was a Tlaxcalan; on this evidence the wheel is so classified. The editions of 1836 and 1944 vary in detail from that of 1907 as does the variant published by Glass (1964).

Copies: See above for manuscripts of the Veytia copies. Anonymous copy, MNA 35-124.

Publication: Chavero, n.d., p. 727; Glass, 1964, p. 182, pl. 135; Veytia, 1836, 1: 109, pl. 7; 1907, p. 49, pl. 7; 1944, 1: 73, pl. 7.

Other: Paso y Troncoso, 1897c, p. 271.

394

Veytia, Codex. Biblioteca del Palacio Nacional, Madrid. Ex–Muñoz collection. Published. Calendrical and ethnographic. Mexico City, D.F. 1755. European paper. Details as to foliation and dimensions (which vary) not determined.

The codex is a copy, by Mariano Fernández de Echeverría y Veytia, of the first 18 figures and corresponding texts of Codex Ixtlilxochitl, part 1 (q.v.), of the drawings of Tlaloc, the Texcoco temple, and Huitzilopochtli from Codex Ixtlilxochitl, part 2 (q.v.), and of part 3 of Codex Ixtlilxochitl (Article 27B, no. 1101). Its importance lies in its copy of the drawing of Huitzilopochtli, now lost from Codex Ixtlilxochitl. In the same volume that includes Codex Veytia is an unpublished copy (f. 59r) of an unidentified calendar wheel, possibly a copy of one of the seven Veytia Calendar Wheels (q.v.). Copies of other documents bound with Codex Veytia and sometimes comprehended under the same title are not relevant to the present census.

Those parts of the codex corresponding to parts 1 and 2 of Codex Ixtlilxochitl have been published in color on two occasions (Librería Echániz, 1937c, and in Veytia, 1944) from a copy by Genaro López. Photographic reproductions of the drawing of Huitzilopochtli and of one of the festival drawings are given in Sociedad Española de Amigos del Arte (1930). J. E. S. Thompson (1941a) reproduces the drawings copied from Codex Ixtlilxochitl, part 2, apparently from the 1937 edition.

Copies: Copy of texts only, also in Biblioteca del Palacio Nacional, Madrid.

Publication: Librería Echániz, 1937c; Veytia, 1944, 2: 339–46, pls. 9–29.

Brief descriptions and other: Kubler and Gibson, 1951, p. 59; Nuttall, 1903, pp. viii-ix; Sociedad Española de Amigos del Arte, 1930, p. 30, no. 348, pl. 58; J. E. S. Thompson, 1941a.

395

Vienna, Codex. Codex Vindobonensis. Codex Vindobonensis Mexicanus 1. Codex Hieroglyphicorum Indiae Meridionalis. Codex Clementino. Codex Leopoldino. Codex Kreichgauer. Nationalbibliothek, Vienna. CVM 1. Published. Ritual-calendrical and historical. Western Oaxaca. Preconquest. Skin screenfold painted on both sides with original wooden covers. 52 leaves. ca. 22 × 26 cm.

The manuscript is believed to have been sent, possibly with Codex Nuttall, to Charles V by Cortés in 1519. A 16thC Latin inscription on the reverse of the manuscript states that it was given to Pope Clement VII by Manuel I of Portugal (died 1521). It was subsequently owned by Cardinal Hipolito de Medici and Cardinal Capuanus (died 1537). It later appeared in Weimar, Germany, about 1650 when a detail was copied by Ludolph. This copy, published by Worm in 1655, is now in the National Museum, Copenhagen. The manuscript was presented to Leopold I of Hapsburg by Johann Georg, Duke of Saxe-Eisenach about 1677. Since that time it has been in the Imperial Library of Vienna (now the Austrian National Library).

The obverse of the manuscript (pp. 52–1;

the 19thC pagination is in reverse order) has been interpreted as ritual-calendrical but also contains mythological genealogies with some emphasis on 9 Wind (Quetzalcoatl), lists of place glyphs and dates, and of persons, gods, or priests. Each of its 10 major sections repeats data pertaining to a ritual or ceremony in which a constant element is fire-making.

The 13 pages of the reverse (the rest of the reverse is blank except for the Latin inscription) present a genealogy that begins two generations before the inception of the first Tilantongo dynasty and continues through the marriage of the third rulers of the third dynasty. This span corresponds to a period from the 8thC through the middle of the 14thC A.D. The probable provenience of the manuscript is Tilantongo (ex-district of Nochistlan, Western Oaxaca).

The history of the manuscript is treated in detail by Adelhofer (1963) as well as by Nowotny (1960) and Lehmann and Smital (1929). Adelhofer cites and quotes the early references by Worm (1655), Lambeck (1679), and William Robertson (1777) as well as other sources derived from these (Nessel, 1690; Kollar, 1769; and others). He also reproduces the Ludolph copy as illustrated by Worm, the engraving of one page of the manuscript given by Lambeck, and the page reproduced by W. Robertson. Four pages of the manuscript were reproduced in color by Humboldt (1810). The history of the Ludolph copy, with an additional datum on the history of the manuscript, is treated by Simons (1963).

The first edition of the manuscript was by Kingsborough (1831–48), based on the copy by Aglio. The photographic color facsimile by Lehmann and Smital (1929) has been reprinted from the same color plates (with different covers and without a facsimile of the page bearing the ownership inscription) by Adelhofer (1963). The 1929 edition was accompanied by a history of the manuscript by Smital and a description and superficial commentary on the content by Lehmann, now outmoded by more recent studies. The Smital-Lehmann commentary was not reprinted with the 1963 edition, which is accompanied by a history and a detailed description of the physical nature of the manuscript but does not treat its content. A reproduction by color photography and a page-by-page commentary is given by Corona Núñez (1964–67).

The obverse of the manuscript has been studied by Nowotny (1948b, 1961b) and its parallels with other sources have been noted by Nowotny (1958), but its full significance has yet to be interpreted. The reverse side has been interpreted by Caso (1951) with poor b/w reproduction. More specialized studies by Nowotny, Röck, Kreichgauer, and others are listed below. Adelhofer (1963) gives an extensive bibliography.

Editions: Adelhofer, 1963; Corona Núñez, 1964–67, 4: 51–183; Librería Echániz, 1944f; Kingsborough, 1831–48, vol. 2; Lehmann and Smital, 1929.

Commentaries: Caso, 1951; Nowotny, 1948b.

Studies: Burland, 1947b, 1966b; Caso, 1963; Kreichgauer, 1917; Nowotny, 1948a; 1956b; 1958; 1960, pp. 33, 70–76, pls. 23–25; 1961b, pp. 47–50, 256–70, pls. 52–58; Röck, 1935, 1936, 1937, 1941.

Other: Anonymous, 1875; Lizardi Ramos, 1953b; Simons, 1963.

Historical references: Humboldt, 1810, pp. 267–70, pls. 46–48; Juncker, 1710, p. 65; Kollar, 1769, p. 965; Lambeck, 1679, p. 660 ff.; Nessel, 1690, p. 163; W. Robertson, 1777, 2: 482–83, plate facing p. 482; Worm, 1655, p. 383.

Brief descriptions: Alcina Franch, 1955, pp. 483–84; Lehmann, 1905a, pp. 266–69.

396

Volador, Códice del. Private collection. Unpublished. Economic (tribute). Central Mexico. 16thC. Native paper. Dimensions unknown.

The manuscript is known through photographs among the Barlow papers in the library of the University of the Americas, Mexico. The photos indicate that it is a vertical tira about 97 × 13 cm. It is divided into 15 horizontal sections; in the largest and center section is a drawing of an Indian climbing a pole, probably a volador ceremonial pole. Items drawn in other compartments are heads of Indians with name glyphs, Spaniards, Spanish monetary units, and other objects. The document is probably a further portion of one of the Gilcrease Fragments (q.v.).

Copies: Photographic copies of the Barlow photos are in LC/HF.

Bibliography: None.

397 (fig. 76)

Waldeck Judgment Scene. Unknown. Published. Unclassified. Western Oaxaca. 16thC. Native paper. 1 leaf. Dimensions unknown.

The manuscript is a fragment that shows a native temple in profile, within which are two men, one upside down with blood streaming from his body. Other figures and a place glyph are drawn outside of the temple. The tentative Western Oaxaca classification is based on a suggestion of Mixtec style.

A lithograph reproduction by Waldeck appeared in the first publication of the Mexican National Museum (Icaza and Gondra, 1827). Waldeck (MS) interprets the manuscript as "representant un jugement."

Copy: Waldeck copy, NLA 1269 (part).

Publication: Icaza and Gondra, 1827, part 1, pl. 3.

Brief description: Waldeck, MS, p. 25.

❖❖❖

X. CRONICA, GROUP. Crónica X is a hypothetical manuscript proposed by Barlow to account for a historical text common to Durán's *Historia de las Indias* . . . (q.v.), Alvarado Tezozomoc's *Crónica mexicana* (a text not treated in this census), and Tovar's *Relación del Origen* . . . (q.v.). According to Barlow, Crónica X was written by an Indian in Nahuatl and illustrated by a series of paintings, the latter now known only through the Durán and the two Tovar manuscripts. As regards the illustrations, the hypothesis has not been properly examined. No student of the question has seriously compared the three series of drawings, which are incompletely and inadequately published.

The main titles directly concerned with Crónica X are cited below; see also Tovar, *Relación*, and Durán, *Historia*, in this census for further comment.

Bibliography: Barlow, 1944b, pp. 534–36; 1945c; 1945e; Bernal, 1947; introduction to Durán, 1964; Caso, 1945a; Kubler and Gibson, 1951, p. 9 ff.

398

Xalapa, Códice de. Mapa del Juego de Pelota. MNA 35-73. Ex–Boturini collection. Published. Economic (property plans). Central Mexico. 1540. Amatl paper. 81.5 × 45.5 cm.

Simple plan of a precinct crossed by lines of footprints, within which is the plan of a native ball court. Spanish texts on the reverse and obverse concern a lawsuit over the property.

Glass (1964) gives brief description and photoreproduction. Mena (1923) also describes it and gives some palaeography of the Spanish texts.

Publication: Glass, 1964, p. 126, pl. 78.

Brief description: Mena, 1923: 53–54, no. 7.

399

Xalbornoz, Juan de, and Juan Mateo, Plan of the Houses of. BNP 82. Ex–Aubin collection. Unpublished. Economic (prop-

erty plans). Central Mexico. 16thC. Native paper. 43 × 48 cm.

The document, probably extracted from some litigative process, shows the plans of two houses, several human figures, the symbols for pesos, and lesser detail.

Brief description: Boban, 1891, 2: 210–12.

400

Xalpantepec, Plainte adressée au Roi d'Espagne Philippe II par les Indigènes de. BNP 113. Ex–Aubin collection. Unpublished. Economic (tribute). Jalpan, Puebla. 16thC. The pictorial sheet, on European paper, forms part of a 44-leaf document.

Not examined. The brief description by Boban (1891) indicates that the document concerns complaints against a native governor; the pictorial element includes depiction of items of tribute.

Brief description: Boban, 1891, 2: 297.

401

Xiu Family, Genealogical Tree of the. In: Xiu Chronicles (also known as Chronicle of Oxkutzcab, Xiu Family Papers, Ticul Manuscript, Libro de Probanzas, Xiu Probanzas, etc.). PML. Ex–Edward H. Thompson and Charles P. Bowditch collections. Published. Genealogical. Mani, Oxkutzcab, or Ticul, Yucatan. 17thC. European paper. On 2 facing pages of the manuscript. Dimensions not determined.

The *Xiu Chronicles* is a compilation of documents, ca. 1608–1817, relating to the authority of the Xiu family, preconquest and colonial rulers of the province of Mani. It contains historical data, titles, petitions for confirmation of hereditary rights, an important one-page chronicle for the years 1533–45 or 1549 copied in 1685, and a version of the Mani Land Treaty of 1557. The only pictorial items are a version of the Map of the Province of Mani (described separately in this census, q.v.) and the Xiu Family tree. The *Chronicles* as a whole has not been published although a photostatic edition has had limited circulation (*Xiu Chronicles*, 1919) and a complete commentary (Morley and Roys, 1941) remains unpublished.

The genealogy depicts nine generations and extends into the 17thC. There is an omission of 18 generations. The tree is shown arising from the loins of a Maya Indian, Hun-Uitzil-Chac, drawn beside his wife. The style and concept are European; some details of costume, etc., are Indian.

The tree is photographically reproduced in Morley (1946) and in a sale catalog from one of Gates' photographs (American Art Association, 1915). The genealogy has been discussed by Morley (1920) and by Gates (1937b), who gives a redrawing. Roys (1957) gives a table of persons shown on the genealogy; Tozzer (1941) quotes from the commentary by Morley and Roys (1941). This is a selected bibliography for the genealogy and omits titles bearing on other documents in the Chronicles or on the Chronicles as a whole.

Copies: See Article 28, Appendix A, for listing of Gates' photocopies.

Publication: American Art Association, 1915, Item 472 and facing plate; Blom, 1928, pl. 2; Gates, 1937b, pp. 120–35; Morley, 1946, pp. 165–67, pl. 22; *Xiu Chronicles*, 1919.

Commentary: Morley and Roys, 1941 (volume and page reference not determined).

Brief descriptions: Morley, 1920, p. 470, note 2; Roys, 1957, pp. 64–65; Tozzer, 1941, pp. 29–30, note 159.

Brief mention: Tozzer, 1921, pp. 203–04.

402

XOCHIMILCO: *Procès entre Francisco de la Cruz Cohuatzincatl, Indio natural de Xochimilco, et Joachim Tecoloatl*. BNP 29. Ex–Aubin collection. Partially published. Genealogical and economic (property plans). Xochimilco, D.F. 1571. 1 drawing

on native paper, 52 × 40 cm., and 15 leaves of Nahuatl text on European paper.

Plan of a native house and drawings of plots of land, maguey plants, and various foodstuffs. Includes a genealogy of approximately 28 Indians, some of whose names are given both by glosses and by personal name glyphs.

Boban (1891) reproduces a photograph of the drawing; the accompanying lawsuit text is unpublished.

Partial publication: Boban, 1891, 1: 399, pl. 29.

❖❖❖

XOCHIMILCO. Three pictorial documents (described separately below) related to litigation between Pedronilla Francisca and Juliana Tlaco, her daughter-in-law, both Indians of Xochimilco, over plots of land, houses, and other belongings. At least one of the documents is described in the unpublished text of the trial and judgment, AGN-T 1525, exp. 3.

403 (fig. 77)

—— *Document concerning Property of Pedronilla Francisca and Costantino de San Felipe*. NLA 1271 (b). Ex–Waldeck collection. Published. Economic (property plans). Xochimilco, D.F. 1575–76. Native paper. 36.5 × 42 cm.

Drawings of plots of land with two place glyphs, cloth, and other items as well as the plans of two contiguous houses. Glosses refer to Juliana and Pedronilla Francisca.

A small photograph is published without comment by McGee and Thomas (1905).

Publication: McGee and Thomas, 1905, plate facing p. 108.

404 (fig. 78)

—— *Genealogy of Pedronilla and Juliana*. NLA 1271 (f). Ex–Pautret and Waldeck collections. Unpublished. Genealogical. Xochimilco, D.F. 1575–76. Native paper. 38.7 × 39.9 cm.

Genealogy of 20 Indians in four generations with only one name glyph. Pedronilla, Felipe, Constantino, and Juliana are identified by glosses.

Bibliography: None.

405

—— *Plan et Titre d'une Propriété sise à Huexocolco.* BNP 33. Ex–Aubin collection. Published. Genealogical and economic (property plans). Xochimilco, D.F. 1575–76. Native paper. 37 × 37 cm.

Drawings of various items of property, including eight plots of land with two place glyphs (Chalchiuhquayaca and Huexocolco) and the plan of a native house. On the right is a genealogy showing relationships between Juliana, Felipe, Costadino de San Felipe, and Pedronilla.

Photographic reproduction and brief description are given by Boban (1891).

Publication: Boban, 1891, 1: 408–09, pl. 33.

❖❖❖

XOCHIMILCO. Two pictorial documents believed to be related to litigation between members of a family named Damian and Pedronilla Francisca, 1576. The inception of this litigation is mentioned in AGN-T 1525, exp. 3, Pedronilla Francisca v. Juliana Tlaco (see previous entries), but the location of the text of this trial is unknown. The two documents are described separately below.

406 (fig. 79)

—— *Document relating to the Descendants of Don Miguel Damian.* NLA 1270. Ex–Waldeck collection. Published. Genealogical and economic (property plans). Xochimilco, D.F. 1576. Native paper. 38.5 × 39.3 cm.

Detailed plans of two native house compounds, one with gardens, and seven plots of land with place glyphs. Includes two-generation genealogy of seven members of the Damian family.

A small photograph is published without comment by McGee and Thomas (1905).

Publication: McGee and Thomas, 1905, plate facing p. 176.

407

—— *Plan de Plusiers Propriétés* [avec des Mesures, des Meubles et des Objets variés]. BNP 34. Ex–León y Gama (?) and Aubin collections. Published. Economic (miscellaneous). Xochimilco, D.F. 1576. European paper. 60 × 43 cm.

The manuscript is divided into seven horizontal compartments. Each contains the drawing of a different member of the Damian family with representations of houses, plots of land with place glyphs, food bins, chests, and other properties. Some of the content also appears in the preceding document.

Boban (1891) gives description and photoreproduction. A small detail is given by León y Gama (1832).

Publication: Boban, 1891, 1: 410–12, pl. 34.

Other: León y Gama, 1832, unnumbered plate, fig. 12.

408 (fig. 80)

Xochitepec, Codex of. Ordaz and Maxixcatzin Papers (part). Nationalbibliothek, Vienna. CVM 3. Ex–Bilimek collection. Published. Economic (tribute and property plans). Tepexoxuma, Puebla (?). 16thC (?). Native paper. 2 separate documents glued together. 96 × 81 cm.

The left half of the manuscript has crudely drawn depictions of 16 Indians seated on *icpallis*, plots of land, turkeys with numerical signs, and other details. One of three Spanish glosses, apparently referring to tribute, is signed by Fray Alonso de Santiago. The right half, in a different style, is a plan of fields and includes over 50 personal name glyphs identifying as many heads.

An old copy of the document, in two parts, with added details that include the names Lic. Juan Dias and Don Diego de Ordas and

Tepe(o?)xuma, is in the García Icazbalceta collection of the UTX (CDG 566 and 567). These form part of the Ordaz and Maxixcatzin Papers of the same collection (CDG 1451), late documents in Spanish treating the origin and descent of various family names. Genealogical trees of the Ordaz family and of Doña Maria Maxixcatzin that are among these papers and in the same style as CDG 566 and 567 are not in the native tradition.

A copy of the Vienna document, owned by Echániz and lacking only the glosses, was published and described by Barlow (1944c) and given its present and probably unjustified title. Following an unpublished description by Ramon Mena, Barlow assigned the document to Xochitepec, Morelos. On the basis of its association with the UTX documents, we have tentatively assigned it to Tepexoxuma, Puebla.

Copies: In addition to the copies mentioned above, a tracing of the right half of the manuscript is in the MNA codex collection (presently uncataloged; no. 21 of the unpublished inventory of 1934; see Glass, 1964). Whether this tracing is based on the Vienna original or the UTX copy has not been determined.

Publication: Barlow, 1944c.

Other: Glass, 1964, p. 25.

409

Xochitepec, Mapa de. National Museum, Copenhagen. Published. Cartographic-historical. San Juan Bautista Suchitepec, ex-district of Huajuapan, Western Oaxaca. 16thC. Skin or native paper. 102 × 92 cm.

At the center of the manuscript is a church and a partially effaced place glyph glossed Xuchitepec. Above this is a row of 20 seated Indians, the first 16 of whom have written Mixtec names and the last four of whom have Spanish names. Surrounding these details are 23 place glyphs, glossed in Nahuatl, presumably representing the boundaries of Xochitepec. At the top are several historical scenes.

Caso (1958e) gives commentary and photograph of the manuscript. The Paso y Troncoso study has been published by Gómez de Orozco (1952; reprinted, 1955). The manuscript was first published by Birket Smith (1946), without commentary.

Publication: Birket Smith, 1946, fig. 349; Caso, 1958e.

Studies: Gómez de Orozco, 1952, 1955.

410

Xochitepec, Plan cadastral de. Unknown. Unpublished. Unavailable. Northern Oaxaca. Physical data unknown.

Lehmann (1905a) classified as Chinantec a document copied by Seler with "Zapotec" hieroglyphs. The copy is not further described, but it may be noted that at the time of Lehmann's reference, glyphs now considered as Mixtec were then considered Zapotec. Both original and copy are now unknown. Cline (1957) speculates that the document may be identified as the Mapa de Xochitepec, in Copenhagen, but since the latter bears Nahuatl glosses, not mentioned by Lehmann, this seems improbable.

Bibliography: Cline, 1957, pp. 293–94; Lehmann, 1905a, p. 280.

411

Xochtlan, Santo Tomas, Pintura de. MNA 35-35. Published. Cartographic-historical. Santo Tomas Xochtlan, Tlaxcala. 18thC. Oil on cloth. 67 × 41 cm.

Late painting showing the church of Santo Tomas Xochtlan, the date 1530, San Buenaventura, and four figures including Juan Maxixcatzin and Juan de Guevara. Short Nahuatl texts around the border have not been translated.

Glass (1964) gives photograph and brief description. Mateos Higuera (1944c) has described it in detail; Gibson (1952) has commented on it.

Publication: Glass, 1964, p. 80, pl. 37.

Brief descriptions: Gibson, 1952, p. 266; Mateos Higuera, 1944c.

240

412 (fig. 81)

Xolotl, Códice. Histoire Chichimeque. BNP 1-10. Ex–Ixtlilxochitl, Boturini, Waldeck (one leaf), and Aubin collections. Published. Historical and genealogical. Texcoco region, Mexico. 16thC. Native paper. 6 leaves (with 10 painted pages) each about 42 × 48 cm., and fragments of a 7th leaf (with 2 fragmentary pages).

Detailed Texcocan history of events in the Valley of Mexico from the arrival of the Chichimecs of Xolotl in a year 5 Tecpatl (1224?) through events leading up to the Tepanec War (1427). Contains extensive genealogical information. Most of the relatively intact pages of the manuscript are also maps of part of the Valley of Mexico.

The document is one of the primary sources for the late 16th–early 17thC historical writings of Fernando de Alva Ixtlilxochitl (Ixtlilxochitl, 1891–92). Boban (1891) reproduces 10 of its pages photographically and comments on it at length. It is interpreted and reproduced in full, together with the incomplete León y Gama copy, by Dibble (1951). Rebus elements from glyphs in the manuscript are listed by Dibble (1940a). Certain genealogical relationships of persons in the manuscript are presented by Espejo and Monzon (1945). A small detail was first reproduced by Aubin (1849, and other editions).

Copies: León y Gama copy, incomplete, BNP 10bis (a). An old copy of plate 2 located in a private collection in Santiago, Chile, has been reproduced and studied by Dibble (1942b) and by Lizardi Ramos (1968); both studies contain commentary bearing on the interpretation of the original. The latter considers the copy to be a falsification. It should be noted that because the copy does not correspond to León y Gama's style, it need not therefore be disassociated with him since he also employed copyists to work for him (see Burrus, 1959, pp. 70–71). For another falsification based on Codex Xolotl see Article 26, no. 901.

Publication: Boban, 1891, 1: 55–208, pls. 1–10; Dibble, 1951.

Interpretation: Ixtlilxochitl, 1891–92, 1: passim, 2: 35–144.

Other: Aubin, 1849; Coy, 1966; Dibble, 1940a, 1942b, 1948, 1965; Espejo and Monzon, 1945; Lehmann, 1906b; Lizardi Ramos, 1968; Robertson, 1959, pp. 141–43, 181–82, pls. 14, 48–49.

Brief descriptions: Alcina Franch, 1955, pp. 453–54; Radin, 1920, pp. 17–18, 41–45.

413

Xoxocotlan, Santa Cruz, Mapa de. Known versions listed below. Unpublished. Cartographic. Santa Cruz Xoxocotlan, ex-district of Centro, Eastern Oaxaca. 17thC. One sheet.

The map is known through five copies apparently derived from two related originals. The copies vary considerably in style and detail. The 1771 copy shows the hills of Monte Alban at the top with stylized pictorial elements, a Mixtec A–0 year symbol and date, and Mixtec glosses. At the bottom are San Antonio de la Cal, San Agustin (Yatareni?), and further hills; at the center is the church of Xoxocotlan. There are Spanish texts with the dates 1660, 1718, and 1771. The 1718 copy bears the title "El cura de Guautla con los Indios de Jocoatlan del Marquesado del Valle sobre tierras del Pueblo. Indios. Año de 1719."

The 1718 copy is mentioned by Orozco y Berra (1871) and by Tamayo and Alcorta (1941). A brief description of the 1686 copy is given by Mazari (1926c). The 1718 and 1771 copies appear to derive from the same prototype; the 1686 copy may derive from a distinct but related version. Known manuscripts are:

1. Watercolor copy of 1718 (58 × 42 cm.), DGMH 1176.

2. Oil copy of 1771 in Pueblo. Photograph in INAH/AF.

3. Oil copy by Villagra from previous copy, Alfonso Caso collection.

4. Oil copy of 1686 (87.5 × 79 cm.), AGN-T 129, exp. 4.

5. Certified copy of 1879 from previous copy, apparently in Xoxocotlan; photograph in INAH/AF.

Brief descriptions: Mazari, 1926c, pp. 348–49, no. 68; Orozco y Berra, 1871, pp. 12–13, nos. 25–26; Tamayo and Alcorta, 1941, pp. 22–23, no. 13.

414

Yahuiche, Santa Maria, Lienzo de.   Pueblo. Unpublished.   Unavailable.   Santa Maria Yahuiche, ex-district of Ixtlan, Eastern Oaxaca.   Early colonial.   Cloth.   140 × 110 cm.

The document is reported, but not described, by Pérez García (1956). It is listed as an unverified Zapotec pictorial by Cline (1966c). Whether or not the manuscript is in the native tradition is unknown, but Pérez García indicates an early colonial date.

Bibliography: Cline, 1966c, app. 2, no. 55; Pérez García, 1956, 2: 295.

415

Yanhuitlan, Códice de.   Academia de Bellas Artes, Puebla, and AGN-V 272.   Economic (miscellaneous).   Yanhuitlan, ex-district of Nochistlan, Western Oaxaca.   ca. 1545–50. European paper codex.   12 leaves and several fragments (Acad. Bellas Artes) and 4 leaves (AGN).   31 × 22.5 cm.

The codex, which is incomplete, treats historical events and economic affairs of Yanhuitlan and Teposcolula. There are drawings in an acculturated Mixtec style of articles of tribute, bins of maize and beans, portraits of Indians and Spaniards, and the churches of Yanhuitlan and Teposcolula. Other pages include a drawing of the Spanish conquest of Tenochtitlan and Mixtec place glyphs.

The Puebla portions of the manuscript, which may once have been owned by José Manso, were published with a detailed commentary by Jiménez Moreno and Mateos Higuera (1940). The four leaves in the AGN

have been published and studied by Berlin (1947).

Copy: Saldaña copy of the Puebla portions, MNA 35-93 (said to be indistinguishable from the original).

Publication: Berlin, 1947, pp. 59–67, pls. A–H; Jiménez Moreno and Mateos Higuera, 1940.

Studies: Anderson and Finan, 1945; Barlow, 1947c.

Brief descriptions: Alcina Franch, 1955, pp. 493–94; Glass, 1964, p. 147, pl. 99; Lehmann, 1905a, p. 266; Paso y Troncoso, 1892–93, 2: 359–64.

416

Yatao, San Lucas, Lienzo de.   MNA 35-122. Published.   Cartographic-historical.   San Lucas Yatao, ex-district of Ixtlan, Eastern Oaxaca. 17thC.   Oil on cloth.   105 × 86 cm.

Occupying most of the lienzo are paintings of 18 Indian couples arranged in two columns. At the top are further Indians, several Spaniards with horses, and lesser detail. There are extensive written glosses with Spanish and Zapotec names. The document lacks specific hieroglyphic elements.

Glass (1964) gives brief description and photograph.

Publication: Glass, 1964, p. 180, pl. 133.

417

Yatini, Lienzo de.   MNA 35-120.   Published. Cartographic-historical.   Eastern Oaxaca. 18thC (?).   Cloth.   160 × 117 cm.

The lienzo presents a crude depiction of the boundaries of an unidentified locality. Glosses, believed to be in Zapotec, suggest an Eastern Oaxaca provenience. The name Yatini is a gloss on what appears to be a mountain.

A brief description and photograph appear in the MNA catalog (Glass, 1964).

Publication: Glass, 1964, p. 178, pl. 131.

418

Yetla, Mapa de.   Pueblo.   Unpublished.

Cartographic. San Mateo Yetla, ex-district of Tuxtepec, Northern Oaxaca. ca. 1811. Physical description unknown.

A reconstruction of cartographic data on the map, based on a copy, has been published by Cline (1961a, 1961b). It shows rivers and communities in the vicinity of San Juan Bautista Valle Nacional. To what extent the original, itself probably a copy of an earlier original, is in the native tradition is uncertain.

Copy: Copy of tracing by Weitlaner owned by H. F. Cline, now in LC, Manuscripts Division.

Description: Cline, 1961a, pp. 60–64, pl. 2b; 1961b, pl. 4.

Long after the foregoing description of the Mapa de Yetla was written, we had occasion in 1972 to see a photograph of the copy owned by H. F. Cline. The map consists only of written Spanish glosses, lines, and a few crosses. It does not have pictorial elements in the native tradition and should not have been included in this census. Cline also owned a copy by Weitlaner of another map of the Yetla region, described by Cline (1961a, pp. 64–65) as "Yetla II." It also lacks pictorial elements other than lines and Spanish glosses. Photographs of both copies have been deposited in the pictorial documents collection of LC/HF. The former (Yetla I, census 418a) is marked "2a"; the latter (Yetla II, census 418b) is marked "2b."

419

Yolotepec, Lienzo de. Lienzo de Amoltepec. Códice Mixteco-Zapoteco Manuel Martínez Gracida. Lienzo Mixteco de Santa Maria Yolotepec. AMNH. Ex–Martínez Gracida collection (?). Published. Cartographic-historical. Santa Maria Yolotepec, ex-district of Tlaxiaco, Western Oaxaca. 16thC. Cloth. Dimensions not determined (published dimensions are in error).

At the top of the lienzo is the glyph for Yolotepec, together with an assemblage of Indians. On other parts of the lienzo are place glyphs, dates, and Indians, some of whom are also shown at the Yolotepec assembly. Another assemblage occurs near the center; a long itinerary, marked by place glyphs and dates, leads from the lower left to the upper right. None of the persons on the lienzo, all of whom are drawn in traditional Mixtec style with calendrical names, can be securely identified in other Mixtec histories. Caso indicates that if one of them is the 2 Rain of the first Tilantongo dynasty, then the principal events of the document occurred toward the end of the 10thC A.D.

A copy of the lienzo made in 1889 (when it was preserved in Santiago Amoltepec, ex-district of Juquila) is reproduced without commentary by Peñafiel (1890). It is photographically reproduced and studied by Caso (1958d). The fanciful commentary and interpretation by Castellanos (1917–18) are unacceptable although of interest as an early attempt to identify Mixtec place glyphs.

Publication: Caso, 1958d; Peñafiel, 1890, vol. 2, pl. 317.

Study: Castellanos, 1917–18.

Brief descriptions: Alcina Franch, 1955, p. 495; Lehmann, 1905a, p. 263.

420

Yolox, Lienzo de. Lost. Published. Cartographic-historical. San Pedro Yolox, ex-district of Ixtlan, Northern Oaxaca. ca. 1596. Cloth (?). Dimensions unknown.

The lienzo is known through an 1832 copy (cloth, ca. 150 × 200 cm.) and a description and translation of its Chinantec and Nahuatl glosses made in Mexico City in 1810, both preserved in the pueblo. The copy exhibits only vestiges of traditional pictorial elements. It depicts Yolox and neighboring communities and gives some local history.

A photograph of the copy and a transcript of the 1810 description are given by Pérez García (1956). Cline (1961a) has discussed its major features.

Publication: Pérez García, 1956, 1: 99–102.

Brief description: Cline, 1961a, pp. 75–77.

Brief mention: Cline, 1957, p. 281, note 23.

421

Yucunama, San Pedro, Mapa de. Lienzo de Yucunama. Pueblo (?). Unpublished. Genealogical. San Pedro Yucunama (Amoltepec), ex-district of Teposcolula, Western Oaxaca. 1585. Physical description not determined.

A positive photostat, measuring 40.5 × 34.5 cm., is owned by Alfonso Caso; the original seems to be on paper. Around three and a half sides of the document are 35 year signs (4 Reed to 12 House). The date, 1585, appears on the manuscript as does the Yucunama place glyph. The latter has been reproduced by Caso (1964a). Near the center are five persons (2 couples and one male) with calendrical names. There is a Mixtec gloss.

Bibliography: Caso, 1964a, fig. 1b.

422

Zacatepec, Lienzo de, no. 1. Códice Mixteco Martínez Gracida de Jamiltepec. MNA 35-63. Published. Cartographic-historical. Santa Maria Zacatepec, ex-district of Putla (formerly Jamiltepec), Western Oaxaca. 16thC. Cloth. 325 × 225 cm.

Scattered across the lienzo are numerous complex place glyphs with hieroglyphic dates and Indians with calendrical names, all in traditional Mixtec style. Most of the major glyphs are connected by roads or chevron bands (considered a representation of warfare). Several rivers are shown. Included within the lienzo is a rectangular frame on which numerous lesser place glyphs are drawn, probably representing some ancient jurisdiction.

The lienzo is reproduced, with 25 photographic details, and described by Peñafiel (1900). A photograph and brief description are in the MNA catalog (Glass, 1964). A study of the manuscript is given by M. E. Smith (1966a).

Copies: Lehmann (1905a) reported a copy obtained by Seler then in the MVBE.

A copy of 1893 is in the pueblo. Peñafiel (1897a) appears to refer to yet another copy. A much later and altered version of the lienzo is described separately in this census as the Lienzo de Zacatepec no. 2.

Publication: Peñafiel, 1900.

Study: M. E. Smith, 1966a.

Other: Peñafiel, 1897a, p. 97; Villagra, 1933.

Brief descriptions: Alcina Franch, 1955, pp. 494–95; Glass, 1964, p. 115, pl. 66; Lehmann, 1905a, pp. 261–63.

423

Zacatepec, Lienzo de, no. 2. Unknown. Unpublished. Cartographic-historical. Santa Maria Zacatepec, ex-district of Putla, Western Oaxaca. 18th–19thC (?). Cloth. 300 × 245 cm.

The manuscript, now known only through a copy of 1893 preserved in Zacatepec, is an extensively altered version of the Lienzo de Zacatepec no. 1 with practically all the historical data and all the calendrical hieroglyphs omitted. A few of the place glyphs are identified by written inscriptions in Nahuatl.

Peñafiel (1900) described the original of this copy. Photographs of the 1893 copy, taken by an INAH photographer, are in the LC/HF collection.

Bibliography: Peñafiel, 1900, p. 2; M. E. Smith, 1966a.

424

Zacatlalmanco, Santa Anita, Codex. MHP. Ex–Pinart collection. Published. Cartographic-historical. Santa Anita Zacatlalmanco, D.F. 1603–04. European paper. 41.5 × 56.5 cm.

Drawings of the Indian governors of Mexico City from about 1536 to 1602, the Viceroy Mendoza, and numerous lesser Indian officials with personal name glyphs. Cartographic detail includes a church within a rectangular plot interpreted as representing the *fondo legal* of Santa Anita, about 1535–54.

The manuscript has been studied and photographically reproduced by Galarza (1962).

Publication: Galarza, 1962.

425

Zapotecos, Arbol Genealógico de los Reyes. Zapotecan Genealogy. Hispanic Society of America, New York. HC 427/46. Ex–Manuel Ortega Reyes of Oaxaca and either Pedro Felix de Silva (Conde de Cifuentes) or Sir Thomas Phillipps collections. Published. Genealogical. Eastern Oaxaca. 18thC (?). Tanned leather (parchment?). ca. 200 × 60.7 cm.

Only briefly examined, the manuscript exhibits drawings of persons in a late style. Some or most of them are in native costume. Approximately 14 couples are arranged vertically and dominate the composition. Glosses in Zapotec include the place names Tlacolula and Zaachila.

A photograph and a brief description have appeared in a sale catalog (Hiersemann, 1913b). The copy owned by Caso is briefly mentioned by Caso (1964a).

Copies: 19thC watercolor copy, 121 × 22 cm., owned by Alfonso Caso.

Publication: Hiersemann, 1913b, pp. 76–80, plate facing p. 72.

Brief mention: Caso, 1964a, pp. 20–21, note 26.

426

Zapotitlan, Códice del Tequitlato de. Códice de Tributos de Santiago Zapotitlan. Apuntes del Tequitlato. MNA 35-59. Ex–Boturini collection. Partially published. Economic (census). Zapotitlan, Puebla (?). 1561. Skin tira painted on one side. 25.6 × 85 cm.

The document is divided into six horizontal rows of house symbols, beside each of which are small circles apparently indicating the number of inhabitants of each house. Glosses in Spanish, Nahuatl, and a Mixtec dialect give names of persons and their civil status. A gloss on the reverse identifies the

manuscript as made by Pedro (?) de Santiago, tequitlato of Zapotitlan. The identification of the Zapotitlan in question is uncertain.

Glass (1964) gives a brief description, illustrates a detail from the manuscript, and cites two unpublished studies of the glosses.

Partial publication: Glass, 1964, p. 110, pl. 62.

Brief description: Mena, 1923, pp. 41–43, no. 2.

427 (fig. 82)

Zolin, Genealogía de. MNA 35-43 (lost). Ex–University of Mexico (ca. 1831). Published. Genealogical. Tlaxcala (?). 16thC. Maguey paper. 44 × 35 cm.

Unglossed genealogy of 14 persons with personal name glyphs. Uppermost person, seated in a house, has a name glyph that may be a quail (zolin).

Glass (1964) gives photograph and brief description. Lithographs of the upper and lower halves of the manuscript by Waldeck are given in Icaza and Gondra (1827).

Copy: Waldeck copy, NLA 1269 (part).

Publication: Glass, 1964, p. 89, pl. 43; Icaza and Gondra, 1827, part 1, pl. 3; part 2, pl. 3.

NOTE. The census numeration through no. 427 was established in 1965. Subsequent documents, nos. 428–434, are in the happenstance sequence in which they were added. They are listed alphabetically in Article 31.

428

Alaman, Lucas, Códice. Unknown. Published. Economic (tribute). Central Mexico. 16thC. Native paper. 1 leaf. Dimensions not reported.

On one side is a short Nahuatl text and drawings of two horses, money, and day signs. Drawings on the other side, in a different and unusual style, show a hill, a pyramidal substructure, a dead person, a day sign, and other details.

Caso and Jiménez Moreno (1966) provide photoreproduction of both sides of the document, brief description, and translation of its Nahuatl text.

Publication: Caso and Jiménez Moreno, 1966.

429

Coatepec, San Bartolome, Lienzo de. Pueblo. Published. Cartographic-historical. San Bartolome Coatepec, Mexico. 18thC. Cloth. 152 × 203 cm.

Paintings on the lienzo depict a church (San Bartolito), surrounding mountains, and neighboring localities; a legend gives the date of 1639. Only the manner of representing a river is specifically reminiscent of traditional artistic forms. The document may derive from an older prototype.

Harvey (1966b) gives description, commentary, and photoreproduction.

Publication: Harvey, 1966b.

430

Huapeán, Códice. AGN-C 1276, exp. 1, f. 75. Published. Miscellaneous (litigative). Zinapecuaro, Michoacan. 1567. Native paper. 20 × 84 cm.

Drawings, with Tarascan and Spanish glosses, of grievances against Alonso Huapeán, cacique and gobernador of Zinapecuaro. Shown are persons in various positions and small circles representing money.

A description and partial photoreproduction are given by López Sarrelangue (1963). The same description and a full two-color reproduction of a copy appear in López Sarrelangue (1965).

Publication: López Sarrelangue, 1965, pp. 98–101, 305–06.

Other: López Sarrelangue, 1963.

431

American Manuscript no. 10, part 8. Lost. Formerly DSB, MS Amer. 10, part 8. Ex–Boturini collection. Unpublished. Economic (tribute). Central Mexico (?). Native (?) paper. 100 × 35 (or 97 × 40) cm. approx.

The manuscript, accessioned by the DSB in 1867, is lost as a consequence of World War II. It is known through a brief description by Guzmán (1936) and four pages of copies of details and Nahuatl glosses by Walter Lehmann in IAI. From these data it is evident that the document represented seated Indian figures and symbols for monetary units.

Copy: Lehmann copy, IAI.

Brief description: Bankmann, 1970, p. 135; Guzmán, 1936, no. 10, part 3 (*sic*).

432

Chalchihuapan, Mapa de. Pueblo. Published. Historical. San Bernardino Chalchihuapan, Puebla. 18th–19thC. Oil paintings on cloth. 101.8 × 252.6 cm.

The painting consists of approximately 15 scenes of varying widths arranged in three horizontal rows. Some of the scenes are very similar to parts of the Mapa de Cuauhtlantzinco (no. 101); the two documents are in some way related.

Castro Morales (1969) provides photoreproduction, line drawings, description, and commentary. The painting is undoubtedly the same as the Mapa briefly mentioned by A. Bandelier (1884 and in White and Bernal, 1960). We have not examined Bandelier, "San Bernardino Chalchihuapan: ein mexikanisches Abenteur" (*National Zeitung*, Berlin, 1886), cited by White and Bernal.

Publication: Castro Morales, 1969.

Brief mention: Bandelier, 1884, p. 143; White and Bernal, 1960, p. 240, note.

433

Tequixtepec, San Miguel, Lienzo de, no. 1. Pueblo. Unpublished. Cartographic-Historical. San Miguel Tequixtepec, ex-district of Coixtlahuaca, Western Oaxaca. 16thC. Cloth. 305 × 248 cm.

The existence of two lienzos from Tequixtepec was reported in a Mexican newspaper in July, 1970. The article (S. Cruz,

1970) provides a very general description and two photographic details of Lienzo no. 1. Both documents were examined in April, 1970, by Ross Parmenter, who had known of at least one lienzo in the town since 1960. A photograph of no. 1 and descriptions of both lienzos were provided by Parmenter for this census. Both lienzos will be treated in Caso's forthcoming *Reyes y Reinos de la Mixteca*.

In traditional Mixtec style, the upper portion of no. 1 has 25 peripherally situated place glyphs glossed in Nahuatl, a large central place glyph, pairs of Indians with calendrical name glyphs, and the single date 6 Reed (1551?). The lower portion has genealogical and historical drawings within rows of rectangular compartments. Many of the pairs of persons also appear in other Mixtec lienzos.

Brief description: S. Cruz, 1970.

434

Tequixtepec, San Miguel, Lienzo de, no. 2. Pueblo. Unpublished. Cartographic-historical. San Miguel Tequixtepec, ex-district of Coixtlahuaca, Western Oaxaca. 16thC. Cloth. 285 × 70 cm.

In more sketchy style than no. 1, this document displays a long genealogy, dates, a Christian church, and a drawing of a ceremony that also occurs in the Selden Roll, the Lienzo Antonio de León, and the Lienzo de Coixtlahuaca no. 2.

Bibliography: See previous entry.

REFERENCES (compiled by Mary W. Cline)

Acevedo López y de la Cruz, 1958
Acosta, 1590, 1962
Acosta Saignes, 1946
Adelhofer, 1963
Aguirre, 1950–51
Aguirre Beltrán, 1940
Alcina Franch, 1955, 1960
Alvarado Tezozomoc, 1878, 1944a
American Art Association, 1915
Anales Mexicanos, 1589–1596, 1949
Anales Mexicanos No. 1, 1948
Anales Mexicanos No. 2, 1948
Anales Mexicanos No. 3, 1948
Anales Mexicanos No. 4, 1948
Anales Mexicanos Uno Pedernal, 1949
Anales Número Cinco, 1954
Anales Toltecas, 1949
Anales Tolteca Chichimeca, 1949
Anders, 1967a, 1968, 1970
Anderson and Barlow, 1943
—— and Finan, 1945
André-Bonnet, 1950
Angulo, 1958, 1959
Anonymous, MS, 1829, 1865, 1875, 1888, 1897, 1935a, 1942, 1944
Antón, 1965
Apenes, 1947, 1953
Aragón y Leyva, 1945
Arreola, 1922

Athearn, 1963
Aubin, n.d.*a*, n.d.*b*, n.d.*c*, n.d.*d*, n.d.*e*, n.d.*f*, n.d.*g*, 1849, 1859, 1859–61, 1875, 1885, 1886a, 1886b, 1886c, 1893
Azcué y Mancera, 1967
Ballesteros Gaibrois, 1948a, 1951, 1964
Bandelier, A., 1884
Bandelier, F., 1932
Bandini, 1791–93
Bangs & Co., 1893
Bankmann, 1970
Barlow, MS*a*, MS*b*, MS*c*, 1943b, 1943d, 1944a, 1944b, 1944c, 1944e, 1944f, 1944h, 1945b, 1945c, 1945e, 1945f, 1946a, 1946b, 1946d, 1946e, 1946f, 1947a, 1947b, 1947c, 1947e, 1948a, 1948b, 1948c, 1948e, 1948f, 1949a, 1949b, 1949c, 1949d, 1949e, 1950b, 1951a, 1954a, 1954b, 1961
—— and Mateos Higuera, MS
—— and McAfee, 1949
Barrios, 1954
Barthelemy, 1798
Batres, n.d., 1888, 1889
Baz, 1899
Beaumont, 1932
Beauvois, 1885, 1886
Beltrami, 1830
Beristáin de Souza, 1883–97
Berlin, 1947

—— and Barlow, 1948
—— and Rendón, 1947
Bernal, 1947, 1962
Beyer, 1910, 1911, 1912a, 1912b
Bibliotheca inlustris, 1842
Bibliotheca mejicana, 1869
Bibliotheca mexicana, 1880
Birket-Smith, 1946
Blacker, 1965
Blom, n.d., 1928, 1936, 1945
Boban, 1891, 1899
Borah and Cook, 1963
Borson, 1796
Böttiger, 1811
Boturini Benaduci, 1746, 1948
Bowditch, 1900, 1910
Brand, 1944
Brasseur de Bourbourg, 1851, 1852, 1857–59, 1864, 1869–70
Bravo Ugarte, 1962
Breton, 1919, 1920a, 1920b
Brinton, 1890b, 1899
——, Phillips, and Morris, 1892
Bullock, n.d., 1824a, 1824b, 1824c
Bunting, 1931
Burland, 1947a, 1947b, 1947c, 1948, 1950a, 1950b, 1951a, 1955b, 1957b, 1957c, 1958a, 1958b, 1960, 1962a, 1965, 1966a, 1966b
Burrus, 1957, 1959
Bustamante, 1829, 1829–30, 1835–36, 1890–96
Cahuantzi, 1939
Capitán, 1911, 1912, 1923
Carbajal Espinosa, 1862
Carrasco Pizana, 1944, 1950, 1964
Carreño, 1950
Carrera Stampa, 1949b
Carrillo y Ancona, 1882
Carrillo y Gariel, 1949
Cartari, 1615, 1626
Caso, 1927, 1928, 1930, 1939a, 1940, 1943a, 1943b, 1945a, 1945b, 1947, 1951, 1952, 1953, 1954, 1955a, 1955b, 1956, 1958a, 1958b, 1958c, 1958d, 1958e, 1958f, 1959b, 1960b, 1960c, 1961, 1962, 1963, 1964a, 1964b, 1964c, 1965a, 1965b, 1965c, 1966a, 1966b, 1966c, 1967
—— and Jiménez Moreno, 1966
—— and Smith, 1966
Castellanos, 1910, 1912a, 1912b, 1917, 1917–18
Castillo, I. B. del, 1906, 1922
Castro Morales, 1969
Ceballos Novelo, 1934
Cédula dada, 1943
Cervantes de Salazar, 1914, 1914–36
Chadwick, 1967

—— and MacNeish, 1967
Chapa, 1957
Charency, 1859
Charnay, 1903
Chavero, n.d., 1877a, 1880, 1882–1903, 1886, 1892, 1899, 1901a, 1901b, 1901c, 1903a, 1903b, 1906, 1964
Cháves, 1865, 1925
Chávez Orozco, 1947
Cicco, 1963
Civezza, 1879
Clark, 1912, 1913a, 1938
Clavigero, 1780–81, 1958–59
Cline, 1957, 1959, 1961a, 1961b, 1963a, 1964, 1966a, 1966b, 1966c, 1968
Codex Abraham Castellanos, 1931
Codex Ixtlan, 1931
Codex Magliabecchiano, 1904
Codex Meixueiro, 1931
Códice de 1576, 1950
Códice Laud, n.d.
Códice Troano, 1930
Códices Indígenas, 1933
Coe, 1963
Collin, 1952
Commission Scientifique du Mexique, 1864
Cook, 1958
Cook de Leonard, 1961
—— and Lemoine Villicaña, 1956
Cordero Mendoza, 1954
Cornyn, 1946
Corona Núñez, 1942a, 1942b, 1946, 1951, 1957, 1959, 1964–67
Covarrubias, 1946
Coy, 1966
Cruz, M. de la, 1964
Cruz, S., 1970
Cuevas, 1913, 1921–28, 1929, 1930, 1956
Dahlgren, 1889
Dahlgren de Jordán, 1954a, 1963
Dark, 1958a, 1958b, 1959
—— and Plesters, 1959
Delafield, 1839
Dibble, 1940a, 1942a, 1942b, 1948, 1951, 1963, 1965
—— and Anderson, 1950–69
Dietschy, 1944, 1960
Dockstader, 1964
Dorez, 1896
Doutrelaine, 1867
Dufosse, n.d.a
Durán, 1867–80, 1951, 1964, 1967
Durand-Forest, 1962, 1971
Durbin, 1969
Echániz, 1954
Echániz, Librería, n.d.a, n.d.b, n.d.c, n.d.d,

1937a, 1937b, 1937c, 1938a, 1938b, 1939a,
1939b, 1939c, 1944a, 1944b, 1944c, 1944d,
1944e, 1944f, 1945, 1946a, 1946b, 1947a,
1947b, 1947c, 1947d, 1949
Ecker, 1966
Ehrle, 1896, 1898, 1900
Emmart, 1935a, 1935b, 1935c, 1940
Eriksson, 1919
Escuela Internacional, 1913a, 1913b
Espejo and Barlow, 1944
—— and Monzón, 1945
Espinosa, I., 1945
Espinosa, M., 1910, 1961
Esteve Barba, 1942, 1952
Estrada, 1937
Evreinov, Kosarev, and Ustinov, 1961
Exposición . . . , 1892
Exposition Universelle, 1867
Fábrega, 1899
Fernández, 1939, 1956
Fernández del Castillo, F., 1925a
Fernández de Recas, 1961
Fewkes, 1893
Flor y Canto, 1964
Förstemann, 1880, 1882, 1886, 1892, 1901,
1902, 1903a, 1903b, 1906
Fortier and Ficklen, 1907
Forty-fourth annual report, 1897
Fuente, 1949
Gabrieli, 1929
Gadow, 1908
Galarza, 1962, 1963, 1964, 1965, 1966
Galindo y Villa, 1895, 1905a, 1923, 1925
Gallatin, 1845
Gamio, 1917
García Abrines and Robertson, MS
García Conde, 1926
García Cubas, 1892, 1897, 1909–10, 1912
—— and Galindo y Villa, 1904
García Granados, 1937, 1939a
—— and MacGregor, 1934
García Gutiérrez, 1939
García Icazbalceta, 1881, 1886, 1886–92, 1954
Garibay, 1948, 1953–54, 1956, 1957, 1959b
Gates, MS, 1909, 1910, 1911, 1924, 1931,
1932, 1933, 1937a, 1937b, 1939a, 1939b,
1940
Gemelli Careri, 1699–1700
Genet, 1928–29
Gibson, 1952, 1956, 1964a, 1964b
Glass, 1958b, 1960, 1964
Gómez de Cervantes, 1944
Gómez de Orozco, 1927a, 1927b, 1937, 1939a,
1940, 1941, 1945a, 1948, 1952, 1955
Gondra, 1846
González de Barcia, 1737–38
Gordon, 1913

Götze, 1743–44
Greenleaf, 1961
Gropp, 1932, 1933
Guerra, 1952
Guevara, 1788
Gurría LaCroix, 1964, 1966, 1967
Guzmán, 1936, 1939b, 1939c, 1949, 1958
Hagar, 1911, 1912a, 1912b, 1912c, 1913
Hagen, 1944
Hamy, 1897, 1899a, 1899b
Haro y Cadena, 1940
Harvey, 1966b
Henning, 1912
Hernández, 1651, 1926, 1942–46, 1945, 1959–
60
Herrera, 1601–15
Hiersemann, 1910, 1913b
Historische Hieroglyphen, 1892
Hochstetter, 1884
Horcasitas, 1959
Hornius (Horn), 1652
Humboldt, 1810
Hunter, 1917
Ibarra de Anda, 1937
Icaza and Gondra, 1827
Iguíniz, 1918
Imbelloni, 1943
Ixtlilxochitl, 1891–92
Jiménez Moreno, MS, 1938a, 1938b, 1948,
1961
—— and Mateos Higuera, 1940
Jonghe, 1906a, 1906b
Josephy and Brandon, 1961
Jourdain, 1889
Jourdanet and Siméon, 1880
Juncker, 1710
Kelemen, 1943
Kelley, 1955
Kelly and Palerm, 1952
Kingsborough, 1831–48
Kircher, 1652–54
Kirchhoff, 1940, 1958
Knorozov, 1963
Kollar, 1769
Kreichgauer, 1915–16, 1917, 1917–18
Krusche, 1966
Kubler, 1948, 1951, 1961
—— and Gibson, 1951
Kutscher, 1961, 1962, 1963a, 1963b, 1964
Lambeck, 1679
Leal, 1953
Leander, 1966a, 1966b, 1967
Legati, 1677
Lehmann, 1905a, 1905c, 1906a, 1906b, 1966
—— and Smital, 1929
Leicht, 1938
Lejeal, 1904

Lemoine V., 1960, 1961
Lenz, 1949, 1950
León, M. de, 1611
León, N., n.d., 1888a, 1888b, 1889a, 1889b, 1903, 1903–04, 1904a, 1905a, 1905b, 1906a, 1906b, 1906c, 1927, 1933
Leonard & Co., 1871
Leonard, 1967
León-Portilla, 1958, 1967a
—— and Mateos Higuera, 1957
León y Gama, 1832
Linné, 1942, 1948
Lips and Deckert, 1962
Lista, 1881
Lizardi Ramos, 1953a, 1953b, 1955, 1968
Long, 1926, 1942
López, A., 1920
López Beltrán, 1966
López Cogolludo, 1688
López de Gómara, 1826
López Sarrelangue, 1957, 1963, 1965
Lorenzana, 1770
Loubat, 1901

McAfee and Barlow, 1945, 1946a, 1947, 1952
McAndrew, 1965
McGee and Thomas, 1905
Madier de Montjau, 1875
Mappa Reinisch, n.d.
Maráin Araujo, 1945
Márquez, 1911, 1912
Marquina, 1960
Martínez, 1606
Martínez Hernández, 1927, 1940
Martínez Marín, 1961, 1963
Mason, 1943
Mateos Higuera, 1944b, 1944c, 1944d, 1944e, 1944f, 1945, 1946a, 1946b, 1947a, 1947b, 1948a, 1948b, 1949a, 1949b, 1949c, 1949d
Maudslay, 1908–16, 1909–10
Mayer, 1844
Maza, 1945, 1959
Mazari, 1926a, 1926b, 1926c
Mazihcatzin, 1927
Medellín Zenil, 1957
Melgarejo Vivanco, 1949, 1953
Melgar y Serrano, 1873, 1875
Mena, 1911a, 1911b, 1913, 1914, 1923
Mendieta, 1870
Mendieta y Núñez, 1949, 1961
Mendizabal, 1926, 1946
Mendoza, 1869
Mengin, 1939–40, 1942, 1945, 1952a
Mercati, 1589
Miles, 1957
Mirabel Lausan, 1937
Mirror of the Indian, 1958
Miyar, 1928

Molins Fábrega, 1956a, 1956b
Monroy, 1946
Moreno, R., 1966
Morley, 1920, 1946
—— and Roys, 1941
Motolinía, 1903
Moxó, 1828, 1837, 1839
Muller, 1958
Muñoz Camargo, 1947a, 1947b
Museo de Artillería, 1856
Nessel, 1690
Nicholson, 1960b, 1961b, 1966a, 1966c, 1966d, 1967
Nicolau d'Olwer, 1952
Nierembergii, 1635
Noguera, 1933b
Nordenskiöld, 1889
Noticias relativas, 1944
Nowotny, 1948a, 1948b, 1955, 1956b, 1957, 1958, 1959, 1960, 1961a, 1961b, 1964, 1968
—— and Strebinger, 1958
Nuevos datos, 1952
Nuevos documentos, 1946
Núñez y Domínguez, 1947a
Nuttall, n.d., 1888, 1901, 1902, 1903, 1911a, 1911b, 1913, 1921

Olivera and Reyes, 1969
Omont, 1899
Orozco, E., 1892
Orozco y Berra, 1867, 1871, 1877–82, 1880, 1897

Paddock, 1959
Paleografía, 1951
Palomera, 1962, 1963
Papillon, 1766
Parke-Bernet, 1953, 1967
Parmenter, 1961a, 1961b, 1961c, 1961d, 1966
Paso y Troncoso, 1882, 1886, 1888, 1892–93, 1896, 1897b, 1897c, 1898a, 1898b, 1905–06, 1905–07, 1912, 1913
Paulinus de Sancto Bartholomaeo, 1805
Peñafiel, 1885, 1887, 1889, 1890, 1895, 1897a, 1897b, 1897c, 1900, 1901, 1902, 1903c, 1907, 1909, 1910, 1914
Pérez, 1859a, 1859b
Pérez Bustamante, 1928
Pérez García, 1956
Pérez Martínez, n.d., 1936, 1938
Picart, 1733–37
Pintura del gobernador, 1878
Pompa y Pompa, 1938
Präkolumbische Kunst, 1958
Prescott, 1844
Preuss, 1936, 1937, 1938, 1948
—— and Mengin, 1937–38
Procesos de Indios, 1912
Pruneda, 1953

Purchas, 1625
Qualli Amatl, 1950
Quaritch, 1880, 1885
Quintana, 1960
Racknitz, 1796
Rada y Delgado and López de Ayala y del Hierro, 1892
Radin, 1920
Ramírez, F., 1956
Ramírez, J. F., 1847, 1855, 1858, 1862, 1898, 1945a, 1945b, 1952, 1953, 1956
Ramírez Cabañas, 1938
Ramírez Flores, 1959
Ramírez Lavoignet, 1953, 1959, 1962
Rauh, 1970
Rea, 1643
Reina, 1924–27
Reko, 1945
Relación de Michoacán, 1869, 1903, 1956
Relaciones de Yucatan, 1898–1900
Rendón, 1952
Rich, n.d.
Rickards, 1913
Riva Palacio, n.d.
Rivera, 1892
Rivet, 1932
Robertson, D., 1954, 1959, 1963, 1964, 1966, 1968
Robertson, W., 1777, 1778
Rodríguez Marín, 1916–25
Röck, 1935, 1936, 1937, 1941
Rojas González, 1940
Roquet, 1938
Rosa, M. G. de la, 1907
Rosado Escalante and Ontiveros, 1938
Rosado Ojeda, 1945
Rosny, Léon de, 1856, 1863, 1869, 1875, 1876a, 1876b, 1881a, 1881b, 1887, 1888
Rosny, Lucien de, 1877
Roys, 1933, 1939, 1943, 1957, 1965
Rubín de la Borbolla, 1953
—— and Spratling, 1964
Ruz Lhuillier, 1944
Sandoval, 1945
Santa Cruz, 1918–19
Sapper, 1897
Saussure, 1891
Schmeider, 1930
Scholes and Adams, 1957
Schoolcraft, 1851–57
Schuller, 1913, 1919–20
Schwede, 1912, 1916
Seler, 1890, 1893, 1895, 1899a, 1899b, 1900, 1900–01, 1901a, 1901–02, 1902a, 1902b, 1902e, 1902f, 1902g, 1902h, 1902l, 1902–23, 1904a, 1904b, 1904c, 1904d, 1904e, 1904f, 1904g, 1904–09, 1908a, 1908b, 1908c, 1913, 1915, 1927, 1960–61, 1963
Seler-Sachs, 1900
Serna, 1892a, 1892b
Siméon, 1888, 1889b
Simons, 1962, 1963, 1967, 1967–68, 1968, 1969
Smith, B., 1968
Smith, M. E., 1963, 1966a
Sociedad Española de Amigos del Arte, 1930
Solís Alcalá, 1949
Somolinos d'Ardois, 1954, 1957
Sotheby and Co., 1935, 1936b, 1939, 1946, 1948
Sotheby, Wilkinson, and Hodge, 1919a
Soustelle, 1937
Spinden, E., 1933
Spinden, H. J., 1913, 1928, 1935
Spineto, 1829
Spores, 1964
Spranz, 1964
Starr, MS, n.d., 1898, 1900, 1908
Steck, 1951
Steininger and Van de Velde, 1935
Stephens, 1843
Tamayo, 1949
—— and Alcorta, 1941
Taylor, 1956
Thevenot, 1672, 1696
Thomas, 1884
Thompson, J. E. S., 1934, 1941a, 1941b, 1950, 1966
Thorndike, 1929–30
Tompkins, 1942
Toro, 1923, 1928
—— and Fernández del Castillo, 1925
Torquemada, 1723
Torres Lanzas, 1900
Torre Villar, and Sandoval, 1967
Toscano, 1943, 1944, 1948
Toussaint, 1936, 1937, 1938, 1948, 1965
——, Gómez de Orozco, and Fernández, 1938
Tovar, 1860, 1944
Tozzer, 1921, 1941
Trimborn, 1959
Tudela, 1948a, 1956, 1960
Twenty centuries, 1940
Vaillant, MSa, MSb, 1939, 1940, 1941
Valadés, 1579
Valentini, 1880, 1893, 1895
Velasco, 1903
Velázquez Chávez, 1939
Veytia, 1836, 1848, 1907, 1944
Villacorta C., 1943b
—— and Villacorta, 1930, 1930–33
Villagra, 1933
Visino, 1864
Vivó, 1946

Wagner, 1944
Waldeck, MS
Warburton, 1738–41, 1744
Warren, D., 1971
Warren, J. B., 1971
Waterman, 1931
Wauchope, 1946
Weitlaner and Castro, 1953, 1954
Weitlaner de Johnson, 1966
West and Augelli, 1966
White and Bernal, 1960
Whorf, 1930
Wicke, 1966

Wieser, 1908
Willard, 1933
Wilson, 1859
Worm, 1655
Wroth, 1949

Xiu Chronicles, 1919

Yáñez, 1942

Zantwijk, 1967
Zavala, 1938, 1952, 1967
Zimmermann, 1954, 1963–65
Zoega, 1797
Zorita, 1909

24. Techialoyan Manuscripts and Paintings, with a Catalog

DONALD ROBERTSON

THE CODEX OF San Antonio Techialoyan (701),[1] now in the Museo Nacional de Antropología de México, became the basis of classification for a group of colonial Mexican manuscripts now known as "Techialoyan Codices." These manuscripts form such a homogeneous unit that no one has ever seriously questioned their grouping. Common elements include the use of native paper and Nahuatl in their texts, the nature of the written text and pictorial components, the style of handwriting, the artistic style, the purpose for which they were created, and the fact that they are all from villages in and around the State and Valley of Mexico.

Although individual items had appeared in the literature earlier (see catalog below), Federico Gómez de Orozco (1933) first treated the manuscripts as a single group. In his study of San Antonio Techialoyan (701) he discussed or mentioned the codices of Cuajimalpa (703), Metepec (704), Zempoala (705), and Ixtapalapa (706), a fragment in Paris (702), one belonging to Sr. Jorge Enciso (707), and two fragments belonging to Don José María de Agreda y Sánchez (735).

It was Robert H. Barlow, in his article "The Techialoyan Codices: Codex H" (Barlow, 1943e), who first set up a system of identifying them with letters of the alphabet. He catalogued the Techialoyan codices A (701) through H (708) and later in subsequent articles carried the series up to the letter P (714), omitting I and O. He also identified Techialoyans R (716) and T (718) and wrote three articles on Techialoyan Q, Codex García Granados (715).[2] Gómez de Orozco (1948) further enlarged the catalog to cover over 24 manuscripts but gave only 19 of them letters, carrying the catalog up to the letter V (720).[3]

[1] Numbers refer to the Catalog of Techialoyan Manuscripts and Paintings at the end of this article. The reader is referred to this catalog for all material pertaining to individual manuscripts.

[2] See catalog for references to the various Barlow articles in which the Techialoyan alphabetical catalog evolved.

[3] Gómez de Orozco (1948) included in addition a manuscript formerly in the Fischer and Phillipps collections, now John Rylands Library Mex. MS 2 (Article 23, no. 204), now known not to be one of the Techialoyan group.

253

In the catalog at the end of this article we list 48 Techialoyan items, using numbers but retaining the original order of the earlier alphabetical catalog. This has been done because of the confusions in the earlier listings and also because numbers are more flexible.[4]

The bibliographic history of individual manuscripts can be complex. Publication includes transcriptions of the Nahuatl text, translations into Spanish, and translations into English. Publication of the pictorial component shows an equal variety, some manuscripts being published by a lithographic process, some in line drawings or tracings, and some photographically, but seldom in color. Publication has ranged from complete editions (701 and 705)[5] to partial publication (715) to fragmentary publication (708). Many manuscripts remain unpublished, with only references to their names appearing in the literature (716).

The Techialoyan manuscripts are in one way the most mobile of all the colonial ethnohistorical sources. Although many are in public collections, enough examples have been in and out of private hands for over 200 years that they continually find their way into the rare book and art markets. Thus locations given in the catalog are more or less fixed for manuscripts in public museum, library, and archive collections, but the location of privately owned ones is potentially subject to change over the years.

Techialoyan manuscripts can be considered under several headings. Their material aspects include the paper they are written and drawn on, the ink and colors used. Their content includes the information conveyed in both the written Nahuatl text and the pictorial component with its written glosses.

THE MATERIAL OF THE MANUSCRIPTS was investigated by Lenz (1949, 1950), who tested four examples, and by Schwede (1916), who tested four others. They both agreed that it is native *amatl* paper made from the bark of the fig tree. The writer, who has examined them, can aver that the material is essentially the same for all.

This material is a coarse-grained, unsized, dark brown amatl paper with a consistency closer to cloth than to the more usual thin but hard lighter-colored amatl paper used in the 16th century. The paper of the Techialoyans is so thick and so poorly compounded that some individual sheets in the course of time have come apart by splitting down the center of the sheet.[6] Another characteristic of the paper is that it tends, because of its softness, to unravel at the edges. As a result many of the surviving pages have been trimmed or at least evened along the edges. In the process, the trimming was often unequal among pages in the same manuscript; this means that the dimensions given in our catalog are more or less approximations or even averages of the present dimensions. In many, if not most, cases both the original dimensions of both height and width were somewhat larger.

In most examples the ink used for the written component and the outlining of the pictorial forms has tended to fade, an indication that it is not the ink of native pre-Columbian or even early colonial manuscripts which still retains its dense blackness. A European ink subject to fading was used, and in some examples letters and even the outlines of pictorial forms were later gone over and reinforced. The colors vary from quite intense (García Granados, 715; Ocoyacac, 733) to extremely faded (Xona-

[4] References to the subsequent catalogs or listings by Alcina Franch (1955, 1956) and Carrera Stampa (1959, 1962–63, 1965) have been omitted from our catalog, as they are based on the earlier catalogs and make no new contributions.

[5] In the case of Zempoala (705) 56 years separated the publication of the pictorial component (Quaritch, 1890) and the text (McAfee, 1946a).

[6] The Codex of Ixtapalapa (706) is a major example where a piece of the non-Techialoyan Codex Huamantla (Article 23, no. 135) was used to repair f. 1 in such a way that both recto and verso sides of the leaf were pasted onto the Huamantla fragment to reinforce the split folio.

catlan, 723). In all cases color seems to have been originally either a dense watercolor or gouache.

THE FORMAT of the usual Techialoyan manuscript consists of sheets of amatl paper tied together in single or double folios or combinations thereof to form a book or *codex* (figs. 83–88). The longest example, Ocelotepec (708), has 27 folios. Often the front and back pages are obliterated by fading or past rough treatment. The *large panel* is another format used in two examples. One in Brooklyn (726, fig. 90) and another in Mexico (720) are both much larger than the pages of a "book" Techialoyan, but their layouts are similar.[7] The third type, of which there are also two examples, is in the form of a long strip or *tira*: Tizayuca (729) and Codex García Granados (715).[8]

The Techialoyan-style *murals* of the Cathedral of Cuernavaca (ex-convento Franciscano) (745) are aberrant and constitute a unique item (fig. 91). However, they surely belong to the Techialoyan corpus on the basis of their graphic style.[9]

THE CONTENT, written and pictorial, is so similar in all codex-type manuscripts that it is clear they follow a single consistent pattern of logic. In the complete or model Techialoyan codex, e.g., Xonacatlan (723), there is a written account in Nahuatl of a meeting in the *tecpan* or city hall of the homonymous village or pueblo. At this meeting the officials of the pueblo gathered to verify the boundaries of the pueblo and its dependencies; *barrios* and even individual fields or *parajes* are defined. In many examples the presence of the *hueytlatocatzin* or viceroy is asserted. Viceroy Antonio de Mendoza (1535–50) is sometimes obliquely referred to by the dates given, sometimes specifically named in the written text. Viceroy Luis de Velasco (1549/50–64) is named in two manuscripts (727 and 744).[10] Putative dates are given in the somewhat cumbersome Nahuatl way of counting rather

than in European numbers and range from 1504, the earliest (Tepanohuayan, 712), to 1596 (Tizayuca, 728), the latest. The meeting, attested to by the signatures of the major persons of the pueblo, pretends to establish boundaries *pro forma legis*. This written component of the manuscript is complemented by the pictorial component.

Pre-Hispanic history takes the form of standing full-length drawings of the ancestral conqueror of the village site and of subsequent native rulers wearing animal skins and carrying weapons (fig. 83). Pre-Hispanic genealogy is to be seen in the form of a genealogical tree or cactus with the heads of descendants of the earlier ancestral ruler displayed in its branches; the genealogical plant rises from the loins or the navel region of the dead ancestor (fig. 84).

Colonial history can include a genealogy (Mimiahuapan, 711, and Coacalco, 743) but appears primarily in pictures of the Spanish military *entrada* showing Spanish soldiers clad in armor (fig. 85) and the Spanish religious *entrada* of monks. Some manuscripts show the cult image of the saint of the pueblo being borne on a trestle carried by the natives (fig. 86). Common is the bust-length figure of an important person under a half-round arched frame. Spanish civil government can be represented by the arms of Spain (fig. 87) or the tecpan (fig. 88), but more often it appears in the form of officials of the village receiving their staves of office and, in subsequent illustrations, bearing them as symbols of the rights conferred upon them by the viceroy (fig. 86).

Description of the village and its lands makes up the largest number of pages in the complete manuscripts and is typically shown by glossed illustrations. These in-

[7] See below under "Graphic style."
[8] For an extended discussion of these formats, see Robertson, 1959, passim.
[9] See below, pp. 262.
[10] For a historical account of the viceroys of New Spain, see Rubio Mañé, 1955.

clude the tecpan (fig. 88), the church (fig. 86), and houses of the main village and of its dependencies. Individual fields appear with their crops, mainly maize, maguey, and *nopal* (cactus). *Monte* (woodlands in the context of these manuscripts) appears as well as claims to fishing and water rights. In these pictorial sections Nahuatl explanations in the glosses commonly accompany the illustrations to define the barrios and village lands.[11]

It can be noted that the order of the contents at present varies from manuscript to manuscript. Essentially the section devoted to the village and its lands is a single unit which can follow or precede the textual units. In cases where an orderly sequence now seems to be disturbed, this may be the result of an incorrect retying of folios which became separated in time.[12]

THE PURPOSE of the Techialoyan codices emerges from the pattern of content in the complete or ideal Techialoyan. It consists of the historical preamble followed by the heart of the matter—pictorial and written definitions and claims to landholdings. Since the manuscripts were prepared for individual villages, they became what have been called "Village Land Books" and perhaps even later substitutions for otherwise missing pre-Columbian and earlier colonial documents to substantiate these village land claims. The primary purpose is reinforced in the manner of early colonial land-claims documents by the historical preamble in which the justification for the claim is made.[13]

Since the codices seem to have been made to be used as legal documents, they were written in Nahuatl, the major Indian language recognized by the viceregal courts, even though the language spoken in certain of the villages was Otomi or Matlatzinca.[14] For examples of manuscripts actually associated with other land-claims documents, see Cuajimalpa (703), Tizayuca (728, 729), Coyoacan (732), Tezcalucan and Chichi-

caspa (744), and, by implication, Ocelotepec (708).

THE LOCATION of the homonymous associated village is often difficult to determine even in more or less complete codices. The problem is compounded by the fact that some of the villages no longer exist. Barlow (1947g) studied Tepanohuayan (712), a village near Tenayuca, which has since vanished. It is especially ironic that San Antonio Techialoyan (701), which lent its name to the group, is identified with a now lost village in the State of Mexico south of Toluca. "Techialoyan" in Nahuatl means "inn" (Spanish, *mesón*). The name is preserved in its Spanish form by the Hacienda del Mesón near San Antonio la Isla.[15]

The location of the village to be associated with each manuscript is much more a matter of conjecture in the case of fragments, the *membra disjecta* of formerly complete manuscripts, which constitute a large number of the items in the Catalog. With the historical preamble text missing the names of barrios are usually not adequate for locating the main pueblo. The names we have used in the Catalog are essentially for purposes of identification and are not always the village names (e.g., Xocotla, 730). In the case of the fragmental Codex of Zempoala (705), however, enough barrios are named to locate the origin of the manuscript in Hidalgo, even though it has only the glossed pictorial content (McAfee, 1946a).[16]

---

[11] Dr. Joaquín Galarza of the Musée de l'Homme, Paris, is currently studying these illustrations in connection with his investigations of colonial Mexican agriculture. See also Schmeider, 1930.

[12] See note 16.

[13] Convenient treatments for the study of land claims in this context include: W. Orozco, 1895; Zavala, 1935; Chevalier, 1963; Gibson, 1964a.

[14] See Robertson, 1960, pp. 110–111, and Weitlaner, 1939, linguistic map facing p. 328.

[15] Basurto, 1901, is a major source for the geography of the archbishopric of Mexico.

[16] Eight fragments of Techialoyan codices have been linked in the catalog to reconstitute in whole or in part three manuscripts divided in the course

In the main all Techialoyan documents are associated with villages in the State and Valley of Mexico.[17] Identified villages are shown in figure 92, to which Table 1 is the key, providing an alphabetical listing of the documents in the catalog with data on the location of identified villages.

THE STYLE of the manuscripts can be considered under two aspects: the written and the graphic components. In each case the style constitutes a defining characteristic of the members of the group and provides information on the vexing question, discussed below, of the time when they were made.

The prose style until now has received little or no consideration. Notes and comments accompanying transcriptions and translations, even recent ones of Byron McAfee, tend to ignore the question of Nahuatl prose style.[18] Although no sustained and consistent attention has been paid to this aspect of the texts in the literature, some provisional statements can be made. The texts are strikingly similar in their common and limited vocabulary. The literary style is quite simple when compared with the more polished and classic 16th-century Nahuatl of Sahagún and his informants. For instance, where Sahagún uses long compound words in complex sentences and literary patterns, the Techialoyan texts use short words and short sentences.

Handwriting similarities parallel the textual similarities of vocabulary and sentence structure. The lowercase unlinked letters used in the manuscripts are written in a rather large, almost childish hand. There are, however, individual variations from manuscript to manuscript suggesting more than one scribe. Key letters for studying these variations seem to be *x, y, p, q, h, tz,* and *ç.*[19]

The graphic style of the drawings has been discussed in the literature (Robertson, 1959, chap. 11; 1960). These earlier discussions, however, were based on a limited

---

of time: 718-714-722, the Codex of Tepotzotlan (Robertson, 1960): 712-709, the Codex of Tepanohuavan; and 702-717-735, the Codex of San Pablo Huyxoapan. Future studies of the fragments might enable us to make more such linkages through recurring names of persons and places, always taking into account that the fragments must be approximately the same size and use congruent handwriting, page formats, etc. A larger study could also detail relations among complete manuscripts by internal cross references of place names common to more than one manuscript; for instance, Xonacatlan is mentioned so often in the Codex of Ocelotepec (708) that it was called Xonacatlan in Boturini's inventory (see catalog).

[17] The main maps used in this study are: Estado de México, Dirección de Comunicaciones y Obras Publicas, n.d., and Eliseo Villegas de San Martín, Road Map of the Valley of Mexico, Comisión Nacional de Turismo, México, D.F., n.d. Other valuable aids for locating the Techialoyan codices include: Basurto, 1901; Memoria, 1893; Sánchez Colín, 1951; Hernández Rodríguez, 1952; Olaguíbel, 1957; Colín, 1963–64, 1966; Gibson, 1964a; and Robelo, Olaguíbel, and Peñafiel, 1966. Zantwijk, 1969, containing 10 published maps of the lands of Tlacopan, covers over half the area from which the Techialoyan codices come.

[18] Byron McAfee, a North American *nahuatlato* living in Mexico City, worked independently. Under the urging of Barlow some of his translations were published in *Tlalocan* (Zempoala, 705; Acatitlan, 709). His transcription and translation of Tepotzotlan (722) was published in Robertson, 1960. Other translations and transcriptions remained in typescript at his death. Their present location is often unknown, but those in McAfee's library, which I know existed in the summer of 1958, are listed in the catalog. McAfee's interest in the manuscripts was in their written rather than their pictorial content; he considered them more as linguistic documents than as literary or historical sources. The first published translation of a Techialoyan text was of San Antonio Techialoyan (701) in 1893 by Faustino Galicia Chimalpopoca, the translator of the Archivo General de la Nación. Another translator of this archive was Francisco Rosales who made mid-19th-century transcriptions and translations, as well as watercolor copies, of Cuajimalpa (703), Tizayuca (728, 729), and Coyoacan (732). Translations have also been made by Wigberto Jiménez Moreno (Tepexoxouhcan and Cuaxochco, 721). Joaquín Galarza is now working on a revision of McAfee's translation of Xonacatlan (723) and for the first time doing certain pages not available to McAfee.

[19] An extended study of this aspect of the texts has been made for the author by James Ramsey, a research assistant supported by the Middle American Research Institute of Tulane University; it will be used for a projected publication of the Tulane Techialoyan Codex of Xonacatlan (723).

TABLE 1–TECHIALOYANS: LISTING AND LOCALIZATIONS

Document	Catalog Number	Location, 1950	Municipio or Delegación	State	Map*
Acatitlan, Santa Cecelia (J)	709	Santa Cecilia Acatitlan	Tlalnepantla	Mexico	L/14-68
Acayuca, San Francisco	734	Acayuca	Zapotlan de Juarez	Hidalgo	K/14-72
Ahuaquilpan, S. Pedro, *see* Huaquilpan	746				
Atlapolco, S. Pedro (panel)	726	S. Pedro Atlapulco	Ocoyoacac	Mexico	M/14-61
Atlinayan, S. Miguel, *see* Atlapolco, S. Pedro	726				
Axoloapan Xoloctlan	737	Santa Maria Ajoloapan & S. Lucas Xoloc	Tecamac	Mexico	L/14-86
Azcapotzalco, *see* Huyxoapan, Fragment 3	735				
Azcapotzalco, Santa Cruz, *see* Huyxoapan, Fragment 2	717				
Calacohuayan, Santa Maria (K)	710	Santa Maria Calacohuayan	Zaragoza	Mexico	L/14-69
Calpulalpan, San Simon	725	Calpulalpan	Calpulalpan	Tlaxcala	L/15-1
Cempoala (E), *see* Zempoala	705				
Chalco, Atenco, Santiago (R)	716	Chalco	Chalco	Mexico	L/14-108
Chichicaspa, Sta. Maria Magdalena, *see* Tezcalucan	744				
Coacalco	743	Coacalco	Coacalco	Mexico	L/14-88
Cohuacalco, *see* Coacalco	743				
Coyoacan	732	Coyoacan & S. Nicolas Totolapan	Coyoacan & Magdalena Contreras	D.F. D.F.	L/14-V L/14-VIII
Coyoacan, *see* Tetelpan	713				
Coyonacazco, *see* Coyotepec Coyonacazco	727				
Coyotepec	747	Unlocated			
Coyotepec, San Cristobal (panel) (V)	720	San Cristobal Coyotepec(?)	Coyotepec	Mexico	L/14-75
Coyotepec Coyonacazco	727	Unlocated			

* Map coordinates and municipio number in key to state maps in Article 1, appendix.

Table 1—(Continued)

Document	Catalog Number	Location, 1950	Municipio or Delegación	State	Map
Cuajimalpa, San Pedro (C)	703	San Pedro Cuajimalpa	Cuajimalpa	D.F.	L/14-VII
Cuaxochco, San Miguel, see Tepexoxouhcan	721				
Cuernavaca Cathedral (murals)	745	Cuernavaca	Cuerna Vaca	Morelos	M/14-2
Cuitlahuac, see Tlahuac	736				
García Granados (tira) (Q)	715	Azcapotzalco(?)	Azcapotzalco	D.F.	L/14-I
Hemenway, see Huixquilucan	724				
Huaquilpan, San Pedro, & San Martin	746	San Pedro Ahuaquilpan	Zapotlan de Juarez	Hidalgo	K/14-72
Huehuetoca, pueblo near	719	Huixquilucan	Huehuetoca	Mexico	K/14-74
Huixquilucan, San Antonio	724		same	Mexico	L/14-63
Huyxoapan, San Pablo (B), Fragment 1	702	Near Azcapotzalco(?)	Azcapotzalco	D.F.	L/14-I
Huyxoapan, San Pablo (S), Fragment 2	717	Near Azcapotzalco(?)	Azcapotzalco	D.F.	L/14-I
Huyxoapan, San Pablo, Fragment 3	735	Near Azcapotzalco(?)	Azcapotzalco	D.F.	L/14-I
Ixtapalapa (F)	706	Ixtapalapa	same	D.F.	L/14-VI
Kaska, see Tizayuca	728				
Matlatzinca, see Tenancingo, 741; Teotla, 739; Zepayahutla	740				
Mazatepec, see Tetelpan	713				
Metepec (D)	704	Metepec(?)	Metepec	Mexico	M/13-42
Mimiahuapan, San Miguel (L)	711	San Miguel Mimiapan	Xonacatlan	Mexico	L/14-64
Ocelotepec, Santa Maria (H)	708	Santa Maria Zolotepec	Xonacatlan	Mexico	L/14-64
Ocoyacac, San Martin	733	Ocoyoacac	same	Mexico	L/14-61
Oztoyaotitlan	738	Unlocated			
Pingret, see Tepotzotlan	714				
Seler's Landbook, see Ocoyacac	733				
Sutro, see Calacohuayan	710				
Techialoyan, San Antonio (A)	701	Hacienda del Meson	San Antonio la Isla	Mexico	M/13-46
Tenancingo	741	Tenancingo	Tenancingo	Mexico	M/13-49
Teotla	739	Teotla	Tenancingo	Mexico	M/13-49

TABLE 1–(Continued)

Document	Catalog Number	Location, 1950	Municipio or Delegación	State	Map
Tepanohuayan, San Bartolome (M)	712	Disappeared; was near Tenayuca	Tlalnepantla	Mexico	L/14-68
Tepexoxouhcan, San Miguel, & San Miguel Cuaxochco (W)	721	San Francisco Tepexoxuca	Tenango del Valle	Mexico	M/13-48
Tepexoyucan, Santa Maria	731	Santa Maria Asuncion Tepesoyuca	Ocoyoacac	Mexico	M/14-61
Tepotzotlan, Fragment 1 (T)	718	Tepotzotlan	Tepotzotlan	Mexico	L/14-73
Tepotzotlan, Fragment 2 (P)	714	Tepotzotlan	Tepotzotlan	Mexico	L/14-73
Tepotzotlan, Fragment 3 (X)	722	Tepotzotlan	Tepotzotlan	Mexico	L/14-73
Tetelpan, Santa Maria (N)	713	Tetelpan	Coyoacan	D.F.	L/14-V
Tezcalucan, San Cristobal, & Santa Maria Magdalena Chichicaspa	744	San Cristobal Texcaluca & Magdalena Chichicaspa	Huixquilucan	Mexico	L/14-63
Tizayuca, San Salvador (codex)	728	San Salvador Tizayuca	Tizayuca	Hidalgo	K/14-70
Tizayuca, San Salvador (map)	729	San Salvador Tizayuca	Tizayuca	Hidalgo	K/14-70
Tlahuac, San Pedro	736	Tlahuac	Tlahuac	D.F.	M/14-XI
Toluca, Santa Maria, see Ocelotepec	708				
Totolapan, San Nicolas, see Coyoacan	732				
Unidentified manuscript	748	Unlocated			
Unidentified pueblo	742	Unlocated			
Unidentifiable pueblo (G)	707	Unlocated			
Xocotla, San Nicolas, & San Agustin	730	Unlocated			
Xoloctlan, see Axoloapan	737				
Xonacatlan, San Francisco	723	San Francisco Xonacatlan	Xonacatlan	Mexico	L/14-64
Zempoala (E)	705	Zempoala	Zempoala	Hidalgo	K/15-66
Zepayahutla	740	Zepayautla	Tenancingo	Mexico	M/13-49

number of contexts and examples. Here we are more concerned with summarizing the characteristics of the Techialoyan group as a whole.

The illustrated pages of the Techialoyan codices are composed either as single scenes (single-level; figs. 83–85, 87, 88) or as two scenes, one above the other (double-level; fig. 86). The major exceptions are the two large panels and the two tiras or long strips. In the large panels, Atlapolco (726, fig. 90) and Coyotepec (720), the scenes are more complex than in the codex pages in their larger number of figures and in their interrelationships. They show a friar seated at a table as the focus of a design depicting numbers of Indians on roads converging toward this center. In this composition a map is suggested as much as a landscape. The two tira compositions are distinct from all others. One, Tizayuca (729), is a long narrow map; the other is a complex land-oriented genealogy in the form of a cactus, Codex García Granados (715).

Space is represented in two main ways. One is landscape where three-dimensionality is strikingly shown. Fields, persons, and houses may appear in the foreground, and mountains rise as a backdrop. The forms are distributed with assurance in a three-dimensional space. The other manner of representing space, although still somewhat related to landscape, is closer to the cartographer's view of the world. Scenes with roads and streams of water are not views of nature but the cartographer's abstract patterns. The Codex of Acayuca in Vienna (734), in which the scene on each folio suggests part of a map, is one example. Interestingly enough, the map accompanying the Tizayuca codex (729) seems to combine these two spatial conventions.

The closeness of style among the manuscripts is such that statements on the quality and use of line, color, human figures, and other forms admit of almost no exceptions.[20] Line is invariably heavy, wide in proportion to its length and in proportion to the figure it defines. It is more broken, however, than the pre-Columbian norm would admit, and it does imply the three-dimensionality of the figure it defines. It is not, in other words, pre-Columbian "frame line" but is closer to the European "contour line." This is especially true in cases where it outlines human figures.

The palette includes blue, green, yellow, orange, red, white, gray, and black; even gold is used on García Granados (715). Color is used to suggest the shading in folds or drapery (figs. 86, 90), but it is not used to suggest shadows under standing figures, nor is it used consistently to indicate shadows on buildings.

The treatment of the human form in the group is remarkably varied. Common to all, however, is the large size in proportion to the pages of the codex (fig. 83). Male and female figures stand, sit, kneel, and appear in three-quarter view (figs. 86, 90). Men in the preconquest history sections wear loincloths or skin robes with fur (fig. 83); women wear skin robes or skirts. This is in sharp contrast with the white trousers, shirts, and garments suggesting the classic tunic worn by men in the colonial sections and the *huipil*-like dress of the women (figs. 86, 90). Men are heavily bearded. They carry a variety of weapons and tools: in the pre-Hispanic sections, *macanas* (native maces), spears, shields (fig. 83), and bows and arrows with quivers; in the colonial sections, spades, staves of office (fig. 86), paddles, saws, fishing poles, and nets.

The human figure is conceived of and thus shown as a unified whole with head, body, and limbs related in a convincing fashion in terms of human anatomy. There is no suggestion of the unitary or additive figure of the pre-Hispanic and early colonial manuscript painter or sculptor. Figural pro-

[20] See Robertson, 1959, passim, for more extended discussion of early colonial manuscript style; see also "The Pinturas (Maps) of the *Relaciones Geográficas*, with a Catalog" Article 6.

portions, however, are reminiscent of pre-Columbian norms: large heads top stocky bodies with relatively short limbs. Quite different from the native tradition is the ease with which the figures seem to sit, to stand, to hold objects, and the ease with which the artist is able to show the three-quarter view, to endow the figures with a three-dimensional plasticity through pose, overlapping, line, and shading (fig. 90).

Architectural forms appear in large numbers. Houses are drawn showing two adjacent walls, but the absence of the vanishing points of traditional European perspective and the lack of consistent patterns of light and shade deprive them of the ability to convey the impression of three-dimensional mass. The *atrios* of churches, even more than the buildings themselves, suggest three-dimensionality.

The tecpan or city hall is the most important and interesting building in the manuscript. Two main types emerge: one in the native tradition, with lintels supported by clearly delineated posts and the colonial one- or two-story arcaded tecpan (see Cuajimalpa, 703; Xonocatlan, 723 [fig. 88]; Tepotzotlan, 718-714-722). More clearly European because of its use of columns and arches, this second type suggests the *cabildo* or *ayuntamiento* buildings common to colonial cities and towns or even specifically the Tecpan of Indian Santiago Tlatelolco.[21]

Geographic elements in the manuscripts are commonly shown as elements of landscape rather than as the signs or "glyphs" of the native tradition. There are examples where the sign for Culhuacan, a leaning or bent hill, is given, but the glossed place name is not Culhuacan (see Cuajimalpa, 703; Xonocatlan, 723). The absence of a consistent system and use of place signs is remarkable and paralleled by the relative scarcity of name signs to identify persons. A series of pages showing fields drawn as long narrow rectangles, some in a vertical, others in a horizontal, pattern, is the main exception; in

these passages name signs do appear sometimes (Tepotzotlan, 718-714-722; Coacalco, 743) but only in the framework of a map or plan (fig. 89).

The main plants shown in the manuscripts are magueys, cactus, the trees of the monte or woodlands belonging to the pueblo, and the main staple food crop, maize. The last is planted either in rows showing stems and leaves or as a series of slightly elongated *taches* more in the manner of a plan than a view of a field.

Water and roads which appear as parallel lines bounding areas of color are in the form of cartographic, not landscape, elements. Interestingly enough, footprints to identify the road and the native convention for water are, with few exceptions, both lacking.[22]

An important addition to the corpus of Techialoyan paintings was made in 1959 when the monumental murals on the walls of the former Franciscan monastery, now the Cathedral of Cuernavaca, were uncovered (745, fig. 91). They depict the martyrdom of San Felipe de Jesús and his companions in Japan in 1597. Until now their Techialoyan quality has not been recognized in print (Toussaint, 1965); the main publication would associate them with a Japanese artist (Islas García, 1967). The remaining paintings occupy large parts of the two side walls of the nave.

Similarity of forms, human, architectural, and geographical, to the Techialoyan manuscript paintings is obvious. The differences are significant but easily explained. Certain differences are due to the diverse subject matter. In addition, the manuscript painter, working with soft amatl paper and at a small scale, had to be more general and less detailed in his delineation of forms than the

[21] Fernández, 1939, is a publication of the Códice del Tecpan (Article 23, no. 303), a 16th-century manuscript with an illustration of the building.

[22] Examples showing these footprints include Ixtapalapa (706), Huyxoapan (702-717-735), Tepexoxouhcan and Cuaxochco (721), and Coyotepec Coyonacazco (727).

muralist working at a larger scale on a good firm and hard surface. We can note, however, that even with the large surfaces, over 8 m. in height and 30 m. in length, the scenes of the martyrdom, the boats paddled over water, and even buildings, all indicate an artist more at ease working at a small scale than one used to painting large-scale murals. In other words, the world of forms in Cuernavaca is too large for a Techialoyan manuscript painting but at the same time too small to be seen properly from the distance the murals themselves require.

THE DATE OF THE TECHIALOYAN MANUSCRIPTS was considered by Barlow to be the date recorded in the texts. An undated manuscript was assumed to come from the 16th century, since dates given in other texts were all 16th century. Gómez de Orozco (1933, 1948) made the same assumption but went even further to suggest they were painted in the 16th-century Franciscan school for Indians at San Jose de los Naturales under the impetus of Fray Padre de Gante.[23]

More recent investigations (Robertson, 1959, chap. 11; 1960) have revised these earlier dates, based on anachronisms of content and style. Demonstrable anachronisms include dates in text earlier than the arrival of Viceroy Mendoza in New Spain in 1535.[24] The two main material aspects of the manuscripts, the paper and the ink, also lead us to discard the dates in text as being accurate dates for the manuscripts. The paper, described above, is in contrast with harder, thinner, and lighter-colored 16th-century examples. The ink is in sharp contrast with the ink of early colonial native-style pictorial documents which diagnostically does not show fading except in written glosses using European ink, which is now turned brown and faded with time. The letters of the texts and glosses are also non-16th century. We have already noted the greater simplicity and limited vocabulary of the literary style of the texts.

It is in the graphic style of the paintings, however, that their non-16th-century date becomes most apparent. Line is heavier and more dynamic in the definition of three-dimensional forms. Color is used to create patterns of light and shade, and the delineation of three-dimensional space is more assured than in the authentically 16th-century documents. The variety of pose and position of the human figure with three-quarter views, overlapping, and the ability of hands to hold and grasp, figures to sit and lean, are all changed from their 16th-century versions by more native-oriented artists. Costume suggests 18th-century neo-classicism; bearded men suggest mestizos more than Indians. Again, the integration of buildings, natural phenomena, people, plants, and animals into landscape visions of the world, however limited the individual scene may be, considered with the strange paucity of personal and geographic name signs or "glyphs," all reinforce our rejection of the early date.[25]

The demonstration through a listing of anachronisms that the Techialoyan paintings are not from the early colonial period then leaves open the question of when they were painted. A determination of the probable date can proceed from the starting point of their purpose: In what period of the history of the colony would such documents have been most needed by Indian pueblos? It can continue from the internal evidence of content and the history of the manuscripts.

During the period from the early 17th century to the first half of the 18th century pressure on Indian agricultural lands from

[23] It is to be noted that neither Barlow nor Gómez de Orozco was acquainted with Tizayuca (728, 729), for instance, dated as late as 1596.

[24] Manuscripts anachronistically citing Viceroy Mendoza and their dates include: 1528, Xonacatlan (723); 1532, Huixquilucan (724); 1534, San Antonio Techialoyan (701), Cuajimalpa (703), Tepotzotlan (718-714-722), and Tepexoyucan (731). One manuscript even bears a date of 1504 (Tepanohuayan, 712), before the arrival of the Spaniards and the introduction of European writing.

[25] Galarza is currently studying the Techialoyan Nahuatl place names and how they are represented graphically.

neighboring haciendas was a real and special peril to villages, especially those with no acceptable documents proving landownership. This was also the time in the colonial period when the Crown attempted to regularize ownership of village lands, as distinct from Crown lands (*tierras baldías*) by the legal expedient of *composición*.[26] Reexamination of land titles and revalidation through composición generally took place in 1631, 1643, 1674, 1716, 1754. This process is recorded in volume 2, Document 6 (dated 1710), of the Codex Kaska now associated with Tizayuca (728). An archival document discovered and described by Herbert Harvey (1966a) clearly describes a Techialoyan manuscript used in a land dispute in 1703 which, it might be noted, was burned by royal officials who said it was a forgery (Tezcalucan and Chichicaspa, 744).

The social stimulus thus was outside pressure on Indian landholdings, and the native response was the Techialoyan codices. Not forgeries in the looser sense, they seem to have been fairly accurate statements. They were thus probably compiled from diverse sources—written and possibly pre-Columbian or early colonial pictorial documents—and oral traditions. Schmeider (1930) has demonstrated the accuracy in this century at least of land nomenclature in the Techialoyan Codex of Cuajimalpa (703). We suggest that field work in other villages would reveal similar accuracy.

The genealogical content of the Codex García Granados (715), according to Barlow, includes persons living as much as six generations after the Conquest.[27] He also said it was made as late as a century and a half after the Codex of Zempoala (705), which he dated ca. 1530,[28] thus placing García Granados as late as 1680. In a letter of November 24, 1946, to George Kubler, Barlow said, "It may be that some of the group are far later than 1530; though the 'Q' of García Granados must be as late as 1700, the style is still recognizable." Barlow did not seem to realize that by placing this manu-

script so late in time, he jeopardized his assumption of the validity of the early dates written in the codices themselves.

The history of the manuscripts provides other clues to their dates. We know, for instance, that there were three and possibly four in the Boturini collection: Ixtapalapa (706), Ocelotepec (708), Tepotzotlan (718-714-722), and Huyxoapan (702-717-735 [?]). They must have been made before 1743, when Boturini was imprisoned and, we can assume, ceased his manuscript-collecting activities (see Article 29, The Boturini Collection).

These data would indicate that the manuscripts were made in a period from ca. 1700 to before 1743. This would mean they were all created within a generation and a half or a single very long generation in the early 18th century.[29]

Since we date the manuscripts between ca. 1700 and 1743, we can attribute the date of the murals of the Cathedral of Cuernavaca (745) within this same period, especially in view of the fact that Vetancurt's description of the building as late as 1697 fails to mention them.

THE IMPORTANCE OF THE TECHIALOYAN GROUP lies in the fact that they preserve for the student of later colonial Indian life a great mass of potential information. They embody what late 17th- or early 18th-century Indians thought about their own colonial past and what they knew about their land tenure.[30] Indirectly, the manuscripts give us pictorial information on agricultural and other technologies for this period. Linguistically they can be used with assurance in

[26] See note 13 for useful sources for the study of landownership in this period, and also McBride, 1923, pp. 56–57.
[27] Barlow, 1945b, pp. 467–468.
[28] Barlow, 1946d, p. 434, note 16.
[29] For a more detailed discussion or arguments regarding the dating of these manuscripts, see Robertson, 1960. Carrillo y Gariel, 1952, discusses a later school of painting in the Toluca area, and from it we can deduce a continuing of artistic activities in this region.
[30] Robertson, 1971.

studies of later rather than earlier Nahuatl. We assume a certain legitimacy in their historical content, although this remains to be tested. We now know they represent a provincial or even folk variation on late baroque themes in the history of Mexican colonial painting. From the point of view of acculturation they show what their maker knew of his remote past and how much knowledge of this past had been eroded through as many as 200 years. Once the Techialoyan manuscripts are more widely understood and individual scholars begin to refer to them, they will become properly known as a large reservoir of information on late colonial Mexico. One can hope this will lead to adequate scholarly publication of this important corpus.

CATALOG OF TECHIALOYAN MANUSCRIPTS AND PAINTINGS

Donald Robertson and Martha Barton Robertson

Where this catalog is in conflict with or leaves out information found in earlier writers, it is because its present authors consider the earlier writer to be superfluous, superseded, or in error. We have translated all unpublished dates as written in Nahuatl and take full responsibility for their accuracy, especially when they contradict published dates (cf. Techialoyan 724). The catalog is based on an almost complete corpus of photographs, microfilms, kodachromes, photostats, xerox, and "copyflow" in the Robertson collection. This corpus will in due course be deposited in Tulane University's Latin American Library; the kodachromes will be added to the Newcomb College art department's slide collection.

The American Council of Learned Societies, the Social Science Research Council, the Guggenheim Foundation, and the Council on Research, Center for Latin American Studies, and the Middle American Research Institute at Tulane University have supported research for this project for over a decade.

We wish to express particular thanks for help in preparing this catalog: to Joaquín Galarza, mainly in problems of paleography and transcription of place names in most of the unpublished manuscripts; to John B. Glass, for bibliography, particularly sales catalogs; to Howard F. Cline, for patience, encouragement, and additional data on locations and references to modern communities; and to George A. Kubler, who put his Techialoyan file at our disposal in 1959. Among officials, librarians, and staffs of institutions holding Techialoyan manuscripts special mention is due Cottie A. Burland, Zita B. de Canessi, Eulalia Guzmán, Gerdt Kutscher, Marjorie E. LeDoux, Clara Penney, Antonio Pompa y Pompa, Edith B. Ricketson, John Barr Tompkins, Robert Wauchope, and Lawrence Wroth. Others who have given help are: Ulf Bankmann, Alfonso Caso, John Galvin, Charles Gibson, Herbert R. Harvey, Doris Heyden, Wigberto Jiménez Moreno, Fernando Horcasitas, Henry B. Nicholson, Ross Parmenter, Fred and Marjorie S. Zengel, and his Excellency Sergio Mendez Arceo, Obispo de Cuernavaca.

KEY:

700. MAIN PUEBLO according to text or *PRINCIPAL BARRIO* if a glossed fragment. (Synonyms) (Letter, if any).

    Repository or collection, city, catalog number.

Physical description: amatl paper unless otherwise indicated, dimensions (height by width), format.

Publication data: text transcription, translation or illustrations (black and white photographs unless otherwise indicated). Partial publication is indicated by numbers of published folios; otherwise publication is complete.

Copy: repository, physical description, publication data. McAfee: refers to D. Robertson's notes of conversations with Byron McAfee, Mexico, D.F., summer 1958 (included to record otherwise unpublished information).

Bibliography: studies of the document.

References: in the literature and catalogs (repository and general catalogs are not included nor are brief and general references).

Ex-coll: past owners (sales of their collections).

Comment: number of folios of text as opposed to glossed illustrations; date given in the MS and reference to viceroy when present in text.

Mod: community, 1950. Map coordinates (fig. 1); municipio number (see Article 1, appendix).

701. TECHIALOYAN, SAN ANTONIO (A).
MNA, 35-65.

20 folios, 26 × 21 cm. (first and last folio in poor condition). Codex, single-level, accompanied by Chimalpopoca transc. (of ff. 2r–10r) and Sp. transl. (whole MS) of 1856.

Pub: Memoria, 1893, pp 567–68 (from 1871 copy of Chimalpopoca Sp. transl. of 1856, ff. 8v bottom [signatures] to end of MS); reprinted by Olaguíbel, 1894, pp. 175–76. Gómez de Orozco, 1933, 37 plates (nonphotographic) of whole MS except ff. 1r, 1v, and 20v (too damaged); Chimalpopoca transc. on pp. 321–22 and Sp. transl. on pp. 322–24; Gómez de Orozco transc. of ff. 2r–8v on pp. 325–27. Gómez de Orozco, 1948, pp. 57, 61–62, 65, pls. 1–3, 7, 9–11 (nonphotographic). Glass, 1964, pp. 118, 199, 202, 208, pl. 68 (of f. 10r).

Copies: MNA/BNA, A. Villagra copy (37 folios, copy on one side only, 32.5 × 24.8 cm.) bound with explanatory notice by

Gómez de Orozco. (COD F1219 T255s). § MNA/AH, Colección Antigua no. 274 (AAMC), no. 26, transc. and Sp. transl. by F. Galicia Chimalpopoca, 1856. § McAfee: transc. and Eng. transl. § See also above.

Bibliog: Robertson, 1959, p. 190; 1960, pp. 112–13.

Refs: Catálogo, 1911, p. 44 (MNA/BNA); Barlow, 1943e, p. 161; Lenz, 1949, p. 163.

Ex-coll: Pueblo of Calimaya in 1856 (MNA/AH, Colección Antigua, no. 274 [AAMC], no. 26).

Comment: First 8 folios are text; date of 1534 given, and Viceroy Antonio de Mendoza is mentioned.

Mod: Disappeared. Location may be present Hacienda del Mesón (Mesón=Techialoyan=Inn) near San Antonio la Isla, ex-district of Tenango, M. San Antonio la Isla, Mexico. M/13-46.

702. HUYXOAPAN, SAN PABLO (B).
BNP, MS Mex. 389 (Ancien no. 6).

2 folios, 45 × 22.5 cm. Codex, text only (poor condition).

Unpublished.

Refs: J. F. Ramírez, 1855, p. 20, no. 6; Gómez de Orozco, 1933, p. 328; 1948, p. 65; Barlow, 1943e, p. 161; Núñez y Domínguez, 1947a, p. 359.

Comment: Text fragment of an incomplete manuscript composed of Techialoyans 702-717-735, San Pablo Huyxoapan; related on the basis of contents, handwriting, dimensions, and tear patterns. Mentions Ixtlahuacan and Azcapotzalco. Includes date of 1545 and page of signatures.

Mod: Near Azcapotzalco, D.F.(?). L/14-I.

703. CUAJIMALPA, SAN PEDRO (C).
AGN-T, vol. 3684, exp. 11 (or exp. 2).

26 folios (first and last folios in poor condition). Codex, single-level, bound with 1865 transc., Sp. transl., and commentary by Francisco Rosales.

Pub: Schmieder, 1930, pp. 30–31, 81 (fig. 7 of f. 20v), 82–83 (Eng. transl. of Rosales

Sp. transl. of text pages only), 168–77 (plates of 42–46 of ff. 1r, 3r, 3v, 8v, and 17r with transc. and Eng. transl.) (nonphotographic). Gómez de Orozco, 1933, p. 328 and facing plate (nonphotographic); 1948, pp. 62, 65, pl. 6. A. Fernández del Castillo, 1952 (Rosales 1865 transc. and Sp. transl. of whole MS and commentary; photographic ed. of 38 pages of illustrations).

Copy: BNP, MS Mex. 419, Doc. 3 (Sp. transl., illus., and transc. of 1865). § McAfee: transl. § See also above.

Refs: Barlow, 1943e, p. 161; Robertson, 1960, pp. 114, 121.

Ex-coll: Pueblo of San Pedro Cuajimalpa, D.F., until 1865.

Comment: Last 6 folios are text pages; date of 1534 is given, and Viceroy Antonio de Mendoza is mentioned. This codex was used as evidence of land tenure. With it in AGN-T are documents from 1538, 1759, 1799, and 1865, among others.

Mod: San Pedro, Del. Cuajimalpa, D.F. L/14-VII.

704. *METEPEC* (D).

Señor Esteban de Antuñano Collection, Puebla (in 1933). Present whereabouts unknown.

Some fragments, physical description unknown.

Unpublished.

Refs: Gómez de Orozco, 1933, p. 328; 1948, p. 65.

Mod: Metepec, Mexico. M/13-42.

705. *ZEMPOALA* (E).

Newberry Library, Chicago, Edward E. Ayer Collection, no. 1472.

16 folios, 27.5 × 22.5 cm. Codex. single-level, accompanied by one-page typescript by E. Seler (general description).

Pub: Quaritch, 1890 (colored lithographic ed. of whole MS). Gómez de Orozco, 1933, pp. 312, 329–30, plate facing p. 329 (f. 15r, nonphotographic). Ceballos Novelo, 1935, p. 8, pl. 5 (f. 2v after Quaritch, 1890). Reed, 1938 (one plate after Quaritch, 1890). Gómez de Orozco, 1948, pp. 62, 65–66, pl. 8 (after Gómez de Orozco, 1933). McAfee, 1946a (transc. and Eng. transl.). Robertson, 1959, pp. 191–93, 195, plates 87–88 (ff. 3r, 10r). Towner, 1970. (ff. 10v, 11r).

Refs: Schwede, 1916, pp. 43–44, no. 5; Barlow, 1943e, p. 161; Robertson, 1960, pp. 112–13, 122.

Ex-coll: Charles Etienne Brasseur de Bourbourg (Brasseur de Bourbourg, 1871, pp. 95, 173–74 [sale]). § Alphonse Pinart (Catalogue, 1883, pp. 95–96, no. 582 [sale]). § Bernard Quaritch, London (Quaritch, 1885, pp. 2896–97, no. 29040; 1886, pp. 2896–97, no. 29040 [catalog]). § Edward E. Ayer (purchased before 1900).

Comment: Glossed illustrations only; no text pages. "Zenpualan" appears on ff. 3v and 4r only. Joaquín Galarza completed field work (winter 1968–69) for a study of this document.

Mod: Zempoala, Hidalgo. K/15-66.

706. IXTAPALAPA (F).

MNA, 35-107.

8 folios, 59.5 × 37 cm. Codex, double-level, upper right corner burned. F. 1r reinforced by a fragment of Códice de Huamantla.

Pub: Gómez de Orozco, 1933, pp. 312–13, 330–31, plate facing p. 330 (nonphotographic; pastiche of figure, houses, church, and glosses from 3 different sections of f. 6v). Glass, 1964, pp. 26, 162, 192, 199, 205, 209, pl. 114 (f. 6r).

Copy: McAfee: black pencil tracing with reconstructed portions of text in red pencil and 4 negative photostats of text folios; his typed transc. and Eng. transl. of 1948 were borrowed by Gómez de Orozco and are now said to be in a private collection in Mexico City.

Refs: Barlow, 1943e, p. 161; Gómez de Orozco, 1948, p. 66; Lenz, 1949, p. 163.

Ex-coll: Lorenzo Boturini Benaduci (Boturini, 1746, VII-13; also Peñafiel, 1890, chap. 12, no. 2-39; Mena, 1918–19, no.

14; Mena, 1923, pp. 59–60, no. 14; P. López 1925, no. 2-39).

Comment: First and last folios are text; date of 1539 is given on f. 8r. F.1, in an advanced state of dilapidation, was split and a fragment of Códice de Huamantla (Article 23, no. 135) pasted between the recto and verso faces of this folio; this hitherto unrecognized Huamantla fragment is the 9th fragment (7th in MNA).

Mod: Ixtapalapa, D.F. L/14-VI.

707. *Unidentifiable Pueblo* (G).

Jorge Enciso Collection, Mexico.

1 folio, 22 × 24 cm. (fragment). Codex, single-level.

Pub: Gómez de Orozco, 1933, pp. 313, 331–32 (transc. and Sp. transl. by Mariano J. Rojas), 2 plates (nonphotographic, of whole MS).

Copy: McAfee: transc.

Refs: Barlow, 1943e, p. 161; Gómez de Orozco, 1948, p. 66.

Comment: Glossed illustrations only.

Mod: Unlocated.

708. OCELOTEPEC, SANTA MARIA (Council House of Santa Maria Toluca) (H).

NYPL, Spencer Collection.

27 folios, 26.7 × 24.2 cm. (Ff. 1 and 27 defective). Codex, single-level. Bound with: (1) Sheet of European paper indicating this codex was used by natives of Miacatlan (*sic*) against an unknown hacienda in a land dispute in 1795, and (2) Spanish transl. of text ff. 1v–6r of ca. 1750. Tipped-in: Thomas Athol Joyce Eng. transl. of 1750 Sp. transl. and of Sp. transl. of glossed illustrations (on small piece of paper tipped on each drawing in 1936 but now missing from MS).

Pub: American Art Association, 1936, pp. 15–20, no. 61 (tracing of f. 5v (text), repro. of ff. 7v and 13r, and Joyce Eng. transl. New York Public Library, n.d., no. 6 (small color repro. of f. 11r).

Copies: MNH/CD, ser. Benjamin Franklin, Rollo X, exp. 2, microfilm (McAfee transc. and Eng. transl.). § McAfee: tracing,

transc. and Eng. transl. § See also above.

Bibliog: Barlow, 1943e; Robertson, 1959, p. 190, n. 5; pp. 194–95.

Refs: Sotheby, Wilkinson, and Hodge, 1919b, p. 92, no. 602; New York Public Library, 1937, pp. 179–80; Barlow, 1948d, p. 383, n. 2; Gómez de Orozco, 1948, p. 66; Robertson, 1960, pp. 112, 121.

Ex-coll: Lorenzo Boturini Benaduci (Boturini, 1746, VII-18; Peñafiel, 1890, chap. 12, no. 4–5; P. López 1925, no. 4–5, as Xonacatlan). § Bernard Quaritch, London. § Mrs. Alice Millard, Pasadena. § Mrs. Milton E. Getz (American Art Association, 1936 [Getz sale]). § Dr. A. S. W. Rosenbach, New York.

Comment: First 6 and last folios are text; date of 1535 given, and Viceroy Antonio de Mendoza mentioned. Miacatlan is not mentioned in the codex.

Mod: Santa Maria Zolotepec, M. Xonocatlan, Mexico. L/14-64.

709. *ACATITLAN, SANTA CECELIA* (J).

Museo Regional, Guadalajara, Jalisco, exhibit no. 96 (formerly in Biblioteca del Estado, Guadalajara).

2 folios, 26.5 × 20.5 cm. Codex, single-level.

Pub: Barlow, 1944g, 1 plate reproducing whole codex, transc. and Eng. transl. by Byron McAfee. Alcina Franch, 1955, no. 46, pp. 428, 468–69, fig. 9 (after Barlow); 1956, no. 46, pp. 12, 52–53, fig. 9 (after Barlow). Zuno, 1957, 2 plates reproducing whole codex.

Refs: Gómez de Orozco, 1948, p. 66; Robertson, 1959, p. 191.

Comment: Glossed illustrations only, no text pages. Belongs to Techialoyan 712, San Bartolome Tepanohuayan, on basis of tops of pages trimmed in double scallops, hole patterns, and Barlow's article (1947g, p. 278) linking them textually.

Mod: Santa Cecilia Acatitlan, formerly a dependency of San Bartolome Tepanohuayan (disappeared), both near Tenayuca, M. Tlalnepantla, Mexico. L/14-68.

710. *CALACOHUAYAN, SANTA MARIA* (Codex Sutro) (K).

Sutro Library, a branch of the California State Library, San Francisco.

3 folios, 47 × 26.6 cm. Codex, double-level.

Pub: La Voz Guadalupana, 1944, 2, repro. of f. 3v (bottom cut off). Gómez de Orozco, 1948, pp. 61, 66, pl. 4 (f. 2v, nonphotographic).

Copy: McAfee: positive photos made from microfilm.

Bibliog: Barlow and McAfee, 1946.

Ex-coll: Adolph Sutro who purchased MS in Mexico in 1880s.

Comment: Glossed illustrations only, no text pages.

Mod: Santa Maria Calacohuayan, slightly west of Tlalnepantla, M. Zaragoza, Mexico. L/14-69.

711. MIMIAHUAPAN, SAN MIGUEL (L).

John Galvin Collection, Ireland.

24 folios, 26 × 21 cm. Codex, single-level, in excellent state of preservation except for fragmentary last leaf; McAfee Eng. transl. is with the codex.

Unpublished.

Copy: Microfilm in MNH/CD, ser. Benjamin Franklin, Rollo X, exp. 3; exp. 4 is McAfee transc. and Eng. transl. § McAfee: transc. and Eng. transl. (see also Barlow, 1947g, 277, n. 1). § See also above.

Bibliog: Barlow, 1947f; Diebold, 1955.

Refs: Guzmán, 1939c, pp. 52–53; Gómez de Orozco, 1948, p. 66; Robertson, 1959, p. 190, n. 5.

Ex-coll: Maggs Bros., London, in 1939 § Robert H. Honeyman, San Juan Capistrano, Calif. § Jacob Zeitlin, Los Angeles (sold to present owner).

Comment: First 4 folios are text. Date of 1544 given on f. 1v; "çe tecpatl" (1 Flint, transl. by McAfee as "1532") appears on ff. 1r, 6r (here clearly a calendrical name of a preconquest forefather), and 17r. "Ome acatl" (2 Cane, transl. by McAfee as "1507") appears on f. 17r. Reference is

made to "Tohueytlatocatzin" ("Our Great Ruling Father" [i.e., Viceroy Mendoza]) on ff. 2r, 2v, and 4v.

Mod: San Miguel Mimiapan, M. Xonacatlan, Mexico. L/14-64.

712. TEPANOHUAYAN, SAN BARTOLOME (M).

Bancroft Library, University of California, Berkeley, Codex Nahuatl C. Mex. MS 470.

15 folios, and 1 fragment (all in damaged condition), 27 × 22 cm. Codex, single-level.

Unpublished.

Copy: Barlow, 1947g, p. 277, n. 1, cites MS transc. of Byron McAfee (should now be in either Barlow or McAfee papers).

Bibliog: Barlow, 1947g.

Refs: Barlow, 1945a, p. 92, n. 3; Gómez de Orozco, 1948, p. 66 (omits this codex and erroneously gives letter "M" to Techialoyan 713, Santa Maria Tetelpan (N); Robertson, 1959, p. 190, n. 5.

Comment: 4 folios of text; date of 1504 given, and Viceroy Antonio de Mendoza mentioned. Techialoyan 709, Santa Cecilia Acatitlan, is part of this codex on the basis of tops of pages trimmed in double scallops, hole patterns, and Barlow's article (1947g, p. 278) linking them textually. San Bartolome Tepanohuayan has now vanished, but was near Tenayuca (Barlow, 1947g, p. 277).

Mod: San Bartolome Tepanohuayan has disappeared but was near Tenayuca, M. Tlalnepantla, Mexico. Santa Cecilia Acatitlan, also near Tenayuca, was a dependency. L/14-68.

713. TETELPAN, SANTA MARIA (Codex Coyoacan) (Títulos del Pueblo de Mazatepec) (N).

JCBL, Accession no. 29022.

14 folios, 25.5 × 23.5 cm. Codex, single-level; first and last folio glued to modern paper. Studies by J. Alden Mason and R. W. Barlow are with the MS.

Pub: Chavero, n.d., p. v (ff. 10v and 11r,

nonphotographic). Wroth, 1945, p.v (f. 5v) (color).

Copy: McAfee: transc. (by Barlow and McAfee, see Barlow, 1948d, p. 383, n. 1).

Bibliog: Barlow, 1948d.

Refs: John Carter Brown Library, 1942, pp. 15–19; Gómez de Orozco, 1948, p. 66 (erroneously gives it the letter "M"); Robertson, 1959, p. 190, n. 5.

Ex-coll: Francisco del Paso y Troncoso (?). § J. Luis Bello (Puebla), stamped signature on outside paper wrappers of codex. § John Wise, Ltd., New York. § Henry Dexter Sharpe, Providence (gave MS to JCBL, 1941).

Comment: 3½ folios of text (front and back of MS probably text also). Date in text is 1545 or 1525 (partly defaced) according to Barlow, 1948d, p. 383, n. 3 Viceroy Antonio de Mendoza is mentioned.

Mod: Tetelpan, Del. Coyoacan, D.F. L/14-V.

714. TEPOTZOTLAN (Fragment of a Village Book) (Codex Pingret) (P).

NLA, no. 1479 (accessioned ca. 1912).

10 folios, 26.7 × 24.5 cm. Codex, single-level.

Unpublished.

Copies: Gates photocopy at BYU. McAfee: photographs.

Bibliog: Barlow, 1949e; Robertson, 1960.

Ref: Gómez de Orozco, 1948, p. 66.

Ex-coll: Lorenzo Boturini Benaduci (Boturini, 1746, III-2; also Peñafiel, 1890, p. 60, and P. López, 1925, p. 18, no. 3–8). § J.-M.-A. Aubin, 1849 (see Boban, 1891, 2:519). § Edouard Pingret, Paris (see Lucien de Rosny, 1875, pp. 223–24; Antiquités Aztèques, 1909, part 2, Item 1 [Pingret sale]). § Charles Chadenat, Paris. § Edward E. Ayer, ca. 1912.

Comment: Second fragment of a complete Codex of TEPOTZOTLAN constructed of Techialoyans 718-714-722; Robertson, 1960, gives complete study. Includes 2 pages of text and glossed illustrations of barrios and fields and woodlands. John

B. Glass called the Pingret association to our attention.

Mod: Tepotzotlan, Mexico. L/14-73.

715. GARCIA GRANADOS, Codex (Q).

MNA, 35-49.

49.5 × 674 cm. Tira.

Pub: Barlow, 1945b (6 plates and 4 figures, line drawings); 1946d (6 plates and 1 figure, line drawing); 1947e (2 plates). Glass, 1964, pp. 94–95, 199, 201, 207, pl. 50 (wheel in center).

Copies: MNA, 35-49A (modern copy by Mateo A. Saldaña). Ref: Glass, 1964, pp. 94, 193. § IAI, full-size tracing by Walter Lehmann. § Ex-Kingsborough and Phillipps (no. 35137) copy. Location unknown. Ref: Sotheby, Wilkinson, and Hodge [Phillipps sale], 1919a, no. 369; Maggs Bros., 1922, no. 1325. § McAfee: transc. and transl. (?); notes.

Bibliog: Hernández Rodríguez, 1966.

Ex-coll: Lorenzo Boturini Benaduci (Boturini, 1746, VI-1) (?) § Emile Dufossé, Paris (Dufossé, n.d.b., inside title page; 1893a, no. 70117; 1893b, no. 72633bis). § Alberto García Granados (purchased in Paris and given to MNA in 1907).

Comment: The three Barlow articles include partial publication of illus., transc., and transl. (aided by McAfee). This codex is unique in form and content, one of the most handsome and elaborate of all the Techialoyan manuscripts; the colors still have a brilliancy lacking in others of the group, enhanced by the use of gold. It contains an extremely complex genealogical tree or cactus drawn up to establish the validity of land claims through doubtful blood connections. The genealogies include both preconquest and colonial persons; in addition, 19 rulers and their pueblos are displayed in the form of a wheel.

It is not possible to say with complete assurance whether this MS was in the Boturini collection or not. However, if it was, it is probably the one Boturini describes as a "lienzo que hice copiar de las Pinturas originales, que se hallan hoy dia en las paredes de los Palacios Tecpanecos de 'Azcapotzalco,' con la Rueda de los Señoríos, que desfrutó este linage." (See Boturini, 1746, VI-1; also XI-1, copia.) This statement is no longer as improbable as it seemed earlier, since mural paintings in a Techialoyan style are now known. See below, Techialoyan 745, Cuernavaca Cathedral Murals.

Mod: Azcapotcalco, D.F. (?). L/14-I.

716. CHALCO, ATENCO, SANTIAGO (R).

BM, Add. MS no. 17038 (accessioned 1847), Dept. of Ceramics and Ethnography.

10 folios, 47.5 × 25 cm. Codex, double-level.

Unpublished.

Copies: Gates photocopies at TU/LAL and BYU. Microfilm in MNH/CD ser. Benjamin Franklin, Rollo IV, exp. 3.

Refs: British Museum, 1864, p. 357; Gómez de Orozco, 1948, pp. 66–67; Barlow, 1948d, p. 383, no. 2; Robertson, 1959, p. 190, n. 5.

Ex-coll: Percy Doyle.

Comment: 4 folios of text; date of 1537 given and Viceroy Antonio de Mendoza mentioned.

Mod: Chalco, Mexico. L/14-108.

717. HUYXOAPAN, SAN PABLO (Santa Cruz Azcapotzalco) (Azcapotzalco Maguey Manuscript) (S).

BM, Add. MS no. 22070 A and B (accessioned 1857), Dept. of Ceramics and Ethnography.

4 folios (A: 2 folios, 46 × 24 cm.; B: 2 folios, 46 × 22 cm.). Codex, double-level.

Pub: Gates, 1935a (page order confused).

Copies: Gates photocopies at LC, NLA (no. 1482), TU/LAL, and BYU. § McAfee: negative photostats and transc.

Ref: British Museum, 1875, p. 584; Gómez de Orozco, 1948, p. 67 (erroneously gives bibliography of this MS to Techialoyan 720, San Cristobal Coyotepec); Lenz, 1949, p. 163.

Comment: 2 folios of text (no. 22070A); Viceroy Antonio de Mendoza is mentioned. This MS belongs with Techialoyans 702 and 735, parts of the incomplete Codex of San Pablo Huyxoapan, on the basis of contents, style, handwriting, dimensions, and tear patterns.

Mod: Near Azccapotzalco, D.F.(?) L/14-I.

718. TEPOTZOTLAN (Fragment d'Histoire Chichimèque) (Tepotzotlan Tzontecomatl) (T). (fig. 84.)

BNP, MS. Mex. 81.

9 folios, 28 × 25 cm. Codex, combination single- and double-level.

Unpublished.

Copy: Microfilm in MNH/CD, ser. Benjamin Franklin, Rollo V, exp. 13 (photostat with Barlow and McAfee transc.).

Bibliog: Boban, 1891, 2: 208–09; Barlow, 1949e, p. 83; Robertson, 1960.

Refs: Schwede, 1916, p. 43, no. 4; Gómez de Orozco, 1948, p. 67.

Ex-coll: Lorenzo Boturini Benaduci (Boturini, 1746, III–2; also Peñafiel, 1890, p. 60, and P. López, 1925, p. 18, no. 3–8). § J.-M.-A. Aubin, 1849 (see Boban, 1891, 2: 519). § "1889 Appartenant à E. Eug. Goupil, Paris" (written on f. 1r). § Mme. E. Eugène Goupil (part of Goupil bequest to BNP, 1898).

Comment: First fragment of a complete Codex of TEPOTZOTLAN constructed of Techialoyans 718-714-722; Robertson, 1960, gives complete study. The content of this fragment (glossed illustrations) is preconquest and colonial history, barrios, and fields of the Pueblo.

Mod: Tepotzotlan, Mexico. L/14-73.

719. *Pueblo near Huehuetoca* (U).

Collection unknown.

Physical description unknown.

Unpublished.

Copy: McAfee: Several pages of photostats.

Ref: Gómez de Orozco, 1948, p. 67.

Mod: Unlocated, near Huehuetoca, Mexico. K/14-74.

720. COYOTEPEC, SAN CRISTOBAL (V).
MNA 35-91.
74 × 96 cm.   Large panel.
Pub: Glass, 1964, pp. 145, 199, 205, 208, pl. 97.
Copy: MNA 35-92, oil on cloth, 73 × 104.5 cm. (18th or 19thC copy); published in Glass, 1964, p. 146, pl. 98.   Enrique Juan Palacios transc. and transl. of glosses and description is in Archivo Administrativo del Dirección, MNA.
Refs: Gómez de Orozco, 1948, p. 67 (erroneously gives to this MS a bibliography belonging to Techialoyan 717, San Pablo Huyxoapan); Lenz, 1949, p. 163; Robertson, 1959, p. 190.
Ex-coll: Emilio Valtón (sold original and copy to MNA in 1936).
Comment: One of two known large panels, an aberrant type, not associated directly with a text.   See Techialoyan 726, San Pedro Atlapolco.   In both a friar is seated writing at a table in front of a building; he is surrounded by seated female Indians before him and standing male Indians behind him.   Each panel has some of the characteristics of a map, since a series of roads converge on the central motif and show Indians walking toward the gathering carrying burdens on their backs.   See Techialoyan 727, Coyotepec Coyonacazco.
Mod: Possibly San Cristobal Coyotepec, Mexico.   L/14-75.

721. TEPEXOXOUHCAN, SAN MIGUEL, and SAN MIGUEL CUAXOCHCO (W).
John Galvin Collection, Ireland.
8 folios, 25.4 × 22.8 cm.   Codex, double-level.   In vol. 1 of 3 volumes, bound with manuscript map locating towns mentioned in the codex.   Vol. 2 contains a Sp. transl. and commentary by Wigberto Jiménez Moreno aided by Miguel Barrios, 1954, and 3 letters from Jiménez Moreno.   Vol. 3 contains a lengthy and detailed analysis and an Eng. transl.

Pub: Parke-Bernet, 1957, p. 6, no. 18; pp. 4 and 13 of codex repro. on frontispiece, pp. 10 and 7 repro. on [5].
Copy: 19thC copy possibly by Aglio in NLA for unpublished vol. 10 of Kingsborough's *Antiquities of Mexico*.   14 plates printed on vellum, 49.5 × 37.5 cm., some water-colored, are of the codex (pp. 4 and 13 of the original are not included in the copy).   § See also above.
Bibliog: Robertson, 1960, pp. 112, 118.
Ex-coll: Lord Kingsborough (*Bibliotheca inlustris*, 1842, p. 91, no. 667 [sale]. § John Howell, San Francisco (sold to present owner).
Comment: No pages of text, glossed illustrations only.   Wigberto Jiménez Moreno assigned the letter "W" to this MS.
Mod: San Francisco Tepexoxuca, M. Tenango del Valle.   M/13-48.

722. TEPOTZOTLAN (X).
JRL, Mex. MS 1 (acquired 1901).
6 folios, 27.3 × 21.5 cm.   Codex, all text.
Pub: Robertson, 1960 (f. 1r facing p. 123; transc. and Eng. transl. by Byron McAfee).
Copies: W. H. Fellowes, Beaconsfield, Bucks., has made transc. and Eng. transl. § McAfee: negative photostats. § Microfilm in MNH/CD, ser. Benjamin Franklin, Rollo IV, exp. 8 (Chimalpopoca transc. from original, 1855, location unknown).
Refs: Gómez de Orozco, 1948, p. 67 (ref. to McAfee photostats); Robertson, 1959, p. 190.
Ex-coll: Lorenzo Boturini Benaduci (Boturini, 1746, III-2; also Peñafiel, 1890, p. 60, and P. López, 1925, p. 18, no. 3–8) § J.-M.-A. Aubin, 1849 (see Boban, 1891, 2:519). § "Coll. E. Boban, Mexico, No. ——" (stick-on label, inner back cover of MS). § Branford. § Earl of Crawford and Balcarres (Bibliotheca Lindesiana).
Comment: Third fragment of a complete Codex of TEPOTZOTLAN constructed of Techialoyans 718-714-722; Robertson, 1960, gives complete study.   In this all-

text fragment, a date of 1534 is given. Mention is made of Viceroy Antonio de Mendoza on f. 1v and "Tohueytlatocatzin ley" ("Our Great Ruler the King") on f. 5v. Robertson assigned the letter "X" to this MS.

Mod: Tepotzotlan, Mexico. L/14-73.

723. XONACATLAN, SAN FRANCISCO. (figs. 85, 87, 88.)

TU/LAL.

15 folios, 32.5 × 25 cm. Codex, combination single- and double-level.

Pub: Frost, 1937, pp. 4–5 (10 photos). Excelsior, 1937, p. 1 (2 photos).

Copy: McAfee: transc. and Eng. transl.

Refs: Gómez de Orozco, 1948, p. 67; Robertson, 1959, p. 190; 1960, p. 119.

Ex-coll: Frederick Starr (Chicago Book and Art Auctions, Inc., 1936, p. 44, no. 1623). § TU/MARI.

Comment: 6 folios of text; date of 1528 given, and Viceroy Antonio de Mendoza mentioned. An edition by Donald Robertson, with McAfee transc. and Eng. transl. (edited posthumously by Joaquín Galarza), is in preparation.

Mod: San Francisco Xonacatlan, Mexico. L/14-64.

724. HUIXQUILUCAN, SAN ANTONIO (Codex Hemenway). (fig. 83.)

PML.

20 folios, 26.5 × 22 cm. Codex, single-level.

Unpublished.

Refs: Peabody Museum, 1898, p. 6; Schwede, 1916, pp. 41–42, no. 2; Harvey, 1966a, pp. 123–24.

Ex-coll: Zelia Nuttall (as of 1893). § Mary Hemenway.

Comment: 7 folios of text; date of 1532 given (Peabody Museum, 1898, date of 1531 is in error) and Viceroy Antonio de Mendoza mentioned. An edition by Herbert R. Harvey is in preparation. John B. Glass first called this MS to our attention and supplied photographs and the Zelia Nuttall provenience.

Mod: Huixquilucan, Mexico. L/14-63.

725. CALPULALPAN, SAN SIMON. (fig. 86.)

BNP, MS Mex. 401.

6 folios, 47 × 22 cm. Codex, double-level, accompanied by three-page 19thC description.

Unpublished.

Bibliog: Exposición Histórico-Americana, 1892, pp. 126–28, no. 830, and Núñez y Domínguez, 1947a, pp. 364–66 both print accompanying description.

Ref: Omont, 1899, p. 64.

Ex-coll: Emperor Maximilian I (gift from Pueblo, July 1864). § Feliciano Herreros de Tejada, Madrid.

Comment: Glossed illustrations only, no text pages. In black leather box elaborately tooled with imperial arms of Mexico. MS bound in red velvet.

Mod: Calpulapan, Tlaxcala. L/15-1.

726. ATLAPOLCO, SAN PEDRO (Aztec Town Record). (fig. 90.)

Brooklyn Museum, no. 41.1249.

74 × 94 cm. Large panel.

Pub: Diffie, 1945, facing p. 227 (left quarter folded under).

Ex-coll: William Randolph Hearst (Hammer Galleries, 1941, p. 305, no. 444-9 sale). § John Wise, Ltd., New York (sold to Brooklyn Museum in 1941).

Comment: See Techialoyan 720, San Cristobal Coyotepec, for comment. Joaquín Galarza suggests adding the name of San Miguel Atlinayan.

Mod: San Pedro Atlalpulco, M. Ocoyoacac, Mexico. M/14-61.

727. COYOTEPEC COYONACAZCO.

Brooklyn Museum, no. 38.3.

9 folios, 42 × 26.8 cm. Codex, double-level.

Unpublished.

Ex-coll: Emilio Valtón (sold to Brooklyn Museum in 1938).

Comment: 2 folios of text. See comment for Techialoyan 747, Coyotepec. "Totecuyo to loyx te pelaxco" ("Viceroy Luis de

Velasco") is mentioned on ff. 1r and 1v. Partly obliterated text (f. 9r) may refer to San Cristobal Coyotepec Coyonacazco; see Techialoyan 720, San Cristobal Coyotepec.

Mod: Unlocated.

728. TIZAYUCA, SAN SALVADOR (Codex Kaska).

HSA, HC 397/433, Doc. 1 in vol. 1 of 4 vols. (since 1956). See comment below.

18 folios, 27.4 × 26.1 cm. Codex, single-level.

Pubs: R. R. Ramírez, 1874, pl. 1–4 (ff. 1v, 3r, 2r, 2v); reprinted in Chavero, n.d., pp. 647–48 (ff. 3r and 2r, nonphotographic). Stargardt, 1911, pp. 1–2, no. I and the two preceding plates (ff. 2r and 3r). Hiersemann, 1911, pp. 81–83, plate facing p. 48 (f. 3v).

Copies: See comment below under vol. 4; BNP, MS Mex. 419, Doc. 5 (19thC copy of the codex—illus., transc. and Sp. transl. —and all accompanying documents).

Ex-coll: Pueblo of San Salvador Tizayuca. § Tribunal Civil de Mexico (? AGN). § Emperor Maximilian I. § Baron Kaska (Stargardt, 1911, pp. 1–2, no. I [Kaska sale]). § Karl W. Hiersemann, Leipzig. § Archer M. Huntington.

Comment: The four volumes of Codex Kaska are bound in blue leather with gold tooling, 1866. Vol. 1 includes Doc. 1, Techialoyan 728, San Salvador Tizayuca; Doc. 2, an Act of the caciques of the Pueblo, 1596; and Doc. 3, Techialoyan 729, San Salvador Tizayuca Map. Vol. 2 includes Francisco Tirso Rosales' 1866 transcriptions of Docs, 4 and 5 (1596), 6 (1710), and 7 (1731). Vol. 3 has originals of Docs. 4–7. Vol. 4 includes Rosales' 1866 description and summary of Docs. 1–7, transc. and Sp. transl. of Docs. 1–3, and watercolor copies of Docs. 1 and 3.

Techialoyan 728, San Salvador Tizayuca, has 5 pages of text at end of MS on ff.

14v, 16v, 17r, 17v, and 18r. "Ze tecpatl" and "ome acatl" appear on f. 17r and also the date 1596, using a system of counting similar to that used in Techialoyan 737, Axoloapan Xoloctlan. "Tohueytlatocatzin" ("Our Great Ruling Father" [i.e., the viceroy]) is mentioned on f. 14r.

Doc. 6 states that in November of 1708 an edict sent from Pachuca required the inhabitants of San Salvador Tizayuca to present their titles proving legal possession of their lands within 30 days. The Pueblo claimed it had already done so in 1596, but paid 100 pesos for a *composición* based on the earlier documents.

Mod: San Salvador Tizayuca, Hidalgo. K/14-70.

729. TIZAYUCA, SAN SALVADOR—MAP (Codex Kaska Map).

HSA, HC 397/433, Doc. 3 in vol. 1 of 4 vols. (since 1956). See Techialoyan 728, San Salvador Tizayuca, comment.

25.4–26.8 × 168.3 cm. Tira.

Unpublished.

Copies: Francisco Tirso Rosales' watercolor copy, transc. and Sp. transl. (1866) in HSA, HC 397/433, vol. 4. § BNP, MS Mex. 419, Doc. 5 (19thC copy of map and all accompanying documents).

Bibliog: Robertson, 1960, p. 114.

Refs: Stargardt, 1911, pp. 1–2, no. I; Hiersemann, 1911, pp. 81–83.

Ex-coll: Same as for Techialoyan 728, San Salvador Tizayuca.

Comment: See Techialoyan 728, San Salvador Tizayuca, comment, especially paragraph 1 (description of contents of accompanying documents) and paragraph 3. This map, though tira in format, shares characteristics with the large panels: Techialoyan 720, San Cristobal Coyotepec, and Techialoyan 726, San Pedro Atlapolco. It shows in the center a church with people in front of it and roads coming from all directions.

Mod: San Salvador Tizayuca, Hidalgo. K/14-70.

730. *XOCOTLA, SAN NICOLAS* and *SAN AGUSTIN* (Codex Petich).

HSA, HC NS 3/8 (since 1956).

6 folios (5th damaged at top; 6th fragmentary), 35.5 × 27.9 cm. Codex, single-level.

Pub: Hiersemann, 1914, no. 8, pp. 10–11, plate facing p. 9.

Copy: IAI (expertise and tracing by Walter Lehmann of f. 1r, 1v, and 2r).

Ex-coll: Petich (?). § Karl W. Hiersemann, Leipzig. § Archer M. Huntington.

Mod: Unlocated.

731. TEPEXOYUCAN, SANTA MARIA.

Dr. Martin Bodmer Collection, Cologny, Geneva.

20 folios, 27 × 23 cm. Codex, single-level (first folio partly missing).

Pub: John Howell—Books, 1961, no. 14 (reproduces ff. 10v and 11r).

Copy: MNA/AH, Colección Antigua, no. 254, Documentos Históricos of F. Galicia Chimalpopoca: Doc. 23, ff. 289r–300r (formerly numbered ff. 220r–222v) are watercolor copies of original codex ff. 6r–10v, 13v?, and 14r (including glosses).

Ex-coll: Alfred Stendahl, Los Angeles. § Jacob Zeitlin, Los Angeles, and Warren Howell, San Francisco.

Comment: First 5 folios are text; date of 1534 given, and Viceroy Antonio de Mendoza mentioned. Herbert Harvey has suggested (personal communication) that the text may not belong to the glossed pictorial section. Seler (1904j, p. 49 and n. 5) refers to text of Techialoyan 733, Ocoyacac, which says that its lands are contiguous with those of Santa Maria Tepexoyucan.

Mod: Santa Maria Asuncion Tepesoyuca, M. Ocoyoacac, Mexico. M/14-61.

732. COYOACAN (San Nicolas Totolapan).

Pueblo of San Nicolas Totolapan de la Magdalena Contreras, D.F.

11 folios. Codex, double-level, accompanied by a volume containing transc., Sp. transl., and watercolor copy of pictorial section by Francisco Tirso Rosales, 1866, and documents of 1563 (Títulos Totolapan granted by Velasco), 1770, and 1866 pertaining to San Nicolas Totolapan.

Pub: Monroy Sevilla, 1964 (poor photographic edition of original, Rosales copies, and accompanying documents).

Copy: See above.

Comment: 4 pages of text, date of 1535 given, and mention of "Tohueytlatocatzin" ("Our Great Ruler" [i.e., Viceroy Mendoza]). Although this MS is associated with documents from Totolapan, Rosales' Sp. transl. indicates that it actually comes from Coyoacan. No prior mention of this MS in accompanying documents. Fernando Horcasitas Pimentel brought the existence of this MS to our attention in 1963, when it was in the Museo Agrario, Depto. de Asuntos Agrarios y Colonización, Mexico, on deposit as evidence in a land litigation. Joaquín Galarza suggests in agreement with Prof. Monroy Sevilla the name San Nicolas Totolapan and in addition Santa Maria Magdalena Atlauitec. Prof. Monroy Sevilla kindly sent us a copy of his publication.

Mod: Coyoacan, D.F. L/14-V. (S. Nicolas Totolapan, Del. Magdalena Contreras, D.F. L/14-VIII).

733. OCOYACAC, SAN MARTIN (Seler's Landbook).

SSPK (before World War II, DSB, MS Amer. no. 7, accessioned 1862 by former Royal Library, Berlin; until 1967 deposited in UBT).

20 folios, 26.5 × 23 cm. Codex, single-level (many pages cropped at bottom).

Pub: Sapper, 1903, p. 57, Tafel II, Abb. 1 (f. 11r, copy). Seler, 1904j, p. 49, n. 5 (short quotation from Nahuatl text). Degering, 1933–34, p. 176, Abb. 15 (f. 7r in color).

Copy: MVBE (30 plates, color, 27 × 22.4 cm.) by Walter Lehmann.

Refs: Schwede, 1916, pp. 40–41, no. 1; Bankmann, 1970, pp. 131–32.

Ex-coll: Carl Uhde (Guzmán, 1939c, pp. 52–53; Bankmann, 1970, p. 131).

Comment: Text on ff. 1v–4v, 19r–20r; date of 1535 given, and Viceroy Antonio de Mendoza mentioned. Colors are more brilliant than in most other Techialoyans. Ulf Bankmann provided the UBT location of this codex and photographs. An edition of the MS is planned with a commentary by Ulf Bankmann and a translation by Anneliese Mönnich.

Mod: Ocoyoacac, Mexico.   L/14-61.

734. *ACAYUCA, SAN FRANCISCO.*
NBV, CVM 11.

9 folios, 21 × 28 cm.   Codex, single-level.
Unpublished.

Ref: Unterkircher, 1957–59, 2: 126.

Ex-coll: Dominik Bilimek.

Comment: No human figures; all illustrations are on the verso of a folio except 8r and 9r. No text pages.

Mod: Acayuca, M. Zapotlan de Juarez, Hidalgo.   K/14-72.

735. HUYXOAPAN, SAN PABLO (Códice Azcapotzalco).
BNMex, MS 1805 (part).

4 folios, 45.5 × 21.75 cm.   Codex, combination single- and double-level.
Unpublished.

Bibliog: Mena, 1918–19, no. 16; 1923, p. 60, no. 16; Gómez de Orozco, 1933, p. 328; 1948, p. 67; R. Moreno, 1966, p. 48, no. 10.

Ref: Glass, 1964, p. 27.

Ex-coll: Lorenzo Boturini Benaduci (?) § José María de Agreda y Sánchez, Mexico.

Comment: Possibly inventoried as ex-Boturini collection in error, as this MS is not listed in any Boturini inventories before Mena, 1918–19. No text pages. This glossed pictorial fragment belongs with Techialoyans 702 and 717, parts of the incomplete Codex of San Pablo Huyxoapan, on the basis of contents, style, handwriting, dimensions, and tear patterns. John B. Glass brought to our attention the existence and location of this codex.

Mod: Near Azcapotzalco, D.F. (?).   L/14-I.

736. TLAHUAC, SAN PEDRO (Títulos de las Tierras de los Indios de Cuitlahuac) (Títulos del Pueblo de Tlahuac).
BAN, Codex Nahuatl A, Mex. MS 468.

9 folios (f. 1 split apart), 23 × 21 cm.   Codex, single-level.
Unpublished.

Copies: Three copies by Faustino Galicia Chimalpopoca are known: (1) BNMex, MS 1735 (1312) (16-64) (14-2-64), 2nd text, f. 8 ff.; ff. 9–12, transc.; ff. 12 15, Sp. transl. (dated April 12, 1856). (2) BNMex, MS 1735 (1312) (16–64) (14–2-64), 3rd text, f. 16 ff. (dated March 3, 1855): ff. 17–19, transc.; followed on f. 19v (2d leaf paginated 19v) by no. I, "Cuauhtli itlacuayan, plano" (watercolor copy dated 1856) (probably f. 1v of original codex) and on f. (unnumbered) recto by no. II, "Plano de Cuitlahuac" (dated 1856) (possibly f. 1r of original codex).   (3) MNA/AH, Colección Antigua, no. 274 (AAMC), no. 25, transc. and Sp. transl. (dated April 25, 1856). § Francisco del Paso y Troncoso copy of 1886. Location unknown. § McAfee: typed transc. and Sp. transl. copied by McAfee from MSS of Paso y Troncoso (1886) and Chimalpopoca (1855–56); microfilm. § MNH/CD, ser. Benjamin Franklin, Rollo 4, exp. 10, microfilm of McAfee... (above).

Refs: Barlow, 1945a, pp. 91–92 and n. 4, Apenes, 1947, p. 18; R. Moreno, 1966, p. 47, no. 9, third item.

Ex-coll: Hubert Howe Bancroft (?).

Comment: F. 1r and v are pictorial, ff. 2–9 are text.   Ff. 1r and 2r mention "Xan Petolo Tlahuac."   Date of June 10, 1561, is given on f. 2r (Chimalpopoca), 1585 on 9r (Galarza). "Tohueytlatocatzin ley caztilan" ("Our Great Ruling Father" [i.e., the king of Spain]) and "Vizoley" (viceroy) are mentioned on f. 5r.

Mod: Tlahuac, D.F.   M/14-XI.

737. AXOLOAPAN XOLOCTLAN.

Sr. Guajardo Collection, Mexico, D.F., ca. 1939. Present whereabouts unknown.

15 folios (last one a fragment). Codex, single-level.

Unpublished.

Copy: TU/MARI Photos MS A (ff. 1r, 2v, 3r, 14v, and 15v missing from photographs).

Comment: This MS was offered for sale to TU/MARI ca. 1939. The first 7 folios are text. The date 1584 is given on f. 1v, using a system of counting similar to Techialoyan 728, San Salvador Tízayuca. "Tohueytlatocatzin" ("Our Great Ruling Father" [i.e., the viceroy]) is mentioned on f. 5r.

Mod: Santa Maria Ajoloapan and San Lucas Xoloc, M. Tecamac, Mexico. Cerro de Xoloc is nearby to the east. L/14-86.

738. OZTOYAOTITLAN.

Sr. Guajardo Collection, Mexico, D.F., ca. 1939. Present whereabouts unknown.

11 folios (poor condition, last folio a fragment). Codex, single-level.

Unpublished.

Copy: TU/MARI Photos MS D (16 photographs).

Comment: This MS was offered for sale to TU/MARI ca. 1939. The MS has no text pages, and the paintings are very crude compared to other Techialoyan paintings. As far as one can see in the photographs, the paintings seem to be on only one side of each folio; the other face seems to be reinforced by a printed Bula de la Santa Cruzada. The pattern is such that each painted page seems to face another painted page.

Mod: Unlocated.

739. TEOTLA (Códice Matlatzinca).

Pueblo of San Pedro Zictepec, state of Mexico.

Physical description unknown.

Pub: See comment below.

Copy: Photographs of each folio are in Biblioteca del H. Congreso de la Unión (Paniagua Jaen, 1943), but Robertson and Galarza were unable to locate them in the summer of 1966.

Ref: Paniagua Jaen, 1943.

Comment: Paniagua Jaen, 1943, pp. 23, 25, repro. two pages from either this MS, Techialoyan 740, or Techialoyan 741, three codices he found in the Pueblo of San Pedro Zictepec. He says all three are on maguey paper (sic) and are dated 1562. His copyist, a painter, could finish copying only one MS because they were run out of Zictepec after eight days. A map of San Pedro Zictepec painted in 1639 is with the codices. Lic. Gustavo G. Velázquez of Toluca was making translations. (Existence of the Paniagua Jaen article reported from Alfonso Caso via John B. Glass.)

Mod: Teotla, M. Tenancingo, Mexico. M/13-49.

740. ZEPAYAHUTLA (Códice Matlatzinca).

Pueblo of San Pedro Zictepec, state of Mexico.

Physical description unknown.

Pub: See comment below.

Copy: Photographs of each folio are in Biblioteca del H. Congreso de la Unión (Paniagua Jaen, 1943), but Robertson and Galarza were unable to locate them in the summer of 1966.

Ref: Paniagua Jaen, 1943.

Comment: Paniagua Jaen, 1943, pp. 23, 25, repro. two pages from either this MS, Techialoyan 739, or Techialoyan 741.

See comment for Techialoyan 739, Teotla.

Mod: Zepayautla, M. Tenancingo, Mexico. M/13-49.

741. TENANCINGO (Códice Matlatzinca).

Pueblo of San Pedro Zictepec, state of Mexico.

Physical description unknown.

Pub: See comment below.

Copy: Photographs of each folio are in Biblioteca del H. Congreso de la Unión (Paniagua Jaen, 1943), but Robertson and Galarza were unable to locate them in the summer of 1966.

Ref: Paniagua Jaen, 1943.

Comment: Paniagua Jaen, 1943, pp. 23, 25, repro. two pages from either this MS, Techialoyan 729, or Techialoyan 740. See comment for Techialoyan 739, Teotla.

Mod: Tenancingo, Mexico. M/13-49.

742. *Unidentified Pueblo.*

Lost. (Formerly DSB, MS Amer. no. 10, Docs. 3 and 4; deposited in early 1940s at Schloss Altmarrin in Pomerania, Poland.)

1 folio each. Probably same dimensions as tracings, below. Codex, single-level.

Unpublished.

Copy: IAI pen-and-ink tracings of both documents by Walter Lehmann, July, 1901 (r and v of the same sheet); Doc. 3 is water-colored (25.5 × 22 cm.); Doc. 4 (26.5 × 22.5 cm.). (Pub: Bankmann, 1970, pp. 134–35, Abb. 1–4).

Refs: Guzmán, 1936 (refers to Docs. 4 and 5); Bankmann, 1970, pp. 133–34.

Comment: Gerdt Kutscher and Ulf Bankmann have kindly supplied information on these two leaves, which show on r and v four pages of illustrations.

Mod: Unlocated.

743. COACALCO (Cohuacalco). (fig. 89.)

Lost.

Physical description unknown.

Unpublished.

Copy: TU/LAL (probably 18thC copy).

10 loose folios on European paper painted on both sides, edges tattered. 29 × 21 cm. Codex, probably single-level, pages numbered. Accompanied by Sp. transl. by Faustino Galicia Chimalpopoca of ff. 3v–10v (5 folios and a half sheet "title page") and Wigberto Jiménez Moreno letter to Frans Blom dated December 11, 1934 (3 folios).

Copies of TU/LAL copy: (1) TU/LAL has typescript of Chimalpopoca Sp. transl. above (11 pages). (2) MNA/CD, ser. Benjamin Franklin, Rollo 4, exp. 1, microfilm of TU/LAL documents and a typed transc. (3) MNA/AH, Documentos Sueltos, ser. 2, leg. 88, no. 2, is a Francisco del Paso y Troncoso copy of a Chimalpopoca copy (which is dated July 31, 1867) and a description of the TU/LAL copy.

Ref: Barlow, 1945f, p. 201, no. 1.

Ex-coll: TU/MARI (1934?–70).

Comment: The old copy at TU/LAL is probably 18thC. Ff. 3r–10v (of the TU/LAL copy, not the lost original) are a copy of the preconquest history and colonial religious entrada sections of a now lost Techialoyan codex. Even though this is a copy, some of the illustrations are so close to those in Techialoyan 718, Tepotzotlan, a nearby town, that the artist of the original codex must have known the Tepotzotlan MS if he was not in fact the painter of both. In addition, f. 1r is so close to f. 1v of Techialoyan 705, Zempoala, an illustration showing "Ixtlilxochitl," that the same relationship can be made; it is glossed "cepohualtecatl." Whoever copied this MS translated the dates from the original Nahuatl into Arabic numbers.

Ff. 1v, 2r, and 2v are not Techialoyan. Ff. 1v and 2r are a mélange of figures, mainly heads, which seem to derive from 16thC MSS; one passage suggests the Mapa Sigüenza (Article 23, no. 290). F. 2v is a symetrically ordered composition drawn on paper originally ruled for eight lines of music.

Mod: Coacalco, Mexico. L/14-88.

744. *TEZCALUCAN, SAN CRISTOBAL,* and *SANTA MARIA MAGDALENA CHICHICASPA.*

Burned by Audiencia of New Spain, 1703, because they considered it fraudulent.

16 folios.

Unpublished.

Copy: AGN/T, vol. 1798 (Sp. transl. and description).

Bibliog: Harvey, 1966a (believes this codex not to have been a Techialoyan).

Comment: Presented as evidence in a land dispute. Four text folios and date of 1555 given. Text states that a delegation of officials from the town had earlier appealed to Viceroy Mendoza to confirm their land titles; Viceroy Luis de Velasco did approve the land titles.

Mod: S. Cristobal Texcaluca and Magdalena Chichicaspa, M. Huixquilucan, Mexico. L/14-63.

745. CUERNAVACA, TECHIALOYAN-STYLE MURALS IN THE CATHEDRAL OF ("Christian Martyrs in Japan"). (fig. 91.)

Lateral walls of nave. 30 m. long × 8 m. high. Murals.

Pub: Cary, 1962 (5 illus.). Toussaint, 1965, p. 250, n. 9 by Xavier Moyssén, pls. 51–52. Islas García, 1967, figs. 10–23 (believes the murals to have been painted by a Japanese artist). B. Smith, 1968, pp. 186–87. Rodríguez, 1969, pl. 45 (color). Almazán, 1971, pp. 22–25 (8 illus.).

Comment: Uncovered in 1959 during renovation work on the Cathedral. Murals depict the Franciscan martyrs, San Felipe de Jesús and 25 religious and lay companions, who set out from Cuernavaca in 1596 and were martyred in Nagasaki, Japan, Feb. 5, 1597. San Felipe was beatified in 1625. Agustín de Vetancurt, writing in 1697 (Vetancurt, 1871, ed., pp. 182–86), makes no mention of these elaborate and handsome murals in his description of the church (at that time still a Franciscan monastery), although other decorations are described in detail. It might be assumed that they were painted after that date.

Mod: Cuernavaca, Morelos. M/14-2.

746. HUAQUILPAN, SAN PEDRO and SAN MARTIN. (San Pedro Ahuaquilpan).

BAN, Codex Nahuatl B, Mex. MS 469.

4 folios and 1 loose folio, 27.5 × 18 cm. Codex, probably single-level.

Unpublished.

Copy: MNA/AH, Colección Antigua, no. 254 (Documentos Históricos), no. 22, ff. 289r–295v (formerly ff. 229r–231v and 304r–307r) by Faustino Galicia Chimalpopoca, August 12, 1858.

Ref: Barlow, 1945a, pp. 91–92.

Ex-coll: Hubert Howe Bancroft (?).

Comment: Four bound folios are text; writing on ff. 3v and 4r is turned sideways. Two different handwritings are present. Date of 1524 is given on ff. 2v, 3r (twice), and 4r; "Tohueitlatocazin ley caztilan" ("Our Great Ruling Father" [i.e., the king of Spain]) is mentioned on f. 4v. The loose folio is the amatl paper of the codex with a sheet of European paper pasted on it. The back of the European paper has a printed text. A view of "Xan Petolo" and "Xan Maltin" is painted on the exposed face. This painting is a copy of a missing Techialoyan page, probably belonging to this MS, or it is possibly another MS (Techialoyan or not).

Mod: San Pedro Ahuaquilpan, M., Zapotlan de Juarez, Hidalgo. K/14-72.

747. COYOTEPEC.

Collection unknown.

10 folios.

Unpublished.

Copy: McAfee: negative photostats.

Comment: The McAfee photostats may be of Techialoyan 727, Coyotepec Coyonacazco (q.v.) in the Brooklyn Museum, or it may be part of that manuscript otherwise lost. A third possibility is that it may be a separate and distinct manuscript.

Mod: Unlocated.

748. Unidentified Techialoyan manuscript (Codex of Boturini).

BAV.

8 folios.

Unpublished.

Comment: Mentioned in catalog notes of Brooklyn Museum Techialoyan 727, Coyotepec Coyonacazco (by Emilio Valtón?). Not found by Robertson in BAV in the winter of 1964–65.

Mod: Unlocated.

REFERENCES (compiled by Mary W. Cline)

Alcina Franch, 1955, 1956
Almazán, 1971
American Art Association, 1936
Antiquités Aztèques, 1909
Apenes, 1947
Aubin, 1849
Bankmann, 1970
Barlow, 1943e, 1944g, 1945a, 1945b, 1945f,
   1946d, 1947e, 1947f, 1947g, 1948d, 1949e
—— and McAfee, 1946
Basurto, 1901
Bibliotheca inlustris, 1842
Boban, 1891
Boturini, 1746
Brasseur de Bourbourg, 1871
British Museum, 1864, 1875
Carrera Stampa, 1959, 1962–63, 1965
Carrillo y Gariel, 1952
Cary, 1962
Catálogo, 1911
Catalogue, 1883
Ceballos Novelo, 1935
Chavero, n.d.
Chevalier, 1963
Chicago Book and Art Auctions, 1936
Colín, 1963–64, 1966
Degering, 1933–34
Diebold, 1955
Diffie, 1945
Dufossé, n.d.b, 1893a, 1893b
Excelsior, 1937
Exposición Histórico-Americana, 1892
Fernández, 1939
Fernández del Castillo, A., 1952
Frost, 1937
Galicia Chimalpopoca, 1893
Gates, 1935a
Gibson, 1964a
Glass, 1964
Gómez de Orozco, 1933, 1948
Guzmán, 1936, 1939c
Hammer Galleries, 1941
Harvey, 1966a
Hernández Rodríguez, 1952, 1966
Hiersemann, 1911, 1914
Islas García, 1967
John Carter Brown Library, 1942

John Howell—Books, 1961
Lenz, 1949, 1950
López, P., 1925
McAfee, 1946a, 1948
McBride, 1923
Maggs Bros., 1922
Memoria, 1893
Mena, 1918–19, 1923
Monroy Sevilla, 1964
Moreno, R., 1966
New York Public Library, 1937, n.d.
Núñez y Domínguez, 1947a
Olaguíbel, 1894, 1957
Omont, 1899
Orozco, W., 1895
Paniagua Jaen, 1943
Parke-Bernet, 1957
Peabody Museum, 1898
Peñafiel, 1890
Quaritch, 1885, 1886, 1890
Ramírez, J. F., 1855
Ramírez, R. R., 1874
Reed, 1938
Robelo, Olaguíbel and Peñafiel, 1966
Robertson, D., 1959, 1960, 1971
Rodríguez, 1969
Rosny, Lucien de, 1875
Rubio Mañé, 1955
Sánchez Colín, 1951
Sapper, 1903
Schmeider, 1930
Schwede, 1916
Seler, 1904j
Smith, B., 1968
Sotheby, Wilkinson, and Hodge, 1919a, 1919b
Stargardt, 1911
Toussaint, 1965
Towner, 1970
Unterkircher, 1957–59
Vetancurt, 1871
Voz Guadalupana, La, 1944
Weitlaner, 1939
Wroth, 1945
Zantwijk, 1969
Zavala, 1935
Zuno, 1957

25. A Census of Middle American Testerian Manuscripts

JOHN B. GLASS

PICTORIAL CATECHISMS known as Testerian manuscripts comprise one of the most curious and distinctive classes of the pictorial manuscripts of colonial Mexico. Although not recognizably in any Indian tradition, they have been included in the corpus of Indian pictorial manuscripts because they were created and have survived in similar contexts. Examples of the type are found in thirteen institutional collections (see Table 1).

The typical Testerian manuscript is a small volume that contains prayers, the articles of faith, or other parts of the catechism, drawn with small mnemonic and rebus figures. Each represents a phrase, word, or syllable of the Christian text. In most of the known examples the figures are drawn between horizontal lines and are read across two facing pages, in boustrophedon-fashion (left to right, then right to left, alternately). Most figures are probably inventions of the mendicant friars without roots in native iconography. Only a very few figures in the extant examples are taken directly from the colonial vocabulary of traditional Indian picture writing. Testerian manuscripts are thus documents for the history of the Church and

TABLE 1—CLASSIFICATION OF TESTERIAN MANUSCRIPTS BY LOCATION AND AVAILABILITY

European Collections

804	Archivo Histórico Nacional, Madrid
806	Biblioteca Nacional, Madrid
807–810	Bibliothèque Nationale, Paris
813	British Museum, London
817	Deutsche Staatsbibliothek, Berlin

Mexican Collections

801–803	Archivo Histórico del I.N.A.H.
830	Museo Nacional de Antropología

Private or Unknown Collections

814	Bullock collection
831	Orozco y Berra collection
835	Romero de Terreros collection

United States Collections

816	Cleveland Public Library
822, 823	Hispanic Society of America, New York
824–826	John Carter Brown Library, Brown University
827, 828	Middle American Research Institute, Tulane University
832	Peabody Museum Library, Harvard University
833, 834	Princeton University Library

Unavailable Manuscripts

805	Aubin, described by
811, 812	Boturini collection
815	Chavero collection
818–820	García Icazbalceta collection
821	Granados y Gálvez, described by
829	Moxó, described by

the missionary effort, for the spiritual conversion of the Indians, and for the history of writing, rather than for political or economic history.

The conversion of the Indians of New Spain to Catholicism was beset by many problems. Not the least of them was the language barrier between the friars and, literally, thousands of Indians requiring instruction in the new faith at one time. An early response by members of the monastic orders was that of preparing paintings to be used as pedagogic devices. Such paintings are described in several early accounts. In his *Historia eclesiástica indiana* Mendieta notes how some friars used paintings illustrating the articles of faith, the ten commandments, the seven sacraments of the Church, or other aspects of Christian doctrine. In his biography of Fray Jacobo de Testera, Mendieta says that Testera brought with him to Mexico a *lienzo*, or painting on cloth, delineating the mysteries of the faith which were explained to the Indians by an interpreter. In another and more detailed account, Dávila Padilla records the use of similar paintings by Fray Gonzalo Luzero.[1]

Fray Diego Valadés attributes the invention of this method of instruction to the Franciscans. Two engravings in his *Rhetorica cristiana* (1579) show these paintings in use. In one of them (fig. 93) a preacher in a pulpit points to painted scenes portraying the stations of the cross. Before him stands a large audience of Indians, with their cloaks knotted over their shoulders. This scene has been copied many times and is most frequently seen in frontispieces to Torquemada's *Monarquía indiana*. An imaginative rendition by Marianus de Orscelar (1625) identifies the preacher as Fray Jacobo de Testera (fig. 94).

The other engraving (fig. 95), which is a view of the grounds around a church, depicts the education of the Indians in an idealized Franciscan setting. In the upper right corner of the atrium a friar points to a large lienzo representing the genesis (*Creatio*

Mundi) before a small gathering of Indians. At the upper left, Fray Pedro de Gante, a famous educator of the Indians, points to a similar panel picturing the mechanical arts, a secular rather than a religious subject. Copies of both illustrations are in the manuscript of Mendieta's history.[2]

Other drawings by Valadés represent the lienzos in this technique of graphic instruction, of which he was a strong advocate. In several, the details, particularly costumes and hair dressings, are notable for their similarity to traditional colonial Indian pictorial manuscripts. The engraving representing the sanctity of Christian marriage and the punishments for its profanation (fig. 96) combines Christian morality and Indian ethnography.

Another aspect of drawings or paintings for religious purposes is described by Fray Toribio de Benavente, who on one occasion required Indians desiring confession to bring drawings of their sins (Motolinía, *Historia de los indios de la Nueva España*, trat. 2, cap. 6; 1858, p. 122). Valadés also refers to the Indians' recording in paintings the subject of their confessions (Palomera, 1962, pp. 67, 308).

The use of religious paintings in instruc-

[1] Mendieta, *Historia eclesiástica indiana*, lib. 3, cap. 29; lib. 5, pt. 1, cap. 42 (Mendieta, 1870, pp. 249–50, 665–66). Both references are repeated in Torquemada, *Monarquía indiana*, lib. 15, cap. 25; lib. 20, cap. 47 (Torquemada, 1723, 3: 69, 489). Dávila Padilla, *Historia de la fundación y discurso de la provincia de Santiago de Mexico*, lib. 1, cap. 81 (Dávila Padilla, 1955, pp. 255–59). The anonymous author (Mendieta?) of the *Códice Franciscano* (García Icazbalceta, 1941, 2: 59–60) also describes the use of paintings in religious instruction. Sahagún (*Historia*, Spanish text, bk. 11, chap. 13 [Garibay, 1956, 3: 359]) makes only the slightest allusion to such paintings.

[2] The relevant passages in Valadés (1579) are given in Spanish translation from the Latin original in Palomera (1962, pp. 274–93, 306–09). On the identification of the signs to which Fray Pedro de Gante is pointing, see Palomera (1962, pp. 134, 276, 293). Palomera (1962) reproduces all the Valadés engravings and Palomera (1963) reproduces the four copies in the Mendieta history from the UTX manuscript. All but one of the Valadés engravings are reproduced by Maza (1945).

tion and as a graphic adjunct to preaching, a practice described by Mendieta, Dávila Padilla, and Valadés and illustrated by the latter's engravings, is traditionally cited by authors who discuss Testerian manuscripts. It seems evident, however, that these paintings were representative or allegorical and should not be confused with the pictorial catechisms painted in mixed mnemonic, rebus, ideographic, and phonetic systems in what is now generally comprehended under the term Testerian writing.

Remarkably little is recorded concerning the picture prayer books in the colonial ethnohistorical literature on Mexico. The fact that they are not mentioned by Valadés is all the more surprising in view of his interest in visual techniques of religious education. In his *Rhetorica cristiana* (1579) he devotes considerable space to Indian picture writing, to the description of religious paintings, and to techniques of memory for learning the scriptures based on pictorial mnemonic aids (Palomera, 1962, pp. 100–08, 274–93, 302–09). His mnemotecnic alphabet for Indians (fig. 97), inspired by the earlier work of Ludovico Dolce published in 1562 (Palomera, 1962, p. 82), reflects this interest.

Only three 16th-century writers have been reported as describing pictorial means of reducing the catechism to the signs of picture writing. They are Las Casas, Acosta, and Mendieta, writing no later than about 1555, 1589, and 1596, respectively.

Las Casas (*Apologética historia de las Indias*, cap. 235; 1909, p. 618) notes an Indian method of representing the Christian doctrine by figures corresponding in voice and sound (in Nahuatl) to the European word. To represent the word *amen*, the natives drew the sign for water (*atl*) followed by the sign for the maguey plant (*metl*) which together (*a-metl*) approximated the word. Las Casas had seen a great part of the Christian doctrine drawn in this manner which could be read by the Indians just as he could read European writing. J. E. S. Thompson (1959, p. 353) gives an English translation

of the passage in which Las Casas describes this example of rebus writing.

Mendieta (*Historia eclesiástica indiana*, lib. 3, cap. 28; 1870, pp. 246–47) recorded the same system and showed how the words *Pater Noster*, as an example, were represented by the drawing of a flag (*pantli*) and a tuna cactus (*nochtli*). He also stated that confessions were recorded by the same means. Mendieta's description is repeated in Torquemada (*Monarquía indiana*, lib. 15, cap. 36; 1723, 3: 101–02).

In the 19th century Aubin described a pictorial catechism in the "bibliothèque métropolitaine" of Mexico and illustrated its first words, *Pater Noster*. These were represented by four figures: a flag, a stone, a cactus, and another stone. The Nahuatl rendition of these four signs is *pantli, tetl,nochtli, tetl* or, in Aubin's transliteration, *Pa-te-noch-te* (Aubin, 1849; quoted in Boban, 1891, 2: 181–82). Unfortunately this manuscript is now unknown (no. 805.)

The possibility that a set of Testerian figures was published toward the end of the 16th century is suggested by the title of a work by Fray Juan Bautista given in a list of his own publications issued in 1606 (García Icazbalceta, 1954, p. 471): "Hieroglíficos de conversión, donde por estampas y figuras se enseña a los naturales el aborrecimiento del pecado y deseo que deben tener al bien soberano del cielo." Since the work is unknown, its actual contents are a matter for speculation. García Icazbalceta (loc. cit.) believed that the reference was to religious engravings and not to anything resembling Mexican hieroglyphs.

The form of rebus writing observed by Las Casas and Mendieta and reported by Aubin is precisely the system used in traditional Indian pictorial manuscripts from Central Mexico during the 16th century, particularly for the representation of toponyms (place glyphs). It is rare to nonexistent, however, in the published pages of the surviving Testerian manuscripts.

The drawings in most of the extant Testerian manuscripts correspond to a less traditional system set down by Acosta (*Historia natural y moral de las Indias*, lib. 6, cap. 7; 1962, pp. 288–90). The description, which I have translated, is in a chapter entitled "Of the nature of the letters and writing used by the Mexicans."

And I have seen, to satisfy myself in this regard, the prayers of the Pater Noster, Ave Maria and symbol, and the general confession [written] in the said manner [by images and characters] of the Indians. Certainly whoever would see it, would admire it. For to signify the words, "I, a sinner, do confess myself," they paint an Indian kneeling at the feet of a religious [priest], as one who confesses. For "to God almighty" they paint three faces with crowns like the Trinity; for the glorious Virgin Mary they paint the face of Our Lady and half the body of a child; for Saint Peter and Saint Paul, two heads with crowns and some keys and a sword. In this manner the whole confession is written by images, and where they lack images, they put characters as in what I have sinned, etc. From this one may conceive the liveliness of the ingenuity of these Indians. Since this method of writing our prayers and matters of the faith was not taught them by the Spaniards, they could not have achieved it unless they had a particular conception of what they were taught. By the same means of painting and characters I saw written in Peru, the confession of all his sins that an Indian brought to confession. Each of the ten commandments was painted by a certain means followed by signs something like numbers that were the sins that had been committed against that commandment.

For this description, Acosta may have had a Testerian manuscript sent to him by Fray Juan de Tovar, along with the manuscript of the latter's *Historia de la benida de los Yndios apoblar a Mexico*. This possibility is suggested by a statement in a letter of transmittal from Tovar to Acosta (English translation from Kubler and Gibson, 1951, p. 78): "And to add to what I have said here, I send to you the orations of the Pater Noster, etc., and of the general confession, and other matters of our faith, as the ancients

wrote and learned them by their characters, which were sent to me by the old men of Texcoco and Tula."

For the Mexican origins of Testerian manuscripts we thus have the evidence of Las Casas, Mendieta, and Acosta. In addition, the signature of Fray Pedro de Gante reportedly occurs on two (different?) examples: on the Testerian manuscript of the Biblioteca Nacional de Madrid (no. 806) and on one of the three examples that were in the García Icazbalceta collection (nos. 818–820). Another, in the Bibliothèque Nationale de Paris (no. 809), is said to bear Sahagún's name. In the absence of any firm dating of the older existing Testerian manuscripts (style, palaeography, paper characteristics), this is sufficient evidence to demonstrate their 16th-century presence in Mexico.

The representation of Christian subject matters both in a systematic way and through picture writing is, of course, not limited solely to Testerian manuscripts. Symbolic, phonetic, and rebus methods of representing the names of saints and Christian festivals have been studied by Galarza (1966), based primarily on occurrences in Codex Mexicanus (BNP 23-24) and Códice Sierra. The undeciphered mixed traditional and Christian signs across the top of pages 52–54 of Codex Mexicanus may represent a Christian prayer or text, possibly related to the passion and crucifixion of Christ (Joaquín Galarza, personal communication; Mengin, 1952a, p. 442).

The name of the 16th-century Franciscan, Fray Jacobo de Testera, has come to be associated with the pictorial catechisms, and the writing which characterizes them is known as Testerian writing. The attribution of the system to Testera rests on Mendieta's and Torquemada's description of his use of religious paintings, discussed above. Aubin (1849; quoted in Boban, 1891, 2: 176–82) was probably the first to use the adjective Testerian but he was careful to distinguish among religious paintings used in preaching, the ideographic-mnemonic system of recording the catechism (as described by Acosta and present in most surviving Testerian manuscripts), and the phonetic-rebus system (as described by Las Casas and Mendieta). Subsequent authors have accepted Testera's connection with the pictorial catechisms, although N. León (1897, pp. 288–89) doubts it. Tozzer (1941, p. 67, note 303) appears to attribute their invention to him. Testera may have introduced the idea of utilizing religious paintings for the spiritual education of the Indians, but there is reasonable historical doubt that he invented the type of manuscript and writing now associated with his name.

While the origins of Testerian manuscripts can be traced into 16th-century Mexico, the possibility of their having had antecedents outside of New Spain has not been investigated. The attempt to convey the written texts of the Church to illiterate heathens all around the world has undoubtedly led to many solutions, among which Testerian writing is but one.

A form of Testerian writing to record the prayers of the catechism has frequently been reported from 19th- and 20th-century Peru and Bolivia among Quechua and Aymara Indians. Ibarra Grasso (1953) illustrates numerous examples of these documents, some prepared by living informants. Miranda Rivera (1958) reproduces a number of South American examples in present-day use. Two specimens, on animal skins, are in the collections of the Peabody Museum, Harvard University. Another, with glosses in Quechua, on paper, is in the library of the Museum of the American Indian, New York. The historical connection between the 16th-century and later Testerian manuscripts from Mexico and the 19th- and 20th-century examples from South America is unknown.

The Mexican manuscripts give evidence from their physical characteristics and glosses that Testerian manuscripts continued to be produced into the 19th century. N. León (1897, 1900) observed that such manuscripts still could be found in the Otomi regions of Guanajuato and Queretaro during the 19th century. To what extent such occurrences were mere preservations and copies of antiquarian interest or were related to their continuing utility is, at present, conjectural. Several extant manuscripts may well have been drawn by the Mexican priest and linguist, Francisco Pérez. An Otomi scholar, Pérez published a translation of an Otomi catechism in 1834. He was known to Aubin, who acquired several manuscripts from him (nos. 807, 808, 816, 833, 834). In addition to these examples made or owned by him, he may be responsible for the glosses on three other manuscripts (John Carter Brown Library no. 3, Peabody Museum Library, and Romero de Terreros collection: nos. 826, 832, 835).

To date, few general studies of Testerian manuscripts have appeared. The first, by Aubin (1849; reprinted in Boban, 1891, 2: 176–82), discusses many pertinent references from the early chroniclers. Orozco y Berra (1877) also discusses many of the same references, describes several Testerian manuscripts, and offers translations of the symbols on two manuscripts. León (1897, 1900, 1968) provides general comments in addition to describing the manuscript which he published (no. 826). J. E. S. Thompson (1959, pp. 352–54) gives superficial generalizations about Testerian writing. More specific articles and translations of particular manuscripts are cited in the census.

Future research on Testerian manuscripts should include a study of the varying styles and differences in particular sets of figures in the 25 available examples. Such analysis might lead to information as to dating, authorship (Indian or European), and provenience. It may be noted that only one Testerian manuscript, that in the Deutsche Staatsbibliothek (no. 817), is reported to be painted on native paper. In addition, this example varies in size and style from all other known manuscripts and uses a highly variant set of symbols. Criteria which may segregate the other manuscripts into meaningful groupings are size (both of the manuscript pages and of the figures), the number of lines of figures to a page, the presence or absence of guidelines intended to accommodate interlinear glosses, and, of course, the particular type of figures. The unpublished Testerian manuscript of the Bibliothèque Nationale, Fonds Mexicains 399 (no. 810), may prove crucial to such investigation.

Further linguistic and symbolic analysis of the pictorial texts is also needed, as well as a more precise definition of the nature of Testerian writing and of its relationship to colonial Indian picture writing (mixed ideographic, rebus, mnemonic, and phonetic). The numerous "translations" of particular Testerian texts that have been made to date (and cited in the census) have served to identify the content of the manuscripts but have contributed little to the understanding of Testerian writing. The studies by Haberly (1963), Soustelle (1936–39), and J. E. S. Thompson (1959) have only initiated such analysis.

The language in which particular Testerian texts were intended to be read also requires attention. It is not known, for instance, if a given Testerian manuscript can be read with equal facility into Nahuatl, Otomi, Spanish, or Latin. It is possible that a somewhat differing sequence of figures may have been required for different languages. A related problem bears on the identity of the particular catechism on which the manuscript or manuscripts were based. Between the 16th and 18th centuries the wording of the catechism was revised, and therefore it may prove possible to identify particular Testerian texts with specific catechisms. N. León (1897, 1900) has touched upon this problem in dating the example he published. The availability of such

revised catechisms in Mexico, not only in Spanish but in the written or printed texts in the relevant Indian languages, will have to be considered. It may be noted that most of the glosses in the extant examples are in Otomi or Mazahua; only three manuscripts are reported as having Nahuatl glosses.

The major problem affecting Testerian manuscripts and writing has to do with their origins. Are they primarily an invention by the friars, stimulated by their knowledge of Central Mexican Indian rebus writing? The characteristics of Testerian writing as we know it today might have been comprehended readily by Central Mexican Indians, since they were accustomed to picture writing. Such an hypothesis, however, fails to explain the presence of a similar system of writing in South America, serving the same purpose, or the comparable picture writing of the 20th-century Cuna Indians in Panama.[3] Neither does it explain the survival of Testerian figures having no roots in native iconography in most of the extant examples or the disappearance of manuscripts bearing the traditional forms reported by Las Casas and Mendieta.

INTRODUCTION TO THE CENSUS

The main previous listing of Testerian manuscripts is that given in a brief notice by Barlow (1943c). It recorded 12 such manuscripts. The same number is also listed by Mateos Higuera (1966, nos. 54–65). The present census includes 23 examples in institutional collections, three published or partially published examples in private or unknown collections, and nine unidentified examples described in the literature since 1743

[3] Writing in Mexico about 1679, the Jesuit lay brother Manuel Duarte (1906, pp. 474–75) observed that the *Pantli-Nochtli* rebus system for recording Christian prayers must have been taught the Indians by the Apostle Saint Thomas (alias Quetzalcoatl) when he preached the gospel in the New World long before its "discovery" in 1492. This diffusionist fantasy at least has the merits of specifying the mechanism for transmission in the first century A.D.!

TABLE 2—TESTERIAN MANUSCRIPTS IN INVENTORIES OF THE
BOTURINI COLLECTION

Census Number	1743 1745	1746	Paper	Number of Leaves	Size	Gloss	Location
817	6-31	25-2	Native	"un pedazo"		-----------	DSB
811	6-32	25-3	European	4	4to	Otomi	-----------
812	6-33	25-4	European	44 or 48	8vo	-----------	-----------
809	6-34	25-1	European	11	4to	-----------	BNP 78

(Table 1). The total number represented is uncertain as there may be some duplication in the entries. Some of the manuscripts in institutional collections are copies and have not been compared with other manuscripts. Published information on most of the extant examples, some of which are wholly unpublished, is insufficient to permit comparison between them and the descriptions of the nine unidentified manuscripts.

Manuscripts in institutional collections are entered alphabetically in the census by the name of the institution, all others according to the name of a person associated with them. The main entry in the census gives information concerning titles, former owners, publication status, number of leaves, and dimensions. The descriptions are largely restricted to bibliographical information. Some further data, particularly catalog references and accession dates, are given in the institutional checklist (Article 28).

The collections of Testerian manuscripts made by Boturini in the 18th century and by Aubin in the 19th century must be mentioned. Those in the Boturini collection present a special problem. Four such documents are listed in the inventories of 1743 and 1745 as well as in the catalog of 1746. These four are noted as missing in the listings of 1823. This information is summarized in Table 2.[4]

Numbers 6-31 and 6-34 of the inventories of 1743 and 1745 may be identified with the example in the Deutsche Staatsbibliothek (Humboldt Fragment 16) and with one of the examples in the Bibliothèque Na-

tionale (Fonds Mexicains no. 78), respectively. Since numbers 6-32 and 6-33 have not been reliably identified, they are entered in the present census as unknown documents. Attempts to identify them with Fonds Mexicains nos. 76 and 77 of the Bibliothèque Nationale by Boban (1891, 2: 172–73) rest on no published facts.

Aubin (1849; quoted in Boban, 1891, 2: 178, 181) stated that he owned five Testerian manuscripts. He identified one of them as the manuscript now cataloged as BNP/FM 78. He then added that after the death of Francisco Pérez he acquired other examples, two with texts in Spanish, one in Otomi, and a fourth in Mexican (i.e., Nahuatl). The manuscripts with Otomi and Nahuatl texts are presumably BNP/FM 76 and 77. The two documents with Spanish texts were not acquired by Eugène Goupil, who purchased the Aubin collection. Boban (1891, 1: 19) reported that two pictorial catechisms were missing from the collection. Available evidence suggests that they are to be identified with the manuscripts once in the possession of Pérez and now in the Princeton University and Cleveland Public libraries (nos. 833, 834, 816).

We have not included in the census the reference by Aubin (1849; quoted in Boban, 1891, 2: 181) to two Testerian manuscripts in the Mexican National Museum (in the

---

[4] Bibliographical information on the inventories of the Boturini collection is given in Article 29. The seventh entry in an inventory of 1771 is a "librito chico que se dice ser cathecismo, por figuras." Nos. 1791-5a, 1791-5b, and 1804-5-3 are catechisms, but their identification remains to be made.

1830s) as they may be represented by examples already in the census. Aubin's description of a symbol on one of them may prove sufficient to identify it.

CENSUS OF MIDDLE AMERICAN TESTERIAN MANUSCRIPTS

801

Archivo Histórico del Instituto Nacional de Antropología e Historia, Mexico. Colección Antigua no. 254 (part). Copy by Faustino Galicia Chimalpopoca. Unpublished.

Various complete and fragmentary copies, in watercolor, ink, and pencil, of pages from one or more Testerian manuscripts are contained in Galicia Chimalpopoca's *Documentos históricos,* a 19thC compilation of miscellaneous copies, transcripts, and translations. Barlow (MS*c*) reports that these occur on ff. 273–74, 280–81, and 286–88. The volume has since been rearranged so that the drawings may now fall on new ff. 239–48. The originals of these copies are unidentified but may correspond to one or more of those listed elsewhere in the present census.[5]

Bibliography: Barlow, MS*c*.

802

Archivo Histórico del Instituto Nacional de Antropología e Historia, Mexico. Colección Antigua no. 776. "Doctrina Cristíana en Geroglíficos." Unpublished. 28 double leaves. 28 × 40 cm.

A very unusual example of a Testerian manuscript (see note 5).

Bibliography: None.

803

Archivo Histórico del Instituto Nacional de Antropología e Historia, Mexico. Colección Gómez de Orozco no. 183. "Códice Catecismo Gómez de Orozco." Partially published. 6 leaves painted on both sides. 15 × 10.5 cm.

The manuscript bears glosses in a native language. A single page is photographically reproduced by Zulaica Garate (1939, plate facing p. 16).

Bibliography: Zulaica Garate, 1939.

804

Archivo Histórico Nacional, Madrid. Biblioteca. Unpublished. 28 leaves.

The manuscript has been very briefly described by Sentenach (1900, pp. 603–04). He reports that it bears the legend "Explicación de la dotrina de los Yndios mucaguas" (i.e., Mazahuas?).

Bibliography: Sentenach, 1900.

805

Aubin, Testerian manuscript described by. Unknown. Unpublished.

In 1849 Aubin briefly described a pictorial catechism, a "Pater fragmentaire," which he said was in the "bibliothèque métropolitaine" of Mexico. He illustrated some of its figures which conform to the *pantli-nochtli* rebus system of rendering the words *Pater Noster.* The document is now unknown. Aubin's (1849, page references not determined) comment and illustration are reprinted in Boban (1891, 2: 181–82) and in Aubin (1885, pp. 29–30).

Bibliography: Aubin, 1849, 1885; Boban, 1891.

806

Biblioteca Nacional, Madrid. "Catecismo de la doctrina cristiana en jeroglíficos." Partially published. 42 leaves. 7.7 × 5.5 cm.

The document consists of two manuscripts bound together. The first, having 34 leaves, has been described as complete. The second has eight leaves from another example and bears the signature of Fray Pedro de Gante. There are apparently no further

---

[5] After this census was completed we were informed by Joaquín Galarza that nos. 801 and 802 are copies of the Testerian manuscript now in the British Museum (see no. 813).

major glosses other than a descriptive title in Spanish.

The manuscript has been studied and two of its pages photographically reproduced by Sentenach (1900). Four additional pages are similarly reproduced by Pérez Bustamante (1928, plate facing p. 96). Photographs of two pages are given in Sociedad Española (1930, no. 266, pl. 39, upper figure). A brief description is given by Paz (1933, p. 5, no. 13). The manuscript has recently been on display in the Museo de América, Madrid.

Bibliography: Paz, 1933; Pérez Bustamante, 1928; Sentenach, 1900; Sociedad Española, 1930.

807

Bibliothèque Nationale, Paris. Fonds Mexicains no. 76. Ex–Pérez, Aubin, and Goupil collections. Partially published. 18 (?) leaves. 21 × 16 cm. (published dimensions of 31 × 16 cm. must be in error).

The manuscript has been briefly described and two of its pages photographically reproduced by Boban (1891, 2: 171–72, pl. 76). Soustelle (1936–39) has studied certain of its linguistic aspects. It apparently has 18 leaves plus two further leaves with notes by Aubin. It is incomplete and, according to Boban, may be missing two leaves at the beginning and perhaps one or two at the end. It has a written Otomi text and Spanish headings.

Bibliography: Boban, 1891; Soustelle, 1936–39.

808

Bibliothèque Nationale, Paris. Fonds Mexicains no. 77. Ex–Pérez, Aubin, and Goupil collections. Partially published. 20 (?) leaves. 21 × 16 cm.

A brief description and a photo reproduction of two pages of the manuscript are given by Boban (1891, 2: 173–74, pl. 77). It has a Nahuatl text and the date 1719. Two leaves of notes in French concerning this manuscript are in BNP/FM 428, part 3.

Bibliography: Boban, 1891.

809

Bibliothèque Nationale, Paris. Fonds Mexicains no. 78. Ex–Boturini, Aubin, and Goupil collections. Partially published. 11 (?) leaves. 21 × 15 cm.

The manuscript has been briefly described and two of its pages photographically reproduced by Boban (1891, 2: 175–76, pl. 78). The same two pages are also reproduced by Robertson (1959, pl. 8). There are Spanish headings and a Spanish gloss identifying some of its drawings. Robertson (personal communication) reports that the date 1832 among other glosses on the cover disguises a Boturini collection inventory number. Boturini attributes the manuscript to Fray Bernardino de Sahagún, and Aubin reports that it bears Sahagún's name and notes (both are quoted in Boban, 1891, 2: 178).

Bibliography: Boban, 1891; Robertson, 1959.

810

Bibliothèque Nationale, Paris. Fonds Mexicains no. 399. Unpublished. Approximately 33 leaves. Octavo.

The manuscript contains Nahuatl texts and drawings of a non-Testerian nature (Article 23, no. 325) and two separate Testerian documents. The first occupies 35 pages and has both Spanish and Nahuatl glosses. The second, on 15 pages, has traditional devices and signs on the lower lines and is not glossed.

Photographs of the manuscript by William Gates are in LC, TU/LAL, and possibly at BYU (see Article 28, Appendix A, for references). A very brief description is given by Núñez y Domínguez (1947a, p. 364).

Bibliography: Núñez y Domínguez, 1947a.

811

Boturini Collection no. 1743-6-32. Unknown. Unpublished.

Four Testerian manuscripts are described in the Boturini collection inventories of 1743 and 1745 as items 31–34 of the sixth section. Two, nos. 31 and 34, probably correspond, respectively, to the example in the Deutsche Staatsbibliothek and to Fonds Mexicains no. 78 of the Bibliothèque Nationale. The two unidentified manuscripts are described here and in the next entry.

Item 6-32 of the 1743 inventory (Peñafiel, 1890, p. 64) is described as "Cuatro fojas útiles de los mismos caracteres de Doctrina cristiana y unos renglones en lengua otomi." In the 1745 inventory (P. Lopez, 1925, p. 42) the four Testerian documents are summarily described together; this particular manuscript is not specifically mentioned. The manuscript is paragraph 25, item 25, of the 1746 catalog (Boturini, 1746, 2: 54). It is described as an original in quarto and as "Unos principios de dicha Doctrina en 4. fojas de papel Europeo, y no continuados. Tienen, ademas de las Figuras, y Cifras, unos pocos renglones en lengua Otomi." The manuscript is not identifiable in later inventories.

Bibliography: Boturini, 1746; P. Lopez, 1925; Peñafiel, 1890.

812

Boturini Collection no. 1743-6-33. Unknown. Unpublished.

The second of the two unidentified Testerian manuscripts in the Boturini collection (see previous entry for general statement) is described in the 1743 inventory (Peñafiel, 1890, p. 64) as Item 33 of the sixth section: "Un librito con toscos dibujos, en papel de Castilla, forrado en una piel, que trata de dichos caracteres, en fojas cuarenta y cuatro." In the 1745 inventory the reference to a "librito entre ellos de a medio octabo" may refer to this manuscript (P. López, 1925, p. 42).

In the 1746 catalog (Boturini, 1746, 2: 54) the manuscript is described in paragraph 25, Item 4, as an original in octavo

and as "Un Librito en papel Europeo de 48. fojas chiquitas. Explica con toscas Figuras, y Cifras la dicha Doctrina." The document is not identifiable in later inventories.

Bibliography: Boturini, 1746; P. López, 1925; Peñafiel, 1890.

813

British Museum, London. Egerton MS 2898. Ex–Felipe Sánchez Solís and (possibly) Baron von Waecker-Götter collections. Partially published. 30 leaves. 24 × 16.5 cm.

The manuscript contains Nahuatl glosses, the date August, 1714, and the signature of a Lucas Matheo. It was acquired by the British Museum in 1911; its contents are outlined in the published catalog (British Museum, 1925, pp. 410–11). It has been described and one or two of its pages reproduced by Orozco y Berra (1877, pp. 212–13, plate facing p. 216, fig. 2). It is treated in a study by Mendoza (1877). The Orozco y Berra illustration has been reprinted a number of times, notably by Blake (1891, p. 83), Chavero (n.d., p. iv), and Cuevas (1921–28, 1: 186). A possibly related item is a copy, by F. Galicia Chimalpopoca, of a catechism by Lucas Matheo also dated August, 1714, formerly in the Ramírez collection (*Bibliotheca mexicana*, 1880, p. 71, no. 513) and now in the Bancroft Library (Barlow, 1943a, p. 198).

An important study of this manuscript is in preparation by Joaquín Galarza. See also nos. 801 and 802.

Bibliography: Barlow, 1943a; *Bibliotheca mexicana*, 1880; Blake, 1891; British Museum, 1925; Chavero, n.d.; Cuevas, 1921–28; Mendoza, 1877; Orozco y Berra, 1877.

814

Bullock Collection. Private collection. Ex–William Bullock, Duke of Sussex (Augustus Frederick, 1773–1843), and Sir Thomas Phillipps collections. Partially published. 35 leaves. 15.24 × 11.43 cm.

Two pages of the manuscript are photographically reproduced in a Phillipps collection auction catalog (Parke-Bernet, 1969, pp. 142–43, no. 1129). The same two pages were previously published in an advertisement for the sale (*Burlington Magazine*, May, 1969, p. xxix). Earlier descriptions are in the Phillipps catalog (Phillipps, 1837–71, no. 12243) and in the sale catalog of the Duke of Sussex collection (*Bibliotheca sussexiana*, 1844, p. 36, no. 400).

The description in the Sussex catalog identifies the manuscript as "brought from Mexico by Mr. Bullock, see his MS note"; the rest of the description is a condensed paraphrase of a description in one of the Bullock exhibit catalogs of 1824 (Bullock, 1824c, p. 49, no. 47). Some of the pictorial manuscripts acquired by Bullock when he visited Mexico in 1823 were from the Boturini collection and on loan to him from the Mexican government (see Glass, 1964, pp. 21–22). The anonymous annotator of the Phillipps sale catalog of 1969 (cited above) states, in connection with Bullock's museum in Piccadilly, that the manuscript was "no. 102 of catalogue." This catalog is unknown to us as is the answer to whether or not Bullock's "MS. note" mentioned in the Sussex catalog survives.

Phillipps gives its provenance as "Bright" —Benjamin Heywood Bright (d. 1843)— but we cannot identify it in the five Bright sales of June 3, 1844–July 7, 1845, or in that of June 18, 1844. As the Bright and Sussex manuscripts were sold in the same year, it may be that Phillipps confused the provenance.

Bibliography: *Bibliotheca sussexiana*, 1844; Bullock, 1824c; *Burlington Magazine*, 1969; Glass, 1964; Parke-Bernet, 1969; Phillips, 1837–71.

815

Chavero Collection. Unknown. Ex–Ramírez collection. Unpublished.

Chavero (1901a, p. 9) describes a Testerian manuscript in his collection as "Una doctrina en figuras, muy antigua y original. Se compone de 8 hojas en ovtavo pintadas con color azul por ambos lados, y con una cubierta de piel muy maltratada. Perteneció al Sr. D. José Fernando Ramírez." The manuscript now in the Hispanic Society of America (no. 823 of this census) may be a copy of this manuscript.

Bibliography: Chavero, 1901a.

816

Cleveland Public Library, Cleveland, Ohio. John Griswold White collection of Folklore and Orientalia. Ex–Pérez and Aubin collections. Unpublished. 14 leaves. 16 × 10.5 cm.

The manuscript includes a complete interlinear translation, in Spanish, in the handwriting of Francisco Pérez.

Bibliography: Sotheby and Co., 1936b, p. 35, no. 239.

817

Deutsche Staatsbibliothek, Berlin, East Germany. American Manuscript no. 1 (part). Humboldt Fragment 16. Ex–Boturini, León y Gama, and Humboldt collections. Published. Native paper. 1 leaf. 35 × 45 cm.

The manuscript is distinguished from other Testerians by its size, native paper, the clustering of symbols, and variant style and symbols. The identification of the paper fiber is discussed by Schwede (1916, pp. 52–54).

The manuscript was published, in color, by Humboldt (1810, p. 283, pl. 57). A b/w natural-size photoreproduction appears in *Historische Hieroglyphen* (1892). Seler (1893, pp. 116–23) gives a detailed commentary. An English translation of the commentary with an added reproduction of a copy is given in Seler (1904f, pp. 221–28, pl. 21). A slight revision of the commentary (Seler, 1902e, pp. 289–99) lacks a full reproduction. See Humboldt Fragments in pictorial census (Article 23) for a general statement concerning the Humboldt collection.

Bibliography: *Historische Hieroglyphen*, 1892; Humboldt, 1810; Schwede, 1916; Seler, 1893, 1902e, 1904f.

818–820

García Icazbalceta Collection. [nos. 1–3]. Unknown. Unpublished.

Three Testerian manuscripts in the Joaquín García Icazbalceta collection were described by Orozco y Berra (1877, pp. 215–16). Three such manuscripts are also listed, but not described, in the published catalog of the collection (Gómez de Orozco, 1927a, p. 87). They were not received by the University of Texas, which otherwise acquired most of the collection. Sentenach (1900, p. 599) reports that a Testerian manuscript in the collection bears the signature of Fray Pedro de Gante, a feature not mentioned by Orozco y Berra.

The first manuscript described by Orozco y Berra has 14 leaves. The second, seemingly by the same author as the first, is described as having six leaves plus 10 "double leaves." The third manuscript also has two parts: the first has 11 leaves and ends with verses in Spanish in honor of the Virgin; the second has 13 leaves. The descriptions contain sufficient further detail to permit identification of the manuscripts when they are found. It is possible that one or more of them may correspond to examples in institutional collections entered elsewhere in the present census.

Bibliography: Gómez de Orozco, 1927a; Orozco y Berra, 1877; Sentenach, 1900.

821

Granados y Gálvez, Testerian manuscript described by. Unknown. Unpublished.

Granados y Gálvez (1778, pp. 10–12) provides an interesting description of a pictorial catechism of 50 or 60 leaves. The Spaniard of his dialogues expresses surprise

that the figures of the manuscript are not "figuras tan horibles, que creyendo fueran algunos embelecos de sus hechizerias y supersticiones." The manuscript, which is now unidentified, included the *Pater Noster* and among its first figures were "unos monillos abrazados de un venerable anciano."

Bibliography: Granados y Gálvez, 1778.

822

Hispanic Society of America, New York [no. 1]. HC 417/50. *Cartilla de geroglíficos de la doctrina cristiana en idioma Otomi.* Partially published. 24 leaves. 21 × 16 cm.

A text in Spanish describing linguistic aspects of this 19th-century manuscript occupies ff. 1–3r and 24r. Half of the first leaf is missing. The drawings are on ff. 3v–23v, and there is an interlinear Otomi and Spanish translation (Otomi only on ff. 15–23). Part of the document is reproduced in a dealer's catalog (Hiersemann, 1913a, p. 12, no. 50, 1 plate facing p. 24). The number D4044377 appears on f. 24v.

The sale catalog description of a manuscript offered by a dealer in Mexico (Blake, 1909, p. 49, no. 665) suggests that it may be the same manuscript. This description is quoted in full:

Cartilla de geográficas (sic) de la doctrina Cristiana en Otomi (the rest of the title page is missing) (18th century manuscript). 46 pp. 8vo. n.d. Instruction in the Christian doctrine by means of hieroglyphs, for the use of some missionary among the Otomi Indians. Every word or phrase is represented by hieroglyphic figures; beneath them are the corresponding words written in Otomi; and, in most cases, the translation in Spanish. Original, very singular and interesting specimen of the manner of instructing the ignorant Indians in the rudiments of the Christian religion.

Bibliography: Blake, 1909; Hiersemann, 1913a.

823

Hispanic Society of America, New York [no.

2]. Wilkinson MS 142. Unpublished. 28 leaves. 21.3 × 15.7 cm.

The manuscript is probably a 19th-century copy. The first leaf bears the glosses "Catecismo en Geroglífico," "in °18–26 hojas," and a modern catalog designation. The Testerian drawings, with only a single word of gloss, occupy ff. 2v through 9r. The remaining leaves are blank. The manuscript was described in the first Paul Wilkinson collection sale catalog as having eight leaves (Anderson Auction Co., 1914, p. 16, no. 142). Many items from that sale were from the Chavero collection; it is conceivable that this manuscript may be a copy of the unidentified eight-leaf Testerian manuscript of the Chavero collection (no. 815 of this census).

Bibliography: Anderson Auction Co., 1914.

824

John Carter Brown Library, Brown University, Providence [no. 1]. Codex Ind. 25. Ex–Mrs. J. H. Pilling collection. Unpublished. 20 leaves. 10.7 × 8 cm.

Examination of the manuscript indicates that four leaves are missing from the present binding, two at the beginning and two at the end. There is some Spanish gloss in the manuscript. A photostatic copy is in the Peabody Museum Library, Cambridge.

Bibliography: None.

825

John Carter Brown Library, Brown University, Providence [no. 2]. Codex Ind. 24. Ex–José María Agreda and George Parker Winship collections. Unpublished. 28 leaves. 15.6 × 11 cm.

The manuscript is in poor condition but has been carefully restored. There are numerous blank pages. On the first leaf is a stamp with a monogram which appears to contain the letters G, M, and C. In correspondence preserved with the document Winship reports that it was purchased from

(José María de?) Agreda (y Sánchez?) in 1895. The existence of the manuscript is mentioned by Tozzer (1919).

Bibliography: Tozzer, 1919.

826

John Carter Brown Library, Brown University, Providence [no. 3]. Codex Ind. 26. Published. Ex–Stavenhagen collection. 13 leaves. 15.5 × 11 cm.

A general commentary and a full reproduction of the 22 utilized pages (ff. 1v–12r) of the manuscript are given by N. León (in English translation, 1900; in Spanish, 1968), who presumably owned it at the time. A shorter version of this work (N. León, 1897) contains a partial reproduction. A few glosses are said to be in Mazahua; others are in Spanish. Sapper (1901) provides a further discussion of the document, based on León's publication. The manuscript was in the possession of a Boston, Massachusetts, art dealer about 1963–68. A 14th and blank leaf was present in 1963.

Bibliography: N. León, 1897, 1900, 1968; Sapper, 1901.

827

Middle American Research Institute, Tulane University, New Orleans [no. 1]. Partially published. 14 leaves. 10 × 7.5 cm.

Two Testerian manuscripts in the TU/MARI collection were cataloged by Gropp (1933, pp. 233–36). One, now missing from the collection, is described in the next entry. The remaining manuscript is the smaller of the two documents; two of its pages are reproduced by Gropp (1933, fig. 3).

Bibliography: Gropp, 1933.

828

Middle American Research Institute, Tulane University, New Orleans [no. 2]. Partially published. 26 leaves.

The larger of the two Testerian manuscripts formerly in the TU/MARI collection (see previous entry) disappeared from the museum gallery in 1957. Two of its pages are reproduced in the announcement of its loss (Wauchope, 1957) and in the catalog by Gropp (1933, pp. 233–36, fig. 2).

Bibliography: Gropp, 1933; Wauchope, 1957.

829

Moxó, Testerian manuscript described by. Unknown. Unpublished.

Writing in 1805, Benito María de Moxó briefly described a Testerian manuscript in his possession: ". . . un catecismo entero de nuestra Santa Relijion, formado por un Neófito, y escrito todo del principio, al cabo con imajenes, ó figuras para uso de sus paisanos, los Indios Otomites. . . ." The manuscript had been found in Xilotepeque and given him by Juan José Pastor. The reference is published in Moxó's *Cartas mejicanas* (Moxó, 1837, p. 75; 1839, pp. 92–93) and perhaps also in the first version of that work (Moxó, 1828).

Bibliography: Moxó, 1828, 1837, 1839.

830 (fig. 98)

Museo Nacional de Antropología, Mexico. Codex collection, MNA 35-53. "Libro de Oraciones." Published. 11 leaves. 15.6 × 11 cm.

A few lines of gloss at the end of the manuscript are in Mazahua. A copy of the manuscript is reproduced in full and in color by Basich de Canessi (1963). Two pages are photographically reproduced by both Kelemen (1937, pp. 137–39, pl. 36) and by Glass (1964, p. 101, pl. 56). Four pages are similarly published by Cuevas (1921–28, vol. 1, plate facing p. 216).

Bibliography: Basich de Canessi, 1963; Cuevas, 1921–28; Glass, 1964; Kelemen, 1937.

831

Orozco y Berra Collection. Unknown. Partially published. 12 double leaves. Sextodecimo.

The manuscript is described by its owner as bearing the inscription "Cartilla de Maria-

no Tullucu." He offers a commentary and a translation of the part of the manuscript which he illustrates (Orozco y Berra, 1877; pp. 202–05, plate facing p. 216, fig. 1).

Bibliography: Orozco y Berra, 1877.

832

Peabody Museum Library, Harvard University, Cambridge. Ex–Edward B. Thompson and Charles P. Bowditch collections. Published. 25 leaves. 16 × 11 cm.

The manuscript is lacking at least two leaves at the beginning and at the end as well as two or more leaves internally. It has Spanish headings and a few glosses in a native language, presumably Otomi.

Two pages of the manuscript are photographically reproduced by Tozzer (1911, pl. 7). A limited photostatic edition is accompanied by a brief discussion of Testerian manuscripts by Tozzer (1919). A line-by-line and picture-by-picture translation has been prepared by R. Thompson (1949). A linguistic analysis of the symbols in one prayer in the manuscript is given by Haberly (1963).

Bibliography: Haberly, 1963; R. Thompson, 1949; Tozzer, 1911, 1919.

833

Princeton University Library, Princeton [no. 1]. Robert Garrett collection. Ex–Pérez and Aubin collections. Published. 26 leaves. 7.8 × 5.8 cm.

The manuscript is one of two Testerian documents that were described as lot 238 in a Sotheby and Co. sale catalog of November, 1936 (Sotheby and Co., 1936b, p. 35). The two manuscripts were purchased by Garrett during the same month through or from the London firm of Bernard Quaritch. Although the second manuscript includes a partial translation of the first, they are entered separately in the present census.

A photofacsimile edition has been published by Griffin (1968). Four pages are photographically reproduced in the sale catalog (loc cit., plate captioned "lot 238").

The manuscript has 51 pages of drawings with the final page blank and unpaginated. There is only one gloss, the word "errata" (?), on p. 31. On one of the preliminary leaves in the present binding is the curious legend "Alaja preciosal cogida al enemigo en Sn. Yago del Cerro."

Bibliography: Griffin, 1968; Sotheby and Co., 1936b.

834

Princeton University Library, Princeton [no. 2]. Robert Garrett collection. Ex–Pérez and Aubin collections. Unpublished. 10 leaves.

The second of Princeton's two Testerian manuscripts, together with the first, described above, formed lot 238 of a Sotheby and Co. sale catalog of 1936 (Sotheby and Co., 1936b, p. 35). It contains a partial translation of the first manuscript into Spanish by Francisco Pérez and copies or originals by Pérez of two separate series of Testerian drawings. Each of the latter occupies three pages and has an interlinear Spanish trans-

lation. The second of these two sets of drawings may be a copy of the two final pages of the Testerian manuscript of the Cleveland Public Library (no. 816). The final words in the manuscript read "Catecismo de geroglíficos Otomi, descifrado por el Presbitero D. Francisco Pérez, Catedrático de esta Universidad, y examinador sinodal de dicho Idioma Otomi. Mexico, Febrero 8, 1837. Francisco Pérez (rubric)."

Bibliography: Sotheby and Co., 1936b.

835

Romero de Terreros Collection. Mexico. Partially published. 21 (?) leaves. Quarto.

Two pages of the manuscript have been published photographically by its owner in a short article devoted to it (Romero de Terreros, 1942; reprinted in N. León, 1968, pp. 47–51). It has Spanish headings and an interlinear Mazahua translation except on the final pages.

Bibliography: N. León, 1968; Romero de Terreros, 1942.

REFERENCES (compiled by Mary W. Cline)

Acosta, 1962
Anderson Auction Co., 1914
Aubin, 1849, 1885
Barlow, MSc, 1943a, 1943c
Basich de Canessi, 1963
Bibliotheca mexicana, 1880
Bibliotheca sussexiana, 1844
Blake, 1891, 1909
Boban, 1891
Boturini Benaduci, 1746
British Museum, 1925
Bullock, 1824c
Burlington Magazine, 1969
Chavero, n.d., 1901a
Cuevas, 1921–28
Dávila Padilla, 1955
Duarte, 1906
Galarza, 1966
García Icazbalceta, 1941, 1954
Garibay, 1956
Glass, 1964

Gómez de Orozco, 1927a
Granados y Gálvez, 1778
Griffin, 1968
Gropp, 1933
Haberly, 1963
Hiersemann, 1913a
Historische Hieroglyphen, 1892
Humboldt, 1810
Ibarra Grasso, 1953
Kelemen, 1937
Kubler and Gibson, 1951
Las Casas, 1909
León, N., 1897, 1900, 1968
López, P., 1925
Marianus de Orscelar, 1625
Mateos Higuera, 1966
Maza, 1945
Mendieta, 1870
Mendoza, 1877
Mengin, 1952a
Miranda Rivera, 1958

Motolinía, 1858
Moxó, 1828, 1837, 1839
Núñez y Domínguez, 1947a
Orozco y Berra, 1877
Palomera, 1962, 1963
Parke-Bernet, 1969
Paz, 1933
Peñafiel, 1890
Pérez, F., 1834
Pérez Bustamante, 1928
Phillipps, 1837–71
Robertson, D., 1959
Romero de Terreros, 1942
Sapper, 1901

Schwede, 1916
Seler, 1893, 1902e, 1904f
Sentenach, 1900
Sociedad Española de Amigos del Arte, 1930
Sotheby and Co., 1936b
Soustelle, 1936–39
Thompson, J. E. S., 1959
Thompson, R., 1949
Torquemada, 1723
Tozzer, 1911, 1919, 1941
Valadés, 1579
Wauchope, 1957
Zulaica Garate, 1939

26. A Catalog of Falsified Middle American Pictorial Manuscripts

JOHN B. GLASS

PERIPHERAL TO THE total body of Middle American Indian pictorial manuscripts in the native tradition are the falsifications. The present catalog of such documents serves to identify a selected number of examples, particularly those specimens that have been published without having been identified as forgeries.[1]

The catalog of falsifications is limited primarily to originals in institutional collections and to originals and copies having a published bibliography. Numerous photographs in various repositories of unlocated originals are thus omitted. Only one of the 63 documents listed does not fit these criteria (no. 939, the Falsified Sahagún Festival Calendar). Twenty-three of the documents in the catalog have been published in whole or in part; 10, without any indication that they were suspect.

Forty of the documents in the catalog are in public repositories, a figure that probably represents only a fraction of the specimens so held. In this casual survey, little effort has been made to pursue reports of further originals located in several institutions. A spokesman for one major museum requested that we not publicize their small collection of falsifications, ostensibly because of the discredit that might be reflected on the collector or donor. Most falsifications in museum collections have been acquired as gifts or as part of larger collections; others may have been purchased in order to remove them from circulation or for a variety of other reasons. Few were acquired initially as authentic specimens.

Some falsifications inevitably find their way into the hands of dealers or auction houses. Depending on their knowledge and ethical standards, they may or may not advise prospective purchasers of the questionable nature of these items. The falsification known as Colección Chavero no. 1 (no. 902), for instance, was described in the catalog of a famous New York auction house

---

[1] Howard F. Cline provided extensive aid in the preparation of this catalog and placed a provisional listing and survey, which he made in 1963, at our free disposition. A memorandum on falsifications prepared by César Lizardi Ramos in 1962 for the Hispanic Foundation, Library of Congress, has also been helpful.

in 1963. When they were advised by us of its questionable nature, the owner withdrew it from the sale.

Archaeologists and museum curators are continually requested to identify manuscripts of doubtful authenticity owned by individuals and dealers. The total number of falsifications that have been examined under these circumstances is unknown but may be numbered in the hundreds. As a result of such inquiry, and from other sources, photographs of falsifications may be found in the collections of various museums and libraries. Often uncataloged, the photographs are usually identified with the name of the owner of the manuscript at the time that the photograph was taken. This transitory datum has little value for identification of the manuscript and would be of doubtful propriety in any published system of nomenclature. In view of the relative unimportance of falsifications, we have excluded photographs of privately owned or unlocated falsifications except when they have been the subject of published reference. Without this and other limitations the catalog would record a considerably greater number of examples.

Two listings of falsified pictorial manuscripts have been published. Blom (1935a) listed 10 "Maya" falsifications; only two of them have been included in the present catalog. Carcer (1948–49, 1949) described 12 falsifications; the five that have been published are relisted herein.

The catalog provides the following data: title or other designation, location, history, publication status, physical description, and bibliography.

Between the authentic manuscript and the outright fraud there is a wide range of documents whose nature is less susceptible to precise definition. Copies may be suspect, particularly when the original or other copies are unknown. If the copy is made on parchment, skin, cloth, or native paper the question of fraudulent purpose is inevitably

raised. The Museum für Völkerkunde in Hamburg, for instance, possesses a copy of Codex Boturini—"Mapa Monclova" (no. 963)—painted on leather. On the reverse are the coat of arms of a 17th-century viceroy and a corresponding date. This document might have been considered a 17th-century copy made for the viceroy, but Prem (1969) has shown that it is based on the 1858 edition of Codex Boturini and on an 1872/73 publication of coats of arms. It may be dated between 1873 and 1896, when it was acquired by the Hamburg museum.

Comparable in some respects to this copy of Codex Boturini is an old copy on parchment of one page of Codex Xolotl (no. 412), the original of which is on native paper. The copy would probably have been recognized as such on stylistic and other grounds even if the original were unknown. It is probable, however, that the copy has been identified mistakenly by former owners in the past as an original. Since the identity and intent of the artist are unknown, the document may be judged as a copy or as a falsification, depending on one's choice of alternative inferences. In this case, fraudulent or not, the copy is of value in reconstructing some details that have deteriorated on the original.

Two falsifications in the present catalog, the falsified version of Codex Colombino (no. 905) and Codex Moguntiacus (no. 923), contain pages copied from the genuine Codex Colombino as well as pages which merely imitate or are inspired by the style and content of that document. In describing Codex Moguntiacus, Mengin (1958a, 1958b) raised the question whether the latter pages might have been copied from lost pages of Codex Colombino. A similar question occurred to me in examining the relationship between the Falsified Drawing of the Conquest of Azcapotzalco (no. 901) and its major source, Codex Xolotl.

It is now known that the lost pages of

Codex Colombino were separated from the original before 1717, and Codex Xolotl was already in its present size in the early 17th century. Caso (in Caso and Smith, 1966, pp. 17–18) has shown that the pages in question in the two documents which derived from Codex Colombino are fraudulent imitations. I have reached the same conclusion with regard to the Azcapotzalco document. The possibility that a falsification may be based on an unknown authentic manuscript should, of course, be considered; the possibility that a relatively recent falsification of this character will be found is small.

Pictorial documents produced during the 17th and 18th centuries, particularly land titles and maps, present more complicated and subtle problems. Iconographic forms of the native tradition or place glyphs may be present but be so greatly altered by the later style of the artist and by degeneration of the tradition that they lead to inaccurate, unrecognizable, or meaningless detail. Such documents may combine contemporary material with information derived from older manuscripts. Although such a document may be authentic and made for a legitimate purpose, the pictorial content and glosses may reveal anachronistic elements and combinations, normally clues to fraudulence. If the document conveys information of an earlier period, only appropriate analysis can test its reliability and authenticity.

The Genealogía de la Familia Mendoza Moctezuma (Article 23, no. 197) is a case in point. The style, forms, material and composition all suggest a 17th- or 18th-century date. The painting portrays genealogical relationships among six prominent preconquest and early colonial Indians that are unsubstantiated by other documents. Since one version of the document forms part of a claim to hereditary rights based on the genealogy, a possible motive for deliberate falsification is present. We do not know if the painting was in existence before such claims were made or if it was made to form

part of the claims. Regardless of the accuracy of the genealogy, however, the document does illustrate the viability of the style and forms of the native tradition at the time it was painted, modified by the extent to which the artist may have believed he emulated older forms. The document may be an original composition, since we do not know to what extent the artist relied upon or copied an older version. Identification of this document as a falsification would not destroy its usefulness as an example of a late product, remotely in the native tradition.

Some of the late extant versions of such manuscripts as the Mapa de Santa Cruz Xoxocotlan, the Lienzo de Tetlama, and the Map of Chichimec History might be suspect were it not for the fact that other versions exist. In the case of the document known as Colección Chavero no. 5, it may be compared with a known prototype. The content of these documents and their glosses are credible. So long as they are recognized as late products and not mistaken for 16th-century manuscripts, they present few problems. Correct dating, even if only approximate, is crucial to the understanding and identification of any source.

Litigation and other legal proceedings have always provided the context for the falsification of genealogies, land titles, maps, and other historical documents. Forgeries made under such circumstances demand far more expert identification than do relatively modern products made to deceive the art collector into believing they are authentic preconquest or colonial documents. The question of false information in a document that is contemporary with its ostensible or purported date of manufacture (and this includes sources of any date) raises problems of historical analysis, historicity, and the nature of valid historical evidence, a very different matter from the expertise of art objects.

The 24 Puebla-Tlaxcala Village Maps in the Library of Congress (no. 937) are late 19th-century forgeries purporting to be of

16th-, 18th-, and 19th-century origin. The artists were convicted in a Mexican court for having forged the maps and the official seals which some of them bear. The validity and scholarly usefulness of the maps for cartographic and other information (as well as for questions of landownership and jurisdictional or boundary claims) are uncertain. To the extent that the documents may be geographically accurate or derive from older sources they may be of value when used with appropriate cautions.

The Techialoyan Codices of the late 17th or early 18th century are a comparable corpus of documents treated separately in this volume by Robertson (Article 24). As with the Puebla-Tlaxcala Village Maps, they were probably made by a group of entrepreneurs who catered to the needs of villages to substantiate landownership claims or questions of community jurisdiction. Despite their questionable origin they are valuable documents; however, their unusual nature must be recognized.

By falsified pictorial manuscript we refer to any relatively recent manuscript which at any given time and place might be identified mistakenly as a genuine preconquest or colonial Middle American Indian document painted in the style and with the iconographic forms of the native tradition. The intent to defraud by the artist or by any subsequent owner or dealer is thus not part of the definition, although motivation and purpose are important factors in the existence of any falsification. Suspect copies and facsimiles of authentic single originals present a special problem; they are best classified on the basis of their individual merits.

The known falsifications of 19th- and 20th-century origin recorded in the catalog vary widely in content and techniques of execution, in the type of manuscript imitated, and in material. Their content includes outright invention based on fantasy and imagination, with little recourse to specific models. Others combine invention with details copied from reproductions of authentic manuscripts, sculpture, or other types of artifacts. It is a characteristic of many falsifications that their content derives from quite disparate sources and cultures. These features are frequently arranged into patterns that have no meaningful structure. In the case of calendrical signs they may be found in meaningless sequences. The most flagrant and readily recognized modern forgeries appear to date from the period after about 1885–1900, when reproductions of such documents as the Lienzo de Tlaxcala and various Maya, Borgia Group, and Mixtec screenfolds first became widely available, either in facsimile editions or in secondary sources. Falsifications based on these sources may be recognized readily by the experienced observer; in most cases little research is necessary to identify the originals on which they are based. Few falsifications have been made with the care necessary to deceive the expert.

The material on which the falsified pictorial manuscripts reported in the catalog are painted includes a variety of substances: amatl paper, imitations of native paper using agave or cotton fibers, parchment, cloth, and various kinds of animal skins. Not in the catalog is a document in a private collection concocted from several published sources and drawn on "European" paper. The owner informs us that the paper exhibits 16th-century watermarks.

Two documents in the catalog are painted on amatl paper, the material of which many authentic preconquest and colonial manuscripts are made. The paper of the Falsified Drawing of the Conquest of Azcapotzalco (no. 901) has been analyzed by Schwede (1916, pp. 44–45) and that of the Falsified Sahagún Festival Calendar (no. 939) specifically for me by two qualified experts. These two specimens are also the "best" of the known falsifications in that they are not immediately recognizable as such. The less convincing Waldeck Calendar Wheel (no. 947) may also be made of amatl paper.

The Falsified Drawing of the Conquest of Azcapotzalco is one of the oldest of the known falsifications, having been acquired by Waldeck in 1831–32. The only other falsifications with comparable suspected antiquity are the Waldeck Calendar Wheel, acquired by Waldeck in 1831, and the manuscript known as Colección Chavero no. 1 (no. 902), which was allegedly owned by Pichardo, whose death occurred in 1812. The Azcapotzalco document portrays an event in the Tepanec War of 1428 A.D., the death of Mazatl at the hands of Moctezuma Ilhuicamina. Also shown are Maxtla and Itzcoatl, rulers of Azcapotzalco and Tenochtitlan, respectively, as well as the place glyph for Azcaptozalco and the *temazcal* or sweat bath in which Maxtla took refuge after his defeat.

For the pictorial content and composition of this falsification the unknown artist drew on the then unpublished Codex Xolotl and on some details from pictorial manuscripts that had been published by Clavigero as early as 1780–81. The narrative content of the depiction may also have been taken from Clavigero (1780–81, 1: 215–19; or any one of six translations published before 1831). For this account Clavigero probably drew upon a Nahuatl historical text known only through its publication and translation in Torquemada's *Monarquía indiana* (1723, 1: 140–41). This particular account of the Tepanec War is the only one that provides the "story" depicted in the drawing.

This falsification is unique in that the artist held original invention to a minimum by adapting authentic pictorial forms to the portrayal of a known event in Aztec history. The calendrical signs and dates that the artist used, however, have no meaningful structural significance, and the style and proportions of the drawing are not those of either preconquest or 16th-century periods of Mexican Indian manuscript painting. Had the artist forged an 18th-century copy rather than imitated a 16th-century manuscript, its identification would have been more difficult.

The Falsified Sahagún Festival Calendar is another falsification distinguished by relatively careful attention to detail. As with the Azcapotzalco manuscript, the artist avoided the invention of pictorial forms by copying an authentic manuscript. In this case, the original was a colonial Nahuatl text with drawings on European paper. The artist rearranged the pictures and texts, placing them on an amatl paper screenfold. Technical analysis of the manuscript identified the sizing as lithopone and one of the pigments as Prussian Blue. Both are 19th-century chemicals, incompatible with a supposed 16th-century amatl paper screenfold. In addition, the artist outlined the drawings in pencil before painting them in. The manuscript which was copied, the Primeros Memoriales (Article 23, no. 271), was virtually unknown (except to a restricted number of scholars) until it was copied by Genaro López for Francisco del Paso y Troncoso about 1893–94. Photographs of the original and color lithographs were printed about 1905 (Paso y Troncoso, 1905–07, vol. 6, part 2) but had little circulation until into the 1920s. These facts bear upon the possible date and authorship of this falsification.

A most curious series of falsifications is painted or drawn on large animal hides. In some instances the hides have not been trimmed into rectangular shapes but preserve parts of the skin extending toward the legs, neck, or tail. From photographs of some of these specimens it is also evident that the hair has not been removed from, or shaved off, the outside. What model for this form the artists had in mind is unknown, the closest Indian artifact being the painted buffalo hides of the North American Plains Indians. The 14 "Zaremba" falsifications (nos. 949–962) are all of this nature. Their content includes invented fantasies and details from a wide variety of sources, many available as reproductions in Chavero (n.d.), published about 1887. Also in this class are the examples entered in the catalog under the names of Lumholtz, Museo de América, Museo Nacional de Antropología, and Parma. It is probable that the Pinart falsifications (nos. 931–933) also belong in this category.

The most notorious group of falsifications is painted on a heavily sized and very coarse brown fiber material that has been reported to be coconut fiber. This identification appears not to have been confirmed by technical analysis. The use of this bizarre material, which in no way resembles any authentic Indian paper, probably serves to identify the product of a single artist or school of forgers. Its use seems to have been reported first by Batres (n.d., p. 10), writing about 1910, whose statement I here translate: "Recently, imitations of pictorial manuscripts of different cultures and of different types are being made. These are true works of art and employ the fiber from the covering or sheath of the coconut as an imitation of the paper used in authentic manuscripts."

Batres published one example of this type of falsification, Códice Fantástico (no. 907). At least six further specimens in the present catalog are of the "coconut" fiber group:

908. Falsified MS purchased from Hans Gadow
917. Codex López
942. Falsified MS purchased from the Sonora News Co.
943. Códice de Comillas
945. Primer Códice de la Granja
946. Cuadro Genealógico de Tulantzinco

Photographs of Codex of Liberec, Codex Moguntiacus, and the falsified ball-court scene of the Royal Ontario Museum (nos. 915, 923, 938) suggest that they may also be made of this material. Carcer (1948–49, pp. 109–12, nos. 2A and 7) reports two additional examples not in the present catalog.

The name of the Mexican artist Genaro López has come to be associated with this type. López is known in more legitimate contexts as the copyist and lithographer for three major publications of pictorial manuscripts published by the Mexican government. The first, under the auspices of the Junta Colombina (Chavero, 1892) reproduced five pictorial manuscripts; Lienzo de Tlaxcala, and Códices Baranda, Dehesa, Colombino, and Porfirio Díaz. Later he was in Spain and Italy, employed by Francisco del Paso y Troncoso to copy the illustrations in the Sahagún manuscripts, Códices Matritenses and the Florentine Codex (Paso y Troncoso, 1905–07). The color lithographs of the Veytia Calendar Wheels (Veytia, 1907) carry his name as lithographer.

Although he did not mention him by name, Paso y Troncoso (in Chavero, 1901c, pp. 3–4) appears to attribute the Colección Chavero MS no. 3 (no. 904) as well as other falsifications to López. Somewhat later Batres (n.d., p. 14) also associates López with falsifications, but again his name is not mentioned (my translation):

One of the most dangerous forgers that there is in the attempt to deceive is a draftsman that a well-known Mexican archaeologist took to Europe as an employee to copy the illustrations of the historical work of Sahagún. I say that he is very dangerous because a multitude of original pieces are familiar to him and have passed through his hands to copy the mentioned work. For that reason he has extraordinary talent for this type of work and for that reason his works are convincing.

A more specific and circumstantial account of Genaro López as a falsifier of pictorial manuscripts is given by Carcer (1948–49, pp. 106–07), quoting Federico Gómez de Orozco, a well-known Mexican bibliophile and historian who had acquired many of Francisco de Paso y Troncoso's papers. Utilizing information from Gómez de Orozco, Carcer attributed eight specific falsifications to López. Two were made of cotton fiber, one of agave paper, and five of coconut fiber. Another manuscript is attributed to López by Blom (1935a).

302

Since Batres, who was a contemporary of both López and Paso y Troncoso, described the coconut-fiber type of falsification without attributing that type to López, the reliability of the attribution of the coconut-fiber type to him rests on uncertain evidence. Although the attribution has entered the folklore of archaeology as a fact, it must be considered an unproven allegation. Lizardi Ramos (preface to Loukotka, 1957) has doubted that the crude forgeries represented by the coconut-fiber examples are compatible with the known artistic abilities that López possessed as a copyist.

Other names that have been associated with falsifications are Miguel Saad as a dealer of Merida, Yucatan; Alfredo Chavero as a gullible collector; and T. A. Willard, also as a collector.

Falsifications will undoubtedly continue to be made so long as there exists a tourist or collector who can be swindled or interested in their purchase. The museum curator and archaeologist will continue to be approached by hopeful owners with requests to authenticate doubtful manuscripts. In recent years we have personally had occasion to inspect about 15 or more fraudulent manuscripts, referred to us for identification. Independent of information supplied by the owners, we were able to determine that two of these had been examined by other archaeologists over 15 years previously. It thus appears that many manuscripts are repeatedly identified—perhaps every time the document changes hands! We know of one archaeologist, a specialist in Maya hieroglyphs, who almost categorically refuses to consider requests to examine newly "discovered" Maya manuscripts. Since authentic colonial pictorial manuscripts have been discovered and will continue to appear, the effort expended in examining new discoveries is perhaps worth the trouble.

CATALOG OF FALSIFIED MIDDLE AMERICAN PICTORIAL MANUSCRIPTS

901 (fig. 99)

Azcapotzalco, Falsified Drawing of the Conquest of. NLA 1271c. Ex–Waldeck collection. Published. Amatl paper. 24.1 × 33.5 cm.

A line drawing of the manuscript is reproduced without comment by Ober (1883 and later editions). Waldeck mentions the document under dates of Oct. 24, 1831, and Jan. 14, 1832, in his unpublished journal (MS in British Museum). Many of its pictorial forms derive from Codex Xolotl. See introduction to this catalog, above, for further comment.

Bibliography: Ober, 1883, p. 139; Schwede, 1916, pp. 44–45; Ternaux-Compans *in* Ixtlilxochitl, 1840, 1: 214; Ternaux-Compans, MS, no. 123; Waldeck, MS, p. 129, no. 123.

❖❖❖

CHAVERO, COLECCIÓN. Under this name Chavero (1901a,b,c) published five pictorial manuscripts. Seler (1901b) denounced nos. 1 and 2 as falsifications. Paso y Troncoso (quoted in Chavero, 1901c, pp. 3–4) denounced nos. 1, 2, and 3. Chavero (ibid., pp. 4–6) defends their authenticity, primarily on the basis of the 19th-century history of nos. 1 and 2. Batres (n.d., p. 7) refers briefly to their publication. For information on nos. 4 and 5, see Article 23, nos. 44 and 167.

902

—— *no. 1.* Mapa de Tlaxcallan. Private collection (the Hearst Corporation as of 1963). Ex–Pichardo, Chavero, and W. R. Hearst collections. Published. Skin. 59 × 87 cm.

Publication: Chavero, 1901a, pp. 13–31, 38–44, pl. 1; Johnson, 1933; Parke-Bernet, 1963, pp. 55, 57, no. 134.

Other: Chavero, 1901c, p. 6; Paso y Troncoso *in* Chavero, 1901c, pp. 3–4; Gibson, 1952, p. 267; Seler, 1901b.

903

—— *no. 2.* Códice Ciclográfico. Unknown. Ex–Manuel Cardoso (ca. 1863) and Chavero collections. Published. Skin. 13 leaves. ca. 20 × 26 cm. (total length, 346.5 cm).

Publication: Chavero, 1901a, pp. 45–49, pl. 2.

Other: Chavero, 1901c, pp. 4–5; Paso y Troncoso *in* Chavero, 1901c, pp. 3–4; Seler, 1901b.

904

—— *no. 3.* Calendario o Rueda del Año. Unknown. Ex–Chavero collection. Published. Skin. 60 × 41 cm.

Publication: Chavero, 1901b.

Other: Chavero, 1901c, p. 6; Paso y Troncoso *in* Chavero, 1901c, pp. 3–4.

905

Colombino, Códice, Falsified version of the.

Códice de la Mixteca. Unknown. Unpublished. Sized native paper screenfold painted on both sides. 14 leaves. 19.5 × 392 cm. (total length).

A watercolor copy of 1912 and a five-page description dated 1916 by Manuel Velasco are in the Peabody Museum Library, Harvard University. Of its 28 pages, 22 correspond to as many pages of Códice Colombino, four pages correspond to published pages of the falsified Codex Moguntiacus (no. 923), and two pages are sheer falsifications based on Códice Colombino. The original was reportedly taken to Europe in 1913.

Caso (in Caso and Smith, 1966) reports the existence of another version of the copy by Velasco and comments on both copies and their relationships to Codex Moguntiacus and Códice Colombino.

Bibliography: Caso and Smith, 1966, pp. 17–18.

906

Contlán, San Bernardino, Mapa Original del Pueblo de. Uncertain. Published.

A certified copy from the early part of this century is in the INAH (Colección de Planos y Mapas, no. 34, leg. 4, no. 1) and was formerly in the INAH codex collection (no. 27 of the 1934 inventory of copies; see Glass, 1964, p. 28). The copy is published in the *Boletin* of the INAH (no. 2, Mexico, 1960, p. 13, fotos 8–9). The original probably has the same origins and characteristics as the 24 Puebla-Tlaxcala Village Maps in the LC (no. 937), to judge from appearance, general style, orthography, and placement of legends on the copy. Some additional data appear to be given by Mateos Higuera (1966).

Publication: loc. cit.

Other: Glass, 1964, p. 28; Mateos Higuera, 1966, p. 13, no. 77.

907

Fantástico fabricado con fibra de la envoltura de coco, adobado con yeso y azúcar y pintado con fuchinas, Códice. Unknown. Published. Single panel of coconut fiber. (Published reproduction is 37 × 46 cm.).

Publication: Batres, n.d., p. 18, second folding plate following p. 30.

Other: Carcer, 1948–49, p. 112, no. 9.

908

Gadow, Hans, Falsified manuscript purchased from. AMNH (1902–22) no. 65-3565. Unpublished. Single panel of coconut fiber.

Bibliography: None.

909

Gomesta Manuscript. Miguel Saad Manuscript. Unknown. Published.

Photographic negatives are in the Peabody Museum, Harvard University.

Publication: Gates, 1935b.

Other: Anonymous, 1935b, 1937; Blom, 1935b; Sorenson, MS; Soustelle, 1935–36.

910

GOTEBORG, ETNOGRAFISKA MU-SEET. *Forged Maya Codex on Parchment.* Partially published. Parchment screenfold. 20 leaves. 15.5 × 17 cm.

Partial publication: Wassen, 1942.

Other: Anonymous, 1946.

911

Hall, Codex. Unknown (possibly in Philo-sophical Research Society, Los Angeles). Published. Agave (?) fiber paper tira. 19.7 × 125.7 cm.

Publication: Dibble, 1947.

Other: Carcer, 1948–49, pp. 110–11, no. 4; Kubler, 1949.

912

Hammaburgensis, Codex. Museum für Völkerkunde, Hamburg. Published. Cotton fiber panel. 61.5 × 58 cm.

Publication: Danzel, 1926a.

Other: Carcer, 1948–49, p. 109, no. 1; Dan-zel, 1926b, 1928.

913

HISPANIC SOCIETY OF AMERICA, New York. Falsified ball-court scene. Unpub-lished. Single panel of deer (?) skin or imi-tation parchment.

The manuscript (together with a separate description in Spanish) was sold to Archer Huntington in 1911 as a modern falsification by the German bookdealer Karl Hiersemann of Leipzig. The painting shows five Indians playing ball in a ball court. It closely re-sembles the falsified ball-court scene in the Royal Ontario Museum (no. 938).

Bibliography: None.

914

JOHN RYLANDS LIBRARY, Manchester. Mexican manuscript no. 3. Unpublished. Not examined (information communicated by Donald Robertson).

Bibliography: None.

915 (fig. 100)

Liberec, Codex of. The Jablonec Codex. Severoceske Museum, Liberec, Czechoslo-vakia. Partially published. Sized coconut-fiber screenfold painted on both sides. 18 leaves. 26.5 × 15.5 cm.

A complete set of photographs is in PML.

Partial publication: Loukotka, 1956, 1957.

Other: Anonymous, 1956; Rodríguez, 1957; Solc, 1956.

916

LIBRARY OF CONGRESS. Unnamed fal-sified pictorial manuscript transferred from Art Department, Colby College, Waterville, Maine. LC, Manuscripts Division, Ac. 13238. Imitation (?) native paper. 28 × 44 cm.

Brief mention: Cline, 1966a, p. 80.

917

López, Codex. TU/LAL. Ex–Martel col-lection. Unpublished. Coconut-fiber screenfold. 32 pages.

Brief mention: Blom, 1935a, no. 3.

918

Loubat, Duc de, False Maya codex, gift of the. AMNH (1901–04) no. 30-9530. Un-published.

Bibliography: None.

919

Lumholtz, Carl, Collection, Falsified pictori-al manuscript of the. AMNH (1896–11) no. 30.3-789. Unpublished. Skin. 73.5 × 63.5 cm.

Bibliography: None.

920

Maya Codex, Another falsified. Private col-lection. Unpublished. Parchment screen-fold. 16 leaves. 7.5 × 9.5 cm.

Bibliography: Brainerd, 1948.

921

Merida, Codex. Unknown. Published. Publication reproduces 12 pages.

Unverified information locates the document in the Southwest Museum, Los Angeles, possibly in the T. A. Willard collection.

Publication: Stacy-Judd, 1940.

922

Merida, Map of. Aztec painting of the siege of Tenochtitlan. Museum of New Mexico, Santa Fe. Sylvanus G. Morley collection. Ex–Miguel Saad collection. Published. Single panel of sized cloth.

Photographic negative in Peabody Museum, Harvard University.

Publication: Blacker, 1965, pp. 144–45.

923

Moguntiacus, Codex. Private collection, Mainz, Germany (as of 1954). Partially published.

The manuscript contains pages based on Lienzo de Tlaxcala, copies of 20 pages of Códice Colombino, and nine pages in a pseudo-Mixtec style based on Códice Colombino. Four of the latter are published by Mengin (1958a) and are similar to pages of the falsified version of Códice Colombino copied by Velasco (no. 905). Caso (in Caso and Smith, 1966) reports that the entire manuscript is a falsification.

Partial publication: Mengin, 1958a.

Other: Caso and Smith, 1966, pp. 17–18; Mengin, 1958b.

❖❖❖

Monclova, Mapa. See no. 963.

❖❖❖

924

MUSÉE DE L'HOMME, Paris. Unnamed falsified pictorial manuscript. Unpublished.

Brief mention: Galarza, 1960, p. 70, note 1.

925

MUSEO DE AMÉRICA, Madrid. Un-

named falsified pictorial manuscript. Unpublished. Single panel of animal hide.

Brief description: Fernández Vega, 1965, p. 151.

926

MUSEO NACIONAL DE ANTROPOLOGÍA, Mexico. Copies of an unnamed falsified pictorial manuscript. Unpublished.

An uncataloged tracing and photograph of a falsified pictorial manuscript painted on animal hide are in the MNA codex collection. The tracing bears stamps of the Exposición Histórico Americana de Madrid of 1892 and the photograph is no. 68 of the 1934 inventory of copies(see Glass, 1964). The location of the original is unknown.

Brief mention: Glass, 1964, p. 25.

927

MUSEUM OF THE AMERICAN INDIAN, HEYE FOUNDATION, New York. Unnamed falsified pictorial manuscript. Unpublished. Single panel.

Bibliography: None.

928

NELSON GALLERY OF ART, Kansas City, Missouri. Unnamed falsified pictorial manuscript. Unpublished. 22 leaves.

Bibliography: None.

929–930

PARMA. R. Museo d'Antichita (Museo Archeologico Nazionale?). "Due Pergamene Messicane." Published. Two separate documents on animal hide, 65 × 45 cm. and 82 × 74 cm.

Publication: Callegari, 1911.

Other: Callegari, 1914.

❖❖❖

PINART COLLECTION. The three items listed below are identified as falsifications solely on the basis of sale catalog descriptions. They are sufficiently detailed to allow identification of the manuscripts.

931

—— [no. 1]. Conquest of Cuetlaxtlan by Montezuma the first in 1457. Unknown. Unpublished. Skin. 76 × 30 cm.

Bibliography: Catalogue, 1883, p. 124, no. 721 (part); Quaritch, 1885, pp. 2898–99, no. 29042.

932

—— [no. 2]. Scenes of Mexican history. Unknown. Unpublished. Skin. 78.5 × 68.5 cm.

Bibliography: Catalogue, 1883, p. 124, no. 721 (part); Quaritch, 1885, p. 2899, no. 29043.

933

—— [no. 3]. Theogonic or genealogical tree representing apparently the succession or relationship of the deities of Mexican mythology. Unknown. Unpublished. Skin. 61 × 38 cm.

Bibliography: Catalogue, 1883, p. 124, no. 721 (part); Quaritch, 1885, p. 2899, no. 29044; 1895, p. 200, no. 1949.

934

Pingret Collection Manuscript no. 2. Unknown (California bookdealer in 1963 and 1969). Published. Skin. ca. 33 × 76 cm.

Pingret Manuscript no. 1 (Lucien de Rosny's numeration) is the Techialoyan Codex of Tepotzotlan (second fragment, no. 714). It bears the number 943 and is also described in the works of 1909 and 1875 cited below. Pingret Manuscript no. 2 bears the numbers 942 and 10 from an unidentified series of catalog numbers. Around three sides are 51 Central Mexican year-bearer day glyphs; in the center are dates, place glyphs, and Nahuatl glosses. Identification of this document as suspect is based on an unpublished memorandum by H. B. Nicholson dated April 15, 1961. A photograph appears in a recent dealer's catalog (Bennett and Marshall, n.d.).

Bibliography: Antiquités Aztèques, 1909, part 2, second item; Bennett and Marshall,

n.d. [1970?], p. 2, no. 9 and facing plate; Lucien de Rosny, 1875, pp. 224–25.

935

Porrúa, Manuel, Códice. Cueros de Porrúa. Manuscrito pictórico de la cultura Maya sobre piel de mamifero. Unknown. Published. Painted on numerous small pieces of animal skin.

Publication: Manuscrito pictórico, 1957.

Other: Bernal and Sodi Pallares, 1958–59; Lizardi Ramos, 1958, 1959; Martínez Paredes, 1958; Ruz Lhuillier, 1958–59; Sodi Pallares, 1958; Stuiver, Deevey, and Rouse, 1963, p. 332.

936 (fig. 101)

PRINCETON UNIVERSITY LIBRARY. Garrett collection. Ex–Gates collection. Unnamed falsified pictorial manuscript. Unpublished. Imitation native paper. 58 × 58 cm.

Bibliography: None.

937

Puebla-Tlaxcala Village Maps, nos. 1–24. LC, Manuscripts Division, Ac. 7828, D. R. 2391. Partially published. European paper. 24 maps of various sizes.

Apparently manufactured between 1865 and 1870, the maps form part of a large corpus of documents entered for evidence in litigation in the District Court of Puebla, 1870–72. The maps include interesting portrayals of buildings, churches, people, etc. Although the maps purport to be of 16th-, 18th-, and 19th-century origin, no particular imitation of the older native tradition is evident. One of the maps is reproduced by Cline (1966a). See Mapa Original del Pueblo de San Bernadino Contlan (no. 906) for a related document.

Partial publication: Cline, 1966a, p. 79, fig. 3.

938

ROYAL ONTARIO MUSEUM, Toronto, Canada. Falsified ball-court scene. Unpublished. Single panel of sized coarse fiber. 48 × 63 cm.

The painting is similar to the falsified ball-court scene in the Hispanic Society of America (No. 913).

Bibliography: None.

939

SAHAGÚN. Falsified festival calendar. Private collection, Ex–H. A. Monday collection. Unpublished. Amatl-paper screenfold. 10 leaves. 19.5 × 159 cm. (total length).

The manuscript is a copy of the first 18 drawings and Nahuatl texts of Fray Bernardino de Sahagún's Primeros Memoriales (Article 23, no. 271). Technical analysis performed at the Museum of Fine Arts, Boston, in 1963 identified the sizing as lithopone and one of the paint pigments as Prussian Blue, both of which are 19th-century chemicals.

Bibliography: None.

940 (fig. 102)

Saville Fragment. Unknown. Unpublished. Bark fiber. 24 × 14 cm.

A photograph of 1901 is among the M. H. Saville papers in the AMNH. Cline (1966c) lists the document as an unidentified Oaxaca pictorial manuscript. The document was subsequently identified as a falsification by both Cline and Caso (personal communications).

Bibliography: Cline, 1966c, p. 124, no. 25.

941

SMITHSONIAN INSTITUTION. Museum of Natural History, Office of Anthropology, archaeology cat. no. 300298. Unnamed falsified pictorial manuscript. Unpublished. Parchment screenfold painted on both sides. 11 leaves. 15 × 11.5 cm.

Bibliography: None.

942

Sonora News Co., Falsified pictorial manuscript purchased from the. AMNH (1910–

35) no. 65-3299. Unpublished. Single panel of sized coconut fiber.

Bibliography: None.

❖❖❖

TLAXCALA, LIENZO DE. *See* Article 23, no. 350. Falsified versions:

943

—— *Códice de Comillas.* Private collection of the Marqueses de Comillas, Santander, Spain. Published. Single panel of sized coconut fiber. 90 × 106 cm.

The painting has three rows with three scenes in each row, corresponding to nine scenes from the Lienzo de Tlaxcala.

Publication: Carcer, 1948–49, pp. 111–12, no. 5, fig. 5; 1949, page reference not determined.

Other: Ballesteros Gaibrois, 1948b, p. 678; Barón Castro, 1949; Gibson, 1952, p. 250; Tudela, 1948b, 1949.

944

—— Dorenberg photographs of a falsified version of the Lienzo de Tlaxcala. Location of original unknown. Unpublished.

The photographs are in the British Museum to which Dorenberg sent them in 1910. Gibson (1952) reports that they correspond to nine scenes of the Lienzo de Tlaxcala.

Brief mention: Gibson, 1952, p. 250.

945

——*Primer Códice de la Granja.* Unknown. Published.

The document is similar in size, physical characteristics, and content to the Códice de Comillas (no. 943).

Publication: Carcer, 1948–49, pp. 107–08, 112, no. 6, fig. 6; 1949, page reference not determined.

Other: Gibson, 1952, p. 250.

946

Tulantzinco, Cuadro Genealógico de. HSA.

Unpublished. Single panel of sized coconut fiber. 82 × 59 cm.

On the reverse of the mounting board is an inscription bearing the putative date of 1705. The manuscript (together with a modern description in Spanish) was sold to Archer Huntington in 1911 by the German bookdealer Karl Hiersemann. A photograph is in the British Museum, to which it was sent by Dorenberg in 1910.

Bibliography: None.

947 (fig. 103)

Waldeck Calendar Wheel. NLA 1271e. Ex–Nebel collection. Unpublished. Native paper. 32 × 36 cm.

The document is mentioned in Waldeck's unpublished journal (MS in British Museum) under dates of 15, 16, and 20 January 1831. A copy, together with a copy of the calendar wheel diagram published by Granados y Gálvez (1778), both by Waldeck, are also in NLA. The original bears some resemblance to a suspect calendar wheel published by Chavero (n.d.).

Bibliography: Chavero, n.d., p. 726; Granados y Gálvez, 1778, plate facing p. 56; Ternaux-Compans, MS, no. 125; Waldeck, MS, p. 101, no. 97.

948

WALLACE, WALTER THOMAS, COLLECTION. Falsified pictorial manuscript. Unknown. Partially published. Skin screenfold. 17 leaves. 26.7 × 16.5 cm.

Apparently the same as no. 2 of Blom's (1935a) list.

Partial publication: American Art Association, 1920, no. 172.

Other: Blom, 1935a, no. 2.

949–962

Zaremba Falsifications, nos. 1–14. NLA. Unpublished.

The documents are on goatskin, deerskin, and parchment. The dimensions range from 74.5 × 85.2 cm. to 200 ×160 cm., although the shapes are irregular. Many skins still have hair on one side. Labels on photographs in the Gates collection at BYU refer to Zaremba, possibly Charles W. Zaremba, author of *The Merchants' & Tourists' Guide to Mexico* (Chicago, 1883). The pictorial elements include outright fantasy and invention as well as details derived from late 19th-century publications, particularly Chavero (n.d.), published about 1887. The originals were found in the NLA basement by H. F. Cline in 1963. Uncataloged, they were considered to be of North American origin. They appear to have been in the NLA since at least 1912.

Bibliography: None.

963

Monclova, Mapa. Museum für Völkerkunde, Hamburg. Ex–Hackmack collection. Published. Skin. 70 × 64 cm.

The painting is a copy of Codex Boturini (Article 23, no. 34) arranged in five horizontal rows in a format identical to the 1858 lithograph of Codex Boturini. On the reverse are the coat of arms of Viceroy Melchor Portocarrero Lazo de la Vega, Conde de Monclova, and the date 1686. Prem (1969), who has published the document, has shown that it is based on the 1858 lithograph and on a publication of 1872–73 (for the coat of arms). It may be dated between 1872/73 and 1896, when it was acquired by the Hamburg Museum.

Publication: Prem, 1969.

REFERENCES (compiled by Mary W. Cline)

American Art Association, 1920
Anonymous, 1935b, 1937, 1946, 1956

Antiquités Aztèques, 1909
Ballesteros Gaibrois, 1948b

Barón Castro, 1949
Batres, n.d.
Bennett and Marshall, n.d.
Bernal and Sodi Pallares, 1958–59
Blacker, 1965
Blom, 1935a, 1935b
Brainerd, 1948
Callegari, 1911, 1914
Carcer, 1948–49, 1949
Caso and Smith, 1966
Catalogue, 1883
Chavero, n.d., 1892, 1901a, 1901b, 1901c
Clavigero, 1780–81
Cline, 1966a, 1966c
Danzel, 1926a, 1926b, 1928
Dibble, 1947
Fernández Vega, 1965
Galarza, 1960
Gates, 1935b
Gibson, 1952
Glass, 1964
Granados y Gálvez, 1778
Ixtlilxochitl, 1840
Johnson, 1933
Kubler, 1949
Lizardi Ramos, 1958, 1959

Loukotka, 1956, 1957
Manuscrito pictórico, 1957
Martínez Paredes, 1958
Mateos Higuera, 1966
Mengin, 1958a, 1958b
Ober, 1883
Parke-Bernet, 1963
Paso y Troncoso, 1905-07
Prem, 1969
Quaritch, 1885, 1895
Rodríguez, 1957
Rosny, Lucien de, 1875
Ruz Lhuillier, 1958–59
Schwede, 1916
Seler, 1901b
Sodi Pallares, 1958
Solc, 1956
Sorenson, MS
Soustelle, 1935–36
Stacy-Judd, 1940
Stuvier, Deevey and Rouse, 1963
Ternaux-Compans, MS
Torquemada, 1723
Tudela, 1948b, 1949
Veytia, 1907
Waldeck, MS
Wassen, 1942

FIGURES

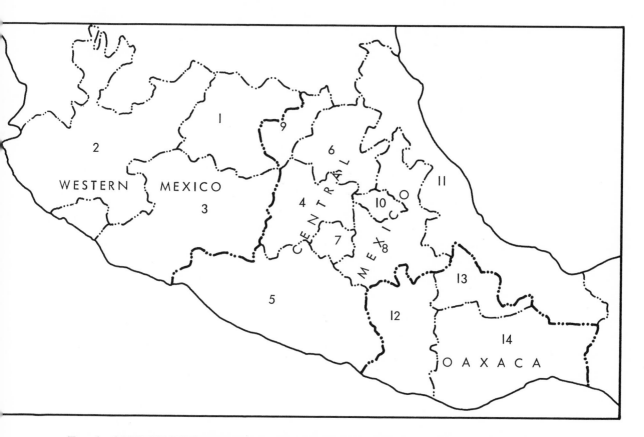

FIG. 1—MAP OF WESTERN MEXICO, CENTRAL MEXICO, AND OAXACA showing regions used in the classification of pictorial manuscripts

Western Mexico
1. (Guanajuato)
2. Jalisco
3. Michoacan

Oaxaca
12. Western Oaxaca
13. Northern Oaxaca
14. Eastern Oaxaca

Central Mexico
4. Mexico and D.F.
5. Guerrero ⎫
6. Hidalgo
7. Morelos
8. Puebla ⎬ Peripheral
9. (Queretaro) ⎮ States
10. Tlaxcala
11. Veracruz ⎭

NOTE: The maps throughout this article were drafted by John B. Glass and redrawn by
Joseph C. Wiedel.

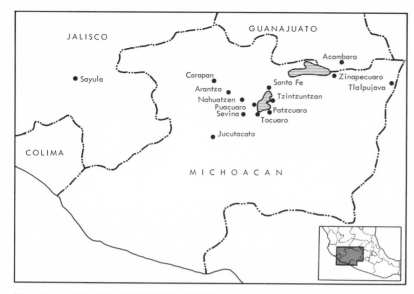

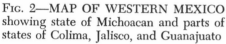

Fig. 2—MAP OF WESTERN MEXICO
showing state of Michoacan and parts of
states of Colima, Jalisco, and Guanajuato

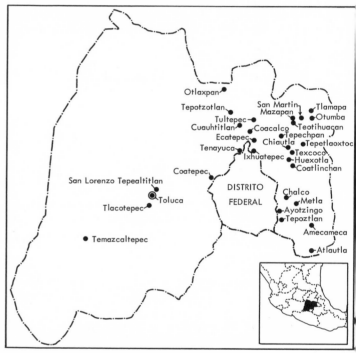

Fig. 3—MAP OF STATE OF MEXICO, CENTRAL
MEXICO

Fig. 4—MAP OF DISTRITO FEDERAL,
CENTRAL MEXICO

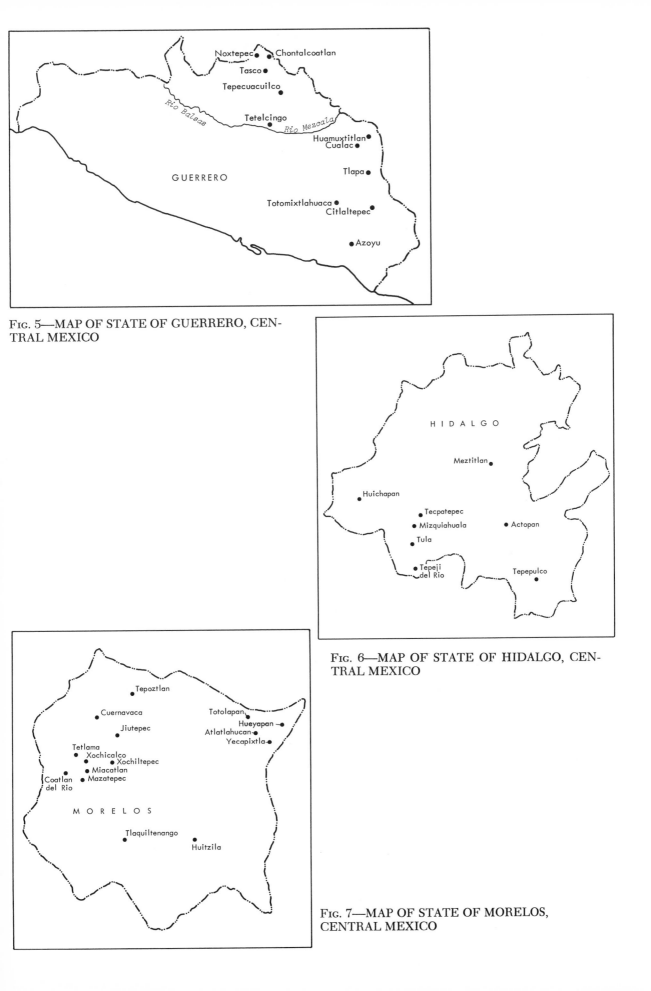

Fig. 5—MAP OF STATE OF GUERRERO, CEN-
TRAL MEXICO

Fig. 6—MAP OF STATE OF HIDALGO, CEN-
TRAL MEXICO

Fig. 7—MAP OF STATE OF MORELOS,
CENTRAL MEXICO

Metlatoyuca

Jalpan

Chicontla

Ixtacmaxtitlan

Tlalancalco
Jopanaque
Huexotzingo
Cholula   Cuauhtlantzingo
Calpan   Puebla   Tepeaca
Chalchihuapan   Tecamachalco
      Cuauhtinchan
Huaquechula   Huitziltepec
  Tepeojuma

Tepexi

Zapotitlan

Coetzala   Acatlan

FIG. 8—MAP OF STATE OF PUEBLA, CENTRAL MEXICO

Tlaxco

MORELOS

OCAMPO

CUAUHTEMOC

Tecopilco
Altzayancan
Xalaxco

Tlaquatzingo   Tlacotepec
Ahuazhuatepec
HIDALGO   Belen
San Matias   Tzompantepec
Quiahuixtlan   Cuaxomulco
Ocotelulco Tepeticpac   Huamantla   Cuapiaxtla
  Tlaxcala

JUAREZ

ZARAGOZA
Santo Tomas
Contlantzingo

EX-DISTRICTS
Towns

FIG. 9—MAP OF STATE OF TLAXCALA, CENTRAL MEXICO

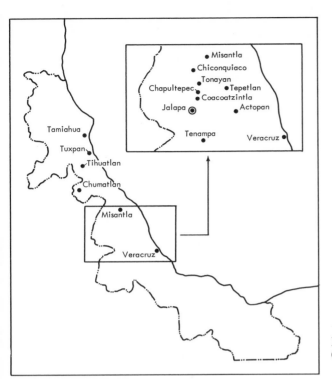

FIG. 10—MAP OF STATE OF VERA-
CRUZ, CENTRAL MEXICO

FIG. 11—MAP OF WESTERN
OAXACA

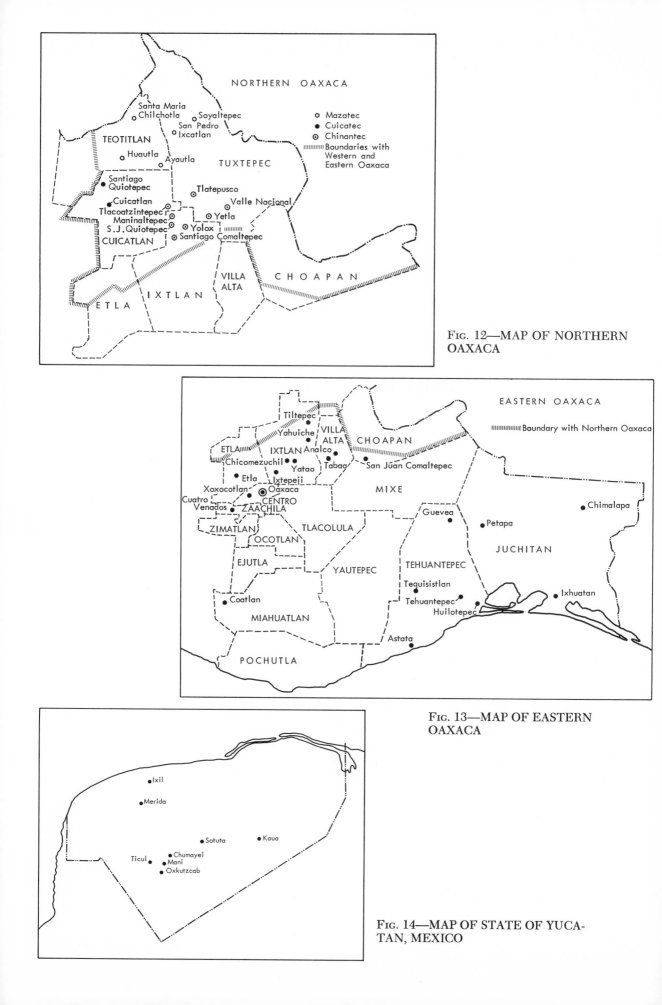

FIG. 12—MAP OF NORTHERN
OAXACA

FIG. 13—MAP OF EASTERN
OAXACA

FIG. 14—MAP OF STATE OF YUCA-
TAN, MEXICO

FIG. 15—ARMAS DE LA CIVDAD DE TESCVCO POR EL SEÑOR EMPERADOR
CARLOS V. AÑO 1551. This is one of the most iconographically interesting examples of
a class of documents (coats of arms) not included in the census. (After an engraving
published by Peñafiel, 1903b.)

Fig. 16—PORTRAIT OF MOCTEZUMA II. The design on the shield is adapted from drawings in Codex Mendoza. (After Thevet, 1584, f. 644r.)

¶ Constituciones del arçobispado y prouincia dela muy ynsigne y muy leal ciudad de Tenuxtitlã Mexico dela nueua España.

FIG. 17—ENGRAVED TITLE PAGE OF A 16TH-CENTURY BOOK PRINTED AND PUBLISHED IN MEXICO IN 1556. The stone and nopal cactus signs at the bottom represent Tenochtitlan and are elements of traditional Indian iconography in an otherwise European heraldic context. (After García Icazbalceta, 1886, pl. XVI, facing p. 62.)

FIG. 18—LORENZO BOTURINI BENADUCI, 1702–1755, collector of Mexican ethno-historical manuscripts. Below his right hand is a copy of the Gemelli Careri Calendar Wheel (Article 23, census, 390). (After Boturini, 1746.)

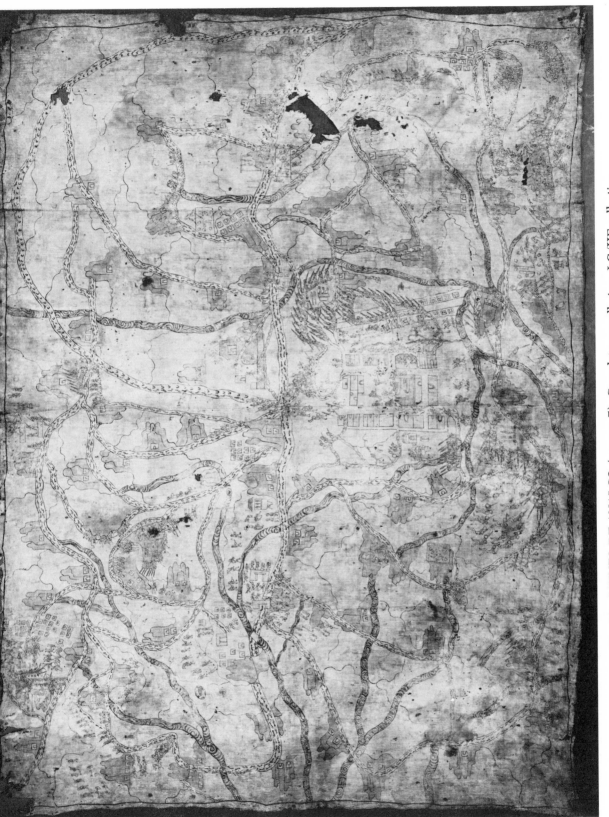

FIG. 19—LIENZO DE ANALCO (census, 7). Complete overall view. LC/HF collection.

FIG. 20—LIENZO DE ANALCO (census, 7). Detail, upper left. The stamp near left center includes the word "Analco." LC/HF collection.

Fig. 21—PORTRAIT OF AXAYACATL (census, 16). Courtesy, Handschriftensammlung Österreichische Nationalbibliothek, Vienna.

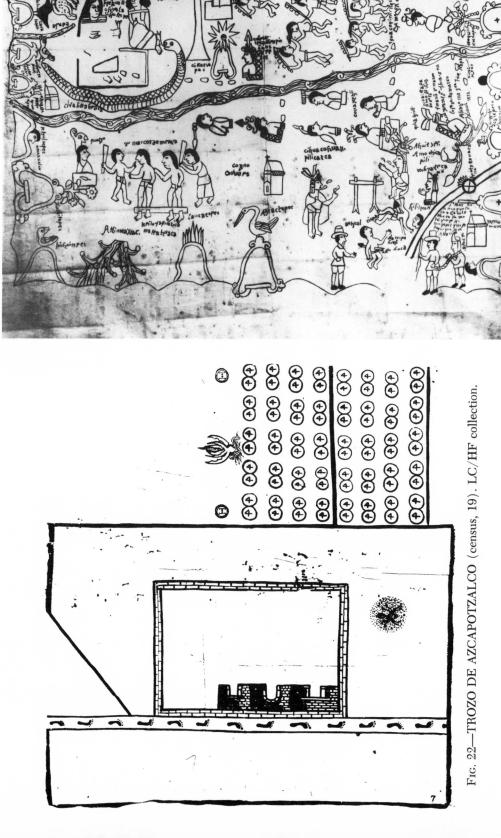

FIG. 23—LIENZO DE AZTACTEPEC Y CITLALTEPEC (census, 23). Unidentified copy. Courtesy, Archivo Fotográfico, INAH.

FIG. 22—TROZO DE AZCAPOTZALCO (census, 19). LC/HF collection.

7

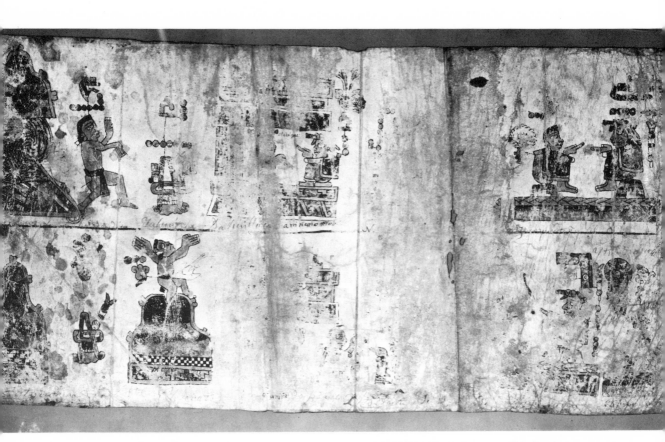

FIG. 24—ADDITIONAL FRAGMENT OF CODEX BECKER NO. 2 (census, 29). LC/ HF collection.

FIG. 25—CÓDICE DE CARAPAN NO. 1 (census, 38). Courtesy, Archivo Fotográfico, INAH.

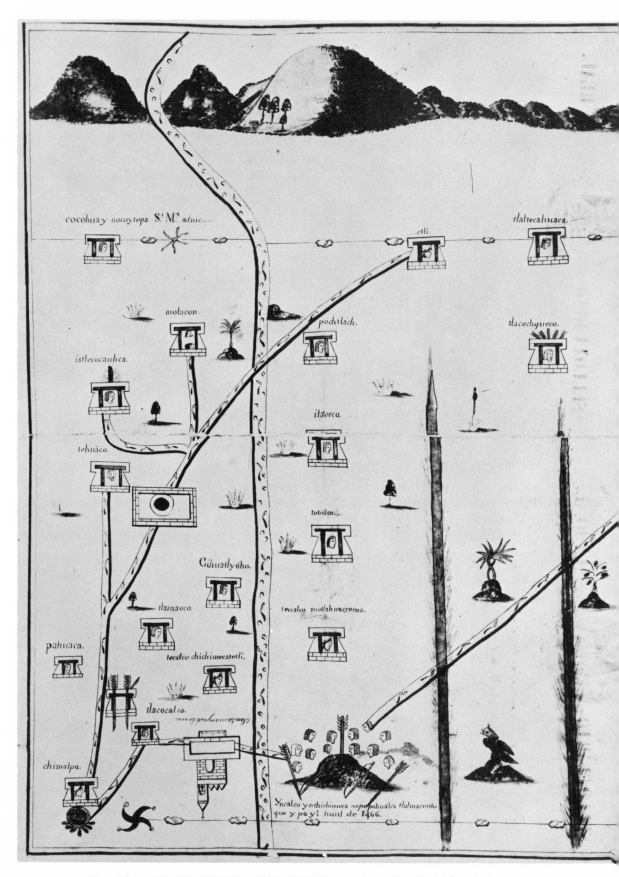

Fig. 26—MAP OF CHICHIMEC HISTORY (census, 46). The Nahuatl gloss at the bottom reads: "Yncalco ynchichimeca nepopohualca tlalmaceuhque ypa yi huitl de 1466." On the reverse is a Mexican government seal (for 1854–58) and a statement that the map is a true and legal copy of an ancient original. It is dated Nov. 30, 1854, and is signed by Manuel María de la Barreda and F. Valenzuela. Courtesy, American Museum of Natural History.

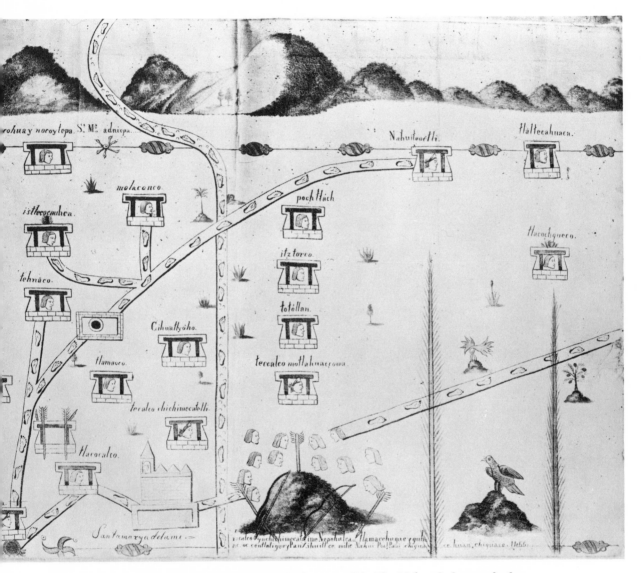

FIG. 27—MAP OF CHICHIMEC HISTORY (census, 46). The Nahuatl gloss at the bottom appears to read: "Ynalco ynchichimecatl ime Nepohulca—tlamacehuque yquh-ac. oc centlaliguey Pan Xihuitl ce. milic Nahui Poal Pani chigua—ce. huan chiquace. 1466." After a photograph in the Gates collection at Brigham Young University labeled "Aztec map of the district of Xochicalco. Copy in oil made by Charles Nebel. 19th century. Canvas, 74 x 59 cm." This label and the dimensions, however, seem to describe Nebel's copy of the Lienzo de Tetlama, BNP 98 (see census, 327). LC/HF collection.

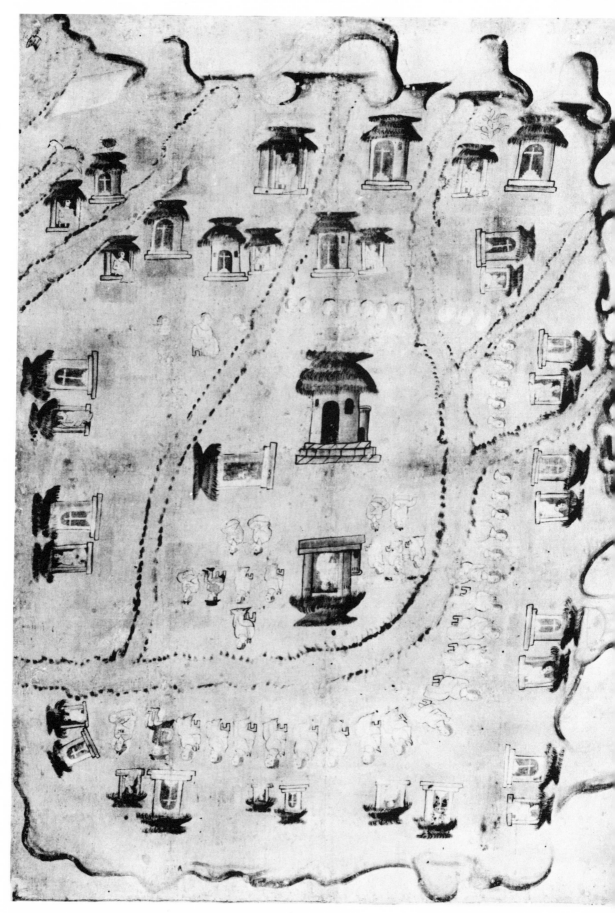

FIG. 28—LIENZO DE LA GRAN CHINANTLA (census, 54). Complete overall view.
Courtesy, Princeton University Library.

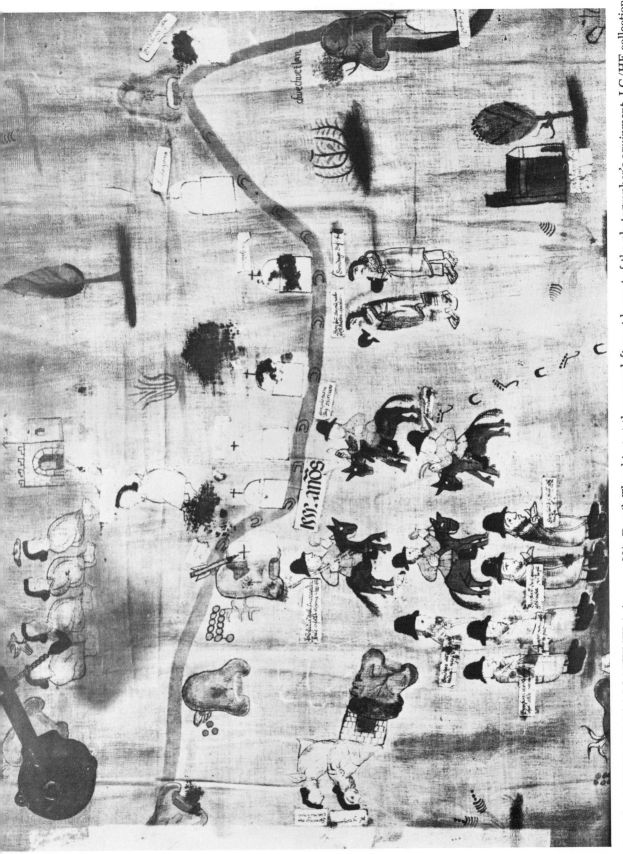

FIG. 29—LIENZO DE COACOATZINTLA (census, 63). Detail. The object at the upper left must be part of the photographer's equipment. LC/HF collection.

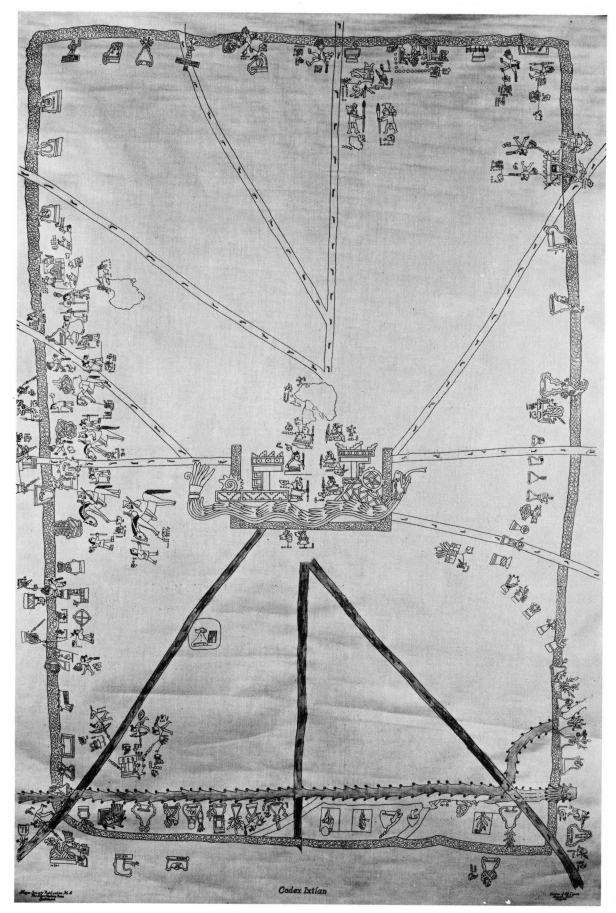

Codex Ixtlan

Fɪɢ. 30—LIENZO DE COIXTLAHUACA NO. 1 (census, 70). After *Codex Ixtlan*, Maya Society Pub. 3, 1931.

Fig. 31—LIENZO CORDOVA-CASTELLANOS (census, 77). After *Codex-Abraham Castellanos*, Maya Society Pub. 5, 1931.

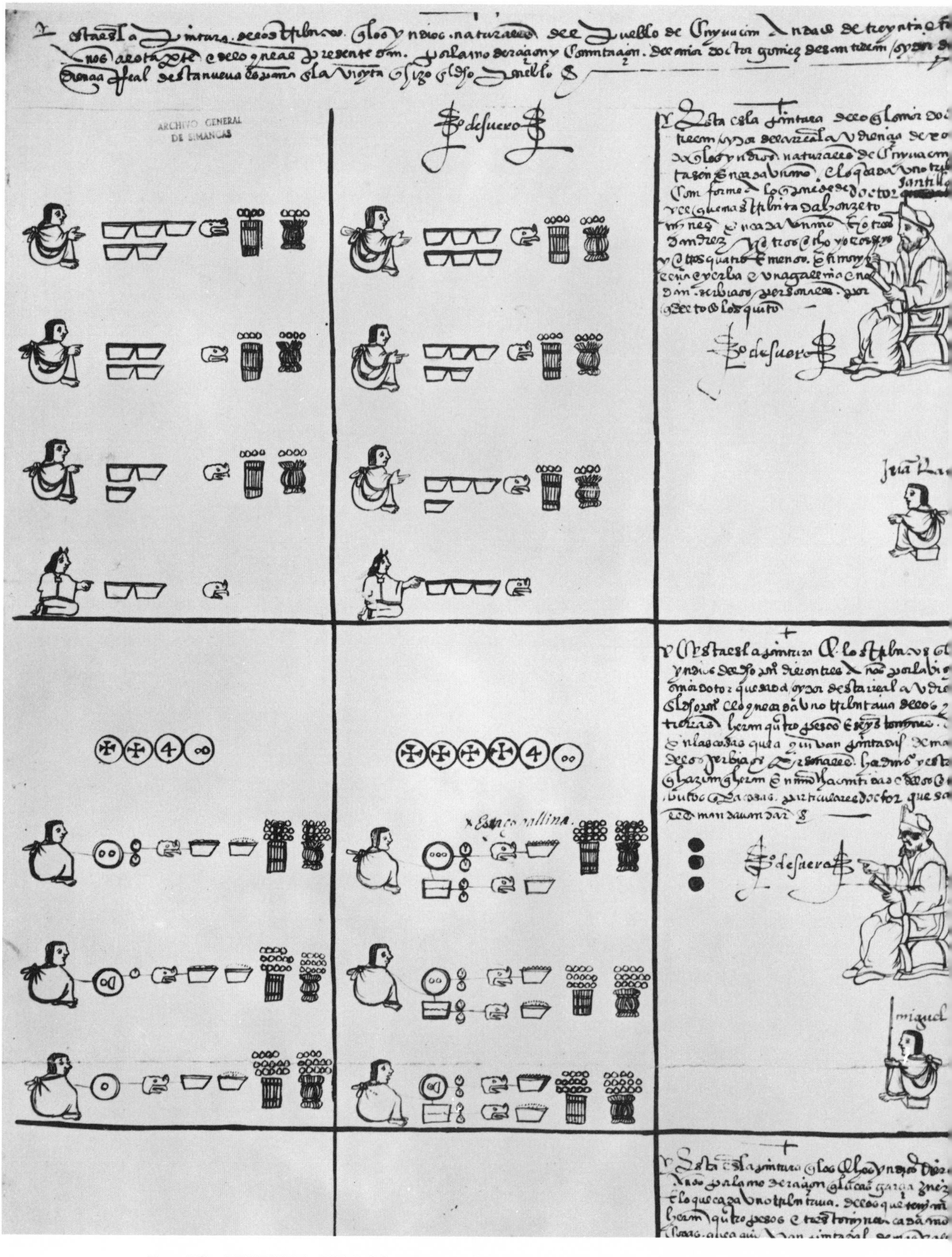

FIG. 32—PINTURA DE LOS TRIBUTOS DE COYOACAN (census, 82). Upper half (*above*). The gloss across the top reads: "Esta es la pintura de los tributos q[ue] los yndios naturales del pueblo de Cuyuacan [h]an dado de treynta e tres/ años a esta p[ar]te e de lo que al presente dan. por la moderación y comutación del señor doctor gómez de santillan oydor de la Au-/diencia real desta nueva españa en la visyta q[ue] hizo en el dicho pueblo." LC/HF collection. Lower half (*opposite*). LC/HF collection.

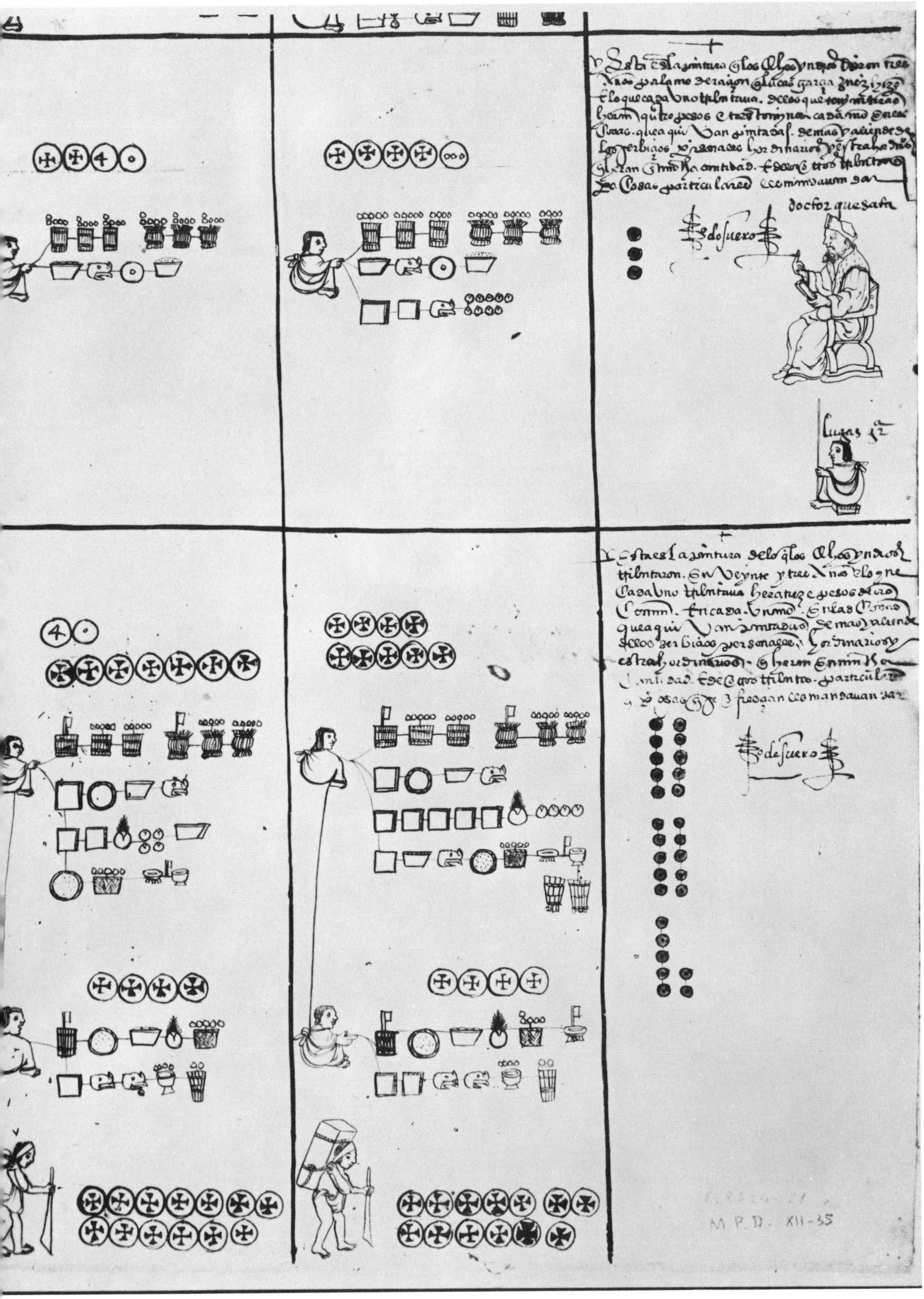
doctor quesada
de Suero
lucas gª
de Suero
M.P.D. XII-35

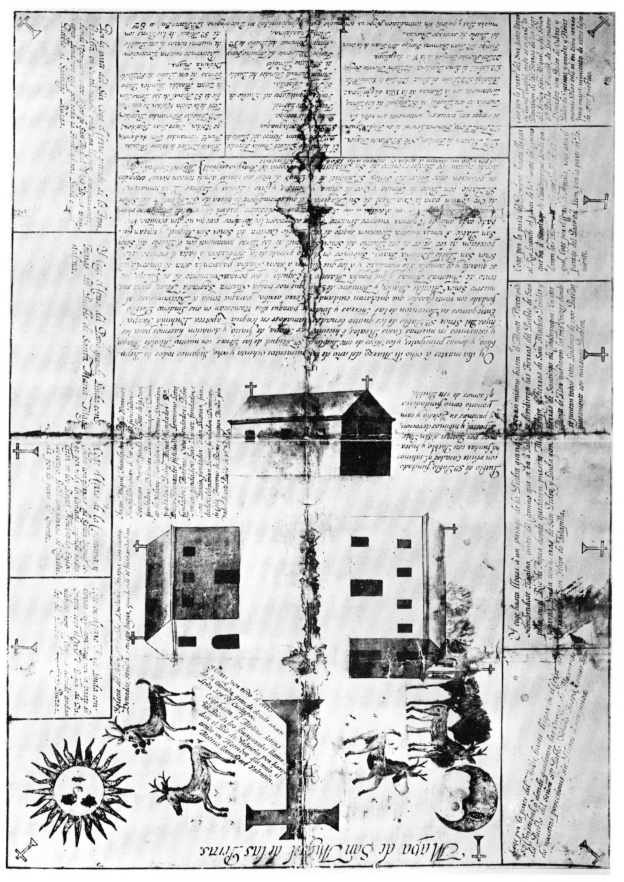

FIG. 33—MAPA DE SAN PABLO CUATRO VENADOS (census, 88). After Steininger and van de Velde. 1935.

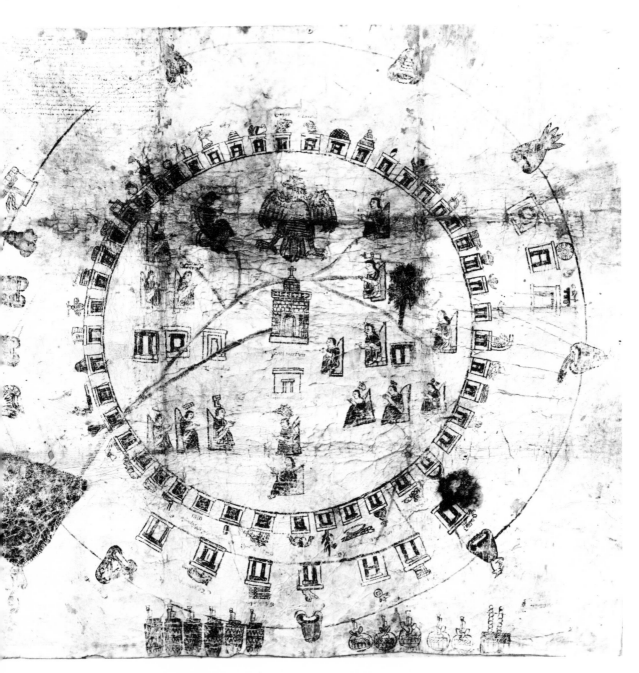

F<small>IG</small>. 34—MAPA CIRCULAR DE CUAUHQUECHOLLAN (census, 90). Courtesy, Handschriftensammlung Österreichische Nationalbibliothek, Vienna.

Fig. 35—MAPA DE CUAUHTINCHAN NO. 2 (census, 95). Detail of the original. Courtesy, Archivo Fotográfico, INAH.

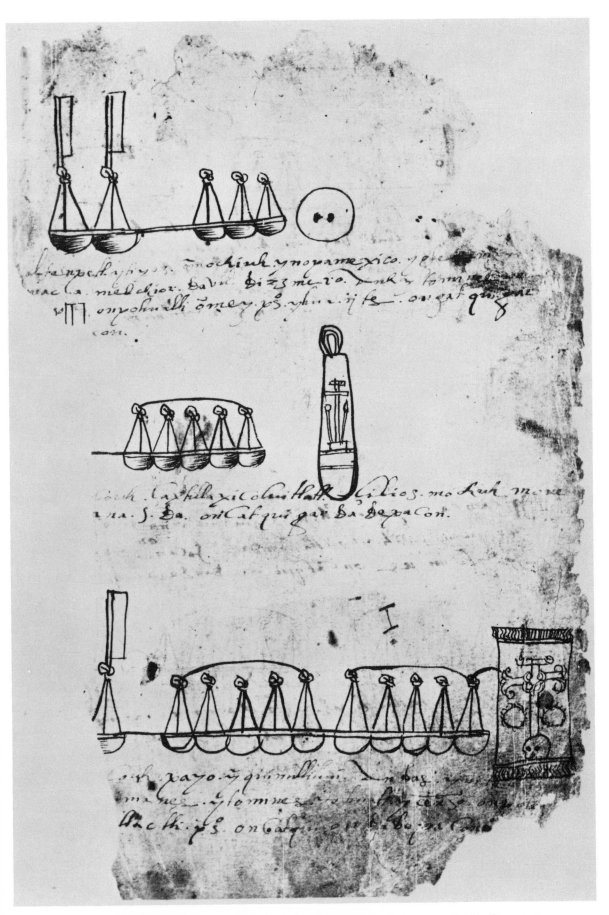

FIG. 36—FINANCIAL ACCOUNTS OF CUITLAHUAC (census, 107). One page.
Courtesy, Edward E. Ayer Collection, Newberry Library.

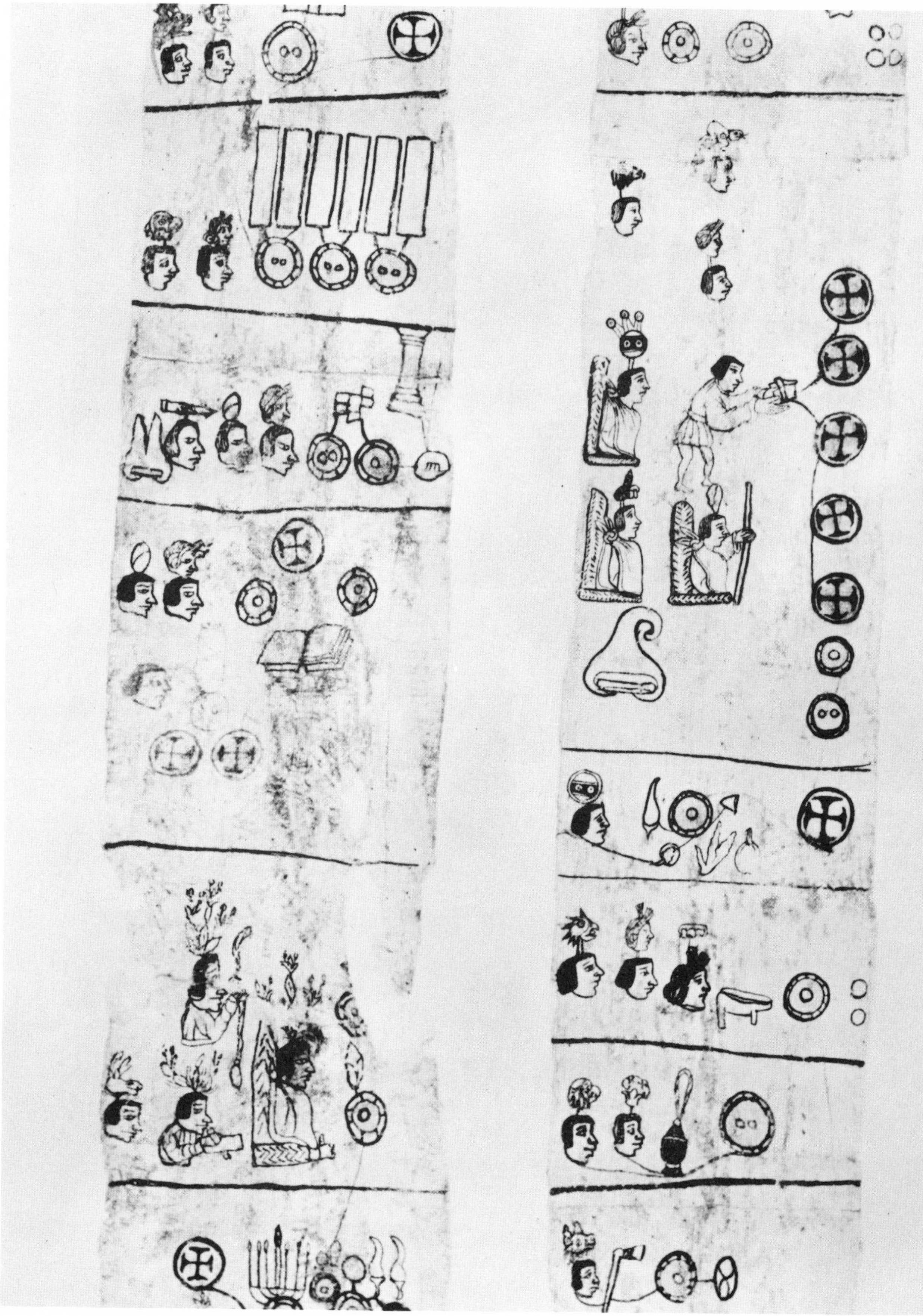

FIG. 37—GILCREASE FRAGMENTS (census, 122–127). Details from two fragments.
Courtesy, Gilcrease Institute.

ATATAPALACATL.

TEOAMATL, VITÆ ET MORTIS INDEX.

TVNA, SIVE NOPALLI
SAXIS INNASCENS.

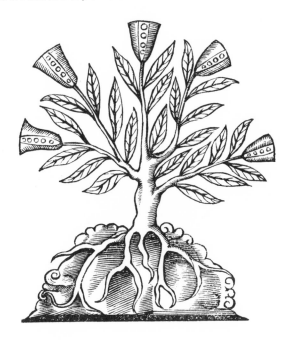

FIG. 38—FRANCISCO HERNÁNDEZ, *Historia de las Plantas de Nueva España* (census, 132). Examples of drawings showing native influence in the use of the rebus signs *tetl* (stone) and *atl* (water). (After Nierembergii, *Historia naturae* . . . , 1635, p. 306 [*Atatapalacatl*], p. 308 [*Teoamatl*], and p. 310 [*Tuna*].) Photographs courtesy of Houghton Library, Harvard University.

Fig. 39—LIENZO DE SAN PEDRO IXCATLAN (census, 162). Courtesy, Princeton University Library.

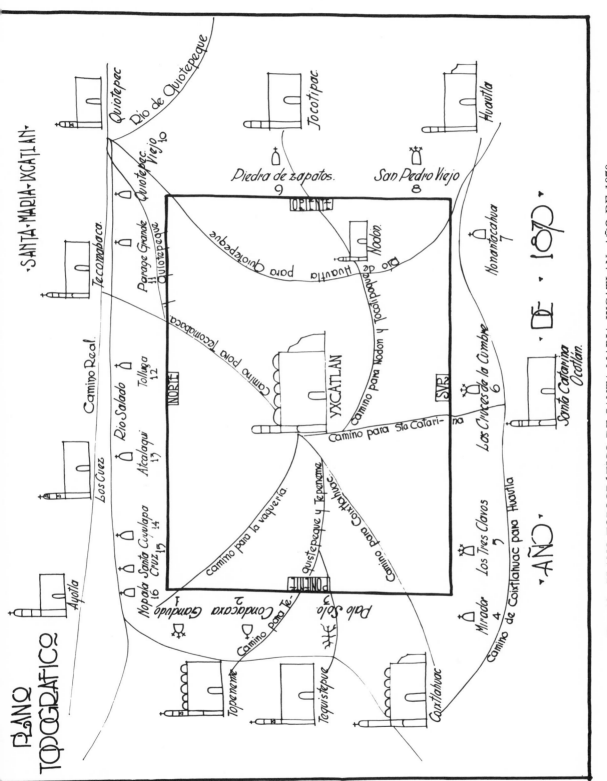

Fig. 40—PLANO TOPOGRÁFICO DE SANTA MARIA IXCATLAN, AÑO DE 1870 (census, 164). Courtesy, Mrs. Irmgard Weitlaner de Johnson, LC/HF collection.

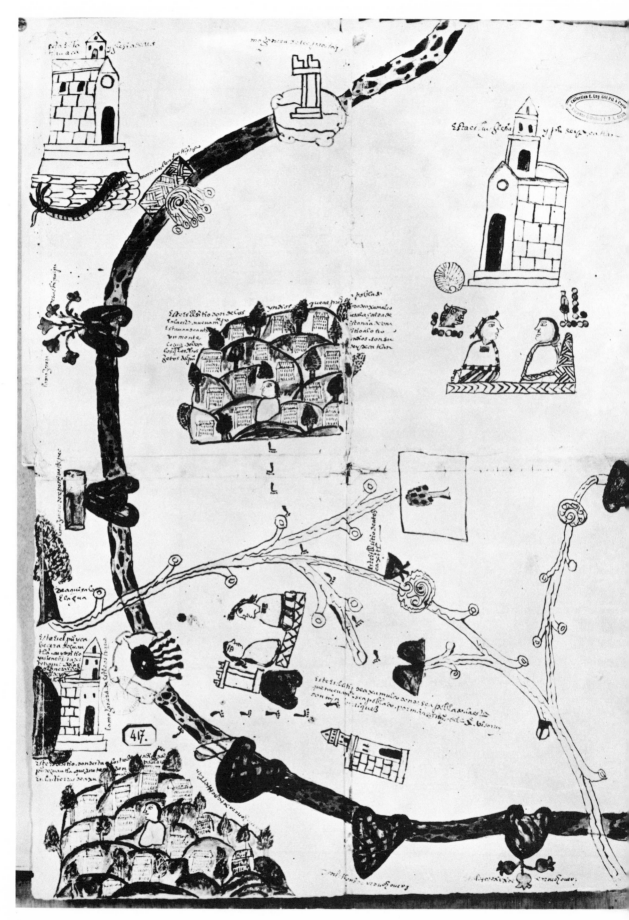

FIG. 41—PLAN TOPOGRAPHIQUE DE SANTA MARIA IXCATLAN, 1580 (census, 165). LC/HF collection.

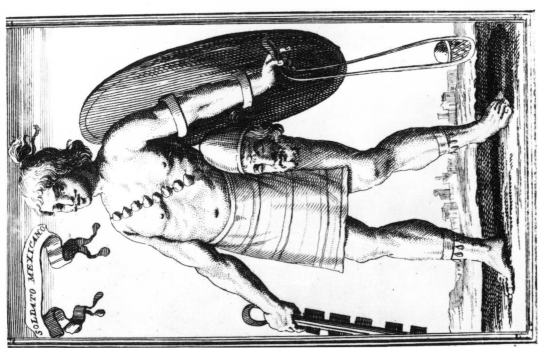

Fig. 43—CODEX IXTLILXOCHITL, PART 2 (census, 172). "Soldato Mexicano." After Gemelli Careri, 1699–1700, vol. 6.

Fig. 42—CODEX IXTLILXOCHITL, PART 2 (census, 172). Portrait of Nezahualpilli, mislabeled "Mouhtezuma IX Re, e 2º di tal nome." After Gemelli Careri, 1699–1700, vol. 6.

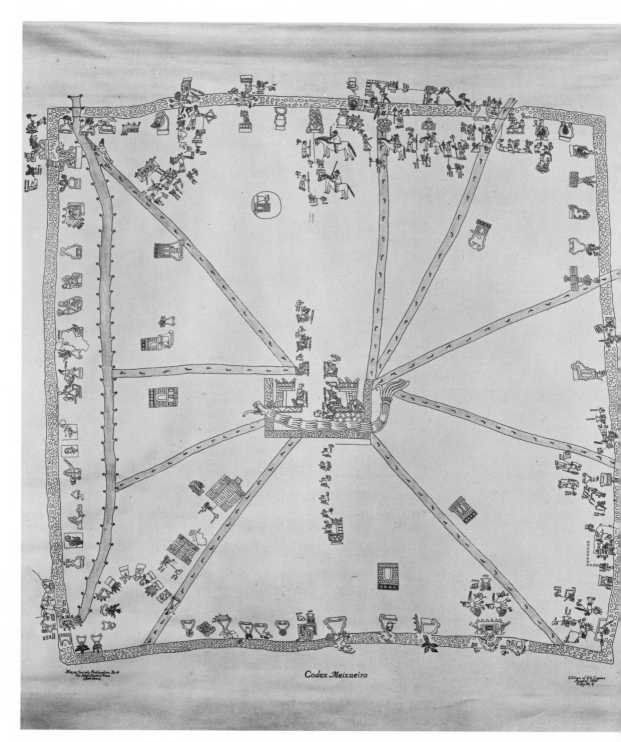

Codex Meixueiro

Fig. 44—LIENZO MEIXUEIRO (census, 195). After *Codex Meixueiro*, Maya Society Pub. 4, 1931.

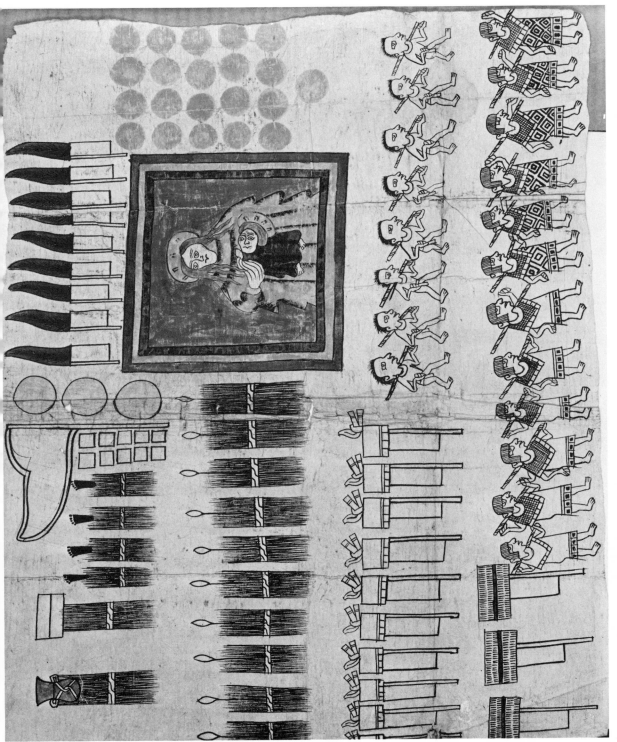

FIG. 45—CODEX MONTELEONE (census, 224). One of the eight paintings in the codex. LC/HF collection.

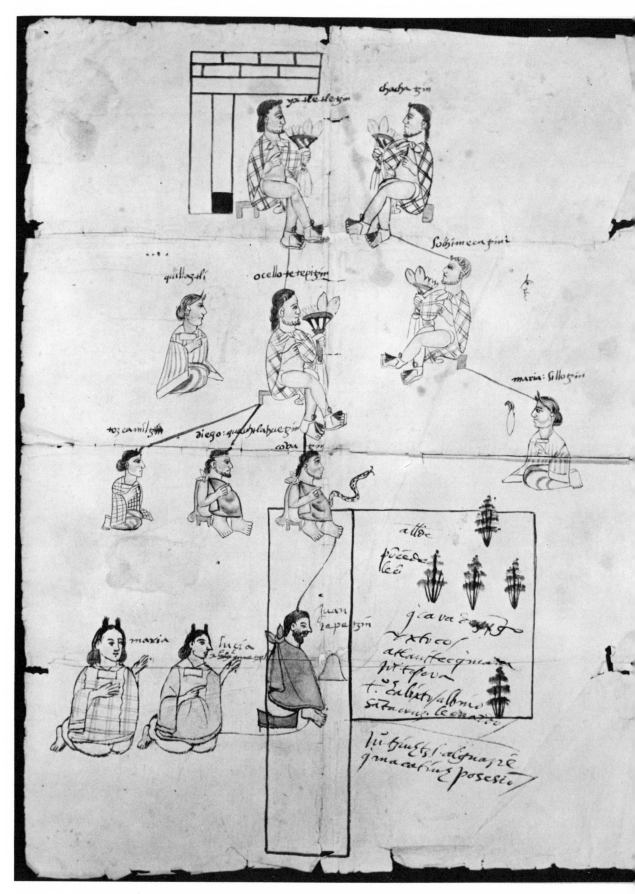

FIG. 46—FRAGMENTO DE LAS MUJERES (census, 226). Names of the persons in this genealogy (left to right, top to bottom) are: Yxtletletzin, Chachatzin, Quillaztli, Ocellotetepitzin, Sochimetzini, Tozcamiltzin, Diego Quauhtlahuetzin, Covatzin, Maria Sillotzin, Maria, Lucia, and Juan Tepetzin. Courtesy, The Brooklyn Museum.

FIG. 47—CÓDICE MURO (census, 228). One page. Courtesy, Fototeca, Museo Nacional de Antropología, Mexico.

Fig. 48—LIENZO DE SANTA MARIA NATIVITAS (census, 232). The numbers "27" and "28" are not on the original. Photograph by Wade Seaford. LC/HF collection.

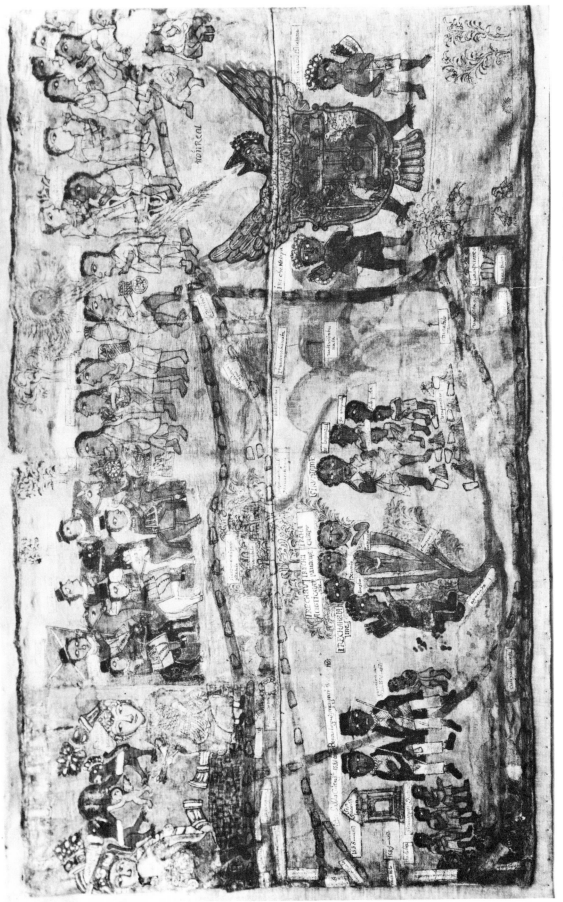

FIG. 49—LIENZO DE PATZCUARO (census, 248). After a photograph in Peabody Museum, Harvard University.

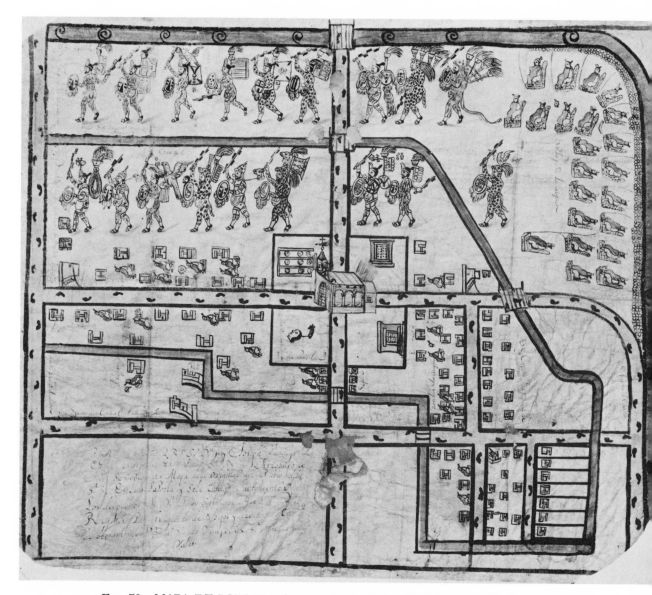

Fig. 50—MAPA DE POPOTLA (census, 254). Codex Vindobonensis Mexicanus no. 2. An eight-line gloss at the lower left identifies it as a copy of 1720. Courtesy, Handschriftensammlung Österreichische Nationalbibliothek, Vienna.

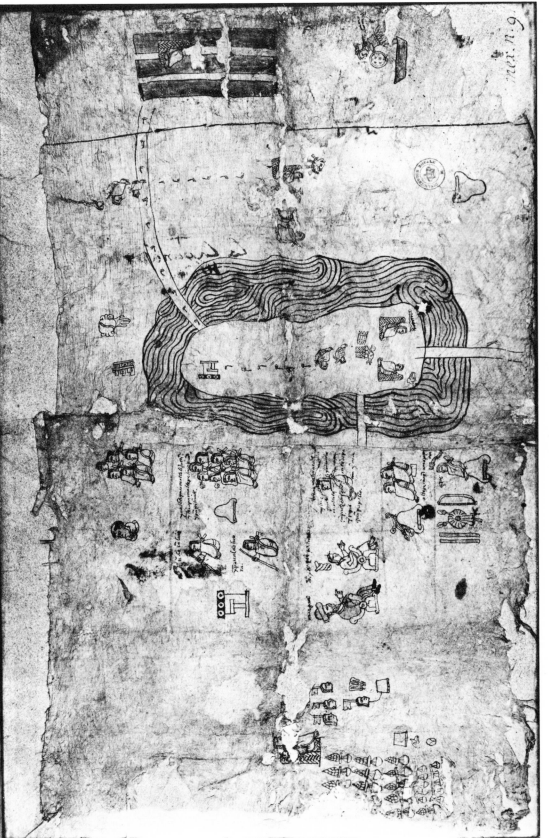

Fig. 51—PIÈCE D'UN PROCÈS (census, 260). LC/HF collection.

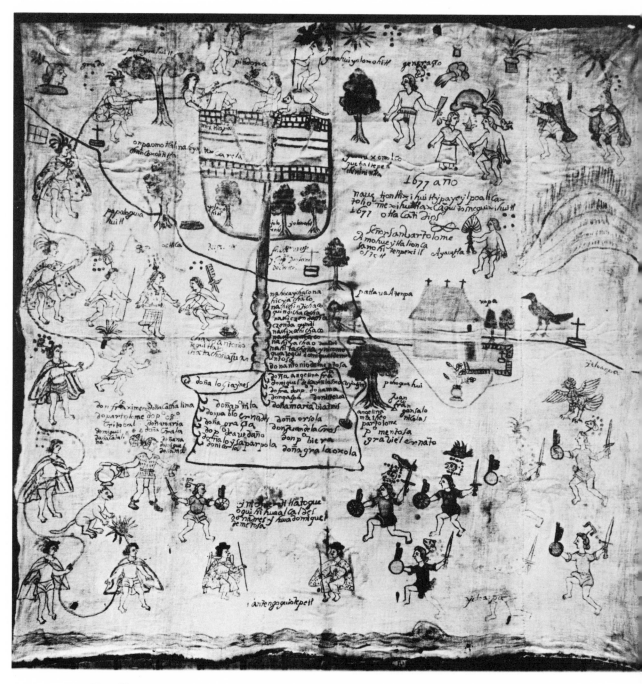

FIG. 52—LIENZO DE QUIOTEPEC Y AYAUHTLA (census, 265). Courtesy, Archivo Fotográfico, INAH.

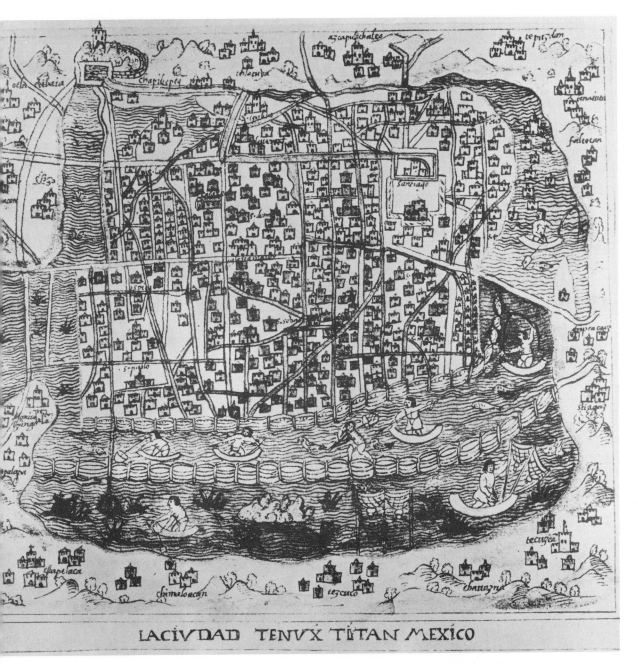

LACIVDAD TENVX TITAN MEXICO

FIG. 53—SANTA CRUZ MAP OF THE CITY AND VALLEY OF MEXICO (census, 280). Partial copy by Alonso de Santa Cruz, about 1556. After Wieser, 1908, pl. 11.

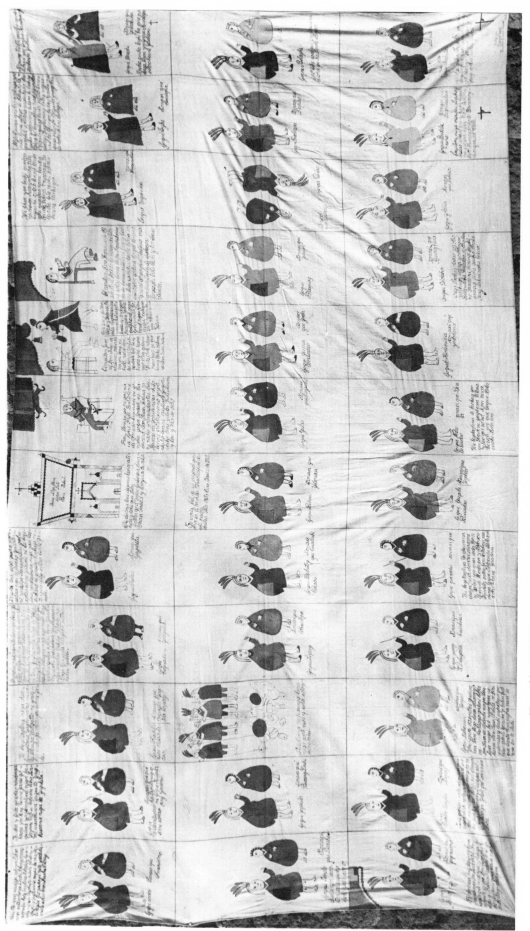

Fig. 54—LIENZO DE SAN JUAN TABAA, NO. 1 (census, 295). Unidentified copy. Gloss in sixth compartment, second row (lacking in MNA 35-114 copy), reads: "Es copia fiel de su original que obra en el archivo Municipal de este pueblo. Tabaa Villa Alta Oax. Nov. 15 de 1933." Courtesy, Fototeca, Museo Nacional de Antropología.

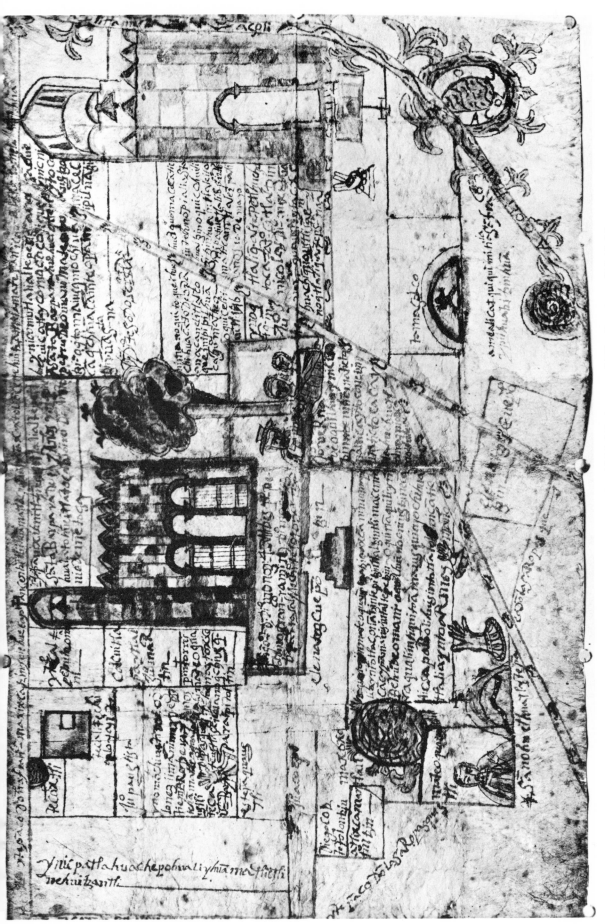

Fig. 55.—MAPA DE SANTA BARBARA TAMASOLCO (census, 298). Courtesy, British Museum.

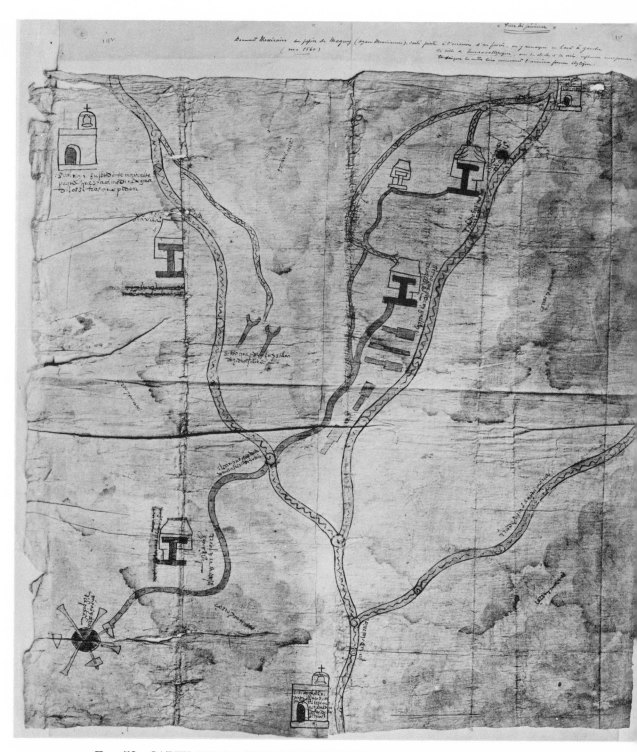

FIG. 56—CARTE DE LA VILLE DE TEMASCALTEPEC (census, 309). Courtesy, Edward E. Ayer Collection, Newberry Library.

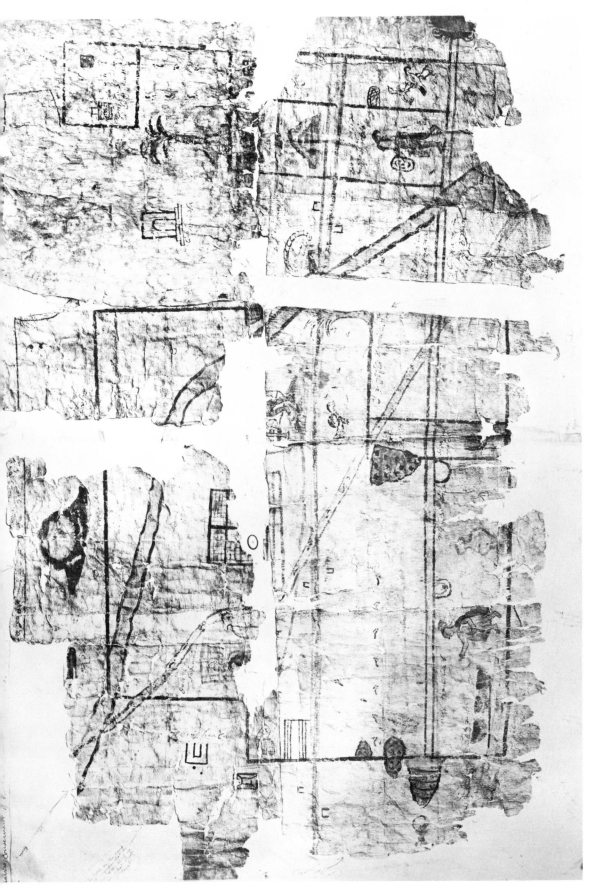

Fig. 57—AYER MAP OF TEOTIHUACAN (census, 312). Courtesy, Edward E. Ayer Collection, Newberry Library.

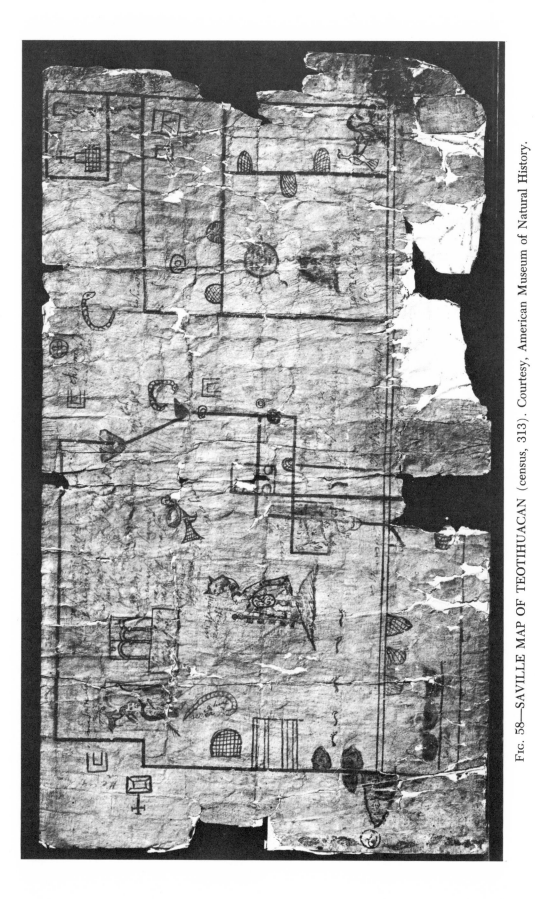

Fig. 58—SAVILLE MAP OF TEOTIHUACAN (census, 313). Courtesy, American Museum of Natural History.

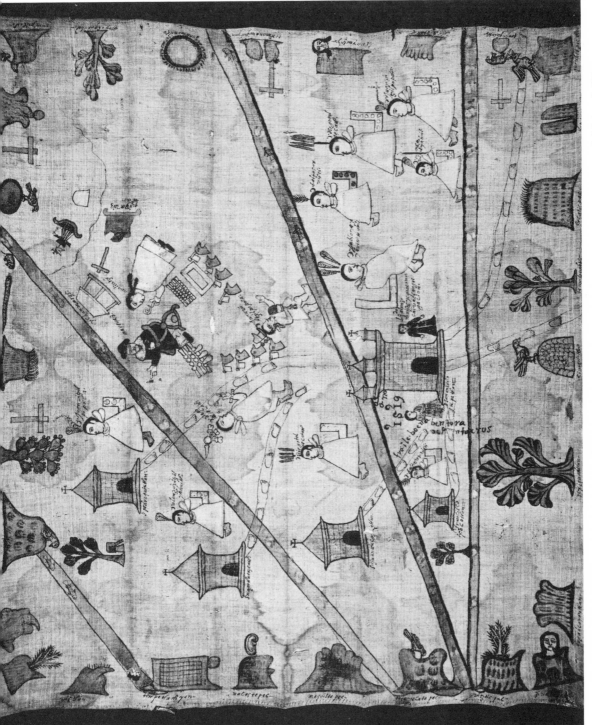

Fig. 59—MAPA DE SAN ANTONIO TEPETLAN (census, 320). Courtesy, American Museum of Natural History.

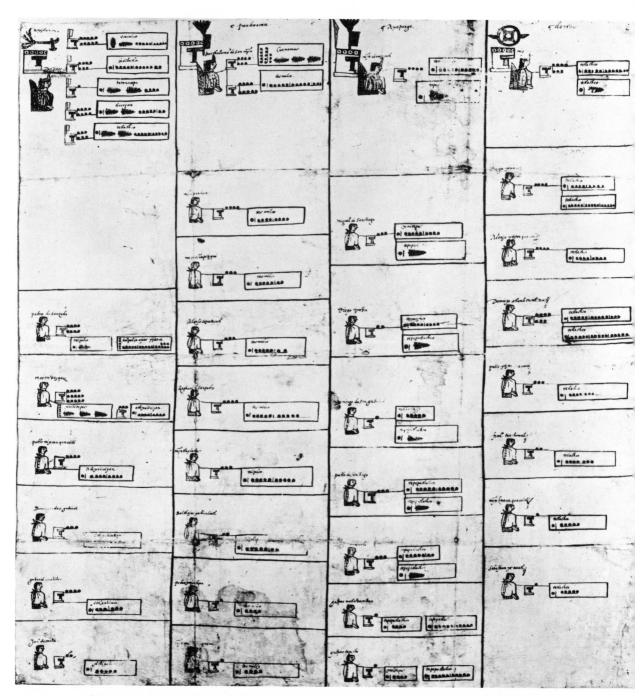

F<small>IG</small>. 60—MAPA CATASTRAL DE TEPOZTLAN, PANHUACAN, AYAPANGO Y
TLANAHUAC (census, 324). Courtesy, Handschriftensammlung, Österreichische Nationalbibliothek, Vienna.

Fig. 61—LIENZO DE TETLAMA (census, 327). "Original," reportedly located in the village of Tetlama. Courtesy, Archivo Fotográfico, INAH.

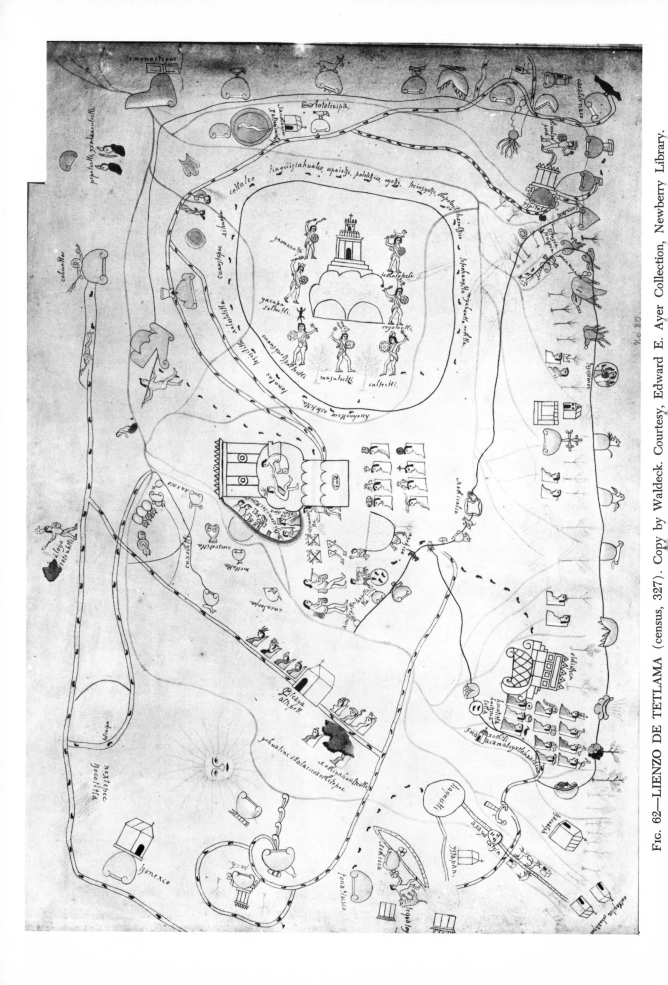

FIG. 62—LIENZO DE TETLAMA (census, 327). Copy by Waldeck. Courtesy, Edward E. Ayer Collection, Newberry Library.

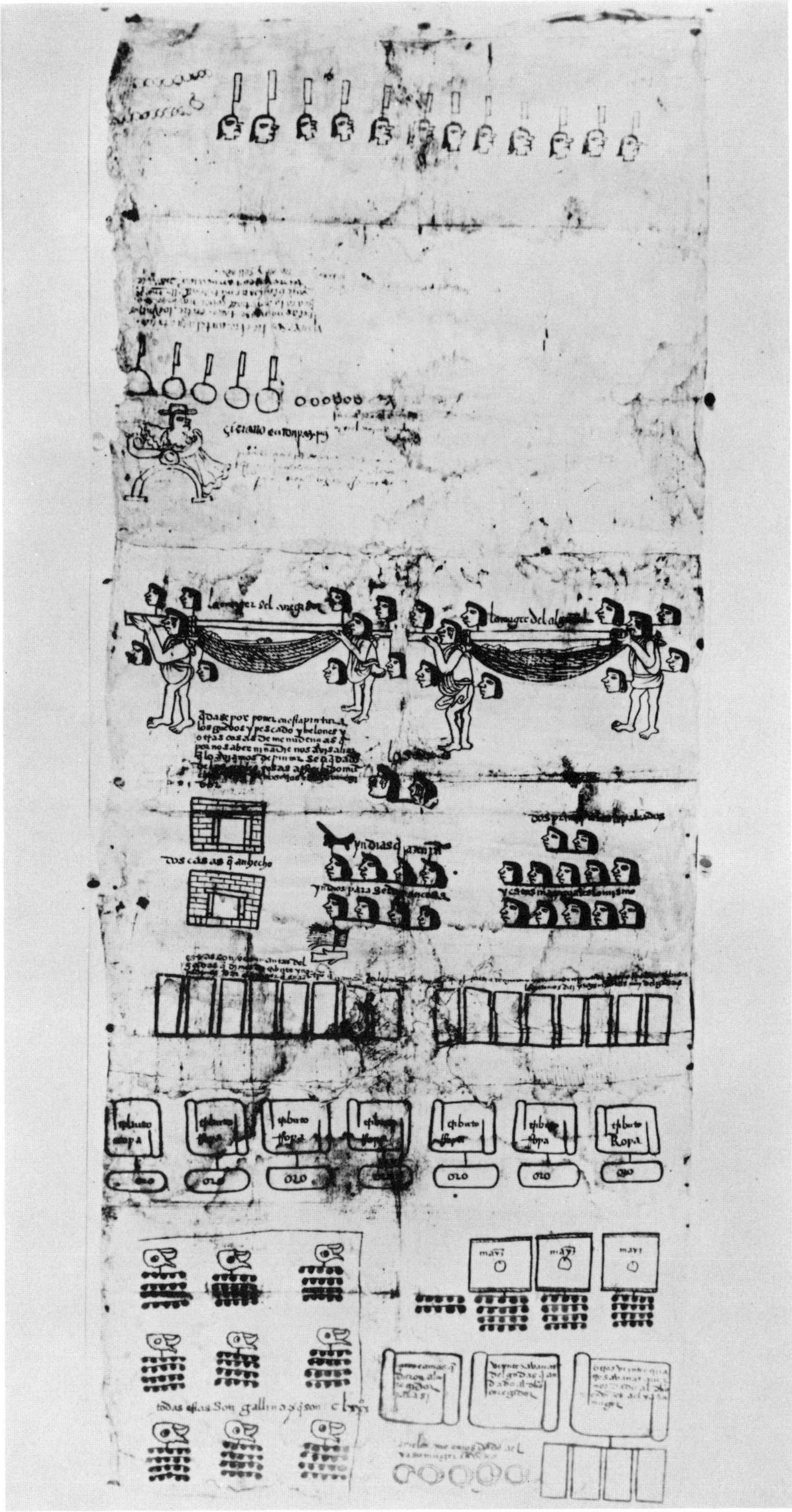

FIG. 63—CÓDICE DE TLACHCO (census, 334). The upside-down gloss above the seated Spaniard reads: "Proceso hecho ante la justicia de las Minas de Tasco entre los yndios de Acala contra el gobernador de dicho pueblo. Va remitido al Illmo. Sr. Virrey desta Nueva España cerrado y sellado." Courtesy, Archivo Fotográfico, INAH.

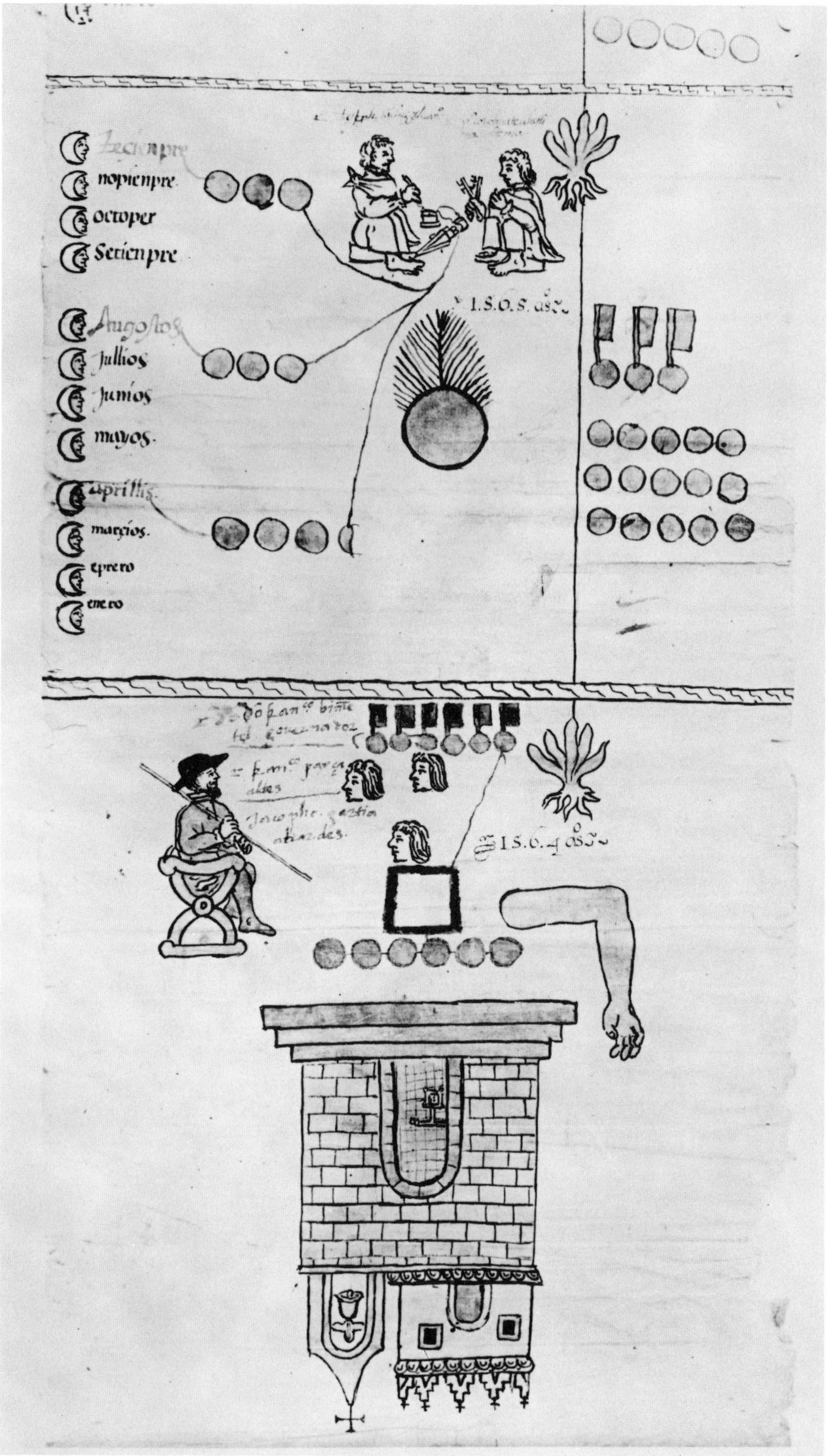

FIG. 64—CÓDICE DE TRIBUTOS DE SANTA CRUZ TLAMAPA, NO. 3 (census, 341). Lowest (1564) and next to lowest (1565) sections. The individual seated on the chair is identified by the gloss as "Don Francisco Pimentel, Gobernador." Courtesy, Fototeca, Museo Nacional de Antropología.

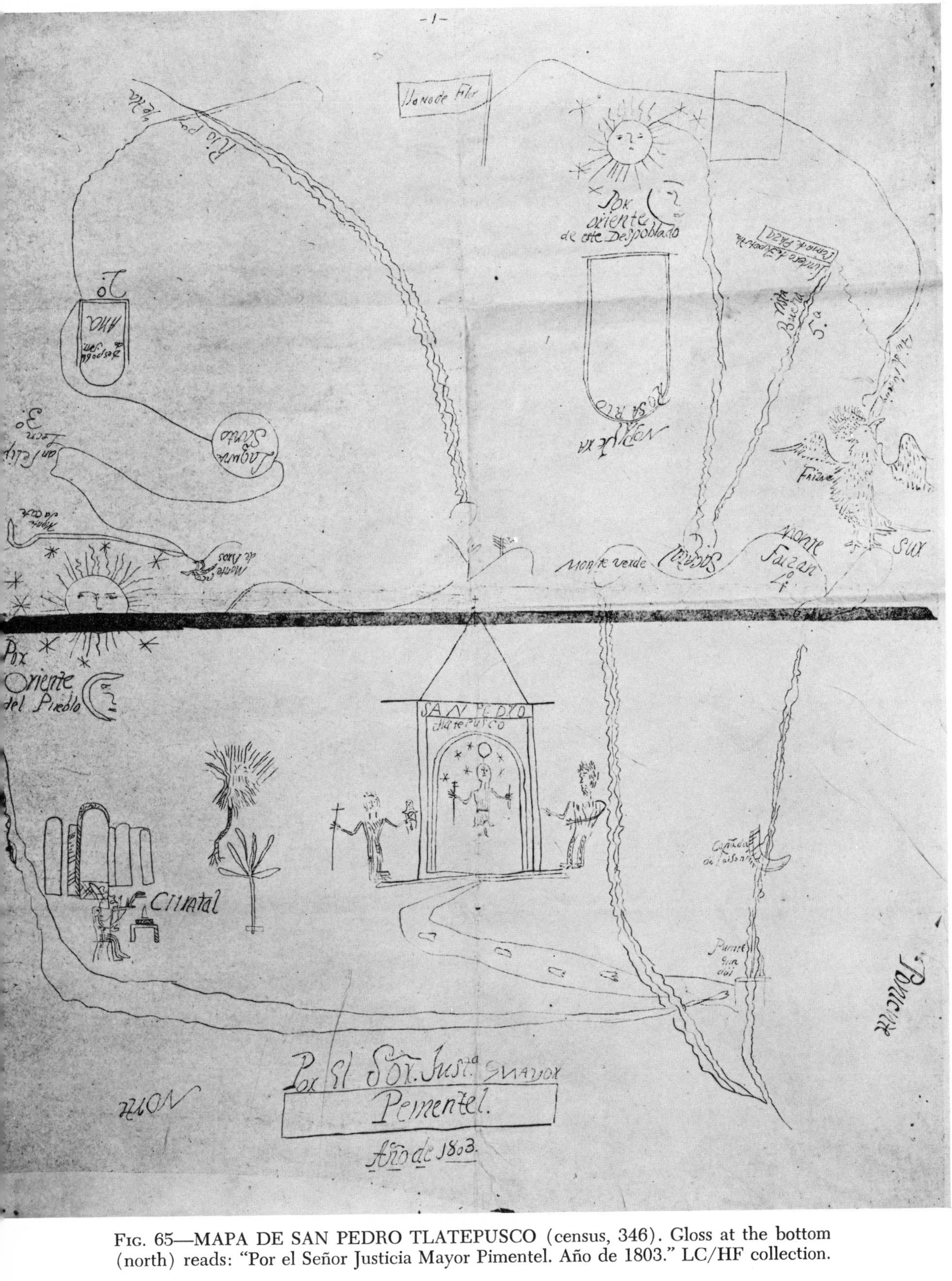

FIG. 65—MAPA DE SAN PEDRO TLATEPUSCO (census, 346). Gloss at the bottom (north) reads: "Por el Señor Justicia Mayor Pimentel. Año de 1803." LC/HF collection.

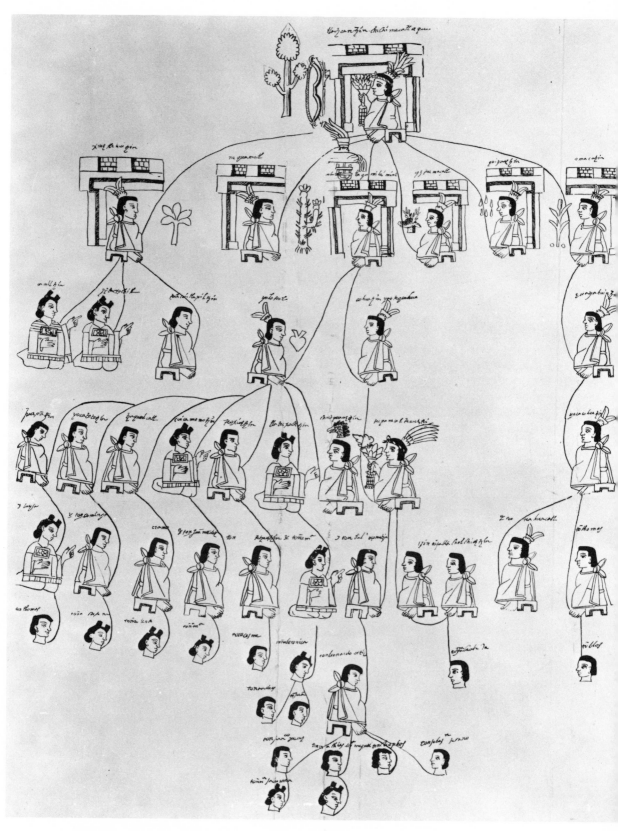

FIG. 66—GENEALOGIE DES TLATZCANTZIN (census, 347). After Lehmann, 1906a, pl. 4.

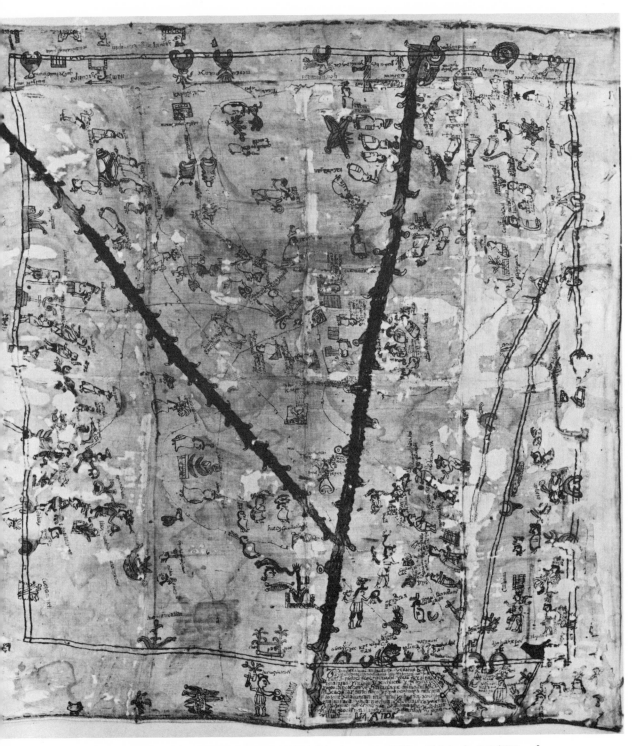

FIG. 67—LIENZO DE TOTOMIXTLAHUACA (census, 362). Original. LC/HF collection.

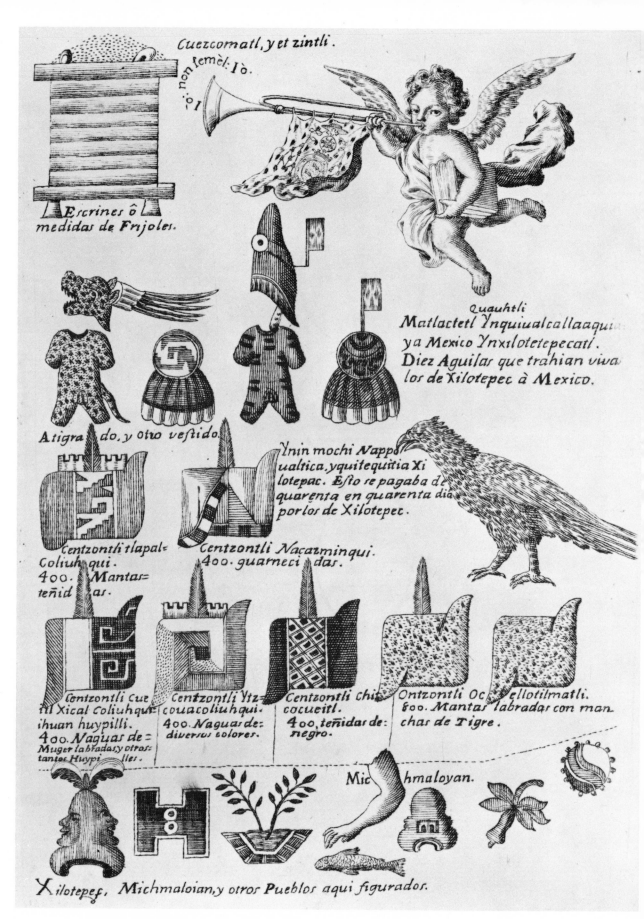

Cuezcomatl, y et zintli.

Io. non femèl. Io.

Escrines ô medidas de Frijoles.

Quauhtli

Matlactetl Ynquiualcallaaqui ya Mexico Ynxilotetepecatl. Diez Aguilas que trahian vivas los de Xilotepec à Mexico.

A tigrado, y otro vestido.

Ynin mochi Nappo ualtica, yquitequitia Xi lotepac. Esto se pagaba de quarenta en quarenta dia por los de Xilotepec.

Centzontli tlapal- Coliuhqui. 400. Mantas- teñid as.

Centzontli Naçacminqui. 400. guarneci das.

Centzontli Cue tli Xical Coliuhqui ihuan huypilli. 400. Naguas de= Muger labradas y otros tantos Huypi lles.

Centzontli Ytz couacoliuhqui. 400. Naguas de= diversos colores.

Centzontli chi cocueitl. 400, teñidas de: negro.

Ontzontli Oc ellotilmatli. 800. Mantas labradas con man chas de Tigre.

Michmaloyan.

Xilotepec, Michmaloian, y otros Pueblos aqui figurados.

Fig. 68—MATRÍCULA DE TRIBUTOS (census, 368). The angel is not on the original manuscript. After Lorenzana, 1770, pl. 11.

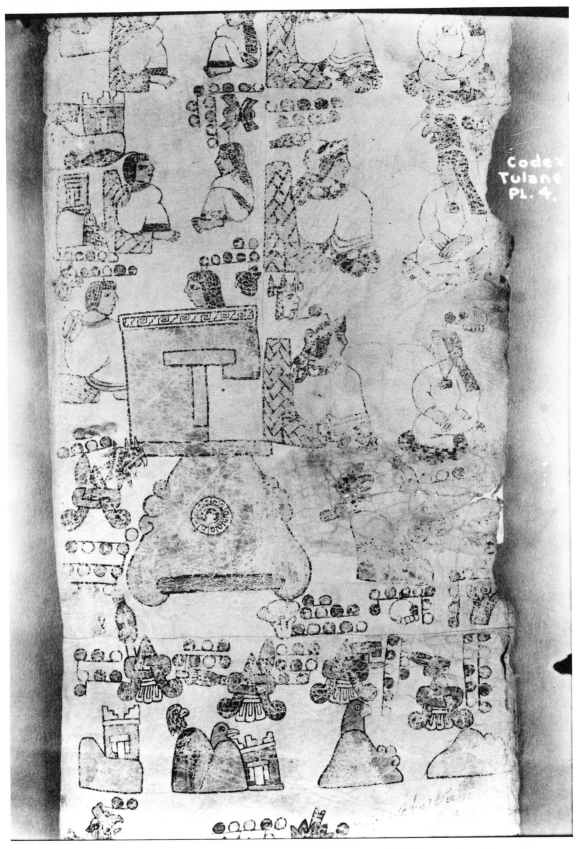

Codex
Tulane
Pl. 4.

FIG. 69—CODEX TULANE (census, 370). Detail. Courtesy, Middle American Research Institute, Tulane University.

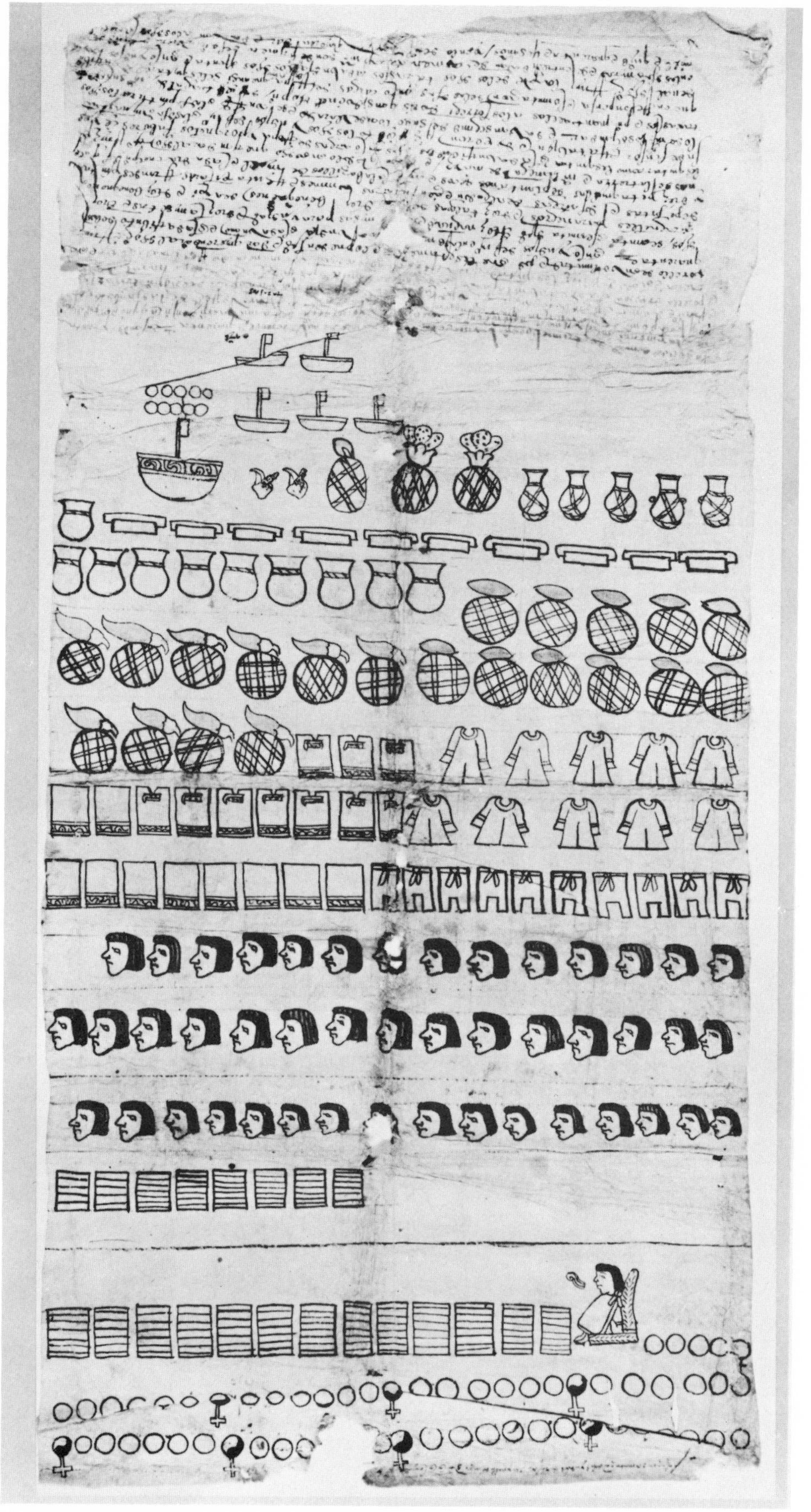

Fig. 70—TRIBUTES OF TZINTZUNTZAN AND TLALPUJAVA (census, 379). Obverse. Reverse contains continuation of written texts, signatures, and the Boturini number, "No. 10, 3 Inventario" (1743–3–10). Courtesy, Princeton University Library.

F<small>IG</small>. 71—MAP OF UNIDENTIFIED LOCALITY (census, 381). Courtesy, Edward E. Ayer Collection, Newberry Library.

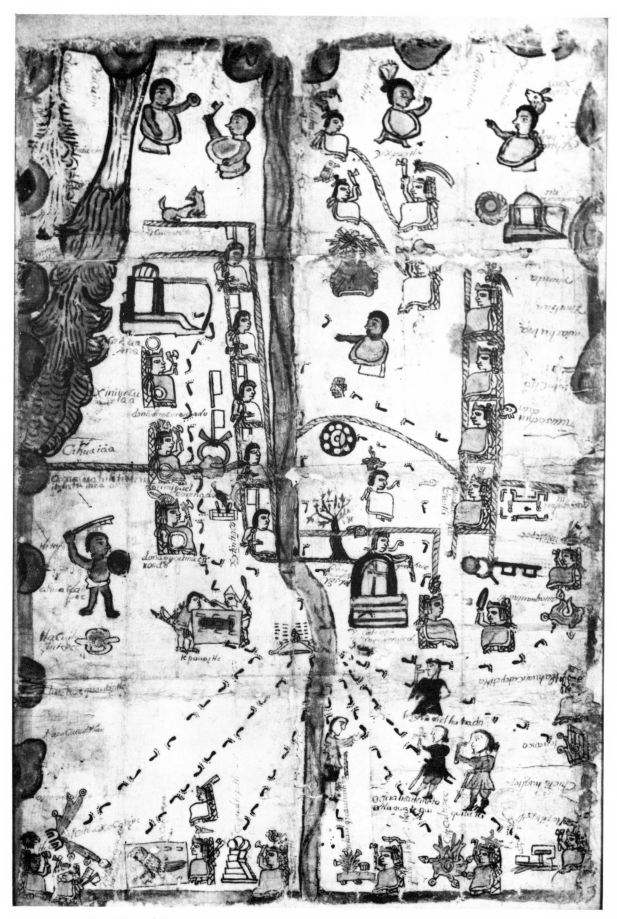

FIG. 72—CÓDICE DE VEINTE MAZORCAS (census, 385). LC/HF collection.

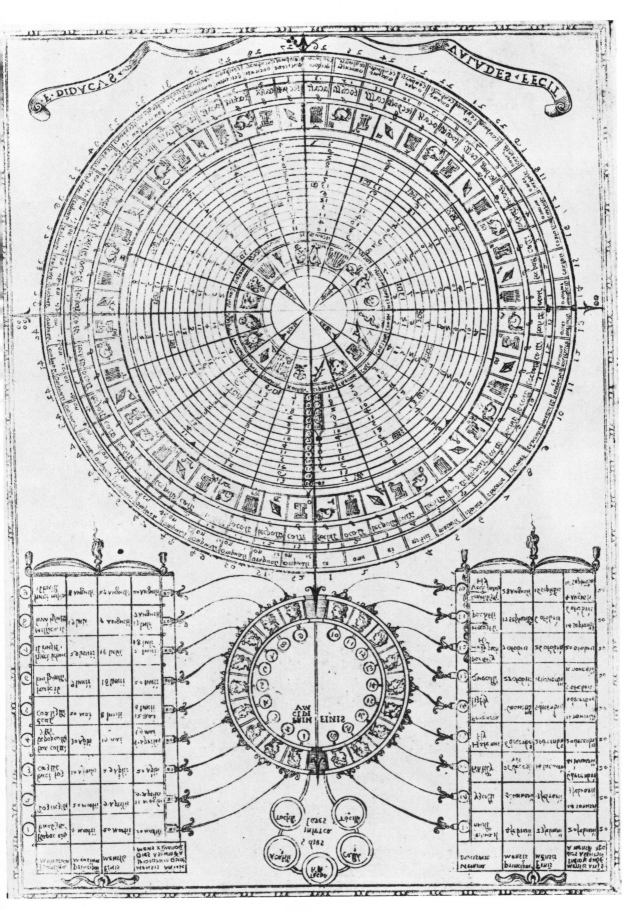

Fig. 73—VEYTIA CALENDAR WHEEL NO. 2 (census, 388). Valadés version.
After Valadés, *Rhetorica cristiana*, 1579.

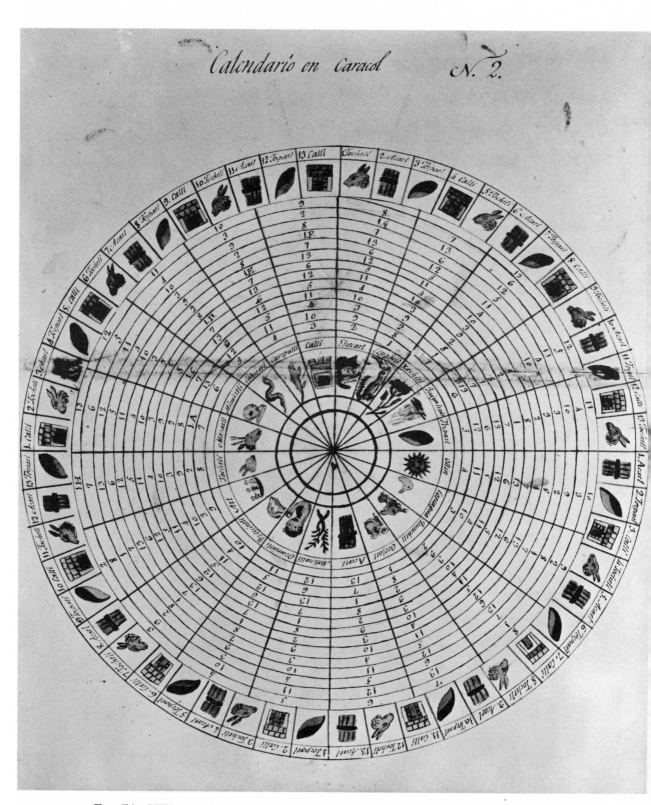

FIG. 74—VEYTIA CALENDAR WHEEL NO. 2 (census, 388). Veytia version. After the manuscript of Veytia's *Historia* in the Library of Congress. LC/HF collection.

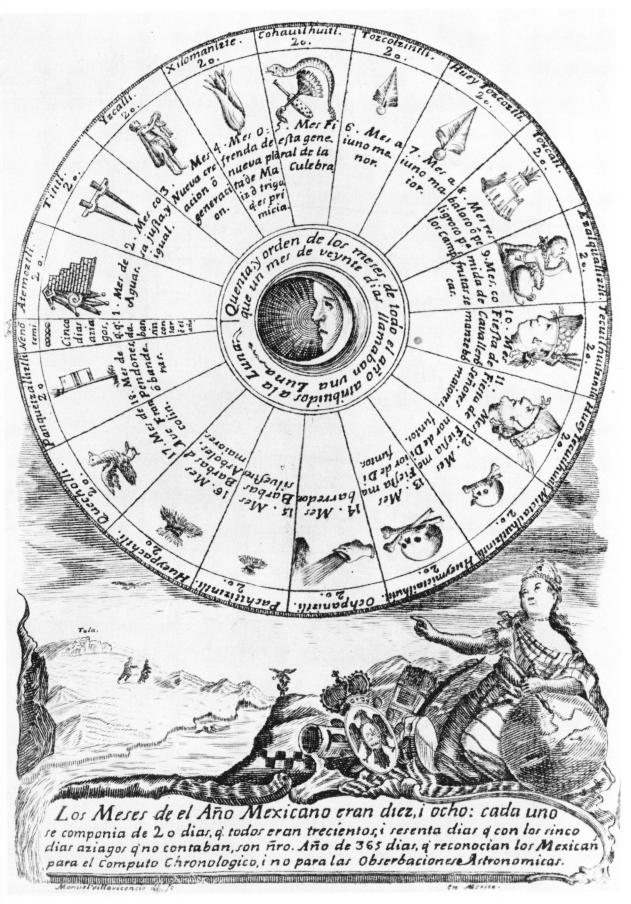

FIG. 75—VEYTIA CALENDAR WHEEL NO. 5 (census, 391). After Lorenzana, 1770, pl. 1.

Fig. 76—WALDECK JUDGMENT SCENE (census, 397). Waldeck copy. Courtesy, Edward E. Ayer Collection, Newberry Library.

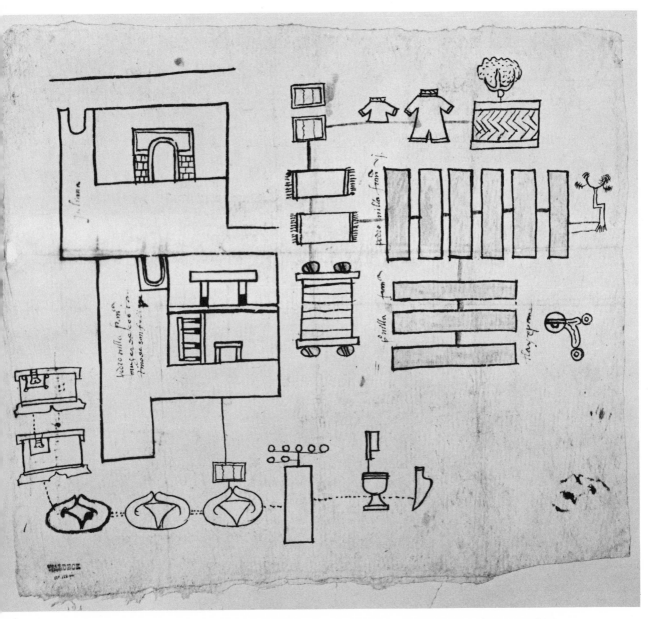

FIG. 77—DOCUMENT CONCERNING PROPERTY OF PEDRONILLA FRANCISCA AND COSTANTINO DE SAN FELIPE (census, 403). Gloss at left center reads: "Pedronilla Francisca muger de Costantino de San Felipe." Courtesy, Edward E. Ayer Collection, Newberry Library.

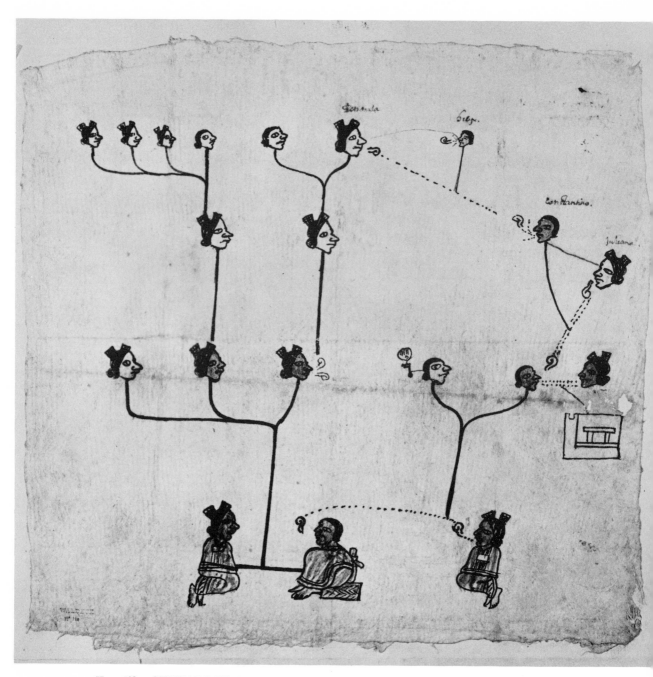

Fig. 78—GENEALOGY OF PEDRONILLA AND JULIANA (census, 404). Glosses, left to right, read: "Pedronila, Felipe, Constantino, and Juliana." Courtesy, Edward E. Ayer Collection, Newberry Library.

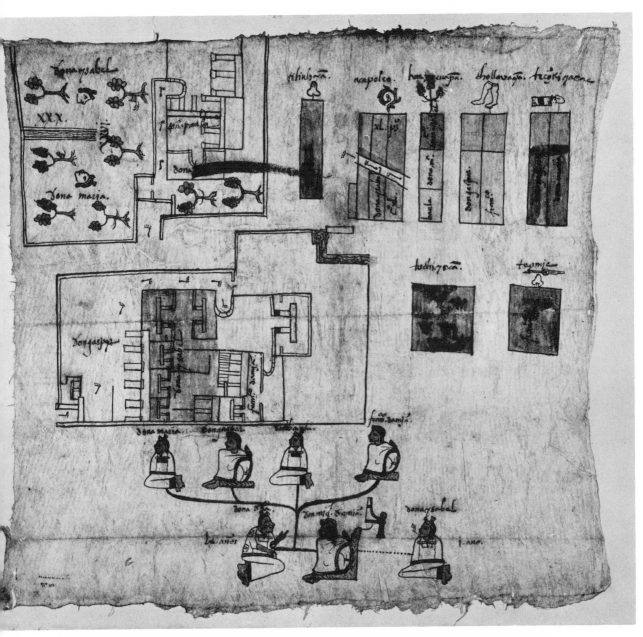

Fig. 79—DOCUMENT RELATING TO THE DESCENDANTS OF DON MIGUEL
DAMIAN (census, 406). Courtesy, Edward E. Ayer Collection, Newberry Library.

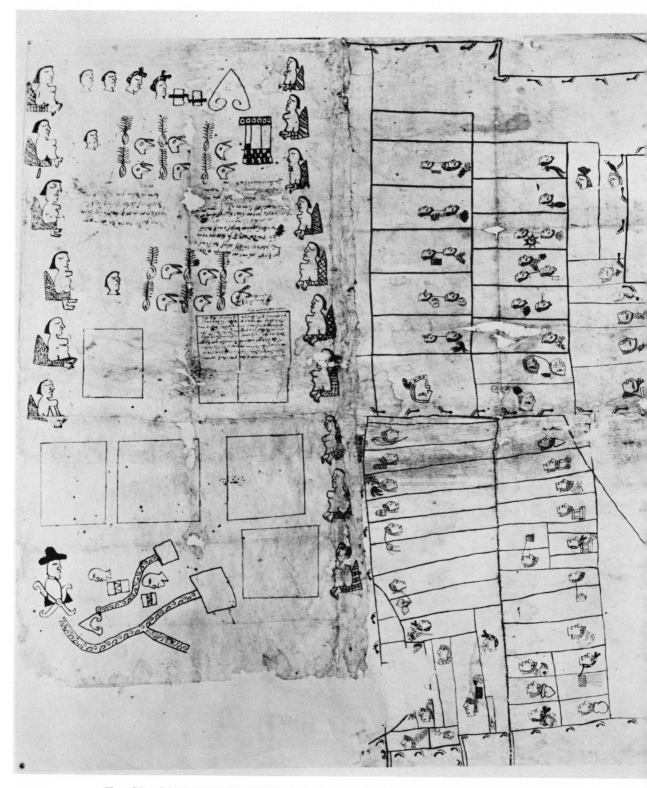

FIG. 80—CODEX OF XOCHITEPEC (census, 408). Courtesy Handschriftensammlung, Österreichische Nationalbibliothek, Vienna.

FIG. 81—CODEX XOLOTL (census, 412). Tracings by Waldeck of selected details from pls. 2 and 3. This is one of two pages of tracings by Waldeck of details from the single leaf of the codex owned by him. Courtesy, Edward E. Ayer Collection, Newberry Library.

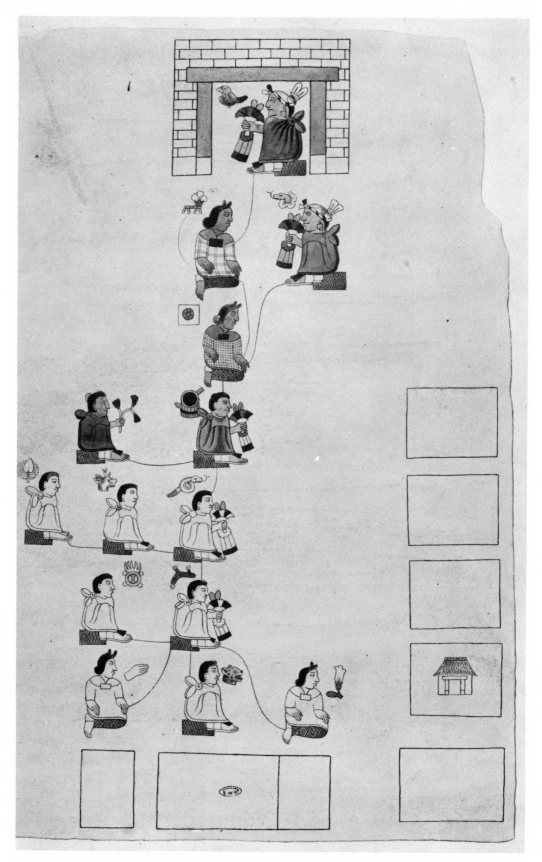

FIG. 82—GENEALOGÍA DE ZOLIN (census, 427). Copy by Waldeck. Courtesy, Edward E. Ayer Collection, Newberry Library.

FIG. 83—HUIXQUILUCAN, TECHIALOYAN 724, f. 3v. Courtesy, Peabody Museum, Harvard University.

FIG. 84—TEPOTZOTLAN, TECHIALOYAN 718, f. 6r. Courtesy, Bibliothèque Nationale, Paris.

Fig. 85—XONACATLAN, TECHIALOYAN 723, f. 6r. Courtesy, Latin American Library, Tulane University.

FIG. 86—CALPULALPAN, TECHIALOYAN 725, f. 1r. Courtesy, Bibliothèque Nationale, Paris.

FIG. 87—XONACATLAN, TECHIALOYAN 723, f. 4r. Courtesy, Latin American Library, Tulane University.

FIG. 88—XONACATLAN, TECHIALOYAN 723, f. 3v. Courtesy, Latin American Library, Tulane University.

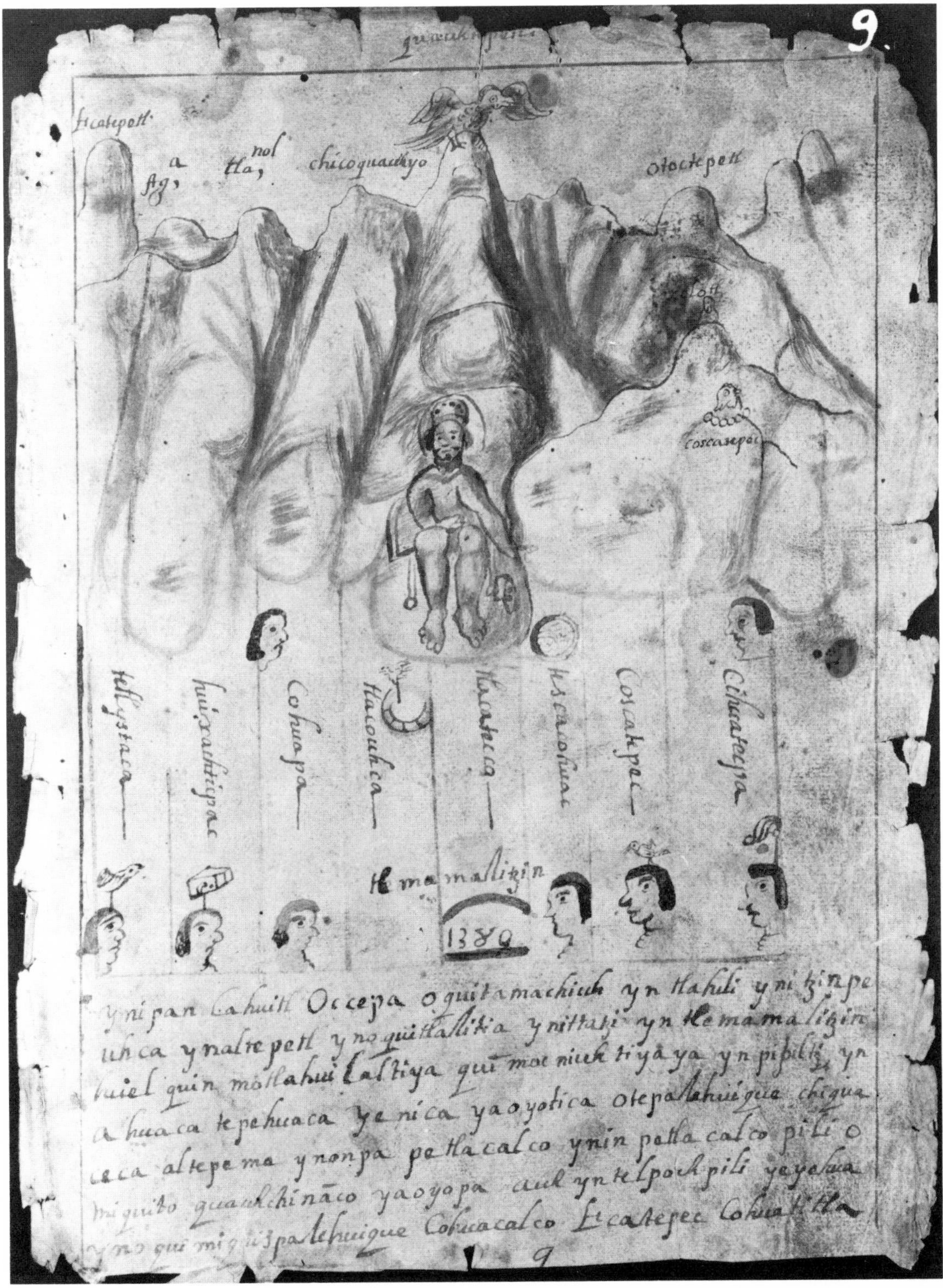

FIG. 89—COACALCO, TECHIALOYAN 743, f. 3r. Courtesy, Latin American Library, Tulane University.

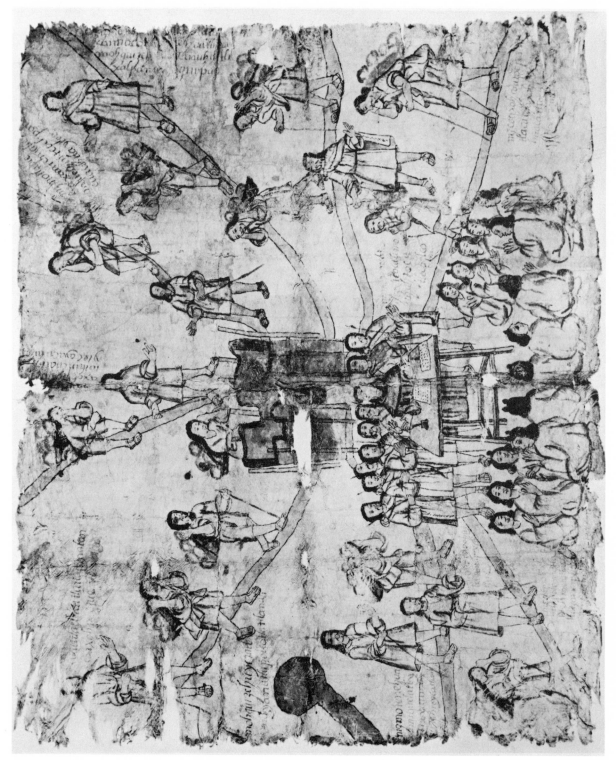

Fig. 90—SAN PEDRO ATLAPOLCO, TECHIALOYAN 726 (panel). Courtesy, The Brooklyn Museum, Ella C. Woodward Fund.

FIG. 91—CUERNAVACA CATHEDRAL, TECHIALOYAN 745 (murals). Courtesy, Bradley Smith, New York.

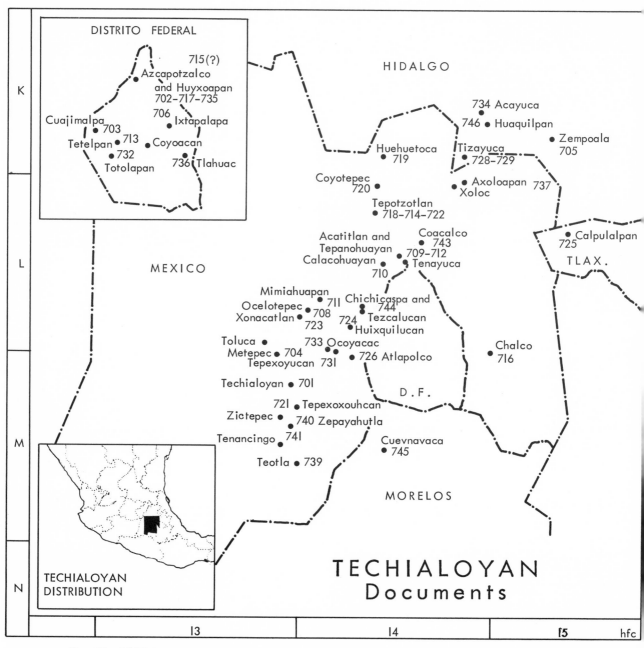

DISTRITO FEDERAL

715(?)
Azcapotzalco
and Huyxoapan
702-717-735
Cuajimalpa   706
703   Ixtapalapa
Tetelpan 713
732   Coyoacan
Totolapan
736 Tlahuac

HIDALGO

734 Acayuca
746 Huaquilpan
Zempoala
705
Tizayuca
728-729
Huehuetoca
719
Axoloapan 737
Coyotepec   Xoloc
720
Tepotzotlan
718-714-722

MEXICO

Coacalco
743
Acatitlan and   709-712
Tepanohuayan   Tenayuca
Calacohuayan
710

Calpulalpan
725
TLAX.

Mimiahuapan
711   Chichicaspa and
Ocelotepec   744
Xonacatlan 708   Tezcalucan
723   724
Huixquilucan
Toluca   733 Ocoyacac
Metepec 704   726 Atlapolco
Tepexoyucan 731

Chalco
716

Techialoyan 701

721
Zictepec Tepexoxouhcan
740 Zepayahutla
Tenancingo 741

D.F.

Cuevnavaca
745

Teotla 739

MORELOS

TECHIALOYAN
Documents

TECHIALOYAN
DISTRIBUTION

13   14   15   hfc

FIG. 92—MAP LOCATING IDENTIFIED VILLAGES IN TECHIALOYAN DOCUMENTS.
Revised by Donald Robertson.

Ignea lingua cadit, Signatus, suscitat orto.
Infantem: pueris forma fit ille crucis.

Iudicii residens infra: stat passio sursum,
Nec uacat Hic lucro, portio parua, suo.

⑧

Hie weist die Zung, wer disen Jung
Erweckt vom todt, vnd der zu Gott,

Die Knaben füert: der passion,
Vnd das gericht, handt da die Cron.

FIG. 94—SIXTEENTH-CENTURY RELIGIOUS INSTRUCTION. Fray Jacobo de Testera (at upper left, misidentified as Alphon. Testera) preaches to the Indians. After Marianus de Orscelar, *Gloriosus Franciscus redivivus*, 1625.

Fig. 95—SIXTEENTH-CENTURY RELIGIOUS INSTRUCTION. Education of the Indians by means of graphic techniques (upper left and right) on the grounds of an idealized Franciscan establishment. After Valadés, *Rhetorica cristiana*, 1579.

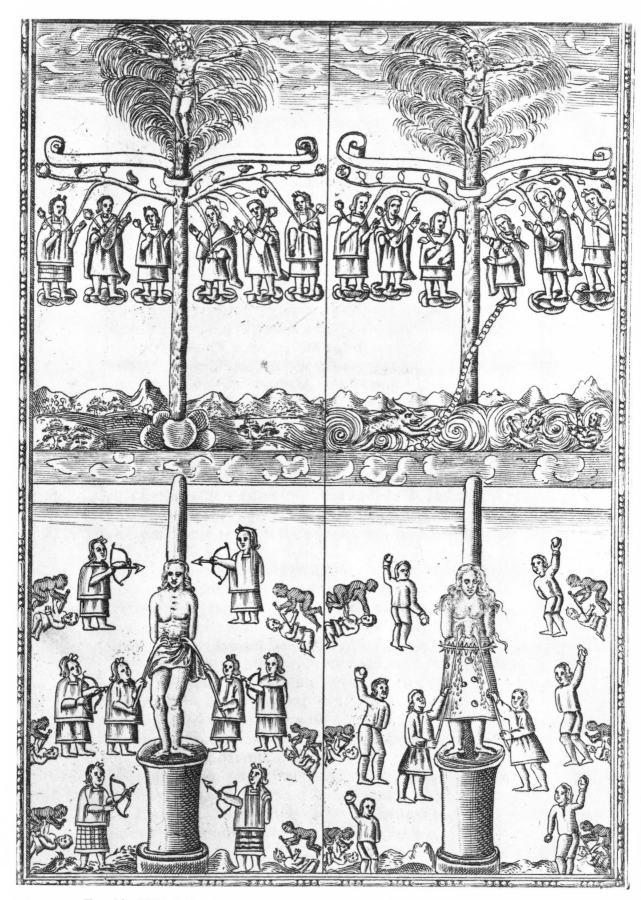

Fig. 96—THE SANCTITY OF CHRISTIAN MARRIAGE AND THE PUNISH-
MENTS FOR ITS PROFANATION. An example of a religious painting used in the
spiritual conversion of the Indians. After Valadés, *Rhetorica cristiana*, 1579.

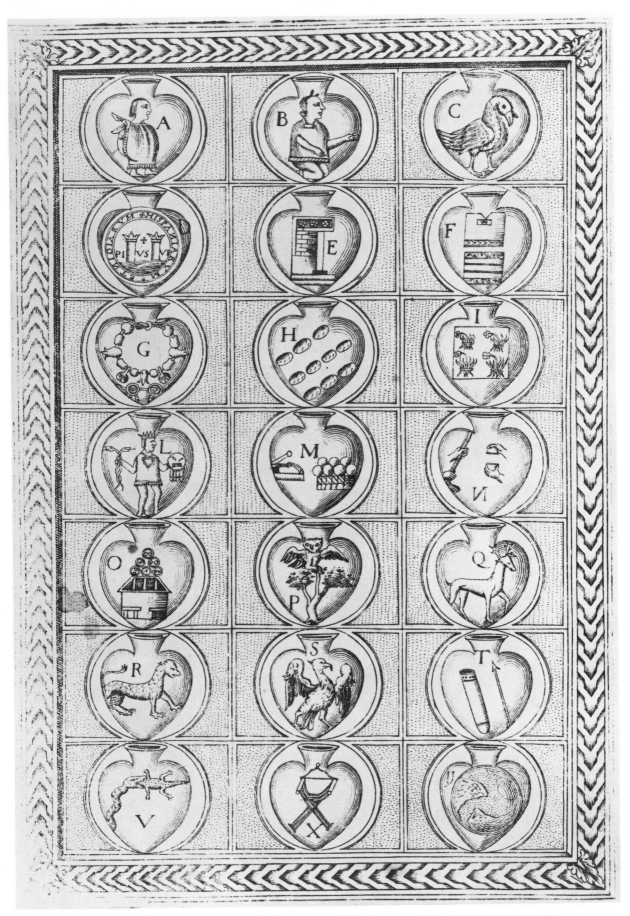

FIG. 97—MNEMOTECNIC ALPHABET PROPOSED FOR THE USE OF INDIANS.
After Valadés, *Rhetorica cristiana*, 1579.

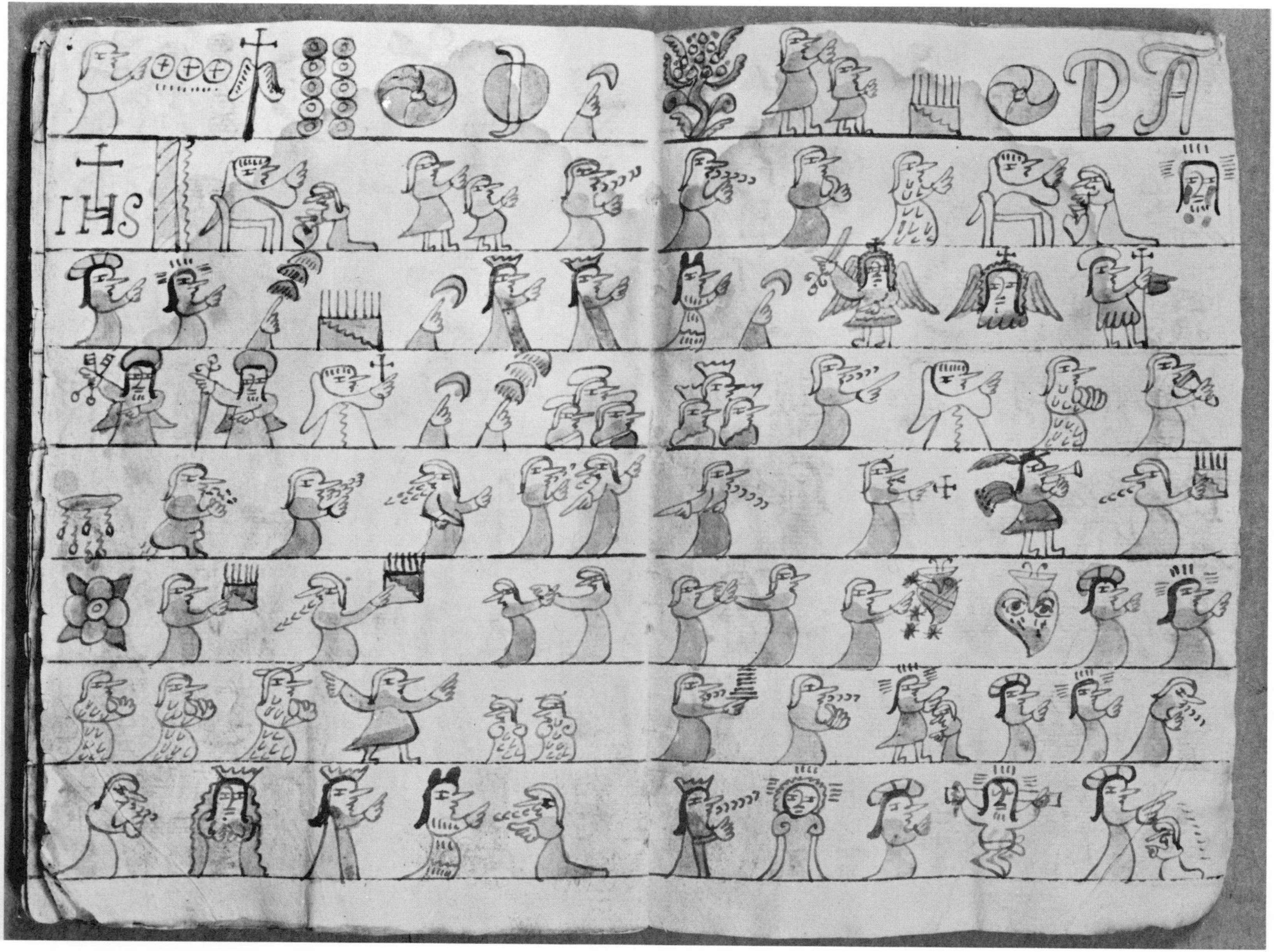

FIG. 98—TESTERIAN MANUSCRIPT. Two pages of the "Libro de Oraciones" (census, 830). Photograph by Juan Guzman (LC/HF collection).

Fig. 99—FALSIFIED DRAWING OF THE CONQUEST OF AZCAPOTZALCO (census, 901).   Courtesy, Edward E. Ayer Collection, Newberry Library.

FIG. 100—CODEX OF LIBEREC (census, 915). One page of a falsified Maya manuscript. LC/HF collection.

Fig. 101—FALSIFIED MEXICAN MANUSCRIPT (census, 936). Courtesy, Princeton University Library.

Fig. 102—SAVILLE FRAGMENT (census, 940). Courtesy, American Museum of Natural History.

FIG. 103—WALDECK CALENDAR WHEEL (census, 947). Courtesy, Edward E. Ayer Collection, Newberry Library.